Mohona Kanjilal was born in Kolkata and spent most of her childhood in Bengaluru. She began her career in Kolkata as a freelance journalist. It was during her stint with the newspapers that she got bitten by the writing bug and ventured into full-time writing after a few years. *A Taste of Time—A Food History of Calcutta* is her third book and first work of non-fiction. Prior to this book, she has authored two short story collections. She is an alumnus of Loreto College in Kolkata, a city that has been her home now for years.

~Praise for *A Taste of Time*~

'[Mohona Kanjilal]'s sweeping scope and her thumbnail histories of various communities make this book something of an instant classic, an invaluable work of reference that is likely to be used by casual quizzers and serious academics alike.'

—Nilanjana Roy, *Biblio*

'Mohona Kanjilal's *A Taste of Time* on the culinary history of Calcutta is *peit pujo* through the written word, aptly depicted on the cover...a motif that knits together the diverse cultures and moments in history that have given Kolkata its present shape and form.'

—Indranee Ghosh, *Hindustan Times*

'With delectable narration bolstered by facts and pleasant stories, the book is never allowed to be relegated to the level of dry culinary dissertations, cookbooks or food guides found aplenty in the market... It is a culinary *tour de force* aiming to journey through the different periods of time in search of origin, evolution and tantalising diversity of innumerable food items, ingredients, food habits and hangout in, around and beyond Kolkata.'

—Manas Das, *The Statesman*

'If you want to read a book about Calcutta that takes you to the vignettes and the history surrounding your favourite dishes and eateries...and if you want to repeat those experiences for yourself, then this is the book for you. In *A Taste of Time: A Food History of Calcutta*, Mohona Kanjilal weaves scholarly accounts of historians and food writers with the everyday fables you hear from a famous panwallah or an old-timer of a club... My only warning is don't read this book before a meal because it will make you ravenous.'

—Shylashri Shankar, *The Telegraph*

A TASTE *of* TIME

A Food History of Calcutta

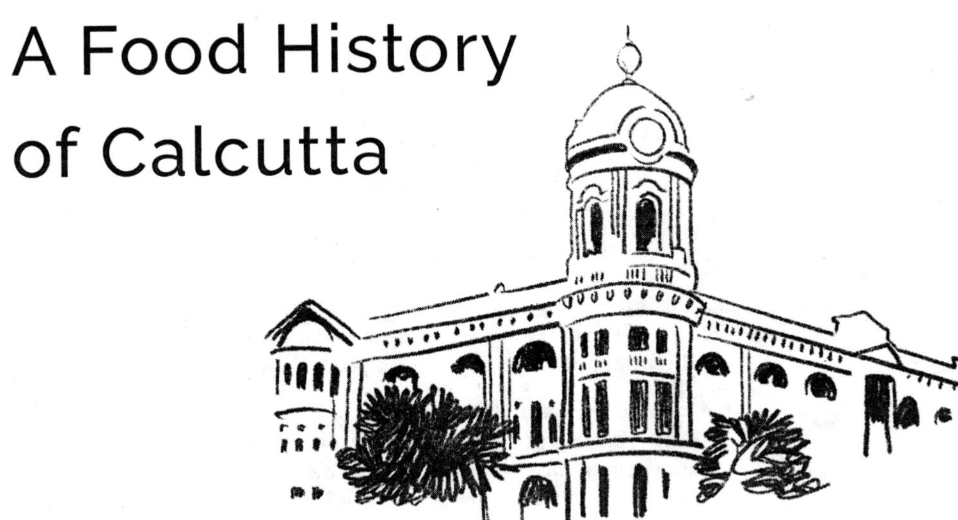

MOHONA KANJILAL

SPEAKING TIGER

SPEAKING TIGER BOOKS LLP
4381/4, Ansari Road, Daryaganj
New Delhi–110002

First published in paperback by Speaking Tiger 2021

ISBN: 978-93-90477-57-9
eISBN: 978-93-90477-69-2

10 9 8 7 6 5 4 3 2 1

Typeset in Adobe Garamond Pro by SŪRYA, New Delhi
Printed at...

To those who love the City of Joy

'Well', he said, 'five hundred rooms, five hundred teapots.
One cockroach. Very good average.'

—Arratoon Stephen,
owner of Grand Hotel, to an irate guest

CONTENTS

Introduction

Cosmopolitan Calcutta

A glimpse of Barabazar, Calcutta, 1945

Source: **Aakriti Art Gallery Pvt. Ltd, Kolkata**

The Founding of Calcutta

In the early seventeenth century, when the British East India Company began making inroads into India, Bengal was under the stable political leadership of the Mughals, though the Portuguese had already established themselves in trade in the port city of Chittagong (Chattogram) and the Dutch were involved in trading activities in the province. Bengal was a very wealthy region and when absorbed into the Mughal Empire in 1576, it was regarded as its wealthiest province. Then a globally prominent trading region, Bengal was regarded by the Europeans as the 'richest country' to trade with and was renowned for its textile (particularly cotton, muslin and silk) manufacturing industry. Unfortunately, it is its enormous wealth that turned out to be Bengal's Achilles heel as it attracted the avarice of many ruling powers. One of these players, Britain, was responsible for draining and bleeding this rich region of its wealth.

When the British reached the Subah (province) of Bengal, they began their trading operations in Baleshwar (Balasore) and Hariharpur (both in present-day Odisha). They developed excellent trade relations with the powerful Sheth and Basak merchant families in Sutanuti, a flourishing village on the banks of the Hooghly, which was already quite important in the textile trade. A relatively unimportant village nearby, lying between Sutanuti and Gobindapur, was then known as Kalikata. The three villages eventually merged to form what would be known throughout the world as the city of Calcutta (in Bengali—and officially, since 2001—Kolkata).

The most widely accepted etymological explanation of the city's name comes from its association with the goddess Kali. Many linguistic variations suggest the goddess's close association with the city, such as Kali-kota (the home or abode of Kali), the Sanskrit Kali-kshetra, (the field or terrain of Kali) and Kali-ghatta (a north Indian distortion of Kalighat, a nearby settlement, which means the riverbank of Kali).

Credit for founding the city of Calcutta has historically been given to Job Charnock, an agent of the British East India Company, who had great faith in the commercial potential of the area. Charnock was born in England around 1630 and came to India in 1655–56. Within two years, he had become a junior member of the Council of Cossimbazar, a commercial town which is today a part of West Bengal's Murshidabad district. Cossimbazar used to be a very prosperous town and a great trading centre in the Subah of Bengal. From Cossimbazar, Charnock was sent to Patna, where he was put in charge of the Company's factory. In 1680, he took charge of the Cossimbazar factory and in 1686, became the Company's agent for all of Bengal.

During Charnock's tenure in India, hostilities between the British and the silk weavers and traders of the Murshidabad area had resulted in the closing down of many British factories in Bengal. Charnock was forced to shift base to Hooghly. But there, too, he faced the ire of Subahdar Shaista Khan, the Mughal Governor of the Subah of Bengal, and had to retreat to the trading village of Sutanuti—his first time staying at the site that would become an important part of the future city of Calcutta. It was during this period that he became convinced of the superior location and advantages of the flourishing textile village. He was convinced that Sutanuti would be the best place to establish the Company's headquarters in Bengal because of its strong military and commercial potential. His stubborn pursuit of this idea ultimately won over the reluctant council of the British East India Company in Madras. In March 1690, they procured permission from Emperor Aurangzeb in Delhi to re-establish a factory in Bengal for trading. The agent set sail for Sutanuti from Madras.

Charnock landed near Nimtala Ghat in Sutanuti on 24 August 1690, and is believed to have hoisted the British flag on the banks of the Hooghly. Calcutta's official birthday was thus considered to be 24 August 1690 for more than three hundred years.

In 2003, based on the findings of an expert committee of five eminent historians, the Calcutta High Court ruled that the city of Calcutta originated through a general process of rural settlement, clusters of which became part of the Company's trading factory in the last decade of the seventeenth century, and grew into a town in the eighteenth century. Historians have also pointed out that references have been made to a certain 'Kalikatah' in some of India's important writings, such as Bipradas Pipilai's *Manasa Vijaya*, which was written in 1495 and refers to a place called Kalikatah and Abu'l-Fazl's *Ain-i-Akbari*, which was written in Persian in 1596, and also refers to a place by the same name. Moreover, one simple founder could not have created the city. In addition to Charnock, people who contributed to the long process of the city's formation, included his son-in-law, Charles Eyre; John Goldsborough, an administrator with the British East India Company; Lakshmikanta Majumdar, who developed the land in the area; the Sheths and the Basaks, who traded with the British from the three villages; and the Sabarna Roy Choudhurys, one of the oldest zamindari families of Calcutta settled in Barisha (historically, one of the oldest boroughs in the city), who sold the villages to the British. Finally, the court ruled that Calcutta cannot have an official birthday—hence giving the ruling on the sobriquet 'Calcutta Birthday Case'.

Regardless of his claim in history, it is indisputable that Job Charnock considered Sutanuti and its neighbouring areas to be an ideal site for the British East India Company's headquarters in India. He recognized that the area provided enough space to accommodate strong fortifications and a rapidly expanding trade centre. Its proximity to the sea made a commercially viable harbour possible. The site was also ideal from a defence point of view as it was protected by the Hooghly on one side and salt marshes and wetlands on the other. It was also well-connected to northern India by plenty of rivers, navigable canals and trunk roads.

Unfortunately, Charnock died within a few years of his landing and never saw the city that he dreamed of become a reality. In his essay, 'The Growth and Development of Old Calcutta', from the book *Calcutta—The Living City: Volume I: The Past* (1990), eminent historian, researcher and author, P. Thankappan Nair, writes, 'The three villages [of Sutanuti, Gobindapur and Kalikata] were part of a khas mahal or imperial jagir (that is, an estate belonging to the Mughal emperor himself) whose zamindari rights were held by the Sabarna [Roy Choudhury] family of Barisha-Behala, in the southern suburbs of modern Calcutta' (p. 11). The zamindari rights of the three villages of Sutanuti, Gobindapur and Kalikata were acquired by Charles Eyre, Charnock's son-in-law and successor, on 10 November 1698, nearly six years after Charnock's death. The deed for the lease of the three villages was drawn up between Sabarna Roy Choudhury's family and the British East India Company at Barisha Aatchala, for a sum of Rs 1,300. This was crucial in binding the three villages together and giving them the structure of a proper city. Gradually, the British East India Company procured the zamindari rights of the thirty-eight villages that surrounded their settlement in Calcutta.

The ambition of the British East India Company, which was actually formed for the purpose of conducting trade with East and Southeast Asia and India, gradually grew beyond merely having trade relations in the region, and was further fuelled by the power vacuum left by Aurangzeb's death on 3 March 1707. He was followed by a line of weak emperors, leading to a series of wars of succession and coups by noblemen. The country was in a state of chaos. The British took advantage of this situation and began raising their own army, and were soon contenders for the control of Bengal. Thus, the Company began to get involved in politics and acted as an agent of British imperialism in India.

On 23 June 1757, the Battle of Palashi (Plassey) was fought between the British East India Company and the Nawab of Bengal, Siraj-ud-Daulah. The nawab's army suffered massive defeat at the hands of the army led by Robert Clive. This gave the British effective control over Bengal. But the most decisive battle was the one fought at Buxar. The British defeated the Nawab of Bengal, Mir Qasim, and the Mughal Emperor Shah Alam II, on 22 October 1764 at the Battle of Buxar (in present-day Bihar). Soon after this battle, on 12 August 1765, Shah Alam II granted the British the diwani rights or the right to collect taxes of the province of Bengal on behalf of the emperor by signing the Treaty of Allahabad. This made the British East India Company the masters of Bengal for generations to come.

In his article, 'The East India Company: The original `corporate raiders' for *The Guardian* (4 March 2015), renowned author William Dalrymple writes, 'It was at this moment that the East India Company (EIC) ceased to be a conventional corporation, trading silks and spices, and became something much more unusual. Within a few years, 250 company clerks backed by the military force of 20,000 locally recruited Indian soldiers had become the effective rulers of Bengal. An international corporation was transforming itself into an aggressive colonial power.'

Murshidabad had been the seat of the nawabs and was the capital of Bengal during the Mughal period. After the British East India Company took over, the British consolidated their hold on the province by shifting the capital to Calcutta. Warren Hastings, the first Governor-General of Bengal, first attempted to make Calcutta the capital in 1772, though his successor, Lord Cornwallis, was the one to finally move the entire administrative machinery in 1790. By the 1850s, Calcutta had been divided into White Town and Black Town. White Town grew around Fort William, which had been built on the original site of Gobindapur, and included areas like Chowringhee and Dalhousie Square. It was inhabited by the British, who lived in European-style mansions built on wide roads. In contrast, Black Town developed around Sutanuti, and was home to the native population, and considerably less glamorous. In November 1858, Queen Victoria's proclamation assuming control of the Government of India was read at the Grand Durbar held in Allahabad. It disestablished the British East India Company, enabled the British monarchy to have direct imperial rule over India and designated Calcutta as the royal capital of British India.

A Taste of Time: A Food History of Calcutta

Calcutta was a city certainly befitting royalty during its tenure as the capital from 1858 to 1911. Law and order were excellent and the city was at the heart of a thriving economy. Migrants from other parts of the country and from foreign lands came to the city, either to share in its prosperity or to escape religious persecution in their homelands. Expatriate communities, including Armenians and Parsis from Iran, Jews from Syria and Baghdad, and the Chinese began making niches for themselves in Calcutta, which was, at this point of time, considered the second city of the British Empire. People from within India also left their homes to explore possibilities in this vibrant city, creating thriving communities of Gujaratis, Marwaris, Punjabis, Sindhis, Oriyas, Biharis and south Indians. Calcutta became a cosmopolitan melting pot, where cultures merged to provide a common platform on which great fortunes could be built.

Modern historians have coined the new term 'Grey Town' to describe the areas where many of these migrants lived, as they did not exclusively belong to Europeans or Indians. These areas were identified with a particular immigrant community, and often featured street names that represented the predominant ethnicity. For example, Bow Barracks is associated with Anglo-Indians, Ezra Street with Jewish migrants, Armenian Street with Armenians and Sun Yat Sen Street held mainly Chinese shops until relatively recently. The presence of such diverse communities gave the royal capital a pulsating and lively atmosphere and made it *the* place to be in the British Empire.

Calcutta's economy soared under the British because of their continuous efforts to develop the city. Administration was strong and the city went through industrial growth on a large scale, affecting its infrastructure and organization and leading to a steady supply of jobs. An important result of this political, economic and social change was the rise of an opinionated and educated Bengali middle class. In the last decades of the nineteenth century, a feeling of national identity began growing among this middle class, many of whom initiated efforts to overthrow the imperialist power. Different levels of political leadership emerged from this class of people, who rose above their regional inclinations and began to think and assume a holistic, national identity. It is around this time that we can see the emergence of some of the greatest revolutionary thinkers and fighters of Bengal.

The cosmopolitan nature of the city brought about a diversity in food that had never been seen before. The white memsahibs who had begun to run households in British India taught their local staff the essentials of British cooking, and the intricacies of handling crockery and cutlery. Appointment of these cooks would be done on the basis of the chitthies or written recommendations from previous British employers. The best cooks were deemed to be the Mogs, many of whom had migrated to the city from Chittagong and Hooghly. They were employed in British households, companies and clubs, alongside the Bihari Muslims and Dacca (Dhaka) Christians. This brigade of chefs travelled every day to Sir Stuart Hogg Market, popularly known as New Market, to buy the groceries and other ingredients they needed.

Sir Stuart Hogg Market has an interesting story of its own to tell. Legend has it that the 'whites' resented brushing shoulders with the locals, disdainfully termed by them as 'natives', in the markets or bazars, and longed for a market, exclusively of their own. Finally, the Calcutta Corporation paid heed to their demand and purchased Lindsay Street, razed the old Fenwick's Bazar (built by Edward Fenwick who held important offices under the Company) located on it, and in its place erected Calcutta's first municipal market, which also happened to be its largest retail market. This market, built in the Victorian Gothic architectural style, was opened in January 1874 amidst much fanfare and the delighted Europeans gave it the provisional nickname, 'New Market'. Everything that could be possibly imagined was available for sale in this market, right from fruits, vegetables, fish, meat, groceries, spices, cheese and confectioneries to crockery and cutlery, utensils, clothes, shoes, flowers and books. Many years later, it was christened 'Sir Stuart Hogg Market' after Sir Stuart Hogg, who had been the chairman of the Calcutta Corporation during the time of the establishment of the market and had provided enough encouragement and support to the plan to build it. But, its nickname, New Market, stuck on to the minds of people and turned out to be the one most widely used.

The liberal lifestyle of the British and other Europeans, as well as the presence of the various communities with their different customs and traditions, gave rise to a new environment. Prolonged exposure of the local Bengalis to this diversity encouraged a progressive, tolerant and experimental outlook, which extended to their eating habits, creating a demand for different cuisines. Many local cooks became experts in European cuisine and their expertise gradually filtered through to the rest of the people who also developed a taste for these dishes. In addition, the culinary practices and food habits of the other communities living in the city, whether indigenous or expatriate, began to blend into the local culinary culture. Over time, these culinary practices, experiments and habits, whether indigenous or expatriate, had a great influence on one another.

A number of eateries opened in Calcutta during this time, specializing in traditional as well as new-found cuisines, both of which were in great demand. Many of these eateries became the favourite haunts of freedom fighters, revolutionary leaders and thinkers, philosophers and litterateurs. Some of the patrons even made anti-colonial plans and wrote seditious literature in these places.

Calcutta After 1911

Politically, the city went through a major change in 1911. At the Delhi Durbar, held in December that year, King-Emperor George V announced the decision to shift the capital of British India to Delhi, due to its central location, its historic importance as the heart of the Sultanate and the Mughal Empire, and the growing political instability of Calcutta. As Delhi had been the seat of powerful empires since medieval times, it was a prominent military and trade centre. In contrast, the increasing involvement of the local Bengalis in nationalist politics and anti-British political propaganda was making effective administration from Calcutta difficult.

The British shift in focus to Delhi had its major repercussions for Calcutta, initiating the gradual decline of the city as an economic power. Major sources of employment began to disappear with the shifting of the government. Coming on the heels of this decision, the First World War (1914–18) also upset the city's economic balance. Suranjan Das stresses that this (the First World War) '[....] led to more acute conflicts of view between the Indians and the British, particularly with regard to the drain of wealth, deindustrialization, rising revenue demands and the stultification of indigenous commerce and industry' (p. 17).

During and after the First World War, the people of Bengal were exposed to dramatically different political movements, all aimed at casting off the shackles of British rule, ranging from Gandhian non-violence to extremist nationalism and communalism, the Congress-led Independence movement, revolutionary terrorism and Hindu revivalist politics. The outbreak of the Second World War (1939–45) had a dramatic impact on the Indian political situation. Das continues:

> 'Calcutta could not remain untouched. The city shared the general national grievance that the Viceroy had unilaterally declared India's participation in the British [w]ar effort without consulting any Indian political party. The German victory at Dunkirk and the fall of France began a new trend among certain Bengali politicians to exploit the British predicament by forging alliances with the Axis powers. This found most concrete expression in [Subhas Chandra Bose's] dramatic escape from Calcutta and his formation of the Indian National Army (INA) to liberate India with Japanese help' (p. 23).

Despite no longer being the centre of power, what happened during that time in Calcutta and Bengal at large continued to shape the fortunes of India. The man-made Bengal famine of 1943–44 was responsible for the loss of more than three million lives. In 1942, when Japan seized Burma during the Second World War, the British not only began hoarding rice in Bengal, but also exporting large quantities of the grain to Great Britain to make up for the loss from Burma, causing a severe food shortage in the province, particularly in the areas that are now in Bangladesh. The British prime minister at the time, Winston Churchill, put in place policies that exacerbated the situation; for example, he is believed to have diverted the supplies of medical aid and food that were being dispatched for the starvation victims to the soldiers fighting the war. Several appeals were made to him by conscience-stricken British officials in India, but Churchill's focus on the war, and well-documented disdain for Indians made him turn a deaf ear to their pleas. He also knew that India, 'the jewel in the crown of the British Empire', was inching close towards Independence and he resented that. As a consequence, Calcutta was overrun with people dying from starvation and malnutrition. Many people became destitute and were labelled as 'famine beggars'; there are documented accounts of how these beggars would search for vegetable skins and rotten fruits to stave off starvation. Some accounts even mention people resorting to eating grass and human flesh for survival. Ultimately, the famine ended in 1944 because of a strong rice harvest, rather than any attempt at good governance by the British, dealing a final blow to the idea that British rule was a form of benevolent patronage.

Meanwhile, attempts to partition Bengal had been made for some time, giving a foretaste of the problems that arose from the Partition of India at the time of Independence. The first attempt to partition Bengal was made in 1905 by Lord Curzon, the Viceroy and Governor-General of India at the time. He considered the province too large for administration, and wanted to increase administrative efficiency by dividing it into the province of Bengal, which would include the modern-day states of West Bengal, Bihar, Odisha (Orissa) and Jharkhand, and parts of Chhattisgarh, and the province of Eastern Bengal and Assam. This action, which was more of a territorial reorganization of the Bengal Presidency, separated the Muslim-dominated eastern areas from the Hindu-dominated western ones. The people of Calcutta, particularly the Hindus, were outraged. They thought the real reason behind this move was the British policy of 'divide and rule' which aimed to turn the people of Bengal against each other on communal lines. Anti-partition agitation pervaded the entire region of Bengal. Finally, to appease the Bengalis, the new Viceroy and Governer-General of India, Lord Hardinge, reunited Bengal in 1911.

However, this paradoxically created some of the conditions that led to the eventual Partition. Lord Hardinge's reunification of Bengal caused much resentment among the elite classes, many of whom were Muslim, leading to the beginning of Muslim separatist politics in Bengal. They culminated in the Great Calcutta Killings, also known as Direct Action Day, the worst communal riots that British India had ever seen. In 1946, the Muslim League called for a hartal or general strike on 16 August to assert its demand for a separate Muslim homeland. The massacre that followed left innumerable people dead and homeless. The riots did not remain confined to Calcutta, but spread to neighbouring regions like Noakhali. They signalled an administrative breakdown, forcing the incumbent Viceroy and Governor-General of India, Lord Wavell, to suggest an early termination of British rule. The slaughter reconciled many Hindus and Muslims to the idea of Partition and the formation of Pakistan as the only alternative to such carnage.

Communal differences notwithstanding, the anti-imperialist mass struggle transcended religious lines, finally winning India its Independence on 15 August 1947. Bengal was divided on the basis of the Radcliffe Line between India and Pakistan, with the predominantly Hindu west becoming a part of India and the predominantly Muslim east, a part of Pakistan. In 1971, East Pakistan finally broke away from Pakistan to establish the independent country of Bangladesh. Meanwhile the Partition had led to the massive migration of Hindus from the eastern parts of Bengal to its west. They left behind stable lives and settled in Calcutta and its neighbouring areas as 'displaced persons' or refugees. However, with time, these displaced persons found their feet in Calcutta by securing different means of livelihood and homes for themselves, and finally, assimilating themselves with its society. This assimilation also led to a change in the culinary culture of the city because when the refugees from East Bengal first arrived in West Bengal, they brought along their culinary practices and food habits and preferences that had always marginally differed from those of the people living in the western part of the state. Over the years, these differences got blended and today, the cuisine of West Bengal has taken on a whole new definition. It is a wonderful combination of the culinary practices and food habits and preferences of the original inhabitants of the land as well as of the new arrivals who are now regarded as its indelible part.

Calcutta's Contemporary Culinary Culture

Calcutta still remains a jewel, although now in the crown of India. The city carries on its legacy as a significant centre of political and social awareness in the country. Various mediums of expression such as periodicals, literature, theatre and cinema, and the grassroot level of creative expression—the jatra (folk theatre), often contribute to fuelling this awareness with their productions. The residents of this city, irrespective of their social strata, are so politically aware that heated discussions on political and social issues in tea shops, coffee houses, students' common rooms and office canteens have become synonymous with the very spirit of the city.

Food has always been an integral part of the lifestyle of the residents of Calcutta and, perhaps unsurprisingly, has also been one of the city's most flourishing business propositions. It is not often that one comes across a city whose people are so enthusiastic about food that it almost borders on passion.

This becomes evident on taking a tour of the city, when one is sure to come across a multitude of endearing sights and sounds that represent food—whether it is the *pani puri* wallah, or rather, the *phuchka* wallah, as the residents of Calcutta prefer to call him, selling his wares at the corner of a road, or the *jhal muri* wallah, selling the spicy puffed rice preparation called jhal muri, or the *ghugni* wallah, serving his customers the semi-dry and spicy preparation of whole yellow peas in bowls made of dried leaves. Scenes of pavement vendors selling cuts of fresh fruits sprinkled with sugar and salt, or hard-boiled eggs dusted with salt and pepper, or charcoal-toasted slices of bread smeared with butter and pepper, are common.

While, on the one hand, one can discover international fast food joints, Italian restaurants, Southeast Asian and East Asian restaurants, on the other, one may come across a multitude of restaurants specializing in the different varieties of Indian cuisine just as easily. At the end of a meal, a customer can buy the good old paan (betel leaf roll) from one of the numerous paan shops dotting the city.

From fancy coffee shops, juice bars, waffle outlets and ice cream parlours selling Baskin-Robbins and Haagen-Dazs sundaes to roadside tea shops, sharbat stalls, sweet shops and ice cream vendors selling the good old orange popsicles and kulfis—Calcutta has it all. The difference may be stark, but the list is endless.

Today, thanks to this endless list of dining out options, the entire city can be called a food hub, with dining options befitting every budget, clientele and rating, serving the best their kitchens can offer. Customers come in a variety, from the bespectacled office-going babu of moderate means to the high-profile spendthrift fashionista. Park Street and Dacres Lane are the two streets that have gained fame as the food streets of Calcutta. While Park Street houses a fair number of posh restaurants, Dacres Lane has become renowned as the mecca of street food in Calcutta.

It should also be pointed out that the zealous interest of the residents of Calcutta in food is not only confined to eating and cooking, but also extends to reading, encouraging many connoisseurs and enthusiasts to write on the subject.

It is a fallacy that geography alone determines the eating habits of a people or the culinary story of a land. Since the British reign, when Calcutta was a flourishing centre of trade and commerce, it attracted immigrants from both far and near. The census superintendent had made an observation in 1911 that only 45 per cent of Calcutta's inhabitants were native Bengalis. Certain areas like Barabazar were magnets for Armenians, Portuguese, Jews, Chinese, Greeks and various migrant Indian communities, who made this market area their own by building houses and setting up shops. This mixed bag of immigrants added their signatures to the culinary history of the city, leaving behind culinary legacies that have both blended with local foods and become signature dishes of Calcutta. They adapted, influenced and, in turn, were influenced by the local culinary habits and practices. This book is an attempt at exploring this culinary evolution specific to Calcutta across a variety of cuisines and time periods.

The book is divided into four sections. The first—European Influences—focuses on the impact of the British and the Portuguese on the culinary habits and practices of the Bengalis in Calcutta and their additions to the native cuisine of the land, ranging from beverages to chops, and cutlets to puddings and confectionery. This section also explores the Anglo-Indian community of Calcutta via the influences on their cuisine and their overall culinary history. It extensively covers the evolution of the hospitality industry in Calcutta as well, which began during the European period with taverns and punch houses, and explores the foray and impact of continental cuisine in Calcutta. The food and signature dishes served in the foremost establishments of Calcutta have also been included throughout the section. The Armenians, who made Calcutta their own, have been a subject of study in this section too, what with their culinary stories and impact on Calcutta's food culture.

Section two, A Culinary Melting Pot, is a detailed study of the culinary histories of other expatriate communities who adopted Calcutta as their home, including the Jews, Parsis and Chinese. It also explores the tremendous influence that Awadhi and Mughlai cuisines have had on the culinary culture of Calcutta, since the time they were brought to the city by migrants from modern-day Uttar Pradesh. I have included these cuisines alongside those of immigrant communities from outside India because they all entered the consciousness of the city during a similar time period, while Calcutta was the heart of the British Raj in India and the cynosure of cosmopolitanism in the country. Conversely, immigrant communities that have not made a significant contribution to Calcutta's culinary scene, or which do not have a noticeable presence in the city anymore, have been deliberately left out. For example, Calcutta once had a sizeable Greek population, comprising mostly merchants trading with the British. Rallis India Limited, which is today a TATA Enterprise and one of India's leading agrochemical companies, has its origin in Ralli Brothers, once the best-known Greek firm in Calcutta. The community left the city after Independence, leaving behind the Greek Orthodox Church, Panioty Fountain and a cemetery. However, since their contribution to the culinary fabric of the city is negligible, I have not explored their history in Calcutta in this book.

The third section explores Bengali cuisine in Calcutta, giving a detailed study of its evolution and influences. It touches upon the minor differences between the culinary practices, food habits and preferences, and the dishes of the immigrants from East Bengal and the inhabitants of West Bengal, living in the city. It also touches upon the popular features of Bengali food, some of the iconic dishes and the slightly offbeat treatment this cuisine gets in some of the bonedi or first families, which includes both the zamindari and aristocratic families, of Calcutta. Despite the abolition of the zamindari system after Independence, the bonedi families have continued with their lavish interest in food, which has been interesting to explore. Finally, the section explores how Bengali cuisine has shattered its old image of being a home-confined cuisine thanks to the efforts of hoteliers and restaurateurs who have turned it into a popular eating-out option, and takes a look at some of the current trends in this ever-evolving cuisine.

The concluding section—Pan-Indian Cuisines—is divided into two parts. The first part briefly deals with migrant communities that have had a strong presence in the city and continue to hold on to their native cuisines, without allowing influences from Bengal to encroach upon their culinary practices. Most of these communities have not influenced the local cuisine much, and only some of their dishes have become popular in Calcutta. However, their presence is strong in the socioeconomic structure of the city and adds to the variety and complexity of the food available. These communities include the Gujaratis, Marwaris, Punjabis, various south Indian communities, Biharis, Oriyas and Sindhis. They came to the city when it was the thriving centre of trade and commerce under colonial rule, and not only added more life to the cosmopolitan atmosphere of Calcutta, but also to the diversity of its culinary culture.

The second part of this section, however, deals with those communities which have made Calcutta their home after Independence, and over here, I have only concentrated on the immigrants from the hills of Darjeeling district. Although, in recent years, Calcutta has witnessed a large influx of immigrants from other hilly regions like Northeast India, I have not explored the communities from the 'Seven Sister States of India' (or rather the 'Seven Sisters and One Brother of India' after the inclusion of Sikkim to the banner of Northeast India), the reason being that the cuisines of the Seven Sister States are yet to become popular. In contrast, the cuisine of Darjeeling district has turned out to be the most popular post-Independence immigrant cuisine in Calcutta.

A Taste of Time—A Food History of Calcutta has attempted to explore as many factors as possible that have lent this city its vibrant culinary scene. To this end, the book also features some of the pre-Independence eateries that continue to be very popular with the public of Calcutta. Their histories, the kind of cuisines they serve, their signature dishes and anecdotes of their famous clientele also serve to highlight the culinary evolution of the city. I have also included some iconic recipes in the book, to bring alive the cuisines, either through their important dishes, influential chefs or essential ingredients.

PART ONE

European Influences

Firpo's confectionery

***Source*: Enrico De Barbieri**

1. The British

The Bengal Renaissance of the nineteenth century marked the beginning of a social reform movement heralded by intellectuals and certain groups who had slowly begun to move away from traditional approaches towards a more liberal path. They shouldered responsibility for bringing about the social and cultural rebirth of the city, and their efforts had a strong influence on the masses. This cultural rebirth extended to their food habits as well. At this point, Calcutta's culinary culture began to undergo a tremendous change, eventually ushering in new cuisines, which grew to be in great demand by the locals.

Various European cuisines left an indelible imprint on the culinary culture of Calcutta. Over the years, they have been moulded and adapted to suit the Bengali palate, leading to a large repertoire of commonly available dishes that owe their origin to various European countries. These do not fit the purist ideals of national cuisines either today, or at the time, but are closer to a fusion cuisine that has both, an undeniably European influence and a local Bengali base.

The British were responsible for introducing certain food habits that have, over the years, become pillars of Calcutta's culinary culture. One of their major contributions was the introduction of beverages to the Bengali table. Tea, coffee and fresh fruit juices are a fixed part of the average Bengali's breakfast spread today because of the British influence. This nation strongly influenced the foods Bengalis ate for breakfast as well, introducing typical preparations of egg, sausage, bacon and bread to the local palate. Chops and cutlets, which are today as essential to a Bengali as rice and fish curry, also owe their popularity to the role played by the British in Bengali culinary history. Today, kiosks in every nook and corner of the city make and sell these fried foods, usually as accompaniments to what many perceive as a quintessentially British meal: afternoon tea. Finally, egg-based puddings, now a fixture on Calcutta's dessert menus, were introduced to the city by the British.

The British not only influenced what Bengalis ate but also how they ate it. Traditionally, meals were eaten sitting on the floor from plates made of either copper or bell metal. The well-to-do, particularly members of the zamindar families, would have their food served on thala-bati (plates and bowls) made of shwet pathor (white marble) or rupo (silver). At grand feasts and festival days, people would eat their food communally, on banana leaves. All of this gradually began to change with the advent of the British. During the British Raj, eating while sitting on the floor was slowly replaced by being seated at a dining table in aristocratic homes. The dining tables and chairs in these homes were made of teak, rosewood and other types of expensive wood. After the British came to Bengal, tableware made of porcelain, bone china, pottery and even enamel was largely imported. During the colonial rule, the aristocratic families began emulating the British and started using cups, saucers and teapots—made of porcelain, bone china and pottery—for tea. Dishes, bowls, serving bowls and other tableware made of the same materials were also used by them. With time, these changes trickled down to the less well-to-do as well. Particularly from the middle of the twentieth century, dining tables and chairs made of less expensive wood and tableware made of pottery began to be seen in middle-class homes.

Breakfast in most Bengali homes traditionally would be *parota* (as paratha, an unleavened fried flatbread made of refined flour, is known in Bengali) or *luchi* (a small, round and puffed up unleavened fried bread made of refined flour), which were eaten with *tarkari* (cooked vegetables). *Muri* (puffed rice), *chire* (beaten rice), whole fruits, milk, and fried sweets like *gaja, jilipi, khaja* and *motichur laddu*s also featured regularly in their breakfast spread. The British generally started the day with a very different meal: eggs with sausage, bacon and hash browns, toasted bread with butter, jam and marmalade, a bowl of porridge, and tea. Bengalis, given their experimental nature, were influenced by these breakfast dishes. Gradually, the complexion of their breakfast spread began to change. Eating bread and eggs for breakfast caught on with them. Bread would mostly be eaten with butter and jam while eggs would largely be eaten boiled or as an omelette. Hard-boiled eggs (sprinkled with salt and pepper) and bread (either plain or buttered) became a favourite combination of the Bengalis. The Westernized lot among them went a step further and included soft-boiled, poached, fried and scrambled eggs in their breakfast menu. Porridge became a common feature at the breakfast table for them and toasted bread was often smeared with butter and marmalade. A cup of tea became a fixture at breakfast for most. But that does not mean Bengalis gave up on their traditional breakfast dishes. Only, it was now often replaced with the British variety.

The strong impact that British food had on the culinary culture of the city led to the growth of many eateries that specialized in the making of this new cuisine. Suddenly, the masses wanted a taste of anything that was British in their attempt to emulate the white sahibs. Entrepreneurs seized this opportunity and many eateries sprang up.

The British and Their Beverages

Juice

Before the arrival of the British, the local people used to consume fruits, whole or sliced. The concept of drinking fresh fruit juices was largely absent. At most, they sometimes indulged in the occasional *daab* (tender coconut water) sold by street vendors. Of course, sharbats, which were introduced into the country by the Mughals in the sixteenth century and popularized by Emperor Babur, were made in the city before fresh fruit juices began to take over. But sharbat (or *sharbot*, in Bengali) is a drink made from concentrated syrup that is prepared from sources like fruits, herbs and even flower petals. Cold water is mixed with the concentrate to make the drink, which happens to be a popular summer cooler. Sometimes, cold milk is used in the place of water for certain sharbat preparations. Spices, lime juice or dried fruits are often mixed into the sharbats. The British introduced the practice of drinking fresh fruit juices at breakfast, tapping into the wide variety of tropical fruits found in India, but orange and sweet lime juices were easily the most popular amongst them. The practice of home juicing began in the city with their advent.

Aristocratic families were the first to pick up this habit from the British and began preparing and drinking fruit juices in their homes as well. The word spread and many adventurous people from different classes began trying this practice until gradually, natural fruit juices became a part of ordinary households and were commonly drunk for pleasure. The widely accepted nutritional value of citrus fruits was lauded and they were deemed to be tastier and much more refreshing to be consumed as juices than being eaten as whole fruits. Soon, it became a general assumption that fruit juices were good for health and they also came to be regarded as a 'patient's drink'. Anyone who fell sick was given a glass of fresh orange or sweet lime juice. The use of other fruits in juices developed much later amongst Bengalis.

Commercial production and sale of fruit juice was largely absent at first. Cashing in on the locals' growing fondness for a glass of refreshing fruit juice, Paradise (now Paramount) was a prominent juice bar to open in the city. It attracted customers in droves and its success set the trend for the other juice bars to crop up over the decades. The city has also witnessed Kapila Ashram, another juice shop housed in an old building on Bidhan Sarani, serve an array of fruit juices to enthusiastic customers. Set up by Hrishikesh Srimani in 1907, it started functioning a few years prior to Paramount. Since its inception, Kapila Ashram has been a small and modest shop. Unlike Paramount, which has proper seating arrangements, customers here had to drink their juices standing on the footpath. Yet, its regular customers simply loved the drinks it churned out. Today, the demolition of the old building has made the future of Kapila Ashram slightly uncertain. As of now, it is a kiosk on Bidhan Sarani that continues to serve juices to its loyal customers.

Paramount: This famous juice bar in central Calcutta has played host to some of the finest intellectuals of Bengal, since it opened in 1918, numbering poets, revolutionaries and professors amongst its clientele. Housed on Bankim Chatterjee Street near College Street (which has earned the nickname of 'boi para' or 'neighbourhood of books', due to the numerous book shops lining the street), it soon became a respectable venue for freedom fighters to meet and thrash out seditious plans of action, all the while maintaining the impression that the juice bar was nothing more than an innocuous place to enjoy a refreshing drink.

Its founder was Nihar Ranjan Majumdar, a physical fitness trainer by profession and one of the first to be drawn into the fruit-juice craze that affected Calcutta. To supplement his income as a trainer, he came up with the idea of starting a juice bar. Always experimental in his kitchen, Majumdar began stirring up combinations of ingredients to create a menu that was healthy while also being strikingly different from the juices one could make at home.

Paramount opened its doors to the public as Paradise, as it continued to be known till 1936. Professors, students and intellectuals visiting College Street flocked to it, intrigued by what the new place had to offer at first, and over the years, became loyal customers.

One of the oldest items served in the juice bar, *daab sharbat* is still the most popular. The recipe was given to Nihar Ranjan Majumdar by the brilliant scientist from Presidency College, Acharya Prafulla Chandra

Ray. Hailed as the 'Father of Indian Chemistry', he established the first pharmaceutical company of India in Calcutta in 1901—Bengal Chemicals & Pharmaceuticals Ltd. Ray frequented the College Street area even after he left Presidency College in 1916 and began dropping in at Paramount. His daab sharbat is a juice made with the water of green coconuts, the tender sweet pulp found inside the fruit, and a few drops of an essence, which Paramount guards as a trade secret. The green coconuts used to make this drink have always been bought from Basirhat in North 24 Parganas, as the ones grown there have the sweetest water and very thin pulp. The recipe has remained unchanged since the days of its invention.

Majumdar followed up the grand success of daab sharbat with many others, based on further experiments in his kitchen. As with most public eating places in that era, popularity depended on word of mouth, and Majumdar's range of juices made from natural fruit extracts, home-made curd, fresh milk and cream, exotic nuts, secret syrups and essences made Paramount the talk of the town. Soon, revolutionary luminaries like Bagha Jatin, nationalist leaders like Netaji Subhas Chandra Bose, politicians like Dr Bidhan Chandra Roy, and literary intellectuals like Balai Chand Mukhopadhyay (who wrote under the pseudonym Banaphool) and Tarasankar Bandyopadhyay were dropping in to sample Majumdar's creations.

The owners of Paramount continue to experiment with different ingredients to add new elements to their menu and the people of Calcutta continue to crowd it around the year. During the summer, customers cool themselves with litchi or tamarind juices, or a glass of either cream lemon or cream green mango. The latter, a sweet and tangy drink, was a favourite with prominent barrister, politician and former chief minister of West Bengal, Siddhartha Shankar Ray. During the rainy season, customers reach out for cream pineapple, while evenings, the year around, are dominated by grapes crush. To make this, green grapes are boiled with sugar at least three times and the pulp is then preserved in a jar for three months before it can form the base of this popular drink. Winters are ruled by the rich flavour of cocoa malai. This completely milk-based drink does not have a drop of water in it and is made with drinking chocolate and crushed ice, topped with a thick layer of khoya (also known as mawa) and sprinkled with dried fruits like cashews, almonds and raisins.

The fruit juices at Paramount have been sought after for decades.

There was a time when firebrand nationalists and university professors in starched dhotis alighted from horse-drawn tongas at Paramount for intellectual discussions accompanied by a few glasses of juice. Over the years, Nobel Laureate Amartya Sen, noted authors Mani Shankar Mukherjee and Samaresh Basu, popular writer and humourist Shibram Chakraborty, well-known poets Shakti Chattopadhyay and Shankha Ghosh, and renowned film-makers Satyajit Ray and Mrinal Sen became regulars at Paramount. Today, the juice bar is the favourite haunt of people from different walks of life like school and college students, office-goers and homemakers. The scene has changed since the original Majumdar's time but Paramount's new customers share the thirst that first pulled Calcuttans to its doors.

Tea

Introducing fruit juice to the Bengali palate pales in comparison with Britain's most important contribution to their beverages: tea. It's practically a cliché to call Britain a nation of tea drinkers: beginning the day with a cup of tea, another at the breakfast table, another at the office, and so on, till the famous afternoon and evening teas. A cup of tea is for all occasions, whether to celebrate or ease nervous tension. But tea is not native to Britain and there is no record of its use before the 1650s. Even after its introduction to the island nation, tea was to undergo many transformations before it became the quintessentially British beverage, cutting across classes and geographies. And ironically, despite the tea plant being native to parts of India, it didn't find purchase here without a great deal of effort, most of it on the part of the British.

As a drink, tea came to Britain only after it had already enjoyed centuries as the undisputed favourite beverage of China. In 1935, the International Botanical Congress, in its sixth session held in Amsterdam, named the genus of the tea plant as *Camellia* and under the International Code of Botanical Nomenclature, the plant as *Camellia sinensis*. The source of Chinese tea is the small leaves of the Chinese tea plant identified as *Camellia sinensis var. sinensis* by the botanist Joseph Robert Sealy of the Royal Botanic Gardens, Kew, in his book, *A Revision of the Genus Camellia*, published in 1958 by the Royal Horticultural Society. Later, in 1962, *Camellia sinensis var. sinensis* was proposed as the species of the Chinese tea plant by the botanist Dr W. Wight.

The Chinese call the beverage 'cha' and drink it without milk and sugar, to enjoy its distinct flavour and fragrance. They drink it in small cups that have no handles and look like tiny bowls. Tea was recommended by Chinese physicians for its health properties. The early accounts of the use of tea focused on its medicinal properties like alleviating digestive or nervous conditions. There are also references of it being used as a stimulant. Tea originated in southwest China during the reign of the Shang dynasty (1600–1046 BCE) where it was used as a medicinal drink. The use of herbs for health care was passed down through oral tradition in China for centuries. In the third century CE, they were presented in a formal manner in the book *Shen Nong Ben Cao Jing*, an ancient Chinese text on herbalism and medicine. The work was attributed to Shen Nong, a mythological deity in Chinese folk religion, revered as the 'Divine Farmer' or 'God of Agriculture'. The invention of Chinese herbal medicine is also credited to him. This ancient book on herbs extolled the medicinal properties of tea. *Shin Lun*, a medical text written by the Chinese physician Hua Tuo in 220 CE, is an early credible record of tea drinking. It extols the virtue of bitter tea as an intellectual stimulant because it made one think better. All of this made the Chinese aware that tea drinking was good for health.

Tea was popularized as a recreational drink and became the national beverage of China under the Tang dynasty (618–907 CE); their reign was considered to be the golden age in Chinese history. Tea drinking was already established in the Chinese court by then, and spread to all levels of society. Tea plantations were established all over China during the Tang dynasty. Lu Yu, the greatest of all Chinese authorities on tea, wrote *Cha Jing*, regarded as the most important manual for tea drinkers in Tang China. Dating to the second half of the eighth century, this book gives advice on the tools needed to harvest and process tea, the equipment needed to brew it, and a list of the tea-producing districts graded by quality. Lu Yu's fondness for tea was so great that it was more than just a beverage for him. This explains the reason behind the number of poetic and reverential descriptions of tea making and drinking in his masterpiece. Thus, from a tasteful drink with a pharmacological purpose, tea became a sophisticated beverage in this dynasty.

In 1107 CE, Emperor Huizong of the Song dynasty (960–1279 CE), a great connoisseur of tea, wrote the book *Da Guan Cha Lun*, which is regarded as a document of great significance on the subject. The book provides a detailed account of the production of tea, its preparation and the spiritual benefits of its consumption. It gives a splendid description of the most sophisticated style of tea ceremony in Chinese history. The treatise explains how to brew tea, rather than merely boiling it in water. It instructs that the water be boiled separately and poured on top of powdered tea (a popular form of tea in the Song dynasty), and then left to brew. Historical records show that the tea industry in China developed during the Tang dynasty and flourished in the Song dynasty.

During the Ming dynasty (1368–1644 CE), the members of the court began to drink tea from fine porcelain handleless cups rather than stoneware, and this became the norm in China. Tea, compressed into cakes, balls or bricks gradually began to be replaced by loose leaves. Another very important invention of the Ming dynasty was the production of black tea. Before the Ming dynasty, there seems to be no record of black tea as the Chinese always drank green tea. Roy Moxham writes in his book, *A Brief History of Tea: The Extraordinary Story of the World's Favourite Drink* (2009), 'Precisely how or why black teas came to be produced is something of a mystery, but they became very popular among the peoples living north of the Great Wall' (p. 54). Although the first variety of tea to find its way from China to the West was green tea, it was black tea that eventually came to dominate western taste.

It was around this time that tea first arrived in the West, alongside the large quantities of porcelain or 'china' that had begun to be shipped there. The Portuguese, who had been traders and missionaries in China since the sixteenth century, were the first Europeans to bring it to their shores. The Dutch followed suit and became the premier tea drinkers of Europe due to their dominion over trade with the Orient. However, the beverage was exorbitantly priced and hence confined only to the wealthy. The consumption of tea soon spread to the fashionable circles of France. Louis XIV (1638–1715) was a tea drinker, and had a teapot made of gold.

The British, in contrast, were slow to discover the joys of drinking tea. The first reference to tea is found in an advertisement in a London newspaper, *Mercurius Politicus*, dated 23 September 1658. It mentions that the China drink, which is approved by all physicians, and called 'cha' by the Chinese and 'tea' by other nations, is sold at the coffee house Sultaness-head in Sweetings Rents by the Royal Exchange, London.

The first London coffee house was established in 1652. By the end of the decade there were many more and by the end of the century, several hundred. These turned into places where men met to transact business and discuss politics. Initially, they sold only coffee but later, also chocolate and tea. The source of the first teas remain unknown. It is not known whether they came from the continent or were brought by people returning from the East.

But, even in 1660, tea remained a subject of curiosity for the public. It was Catherine of Braganza, the daughter of King Juan IV of Portugal and wife of King Charles II, who made tea drinking a fashion at the English court because she was a tea addict. Along with her immense dowry, she had brought other goods with her, like sugar, spices and a chest of tea, to England in 1662. From the court, the use of tea spread to the elite, fashionable society and became the drink of the wealthy. Sometime between the late seventeenth and early eighteenth centuries, sugar was added to tea in the elite circles. Sugar was a luxurious commodity that Britain imported from its colonies in the West Indies. It was mainly used by the rich as a flavour enhancer in foods. Sugar made tea taste better because it reduced its bitterness.

Initially, during the seventeenth century, small quantities of tea were imported into Britain by the British East India Company. Moxham elaborates on the same,

> In 1664 the Company placed its first order—for 100 lbs of China tea to be shipped from Java. Annual imports remained in three figures until 1678, when 4,713 lbs were imported. This glutted the market for a number of years, until in 1685, 12,070 lbs were brought in, which saturated the market again. This pattern of larger and larger imports, interspersed with stagnant years of oversupply, continued until the end of the century. In 1690, 38,390 lbs of tea were imported, but in 1699 only 13,082 lbs. (p. 19)

Tea was sold in Britain at auctions. The alternate pattern of oversupply and shortage of tea made its auction price fluctuate widely. It was also heavily taxed. All of these factors affected its retail price. Records suggest that at the beginning of the second half of the seventeenth century, tea was retailed at about £3 per lb, and by the end of the century, the price was nearer £1 per lb. This confined significant consumption of tea to the wealthy because at that time a skilled craftsman would have been lucky to have made £1 a week, and a labourer, 40p.

But despite the resulting high prices, the use of tea spread from the court and the elite fashionable society to the middle class. Apart from its soothing taste, specialists in the field of medicine thought that tea was a good drink to cure colds and fluxes, which made more people try it out. In the eighteenth century, the rise in demand for tea in Britain was phenomenal. It has been difficult to identify the reason behind this. Britain took to tea with such enthusiasm that it outdid all other European nations. But legitimate taxed tea was beyond the means of most people. As a result, it now began to be smuggled into the island nation. The notorious and well-organized Hawkhurst Gang (1735–49) took extraordinary risks to procure and sell it to personal contacts, shopkeepers or hawkers. They had the tacit support of the public, which wanted to drink this wonderful beverage without having to pay a heavy tax. Organized crime took over and legitimate dealers protested loudly. The desire for cheap tea was also met by adulteration. Tea was adulterated with leaves that had already been brewed (and then dried on hotplates) or with leaves from other plants. Since these leaves did not make convincing liquor, many colouring agents were added.

The British made their tea differently from the Chinese. When tea was introduced to Britain, people mostly consumed green tea. But, by the end of the eighteenth century, black tea began selling better. Green tea was mostly adulterated with hawthorn leaves and poisonous copper dyes were used in it. This caused grave concern and the tea-loving public began switching over. Now milk began to be added to tea. Quite a few reasons are shown for this but the most plausible ones could be the taste and price of the beverage. Black tea tasted better with milk. Milk was also a cheap commodity. Since tea was a much sought-after, expensive drink, the less well-to-do section of the society would fill a good portion of the cup with milk. In contrast, the affluent would add only a splash of it to their black teas.

Moreover, the British government had colonized the Caribbean Islands in the seventeenth century so that they could set up sugar plantations there. This was because sugar was becoming a very popular commodity in Britain. By the eighteenth century, the price of sugar had dropped in Britain and all levels of society could buy the product, most of which initially went into tea. Tea, milk and sugar became a popular combination all over the nation. Initially, teaware was imported from China into Britain. But, since the British liked to drink tea piping hot, they had always found it difficult to handle the bowls. It was not until the eighteenth century, that they began making their own tea bowls with oriental scenes and motifs that were often copied from Chinese imports. It was around this time that a small matching dish was invented to hold the bowl. A century later, a handle was attached to the tea bowl. This gradually evolved into the more refined form of cup and saucer as we know it today.

Meanwhile, tea smuggling was causing severe damage to the profits of the British East India Company. Throughout Britain, people were drinking more and more tea. But official tea imports showed no sign of increase. The number of licensed tea dealers dropped significantly. The only remedy was to lower the taxes and sell legal tea at very reasonable prices. The British Parliament finally paid heed. William Pitt the Younger, who had become prime minister in 1783, decided to slash the tax on tea. The Commutation Act of 1784 reduced the tax on tea from 119 per cent to 12½ per cent. Soon, tea smuggling was a thing of the past and tea had become an everyday beverage for all levels of the society.

By the nineteenth century, tea imports in Britain grew to over thirty million pounds each year and the import duty on tea accounted for 10 per cent of the British government's entire revenue. The British also imported other exotic Chinese goods like porcelain and silk. In contrast, China was not interested in buying anything from the island nation. Moreover, it accepted only silver in trade. But, by the late eighteenth century, the British were unable to afford this silver because of the Anglo-Dutch Wars (1652–1784), which led to its severe shortage and created a chronic trade imbalance with China.

So, the British came up with an alternate strategy of counter-trading opium against Chinese tea. Opium was used by the Chinese for medicinal purposes since the seventh century, when Arab traders introduced it into the country. It was taken orally and in limited quantities to relieve stress and pain and induce sleep. But, over the years, many people got addicted to opium and began using it as a recreational drug. In the seventeenth century, the practice of smoking tobacco spread from North America to China. Smoking tobacco mixed with opium in pipes became a popular practice, increasing the demand for the narcotic drug.

Arup K. Chatterjee points out, 'To counter smuggled tea, on the one hand, and the increasing Chinese demand for silver on the other, the British responded by growing opium in India—largely in Bengal, Patna, Benares and the Malwa plateau—and smuggling it into China, in exchange for their beloved beverage.' They exported this opium and sold it to China. With the profits earned, they bought Chinese luxury goods like tea, porcelain and silk, which were in great demand in their nation. This tactic proved to be lucrative and the opium trade increased the demand among the Chinese addicts for the drug, now tilting the trade balance in favour of Britain.

But opium addiction was so severe in China that it became a

menace. The Daoguang emperor of the Qing dynasty made opium trade illegal in the country. The death sentence was advocated for addicts and ruthless action would be taken against all opium sellers, including foreign merchants. The British East India Company reacted by auctioning off its opium to small traders who smuggled it into China. In the late eighteenth and early nineteenth centuries, rampant smuggling of opium was taking place and the British East India Company became the leading supplier of the illegal drug to China, via India.

In July 1838, Imperial Commissioner Lin Tse-hsu wrote a memorial to the emperor, recommending draconian measures to be taken against dealers and smugglers. In January 1839, on being given permission, he set out on a journey from Peking (Beijing) to Canton (Guangzhou) with a small staff to deal with the situation. On reaching Canton, he ordered the foreigners to surrender all the opium in their possession, otherwise he would confiscate their property and execute some of them. Most of the opium belonged to British and Parsi firms and they agreed to surrender. Moxham informs: 'All together, 20,283 chests of opium, valued at $9 million, were dumped into the sea' (p. 69).

This made the British belligerent and they declared war, infamous in Chinese history as the Opium Wars—First Opium War (1839–42) and Second Opium War (1856–60)—in which the Qing dynasty (1644–1912) suffered a humiliating defeat. The trade treaties forced the Chinese to open up ports to the British so that they could trade in almost everything, including opium. The Treaty of Tientsin signed between Great Britain and China in 1858 in the city of Tientsin (Tianjin) during the Second Opium War legalized the import of opium.

The British East India Company now wanted to avoid future disturbances in the tea market and also bring an end to China's monopoly over tea. But long before the Opium Wars, British tea cultivators were keen to have Chinese tea and techniques brought to India. The Company ships would frequently bring the tea plants into the country in the eighteenth century. Colonel Robert Kyd of the British East India Company was interested in horticulture and in 1786, founded the botanical garden in Calcutta and experimented with transplanting Chinese tea plants in the city as early as the 1780s. Jayeeta Sharma, in her essay 'Making Garden, Erasing Jungle: The Tea Enterprise in Colonial Assam' from the book *The British Empire and the Natural World: Environmental Encounters in South Asia* (2010), mentions that Kyd's efforts were, '[...]in the spirit of the renowned botanist Sir Joseph Bank's dictum that eastern India might be a suitable habitat since the plant grew best between 26th and 30th degree latitudes' (p. 120).

But, at that point of time, the British East India Company was indifferent to these efforts because it enjoyed a profitable tea trade with China. But, when the trading monopoly of the Company got abolished in keeping with the Charter Act of 1833 (a result of the Industrial Revolution in England that ushered in the era of laissez-faire), it had to change its stance. Sharma elaborates on this:

> The abolition of this monopoly crucially served to move the quest for tea from a domain of disinterested (and thus impractical) science to that of an all-important commerce. After 1833, the pendulum swung so far that the East India Company's directors began objecting to the members of its medical corps conducting 'agricultural or horticultural experiments' or enquiring into 'matters connected with natural history'. According to them, these would not aid the cause of 'the peculiar question of the practicability of cultivating the tea-plant with a view to its manufacture as an article of commerce'. (p. 120)

Now the plan was to grow tea under the British flag, rather than importing it from China. Oriental tea was of superior quality and there were fears that the British tea would fail to find the unique soil and climatic qualities that the Chinese plant enjoyed. But these fears were gradually put to rest as botanists gathered more information. The British believed that it would be a fallacy to assume that China was the only country that could grow tea. The Japanese, Brazilians and the Burmese had cultivated tea with success. The botanist Dr Clarke Abel, who had accompanied Lord Amherst (Governor-General of India, 1823–28) to China in 1816, had made the observation that tea plants grew best on the sides of mountains. Fortunately, the Burma and Nepal wars had brought large tracts of the Himalayan foothills into the Company's hands.

Tea plants had grown wild in the jungles of upper Assam in the Northeast region of India. The locals drank an infusion of the dried leaves but it was not brewed in any particular manner. The leaves of the plant were also consumed as a green vegetable, eaten with garlic and oil. In 1595, this fact was corroborated by the Dutch traveller Jan Huygen van Linschoten in his book, *Discours of Voyages*, which had details about his adventures in the East Indies. An English edition of the book was published three years later. It was as early as 1823 that Maniram Dutta

Baruah, an Assamese nobleman and a loyal ally of the British East India Company, informed the Scottish trader Robert Bruce about the tea plant being grown and consumed by the Singpho tribe of Assam. In the same year, he guided Bruce to the Singpho chief, Bessa Gaum. The Scot took away with him samples—both seeds and plants—from the meeting and planned to have them scientifically examined. Unfortunately, he died before the experiment could happen. Just before his death in 1824, he had informed his brother, Charles Alexander Bruce, about his discovery. Since Charles was a Company soldier posted in Assam, he collected the leaves and seeds of the tea plant and dispatched them to the Company's botanical garden in Calcutta for examination. But his discovery was not taken seriously and hence, not pursued.

It was a decade after Robert Bruce's discovery, when the British monopoly on Chinese tea trade had ended, that the colonialists began to sincerely consider the idea of establishing major tea plantations in India. Lord William Bentinck, then Governor-General of India, set up the Tea Committee in 1834 with the purpose of achieving this goal. The tea plant, which was indigenous to upper Assam, was now brought to official consideration and declared a very important and valuable discovery. Most of the information about the plant was supplied by a military officer, Lieutenant Andrew Charlton, who was posted at Sadiya in upper Assam. He dispatched both the seeds and the leaves of the plant to Calcutta. On examination, the Assam tea plant was declared to be a proper *Camellia* species. A scientific delegation was sent to Assam in 1835, headed by Dr Nathaniel Wallich (superintendent of the Calcutta Botanical Garden), along with another well-known botanist, Dr William Griffith, to confirm the existence of the tea plants and thoroughly examine them once again before any decisive measure could be taken regarding their cultivation in that part of the country. They also had to assess whether the soil and climatic conditions in Assam would be suitable to set up a tea industry, which areas would be best for cultivation and whether it was necessary to import seeds from China. The members of the delegation found the region to be suitable for tea production. But, on closely examining the plant, Dr William Griffith declared it to be of a 'junglee jaat' (wild variety) with very broad and thick leaves, and hence, unsuitable for the refined British palate. The only alternative was to import seeds from China.

The British East India Company brought enough seeds from China to India for trial. These seeds were distributed widely throughout the country to see where they grew best. Since Charlton was called away to subdue a rebellion in which he was badly wounded and sent out of Assam as an invalid, Charles Alexander Bruce became a pivotal figure in Assam tea for years. In 1836, he was appointed superintendent of tea forests and given the authority of setting up plantations in the region. He planted the Chinese seeds in the experimental nurseries set up by the Company in various places in upper Assam, like Jaipur, Chabua, Chota Tingri and Hukanpukri. At Sadiya, there were two nurseries: one for Chinese tea and another for indigenous Indian tea. But the experiments with the Chinese seeds ultimately failed and were abandoned in favour of the hardier and more productive indigenous variety, identified by Joseph Robert Sealy in his book as *Camellia sinensis var. assamica*. In 1962, Dr W. Wight proposed *Camellia sinensis var. assamica* as the species of the Assamese tea plant. By 1826, Assam had fallen into the Company's hands and was made a part of the Bengal Presidency. This enabled the British to convert wastelands in the region into cultivable lands that were now used for planting and cultivating this indigenous variety of tea. Indian tea was first shipped to London in December 1838. The British were overwhelmed when a trial consignment of tea arrived at the London tea auctions in January 1839. Not only was the beverage drinkable but it also meant that they would now be able to grow their own tea. This positive feedback encouraged the production of the indigenous variety to be taken up on a commercial basis. The Assam Company, the oldest commercial tea company of Assam, was formed in England in 1839. Its headquarters was at Nazira in Assam. Charles Alexander Bruce now began working for the company. This was very essential for the company as he was the only senior employee who had a thorough knowledge about the cultivation and manufacture of tea in Assam. Large tracts of forest land were chopped down and converted into tea plantations, which were known as tea forests. In 1840, Charles Alexander Bruce, in his reports to the Assam Company, pioneered the use of the term 'garden' to describe these plantations and tea forests came to be known as tea gardens.

Initially, tea was produced in Assam with the purpose of export. The company was successful in its operations and, over the years, there was a consistent improvement in the quality of tea sent to Britain. Arani Saikia in her thesis 'Food Habits in Pre-colonial Assam' for the *International Journal of Humanities and Social Science Invention*, points out that '[...] by the mid-nineteenth century Assam was developed as an agricultural estate of tea-drinking Britain' (p. 4). The monopoly of the

Assam Company over tea cultivation and production came to an end in the early 1850s when a number of small tea estates opened up in the region. Many of these units were started by the British employees of the Assam Company. In 1859, the Jorehaut Tea Company was established in Jorhat, Assam. This company expanded its business by taking over several of the existing small tea gardens. By the end of 1859, in addition to these two companies, there were fifty other tea estates in Assam.

The white empire builders did not just concentrate on developing Assam as a tea growing region but invested their efforts in another place closer to home. This place was Darjeeling, a mountain hamlet of Sikkim, which was leased to the British East India Company in 1835 by the chogyal (monarch) of Sikkim. Under their administration, the once virtually deserted hamlet developed into a beautiful hill station. Since Darjeeling was so close to Calcutta, the administrators now abandoned far-flung hill stations and began spending their tropical summers at the place.

In 1839, Dr Archibald Campbell, a civil surgeon with the Indian Medical Service, was appointed as the first superintendent of Darjeeling. He, along with Lieutenant Robert Napier (later Lord Napier of Magdala), began working on the region and developing it into a hill station. Dr Campbell was not only a keen horticulturist who experimented with various plants in his own garden but was also the first person to experiment with tea planting in the area. In 1841, he planted seeds of the Chinese tea, which he had bought from the Kumaon region (in present-day Uttarakhand), in the first ever trial plantation near his residence at Beechwood. This experiment was very successful. Dr Joseph Hooker, the eminent British botanist, reported that these tea plants might be cultivated at great profit in the region, encouraging the British East India Company to pursue the matter seriously.

In 1845, an experimental nursery was set up by the Company and in 1847, a proper one at Lebong. In 1856, commercial cultivation of tea began in the region, inducing many British planters to settle there. In the same year, Captain Samler became the first tea planter in the region by starting the Alubari Tea Garden under the management of the Kurseong and Darjeeling Tea Company. A number of companies were formed to engage in tea plantation in Darjeeling and soon, several tea estates came up. Darjeeling Tea Company Limited, incorporated in 1864, was one of the largest tea concerns. It was located in Calcutta and had its headquarters in London. By 1891, there were 164 tea planters in Darjeeling.

Today, thanks to the British, India is the largest tea-producing country in the world after China. The British not only introduced tea plantations in Assam and Darjeeling but also initiated tea production in other regions in the northeast, north and south of India. The most distinctive variety to come out of these other regions is the highly flavourful Nilgiri tea, named after the Nilgiri Mountains in south India, where it is grown. This tea has a wonderful blend of delicate floral notes and crisp briskness. But Assam and Darjeeling teas remain the finest and most prominent of Indian teas. Today, Assam is the largest tea-producing state in India and is renowned for its quality of tea. Assam tea is a full-bodied variety with a bright colour, strong brew and malty flavour. It is harvested twice, in 'first flush' and 'second flush'. Its second flush variety, also known as 'tippy tea' because of the gold tips that appear on the leaves, is the more popular one. In contrast, Darjeeling tea is thin-bodied and light coloured with a rare taste. Some of its second flush varieties have a distinct flavour, which is described as 'muscatel' by the tea industry. The exclusivity of Darjeeling tea lends it the sobriquet, 'Champagne of Teas'. To fully savour its unique flavour, it is advised to drink Darjeeling tea without milk.

The growing British consumption of Indian tea encouraged constant expansion in the industry. The number of plantations increased. By 1888, the export of tea from Assam, Darjeeling and other mountain regions to Britain surpassed that of China. Arup K. Chatterjee writes, 'By 1888, Indian tea exports into Britain were over 86 million pounds, exceeding China's 80 million pounds.' Author Erika Rappaport mentions in her book, *A Thirst for Empire: How Tea Shaped the Modern World* (2017) that the virtues of Indian tea were extolled in Victorian London to highlight China's backwardness and deceit. Large volumes of adulterated Chinese tea were seized by the Customs and thrown into the Thames. In contrast, Indian teas were advertised to be more wholesome and aromatic than Chinese teas. They were declared to be purer, stronger, cheaper and better in every respect. The Darjeeling and Assam varieties were packed in ostentatious wooden boxes and sold by tea stores in London.

Back in India, the British government's decision to introduce tea to the Indian consumer came much later. Philip Lutgendorf, in his essay 'Making tea in India: Chai, capitalism, culture', for the academic journal *Thesis Eleven: Critical Theory and Historical Sociology*, 113(1): 11–31, (December 2012) writes,

> The tea[…] was intended solely for export to the West, though it passed through the port and (after 1861) the auction market of Calcutta, where a tiny fraction of the native population—principally the Anglophile *bhadralok* elite as well as 'office babus' employed by British firms—began to partake of the foreign beverage, produced by steeping in china pots and usually supplemented by hot milk (considered essential to reduce the 'bite' of the strong-liquoring Assam leaves) and sugar. (p. 13)

However, the fluctuating auction prices at London and the inherent difficulties of long-distance transport would occasionally make the planters and officials of the British East India Company muse over the possibility of a domestic market for the product. In 1901, Viceroy Curzon commissioned an experiment to introduce tea to Indians in select areas. But, despite modest success, the effort was abandoned in 1904. The Indian Tea Association, founded in 1881, mentioned in its annual report that despite three years of effort, the results were not good enough to indicate a promising market in India. An already well-established cultural preference for other traditional beverages like sharbats made the general public baulk at the prospect of trying it out.

Lutgendorf further mentions, 'Advertising during the first three decades of the twentieth century […] was largely aimed at resident Britishers and the Anglophone elite who aspired to their lifestyle. It celebrated tea as a natural product of a colonized and "tamed" jungle, raised in geometrically arrayed and manicured "gardens" and picked by dark-skinned, subaltern women, who offered it at a gleaming white table to equally white consumers […]' (pp. 13–14). As long as the financial returns from the exports were profitable, there was little inducement to pursue a domestic market that would inevitably yield a lower return.

Viceroy Curzon introduced the Tea Cess Bill in 1903 to tax the Indian tea trade, raise a fund and promote marketing. The Tea Cess Committee made sporadic and small-scale attempts in select public venues to promote tea. The first and most important place where these experiments were conducted was the Indian Railways. Not only were free cups of prepared tea distributed to the public at the Howrah railway station in Calcutta, but paper packets of tea (of such quality that would not find favour at auctions) were sold to them for one pice (a monetary unit of very low denomination in British India). The British method of brewing tea—by pouring boiled water onto the tea leaves in a china teapot, straining the liquid into a teacup after it had brewed, and adding some milk and sugar to it—was also demonstrated to the public in the tea stalls set up at the railway station at Howrah. Despite these efforts, by 1930, only a small fraction of the Indian population had developed an affinity for tea and more than 90 per cent of the crop continued to be exported.

It was only with the onset of the Great Depression, which began in 1929, that the domestic market suddenly began to seem more appealing. International tea prices dropped sharply in the early 1930s. By 1935, planters were faced with the problem of unsold, surplus tea of more than a hundred million pounds. Around this time, the Tea Cess Committee was reorganized as the Indian Tea Market Expansion Board, a precursor to the present Tea Board of India. Armed with an expanded budget, it embarked upon the largest and most aggressive marketing campaign in the history of the Indian tea industry. Lutgendorf, detailing the campaign, writes, '[…] "tea propagandists" were now dispatched in the hundreds, sometimes in motorized "tea vans", equipped to dispense millions of cups of free tea and comparable numbers of "pice packets", and to display colourful, vernacular-language signage produced by leading commercial artists' (p. 15).

Enamel placards were put up at railway stations, markets and festivals that not only advertised tea and its health benefits but also gave detailed instructions on the correct British method of brewing it. Demonstration teams were also present at these places for the same purpose. In the 1930s and 1940s, vehicles decorated with large kettles travelled to the urban and semi-urban areas of Bengal to advertise tea and demonstrate its method of preparation. Tea was now touted as a medium for women's awakening. It was advertised as a progressive and empowering tool for smart, modern homemakers, who understood the importance of good nutrition and domestic hygiene. The Indian Tea Market Expansion Board urged factory owners and office managers to offer afternoon tea breaks to workers that would result in a more alert and productive workforce. Keeping in tune with the spirit of the Independence movement, tea was now championed as India's national beverage that unified the country's diverse religious, linguistic and caste groups.

This campaign created tremendous awareness among the public about tea. The marketing strategy of offering free samples of prepared tea and low-priced single-use packages was so successful that it was adopted by private tea companies like Brooke Bond, Lipton and A. Tosh & Sons. Brooke Bond (founded in England in 1869 by Arthur Brooke) and Lipton (a British firm founded by Sir Thomas Johnstone Lipton that ventured into tea business in 1888) were the two foreign companies, which dominated the tea trade in India in the twentieth century. Brooke Bond carts would travel around Calcutta and make free tea for those who were interested in trying out the beverage. Free samples of packaged tea were also distributed by these two companies in the villages. Indian firms like A. Tosh & Sons (founded in Calcutta in 1897 by Ashutosh Ghosh and his eldest son, Prabhash Chandra Ghosh) capitalized on the 'Be Indian, Buy Indian!' sentiment and marketed their tea as a swadeshi product.

Unsurprisingly, with so much advertisement, drinking tea caught on with the locals of the city. Bengalis began calling it 'cha'. On witnessing this growth in tea consumption, many local entrepreneurs ventured into the business of selling tea leaves. Inspired by the British, local vendors, armed with stoves and kettles, began selling tea on the platforms of the historic railway station at Howrah and even on the roadsides, serving the beverage in small glass tumblers. However, the majority of the locals made tea by boiling the leaves with milk, sugar and spices like pounded ginger or crushed green cardamom pods. The quantity of milk used in the preparation was far more than the British could have ever imagined. It has been difficult to trace the source from which this method of tea-making originated—whether it was the roadside or the railway platform tea vendor or the overburdened homemaker. But it horrified the British because they had failed to teach the Indians how to make the beverage the 'correct way'.

It was only the city elite who made tea the British way and the variety that was preferred for this method was the 'Champagne of Teas'. Since Darjeeling tea is a light-coloured and thin-bodied variety that is best taken without milk, it made no sense to boil it with milk, sugar and spices. It is too fine and upscale in quality, flavour and aroma to be treated in that manner. In contrast, Assam tea is a robust and full-bodied variety that is too strong to be taken without milk. The prices of these teas are also another very important factor that determined the customer base. Compared to Assam tea, the Darjeeling variety is difficult to grow. The soil and climatic conditions, and the high altitude in which it is grown, give it a lot of flavour but make its growth slow. Darjeeling tea also has a shorter harvesting season and is produced in smaller quantities. All of these factors, along with the fact that it is better in quality, have made it the more expensive one. In contrast, Assam tea has always been more accessible price-wise and the preferred variety for most who make tea the Indian way. In 1903, Brooke Bond launched Red Label in India, which is still a popular brand of Assam tea.

Dust tea, the lowest grade of tea, is the fine powder or extremely small particles that are left over from processing Assam tea. This grade of tea was preferred by the roadside or railway platform vendors because not only was it inexpensive but also worked best when boiled. It was a wise strategy for tea companies to market this grade of tea, keeping in mind the Indian habit of boiling tea. Its low price also helped in reaching out to homes of low-income groups. Brooke Bond's Kora Dust was the first brand in this grade of tea to be introduced into the market. Sold in paper packets, it was marketed aggressively by the company, particularly from the 1930s, mostly in smaller municipalities and rural areas.

Bengalis began to have the beverage at all hours and for most, the day began with a cup. Tea, infused with the juice of ginger, now turned into a home-made remedy to give some relief when feeling under the weather with a cough, cold or sore throat. Bengalis also began emulating their colonial masters by taking the beverage at 4 p.m., often accompanied with biscuits. This daily ritual, known as 'bikel chaar-ter cha', grew in popularity all over Bengal, cutting across the different levels of society. It became as important a ritual for the Bengalis as it was for the British.

Bengalis also had their own version of afternoon tea, which was known as 'jalkhabar'. The concept of afternoon tea was first introduced in England by Anna Maria Russell, the duchess of Bedford, before becoming widespread in Britain. Dinner at her home was served fashionably late at 8 p.m. This long gap between lunch and dinner made her feel hungry. One day, sometime in the early 1840s, while at Woburn Abbey, which is the country estate and family seat of the duke of Bedford, the duchess, in an attempt to quell her hunger pangs, ordered her maid to bring her a pot of tea at 4 p.m. with accompaniments like bread and butter, and cakes. This developed into a daily ritual and soon, she decided to invite her friends over, who were equally enthusiastic about the idea. Thus, a new social event called 'afternoon tea' was born.

The duchess, a prominent figure in London's aristocratic society, was a lifelong friend and lady-in-waiting to Queen Victoria. On returning to London, she introduced the concept to the queen, who took an instant liking to it, and also began taking tea in the afternoons with slices of a cake, which came to be famously known as the Victoria Sandwich. Named after the queen, this circular-shaped cake was made of eggs, butter, refined flour and sugar. A layer of jam was spread over one half of the cake and the other half was placed over it. Served in slices, this basic cake, which was a favourite of the queen, evolved into the Victoria Sponge as we know it today.

Thus, Queen Victoria became an influential supporter. This royal endorsement made the trend popular and afternoon tea became a fashionable event for the elite and upper class women, who turned it into an elaborate affair that now extended from the afternoon to the evening and included accompaniments like delicate sandwiches, cakes and sweet pastries. Gradually, this practice spread throughout England and the rest of Britain. Scones, served with strawberry jam and clotted cream, which are today essential to the afternoon tea spread, were introduced in the twentieth century.

The concept of jalkhabar always existed among Bengalis who have the habit of eating their dinner very late in the evening. To fill the gap between lunch and dinner, they would have jalkhabar or snacks early in the evening. These snacks included local varieties of savouries and sweets. When tea became popular, it was often served with jalkhabar. Thus, both the concepts of bikel chaar-ter cha and jalkhabar are prevalent in Bengali society.

While writing about the evolution of tea in India, with a special focus on the eastern part of the country, it becomes necessary to mention a manufacturing process that revolutionized the Indian tea industry. Tea leaves that were further broken down into smaller particles could be brewed rapidly. This led to a growing preference among consumers for this type of tea.

So, in 1930, Sir William McKercher, a Scottish engineer, who was the superintendent of the Amgoorie Tea Estate in Assam, invented a machine to 'crush, tear and curl' (or, more accurately, as the machine developed, to 'cut, tear and curl') the large Assam leaf into tiny fragments, using serrated stainless steel rollers. He had been experimenting with leaf-crushing machines at Amgoorie for quite a few years prior to his invention. This new method was in contrast to the orthodox one in which the whole leaf was lightly rolled to break down its cellular structure. The device came to be known as the 'CTC' machine. Tea manufactured by this machine also produced stronger liquor. However, it was hardly used by planters for the next three decades because it was cumbersome, expensive to operate and prone to breakdowns.

According to Lutgendorf, it was in the late 1950s that Indian engineers of the Calcutta-based Small Tools Manufacturing Company redesigned McKercher's CTC machine, overcoming the flaws that had led to its failure. Although this new design was patented by the company, it was quickly pirated by other firms. Over the next two decades, the orthodox method of manufacturing Assam tea steadily declined and was gradually replaced by the CTC method. Soon, 'CTC tea' became synonymous with Assam tea and was available in a range of particle sizes, from rice-sized nuggets to dust.

Over the years, black tea, commonly known as *liquor cha* in Bengal, has become popular. The Anglophiles or brown sahibs often add a slice of lime or 'lebu' to black tea. In contrast, black tea flavoured with lime juice, a special spice mix, sugar and very little rock salt or 'bitnoon' has become the favourite of Bengalis. This version, known as *lebu cha*, is mostly sold by vendors.

Cha also became an indispensable part of the Bengali adda culture. An adda can be best described as a lengthy conversation between two or more persons that is casual in nature. It can take place at home or a public venue. When tea became popular, the adda became incomplete without it. Bengalis, spending hours, discussing everything under the sun, over countless cups of tea, became a common sight all over Bengal.

Cashing in on the popular combination of cha and the adda, small restaurants that served tea and snacks began opening up. These restaurants became popular with the public. Families, friends, students, professionals and people from different walks of life began taking breaks from their routine lives and met at these restaurants to engage in some engrossing adda over tea and good food.

It was a common feature for many of these restaurants to have plywood-partitioned, curtained cabins in which families could dine in privacy. Some of the restaurants, which had this arrangement, had the word 'cabin' attached to their names. Gradually, the word 'cabin' came to be loosely associated with small restaurants.

Even today, it is a common sight in Calcutta to come across people, whether young, middle-aged or old, huddled together in restaurants or other public venues, discussing politics or scandals over cups of steaming tea. So, the Bengalis owe their craze for tea to the British, who have successfully managed to convert them into a community of passionate tea-drinkers. Just like their erstwhile colonial masters, Bengalis now simply need an excuse to drink the beverage.

Favourite Cabin: The first tea shop to come up in the city was Favourite Cabin on Surya Sen Street. Gour Chandra and Nutan Chandra Barua were brothers who lived in a small village in the district of Chittagong. After a serious outbreak of cholera killed their parents, Gour left for Calcutta in search of a job. He found one in Sangu Valley, a popular restaurant in Wellington Square. Established around 1915, this was the first branch of the Sangu Valley chain of restaurants in Calcutta. Gour began working there as a cabin boy (a term used in those days for waiters). It was then that the idea came to him: of opening a tea shop that would also serve accompaniments like biscuits, confectioneries and well-done toasts. At that point of time, such a notion was uncommon. But Gour Chandra Barua had great faith in his idea. He wanted to capitalize on the growing visibility of the beverage and decided to take the risk.

Favourite Cabin was set up on Vivekananda Road and Chitpur Road crossing by Gour Chandra Barua. Nutan Chandra Barua joined his brother in Calcutta a few years later. Another branch of Favourite Cabin was opened in 1924 on what is now Surya Sen Street. The untimely death of Gour Chandra Barua led to the closing down of the first Favourite Cabin because Nutan found it difficult to manage the two places at the same time. The Favourite Cabin on Surya Sen Street continued functioning, withstanding stormy political changes and the passage of time, to become the favourite tea hub of the residents of central Calcutta.

Customers found the serving of tea with 'Ingrej ishtyle' accompaniments like biscuits, bakery cakes, plum cakes, hard cakes, chocolate cakes and Swiss rolls quite exciting and sophisticated. The menu also offered some familiar local favourites to make them feel at home: crunchy buttered toast, either sprinkled with granules of sugar or dusted with pepper. The word spread and Favourite Cabin became inundated with customers.

Favourite Cabin soon turned into a popular hub for freedom fighters. Having 'garom cha' in the quaint atmosphere of the tea shop and discussing politics became a habit for revolutionaries like Lokenath Bal, Ganesh Ghosh, Ambika Chakrabarty and Kalpana Datta. Netaji Subhas Chandra Bose was a regular at the tea shop when he was a student of the nearby Presidency College. The solitary Table Number Four next to the window is revered even now as the place where he and the renowned poet, Kazi Nazrul Islam, would sit and sip cha for the price of two paise. It was the poet's favourite spot in the tea shop and Netaji would be the audience for his poems and songs. Surya Sen, who became infamous to the British government when he raided their armoury in Chittagong on 18 April 1930, also visited Favourite Cabin a few times. Mirzapur Street, which houses Favourite Cabin, was rechristened Surya Sen Street after Independence.

The tea shop was also the meeting place for the members of the Kallol literary circle. *Kallol* was a literary magazine that began publishing in 1923 and lasted for only six years. But within that short period of time, it turned into a powerful literary force that created a major impact in Bengali literature. The name is also used to refer to the group of fiery young intellectuals who regularly contributed to the magazine. Many from this group of talented young authors went on to become major figures in Bengali literature in the future. Kallol had renowned authors like Achintya Kumar Sengupta, Kazi Nazrul Islam, Buddhadeb Basu, Jibanananda Das and Premendra Mitra as members. In his 1937 memoir of those times, titled *Kallol Yug* (The Kallol Era), Achintya Kumar Sengupta has mentioned that Kallol would have been incomplete without Favourite Cabin because it was the daily haunt of the group. They would spend hours at the tea shop on Mirzapur Street, sitting in a circle around the marble-top tables, discussing and debating various topics.

The room facing the entrance was used by the general public. Nutan Chandra Barua always occupied the seat at the cash counter near the entrance, in order to keep a lookout on behalf of the revolutionaries, who often came in disguise. The innermost room closest to the kitchen was perpetually occupied by freedom fighters. The middle room next to that was usually haunted by litterateurs and journalists. Whenever Barua got a whiff of the police, he would signal in a code language and the men in the innermost room would escape from the back door. Not a single freedom fighter was ever caught at Favourite Cabin.

The tea shop was a trendsetter during the Raj and continued doing brisk business even after the British left the country. It has never seen a fall in customers. Today, it is renowned throughout the city for its historical importance. On walking into the tea shop, one sees walls with peeling paint and rickety tables where customers peruse newspapers like *The Statesman* and *Anandabazar Patrika*. The owners believe that drinking tea goes well with the reading habit. The appetizing aroma of baked bread floats through the air. The history of the place and its relaxed atmosphere make customers want to return to it time and again to banter over 'the cup that cheers but not inebriates'.

Coffee

With the tremendous popularity enjoyed by tea in the Bengali community, there seemed to be no room for any other beverage to make an entry in the market. That is, not until the British started making concerted efforts to promote coffee in the twentieth century.

Unlike its more popular counterpart, coffee was not indigenous to India. The history behind its discovery is an ambiguous one. Although there are many legendary stories, historians have found it difficult to choose a single one because they are unsure of their veracity. The one that is most popular is that the coffee cherry was chanced upon Kaldi, a goatherd in Ethiopia, formerly known as Abyssinia. Although many estimate that the event took place in 850 CE, no one is exactly sure about the date. One day, while herding his goats in the forests, Kaldi observed that on eating the bright red berries of a certain tree, the animals became so energetic that they had difficulty sleeping that night. He then sampled some of these berries and felt their energizing effects. The excited goatherd took them to the nearest mosque and showed them to the Islamic priests, recounting his experience.

But the chief priest did not approve of Kaldi's discovery. He condemned the berries as the work of the Devil and threw them into the fire where they began getting roasted. This was the world's first roasted coffee. A wonderful smell emanated from the seeds, also known as beans, within the roasted berries. This aroma of fresh roasted coffee beans filled the mosque, tempting the priests to ground them and then dissolve the powder in boiled water, creating the world's first prepared coffee. On consumption, the priests realized that the drink kept them awake and alert through the long hours of evening prayers. The news about the aromatic and energizing coffee cherry now began to spread. Although the veracity of this story is doubted, it is a fact that the coffee plant is native to Ethiopia, where it grew wild. There is a strong possibility that around the time this legendary story takes place, Ethiopians had discovered the stimulating effect of coffee cherries and began consuming them as a drink.

Within a century, coffee entered the Middle East. But no one is really sure how it happened. There are hints that Islamic priests would consume it as a drink. However, there is evidence of written materials by learned men from the Islamic world extolling the virtues of coffee. Many scholars are of the opinion that the first person to mention the properties of coffee beans was the Persian polymath, Abu Bakr Muhammad ibn

Zakariya al-Razi (865 CE–925 CE), or simply Rhazes (as he is known in Latin), in his most important medical work compiled posthumously, *Kitab al-Hawi fi al-tibb* (The Comprehensive Book on Medicine). In this multivolume medical encyclopaedia, which was translated into Latin in 1279 CE, he wrote that coffee had hot and dry properties, and was very good for the stomach. He used the Arabic words 'bunn' and 'buncham' to describe the plant and the beverage respectively. The Persian physician and philosopher, Abu Ali al-Husayn ibn Abd Allah ibn Sina (980 CE–1037 CE), popularly known in the Western countries as Avicenna, describes the unique effects of coffee in his multivolume encyclopaedic book, *al-Qanun fi al-tibb* (The Canon of Medicine), published in 1025 CE and considered to be an authoritative piece of work on medicine for centuries. He is known to have prescribed coffee as a medicine because he was of the opinion that it revived the body and imparted an excellent smell to it. He also believed that coffee cleaned the skin and dried the humidity under it. Like Rhazes, he uses the words 'bunn' and 'buncham' in his text.

After these two medical texts, history becomes silent on coffee. It is believed that a few centuries later, Yemeni traders, on their return from Ethiopia, brought coffee seeds to their homeland. The Sufi priests in Yemen would grow the coffee plants in their gardens. They would make a form of wine from the pulp of the fermented coffee cherries, which they called qishr. However, the first evidence of the drink, as it is made today, was found in the fifteenth century. It is not known who first invented it or where it was invented. But there is enough evidence to indicate that the Sufi priests in Yemen would drink the beverage to stay awake for their night devotions, calling it qahwah and turning it into a useful prayer aid. Therefore, Yemen can be regarded as the first place in the world where coffee cultivation began. From a religious aid, it soon turned into a popular drink in the country, giving rise to a flourishing industry. Since the Quran, the central religious text of Islam, forbids the consumption of intoxicants like alcohol, coffee was looked upon as a stimulant by all those Yemenis who were enamoured by the drink.

Within a century, coffee consumption spread from Yemen, across the Arabian Peninsula and into the rest of the Middle East. People, in both the North African and Middle Eastern regions, were drinking coffee, which was sourced from the Yemeni port city of Mocha. The name, 'Caffe Mocha', which is used by coffee shops across the world today for a certain preparation of coffee, is derived from this port city. The Yemenis were very protective of their coffee industry. Sale or trade of raw and fertile coffee beans to foreign lands was prohibited. Only roasted coffee beans would be shipped.

Coffee lovers not only enjoyed drinking the beverage in their homes but also in public coffee houses. Coffee houses first came up in the Islamic holy city of Mecca (in modern-day Saudi Arabia) and from there, the concept spread to the rest of the Middle East. It is difficult to identify exactly when they began coming up but by the early sixteenth century, they were commonplace in Mecca. At these comfortably furnished coffee houses, men from different strata of society would meet and engage in discussions and debates, read, watch performances and play chess. It was a public venue where they could mingle and exchange ideas, and even conduct business, over plentiful cups of the beverage. Although, throughout the sixteenth century, coffee continued to gain popularity in the Middle East, there were mixed reactions to the beverage and not everyone approved of it. This was particularly true for the orthodox Imams, the worship leaders of mosques, who frowned upon its stimulating effects, which came from the chemical substance called caffeine found inside the plant. The coffee houses also became a bone of contention for the Muslim orthodoxy because social taboos like prostitution and astrology were allowed in them. They became centres of political activity, where political sentiments were expressed freely and this disturbed the rulers. This led to both the beverage and coffee houses being banned in many places on several occasions. But coffee had many supporters, including powerful leaders like Suleiman I, the sultan of the Ottoman Empire, who enjoyed drinking the beverage. These powerful men lifted many of the bans and advocated the acceptance of coffee in Islam.

Coffee consumption remained confined to the African and Islamic world in the first half of the sixteenth century. Europeans had their first encounter with coffee in Malta. The Great Siege of Malta took place in 1565 CE when the Ottoman Empire tried to invade the island of Malta, which was then held by the Knights Hospitaller (a medieval and early modern Catholic military order). The victorious Knights, who had successfully resisted the Ottoman Turks, found some of the captured slaves preparing coffee and tried out the drink themselves. In 1573 CE, when the German physician, botanist and traveller, Leonhard Rauwolf, was in Aleppo (in present-day Syria), he described coffee in his travel book as a drink that was as black as ink and praised its usefulness as a remedy for diseases, particularly those of the stomach. But it was only during the last two decades of the sixteenth century that coffee found its way into mainland Europe through the Venetian merchants when they increased their trade with the Muslim world. Europeans now began drinking coffee and many took a liking to the beverage. But most of the orthodox Christians disapproved of it and called it a bitter drink of Satan.

This controversy lasted till 1600 CE, when Pope Clement VIII, whose reign was marked by a long-drawn conflict with the Ottoman Empire, became the first pope to drink the beverage. Although, he was pressurized by his advisors to denounce coffee, he declared that it would be a pity to let go of it because he found it to be very delicious. He is believed to have blessed the coffee bean and declared the beverage to be a Christian drink. The pope genuinely believed that coffee would be better for people than alcoholic beverages. After this, coffee became a very sought-after commodity in Europe. Although in the early part of the seventeenth century, coffee was imported into Europe mainly through the Venetian merchants, later, the trading companies focussed on importing it from the Arab countries. In Europe, the first coffee houses appeared in Venice in the early part of the seventeenth century, followed by many more across the continent. The oldest recorded coffee house in Venice was set up in 1645 CE.

Although the Yemenis had always tried to safeguard their coffee production, they could not protect it forever. Several attempts were made to break Yemen's monopoly over the commodity by smuggling coffee plants or raw and fertile coffee beans out of the country. But all of these attempts failed. The myth that coffee could not be grown outside Yemen was broken by the Dutch. In 1616 CE, the Dutch cloth merchant Pieter van den Broecke, who was in the service of the Dutch East India Company, successfully smuggled coffee plants from Mocha to the Netherlands. He took them to Amsterdam, where they began to thrive in greenhouses, and produced healthy coffee bushes. The coffee plant grows well in tropical and equatorial regions. In 1658 CE, the Dutch began coffee cultivation in Dutch Ceylon (Sri Lanka) and later, in Dutch Malabar in southern India. In 1699 CE, they sent a shipment of seedlings from the Malabar region to their colony in Batavia (now known as Jakarta), located in the northwestern coast of Java, an island in Indonesia. They successfully set up coffee plantations from these seedlings in the region. Thus, Yemen's monopoly over coffee production was finally broken. The Dutch began trading coffee across Europe in the eighteenth century. Their coffee production in Java was so successful that over half of the coffee consumed in Europe came from the island. This eventually earned coffee the nickname of 'java'.

One of the highlights of Europe in the eighteenth century was the Age of Enlightenment, an intellectual and philosophical movement that took place in the continent. Many of the Enlightenment thinkers met at the coffee houses to discuss burning issues like social, political and religious reforms over cups of coffee. Coffee became synonymous with the intelligentsia. The French Enlightenment writer, philosopher and historian, Voltaire, was an extreme coffee addict. It is believed that he drank fifty to eighty cups of coffee in a day. The European monarchs would make many attempts to curb rebellious and seditious talks and activities during this period. King Charles II of England, particularly, made coffee houses his target because he felt that they were political in nature and provided the perfect platform for plotting treason and sedition. On December 1675 CE, he passed a proclamation banning coffee houses and coffee. But many of his ministers overturned the ban on January 1676 CE because they were coffee lovers themselves.

Coffee was introduced to the Americas in 1723 CE by the French naval officer, Gabriel de Clieu. In 1714 CE, the mayor of Amsterdam had gifted King Louis XIV coffee plants from Hortus Botanicus, the botanical garden in Amsterdam. The plants were grown and propagated in a greenhouse in Jardin des Plantes, the oldest botanical garden in Paris. These were the only known coffee plants in France at that time. It is believed that de Clieu managed to steal seedlings from these plants and transport them across the Atlantic Ocean to the Caribbean island of Martinique, which was then a French colony. This led to an abundance of coffee trees on the island within a decade. The success of the coffee plantations in Martinique encouraged other French islands to take cuttings or seedlings from them. Coffee plantations gradually spread to the rest of the Caribbean islands, South America and Central America.

Tea was the popular drink of the North Americans till the American War of Independence (1775 CE–83 CE) took place. Ironically, tea acted as a catalyst in this war because the taxes on the commodity had become a bone of contention between Britain and its North American colonies. The Boston Tea Party was a political and mercantile protest against this taxation policy of the British Parliament. A large group of men, belonging to a secret political organization of patriots called the Sons of Liberty, boarded three docked ships in Griffin's Wharf in Boston Harbour on the night of 16 December 1773 CE and threw 342 chests of British East India Company tea into the water. This incident, which became famous in history as the Boston Tea Party, was the first major act of defiance by the colonists against the British rule. Tea now became a symbol of British subjugation. The Boston Tea Party was a symbolic rejection of that subjugation. It was an event of utmost significance that played an important role in setting the stage for the revolutionary war that was fought between Britain and its Thirteen Colonies in North America.

In these circumstances, switching to coffee became a patriotic duty of the Americans. But it was in short supply, making it an expensive drink. Hence, its consumption was confined only to the nobility and the wealthy. It is here that Brazilian coffee steps in. Brazil had been a colony of Portugal from the early sixteenth to the early nineteenth centuries. It was the Portuguese who wanted to begin a coffee industry in the country but could not obtain seeds from the neighbouring French Guiana because its Governor, Claude Guillouet d'Orvilliers, was not willing to share them. Brazilian coffee, which would grow to become a billion dollar industry in the future, owes its existence to a romantic liaison that took place in French Guiana. Legend has it that in 1727 CE, the Brazilian army officer Francisco de Melo Palheta, was sent on a diplomatic mission to French Guiana to resolve a border dispute. He was also given another secret order, which was to obtain a few of the closely guarded coffee seeds. On arriving in French Guiana, the handsome and suave Palheta set his eyes on Madame d'Orvilliers, the Governor's wife, who was captivated by his good looks. His amorous exploits paid off and in the closing banquet, she gave him a large bouquet of flowers, inside of which were buried a few coffee seedlings. These seedlings laid the foundation of the hugely successful Brazilian coffee industry.

Coffee was initially produced in Brazil for domestic consumption. But, when the demand for it began to rise in America and Europe in the early nineteenth century, it led to an expansion of plantations in the country. Coffee now became Brazil's largest export. By 1840, production in the country had increased so much that it became the largest coffee-producing nation in the world. The surplus production made the commodity more accessible price-wise. Coffee now became the popular choice in America because Brazil had made it a beverage of the masses.

In 1737 CE, the eminent Swedish botanist Carl Linnaeus proposed the genus *Coffea* for the coffee plant. The two main species of the plant that are traded commercially are *Coffea arabica*, a name bestowed by Linnaeus, and *Coffea canephora var. robusta*, which was discovered in the second half of the nineteenth century. The coffee beans, which crossed the Red Sea, from Ethiopia to Yemen, took on the name 'Arabica'. The source of the Arabica beans is the *Coffea arabica* plant. Today, Arabica is the dominant bean, accounting for nearly 80 per cent of the world's coffee production. It is of better quality, more aromatic and sweeter, with just a mild hint of bitterness. It has a slight and pleasant acidity. The source of the Robusta beans is the *Coffea canephora* plant, an inferior variety that is grown at lower elevations. It is a hardier plant, which is easy to grow and maintain. It produces a higher yield and is more disease resistant. The bean has a higher amount of caffeine and a more astringent flavour. Moreover, since its production cost is cheaper, it is the preferred variety of large commercial companies and used mostly to make instant coffee and espresso. In contrast, Arabica is largely used in gourmet coffee shops. Presently, Brazil is the leading producer of Arabica coffee while Vietnam, of the Robusta variety.

In the denouement on the history of world coffee, it is important to mention the introduction of milk and sugar into the beverage. The Arabs drank unsweetened black coffee. Sugar was first added to coffee around 1625 CE by the Egyptians. It is also believed that in the aftermath of the Battle of Vienna, which took place in 1683 CE, milk began to be added to coffee. The battle was the second failed attempt by the Ottoman Empire to capture the imperial city of Vienna. The legendary story connected with this battle is that the residents of Vienna discovered bags of coffee, which were left behind in the abandoned encampment by the retreating Ottoman Turks. These supplies were used to open Vienna's first coffee house, in 1683 CE, by the merchant Jerzy Franciszek Kulczycki. He is not only credited for introducing coffee consumption in Vienna but also for changing the way the world drank coffee. Austrians found the taste of black coffee too bitter. So, Kulczycki began adding both milk and honey to coffee with the hope that it would lure customers away from beer and wine. Although no one is quite sure about the veracity of this story, it is a fact that by the eighteenth century, Europeans were drinking coffee with milk and sugar.

This brings us to the conclusion of the fascinating story of coffee, a drink that has travelled between countries, taking on different names along the way like the Arabic qahwah, the Turkish kahveh, the Italian caffe, the Dutch koffie, the French café, and finally, the English coffee, to become a sought-after beverage.

The Story of Indian Coffee

Besides the Dutch cloth merchant, Pieter van den Broecke, there was another person who was successful in smuggling coffee out of Yemen. This person was the Indian Sufi saint, Baba Budan, and it is with him that the story of Indian coffee begins. The event takes place sometime in the seventeenth century, although it is difficult to identify the exact year when it happened.

Baba Budan, as he was popularly known, lived in Chikmagalur (now in Karnataka) in southern India and was revered by both the Hindus and the Muslims. Legend has it that on his return from the Hajj in Mecca, he had to travel through Mocha, where he tasted qahwah and enjoyed it tremendously. Keen to experiment with growing coffee himself, Baba Budan secretly brought back seven (a sacred number in Islam) raw and fertile coffee beans by strapping them across his chest, hidden underneath his long flowing robes. He planted them in the courtyard of his hermitage, on the hills of Chikmagalur, where the plants remained a garden curiosity for a considerable period of time. Gradually, the locals of the area, intrigued by the coffee plant, began growing it as a backyard planting. This area, now known as Baba Budangiri (Baba Budan Hills), has become famous as the birthplace of Indian coffee and houses the shrine of the saint.

The coffee plant remained confined to backyard planting till the Dutch and the British stepped in. Coffee plantations in India began with the Dutch East India Company, when, in the second half of the seventeenth century, they chose to grow coffee in the Malabar region in southern India. But this attempt was not very successful. The credit for commercializing coffee production in India goes to the British entrepreneurs, who appeared on the scene in the eighteenth century and found that the climatic conditions in the hilly regions of south India were ideal for the cultivation of the Arabica crop. They began conquering the hostile forest terrain and setting up coffee plantations mainly with the objective of export. The first commercial venture was successful, which led to more British entrepreneurs taking to the coffee plantation business. This eventually resulted in the proliferation of coffee plantations across the region. The coffee produced was mainly exported for British and European consumption.

However, the domestic consumption of coffee was not to be left behind. The British in India not only took the beverage in the privacy of their homes, but, by the middle of the nineteenth century, they were being served coffee in many of the upscale British clubs and other establishments that had come up in India. The British, particularly, enjoyed drinking their after-dinner coffee, served strong and black, and sometimes sweetened, in beautifully decorated demitasse cups that were placed on matching saucers. A local market for the Indians was also developing around this time. Since coffee plantations had spread across south India, it is obvious that the locals of the region were among the first Indians to enjoy the beverage. By the end of the nineteenth century, coffee began to enter the urban middle-class south Indian households. They would prepare the beverage by boiling the coffee powder with water, milk and sugar. But it was still a rare commodity in north India, where, in comparison to tea, it was a novelty to the majority of the urban middle-class households.

Initially, it was *Coffea arabica* that was popularly cultivated. But a serious infestation to this species caused by coffee rust (a foliar disease of coffee plants caused by fungus) led to *Coffea canephora var. robusta* being introduced to the plantations at the close of the nineteenth century.

However, the industry suffered a huge setback during the Great Depression. The world market had shrunk, leaving the coffee estates with unsold surplus production. There was also a great slump in the price of coffee. The Indian coffee industry was on the verge of ruin. Estate owners found coffee cultivation to be a losing proposition and many abandoned their plantations. The coffee producers approached the Government of India for the protection of their interests. The government stepped in by passing the Indian Coffee Cess Act, 1935 (XIV of 1935) and setting up the first Indian Coffee Cess Committee in November 1935. The task of this Coffee Cess Committee was to promote the sale and consumption of Indian coffee in India and abroad. The committee started the Indian Coffee House chain for this purpose, opening the first outlet in 1936 in Churchgate in Bombay, and another one soon after, in Hyderabad. By launching the coffee houses, the committee aimed at creating a market for coffee at home. This chain, run by the Government of India, soon began to garner popularity and played an important role in spreading coffee drinking from south India to the rest of the country.

But once again, the coffee industry in India went through a financial crisis during the Second World War (1 September 1939–2 September 1945). The Coffee Cess Committee could not deal with the problem effectively. This time, to retrieve the situation, the Coffee Board of India was set up by an Act of the British Parliament (Coffee Act VII of 1942) in 1942. The Coffee Board of India was placed under the administrative control of the ministry of commerce and industry. The main objective of the Board was to promote the sale and consumption of Indian coffee in India and abroad. It was also allocated other responsibilities like looking into the growth of the Indian coffee industry, its trade and labour interests, and the interests of the consumers. In the course of the 1940s, there were at least fifty India Coffee House (later called the Indian Coffee House chain) outlets dotted all over British India, including two in Calcutta. By the late 1940s, the Indian Coffee House chain soared in popularity and in the early 1950s, it had as many as seventy-two outlets all over the country.

Bhaswati Bhattacharya, in her book, *Much Ado over Coffee: Indian Coffee House Then and Now* (2018), writes about the Indian Coffee House (ICH) chain:

> One major difference between the other existing spaces of socialization on the one hand and the ICH on the other was that while most of the eateries and tea-shops accessible to the average middle class were small, private local enterprises, working under the Coffee Cess Committee and later the Coffee Board, the ICH was a pan-Indian initiative on behalf of the coffee capitalists directly aided by the state for the public to come together and take to the consumption of coffee. (p. 65)

Before the launch of the Indian Coffee House chain, no effort had been made to promote coffee in India. Although coffee houses did exist in Madras and Calcutta in the eighteenth century, they catered only to the whites and Indians were barred from entering them. The domestic market for coffee was also fragmented. So, the government thought that the most effective way it could introduce and popularize coffee among the potential domestic customers was to start a chain of coffee houses.

So far, in the northern cities of India, coffee had been available in the upscale colonial hotels and restaurants, making some upper-class Indians familiar with the beverage. The less well-to-do, in contrast, might have tasted coffee in the cafés and hotels opened by the migrant south Indians. But, by making coffee available at a subsidized price, the Coffee Board of India made it possible for the majority of the urban middle-class north Indians to have access to the beverage that had so long been the preserve of a few.

Unsurprisingly, after India gained independence, coffee was not high on the priority list. By the middle of the 1950s, the Coffee Board of India had decided to close down many of the coffee houses. They felt that enough had been done on their part to promote coffee in the country. Several Indian Coffee House outlets that had begun under its aegis were shut down and many employees lost their jobs. Popular communist leader, A.K. Gopalan, who hailed from Kerala, stepped in as a messiah for the jobless workers at these places and motivated them to take matters into their own hands. Their movement compelled the Board to hand over the outlets to the workers, who formed cooperative societies and renamed the network, Indian Coffee House. The first Indian Coffee Workers' Cooperative Society Ltd was formed in Bangalore in 1957. The first two Indian Coffee House outlets were also opened in the same year in Mahatma Gandhi Road in Bangalore and Connaught Place in New Delhi.

Today, the Coffee Board of India, with its headquarters in Bangalore, continues to operate twelve Indian Coffee Houses throughout the country, from where they also sell their in-house brand of coffee, the 'India Coffee'. Several of the workers' cooperative societies run the rest of the network as the restaurant chain, Indian Coffee House. Today, this chain has around 400 outlets and associate canteens across the country with Kerala alone being home to fifty-one of them. The branch on Bankim Chatterjee Street in Calcutta was one of the outlets shut down for some time after the Board's decision to downsize the operation. It was taken over by the Calcutta chapter of the Indian Coffee Workers' Cooperative Society Ltd. Nevertheless, both the India Coffee House and the Indian Coffee House outlets have become ideal meeting places to indulge in coffee and conversation in an unrushed atmosphere.

Over the years, Karnataka, Kerala and Tamil Nadu have emerged as the major coffee-producing regions in the country. These three states in south India are regarded as the traditional coffee growing areas. Over 70 per cent of India's coffee production comes from Karnataka, and its biggest contributor is Chikmagalur, which has earned the sobriquet 'Coffee Land of Karnataka'. Coffee production has also spread to other non-traditional areas like Andhra Pradesh, Orissa and the Northeast.

Indian coffee is shade-grown, which means that the coffee plants are grown under a canopy of trees. The shade trees prevent soil erosion, enrich the soil by recycling nutrients from the deeper layers and protect the coffee plants from seasonal fluctuations in temperature. The two main varieties of coffee produced in India are Arabica and Robusta. While the former is grown in higher altitudes, in cool climatic conditions, the latter is more suited to lower elevations and hot and humid climate. Usually, the coffee powders manufactured in India are a blend of both the varieties. The Arabica variety imparts a nice flavour to the coffee while the Robusta gives it a strong body.

Another type of coffee is the Monsooned Malabar, an exclusive variety from the Malabar Coast of Karnataka and Kerala. Not many Indians know about this variety, which originated during the British colonial rule, and has a strong following in Europe and the United States of America. It was discovered by accident in British ships sailing from India to Europe during the monsoon months. The big ships had to sail around the Cape of Good Hope to reach Europe and the journey would take nearly six months. This was before the Suez Canal was constructed in 1869. While the wooden vessels sailed around the Cape of Good Hope, the rains, humidity and winds caused the raw and fertile green beans to ripen and turn into a shade of aged-pale yellow. The coffee powder, made from these beans, had a pungent and musty flavour, and developed a heavy-bodied brew, which the Europeans seemed to prefer.

However, the opening of the Suez Canal, which created a fast-track shipping route between Asia and Europe, and improvement in means of transportation, reduced the length of these journeys. As a result, the coffee beans stopped going through any kind of transformation because of less exposure to the climatic conditions. The Europeans discovered that the coffee they were drinking had lost the flavour that they were used to and began demanding the aged coffee. So, coffee cultivators decided to replicate the process on the Malabar Coast manually. They devised an alternate method, known as Monsooning, which would reproduce the conditions experienced on sea. The harvested coffee beans were exposed to the monsoon rains and winds of the coast, causing them to swell double in size, turn pale and brittle, and lose some of their inherent acidity (found in the Arabica and Robusta varieties). The coffee powder, made from these beans, had a bold and earthy flavour, and was given the name, Monsooned Malabar.

Sanchari Pal, in her article, 'Care for Some "Monsooned Malabar"? You'll Love This Celebrated Coffee!' for *The Better India* (14 May 2018), writes, 'Over the years, Monsooned Malabar has become a much-in-demand component in several fine espresso blends (especially in the Scandinavian and German speciality roasted blends) to which it lends weight, body and its unusual chocolatey flavour. It is also sought by major international brands such as Nestle Nespresso, Benecke Coffee and Grecof.' In Calcutta, the Promenade Lounge at Taj Bengal, a premier five star hotel, serves its customers a select variety of tea and coffee. In this fine collection is the exclusive 'Indian aged monsoon malabar', which a connoisseur can indulge in with cookies and sandwiches.

Over the years, south India has also become famous for the way it prepares the beverage, known as the south Indian filter coffee. It is made by mixing the infusion, obtained from percolation brewing of finely ground coffee powder, with boiled milk. The brewing is done in a traditional coffee filter that is made of stainless steel. No one is sure how or when this coffee filter, which can be regarded as the Indian version of the French Press or the Coffee Plunger, originated. The coffee is served in a stainless steel tumbler that is placed on a wide bowl made of the same material. This bowl, known as the dabarah, functions as the saucer and is used to cool the coffee. This is done by pouring the hot coffee back and forth between the tumbler and the dabarah till it cools down to a temperature warm enough to be sipped. The action also helps in mixing the sugar into the coffee just in case it has been added after the beverage is prepared. The hot coffee, which is collected in the dabarah, is poured bit by bit into the tumbler and drunk.

Today, India is the sixth largest producer of coffee in the world. Nearly 80 per cent of its coffee production is reserved for export. Indian Robusta coffee has particularly carved a niche for itself in the international market. India is able to bask in this glory because of an adventurous Sufi saint who could have never imagined that his small step would leave behind such a gargantuan imprint.

Two Coffee Houses, Both Alike in Dignity

India Coffee House, on Chittaranjan Avenue (formerly Central Avenue), was one of the two venues originally selected by the Coffee Board of India in Calcutta, the other being the Albert Hall Coffee House on Bankim Chatterjee Street. While the latter split from the Board and formed its own Indian Coffee Workers' Cooperative Society Ltd, the coffee house on the upscale Chittaranjan Avenue remained under the control of the central government.

India Coffee House: Established in 1942, India Coffee House was partitioned into two: the House of Lords and House of Commons, following the British parliamentary system. Coffee in the House of Lords was priced 25 per cent higher than in the House of Commons, and was always served with the full paraphernalia: a coffee pot, sugar bowl and tongs, cream pitcher and the matching delicate coffee cups and saucers. In his essay, 'A Spell in Hindustan', compiled in the book *Sahibs Who Loved India* (2010), the late British journalist Philip Crosland, who had a very successful career in the Calcutta-based leading English-language newspaper, *The Statesman*, wrote about his experiences at the India Coffee House, 'In the Commons, your coffee was brought to you with the milk already in it; you merely added the sugar. In the Lords, milk, sugar and coffee were produced on a tray in their separate receptacles and the customer paid for this refinement' (p. 71).

The better quality of service in the stately House of Lords attracted the upper class to it. They did not mind paying a high price for their coffees and snacks as long as they were able to dine in the comfort of this section. Many eminent personalities from the political, bureaucratic, literary, artistic and other fields once had their coffees here. Philip Crosland continues, 'In the Commons there was pandemonium. The Upper House was appropriately sedate. A table near the door was almost invariably occupied by the Chief Secretary to the West Bengal government, whose name I have forgotten, immersed in the *Statesman* crossword. In the centre of the room was a galaxy of talent from an advertising agency. One of their number would be Satyajit Ray, yet to find fame as a film-maker, but a quarter way through the making of *Pather Panchali*' (p. 71). Besides Ray, renowned actor and theatre personality, Utpal Dutt, and noted film critic and historian, Chidananda Das Gupta, were regulars at the India Coffee House. While the former, known for his strong faith in Marxism, chose the House of Commons, the latter preferred the aristocracy of the House of Lords.

But, over the years, the House of Lords witnessed a decline in the footfall of customers possibly because of overcrowding, traffic snarls and concomitant problems that gradually developed in the area. This made the House of Lords a commercially unviable proposition and ultimately led to its closure in 2006.

Now the House of Commons operates on its own, though it is no longer known by this name. Students, professors, office goers and people visiting the area often drop into India Coffee House for a cup. India Coffee House has always been a favourite with the journalists of *The Statesman* as its office is located in the vicinity.

There was a time when coffee and its accompaniments like sandwiches, cakes and nuts were served by liveried and turbaned waiters at the place. Although these grand uniforms have been done away with, the food is still delectable. Different preparations like hot black coffee, milk coffee, iced coffee and cold cream coffee are served to customers along with snacks of British and Indian origin. Fluffy omelettes and flaky patties are a reminder of the legacy left behind by the British, as are the vegetable, cheese, chicken and egg sandwiches, and cutlets. Chicken, egg and mutton rolls are spicy fusion dishes that have a base of British culinary techniques with a pinch of Indian flavours. The popular south Indian idlis, vadas and dosas add a typically Indian touch to the menu, alongside fried snacks like onion and vegetable pakoras. Packaged coffee powder is sold from the counter and bought by hotels, restaurants, coffee outlets and even coffee aficionados.

India Coffee House has had a long innings and is still going strong. One of the few central government-owned coffee houses still functioning in the country, it attracts a large number of customers every day.

Indian Coffee House: Popularly known as College Street Coffee House, and earlier as Albert Hall Coffee House, its history is interwoven with that of Calcutta in a complex manner. Founded in April 1876 by noted philosopher and social reformer Keshub Chandra Sen, Albert Hall did not turn into the landmark coffee house that it is now until sixty-six years later.

An educated and cultured man, Keshub Chandra Sen was one of the distinguished members of the Brahmo Samaj sect. He belonged to a wealthy family and owned many plots of land and properties in Calcutta. In 1870, Sen visited England and was granted an audience with Queen Victoria. He had been toying with the idea of converting his residence on Bankim Chatterjee Street into a meeting place for the intelligentsia. After returning from England, he decided to name this residence after the late Prince Albert, Queen Victoria's husband. The inauguration of Albert Hall took place in April 1876 in the presence of an august audience, and it was soon to become an institution in itself. Albert Hall became a meeting place for the intelligentsia and many important political meetings and discussions took place at the venue. It is believed that Surendranath Banerjee founded the Indian National Association (also known as Indian Association) here, in 1876. The first Indian National Conference, which took place here in 1883, is said to have paved the way for the formation of the Indian National Congress in 1885. Netaji Subhas Chandra Bose attended a few political meetings held in this place. Albert Hall was also famous for being a secret meeting place of the swadeshis. Books and papers on swadeshi strategies were kept here and its secret doorways and passages were used by freedom fighters to escape whenever the police conducted raids. After the requisition of Albert Hall by the Government of India, the Coffee Board converted it into a coffee house in 1942. Albert Hall now became India Coffee House and began to be frequented by people from different walks of life like intellectuals, litterateurs, artists, academicians and students who would drop into the place for hours of stimulating adda over plentiful cups of coffee. The place was also popularly known as Albert Hall Coffee House.

But, when the Coffee Board of India decided to down its shutters in 1958, employees and customers alike objected strongly to the idea. The jobs of the workers were at stake and the customers were appalled at the thought of losing such an integral part of modern Indian history. The regular coffee house goers wrote a letter to the incumbent chief minister, Dr Bidhan Chandra Roy, imploring him to save the heritage place and claiming that India Coffee House was no ordinary coffee shop. Aviram Mullick, a close associate of Dr Bidhan Chandra Roy, came to the rescue and acquired ownership of Albert Hall. The workers of India Coffee House decided to take over the running of the place themselves and formed the Indian Coffee Workers' Cooperative Society Ltd for this purpose. India Coffee House on Bankim Chatterjee Street now became Indian Coffee House and the cooperative society became the tenant of Aviram Mullick. In 1992, the government of West Bengal took over the ownership of Albert Hall.

Over the years, this Indian Coffee House has come to be popularly known as College Street Coffee House because of its proximity to College Street. Since College Street is such a popular landmark in that area, it was easier for the customers to identify this iconic coffee house with the iconic street, which takes its name from the historic Presidency College located on it. Today, College Street Coffee House owes its popularity to its huge academic customer base and its long history of being visited by the intelligentsia. As can be seen in the passion with which Calcuttans fought to keep the place open, it is clearly much more than just a coffee shop. College Street Coffee House has been a centre for intellectual and artistic discussions and political movements. Noted film-makers Satyajit Ray, Mrinal Sen and Ritwik Ghatak, veteran actors Aparna Sen, Soumitra

Chatterjee and Utpal Dutt, renowned economist Amartya Sen as well as eminent litterateurs Sunil Gangopadhyay and Samaresh Majumdar, have all been regulars. Sunil Gangopadhyay would often fall short of money in his impecunious days and leave his black umbrella as credit at College Street Coffee House, until he could reclaim it the next time. During the Naxal Movement days of the 1960s and '70s, College Street Coffee House was a favourite meeting place of the Naxalites in Calcutta. The former chief minister of West Bengal, Buddhadeb Bhattacharjee, was also a regular fixture here during his student days at Presidency College.

A winding wooden staircase leads to the first floor, which has a large dining area. On the floor above is a semicircular balcony, from where people can look down on the action below. Waiters in starched white uniforms with broadbelts and fancy headwear—as they wore in the days of the Raj—dot the floor, carrying coffees and food that seem to be equally suspended in time. The days of black coffee, known as Infusion here, are clearly not over, though it has been joined by the famous bittersweet milk coffee and the creamy, lathered cold coffee. Traditional British food like chicken stew, buttery grilled or baked fish, and crunchy fish fry are popular dishes, as is the classic chicken roast and versatile grilled chicken.

So great is the aura of College Street Coffee House that it has even made itself a fixture in movies and songs. Renowned singer, Manna Dey, known for lending his golden voice to many Hindi and Bengali film songs, sang:

> '*Coffee Houser sei adda-ta aaj aar nei*
> (Coffee House's adda is no longer there today)
>
> *aaj aar nei*
> (no longer there today)
>
> *Kothai hariye gelo sonali bikel gulo sei*
> (Where have those golden evenings gone? They are)
>
> *aaj aar nei'*
> (no longer there today)

The lyrics of this iconic song were composed and scribbled on the back of a College Street Coffee House bill by lyricist Gouri Prasanna Mazumder and the music contributed by Suparna Kanti Ghosh, while the three music geniuses were having an engrossing adda at the famous venue.

Paramount, Favourite Cabin, India Coffee House and Indian Coffee

House are legendary joints that represent the colonial culture of the city. The British left their royal capital a long time ago, but the contribution they made to its culinary culture via their beverages has come to play an important role. The average person's affinity for these beverages has made these restaurants so popular that they are still filled with customers eager for a sip of their favourite rose malai juice, sweetened milk tea, cold cream coffee or infusion coffee. The advent of the beverage culture in the city can be seen in the histories of these four restaurants, and their success created opportunities for other entrepreneurs to set up places on similar lines in the future, laying the foundation of Calcutta's love affair with drinking as well as dining out.

Chops and Cutlets

Chops and cutlets are an integral part of Calcutta's culinary culture and owe their origin to British cooking. Chops are round, oval or oblong, based on the traditional potato croquette, which was a regular teatime accompaniment at British tables. Cutlets, in contrast, are flat or rectangular in shape and do not use potatoes as binder. When the British began setting up homes in the royal capital, they tried to stick to their original dishes as far as possible. However, they had to depend on what was available in the local markets without making too many alterations to the recipes. Some tea-time snacks, ostensibly meant for British masters, were given a personal touch by their Indian cooks. What evolved was a spread of fried delicacies based on the croquettes and cutlets, but with a distinctly Indian flavour.

From the second half of the nineteenth century these modified recipes gradually spread to the local Bengalis who began following the cooks working for the British by not only making their versions of croquettes but also calling the final product 'chops'.

These are very different from the chops made in Britain, which refer to a slightly thick chunk of meat (usually lamb or pork). There are quite a few types of chop cuts sourced from different parts of the animal but the most popular ones are rib chop and loin chop. These chops can be boneless or with bones. A bone-in rib chop has a rib bone jutting out at one end, indicating that the chunk of meat has been cut from the ribs of the animal. Many prefer to have their rib chops Frenched, which means that some of the meat, fat and membranes that connect the individual rib bones in a rack of meat are removed by a few inches. This exposes the bones and gives them a clean look. Often, a rib chop may have more than one Frenched rib jutting out of the meat. In contrast, a bone-in loin chop does not have any exposed bone. A thick T-shaped bone runs through the chunk of the meat. It is larger in size and has more meat than a rib chop.

Since red meat is flavourful, it does not require too many spices. The chops are coated with a marinade of oil, salt, ground black pepper, garlic and herbs. They are thoroughly marinated before being grilled, roasted, broiled or pan-fried. Chops are meals in themselves and served with vegetables (steamed, sautéed, grilled or roasted) and potatoes (boiled, mashed, sautéed, grilled, roasted or as a dauphinoise).

Croquettes, in contrast, have mashed potatoes as their main base, to which ingredients like cheese, ham, bacon and vegetables are added, alongwith herbs and spices. This mixture is then moulded into cylindrical, round or oval shapes, which are dusted with refined flour, dipped in a batter of whisked eggs, coated in breadcrumbs and deep-fried. The same technique is used to make Bengal's 'chops'. The potato plays the role of a binder in croquettes as it holds all the ingredients together while they are being fried. Plain potato croquettes are also popular. These feature the potato as the main ingredient besides spices and herbs. However, in the case of fish or meat croquettes in Britain, instead of mashed potatoes, refined flour is mainly used as a binder. But the cooks working for the British in Bengal preferred using the potato as a binder for all types of croquettes, whether vegetarian or not, and called them chops. Some food historians like Bridget White-Kumar, regarded as the doyenne of Anglo-Indian cuisine, suggest that perhaps the cooks who worked for the British found it difficult to pronounce the word 'croquettes' and called them 'chops' instead.

There are a variety of chops available. The simple vegetable chop is made with grated beetroots and carrots to which mashed potatoes, a variety of local spices, finely chopped coriander leaves and fried peanuts are added. Many Bengalis prefer to keep the making process completely vegetarian by replacing the egg wash with refined flour batter. Some even coat the chop with poppy seeds instead of breadcrumbs for enhanced taste. While the popular *mochar chop* is made with the mashed blossoms of the banana tree, the much-liked *enchorer chop* uses mashed unripe jackfruit. These two chops have, over the years, turned into delicacies served in upscale Bengali restaurants. Non-vegetarian chops include the aromatic mutton (as goat meat is widely known in India) chop and the delicious fish chop, which is popularly made with rui (a variety of carp, commonly known as rohu in India), katla (another variety of carp) or aar (long-whiskered catfish). These chops have minced mutton or mashed fish meat as the main ingredient, along with mashed potato.

A cutlet generally refers to a small and flat piece of meat on a single bone. This meat is mostly taken from the rib and the bone is often Frenched. The traditional British recipe of a cutlet is to coat the meat with oil and salt, and then either grill or roast it in an oven. Cutlets are also meals in themselves and served, just like chops, with the same preparations of potatoes and vegetables. (The most popular variety in Britain is the lamb cutlet.)

However, in India, a cutlet refers to a thin slice of tender and boneless meat, which the British used to cook in a manner similar to the European schnitzel: the thin slab of meat was pounded flat with a mallet and seasoned with salt and pepper before being dusted with refined flour, dipped into whisked eggs, coated with breadcrumbs and, crucially, deep-fried till golden brown. Instead of a schnitzel, the end product was called a 'cutlet'. Expert opinion on the reason behind applying such a technique, which became ingrained in the Indian culinary culture, is divided. The most plausible one could be that since only rudimentary ovens existed in the city, the memsahibs and their cooks may have found it easier to fry the meat slabs instead of roasting or grilling them. Here again, the cooks perhaps found it easier to pronounce 'cutlet' than 'schnitzel' and thus, the word came to be used. And staying true to their culinary practices, these local cooks began coating the meat with spices as well.

Today, chicken, mutton, bhekti (barramundi) and prawn cutlets are all widely available throughout Calcutta. Vegetarian cutlets (usually made with raw banana, unripe jackfruit or banana blossoms) are rare and greatly overshadowed in popularity by the non-vegetarian ones. Chicken cutlets in Calcutta were traditionally called 'fowl cutlets' while fish cutlets are known as 'fish fries'. Usually, chicken cutlets are made with chicken breasts and boneless fish is used for fish fries. The British preferred bhekti because it was boneless, could be easily cut into fillets and also tasted good, making it a popular choice for cutlets. This popularity has continued and today, for Calcuttans, bhekti has become synonymous with fish fry. In the case of both chicken cutlet and fish fry, the meat is rubbed with lime juice and salt after being pounded flat, marinated in ginger-garlic-onion pastes, and seasoned with red chilli powder. Mutton cutlets are given a similar treatment, but the minced meat is usually cooked with chopped green chillies and garom mashla (as garam masala, a combination of green cardamoms, cinnamons and cloves, is known in Bengali) in addition to the various pastes, and then kneaded with slices of bread dipped in water. Even in chicken cutlets, instead of breasts, mince is often used. Sometimes, a customer can find 'Diamond Fish Fry' listed in the menu of a cabin in Calcutta. This is a fillet of bhekti shaped like a barfi, which is called a diamond cut, and marinated with extra spices and herbs. In all cases, they are dusted with refined flour, given an egg wash and a coat of breadcrumbs and, thus attired, are deep-fried.

Bengalis enjoy eating chops and cutlets with fresh vegetable salads that generally include finely sliced onions, cucumbers, carrots and beetroots. Sauces are essential condiments served with these fried snacks and the most commonly used ones are kasundi and tomato ketchup. Kasundi is the Bengali version of table mustard that is made of a spicy paste of mustard seeds, which includes raw mangoes, and mustard oil. While the British would reach out for Colman's Mustard, their favourite brand imported from England, to enhance the taste of chops and cutlets, Bengalis always found the sharper and more pungent kasundi appealing. From being the sine qua non component of every Bengali kitchen, the popularity of this sauce has spread to the other communities living in the city. A bottle of kasundi can now be seen in most Calcutta homes.

Chacha's Hotel: This iconic restaurant's signature dish has always been the fowl cutlet. The oldest of the fried food joints in the city, dating back to 1875, the restaurant had a humble beginning as a small tea stall on Gour Mohan Mukherjee Street in north Calcutta. It was run by an old Muslim gentleman whose customers fondly called him chacha (uncle).

Chacha developed a fondness for a young man who worked in this tea stall. When he left Calcutta, he sold the stall to this man, one Goshai Das Patra. But, not content to simply run a tea stall, Das Patra decided to open a food stall and began selling mutton chops and fowl cutlets. At first, the stall did not have a proper name, but was popularly called Chachar Hotel (Chacha's Hotel) by customers. By the time a name was required to be registered, 'Chacha's Hotel' seemed a natural choice.

Goshai Das Patra's innovative manner of cooking the fowl cutlet appealed to his customers. Instead of adding the usual ginger-garlic-onion pastes and finely chopped green chillies to the chicken mince, the restaurateur used an assorted variety of ingredients like black pepper, cardamom powder, garom mashla and Worcestershire sauce. The recipe was tremendously popular among his original customers and even now, the owners of the restaurant have made no change to it. The fowl cutlet continues to be the most ordered fried snack in Chacha's Hotel.

Chacha's Hotel can boast of many prominent patrons, including Netaji Subhas Chandra Bose, who was a regular customer. Long after the country won its independence, the restaurant shifted to Bidhan Sarani (formerly Cornwallis Street) in north Calcutta. Uttam Kumar, who later became the superstar of Bengali cinema, frequented that eatery often in his days as a struggling actor. Among the later generation of actors, Mithun Chakraborty was a regular visitor before the Bombay film industry beckoned him westwards. Celebrated Hindustani classical music exponent Pandit Bhismadeb Chattopadhyay, the legendary Manna Dey, renowned Bengali actor Chhabi Biswas, prolific Bengali actress Chhaya Debi, prominent cricketer Pankaj Roy and popular authors Shibram Chakraborty and Mani Shankar Mukherjee, who writes under the pseudonym, 'Sankar', have also been seen at Chacha's Hotel.

Dilkhusha Cabin: Ask anybody in Calcutta, 'What is the best place for kabiraji cutlet?' and the prompt reply will be, 'Are you talking about Dilkhusha?' Dilkhusha Cabin has been serving British fried foods on Harrison Road (now Mahatma Gandhi Road) in Central Calcutta since August 1908 and is famed for its two signature dishes: *kabiraji cutlet* and *deemer devil*.

Kabiraj literally means an Ayurvedic doctor in Bengali. No one is really sure how the word 'kabiraji' came to be applied to a cutlet. There is a general belief that it has no connection with a doctor and is derived from the English word 'coverage' because the cutlet is wrapped in a crispy 'eggs cover'. Invented and named by the local cooks working for the British in Bengal, kabiraji cutlets are essentially non-vegetarian and popularly made with fish, prawn, chicken or mutton. The cover is made with eggs that have been whisked together with some cornflour and salt. This batter, with the quick to and fro vertical movement of the fingers, is spread in fine strips on hot oil to form a delicate mesh. The fried cutlet is coated with an egg wash and placed on the middle of this mesh, which is folded over it. The cutlet is fried till its cover becomes crispy, giving it a delicious taste and frilly appearance. Dilkhusha Cabin serves all the four varieties of kabiraji cutlet.

Deemer devil (not to be confused with the modern preparation of devilled eggs) is the Bengali version of Scotch eggs. In the case of

Scotch eggs, hard-boiled or soft-boiled eggs are encased in a seasoned meat mixture. Sausage meat (usually pork or beef) is preferred for this preparation. The meat is seasoned with ingredients like salt, ground pepper, mustard (usually powdered), ground nutmeg and chopped herbs (usually parsley and chives). The encased eggs are dusted with refined flour, dipped in an egg wash and coated with breadcrumbs. They can be baked or fried till the meat is cooked and the eggs are golden brown.

But naturally, the cooks working for the British in Bengal spiced up the Scotch egg. The minced meat (usually mutton) is cooked in oil with a variety of local spices like bay leaves, finely chopped onions, ginger, garlic and green chillies, ground cumin, coriander, turmeric, dried red chillies and garom mashla, chopped coriander leaves and salt. Hard-boiled eggs (or *deem* in Bengali), cut into halves, are largely preferred for this preparation. The halved eggs are encased in this cooked meat mixture and the procedure of flour-egg wash-breadcrumbs is followed. The cooks preferred frying the eggs, a technique they were more comfortable with than baking. The halved eggs were also often encased in a mashed potato mixture (cooked in oil with onions, spices and herbs), coated with the necessary ingredients and fried. This potato encased version is also called egg chop. The minced meat encased version is popularly served in eateries like Dilkhusha Cabin. The chefs at this restaurant lend a special touch to their preparation of deemer devil by making the unexpected addition of a few drops of vanilla essence to the minced mutton mixture.

Through the decades, members of the royal families of the city and prominent academicians would drop in at the restaurant for engrossing sessions of adda over the fried food. Dilkhusha Cabin was once a favourite of Bengali poet Kazi Nazrul Islam and writer Shibram Chakraborty.

The current owner, Utpal Basu, is unaware of the names of the people who set up the restaurant. All that he knows is that it was established by the grandparents of his late uncle, Chunilal Dey. Chunilal and Meera Dey's son Samir Dey ran the restaurant after the death of his parents, but he suffered a stroke and passed away. Since he was a bachelor, the responsibility of running the restaurant fell on Utpal Basu, who used to be an employee in the restaurant. From the beginning, the restaurant has been a family-run business.

The decor of Dilkhusha Cabin is reminiscent of the bygone era. A crowded entrance leads customers into a spacious restaurant, filled with colonial furniture that is still seen in some of the old eateries of Calcutta. Burma teak wood chairs and marble-top wooden tables with carved legs furnish the eatery. A big, wood-framed Belgian glass mirror, which often attracts unwanted prospective buyers, adorns one of the walls. The restaurant also has the cabin system of seating arrangement for customers preferring privacy.

Today, the restaurant is frequented by both the old and the young, eager to sample the delicious legacy of colonial Calcutta.

Allen Kitchen: Known as Allen Saheb-er dokan in the Company days because it belonged to a Scottish gentleman named Allen, this evening snacks stall was housed in Sir Charles Allen Market on Upper Chitpur Road (now known as Rabindra Sarani) in north Calcutta.This municipal market was named after Sir Charles Allen (not to be confused with Allen Saheb of 'Allen Saheb-er dokan'), who was the chairman of the Calcutta Corporation from 1905 to 1909. Allen Market, as it is popularly known, was opened to the public in 1910. The exact year of the opening of Allen Saheb-er dokan is not known to the current owners. Eventually, Allen Saheb left the country, gifting the eatery to his employee, Jiban Krishna Saha, who took charge of a menu covering a range of chops and cutlets. The most prominent item then, as of now, was the prawn cutlet.

A branch of the original eatery was opened on Jatindra Mohan Avenue in north Calcutta in 1958. But this time, it was a small restaurant, decorated with wooden chairs and tables with marble tops that opened every evening to curious customers. Christened Allen Kitchen, it gradually became so renowned for its food that it turned into a landmark restaurant in that area. By now, the Allen brand had become a family-owned restaurant business. The success of their restaurant prompted the owners to down the shutters of Allen Saheb-er dokan and focus on their new eatery, which continues even today.

Over the years, the juicy prawn cutlet, cooked in ghee and served with vegetable salad and kasundi, has become Allen Kitchen's signature dish. Butterflied tiger prawns are marinated in a secret spice mix and served as piping hot cutlets to eager customers. Despite its small size, the restaurant often attracts an elite clientele, who feel that this is the place for superlative fast food, leaving new entrants like KFC and McDonald's in the dust.

Basanta Cabin

Brothers Basanta, Sushil and Sudhir Kumar Ray set up a small tea shop in the College Street Market complex. This was the humble origin of the famous Basanta Cabin, which was to become the intellectual hub of Calcutta in the days before Independence. This eatery did not boast of a particular signature dish but became popular for its delectable chops and cutlets that customers took with tea and coffee.

The office of Abhay Ashram (a social welfare organization based on swadeshi ideals) used to be on the first floor of the College Street Market complex. Netaji Subhas Chandra Bose, his elder brother Sarat Chandra Bose and Shyama Prasad Mukherjee (founder of the Bharatiya Jana Sangh), among other great nationalists, would visit this place to attend meetings. Beverages and snacks for these meetings would be supplied by the Basanta Cabin, which was housed below. Although this particular eatery, inside the market complex, has now closed down, its first branch was opened on the same street in 1931. Today, Basanta Cabin's branches in College Street and Hedua (just across Scottish Church College) are still thriving. Renowned painter Ganesh Pyne, and celebrated actors Uttam Kumar and Basanta Choudhury, were regular patrons of Basanta Cabin.

Mitra Café: Mitra Café was set up by Ganesh Mitra in 1920, on Jatindra Mohan Avenue. He was unable to run it successfully, and two years after opening, he gave it to his childhood friend, Sushil Roy, who retained his close friend's name for the café.

Well known for its range of chops and cutlets, Mitra Café's signature dish is its brain chop, a delicacy that is difficult to come across in the other eateries of Calcutta. Although the recipe is a trade secret, one can get a rough idea of what goes into the dish. A goat brain is blanched in water, boiling with salt and turmeric, and then chopped and marinated with vinegar or lime juice for a short period of time. The marinated pieces are mixed with the pastes of ginger, garlic and green chillies, salt, crushed black pepper, powdered cinnamon and secret spices. These are then shaped into chops, dipped in an egg wash, rolled in finely ground breadcrumbs and deep-fried. Unsurprisingly, just the way crumbed and fried brain cutlets were popular with Calcutta's British, this delicious chop, which has been served in the restaurant from its early days, is popular with all the hardcore non-vegetarians of the city.

Mitra Café is also one of the very few eateries in Calcutta that serves the Afghani cutlet. The British enjoy eating chops and cutlets smothered in slightly thick gravies. The cooks working for them in Bengal would replicate this recipe with crumbed cutlets. The Afghani cutlet is similar to this dish. The crumbed cutlet used in this recipe is covered in rich, thick and spicy gravy. In Mitra Café, this dish is made with fish, prawn, chicken and mutton cutlets. Although the popularity of its Afghani cutlets cannot equal that of its brain chop, the rarity of this dish in the other eateries of Calcutta makes it worth mentioning here.

Since its early days, Mitra Café has been an evening joint. The restaurant is close to the Star Theatre and veteran Bengali actors like Uttam Kumar and Soumitra Chatterjee would often drop by for a quick bite after a theatre show. Even now, Mitra Café is packed every evening with people from north Calcutta. Professionals and commuters passing that area often drop in. The restaurant is also frequented by gourmets from all over the city who are keen to try out its fare. Every little aspect of the small eatery is a reminder of colonial Calcutta, right from the décor of wooden chairs and marble-top wooden tables and the crockery and cutlery—with each pristine white plate having the words 'Mitra Café' embossed at one corner, near its edge, in bold blue letters and the word 'Restaurant' scribbled underneath them in red—to the fried snacks that are still so popular among the customers.

Anadi Cabin: Revered throughout the city for its *moghlai parotas*, Anadi Cabin entered the list in 1924. Located on Chowringhee Road (now Jawaharlal Nehru Road) in central Calcutta, the eatery was established by Balaram Jana. He named it after his elder brother Anadi, who had died an untimely death at the age of twenty-two. Under the supervision of Balaram and his son Adikanta, the chefs at the restaurant cooked fried snacks of superlative quality for the customers. In its early days, *dhakai parota*, *kosha mangsho* (mutton cooked in rich, thick and spicy gravy) and tea were served in the eatery. But, within a few years since its opening, it discontinued the traditional dhakai parota and began serving the popular chops, cutlets and moghlai parota instead. Although the small joint served chops and cutlets, over the years, its signature dish became its moghlai parota.

Dhakai parota is a round, layered and puffed up unleavened fried bread that is made of refined flour. This crispy and flaky parota has a big hole at its centre and is generally eaten with a sweet and slightly spicy preparation of chholar dal (split Bengal gram), cooked with small and thin pieces of fried coconut. The history behind the origin of this parota is obscure. No one knows who invented it or in which year or period of time it was first made. There is a popular theory that it originated in

Dhaka (now the capital of Bangladesh) in undivided Bengal and hence, the name came to be used. But there is no strong evidence available to support this theory and many reject it, believing that the name was used as a promotional gimmick. Dhakai parota, which is also eaten with kosha mangsho, found favour among the city folks for a long time, till a new dish began gaining tremendous popularity: the moghlai parota.

Like the dhakai parota, no one is exactly sure how and when the moghlai parota originated. There are quite a few theories afloat and one of them is that this parota originated in the Mughal period. 'Moghlai' is the Bengali variation of the word 'Mughlai', which is used to describe the cuisine brought to India by the Mughals in the sixteenth century. There is a general belief that this parota originated during Mughal Emperor Jahangir's rule. Jahangir, who ruled from 1605 until his death in 1627, got bored eating simple parathas made with keema or minced meat and commanded his chef Adil Hafiz Usman to come up with a new variety within ten days. On the ninth day, Usman made zabir-fala or anda-roti ('zabir' is egg and 'fala' is bread in the Pahlavi language). Jahangir was delighted and gifted Usman 1,001 gold coins.

Usman, who belonged to Bengal (Burdwan was his hometown), did not share the recipe with anyone except his son. This son, Farogh, experimented with the recipe in Burdwan and further refined it. The recipe, which he finalized, came to be known as the moghlai parota. He then shared it with his seven sons who kept it confined within the family for a long time. It was the descendants of the family who spread the dish when they began working as chefs in nineteenth-century Calcutta.

Another theory is that the cooks of Bengal, to dress up their invention in an exotic Mughal garb, thought of the name as a promotional gimmick. Whichever may be the real one, it is a fact that the moghlai parota became a very popular snack during the British rule, enjoyed by both the Bengalis and the British.The dhakai parota was replaced by the moghlai parota at Anadi Cabin because it was very much in public demand. Another reason behind the replacement was that the dhakai parota was too time-consuming to make. This tedious method along with the change in consumer preference has nearly driven out the dhakai parota from the local sweet shops and eateries that once made them and almost turned it into a lost recipe. The cooks in Anadi Cabin excelled in the art of making the moghlai parota and the dish soon became a bestseller. To make the parota, a big ball is cut out from the refined flour dough and rolled into a large, thin round. At the restaurant, instead of minced meat, the filling is made of finely chopped onions, carrots, green chillies, ginger and coriander leaves. Chopped raisins and grated coconut are also added to it. This filling is then seasoned with salt and mixed with breadcrumbs. The mixture is placed in the middle of the round dough. Whisked eggs (the restaurant gives the option of choosing between duck and hen eggs) are poured into this mixture, blended well with it and spread over the dough. The parota is then folded into a rectangular shape and fried in smoking oil. A hearty meal at the restaurant includes the parota, *alur tarkari* (a dry potato preparation), salad, and tomato sauce as condiment. It is very filling while remaining light on the pocket—a sure-fire hit.

The proximity of the eatery to Sir Stuart Hogg Market, or New Market, ensures that there is a regular flow of customers. In fact, it is difficult to find Calcuttans who have not been to Anadi Cabin to sample its moghlai parotas. The eatery is a favourite haunt of both the old and the young, who frequent it for this delectable dish as well as its crumbed and fried cutlets.

Barua & Dey Fast Food Centre: Mog is an Arakanese tribe from Burma that lived in the Chittagong region of undivided Bengal. Buddhist by religion, they were excellent cooks and often employed for their culinary skills on the Arab ships that traded with Southeast Asia. They also worked as deckhands on these ships. Their culinary prowess made them rule the kitchens of the households and clubs of British Calcutta. Largely employed by the whites, they became experts in the continental style of cooking. Among the locals, old-timers who have been lucky to have tasted the meat loaves, chops, cutlets, pancakes and puddings made by them, claim that these are worth remembering.

Many of them improved on the tutelage of their masters to come up with creations that deftly combined European influence with a local base. One of these is *pantara*s, a sleek, rectangular fried snack that is made by filling a crepe, prepared with the batter of refined flour, with a spicy mutton or chicken mince. The filled crepe is then rolled and both its ends are tucked inside. It is given an egg wash and a coat of breadcrumbs before being deep-fried till golden brown. Pantaras was a favourite afternoon tea snack of the British in Calcutta and continues to be popular in the Anglo-Indian households of the city. It is still served in the colonial clubs of Calcutta at teatime. Pantaras is believed to be the modified version of the French dish popular with the British, crepes au poisson.

Nakul Chandra Barua was a Mog cook of some renown in the city whose work experiences included a stint at the famous Great Eastern Hotel. While he was still working in this hotel, the secretary of 'Theta-Feta Club', a local bridge club meant for the modern Bengali that was set up in the Shyambazar area of north Calcutta, lured him with a lucrative offer. Barua, now in charge of the club's canteen, churned out chops, cutlets, roasts and a variety of delicacies for its members. He excelled in the making of pantaras.

But, when the club closed down, Barua decided to start his own venture. Around 1935, he opened a shop just opposite to it from where he sold chops, cutlets, fish finger, fish roll, deemer devil and mutton pantaras to a local clientele. Although the shop was christened Barua & Sons, it was popularly known as 'Mamar Dokan' as Barua had been fondly called Mama (uncle in Bengali) when he was working in the canteen of the club. The shop had a change of address in between before shifting to its present location, which happens to be very close to the Shyambazar Metro Station. In 1984, Nakul Chandra Barua's son Bidhu Bhushan got into a partnership with Phatik Chandra Dey. The shop became a joint venture between two families—the Mog Baruas and the Bengali Deys—and was rechristened Barua & Dey Fast Food Centre in 1990.

Although now, a few eateries can be seen serving pantaras, this small shop in Shyambazar is famed to be the first one in the entire city that began making the fried snack. In its early days, the family members of Barua would be seen making piping hot mutton pantaras for curious customers, who were eager to try them out. It did not take long for the fame of their pantaras to spread throughout Calcutta, marking Barua & Dey Fast Food Centre as the only shop in the city that offered this fried snack for a considerable period of time.

In the period before Independence, there were many establishments in the city that were run by Mog cooks. Nearly all of them closed down because the modern generation was not interested in continuing with this kind of business. Today, despite the fact that Mogs are still living in the city, Barua & Dey Fast Food Centre boasts the presence of the last professional Mog cooks in Calcutta. And it continues making mutton pantaras of superlative quality that attract a constant rush of customers not just from north Calcutta but also from other parts of the city.

This list of restaurants serving fried snacks, the majority of which were set up before Independence, is not exhaustive but only includes the most popular ones. Each of these prominent restaurants, along with others, has been responsible for the commercial availability of chops and cutlets in the city. Since centuries, these small restaurants have carried forward the legacy of the British by serving their fried snacks. As Bengalis have adopted the British practice of taking tea with snacks, most of these joints have the beverage listed in their menus. Also, the manner in which the food is served is a reminder of the adab qaidas or etiquettes handed down by our erstwhile colonial masters, which these modest and unpretentious eateries have continued with. Along with salads and condiments, they serve the fried snacks not only in the proper crockery but also with the right kind of cutlery such as forks and knives—just the way the colonialists would have liked it—and customers from different strata of society can be seen eating the food, perfectly or awkwardly, with these dining tools.

Most of these restaurants have remained loyal to the fried food recipes that percolated from the kitchens of the British, but at the same time, they have added their personal touches and come up with innovations that are very tempting. A few, like Anadi Cabin, started out with recipes that were in vogue at the time but later shifted to alternatives that had grown in popularity. Conversely, some recipe variations have failed the test of time. Cream cutlet, for example, which was usually made with either chicken or mutton had sour cream in it. According to hearsay, a bite into this cutlet would fill the mouth with soft and delicious cream. The method of making this concoction is, unfortunately, lost.

Puddings

Along with their fried snacks and beverages, the British also brought puddings to the Bengali table. Puddings were a traditional dessert, and the recipes for warm and fluffy egg-based puddings were carried by British memsahibs and taught to the local cooks. Various types of puddings were soon commonplace items in the kitchens of the all-white clubs of Calcutta.

Local aristocratic families and the brown sahibs and memsahibs were the first to bring the habit of rounding off a meal with servings of these sugary puddings into Bengali households. This happened in the second half of the nineteenth century, almost around the same time as the spread of chops and cutlets. Beginning with the aristocrats and Anglophiles, who were, most of the times, the first to emulate their colonial masters, the habit was gradually picked up by the public.

Bread-and-butter pudding, crème caramel and tipsy pudding were extremely popular in the colonial period, and while the first two continue to be made and served across Calcutta, tipsy pudding is no longer commonly made.

Tipsy pudding is the alcoholic version of the English dessert known as trifle. The latter uses fruit juice instead. The halved pieces of a sponge cake are soaked in rum, sherry, brandy or sweet wine and then layered in a glass bowl with a mixture of fruit jam, marmalade and fruit jelly. A layer of thick custard is spread on top of the whole and the final spread of fruit jam, marmalade and fruit jelly mixture, applied over it. Thick whipped cream is smoothened over the fruity surface, and slivered almonds are sprinkled on the top. The alcohol content in the pudding is evident in its name and the dessert is truly supposed to make one feel slightly off balance.

The popularity of these British creations fired the imagination of local entrepreneurs. Some of them even made their own versions of the dish. For instance, *narkeler* (coconut) pudding and jilipi (jalebi) pudding are two fusion creations that were popular among the members of the Tagore family. Over time, restaurants began specializing in fried foods and puddings, which, due to their common British origin, were invariably served together. These eateries popularized an entire spread of British snacks and puddings, bringing their recipes into the kitchens of the royal capital and making them an inextricable part of Calcutta's culinary culture. Kiosks in every nook and cranny of the city prepare chops and cutlets today and entrepreneurs have even come up with recipes of their own. Puddings, on the other hand, are still very exclusively made, and increasingly confined to home kitchens. Most fried food joints have done away with European puddings, as making them is a slow and time-consuming affair.

Cabin-style Puddings

Mitra Café: This is one of the few old-school fried food joints that has retained the British dessert in the form of a *chhanar pudding*, which used to be served in most of the old cabins of Calcutta. This signature pudding of Mitra Café, which is old as its brain chop, is a two-layered affair made of chhana (as chhena or casein is known in Bengali), eggs, milk, sugar and vanilla essence. Chhana imparts a delicate and smooth texture to the pudding. The top layer is a sunny yellow, and one beneath is pristine white. The pudding is served topped with swirls of chocolate sauce. Unsurprisingly, it comes a close second in popularity to the chop.

Regent Restaurant: Popularly known as Regent, the restaurant was set up in 1935 in Chowringhee Place in the Sir Stuart Hogg Market area by Biswanath Mukherjee. The restaurant has the distinction of having catered for the cricket matches held in Eden Gardens by not only putting up stalls for the audiences but also serving lunch to the players. It enjoys the privilege of having been the appointed caterer for the matches sponsored by the Maharaja of Cooch Behar, Jagaddipendra Narayan, at the iconic stadium. The late king was an avid sportsperson and a good cricketer who led the Bengal cricket team for many years and would often organize and sponsor cricket matches.

Its proximity to Sir Stuart Hogg Market made the eatery very popular among the British and Anglo-Indians who were regular shoppers there. Another reason for its popularity was the colonial food, including chops, cutlets and puddings, which had been served in the restaurant since its inception. In fact, there was a time when, to cater to the pudding craze, bread pudding, custard pudding and fruit pudding were whipped up by the restaurant's Muslim and Goan cooks.

Perpetually overflowing with customers, the restaurant today, in an attempt to keep the legacy of the British alive, serves a 'Special Pudding', whose main ingredients are sandwich bread, eggs, milk, sugar, chhana, vanilla essence, cashew nuts and raisins. This slender block of delicious pudding takes the customers back to the colonial times when the palate for the dessert began to develop.

Film-makers Mrinal Sen and Satyajit Ray, cricketer Pankaj Roy and writer Samaresh Majumdar belong to Regent's list of celebrity customers. For the general public, the presence of Regent in the Sir Stuart Hogg Market area is a nostalgic reminder of an earlier era, which has become ingrained in the city's history.

2. Hospitality Industry and Continental Cuisine in British Calcutta

British cuisine made up a large part of what was often called 'club food', referring to the food served even today in the once all-white clubs throughout India. Roasts, stews, bakes, sandwiches and white bread, fish and chips, cutlets, croquettes, sausages, bacon, ham, egg variants, puddings, custards, etc. are all legacies left behind by the British. In

> recent years, full-fledged continental cuisine has made a mark for itself in the country. But the British food, along with a few dishes of the other European countries, which largely made up continental cuisine in India at one point of time, still flourishes, especially in Kolkata, where nostalgic memories of the Raj linger on in many old eateries and restaurants that have been serving it over many years.
>
> —Bridget White-Kumar, food historian

The introduction of continental cuisine in Bengal can be traced back to when Europeans stepped on its shores, bringing along their food habits and culinary practices. But, when did continental cuisine begin to make its presence felt in Calcutta? The process was a gradual one and quite complex. It took more than a century, since this alien cuisine began to be commercially available, for the locals to develop an affinity for it.

Initially, the cuisine was confined to the homes of the European settlers like the Portuguese and the Dutch who had arrived in Bengal before the British (the French, Danes and Austrians arrived later). Even when the British developed Calcutta and made the city their home, there was no effort on their part to spread their home cooking. Continental cuisine stepped out of the homes of the white settlers only when some enterprising Europeans began establishing taverns in the seventeenth century.

The spread of continental cuisine in Calcutta had a methodical pattern. It began with the local cooks working in British households. The establishment of taverns, boarding houses and colonial clubs made this cuisine move out of the confinement of homes and reach a wider European audience. European hotels and restaurants took over from here and blazed the trail by making this cuisine commercially available to Europeans as well as upper-class Indians and Anglophiles. The fancy restaurants that came up on Park Street during the Company Raj period added a touch of glamour to the cuisine. Finally, after Independence, local restaurateurs picked up the threads and made continental cuisine accessible to the masses by setting up restaurants. Today, continental cuisine is no longer an alien fare to the people of Calcutta and has become one of the regular eating-out options.

Taverns

In the early days, Europeans reached India via the overland route across Asia Minor and Persia. But, once they discovered a sea route to India, it became the most convenient way to travel to the country. The journey was hard, the sea route, difficult and dangerous, and the food and water often got spoiled. But the voyage was not always the worst part of the journey. Newcomers would be filled with anxiety about where they would stay once they reached the city and the kind of accommodation they would find. The establishment of taverns must have come as a boon to these weary travellers.

If the British sailing to Calcutta did not have acquaintances in the city, they usually stayed in taverns before they found permanent residences. This was when hotels were yet to arrive. The English travel writer and poet Emma Roberts, in her book *Scenes and Characteristics of Hindostan, With Sketches of Anglo-Indian Society* (1837) writes, 'Formerly, strangers visiting Calcutta were dependent upon the hospitality of the residents, or were compelled to take large unfurnished houses, there being neither lodgings nor hotels for the reception of guests' (p. 3). Prior to the opening of taverns, it was common to find the new arrivals staying on budge-rows moored at the river ghats in Calcutta for a week at a time. A budge-row (the anglicized expression of the Hindi word 'bajra') is a large boat with accommodation facilities, used for journeying on the rivers. With the development of the city, the establishment of taverns became a necessity. Some were frequented by the well-to-do, who hosted public dinners in these places. There were also taverns of modest description, admitting all and sundry, and generally filled with an abundance of people. Some were also set up in the suburbs of the city, alongside the river. Taverns, which served punch to their boarders and visitors, were known as punch-houses. Many, particularly the seafaring persons, indulged in large quantities of punch, the drink that was made at these places. During this time, Calcutta was not only swarming with European sailors, but also taverns and punch-houses to shelter them on their arrival. Punch is a drink of low alcohol content served communally in large and wide bowls. The credit for its discovery goes to those sailors and employees of the British East India Company, who were among the early arrivals in India, where it originated. On finding an abundance of spirits, sugar and limes upon their arrival in the country, these early settlers made ample quantities of this drink, which was introduced to England in the early seventeenth century and from there, to the other European countries.

Along with lodging facilities, the taverns provided food. The English lawyer William Hickey's *Memoirs* was among the bestsellers of 1919; in this book he paints a vivid picture of life in Calcutta and Madras, among other places, in the eighteenth century. Hickey had arrived at Hooghly on 1 November 1777. From there, he sailed for Calcutta, and on the way, stopped at a tavern close to Culpee (an anchorage towards Calcutta, near Diamond Harbour), where he spent a night. He describes his stay at this tavern:

> In about an hour and a half after our arrival we had served up some very excellent fish, tolerable fowls, with plenty of eggs and bacon, and, what was a prodigious luxury to me who had been so long without it, capitally good bread[...] At eight I arose, and did ample justice to the hot rolls, tea, and coffee. At ten, the tide suiting, we re-embarked in our unaccommodating vessel, taking with us a plentiful supply of cold fowls and other articles of food. (pp. 118–19)

Passengers of every class resided on the shore during the ship's detention, often indulging in dinner at the taverns, where they could even have beefsteaks and claret, which tasted better than the food served on the deck.

Job Charnock is believed to have been very interested in Calcutta's taverns. He frequented a punch-house maintained by a certain Hill, secretary and captain of the soldiers, and often played billiards there. There are records of an Apollo Tavern in Lal Bazar where the President and Governor of Fort William held a consultation on 12 December 1748. An advertisement has been found of Tresham's Tavern, set up by J. Tresham in 1785, when it shifted base from Meredith's Lane to Cossitollah Bazar on Cossitollah Road (subsequently renamed Bentinck Street). In this advertisement, the owner states, 'Ladies and Gentlemen may be furnished with Dinners, Suppers, or Cold Collation, on the shortest notice. Biscuits of all kinds, tarts and tartlets fresh every day.' He also advertised a list of all those food items that could be taken to sea or while travelling up-country:

> potted beef, veal, mutton, ducks, geese and pigeons, collard beef, pork, and small pigs, fish coreach, minced meat, plum cakes, jams and marmalades of all kinds, preserved butter, eggs and milk, milk-punch, etc., etc.

J. Tresham guaranteed a shelf life of six months for these items. The tavern-keeper lured his customers by promising them complete attendance and 'turtles dressed at home and abroad'.

The owners advertised their taverns, particularly the hearty meals that were served. A certain Robert Rishton wished to acquaint the 'Gentlemen of the Settlement' that he had opened a tavern in Radha Bazar next to Fivey's Europe Shop, with the unique selling proposition of serving 'oysters every week'. This advertisement was featured in James Augustus Hicky's *Bengal Gazette* on 10 February 1781. Nicholl's Tavern was well known for its fowls and oysters, and a tavern called London Hotel, for its meals (exclusive of the wine and dessert) and entertainment for the moderate price of a gold mohur a head.

Francis Le Gallais, an old hand in the tavern business of Calcutta, often catered dinners for Government House functions and important personalities. There is an account of a large gathering of respectable and well-known personalities who dined in his tavern, Le Gallais, on turtle, turkey and 'other good things' on New Year's Day in 1789. The gathered company then toasted the occasion twenty-four times. The accompanying Grenadiers of the European Regiment of Fort William fired volleys of blank cartridges out of the windows after each toast. St Andrew's Day Dinner, probably the first held in Calcutta, took place in his tavern in 1792. It is believed that it was in his tavern, in the same year, that a meeting was held with the purpose of raising subscriptions for the 'erection of a public building' where the inhabitants of the settlement could gather. This eventually led to the construction of the Town Hall.

In 1780, the Harmonic Tavern in Lal Bazar reigned as the most exclusive in White Town. It was a splendid-looking building and the best of British society gathered here. Mrs Warren Hastings was a patron. The select crowd of gentlemen who gathered here gave a concert, ball and supper during the cold season in alphabetical rotation, once a fortnight. Major Harry Hobbs, in his book *Calcutta Taverns and Hotels—Volume I* (1988), mentions the famous 'Bread and Cheese' bungalow located at the far end of Bowbazar, which reached the heights of popularity in 1776. At the same time there were the not-so-exclusive taverns in Dacres Lane and Khidderpore, where the meals consisting of chickens, ducks, boiled (buffalo) beef with roast gravy, mutton chops, cheese, milk, overripe bananas and other items were enough to stuff a boarder.

'Clubs and Cows', Boarding Houses and Hotels

From the 1800s, boarding houses, hotels and eateries were opened in the city by Europeans. Billiard tables were kept in these places and liquor of various kinds sold in them. In *Calcutta Taverns and Hotels—Volume II*

(1987), Major Hobbs writes, 'Some years ago a contributor to one of the Calcutta papers told the story of Mrs Box who, he said, introduced the boarding house system to Calcutta' (p. 386). Although this claim cannot be confirmed, it is definitely true that she was a very prominent owner of boarding houses in the city, who appeared on the scene in 1867 and ruled for thirty years. She had eight boarding houses in places like Camac Street, Middleton Row and the surrounding areas. Mrs Box's boarding houses were not meant for everybody. She catered to the top drawer of British Calcutta's society—gazetted officers and their families—for whom she provided scrupulously clean lodgings and good food. One of them was even more select than the others and was visited by the secretaries to the government and their wives, Members of Council and the General Officers from the army headquarters. But the Box boarding houses were very much in demand and Mrs Box soon widened the circle from 'Gazetted Officers Only' to 'On the Government House List'. Despite this, the snobbery remained and there was now a rush of bara sahibs and their wives to her establishments.

Closely following Mrs Box was Mrs Annie Monk, the Irish widow of a soldier with a shrewd capacity for business. It is believed that no Calcutta businesswoman was more popular in those days than her. She took in lodgers at her boarding houses and provided them with comfortable rooms, hot and cold water, and scrumptious meals, with the provision for arranging private dinners and suppers on request. Mrs Monk's boarding establishments in Calcutta were spread all over White Town and included Palms' on Middleton Row, Hamilton House on Theatre Road, Outram House, Lansdowne House and an establishment at No. 15 Camac Street. Her boarding houses in Chowringhee were heavily patronized as they were near the business quarter. These houses were later converted by the Armenian real estate baron, Arratoon Stephen, into the imposing Grand Hotel. The No. 8 plot on Harrington Street was occupied by Mrs Annie Monk's popular boarding house for a very long time until another Armenian real estate baron, Johannes Carapiet Galstaun, erected the Harrington Mansion on it. In *Calcutta Taverns and Hotels—Volume II* (1987), Major Harry Hobbs mentions that there were moderately priced boarding houses on Dacres Lane and around New Market, and pleasant ones on Kyd Street. In stark contrast, the boarding houses on Dharmatala Street provided the boarders with watery soup, stiff bread, tough beef and puddings that resembled a stodgy mess.

The British began establishing clubs in Calcutta. These became platforms for social interaction among them and were sometimes dedicated to a particular interest or activity. There were clubs that enabled members to enjoy items that might otherwise be too expensive and troublesome to obtain, like mutton clubs, cheese clubs, ice clubs, bread clubs and draught beer clubs. The beef of the city was held in high regard by the sahibs. They felt it was the best in the world and highly praised the quality of Calcutta's beefsteaks. Perhaps, this is the reason Calcutta had a Beefsteak Club that survived for nearly fifty years. It languished for some time, was revived in 1827, and gradually faded away.

Calcutta is believed to be the birthplace of clubs in India. There were so many exclusive white clubs in Calcutta at one point of time that it prompted an American writer to comment that Calcutta is 'a city of clubs and cows'.

The social clubs, where the sahibs and memsahibs gathered to mingle, were popular for the food that they served. In *Calcutta Taverns And Hotels—Volume II* (1987), Major Hobbs mentions a certain Reform Club. The kitchen of this club was ruled by a French chef for some time. He soon became famous for turning out salads that were sheer masterpieces. When a member asked him about the secret behind them, he is believed to have replied in jest that when he finished preparing and dressing the plate, he would chew a little clove of garlic between his teeth and breathe gently over the whole food. The United Service Club (established originally as the Bengal Military Club in 1845) on Chowringhee Road had membership reserved exclusively for men from the Indian Civil Service and Military Service before financial considerations led it to open its doors to people from other government services. It was an excellent institution in all respects, including the food that it served, and was believed to have a magnificent billiards room. Around 1949, the club closed down and the building is currently occupied by the Geological Survey of India.

Games, concerts, dancing and other entertainments were organized in the clubs to provide amusements on dull evenings. For example, the members of the United Service Club would organize garden parties on the club lawn once a week during winters. Looked upon as one of the society functions of Calcutta, these parties were held in the evenings from 5 to 7 p.m. and always had a band in attendance to brighten and enliven the proceedings. They were a part of the entertainment activities that took place throughout the year at the club premises. Some of the prominent clubs in the city during the Company Raj period were the

Calcutta Cricket and Football Club (estd. 1792), Bengal Club (estd. 1827), Royal Calcutta Golf Club (estd. 1829), Royal Calcutta Turf Club (estd. 1847), Saturday Club (estd. 1875), Tollygunge Club (estd. 1895) and Calcutta Club (estd. 1907). According to the rules laid down by the clubs, members had to follow proper dress codes and conduct, modelled on the British upper classes, when they were in their premises.

Generally, Mog, Bihari Muslim and Dhaka Christian khansamas or cooks dominated not only the kitchens of British households but also of the clubs. Besides their native fare, the British were equally fond of Italian, French and Swiss cuisines. Traditional recipes were handed to the khansamas by the British, and they became experts in making these dishes. The memsahibs came to rely on their competence so much that they did not have to think about the possibility of burnt puddings and custards anymore while sending out dinner invitations. The khansama could now make the best hors d'oeuvres and soups, cook the fish, shellfish and meats to near perfection, and churn out delicious desserts from soufflés to transparent caramelized sugar baskets filled with fruit salad and cream. The finest of wines were brought out from the bottlekhana, as the pantry was called, and served in delicate glasses by bearers or waiters. Constantly on their feet, these well-trained bearers waited on the table, changing the plates after every course and serving the guests after-dinner coffee and expensive cigarettes—all under the watchful eyes of the khitmatgar or steward.

The exclusive clubs, predominantly scattered over White Town, served the foods that were trendy in contemporary Britain and the rest of Europe. Consommés, stews, meat pies and roasts, and juicy pork chops formed a part of the fare offered at these clubs. Soufflés, bread-and-butter puddings, crème caramels and tutti-frutti desserts wrapped up the scrumptious and hearty meals. The British followed the tradition of having either bara or chota pegs of their favourite hard drinks in the cosy club bar, after which, they ate their dinner in the dining hall. Before wrapping up on the clubs of Calcutta, let us take a look at some of the dishes they served, as described by authors Minakshie Das Gupta, Bunny Gupta and Jaya Chaliha, in the chapter 'Firinghee Flavours', from their book *The Calcutta Cookbook: A Treasury of Recipes from Pavement to Palace* (1995): A typical luncheon served at the Bengal Club included the choice of bhekti Normandie or steak and kidney pie or a cooked leg of ham in pineapple and cherry sauce and apple pie while cold collations, roasts and au gratins, among other dishes, often featured in its Friday luncheon spread. Mince pies and roast turkey defined the Christmas lunch at the club. Shashlik and chicken à la Kiev were specialities of the Saturday Club. Stewed turtle soup and minced partridge pies were runaway hits at the Calcutta Club, which also took pride in making the best Steak Romaine in the city—a dish best described as 'a fairly thin slice of grilled beef, on top of that grilled ham, on top of that mushrooms and on top of that a good appetite'. The Royal Calcutta Golf Club was a close competitor and claims to have once made the best steaks in the royal capital. Members of Tollygunge Club, a splendid country club set up on vast acres of land, after a round of golf, would treat themselves to hot drop scones served with jam or paté. Sometimes, balls at the club featured barbeque dinners. On these occasions, whole sheep were roasted on turning spits and whole roasted suckling pigs, with apples stuck in their mouths, were laid on tables.

The hospitality industry in Calcutta was growing. In 1845, there were twenty-five wine merchants and fourteen bakers and confectioners in the city. B. Smythe & Co. was supposedly one of the largest wine and spirit merchants in those days. The Europeans took to alcohol with more enthusiasm after the introduction of ice from North America. Before 1833, ice was a rare commodity in India. In Bengal, ice was procured in the winter months from Chinsurah, now a town in West Bengal's Hooghly district. It was called 'Hooghly Ice' because it was made by freezing the river's waters in shallow pits. This ice was more like slush and filthy and unfit for consumption. Finally, in the nineteenth century, the British East India Company decided to make arrangements for the regular supply of ice for all seasons. The year 1833 was a memorable one for Calcuttans when ice or burruf, covered with fly ash and salt, and packed in jute, arrived aboard the *S.S. Tuscany* from Massachusetts. A large number of American apples came with the cargo and these were placed on top of the huge blocks of ice.

Frederic Tudor, an enterprising businessman from Boston, had taken up this project and arrived in Calcutta with the ice. The excitement of Calcuttans knew no bounds. Soon, ice glittered on Calcutta's tables, filled its butter dishes and floated in goblets of water. Dinner invitations were sent out to taste claret and beer cooled by this American import. Over the years, as trade increased, the American ice, which always arrived with the much-in-demand American apples, was preserved in Ice House. Built by Tudor, the entrance of this building faced Church Lane in Dalhousie Square. Anyone who could afford an icebox now invested in one of those zinc-lined wooden contraptions. In the chapter 'Firinghee Flavours' from their book *The Calcutta Cookbook: A Treasury of Recipes from Pavement to Palace* (1995), the authors write, 'Calcutta's banqueting tables took on an arctic hue with peaks of ice and ornately sculpted swans bearing caviare. Cold soufflés, aspics, mousses and galantines were washed down with plenty of chilled loll shrob (red wines)' (p. 158).

Tudor Ice Company made a fortune shipping ice cut from the lakes and ponds of Massachusetts, a state that has the climate necessary for producing natural ice in excess. Unlike the Hooghly Ice, this one was pure. The company also transported ice to Bombay and Madras, and had a similar Ice House set up in each city. Tudor was the pioneer of the international ice trade and made such grand profits from it that he eventually came to be known as 'Boston's Ice King'. The import of American ice into Calcutta continued for a long time. Ice factories were first established in the city in 1878 with the formation of the Bengal Ice Company and in 1882, with the Crystal Ice Company. Later, these two companies merged and formed the Calcutta Ice Association Ltd. Thus, Bengal became self-reliant and started manufacturing its own artificial ice.

Hotels had cropped up in the city but there was a great deal of variation when it came to quality. Major Hobbs noted, 'The difference between hotels is amazing. One may be like that bamboo-and-mud basha in Gariahat, exalted by the title of the "Glutton's Hotel", or it may be such luxurious magnificence that it is necessary to be almost a millionaire to sleep in the garret' (p. 506, *Calcutta Taverns and Hotels—Volume II* [1987]). The daily fare in those modest dwellings, which conferred upon themselves the title of hotels, was potato chops, minced meat and soda water. Hobbs continues, 'soda water from Scheppe & Co. in stone quarts and pints was on the market in Calcutta in 1810' (p. 181, *Calcutta Taverns and Hotels—Volume I* [1988]). Locally made soda water was also available and many British men preferred the Calcutta sodas which were stronger and had more fizz. Most of the hotels had bars and the main attraction in these bars was the barmaids. They came from lower middle-class homes in Britain to work in Calcutta on six-month agreements; some stayed longer, while most got married.

Some hotels stood out from the rest in terms of quality. Bristol Hotel, Continental Hotel and Adelphi Hotel were the front runners in the Calcutta hospitality industry. Bristol Hotel, formerly known as Hotel d'Europe, was located in Chowringhee. The food there was of excellent quality. Its unsurpassable fillet steaks and tiffin spread, of eighteen items with unlimited helpings, saw a rush to visit its portals. One of the attractions of the hotel was an all-female Austrian string band. The hotel soon became a fashionable resort. Hotel Continental, also in Chowringhee, was renowned for its excellent food and clean kitchens, which made it a popular resort where some of the best public dinners were served. The Adelphi Hotel on Waterloo Street was a fine hotel with lofty rooms on the first floor, a well-stocked bar with best quality wines and liquors, and excellent food. The hotel was particularly known for its corned and spiced beef, and the general belief was that it was difficult to come across beef brisket and corned or spiced rump as good as those made at the Adelphi. Its star culinary attractions were the hot and cold suppers available at all hours and the weekly supper every Saturday, which lasted from eight in the evening to one in the morning. The ship captains often made the Adelphi Hotel their headquarters, filling its bar and dining room. Skittles was the favourite game in Calcutta in the 1880s. Besides having splendid billiard saloons, the hotel had the best skittle alley, which only added to its popularity.

But the jewels in the crown were Spence's Hotel, Great Eastern Hotel and Grand Hotel. These three hotels left a lasting impression on the hospitality industry of British Calcutta. They were classy, luxurious and extremely popular among the residents of the city, making them the subject of literature and discussions for many years, even after colonialism ended in India.

Spence's Hotel, established in 1830, was the first hotel to have started in Calcutta. The founder of the hotel, John Spence, originally hailed from Paisley in Scotland. He came to India alone and made a considerable fortune here. Originally, the hotel was located just across the road from the West Gate of Government House (now known as Raj Bhavan) in Dalhousie Square. During its history, the hotel had a few changes of location, but its final address was Wellesley Place. It was a first-class hotel for travellers and residents of the city, and was particularly noted for its extreme cleanliness. The fame of Spence's began to spread within a few years after its establishment. George William Johnson, author of *The Stranger in India; Or, Three Years in Calcutta* (1843), wrote that people leaving England were advised to keep a note ready so that as soon as their ship reached 'Kedgeree' (a point on the Hooghly, halfway between Calcutta and Sagar Island, and a place where the river widens into a basin), it would be dispatched by the post office boat, which would come alongside, to Mr Spence, requesting him to reserve rooms for them. British civil servant, barrister and ornithologist, Douglas Dewar, in his book *Bygone Days in India* (1922), described the arrival of a sailing ship in Calcutta in 1840: 'At length the traveller finds himself ashore[...] [and] having tumbled into a palanquin, as primed by a fellow-voyager, shouts, "Barra potch khana"', which is the name by which all the bearers know Spence's Hotel[...] It is managed by the proprietor, John Spence, who may fairly be said to have originated hotels in Bengal' (p. 271). John Spence had, very quickly, earned the reputation of housing and feeding his guests well. An account has been found by a cadet, who arrived in Calcutta in 1835, after spending eight long months on voyage on a country ship. He had survived those months on board on salted beef, hard biscuits and stinking water. After checking into Spence's Hotel, he wrote about his gastronomic experience,

> And then, dear reader, picture to yourself a snow-white table cloth on which was drawn up in beautiful array, ham, eggs (fresh for a change), a superb kind of fish from the salt-water lakes called a becktee or cockup, fried, boiled rice, muffins, tea, coffee etc. Plantains, radishes, small prints of butter in a handsome cut-glass vessel of cold water, and a bouquet of flowers in the centre gave a most cool and refreshing appearance to the table.

There is also an account of two cadets who, on their arrival in Calcutta in 1845, checked into Spence's Hotel and found themselves in a long room 'where some dozen or fifteen gentlemen were engaged in consuming cold meat, hot potatoes, and bottled beer'. An advertisement of Spence's Hotel, which appeared in *The Statesman* in February 1885, mentions the shipment of 'Fresh English Grapes, Filberts, and Brazil Nuts', and even 'Fresh Oysters', that would be served every 'Wednesday, Thursday and Saturday'.

The ownership of Spence's Hotel changed hands many times. One of the owners after John Spence is believed to have installed a lift that was wound up by a 'coolie', making Spence's Hotel the first place in Calcutta to enjoy such a facility. The hotel also enjoyed the distinction of being one of the first British concerns to recognize the value of cooperation with Indians in business. In *Calcutta Taverns and Hotels—Volume II* (1987), Major Hobbs mentions that in the 1860s, Babu H.L. Mitter was one of the directors of the hotel, perhaps the first Bengali to hold such a position in a European business house in India. The hotel would often advertise in the newspapers about its clean and comfortable rooms, delectable food, dining and billiard saloons, and in later years, its American bar and lounge.

For a long time, Spence's Hotel was the favourite haunt of people from different walks of life. Businessmen, married couples, families and many more often visited 'Eeshpen Hotel' to enjoy good food in quiet surroundings. Spence's hotel was the centre of social life in Calcutta and became renowned as a family hotel. Many well-known people of the city made it their permanent home. The eminent Bengali poet and dramatist of the nineteenth century, Michael Madhusudan Dutt, is believed to have once stayed in this hotel. In later years, Spence's Hotel was the inspiration behind the very successful novel *Chowringhee* (1962), written by the popular Bengali author Mani Shankar Mukherjee. The luxurious hotel was called 'Shahjahan' in his novel, which was later made into a blockbuster Bengali film.

Nobody knows the cause or date of John Spence's severance from the hotel he founded. Local history is also silent about how he spent the remaining years of his life, or even whether in India or elsewhere. Although Spence's Hotel no longer exists (no one knows why or when it was closed down), John Spence will always be remembered for doing a great service to Calcutta by being the first person to establish a hotel in it.

The Great Eastern Hotel, first known as Auckland Hotel, was established in 1841 by David Wilson on Old Court House Street. The name of the hotel was changed to Great Eastern Hotel in 1858. Besides being a first-class luxury hotel, Great Eastern was the first to pioneer the concept of multiple shops on its premises. On the ground floor of the building was a variety of shops, which were all owned by the hotel and sold all sorts of goods. This prompted the famous war correspondent, Sir William Howard Russell, who arrived in Calcutta at the end of January in 1858, to comment,

> In one large house there is an attempt to combine a tailor's, a milliner's and dressmaker's, a haberdasher's, a confectioner's, a hardware man's, a woollen merchant's, a provision dealer's, a grocer's, a coffeehouse-keeper's establishment, with a hotel and other trades and callings. (pp. 240–41, *Calcutta Taverns and Hotels—Volume I* [1988])

These departments were managed by men who 'dressed to perfection' and smoked handsomely carved pipes or the finest cigars. In *Calcutta Taverns and Hotels—Volume I* (1988), Major Hobbs writes, '[…]a man could walk in at one end, buy a complete outfit, a wedding present, or seeds for the garden, have an excellent meal, a full peg for ten annas, and if the barmaid was agreeable, walk out at the other end engaged to be married.' (p. 244)

William Walker published a series of letters reprinted from *the Times of India*, with the title, 'Jottings of an Invalid in Search of Health, Comprising a Run Through British India and a Visit to Singapore and Java' in 1865, under the pseudonym Tom Cringle. He had paid his first visit to Calcutta in 1863. His observation of the Great Eastern Hotel read as:

> […]it has its coffee rooms, billiard rooms, dining rooms, bed rooms, wine cellars, and every description of provisions which travellers will do well to select from for a journey. They have a steam engine to grind coffee […]. The coffee room is nicely furnished (as are the whole of the different departments)[…] (p. 10).

Though the concept of multiple shops was unique, it was ahead of its time and not very successful. It took the directors a very long time to realize that the combination of shops and hotel keeping was not a paying proposition. The concept was abolished, though it is not exactly known when.

The hotel had a splendid appearance and went through quite a few architectural and structural changes and improvements with time. But its decor was always sophisticated and kept getting better with these changes. The final appearance of the hotel was striking. Its walls were embellished with dados of brightly coloured tiles and the floors, paved with black and white marbles. The doors were of the latest designs and had polished brass handles and fittings. The bedrooms were large and tastefully done while the bathrooms were clean with modern and up-to-date sanitary fittings. A large dining hall, spacious billiard saloon and modern lounges gave added appeal. The cherry on the cake was the grand arcade with a spacious verandah on the top, which overhung the footpath of the hotel. This was one of the best features of the Great Eastern.

Great Eastern Hotel offered a breakfast spread of fresh fruits, fruit juices, warm and cold cereals, eggs, sausages, bacon, ham, grilled tomatoes, hash browns, devilled kidneys, breads, herb butter, jam, marmalade, tea and coffee. Meals at the hotel included a variety of dishes like soups, cold meats, pies, roasts, steaks, puddings and soufflés. Often a curry was also included in the fare. Brunches at the Great Eastern Hotel were something that many looked forward to. The hotel followed a tradition of serving drive-in meals to people who pulled up outside on the street in gharries or vehicles. A place was reserved near the hotel entrance for this purpose. These customers could avail of the one-rupee tiffin service, which included a plate of the basic steak or chop, bread, two vegetables and a full peg. There are written accounts of special Sunday tiffin at the hotel; for example, half a dozen choice spirits, hors d'oeuvres, turtle soup, pâté de foie gras, asparagus and ices washed down with extra dry champagne or consomme royale, chicken liver or prawn paté, asparagus and green mango ice washed down with champagne. Sometimes, the regular fare included potatoes boiled in their jackets, boiled beef and aubergines, and a curry. Great Eastern Hotel was famous for its smoked hilsa, a delicacy prepared with the most favoured fish of Bengal whose meat has a great taste. This boneless creation was completely of European conception because robbing the hilsa (Indian shad or ilish in Bengali) of its bones is alien to the Bengali culinary practice.

A menu card of the hotel, dated 1 February 1928, has the following dishes listed in it for lunch: jelly consommé in cup, longchamp soup, fried fillets of beckti with tartare sauce, prawns a l'Americaine with Creole rice, sheep's brain grenobloise, steak and kidney pudding, braised chicken printanier, and roast leg of pork with apple sauce and puree of peas. The menu mentions that a diner has to wait ten minutes to be served: grilled tournedos nicoise, grilled sheep's kidney on toast with Darjeeling cabbage and brinjal marseillaise or mutton korma curry. The cold buffet spread in the menu includes chicken salad, roast mutton, fowl galantine, chicken patties, pork brawn, stuffed veal, roast chicken, sirloin of beef, ox tongue, game pie, boiled round of beef and mousse of ham in aspic with assorted salad. A diner is spoilt for choice between apple flan Chantilly and nougat ice cup for dessert. The luncheon is rounded off with cheese, fruits and mocha coffee.[1]

The Great Eastern Hotel did thriving business and became a popular destination in Calcutta for the local residents, tourists, businessmen,

1. Courtesy: Society for the Preservation of Archival Materials and Monuments of Calcutta.

dignitaries and celebrities. People flocked to it for its classy ambience, great food and plush accommodation. The popularity of Spence's and Great Eastern encouraged Dave Carson, a local humorist, who flourished in the late nineteenth century, to sing:

To Wilsons, or to Spence's Hall
On holiday I stray;
With freedom call for mutton chops
And billiards play all day;
The servant catches from afar the hukum,
'Jaldi jao,
Hi Khitmagar, barandy, shrab, Bilaitipani lao…'

The splendour and glory of Great Eastern Hotel continued even after Independence. But, unfortunately, its business went into a decline during the Naxal era. Its deteriorating condition made the state government take over the management control of the hotel in 1975. But soon it became engulfed in trade union problems which further affected business. Ultimately, the state government sold the hotel to the private company, Lalit Suri Hospitality Group, an enterprise of Bharat Hotels Limited, in 2005. For many years the hotel remained closed because it underwent extensive renovations, reopening in 2013 as The LaLiT Great Eastern Kolkata.

Today, the building is registered as a heritage structure, and despite the renovations, some of its early features like the facade and the grand staircase have been retained. In her article 'Heritage with High Tea' for *Outlook Traveller* magazine (22 April 2018), Uttara Gangopadhyay writes, '[…]old artefacts such as bread moulds and charcoal-irons have been converted into flower pots. Old German-silver water jugs monogrammed GEH serve as plant holders. Some of the old furniture that could be salvaged [are] being used as corner pieces across the hotel. An eclectic collection of old statues, tea dispensers, decanters, liquor bottles and other bric-a-brac can be found […]. One of the surprises waiting in store in the Atrium Lobby [are] two large iron cages, their use left to the visitor's imagination—probably used during cabaret performances at the Maxim's, the older hotel's famous bar and restaurant.[…] the piano, again from Maxim's, […]sits in a corner of the main lobby. Manufactured in Hamburg by M.F. Rachals & Co., it was restored by Braganza and Co. of Free School Street in Kolkata. It is in perfect playing condition. The final stop has to be the bakery[…].

The old oven, a fair-sized room, has now been redesigned as a private dining area. In deference to the legacy, a part of the old brick wall has been left exposed. The Baker Perkins machineries used by the old bakery have been strategically placed as decorative pieces.' Copies of old advertisements dating back to the days of the establishment of the hotel are displayed on one wall. The pub has been named Wilson's, as a tribute to the Englishman, who founded this iconic hotel.

The Great Eastern Hotel is deeply linked with Calcutta's antiquity and there are many interesting stories surrounding it. Beneath its modern appearance and amenities lie buried layers of history, which, if dug up, can richly enlighten the future generations of this city.

Grand Hotel: When Mrs Annie Monk was no longer able to handle the business, she packed her bags and sailed back to Ireland. The Armenian real estate baron Arratoon Stephen bought over her boarding house complex, and by the early twentieth century, had converted it into an imposing hotel. He named it Grand Hotel after Colonel Grand, whose mansion it had once been, before Mrs Annie Monk made a boarding house of it. The hotel made a mark in the city, thanks to the luxurious comfort it offered its guests. Stephen advertised the hotel as 'A Home to all who are away from Home'. Under his reign, Grand Hotel became renowned as the first up-to-date hotel in Calcutta, complete with all modern amenities. A 1927 advertisement of the Grand Hotel lists some of its attractive features:

Wonderful view, overlooks maidan and river
Under English management
Four dining rooms accommodating 1000 guests
Banqueting room seating 400
Three kitchens under the supervision of French chefs
Fruits and vegetables from our own gardens
Pure fresh water from our own tube wells
Largest and best appointed ball-room in the East
Three orchestras—Sunday morning concerts,
Rates: Rs 15—per day to Rs 100—per day inclusive.

As in every hotel, there were minor mishaps now and then. But that did not tarnish the reputation of Grand Hotel because overall, its management was excellent. Arratoon Stephen's wit and charm also helped matters. He had once been a successful jeweller and had enough experience in dealing with aristocratic and wealthy customers. Known to use polished courtesy as a weapon to deal with rudeness, Stephen solved minor mishaps with his gift of the gab. Once, as the inside story goes, an irate guest rushed into the hotel office and demanded Stephen's explanation for the presence of a cockroach in his early morning tea. The cockroach, as big as his thumb, was scalded to death on top of the tea leaves in his teapot. The guest was appalled that he was being fed such muck in a first-class hotel. While he was hurling abuses at Stephen, the hotelier calmly put on his glasses and took a good look at his angry guest. 'Well', he said, 'five hundred rooms, five hundred teapots. One cockroach. Very good average' (p. 335, *Calcutta Taverns and Hotels—Volume II* [1987]).

Stephen installed a hydraulic lift in the hotel, becoming the first person in Calcutta to do such a thing, and was also the first hotelier in India to bring an orchestra from England to perform in his hotel. Grand Hotel became the favourite haunt of the Europeans in Calcutta who, along with the aristocratic brown sahibs, dined on soups, cold cuts, roasts and perhaps even curries, followed at times by bread-and-butter pudding. A luncheon menu card of the hotel, dated 6 January 1946, offers a five course meal for three rupees. The meal includes a choice of consommé premiere or mulligatawny soup, chateaubriand garni with vegetables and potatoes or kofta curry and peas pulao, a cold buffet choice of Hunter's spiced beef, boar's head, Swiss sausage or steak and kidney pie along with assorted salads and pickles. Delicious coconut puffs and custard is offered for dessert. This hearty meal is rounded off with fruits and coffee.

The hotel was famous for its annual New Year's Eve party. Bachi J. Karkaria, author of *To a Grand Design* (2009), writes, 'Not unsurprisingly, the grandest night at the Grand was New Year's Eve. The great dining room's chandelier was ablaze, its myriad facets finding counterpoint in the diamonds that glittered on a hundred milky throats; the sparkle of the crystal was outmatched by that of the conversation; the liquor flowed; the tables groaned, and the women gushed with delight over the gifts that "darling Arathoon" had placed on each table. Not just the paper hats and squeakers that have survived into our less generous times, but Italian dolls dressed in lace and taffeta, porcelain figurines, French perfume. The men were no less excited over their presents; silver snuff boxes were nothing to be sneezed at, less so, the cigarette cases, or perhaps, even a cigarette holder in gold. A champagne bottle wedged in ice was on each table—on the house. As the clock above the band began to chime out the old year, the corks popped, the strains of "Auld Lang Syne" flowed out and voices rose, if not in tune, certainly in high spirits. But that was not all. Before the clock had stopped ringing out, twelve piglets were released into the ballroom; there followed a mad scramble as the men tripped over their tails and the women over their high heels to catch one of them. Finders were keepers, and the squealing little fellow ended up as the traditional suckling on New Year's Day for whoever had been swift enough and sober enough to have caught one.' (pp. 15–16)

But, unfortunately, Grand Hotel's good fortune did not continue forever. It is believed that Stephen had doubts about the purity of the drinking water in his hotel, and even put up notices in every room, warning guests about it. Instead of drinking water, he began selling soda water to the most affluent in his hotel, for two annas a bottle. But there was something prophetic about his notice. A decade after Arratoon Stephen's death, by some mischance, the Grand Hotel water gave a large number of its guests enteric fever, killing as many as six persons. This incident happened in 1937. Although the rest of the guests recovered, the hotel under the Stephen banner did not. While those who had booked rooms panicked and made cancellations, fear drove away potential customers. This sudden loss of a carefully built-up reputation over the years, prompted the incumbent owner, Stephen's son-in-law, to shut down the hotel in the same year. The massive gates of the hotel opened once again on 21 December 1938 when hotelier Mohan Singh Oberoi, who had begun his career as a guest clerk in Cecil Hotel in Simla, with a salary of Rs 60, took over the Grand Hotel.

As Bachi J. Karkaria writes, '[....] it was almost an enactment of the Sleeping Beauty story. The magic kiss injected life into the hotel that had lain in slumber and shame. Everyone and everything was reactivated as though at the press of a button, taking up where each had left off, as if the last 12 months had been only a bad dream' (p. 44). The silver was polished again, the dust covers removed from the chandeliers and sofas, the crystal and porcelain washed, and the old staff brought back. Most importantly, the water pipes were ripped out and replaced with a modern and fool-proof plumbing system. All these efforts paid off and the Grande Dame of Chowringhee was back on her feet.

Since its resurrection, the Oberoi Grand, as the hotel is now known, has never looked back. Undoubtedly, the finest hotel in Calcutta, its name has become synonymous with luxury and fine living. A symbol of sedate grandeur, its magnificence makes it a prized treasure of Calcutta. So grand is this hotel that its name evokes a feeling of awe in Calcuttans, who are proud that this piece of majesty belongs to their city.

In the taverns, boarding houses and clubs, occupancy was reserved for the white folks. But the scenario began changing with the establishment of hotels. Business compulsions induced proprietors to open the doors of their hotels to Indians, as long as they could pay for their lodging and meals. This gave the residents of the city the opportunity to enjoy European hotel life. There were moderately priced hotels for the middle class and luxurious hotels for the upper class. People travelling to Calcutta, from overseas or within the country, stayed at these hotels and sampled their fare. The upper class generally stayed at Spence's Hotel, Great Eastern Hotel or Grand Hotel. It also gave them an exposure to a new kind of cuisine. The Bengali business community was fast to catch on and make the most of them, quickly becoming connoisseurs of European foods and French wines.

European Restaurants During the Raj

Along with the various hotels, many restaurants appeared on the scene that catered to different categories of customers. These were set up by Europeans and were also open to everybody. But among this entire lot were two establishments that carved a niche for themselves in the culinary scene of Calcutta—Federico Peliti and Firpo's. An upper-class air pervaded both these restaurants that stood out for their food and ambience in British Calcutta.

Federico Peliti was a reputed name in the confectionery and restaurant business in British Calcutta. Popular for the excellent food that it served, its posh, upmarket and classy ambience attracted the upper class. This confectionery and restaurant, popularly known as Peliti's, was opened by Chevalier Federico Peliti, who was an excellent chef, baker and confectioner as well as a restaurateur, hotelier and amateur photographer in British India. Of Italian origin, Peliti was born in 1844 in Carignano, a small town in Turin. He settled in Calcutta as the chief confectioner in the service of Richard Southwell Bourke, Sixth Earl of Mayo, when he became the Viceroy of India in 1869. He joined the Viceroy's staff after winning a confectionery competition, arranged by Lord Mayo himself, in the same year in Turin, a city famous for its strong confectionery tradition. The Viceroy wanted some of the finest chefs and confectioners to work for him and Peliti's appointment was the first of its kind in Government House. But Lord Mayo was stabbed to death by a convict named Sher Ali Afridi, while on an inspection tour of the convict settlement in Port Blair in the Andaman Islands in 1872. The untimely death of his patron compelled Peliti to fend for himself. It was then that the Italian decided to set up his own establishment in Calcutta.

After a failed partnership with Thomas O'Neill, with whom he had opened a confectionery called O'Neill & Peliti on Bentinck Street, he began his own independent venture in Chowringhee in 1875, which was no longer just a confectionery but also included a restaurant. But differences with his Jewish landlord prompted him to change the premises of his establishment to Esplanade Row (East) in 1881. Within a decade, the Italian master chef was able to make a huge success of this establishment, and it became the favourite haunt of the business fraternity of the nearby Clive Street (the commercial district of Calcutta), who frequented the restaurant every Friday during lunch hours. The confectionery and restaurant continued to function at this address till nearly the end of 1902, when it shifted base to larger premises on Government Place (East) in Dalhousie Square. The external and internal appearance of this restaurant, which stood opposite to Government House, was as excellent as its new surroundings. The ground floor had a café and a department that stored all kinds of delicious confectionery, groceries, wines and spirits. These were the best known of European and American delicacies, dominated by the choicest Italian products. While the ground floor was nicely decorated, the upper floor was classy. In the chapter 'Commercial Calcutta' from his book *Seaports of India and Ceylon* (1928), Allister Macmillan describes this section of the restaurant, 'It is, however, the spacious sections on the upper floor that have made Peliti's so popular amongst people in Calcutta who can appreciate the combination of art and utility therein exemplified in every detail. The pleasure of lunching, dining, or having afternoon tea at Peliti's is greatly enhanced by the delightful comfort and goodness of everything pertaining to the service, menu, and all those innumerable little things that are never absent in any first-class restaurant. The tables covered with spotless linen, the glittering spoons, cutlery, and tableware, the charming decorations, especially the coloured electric lights over each table in the form of baskets of fruit and flowers, and the excellence of the orchestra, all combine to make a visit to Peliti's very pleasurable. There is dancing at Peliti's every evening between tea and dinner all the year round. In the hot season Thursdays and Saturdays are the nights appointed for dinner dances; but in the cool season all the dinners at Peliti's are dinner dances. On gala nights the scene there is exceedingly joyous' (pp. 102–03).

Besides whetting the British appetite for dining and entertainment by organizing musical performances by orchestras in his restaurant, Federico Peliti served his customers delicious confectioneries of superior quality, an exclusive assortment of wines and liquors, and a variety of European delicacies. He kept his restaurant well-stocked with the best brands of wines, spirits and beers. His mince pies were believed to be of only one quality—'the best'—and he supplied his customers with the Best Red Gate Hams and Bacon, in canvas or cooked. But the emphasis was on Italian preferences like Turin's vermouth, Asti Spumante, risotto alla Milanese, agnolotti toscani, maccheroni di Napoli and Neapolitan gelato. Passionate about his work, Peliti spent years researching on food and liqueurs. He kept experimenting and came up with new and original recipes. One such recipe was that of a unique kind of white vermouth, which he made with Indian spices, for the Prince of Wales, Albert Edward (later King Edward VII), when he visited Calcutta in December 1875 during his historic tour of India. The drink tasted exceptional and the prince took a great liking to it. Since 1877, this original recipe went into production, especially to be supplied to the English Royal House at the request of the prince. Branded as 'Peliti's', this exclusive vermouth also won medals at international exhibitions in Calcutta, Turin and Paris.

Peliti's was also well-known for its excellent catering service and the great food that it supplied on such occasions. Thus, the firm was appointed as the Manufacturing Confectioner and Court Caterer by Royal Warrant to His Majesty the King, in addition to holding similar warrants from successive Viceroys of India and Governors of Bengal since the time of Lord Mayo.

Federico Peliti catered for private dinners on or off the restaurant premises, public dinners, luncheons, balls, soirees, afternoon parties, wedding receptions and other entertainments 'at the shortest notice' and in the most exclusive and classy manner. The best of refreshments was supplied by the restaurant in 'first class style only'. Peliti's catering business flourished and it also took orders from all over British India, including Burma. A menu card, dated 18 January 1931, has been found, which shows Peliti's catering lunch at a certain Jodhpur Club in British Calcutta. The following dishes were on offer: beckti norvegienne, steak and kidney pie, cold turkey and ham, pressed beef, pressed tongue and spiced rump salad. While chilled Beck's beer was available as the perfect accompaniment, delicious apple and black currant pie and hot coffee wrapped up the filling meal.

Peliti's is also the birthplace of the Rotarian movement in India. It is at a lunch meeting at Peliti's that the roots of the Rotary Club of Calcutta can be traced. While on a business trip to the United States of America, expatriate businessman R.J. Coombes was very impressed with the philosophy and ideals of Rotary International. He returned to Calcutta in 1919, with authority from the organization, to set up a club in Calcutta. He managed to garner the interest of a few of his European friends, mostly Freemasons, and at a luncheon meeting of about forty-five men, a formal resolution was passed to set up a Rotary Club. After Coombes had obtained the permission to start a Rotary Club in Calcutta, its first meeting was held at Peliti's, with a membership of twenty, on 26 September 1919. The club charter was received on 1 January 1920. Today, the Rotary Club of Calcutta, which happens to be the oldest in India, is responsible for ushering in the movement in the country.

The king of Italy had made Federico Peliti a chevalier in 1889. In his later years, he went back to Carignano, bought a property and settled down there. He eventually died in his hometown in 1914. Peliti was blessed with a large family and had many sons. Before his move to Carignano, he had handed over the management of his confectionery and restaurant in Calcutta to his sons Edoardo and Giuseppe. The establishment at the Government Place address was run successfully by them. They were able to maintain its reputation as a very exclusive and elegant place that served food of first-class quality, for many years to come.

The glory of Federico Peliti faded away with the end of the British Raj. It has been difficult to gather concrete evidence regarding the date and reason of its closure. There are many conflicting theories surrounding its final days. There are reports that the ownership of the restaurant changed hands in the 1930s. It was taken over by Firpo's, which continued to run the place till sometime in the 1940s, when it was finally closed down. On the other hand, there are reports that mention nothing about the takeover by Firpo's. These simply claim that Peliti's downed its shutters either just after Independence or sometime in the 1950s. Whatever maybe the truth, Federico Peliti (both the genius and his establishment) is sorely missed. Calcuttans long for the day when another magician, with the aura of the multitalented man from Carignano, will make this city home and create the same magic that has embedded the name of Federico Peliti in the culinary history of Calcutta.

But there was also another name that created quite a stir in the culinary scene of Calcutta. If any European restaurant in British Calcutta could come close to the success achieved by Federico Peliti, then it had to be Firpo's. This posh restaurant became so well known for its classy ambience and good food that it soon turned into a fashionable meeting place and the favourite haunt of the European community.

Angelo Firpo, a chef and confectioner from Genoa in Italy, had been a staff member at Peliti's. After gathering enough experience by working under the great Peliti, he set up his own restaurant-cum-confectionery. Firpo's, which was established in 1917 in Chowringhee, had tables with expensive crystal and polished silverware, served by liveried waiters. The high society and glitterati of Calcutta dined here. The place became such a great success that it left a lasting impression on the city, even years after Independence, with generations having heard of the glorious days of a restaurant called Firpo's.

A three-course luncheon menu card, dated 30 March 1945, shows the spread for the day. It begins by giving the option of choosing between consommé frappe and Scotch broth. A diner can then move on to any of the following dishes: fried fillets of pomfret with tartare sauce or prawn mayonnaise, roast lamb, new potatoes and green peas or sausages and mashed potatoes or cold meats, roast fowl and ham or roast duck, roast sirloin of beef, roast pork, roast lamb, roast saddle of mutton, pressed beef, spiced rump, Melton Mowbray pie, steak and kidney pie or chicken and ham pie. The meal is rounded off with gâteau mille-feuilles, coffee and fruits. This luncheon was served for a princely sum of two rupees and twelve annas. The menu also has the à la carte options of steak and kidney pudding or hamburger steak and onions, each dish priced at one rupee and eight annas. A lunch of minestrone soup, chicken vol-au-vents and vanilla ice cream, topped with hot chocolate sauce and a wafer of biscotti, was also available for the same price. The upscale restaurant gained a reputation for its smoked ilish, a dish much liked by the Europeans.

A sample menu of the Christmas spread at Firpo's included dishes like chilled asparagus, chilled artichoke bottoms, pâté de foie gras, turtle soup, homard thermidor, roast turkey breast stuffed with ham, and plum pudding. In keeping with tradition, brandy would be poured on the pudding and the whole dessert set alight, sometimes by the suave restaurateur himself, for special guests. A bottle of Scotch whisky and a tin of Firpo's in-house chocolates were kept at the centre of each table amidst the paper hats, crackers and bugles.

Like his former employer, Chevalier Federico Peliti, Angelo Firpo also understood the need to combine entertainment with fine dining. An advertisement in *The Statesman* newspaper on December 1925 reads: 'Dine at Firpo's Tonight, Chat Noir Souvenir Ball'. The orchestra at Firpo's was a huge band consisting of trumpets, saxophones, trombones and a complete string quartet with drums. Debonair men and elegant women from the upper-crust of society swayed graciously to the music played by this orchestra on the full-sized dance floor. These well-bred men and women were treated to as many as six cabarets on a single night at the grand Lido Room in Firpo's. It was in this room that Bengal's first cabaret dancer of colour made her debut in the 1960s. The young seductress Arati Das mesmerized audiences at the Lido Room so much with her sensuous moves that she quickly became the star attraction at Firpo's. Thus, Firpo's created history by introducing the sensational Miss Shefali to Calcutta. She was famous by her stage name and went on to rule Calcutta's cabaret scene throughout the 1960s and '70s, performing at the best of hotels and restaurants, and eventually earning the title 'Queen of Cabaret'.

It is believed that Angelo Firpo, who had climbed up the social ladder to become a prominent member of Calcutta's high society, passed away in England in 1948. Before leaving India, he sold his restaurant with the hope that the new owners would be able to maintain the same standard of service and food that Firpo's was renowned for. But this did not happen. Problems began arising from the late 1960s, when the onset of the Naxal Movement shook Calcutta to the core and created a turbulent atmosphere. During this time, the business of Firpo's was on the downslide. Matters became aggravated with labour problems in the 1970s. The situation in the restaurant became so dismal that even its loyal followers stopped making visits, leading to its eventual closure. In 1977, the owners of Firpo's appealed to the state government led by the Indian National Congress for permission to convert the building of the restaurant into a commercial market complex. But the appeal was turned down. Then the Left Front came to power in West Bengal in June in the same year. The owners approached the new state government and permission was granted. The restaurant was erased from the history of Calcutta and in its place now stands Firpo's Market.

The demise of both of these premier restaurants was unfortunate. However, the success of Federico Peliti and Firpo's left a lasting impression and encouraged many local entrepreneurs to pick up the threads after Independence and strive to keep their legacy alive by setting up establishments that not only specialized in the same kind of cuisine but also provided customers with a similar quality of food, service and ambience.

Continental Restaurants in Modern Calcutta

Some of the best fine dining restaurants specializing in continental cuisine arrived with the development of Park Street, which grew into a fashionable avenue during the twentieth century. These restaurants were responsible for popularizing the cuisine on a scale larger than even the hotels could achieve. But in its early days, Park Street was a far cry from the glamorous stretch it later became. It was infamous as the Burial Ground Road. The stretch was a wasteland used for carrying corpses to the cemeteries nearby. There was not a single shop on this deserted road. Only a few residential houses stood on it. The German orientalist and scholar of Persian language and literature, Heinrich Blochmann, also known as Henry Ferdinand Blochmann, who documented the history of Calcutta and its streets during the eighteenth century in his book *Calcutta During Last Century* (1868), mentions that Park Street had about ten houses standing on it.

But, on Middleton Row, a relatively small street, which is a bylane off the main thoroughfare that is now Park Street, stood the palatial residence of Sir Elijah Impey, the first chief justice of British India, who ran office effectively from 22 October 1774 to 3 December 1783. A deer-strewn garden, which eventually came to be known as a deer park, surrounded this residence. Park Street earned its name from this deer park. Although it isn't clear when this happened, it can be assumed that it was sometime during Impey's tenure because of the association with the deer park. The area covered by the residence and its garden was massive, and included the grounds on which Loreto House School and College now stand. It was only in the late nineteenth and early twentieth centuries that the wealthy Armenians of Calcutta, many of whom had ventured into the real estate business by then, began to buy plots along Park Street and filled the stretch with stately buildings, eventually turning it into an upscale locality. They even developed its adjoining areas by constructing large and impressive buildings in them.

Hall & Anderson, the first departmental store in Calcutta and the finest in India, was housed in a grand and imposing building that stretched from the corner of Park Street to that of Chowringhee. Opened to the public in 1925, it was the first shop to come up on Park Street. Here, customers could buy anything from clothes to kitchenware, crockery, cutlery, glassware, ironmongery to furniture, carpets, curtains and linen. Upmarket restaurants specializing in continental cuisine sprang up all along the stretch, along with salons, tailoring shops, pharmaceutical shops, jewellery shops and general stores, in the early twentieth century. The road also housed some important institutions like The Asiatic Society, Archbishop's House, St Xavier's School and College (where the Sans Souci Theatre once stood) and other business establishments. The long stretch and its upmarket vicinity were locales where many of the affluent Indians and landed gentry, stifled by the orthodox environment of north Calcutta, set up residences. Thus, Park Street turned from a desolate and dreary road into a vibrant thoroughfare.

> But the boom in continental cuisine in Park Street happened, to a great extent, after Independence, when local restaurateurs, greatly influenced by the efforts of the European restaurateurs and encouraged by their success, began opening restaurants specializing in this fare. In the post-Second World War period, the government decided to liberalize the use of foreign exchange by the hospitality industry. This led to a surge in the entertainment activities in the restaurants and hotels of Calcutta. Foreign bands and nightclub acts became common. Flamenco, tango, rhumba and can-can dancers were signed up by hotels and restaurants striving to furnish their guests with the best. The Grand Hotel, Great Eastern Hotel and Firpo's now competed with each other to provide the perfect entertainment. In the chapter 'Tables Turn', from the book *The Calcutta Cookbook: A Treasury of Recipes from Pavement to Palace* (1995), the authors elaborate, 'Night clubs mushroomed in and around Chowringhee with Las Vegas-like names such as Ace of Spades, King of Clubs, Puerto Rico and Club 60. Daddy Mazda's Golden Slipper remained one of the most popular night clubs till the 1960s.' (p. 344)

The restaurants on Park Street were not to be left behind. Cabarets, jazz and good food came to define this stretch. The legendary jazz singer Pam Crain made her debut in Park Street in 1956, in the restaurant Mocambo, which was then a very posh nightclub. Over the years, her talent earned her a large following and the title 'Queen of Park Street'. Trincas, a very well-known restaurant on the same street, also hosted live

Western music. This was the place where another legendary singer, Usha Uthup (then Iyer) made her debut in Calcutta's entertainment scene in 1969. In contrast to Pam Crain, who wore glamorous dresses while performing and had her hair done in perfect Western styles, Uthup's trademarks were her beautiful saris and the strings of flowers clipped to her long hair that was always tied at the back. Both the ladies were outstanding singers who performed with aplomb.

Even Biddu Appaiah, who later based himself in England and found international success and fame as a composer and music producer, performed at Trincas in the early stages of his career. He was then a lead member of a band called Trojans and later, performed as the Lone Trojan. This was sometime in the 1960s, much before he left for England in 1967. Some of the most noteworthy achievements of his career are producing the worldwide smash hit disco single 'Kung Fu Fighting', sung by the Jamaican vocalist Carl Douglas, and launching the careers of the late Pakistani pop sensation Nazia Hassan and her brother Zoheb by producing their debut album *Disco Deewane*.

Another great figure in the Western music scene of Park Street was the jazz guitarist Carlton Kitto. He made his debut in Calcutta's nightlife in the early 1970s as a member of the band Jazz Ensemble in the upscale restaurant Moulin Rouge on Park Street. Praising Kitto in his article, 'The chords that bind' for *The Hindu* (3 December 2016), Akhil Sood writes, 'He's considered one of the foremost proponents of bebop jazz in the country, a true legend of the form, whose legacy spans decades. [...] he was a central figure during the glory days of jazz in the Calcutta of the '70's [...]. The city's famed Park Street, at the time, was the hub for this music, jazz blaring out from practically every club around—Trincas, Mocambo, Moulin Rouge, Blue Fox.'

And, of course, one can't forget the legendary Marie Sampson, considered to be one of the finest jazz vocalists, who performed at many of the Park Street outlets. And neither can one forget Delilah at Moulin Rouge, Brenda Lilley at Blue Fox and her sister Fay at Magnolia—all well-known talents who lit up the surroundings with their strong vocals.

When it came to food, Skyroom and Blue Fox were the two post-Independence restaurants on Park Street that stood out for the fare they offered to their customers. Out of the two, the former was more renowned for its superlative dishes.

The elegance of Skyroom, which opened in 1957, beckoned the privileged who were attended by polite and respectful waiters in the finest attire. Once the diners had placed their orders, they were served pistachios, biscottis and creamy coleslaw salads on cabbage leaves as special treats. As long as the restaurant functioned, it held the reputation of serving the best continental food in the city. Like the legendary Great Eastern Hotel and Firpo's, Skyroom's smoked hilsa was perceived to be of sheer excellence. The restaurant served its customers this dish with the roes as well. Its chefs made a variety of appetizing salads and delicious soups like French onion and cream of asparagus. Patrons vouched for its cream of tomato soup, which they believed was the best in the city. While diners marvelled at the perfectly cooked pork chops, they drooled over the soft bangers and creamy mash. Chicken tetrazzini and bhekti mayonnaise were some of its most popular dishes. A dig into the chicken steak, with a delicious steak sauce poured over it, and served with French beans and potatoes, would convince a diner that it was not possible for any other restaurant to make it as well as Skyroom had.

Skyroom did not serve alcohol to its customers. But that hardly mattered because its patrons were more than happy with its delicious continental spread, mocktails and soft drinks. The most popular drink was the in-house lemonade that was served in Codd-neck bottles. Children were especially fascinated by these bottles as they opened with a loud pop. They even brought out the child-like enthusiasm in adults. Eminent novelist Sankar, who visited the restaurant often, gives further details about it in his article, 'Ray and his grilled fish', for *India Today* (4 September 2008): 'The lemonade bottles with nineteenth century bullets were a hit for many to pick up as souvenirs; among them, Satyajit Ray, whose favourites were Chicken Sicilian without Asparagus and Grilled Fish. An equally fascinating fan was Suchitra Sen, who made frequent but quiet visits. So did many Bombay superstars.'

Noted musician and food columnist, Nondon Bagchi, further eulogizes the fare in his article, 'Yesterday once more' for *The Telegraph* (14 March 2006), 'The main courses that day were Baked Bekti in a tomato-based sauce and Chateaubriand Steak with Mushroom Sauce (a sublime affair). The accompaniments that went with these dishes, vegetables like peas, beans and carrots lightly boiled and then glazed by tossing them in butter, or mashed potatoes, were as inviting as the main items.'

It is believed that Skyroom introduced the much loved Black Forest cake to Calcutta. A variety of inviting desserts, like Black Forest pudding and baked Alaska could be found on its menu. The restaurant's chilled fruit cups and coffee hour specials, like cheese balls, asparagus rolls and prawn patties had their own fan following. But the signature dish of Skyroom was its prawn cocktail. Its quality made it so legendary that it was often packed in ice for the former prime minister of India, Indira Gandhi, who was very fond of it, and flown to her residence in New Delhi.

Unfortunately, the restaurant, which reached the pinnacle of success despite a 'no crooner or cabaret' policy and solely on the strength of its food and service, had to down its shutters in 1993 because of some internal problems.

Blue Fox, too, had its large share of admirers. One of them was the renowned Indian film music director, R.D. Burman. A contemporary of Skyroom, the restaurant was famous for two things: its continental cuisine and live Western music, particularly jazz. Evenings at the restaurant were set ablaze by the crooning of Pam Crain while diners dug into their chickens à la Kiev, lobster thermidors, gratins and baked dishes. The glamorous songstress belted out numbers to the music played by the renowned jazz artist, Louis Banks, known as the 'Godfather of Indian Jazz', and the legendary jazz saxophonist, Braz Gonsalves. Together, they were known as the Louis Banks Brotherhood. Unfortunately, like Skyroom, this upscale restaurant too, had to down its shutters.

The two restaurants still functioning from the early days of Park Street are Flurys and Magnolia. Although Flurys is essentially a confectionery shop and tea room, it has always offered a good spread of continental cuisine as well. The patrons often indulge in the tea room's creamy fisherman's pie, grilled pork chop with cabbage mash, apple sauce and jus, grilled marinated chicken thighs with warm potato and bean salad, and chilli con carne with steamed rice, sour cream and salsa.

Magnolia: Magnolia opened as a soda fountain joint at the exact location where it stands today on Park Street. Set up in 1942, this soda fountain joint was very popular among the American GIs posted in Calcutta during the Second World War, many of whom resided in the nearby Grand Hotel. British and American personnel flocked to Magnolia for its soda pops, ice creams, sundaes and milkshakes. In the chapter 'Tables Turn', from the book *The Calcutta Cookbook: A Treasury of Recipes from Pavement to Palace* (1995), the authors describe those times,

> An invasion of British and American armed forces put the city into fourth gear. Those who returned as tourists after the war remembered

> Claire Ross, the American manager of Magnolia's, the first soda fountain on Park Street. [...] The sixty-plus recollect the thrill of ordering soda pops and multi-coloured milk shakes in their student days in institutions of learning within walking distance of Magnolia's (p. 344).

Those were the times when branded ice creams had not yet arrived in the country. Most restaurants, including Magnolia, made their own in-house production of the dessert. When the royal family of Nepal, the Ranas, took over Magnolia in the early 1950s, they began selling its ice cream popsicles to the public in bright yellow handcarts, the name painted in blue on the side. It was Magnolia ice cream that made the restaurant a household name in the city.

The Ranas did away with the soda fountain business and converted Magnolia into a full-fledged restaurant serving continental dishes. This found a lot of favour among the Europeans who still lived in the city and the brown sahibs who were influenced by the European culture. They flocked to the restaurant to dig into chicken supreme de volaille, grilled lamb chop, fish Florentine and prawn Newburg. During Christmas, the restaurant presented its patrons a selection of whole turkey with their choice of sauce, whole roast rabbit and Christmas pudding with brandy sauce. The restaurant grew so popular that it was dubbed 'Mag's' by the continental cuisine-loving public who thronged it for their share of the classic spaghetti bolognese or grilled chicken chipolata. The 1950s also witnessed songstress Patricia Tarley crooning Mag's to its popularity as she belted out numbers of Frank Sinatra and Tony Brent to a loyal following.

Over the years, the ownership of the restaurant changed hands many times. Currently, it is owned by businessman Charles Mantosh, who owns a few more eateries on Park Street and the nearby Russel Street. Belonging to a business family that is very well known in Calcutta, he has continued with the traditional continental dishes that made Magnolia so popular in the first place. Although, after the invasion of branded ice creams, the restaurant's in-house ice creams and ice cream carts gradually became a thing of the past, yet, even today, they remain wonderful memories for many from the older generation. Magnolia has continued as one of the popular eateries on Park Street and despite becoming a multicuisine restaurant that also serves north Indian and Chinese food, its thrust still lies on continental cuisine, serving a large variety of delectable dishes, reminiscent of the Raj.

In the 1980s, the entertainment scene in Park Street began to peter out because the Left Front government disapproved of such bourgeois indulgences and raised the entertainment tax. Musicians, singers and dancers, who used to perform in restaurants on this amazing thoroughfare, quietly packed their bags and retreated. Trincas and Someplace Else (the bar at the Park Hotel) are the only two places on the street that still have live music. But the food still continues to attract diners in droves to Park Street. Although most of its continental restaurants have now become multicuisine, the focus is still on food from the European countries. Converting the menu into a multicuisine one is only an attempt to expand the customer base. But that does not mean the number of continental food lovers in this city is small. On the contrary, this number is increasing with time, and more restaurants specializing in this cuisine are coming up not only on Park Street but also in other parts of the city. Hotels and clubs, whether old or new, keep adding options to their continental menu.

It is superfluous whether entrepreneurs make their restaurants multicuisine or strictly continental. What is important for continental food lovers is the stress given to maintain the authenticity of the dishes. Even today, decades later, when a diner walks into Mocambo, he will feel the old world charm of the years gone by not only in the decor and ambience, but also in the food served. As Somini Sengupta writes in her article, 'Calcutta: Mocambo' for the *New York Times* (28 August 2008),

> Mocambo is still an odd jumble of Europeanisms: a mural of faux Degas ballerinas, red vinyl banquettes, red silk lampshades hanging like upside-down tulips, cigarette smoke rising from the tables. Fish a la Moutarde is grilled beckty, a Bay of Bengal delicacy, drenched in a spicy mustard sauce, whose virtues a Bengali can croon about. Angels on Horseback is chicken wrapped in bacon. Fish a la Diana is indulgence itself: beckty, stuffed with prawn and cooked in cream.

So, it does not matter if the entertainment has stopped. The turnover from continental food alone is good enough for entrepreneurs to continue serving it.

3. Portuguese Influences

Confectionery Crusaders

The Portuguese were the first Europeans to establish themselves in the region, thanks to their mastery over the sea routes. In the 1500s, much after the Portuguese explorer, Vasco da Gama, arrived at the Port of Calicut on the Malabar Coast in 1498, the Portuguese began to make inroads into Bengal, a region then reputed to be the wealthiest in the Indian subcontinent. Private traders and merchants as well as the official representatives of the kingdom of Portugal would come to Bengal regularly. However, it was in Chittagong that they made their first base, starting with a factory that was set up in 1517. Currently a part of Bangladesh, Chittagong was the largest and most thriving seaport of undivided Bengal. This made the Portuguese refer to it as 'Porto Grande de Bengala', meaning the Grand Harbour of Bengal, a term that was often simplified to 'Porto Grande'. In 1528, they were given permission to establish factories and customs houses in the port city, which marked the beginning of their journey in Bengal.

In 1536, Portuguese traders procured a firman (written permission) from Sultan Ghiyasuddin Mahmud Shah of Bengal to trade in the area surrounding the Hooghly. Trade was not the only ambition of the Portuguese; many of them had the intention of converting the Hindus and Muslims of the region to Christianity, as they believed that it was the only religion that could offer salvation.

Around 1579, Portuguese traders were given a firman by Mughal Emperor Akbar, who had annexed Bengal in 1576, to build a town in the province. They chose Hooghly, or Ugulim, as it is called in Portuguese, because it was positioned at the mouth of the river and offered a good harbour. They established a town towards the north called Bandel, derived from the Persian word 'Bandar', which means port. Over time, they kept expanding their settlement along the banks of the river and the entire area around present-day Hooghly became a Portuguese stronghold. The settlement flourished and by the early seventeenth century, the Portuguese held a formidable position in trade in Bengal.

Permission was also given to Captain Pedro Tavares to preach his faith publicly and for the construction of churches. In 1599, the Order of the Augustinians built a church in Bandel and named it Basilica of the Holy Rosary. This church is more popularly known as Bandel Church now, and is believed to be the oldest Christian church in West Bengal. Portuguese priests began to forcibly convert the local inhabitants to Christianity and by 1603, there were around 5,000 Catholics in Ugulim, including those of mixed Portuguese and Indian descent. By 1680, there were at least 20,000 Portuguese in Bengal, although only 3,000 of them were fully Portuguese; the rest were known at the time as Mesticos (people of mixed blood). A majority of them lived in Hooghly and the rest were spread over Satgaon, Chittagong, Banja, Dhaka and other places.

The Portuguese were experts in the baking of breads, cakes and pastries. They would also make a wonderful spread of desserts, using locally available ingredients like mangoes, oranges, lemons, ginger and pickles. They indulged in a life of luxury in their strongholds, dressing up like the local nawabs and engaging a retinue of dancing girls, seamstresses, cooks and confectioners.

On the flip side, the Portuguese were also infamous for piracy along the rivers of Bengal. The Portuguese pirates of Chittagong were known as 'Firingis'. They captured the Mogs and employed them as servants. Under their Portuguese masters, the Mogs became expert bakers and confectioners. It is believed that the moiras (Bengali confectioners and sweet-makers) of West Bengal learnt the art of making chhana from the Mog cooks who were employed by the Portuguese based in Hooghly.

From Cheese to Chhana

Bengal is famous throughout the country for its sweets. Bengalis adore their mishti (sweets) as much as their maachh (fish). Partha Pratim Ghosh, one of the owners of the prominent confectionery chain, Dwarik's Grandsons, explains:

'What makes Bengali sweets different from those of the rest of the country is that chhana is used as the main ingredient in them, while most of the rest of India relies on khoya, a milk solid prepared by boiling full-cream milk till it condenses to a thick paste, which is then cooled down to a hard mass. Bengali sweets are more perishable because chhana is soft and full of moisture; the sugar in them actually plays the role of a preservative.'

Bengali confectioners are very creative. They add an assorted variety of ingredients to the sweet chhana paste and also give it different shapes. What the Bengali sweet lover gets on a platter are sweets of different tastes, shapes, sizes, colours and textures, but whether it is *sandesh*, *rasogolla* or *rasomalai*, or *pantua*, *langcha* or *malpoa*, the shelf life of Bengali sweets is a short one.

However, contrary to popular belief, chhana was not the invention of the moira. It has its roots in Portuguese cooking. The Portuguese made a certain kind of cheese that became popularly known as Bandel cheese. It was made by curdling cow's milk using an acidic agent like lime juice or vinegar. The whey was then drained from the cheese by keeping the lumpy paste in pots, which had many small holes in them. The dried and crumbly cheese, or chhana, was flavoured with salt, which was the only preservative used. It was then kneaded and shaped into small and thick ovals or circular discs. These were available in two varieties: plain and smoked.

Before the arrival of the Portuguese, the traditional sweets of Bengal were given the generic name of *monda-mithai*. Monda were milk-based sweets made of khoya, sweetened with gur (jaggery) or sugar and shaped into balls. Grated coconut or khoi (popped rice) or murki (khoi coated with gur) was often added for an extra texture and taste element. Mithai were flour or lentil-based sweets, sweetened with jaggery or sugar.

Simple sweets made of coconut like *narkeler naru* (coconut laddu) and *narkeler takti* (coconut and milk solid fudge) were equally popular. *Naru* was also made with chholar dal (split Bengal gram), til (sesame seeds) or shooji (semolina). *Ananda naru*, prepared during auspicious occasions like weddings, was made with rice flour, coconut and jaggery. Fried in mustard oil, these sweet balls were often studded with sesame seeds. *Moa*, a sweet ball made with puffed or beaten rice and jaggery, has always been well-liked. Bengal also has the tradition of making extremely simple sweets like the tiny *phulbatasha* or the larger *batasha* called *pheni*, *nokuldana*, *kadma* and *mathh*, which are nothing but sugar lumps that often form a part of ritualistic offerings.

Bengali medieval literature, particularly the *Mangal Kavya*, which is a vast body of narrative verses composed between the thirteenth and eighteenth centuries, mostly in praise of folk deities by authors from different parts of Bengal, has quite a few references to the sweets commonly made in Bengali households. Mukundaram Chakrabarti's *Chandimangal* (a subgenre of *Mangal Kavya*) is filled with accounts of sweet dishes like those made of condensed milk or kheer, *meetha petha* or sweet cake made of rice flour and cooked in milk, sesame porridge, *kheer puli* or rice flour dumpling stuffed with sweetened grated coconut and stewed in sweetened milk, and gourd cooked in milk and flavoured with fennel seeds.

Khaja, *gaja*, *malpoa*, *sarbhaja* and *sarpuria* (earlier known as *sarpupee*) were also popular sweets in those days. In sarbhaja and sarpuria, the main ingredient is sar, which is the rich cream that floats on top of milk when it is boiled. It is believed that the origin of these two sweets was in the city of Krishnanagar in the Nadia district of Bengal. The ingredients of both are more or less the same, but the difference lies in the method of cooking. Sarbhaja is deep-fried while sarpuria is baked.

A fried sweet called *kundalini* was very popular among sweet lovers. The modern version of this sweet is known as jilipi. *Karpurnalika*, now known as *labango latika*, was also popular. Kheer mixed with sliced mangoes, sweet yoghurt and *dugdhalaklaki* were often made in households. Eminent food historian Chitrita Banerji is of the opinion that the last is a predecessor of the present-day Bengali rabri in which the rich and fatty sar is skimmed off the milk, piled in layers, allowed to rest until firm, and then cut into squares and stewed in sweetened milk.

Payesh (creamy rice pudding) and *pithe* (rice flour cake) are still made in homes today. Payesh is made by cooking rice and milk to a thick and creamy consistency. It is sweetened by adding date palm jaggery or sugar. Green cardamom is sometimes added to the cooking for additional flavouring. Also referred to as *paramanno* (literally meaning best rice), it is considered to be an auspicious dessert, making it an important part of ritualistic spreads and the ideal offering to the deities. But the main component of payesh does not always have to be rice. Ingredients like semolina, rice flakes, young bottle gourd, sweet potato, jackfruit seeds and even luchi have often been stewed in sweetened milk to make this dessert.

Bengali cuisine boasts of a staggering variety of pithes. Also called *pitha*, these are largely sweet in taste, although there are savoury pithes too. Date palm jaggery is one of the vital ingredients in the preparation of pithe. Preference is always given to it over sugar. Pithes are largely rice flour-based cakes. A variety of ingredients are used in the preparation like rice flour, semolina, khoya or kheer, milk, date palm jaggery or sugar, and grated coconut. Wholewheat flour or atta was also an important ingredient that got gradually replaced with refined flour or maida since its introduction to India by the Muslim traders and rulers. Some are also based on lentil pastes and mashed sweet potatoes. The fifteenth-century poet Bipradas Pipilai, who wrote *Manasa Vijaya* (another version of

Manasamangal Kavya), mentions a variety of sweet dishes made of rice, legumes, semolina, milk solids and jaggery. Some of these are *ashke pithe*, *mug samli* and *dugdha chusi*—all varieties of pithe. Pithes may be fried, steamed, cooked in milk or fried and soaked in sugar syrup.

Gokul pithe, *rasbora pithe*, *puli pithe*, *bhapa pithe* and *ranga alur pithe* are some of the popular varieties. But the most popular pithe is the *patishapta*, which is a stuffed and folded sweet crepe. To make *patishapta pithe*, milk and date palm jaggery, or sugar, are added to rice flour and semolina. This batter is used to make the crepe. Maida is often added to this batter. A sweetened filling of khoya and grated coconut is arranged vertically on the fried crepe. The crepe is then folded and fried for a few more seconds till it turns light brown.

The tradition of making pithes in Bengali households is a time-honoured custom that is especially observed on the occasion of Makar Sankranti, the harvest festival of Bengal held on the last day of Poush, which is the first month of winter in the Bengali calendar, extending from the middle of December to the middle of January. This also lends the festival the names of Poush Sankranti and Poush Parbon (parbon means festival in Bengali). However, the celebration is a three-day affair that begins on the day before Makar Sankranti and ends on the day after. A variety of sweets are made in Bengali households on these days. Since Bengal abounds in paddy fields, it is customary for Bengalis to use the freshly harvested rice to make pithes. In fact, pithe has become so synonymous with this festival that it is also known as Pithe Parbon.

Bengal is also the land of plenty of date palm trees. These trees are the source of dates or khejur and date sap or khejurer ras, which is extracted from the soft trunk of the topmost part of the tree. The extraction is done in winter, when the sap develops into a rich and thick brown liquid. The khejurer ras is slowly boiled in large vessels over wood or charcoal fires to make date palm jaggery or khejurer gur. This gur is more popularly known as nolen gur or notun gur (meaning new jaggery) since winter marks the arrival of the date palm jaggery into the market, which is then used in a variety of sweet preparations from sandesh to rasogolla to payesh, lending these creations the names of *nolen gurer sandesh*, *nolen gurer rasogolla* and *nolen gurer payesh*. Nolen gur is available in the following consistencies: liquid, grainy liquid and solid. The gur in the liquid form is known as jhola gur while the solid chunks are known as patali gur. The end of winter brings to a close the date palm jaggery season. However, patali gur can be stored for a few more months after winter, mainly with the help of refrigeration. This gives it a longer shelf life.

The advent of chhana revolutionized the Bengali sweet landscape. This new ingredient fired the sweet-makers' imaginations. They began experimenting with the soft pliable paste and created varieties of innovative sweets. The French physician and traveller, François Bernier, who lived in India from 1658 to 1669 opined that Bengal was celebrated for its sweetmeats, especially in the places that were inhabited by the Portuguese, and the Bengalis were skilful in the art of preparing such sweets, which were articles of considerable trade. By the middle of the nineteenth century, moiras across the region, were using chhana as the main ingredient in sweet-making.

Nitai Ghosh, owner of the renowned Chittaranjan Mistanna Bhandar, a confectionery shop, which opened in 1907, says, 'Family-owned animal husbandry business was a common feature in the Hooghly district. The village milkmen were often left with unsold milk that turned sour. They did not want to waste this surplus milk and thought of an alternative use for it. The result of their innovative thinking was home-made sweets. Earlier, the milkmen would make sweets out of khoya but soon, they switched to chhana.' To make chhana, milk was heated slowly in a large pot, and when it began to boil, a little lime juice or vinegar was added to it. The milk was again brought to a boil and then simmered until it curdled. The curdled milk or chhana was put inside a large muslin cloth, squeezed and then put under a heavy wooden block till all the whey got drained. It was then kneaded with sugar or date palm jaggery to make a smooth, pliable and palatable paste. This sweet paste went on to become the foundation of Bengal's iconic sandesh. Some of the early confectioners of Calcutta came from Hooghly, leaving their villages behind.

Solidly Sandesh

In his essay, 'The Food and Sweets of Calcutta', from the book, *Calcutta—The Living City: Volume II: The Present and Future* (1990), Pratap Kumar Roy points out, 'The primary sense of the Bengali word *sandesh* is "news" or "a message". Some scholars derive the name of the sweet from the old practice of sending food, particularly sweets, with messengers. That the name has attached itself to a special kind of sweet, may be a sign of exceptional regard, a reflection of the purity [and] simplicity of its preparation' (p. 339). It is a fact that sandesh gradually became the most popular sweet to be associated with news, particularly of the good kind. Bengalis began gifting sandesh on auspicious occasions or while delivering good news, turning it into a common practice.

It may come as a surprise to many that the sweet is mentioned in *Chaitanya Charitamrita*, the biography of the saint and founder of Gaudiya Vaishnavism, Sri Chaitanya Mahaprabhu, which was written in the sixteenth century by Krishnadasa Kaviraja Goswami. But Chitrita Banerji is quick to point out that the sandesh of those times were sweetened pellets of khoya kheer and not the chhana-based sweetmeat of today.

It is in Guptipara in Hooghly that sandesh first got its name. Earlier, sandesh did not have any name or form. It was available as a sweet paste, known as *makha sandesh* (sandesh mixture), which was made by lightly cooking chhana, mixed with sugar or nolen gur, over low heat. Guptipara is also the place where the legendary Bhola moira's ancestors lived. Bhola moira was a confectioner and had a sweet shop of his own in Bagbazar in north Calcutta. But more than his sweet-making skills, he was famous for his kabigaan or folk songs. The famous musical duel between Bhola moira and Antony Firingi, the Bengali singer-writer and folk poet of Portuguese descent, has been immortalized in Bengali literature, theatre and cinema. Born as Hensman Anthony, the latter was popularly known as Antony Firingi because the word 'Firingi' gradually came to be associated with Portuguese nationals who had settled in Bengal and with those of mixed parentage (with one parent Indian and the other one Portuguese). It is in Guptipara that sandesh graduated from the sweet paste of makha sandesh to the more defined *gupo sandesh*, a rudimentary form of the sweet, made with chhana and sugar, and shaped into a small ball.

In the nineteenth century, gupo sandesh was improved upon and fruit pulp-based sandesh, like *kamranga* (star fruit) and *aam* (mango) *sandesh*, were made. The more refined *narompaak* and *korapaak* forms were also created during this time. Chhana, which is cooked on low heat for a short time takes on a soft (narom) texture. It is then set aside to cool and given different shapes with the help of chhaanch or moulds. Sandesh made by this method is called narompaak. When chhana is cooked for a long time, it takes on a harder (kora) texture, which is how korapaak is prepared. A steamed version of sandesh was also made with a smooth paste of sweetened chhana that came to be known as *bhapa sandesh*.

Slowly, moiras began creating more innovative types of sandesh flavoured with essences, fruit pulps, syrups, coconut and even nolen gur. They were cooked to different levels of consistency. Wooden, clay and stone moulds were used in households and shops to form the different types of sandesh into conch shell, fish, butterfly, peacock and elephant shapes. They were also shaped into fruits like custard apple and mango, and flowers like the lotus and rose, and given different geometrical patterns. Food colour was often added and fancy names were given to these sweets, either to specify the ingredients that went into their making or as marketing gimmicks. Examples include *manohara* (captivator of the heart), *pranohara* (captivator of the soul), *dilkush* (joy to the heart), *madhuja* (born of honey), *abak* (wonder), *parijat* (heaven's blossom) and *paradise sandesh*.

Bengalis observe the tradition of exchanging a large number of gifts, beautifully packed on trays, on the morning of their wedding day. These gifts are called tatwa. This exchange takes place between the families of the bride and the groom. According to custom, sweets are an important part of these gifts. In the early days, the skilled moiras of Bengal, with their abundant creativity, would also make beautiful images out of khoya for the purpose of tatwa like a large butterfly or a fish, generally considered as auspicious symbols in Bengali weddings. Elaborate creations included figures of the bor-bou (Bengali bridegroom and bride) dressed in their wedding attire, or a buro-buri (old married couple), signifying that the marriage will last a lifetime, or a palki (palanquin), the traditional mode of transport in Bengal, carried by men. These creations were expensive and more of an upper-class indulgence. When sandesh appeared on the scene, many began including it in the sweets that were gifted as tatwa. With the development of this trend, moiras gradually started reproducing these images with korapaak sandesh. Today, images made of sandesh are commonly seen as part of tatwa. They are no longer confined to the upper class and are more popular than those made with khoya.

Over the years, Bengal's moiras, who are never afraid of experimenting, have come up with more modern creations like chocolate and strawberry sandesh, and other varieties, infused with synthetic flavours, that die-hard conservatives often sneer at. Sandesh is the most versatile Bengali sweet and the highest number of experimentations has taken place with it. As Pratap Kumar Roy sums up, '[...] it is in the sandesh, with its unending range of flavours, shapes and textures that Bengali confectionery achieves its highest glory' (p. 339).

Syrups and Sweets

Raser mishti, or sweets with syrups, and *bhaja mishti*, or fried sweets, were a later entry. Raser mishti are generally chhana-based and cooked in sugar syrup like rasogolla, rasomalai, *chamcham* and *malai chop*. They may be served in different ways. While rasogolla is served in sugar syrup, chamcham and malai chop are stuffed with sweetened khoya mixture, laced with saffron. Rasomalai, on the other hand, is made of soft and sweet chhana balls immersed in sweet cardamom-flavoured milk, laced with saffron and garnished with chopped pistachios. In contrast, although the main ingredient in bhaja mishti is chhana, it also includes other ingredients that are equally important in its preparation like khoya, refined flour and semolina. The final product is deep-fried and soaked in sugar syrup. *Pantua,* langcha, *ledikeni, chhanar jilipi* and *kalo jaam* are some examples of bhaja mishti. Sandip Sen, one of the directors of Sen Mahasay Private Limited, which runs the successful confectionery chain, Sen Mahasay, adds, 'Over the years, with the advancement and refinement of sweet-making, moiras have come to their own conclusions regarding the techniques and ingredients that work best. Some opine that sweets cooked over wood fires taste better than those cooked over coal. Many also believe that the quality of cow milk is far superior to that of buffalo milk. But adding a little bit of buffalo milk to the cooking gives more body and better texture to the sweets.'

Sweet Evolution

When Calcutta became the royal capital, the economy of the city thrived under British rule. A new middle class evolved, educated and professionally qualified, working as doctors, lawyers, clerks and in other professions. The cosmopolitan milieu of the city, furthermore, exposed them to many fine tastes and pleasures. Their good jobs gave them disposable incomes, which they could now spend on better lifestyles. This prompted many moiras in the late nineteenth century to leave their villages in Hooghly and nearby areas, and settle in thriving Calcutta. Most of them set up shops in north Calcutta or Black Town.

The moiras competed with one another and created new recipes to attract their customers' attention. They adopted new and finer techniques in sweet-making that improved the quality of their wares. These recipes have, over the years, spread across Bengal and been improved upon by succeeding generations. But some of these traditional recipes are lost in the annals of history, and modern sweetmeat artists do not know how to make them. For example, *Empress Gaja*, a sweet dedicated to Queen Victoria, is now lost to us, and the present owners of Naba Krishna Guin, a confectionery shop set up in colonial times, are unaware of how to make this sweet, although they know that the founding fathers of their shop once specialized in its production.

The six most important sweet-makers, who were among the earliest to come to the royal capital, were Paran Chandra Nag, Mahesh Chandra Dey, Nobin Chandra Das, Dwarikanath Ghosh, Ashutosh Sen and Ganguram Chaurasia. These six sweetmeat artists set up shops that created history in the city, either with their innovative creations or the superior quality of their products.

Bhim Chandra Nag: Housed on Nirmal Chandra Street in the Bowbazar area of central Calcutta, this sweet shop was opened by Paran Chandra Nag, a moira from the Janai village in Hooghly. In 1826, he set up a small shack selling sandesh near Bowbazar Market. Despite the fact that sandesh lacked the variety it can boast of today, Paran Chandra Nag's offerings stood out because of their superior quality. The shack that sold mouth-watering sandesh soon became renowned as 'Paran-da's Shop' and the reputation of his sweets grew through word of mouth.

Paran-da's untimely death at the age of forty-eight compelled his only son, Bhim, to shoulder responsibility for the shop at an early age. Bhim was aware of the techniques that went into sandesh-making, having assisted his father for a long time. During his tenure, the sandesh market of Calcutta went through a transition. New varieties of sandesh were being created by sweetmeat artists all over the city. Bhim Chandra Nag would not be left behind in the race. He began adding new elements like cashew nuts, pistachios, almonds, rose water and saffron to the sweetened chhana. The result of his experiments was the creation of unique sweets that caused quite a stir among his customers. Bhim Chandra Nag's son, Ashutosh Chandra Nag, took over when his father was unable to continue and carried on his legacy of experimentation. Ashutosh Chandra Nag is given credit for naming the shop 'Bhim Chandra Nag' after his father's demise, and for building a concrete shop in place of the shack.

This shop invented the *Sakuntala sandesh* and *Nehru sandesh*. Other varieties of sandesh like dilkush, *peshawari* and paradise were also invented in the pre-Independence era, with each sweetmeat shop claiming to have invented them. While the veracity of this claim cannot be confirmed, it is an accepted fact that Bhim Chandra Nag created the Nehru sandesh when Jawaharlal Nehru's father, Motilal Nehru, the renowned lawyer and leader of the Indian National Congress, visited Calcutta in 1928. A feast was arranged in his honour and Bhim Chandra Nag was asked to make the sweets for the occasion. Nehru sandesh was the result of this request. The sandesh is green in colour and made of sweetened chhana mixed with ground pistachios and ground almonds. Its production has been discontinued because of the high cost of the ingredients and the time-consuming procedure. Today, one can buy Nehru sandesh from Bhim Chandra Nag only by placing a special order. The production of Sakuntala sandesh, another colonial-era sweet that the shop once made, has been stopped for the same reasons. In this raisin-topped sweet, the chhana is mixed with ground cashew nuts and saffron strands that have been soaked in rose water. Bhim Chandra Nag also created other varieties of expensive sandesh like *badshah bhog* and *paritripti*. The former is high in saffron content while the latter, in pistachios and green cardamoms. The shop once made *Victoria*, an oval-shaped sandesh named after the queen that had three different colours in it—yellow, pink and green. The original sweet was so big in size that a kilogram of it would be only twelve pieces. Sweets by Bhim Chandra Nag were once a great favourite of Rani Rashmoni, the highly spiritual widow of zamindar Rajchandra Das (Marh) of Janbazar, who was responsible for building Dakshineswar Kali Temple and appointing Sri Ramakrishna Paramahansa as its chief priest. *Abar khabo* was her favourite sandesh, and she regularly bought fifteen kilograms of it for the presiding deity of the temple, Bhavatarini Kali. After the worship was over, the Abar Khabo prasad (devotional offering shared among devotees after worship) was distributed by Sri Ramakrishna Paramahansa to his favourite disciple Naren (Swami Vivekananda), and other devotees.

Bhim Chandra Nag is also regarded as the inventor of ledikeni. This bhaja mishti was the result of a birthday wish. Lord Canning was the Governor-General and first Viceroy of British India from 1856 to 1862. His wife, Lady Canning, ordered the confectioner to make a unique sweet for her birthday party. Bhim Chandra Nag spent days experimenting in his kitchen and came up with a rich brown sweet that was spherical in shape and soft and syrupy. The sweet was a huge success with the Vicereine and her guests. From then on, it became known as *Lady Canning* after its patron. Over the years, the name got corrupted to *Lady Kenny* and eventually to ledikeni, and continues to be a popular fried sweet made by all sweet shops today.

Bhim Chandra Nag enjoyed the patronage of eminent personalities like Acharya Jagadish Chandra Bose, Meghnad Saha, Raja Ram Mohan Roy, Rabindranath Tagore, Maharshi Debendranath Tagore, Prince Dwarakanath Tagore, Ishwar Chandra Vidyasagar, Acharya Prafulla Chandra Ray, Deshbandhu Chittaranjan Das, Dr Bidhan Chandra Roy and Sir Ashutosh Mukherjee. For some time, a sandesh known as *ashu bhog* was made in the shop as a tribute to the regular patronage of Sir Ashutosh Mukherjee, the renowned educationist and jurist. He would stop by every afternoon in his horse-drawn carriage on his way from the High Court to the University of Calcutta and order two baskets of sweets for his family from the shop.

The shop's sales have not sagged, but continue to multiply with time. The family continues to experiment and create specialities like *alphonso mango sandesh* (made with sweetened chhana, rose essence, the pulp of alphonso mangoes and finely chopped pistachios), *green mango sandesh* (sweetened chhana and green mango essence), *paan sandesh* (designed and coloured like a betel leaf roll, stuffed with finely chopped cashew nuts and served chilled), *padma sandesh* (with the imprint of a lotus) and *ganga jamuna sandesh* (a half layer of chocolate flavoured chhana and a half layer of saffron flavoured chhana). The shop still stands at the same spot where the small shack was opened in 1826.

Girish Chandra Dey & Nakur Chandra Nandy: This iconic sweet shop had a humble start as a small shack, set up in 1844 on Ramdulal Sarkar Street (then known as Maniktala Street) in north Calcutta by Mahesh Chandra Dey. Dey had left his village in Hooghly district to try his luck in the big city. The shack soon became very popular in the neighbourhood for its delicious confectionery.

Girish Chandra Dey, the son of Mahesh Chandra Dey, inherited his father's sweet-making skills. He had a daughter, who married Nakur Chandra Nandy, a young man from the neighbourhood. Dey was very fond of Nandy and this made him arrange the union. Although his son-in-law also hailed from Hooghly district, which was the hub of moiras, he was not at all involved in the sweet-making profession. It was at his father-in-law's insistence that Nandy joined the business, learning the tricks of the trade and eventually, becoming an even better confectioner than his teacher. It is widely believed that Nandy gave succeeding generations of Calcutta's sweet-makers a direction for their craft. He perfected the proportions of chhana and sugar, the essential ingredients in Bengali confectionery, and his measurements were even emulated by the other moiras of his time.

After he passed away in 1924, his sons named the shop Girish Chandra Dey & Nakur Chandra Nandy, in homage to the collaboration between the father-in-law and son-in-law. The shop specializes in dry sweets and is famous for its collection of sandesh today. One of the most remarkable features of its sandesh is that it is so soft that it simply melts in the mouth. The secret behind this softness lies in the way the chhana in the shop is processed. Most confectionery shops place heavy wooden blocks on the chhana to completely drain out the whey. The owners of Girish Chandra Dey & Nakur Chandra Nandy believe that completely draining out the whey also squeezes out the fat content of the chhana, which is necessary for softness in sandesh. Karigars (workers) in the shop spend a lot of time hand-processing the chhana. Though an arduous task, it gives the sandesh a superior quality in comparison to that of other shops.

Girish Chandra Dey & Nakur Chandra Nandy was a pioneer in introducing the *narompaak jalbhara sandesh*, in which the juicy filling is covered with a soft layer of chhana, a deviation from the korapaak version that has a hard chhana covering. Their jalbhara sandesh has dried fruits, which makes the confection unique and very popular among customers. A chocolate version of the jalbhara sandesh is also made. The shop's nolen gur sandesh varieties are very popular in winter, particularly the nolen gur-filled jalbhara sandesh (both the narompaak and korapaak versions) where the soft and gooey filling of liquid jaggery fills the mouth with an exquisite flavour. Some of the traditional sweets, like *golapi pera*—a slightly flat disc made of sweetened khoya, flavoured with rosewater, with a slight depression at the centre that is decorated with a rose petal, *malai roll*—a cylinder made of a firm sheet of sar and stuffed with sweetened khoya, *kanchagolla*—a sweet ball of chhana coated with finely grated khoya, and *chandrapuli*—a half-moon made with a sweetened mixture of chhana, khoya and grated coconut, flavoured with green cardamom powder, have been made in this shop since its early days. Some of its signature sweets include *chocolate sandesh, gurer narompaak jalbhara*, parijat sandesh and *mousumi sandesh*. In mousumi sandesh, the chhana is mixed with grated coconut and a variety of nuts, and sweetened with nolen gur, making it a winter sweet. Parijat sandesh is made with sweetened chhana, finely chopped pistachios and other nuts. To give chocolate sandesh its flavour, chocolate sauce is mixed with the chhana. The shop also sells white and dark chocolate sandesh as well as *chocolate shingara*, a chocolate-flavoured sweet shaped like a samosa, which is as popular as its *sandesh shingara* that comes stuffed with dried fruits. Flavoured varieties of sandesh are a huge success with the shop's customers whether it is *rose sandesh*, which is made with sweetened channa, lightly laced with rose water and decorated with a rose petal on the top, or *butterscotch sandesh*, made with sweetened channa infused with butterscotch sauce and embedded with small and crunchy pieces of crushed butterscotch praline. *Black Forest* and *coffee flavoured sandesh* are also runaway hits.

Fancy names have been given to some of the other creations, like *sourav sandesh* and *sandhek*. While the former, named after the celebrated cricketer from West Bengal, Sourav Ganguly, is made with sweetened chhana and chopped pistachios, and coated with sugar granules, the latter is a sandesh shaped and designed like a cake. Bijaya Dashami, is a social custom of visiting relatives, friends and elders with sweets observed by Bengalis after the immersion of the idol of Goddess Durga in the river that brings the festival of Durga Puja to an end. For this occasion, the shop makes *chandan sandesh*; drops of chandan or sandalwood essence are added to the sweetened chhana, giving the sandesh the delightful smell of sandalwood.

Girish Chandra Dey & Nakur Chandra Nandy is known for constantly upgrading its sandesh collection and adding new varieties that take its loyal customers by surprise. Fruit-flavoured sandesh is a new addition to its collection and includes varieties like mango, green mango, apple, green apple, strawberry, lebu (lemon), litchi, pineapple, blackcurrant, kanthal (ripe jackfruit), orange, mulberry and kiwi. A sandesh shaped and designed like a pigeon, with pink feet and beak, tiny black eyes, and delicate designs on its pristine white body and tail, is another innovative addition that speaks volumes for the expertise of the sweetmeat artists of the shop. Over the years, Girish Chandra Dey & Nakur Chandra Nandy has become such a trusted name that when, Hillary Clinton, who was then the US Secretary of State, visited Calcutta in 2012, she was presented one hundred pieces of kanchagolla and one hundred pieces of parijat sandesh from the shop by Mamata Banerjee, the chief minister of West Bengal. This sweetmeat shop has also catered sweets for the wedding reception of superstar Amitabh Bachchan's son Abhishek Bachchan and Bollywood queen, Aishwarya Rai. The confectionery shop once enjoyed the regular patronage of renowned personalities like the great saint Sri Ramakrishna Paramahansa, Swami Vivekananda, eminent theatre artist Girish Ghosh, Mahanayak Uttam Kumar and acclaimed film director Satyajit Ray. The many awards that Girish Chandra Dey & Nakur Chandra Nandy has won in high-profile sweetmeat competitions confirm that when it comes to quality sandesh, no other shop in the city comes close.

K.C. Das: Thanks to this shop, the popularity of rasogolla has now crossed the boundaries of Bengal and spread itself, with sweetmeat artists across the length and breadth of the country specializing in the making of this sweet.

However, as we are all aware, rasogolla is a controversial sweet. The Oriyas claim that 'rasagola' originated in the kitchen or rosaghara of the Shree Jagannath Temple in Puri, the temple city of Orissa. Although the exact year has never been documented, food historians from Orissa have identified the twelfth century as the probable period of its invention.

But the sweet was known as khira mohana. The legendary story goes that Lord Jagannath offered this sweet to his consort Goddess Lakshmi after his return from Shree Gundicha Temple on Niladri Bije to pacify her because he could not take her along during the annual Ratha Yatra or the ritual chariot ride. As a result, it became customary to offer this sweet to Goddess Mahalakshmi as bhog (devotional offering) during Niladri Bije, which is the last day of this ten-day Chariot Festival. Unlike the usual white rasagola, khira mohana is a slightly flat and round sweet that is brown in colour and less spongy. The brown colour is because the chhena (as Oriyas call chhana) balls are boiled in raseni (sugar syrup, also known as sira) for long. Rasagola is claimed to have descended from this sweet.

But this claim is contested by other food historians from Bengal, who suggest that as chhana, the main ingredient in rasogolla, came to the country with the arrival of the Portuguese, it is quite unlikely that rasogollas were made in Puri as early as the twelfth century.

This prolonged tug of war between the two states about who invented the sweet first has ultimately ended in a draw. In 2017, West Bengal's rasogolla was granted the GI (Geographical Indication) tag and is now known as *Banglar Rasogolla* (Bengal's Rasogolla). Two years later, Orissa's rasagola was also granted the GI tag and is now known as *Odishara Rasagola* (Orissa's Rasagola). The difference lies in the belief that the two variants are separated by colour, texture, taste, juice content and method of manufacturing.

If we leave the controversy aside, it is believed that in the nineteenth century, crude versions of the sweet could have been made by some moiras in Bengal, which obviously lacked the finesse and the refined taste that would define the later version. But it is a confirmed fact that the round, spongy and syrupy milk-white rasogolla that is so famous today was the invention of the legendary Nobin Chandra Das, the founding father of the iconic confectionery shop, K.C. Das.

Nobin Chandra Das's ancestors were originally Vaishnavs, who worked as moiras, and made sweets like payesh, monda, *mohan bhog* and malpoa as mistanna bhog (devotional sweet offering) in the vien (a place reserved for sweet-making) at the ashram (spiritual hermitage) of the revered guru Sri Chaitanya Mahaprabhu in Nabadwip, located in Nadia district of West Bengal. Many generations later, the family became full-time sugar merchants of considerable social standing in the district of Burdwan. Eventually, they made Calcutta their home and settled down in Bagbazar in a joint family set-up. Nobin Chandra Das's family became well-known and respectable sugar merchants in Calcutta. After the death of his father, Madhusudan Das, Nobin Chandra Das decided to return to the profession of a moira. This caused an unpleasant stir in the extended family. Moiras were looked down upon by upper-class society. But Nobin Chandra Das had a knack for making sweets, so the choice came naturally to him. Das worked in a mishtir dokan (sweet shop) in north Calcutta for a couple of years to hone his skill and gain experience before venturing out on his own. He opened a sweetmeat shop in Jorasanko in north Calcutta in 1864 along with a friend, but the shop closed down after a year because of mismanagement of funds. He was more of a confectioner than a businessman. Refusing to be bogged down by his failure, he started another shop, this time completely on his own, in Bagbazar in 1866. This second venture proved to be a stable one, which laid the foundation of his future success.

Sweet-making in those days was mostly confined to sandesh and customers yearned for some kind of novelty in sweets. It was at this opportune juncture that Nobin Chandra Das came up with the idea of the spongy rasogolla. His shop at Bagbazar was a hangout for old folks who would drop in to have sandesh and indulge in some adda over sweets. Some of them suggested that he come up with a sweet that would be thirst-quenching. They were of the opinion that sandesh was a dry sweet, which satisfied hunger, but did not quench thirst.

Taking their suggestion seriously, Nobin Chandra Das began

experimenting. In the course of this, he invented a sandesh that was round in shape and made of sweetened chhana and khoya, mixed with chopped pistachios, laced with saffron and topped with a raisin. He thought the apt name for such a rich and unique sandesh should be *Baikuntha Bhog*, as its divine taste made it truly fit to be served at Baikuntha, the celestial abode of Lord Vishnu. Over the years, the sweet became popular with the monks of Ramakrishna Math, located in Bagbazar.

It was in 1868 when Nobin Chandra Das finally made the spongy rasogolla, a sweet that subsequently became so popular that it drove its crude versions to extinction. At first, he cooked small balls of chhana in thick sugar syrup on low heat till they doubled in size and completely soaked up the liquid. After this, he immersed the balls in lukewarm water for some time and then put them in thin sugar syrup. The sweet chhana balls turned out soft, fluffy and juicy, and he served them cold with some of the syrup. Nobin Chandra Das christened this unique creation, rasogolla, a name derived from the words 'ras', which means juice, and 'gol', meaning round. Thus, a legendary sweet was born.

But it took another ten to twelve years for his creation to reach the heights that it finally achieved. The credit for popularizing Nobin Chandra Das's spongy rasogolla goes to Rai Bahadur Bhagwandas Bagla, a wealthy Marwari businessman. One day, while travelling with his family, one of his children became thirsty. At that moment, his horse-drawn carriage was passing by Nobin Chandra Das's shop. The businessman stopped his carriage and requested for some water. The sweet-maker gave the child water to drink along with a free rasogolla. The child loved the sweet so much that he asked for more. Everyone in the carriage, including Rai Bahadur Bhagwandas Bagla, had many rasogollas, and the businessman even bought large quantities of the spongy sweet to take home. He spread the word about the sweet and its creator in his community and many Marwaris began dropping into the shop. This marked the beginning of the popularity of Nobin Chandra Das's rasogolla.

Nobin Chandra Das used natural fruit pulp in his creations, and the *ata* (custard apple) *sandesh* and *kanthal sandesh* are two of the more famous varieties. These have been recreated in other Bengali confectionery shops by succeeding generations of sweet makers.

Abar khabo, a sandesh made of sweetened chhana and khoya laced with green cardamom powder and rose water, owes its existence to Nobin Chandra Das. Dhiman Das, director of K.C. Das Pvt. Ltd, elaborates, 'Nobin Chandra Das's creative endeavours were limitless. When Maharani Swarnamoyee Debi of the Cossimbazar royal family complained that there were no sweets left in the market to excite her appetite, he came up with a delectable sandesh. After sampling it, the lady said, "Abar khabo!", which means, "Want to eat it again!", the name that this sandesh goes by till today.' It continues to be a popular sweet sold by most of the Bengali confectionery shops. Another famous invention is the *dedo sandesh*, which is still monopolized by the K.C. Das brand. This particular sandesh was a favourite of Ma Sarada Debi, the consort of Sri Ramakrishna Paramahansa, and even today, large quantities of it are sent to the Dakshineswar Kali Temple from the K.C. Das factory as her mistanna bhog.

Nobin Chandra Das died in 1925, leaving his business in the able hands of his wife, Kshirodmoni Debi, who was the granddaughter of Bhola moira, and their son Krishna Chandra Das. Descendants of Nobin Chandra Das believe that since he had never been business-minded, it was Kshirodmoni, who took care of the accounts and put an end to her husband's unprofitable habit of giving sweets to customers without taking any money in return.

After 1868, 1930 was another remarkable year in which three important events in the history of Bengal's sweetmeat industry took place: the invention of the iconic rasomalai, the canning of rasogollas and the opening of 'Krishna Chandra Das Confectioner'.

Krishna Chandra Das was responsible for inventing the rasomalai—soft and sweet chhana balls immersed in sweet cardamom-flavoured milk. In the same year, he opened a new shop in Jorasanko, where his father's first attempt at business had failed miserably, and named it 'Krishna Chandra Das Confectioner'.

During the Company Raj period, European food was often sold in the market in vacuum-packed cans. This gave Krishna Chandra Das the unique idea of selling rasogollas in a similar fashion. Krishna Chandra Das had graduated from Rajabazar Science College and was more interested in the scientific aspect of sweet-making than the day-to-day affairs of the shop. In 1930, he made the bold move of introducing rasogollas in vacuum-packed cans at the shop in Jorasanko. He also began selling them at his father's shop in Bagbazar. Although he never made any attempt to advertise this, the word about his new method of packaging spread. When people visiting the shops saw the cans, they bought some out of curiosity while those visiting the city would buy them for their families and friends back home. Canning of Indian confectionery was unheard of before this and it is believed that Krishna Chandra Das was a pioneer in this regard. Sadly, he died of throat cancer within four years of the opening of the shop, leaving the business in the hands of his son, Sarada Charan Das.

In 1935, the enterprising Sarada Charan Das opened a new shop in his father's name at Esplanade Row (East) in central Calcutta. This was his first attempt at expanding the business and the Esplanade shop remains the most popular branch of K.C. Das in Calcutta today. Sarada Charan Das can be given credit for moving away from the traditional norms that had characterized the previous shops. His first step was to abbreviate the name of Krishna Chandra Das Confectioner to the crisper and anglicized K.C. Das, which gave the brand an international feel. His second was to install a seating arrangement inside the Esplanade shop, where liveried employees attended customers, to give the place the look of a restaurant instead of a simple sweetmeat shop—groundbreaking concepts in those days as far as local confectionery shops were concerned. His third significant step was to package sweets in white cardboard cake boxes lined with butter paper instead of traditional leaf packing.

In the early 1970s, he introduced a sugar-free version of sandesh to satisfy the sweet tooth of the growing number of diabetics, a groundbreaking innovation that eventually caught on with other confectioners and came to be popularly known as 'diabetic sandesh'. He also invented the *amrita kumbha sandesh*, which was an exciting departure from conventional sandesh in both design and taste. In Sanksrit, 'amrita' means 'nectar' or 'ambrosia' and 'kumbha' means 'pitcher'. This is a pitcher-shaped sandesh that has a hollow at its centre. It is covered with a lid on the top. The pitcher as well as the lid is made of sweetened chhana that is infused with a few drops of ice cream essence. The inside is filled with creamy chhanar payesh. Amrita kumbha sandesh remains the speciality of K.C. Das.

His other noteworthy introductions are *ice cream sandesh* and *sandesh cake*. The former, inspired by the Western dessert, was an innovative attempt to serve a delicious piece of steamed sandesh chilled like an ice cream. This was done by refrigerating it for a few hours. Needless to say, it became tremendously popular, especially among children. The concept caught on and other confectioners began recreating it. This square-shaped sandesh, which generally comes topped with finely chopped pistachios, is made of a blend of sweetened chhana and cream to which a few drops of vanilla essence are added. Over the years, confectioners have experimented with this basic recipe and added a lot of variety to it. Another unconventional thought was giving sandesh the shape and design of a cake. Named sandesh cake, it was the result of an attempt to lure customers away from its Western counterpart. The effort has been successful. This modern innovation, which is now replicated by other confectionery shops, has become a much sought-after fancy replacement for the conventional cake on celebratory occasions. Today, sandesh cake is available in different sizes, shapes, flavours and designs.

Sarada Charan Das was a man with a scientific bent of mind. His biggest contribution to the industry has been the conception, design and implementation of the process of using steam generated from a boiler and passing it through steam-jacketed pans. This method replaced the traditional one of using coal or wood fire stoves and conventional woks to make rasogollas. 'It is hygienic and faster than the old method, enables the equal distribution of heat and makes the boiling better,' explains Dhiman Das, 'Rasogollas made over wood fires smell of wood, have a reddish tinge to them and are not as spongy as those made with steam. Except for fried sweets, which we make over gas fire, everything else, including the pasteurization of milk, is done with steam.'

In 1935, Sarada Charan Das introduced savouries at the Esplanade shop like *radhaballabhi-alur dom*, *nimki*, *shingara* and *kochuri*. It was these savouries that helped this shop sail through the tough time after the stringent Milk Trade Control Order was passed by the government of West Bengal, under the chief ministership of Prafulla Chandra Sen, in 1965. While most sweet shops in Calcutta closed down during this period because of the scarcity of milk, the Esplanade branch of K.C. Das managed to continue with its business.

During this difficult period, which lasted for two years, full-fledged research was carried out in the in-house laboratory of K.C. Das that had been converted into a private limited company in 1946 by Sarada Charan Das. The researchers at the laboratory, set up on Chitpur Road by the confectioner, carried out microbiological research on milk and related products for the company. They tried to come up with an alternative plan for making sweets and began experimenting with soya bean milk as the possible solution. Although, during this time, sweets made out of soya bean milk were commercially produced, their quality did not match the standard of the company. So, when the government withdrew the order, these sweets were discontinued.

While this difficult phase lasted, Sarada Charan Das also began looking for places outside West Bengal, where he could set up a factory and a shop, so that the repertoire of K.C. Das sweets could be extended to customers beyond the state. He began an extensive southern campaign and ultimately chose Bangalore for its cool climate and quality of milk. In 1972, he set up a factory and shop of K.C. Das in Bangalore and St Marks Road soon became a sweet landmark for the locals of the Garden City because it housed this first retail outlet. In fact, K.C. Das is the first Bengali confectionery shop to have a branch outside West Bengal. In the early 1980s, Sarada Charan Das set up a research and development (R&D) centre in Bangalore that is recognized by the department of science and technology of the Government of India. The unit is affiliated to Bangalore University and carries out research work on milk and related products. This attracts postgraduate students from universities across the country, whose field of study is milk, to carry out research projects at this facility.

The cottage technology that was once adopted for making sweets in Nobin Chandra Das's shop in Bagbazar has, over the years, made way for a full-fledged business that makes high quality Bengali confectionery in a modern, scientific and hygienic manner. The company plans to dot the country's map with its outlets and is on an expansion spree. At present, it has seven outlets in Calcutta and many more in Bangalore. Thus, a creative genius, who was disparaged by his extended family for wanting to be a moira, laid the strong foundation upon which his successors built an iconic company that stands tall today.

Dwarik's Grandsons: An interesting story that circulates in the corridors of this famous confectionery shop is that once, when the Bard of Bengal, Rabindranath Tagore, tasted the sweetmeats made by Lilabati, the wife of the renowned Bengali author, Banaphool, he is believed to have said, 'The sweets you have made are very tasty. In Calcutta, I know of only one shop that makes such tasty sweets, and that is Dwarik's.'

Dwarikanath Ghosh, the founding father of Dwarik's Grandsons, left Nijabalia, his village in Howrah district, with the intention of starting a confectionery business in Calcutta. He began his career in the city as a karigar in a sweet shop in Chorbagan in north Calcutta. Five years later, when he had saved enough funds to venture out on his own, he set up his own sweet shop in 1885 at the Shyambazar and Shyampukur Street crossing. At first, he began his business with the basic version of narompaak and korapaak sandesh, *makha sandesh*, *danadar* (balls of chhana cooked in sugar syrup and coated with sugar granules) and *mishti doi* (sweet yoghurt). Gradually, he added more varieties of sweets to his collection like *rabri*, rasogolla and pantua. Pantua is a rich, dark brown and syrupy sweet made of chhana, khoya and refined flour. These ingredients are mixed together with green cardamom powder and kneaded into a dough. Balls, made from this dough, are deep-fried in ghee and soaked in thick sugar syrup. Dwarikanath Ghosh made perfect pantuas that became popular with his customers.

Dwarikanath Ghosh was not an inventor. He was a refined sweetmeat artist who knew how to proportion his ingredients well enough to make sweets of superlative quality that spoke for his workmanship. Although many moiras left their villages in the outskirts and made Calcutta their home in the days of the Company Raj, only a select few made it to the list of top confectioners. Dwarikanath Ghosh was one of them. Word spread about Dwarikanath's confectioneries and the customers of north Calcutta flocked to the small shack to taste the juicy and scrumptious sweets, returning home with happy hearts. The turnover from his business increased so much that the confectioner soon had a proper shop built in place of the shack and named it Dwarikanath Ghosh & Sons. But for its loyal customers, the name was always the short and sweet Dwarik's.

Over the years, the reputation of Dwarikanath Ghosh & Sons crossed the borders of north Calcutta and spread across the city. It turned into a brand name that became synonymous with high-quality Bengali sweets. The confectioner had a large family of three sons and two daughters. His sons were enterprising enough to consider the prospect of expanding the business. From the 1920s, they gradually began opening branches across the city. Eventually, these shops came to be known as 'Dwarik's Grandsons', which has turned into a household name when it comes to traditional Bengali sweets. Customers throng the shops for their spongy and syrupy *rajbhog*, which is a bigger version of rasogolla, fresh *kanchagolla*, bolster-shaped langcha or coiled chhanar jilipi. But the most sought-after item at Dwarik's Grandsons, also popularly known as Dwariks, has always been mishti doi, which connoisseurs feel is of superlative quality. There was a time when an ice cream sharbot, a creamy concoction of milk, vanilla essence and crushed green cardamom, was made at these shops, but this has now been discontinued.

A walk into any of the Dwarik's and one can see a range of traditional Bengali sweets displayed on trays at its counter. To take examples, the shops make lip-smacking *darbesh* and *chitrakoot*. Partha Pratim Ghosh, owner of the Shyambazar branch of Dwarik's Grandsons, shares his recipe of darbesh, which is a round and orange-coloured sweet made of boondis or round droplets of gram flour batter to which some mud apple (chikoo or sabeda) powder and saffron essence are added. This batter is passed through a perforated ladle and fried in ghee in a wok. The fried boondis are then soaked in sugar syrup, laced with green cardamom or rose essence. This process makes them double in size. After this, the boondis are mixed with grated khoya, nutmeg (jaiphal) powder, mace (javitri) powder, cashew nuts and raisins, and shaped into colourful balls that are not only attractive to look at, but also very appetizing. Chitrakoot is a square-shaped fried sweet made of chhana and khoya to which some maida is added. These ingredients are kneaded together into a dough. Balls pinched from this dough are flattened into squares. These squares, with incisions made on them, are fried in ghee to a deep brown colour and soaked in sugar syrup, laced with green cardamom. The sweet is served sprinkled with grated khoya

From the 1930s to the 1950s, stalls of Dwarik's were put up at the Howrah and Sealdah railway stations. Sweets of this heritage brand were also catered during this time to the Indian railways. Sir Ashutosh Mukherjee, Shyama Prasad Mukherjee, Dr Bidhan Chandra Roy, and the renowned stars of early Bengali cinema, Pramathesh Barua and Kanan Debi, were customers of Dwarik's. Mani Shankar Mukherjee, the popular Bengali author, mentioned Dwarik's in his works.

Many years have gone by since the end of the Company Raj and the inception of this iconic sweet brand. But the magic that Dwarikanath Ghosh created continues to live in the hearts, minds and taste buds of Calcuttans through Dwarik's Grandsons. Little did the young sweet-maker know when he abandoned his rural life and arrived at the royal capital that one day, he would rise to prominence in his profession in this cosmopolitan city and pave the way for his descendants, who would continue to keep his legacy alive with their exemplary sweet-making skills.

Sen Mahasay: Sen Mahasay, another household name in Bengali sweets, was set up in 1885 by Ashutosh Sen on Sibdas Bhaduri Street in Fariapukur, a neighbourhood of Shyambazar in north Calcutta. Ashutosh Sen left his village in Hooghly district and migrated to Calcutta, where he took up a job as a goldsmith so that he could save enough money to turn his passion for sweet-making into a full-time profession. Around the age of forty-five, he began his own confectionery shop in a shack on Sibdas Bhaduri Street. Since he had no children, Ashutosh Sen handed over the confectionery shop to his nephew, Nilmoni Sen, in his old age.

'The idea of naming the shop after our surname and adding mahasay to it was given to Nilmoni Sen by the renowned author, Sarat Chandra Chattopadhyay, and poet, Nabinchandra Sen,' explains Sandip Sen. 'In those days, the office of Bichitra Press was at Fariapukur. These great personalities would sometimes drop into the sweetmeat shop after visiting the press. Since in Bengali, "mahasay" means "sir", people would now know us as Sen Mahasay and not just as moiras.'

The shop started with narompaak and korapaak sandesh and gradually shifted to making golapi pera and more innovative varieties of sandesh like *ratabi sandesh*, peshawari sandesh and manohara sandesh. Ratabi sandesh is a korapaak sandesh that is shaped like a pera. It is a slightly flat disc made of the following ingredients: chhana, sugar, pistachios, cashew nuts, green cardamom powder and saffron strands. The sandesh has a slight depression at the centre that is embedded with finely crushed pistachios. Peshawari sandesh is made of sweetened chhana infused with rose water and saffron strands while manohara sandesh boasts of pistachio content and also of the aromatic flavour of green cardamom. In the latter preparation, the sweet ball of sandesh is covered with thick sugar syrup and kept aside till the liquid solidifies and forms a crunchy coating on the surface.

Raser mishti like *kheer kadam* and bhaja mishti like *kalo jaam* were introduced much later into the shop. Kheer kadam (also known as *ras kadam* or *khoya kadam*) is a small, round sweet coated with grated khoya. Its centre is filled with a miniature rasogolla that is drained off its excess syrup. The covering of the sweet is made of khoya that has been mixed with powdered sugar and kneaded into a smooth dough. A small portion is taken from this dough, flattened against the palm and stuffed with the rasogolla. As a final touch, the sweet is rolled over a bed of grated khoya.

Kalo jaam is a round, fried sweet, black in colour, made of chhana, khoya and refined flour. These ingredients are kneaded together into a smooth dough with some sugar, cardamom powder and ghee. Balls made from this dough, are deep-fried at a high temperature. The sugar in the balls caramelizes and gives them their characteristic black colour. They are then soaked in sugar syrup, laced with green cardamom. Kalo jaam is served sprinkled with grated khoya.

Gradually, the fame of Sen Mahasay spread beyond Shyambazar to the rest of north Calcutta. The sweets of the shop began to be sought after both by eminent personalities and common people alike. In turn, the owners became more and more creative with their sweet-making. Over the years, they came up with unique varieties of sandesh that were given different flavours and shapes, and even fancy names. For example, they created *vanco sandesh*, a two-in-one variety that was half flavoured with vanilla essence and half with chocolate, *babu sandesh*, a triangular shaped creation with a high saffron content and coated with edible silver leaf, *pastry sandesh*, a variety that looks like pastry and is filled with cashew nut and topped with its dust, *baisakhi sandesh*, a square-shaped sandesh that is stuffed with cashew nuts and has three colourful shades in it—yellow, green and white, and the round, green-coloured, pistachio-based *monmatano sandesh* that is stuffed with cashew nuts and also topped with one. *Jai Hind*, an oblong-shaped, tricoloured sandesh that bears the colours of the Indian flag in three separate strips, was introduced in 1947 on Independence Day. It has the imprint of the Ashoka Chakra at the centre. This sandesh does not feature in the regular collection of the shop and is made only on Independence Day, Gandhi Jayanti and Republic Day. So, whether it is the oblong-shaped *manthan* or the barfi-shaped *aparupa*, Sen Mahasay has always been well-known for its diverse sandesh creations.

Today, Sen Mahasay operates a large business in Calcutta. The confectionery shop that began as a small shack on Sibdas Bhaduri Street has become a retail chain with branches spread across the city. The superior quality of its sweets has made this confectionery chain so well-known that it is near impossible to come across a resident who has not heard of it.

Gangurams: With a reputation that spans over a century, Gangurams is a name to reckon with in the sweetmeat industry of Calcutta. Set up in 1892 by Ganguram Chaurasia, Gangurams (as the brand is widely known) has served its lip-smacking sweets even to distinguished foreign dignitaries on their visit to Calcutta like Queen Elizabeth II, Nikita Khrushchev, Nikolai Bulganin and Zhou Enlai. This is a giant leap for a confectionery business that had a humble beginning as a small shop set up by a young man, who came from a village in Varanasi district at the age of eighteen, and began work as a confectioner in the kitchen of the zamindar, Raja Kamala Prasad Mukherjee. Though Ganguram Chaurasia's family was into agriculture, the halwai discovered his knack for sweet-making early in life. This made him give up the family profession and come to Calcutta, a city that had gained a reputation as the sweet hub of the country, to earn a living in the sweetmeat trade.

Raja Kamala Prasad Mukherjee was pleased with the work of his halwai and after six months of service, gave him one hundred square feet of land in his zamindari, on Vivekananda Road, a neighbourhood of Maniktala in north Calcutta, to start a shop. Ganguram Chaurasia began work in his shop (at that time, just a shack) by making halwa-puris cooked in pure ghee. When his halwa-puris started selling well, Chaurasia gradually added more varieties of sweets like sandesh, rasogolla, *mihidana*, *bonde*, mishti doi and *chhanar pulao* to his collection. After ten years of successfully running his business, he converted the shop from a shack into a proper building and named it Ganguram & Sons. Ganguram Chaurasia's sons grew into capable men who were also interested in the business. They expanded the first shop and opened branches in six other localities of Calcutta.

Over the years, Gangurams has become a very large business that is no longer confined to the shop on Vivekananda Road and its first six branches. It is the largest retail confectionery chain in Calcutta with several branches spread across the city that are run by the enlarged family of Ganguram Chaurasia. It also has a large number of franchise shops under its wing. Gangurams has expanded its customer base by retailing its sweets through leading supermarket chains and at its own stalls put up in Howrah, Sealdah and Kolkata railway stations as well as supplying them at the meetings and conferences of corporate houses and government organizations.

What is appealing about the history of Gangurams is that it has its roots in a shop that was set up in pre-Independent Calcutta by a non-Bengali, who specialized in making Bengali sweets, making it the first of its kind. It was only much later that this confectionery chain began including north Indian sweets in its collection. Today, Gangurams has a large customer base of both Bengalis and non-Bengalis, who flock to the shop for its rasomalai, *chhanar payesh*, *amriti*, *malai chamcham*, *sitabhog*, *chhana toast* and sandesh or gulab jamun, rabri, *barfi*, *kesaria pera*, *soan papdi*, laddu and *kalakand*. In winter, the rich fragrance and inviting looks of the cardamom-khoya-dried-fruit-laden *gajar ka halwa* on the shelves of Gangurams is as tempting as its collection of delicious *nolen gurer mishti*.

Milk Crown and *Indrani* are the two sweets that are the specialities of Gangurams. They were introduced during the 1970s and both are chhana-based. The latter has an edge in popularity. Indrani is a dessert that resembles rasomalai but is creamier. Miniature rasogollas made of buffalo and cow milk are drained off the excess sugar syrup and placed in a cup over which sweet milk cream, laced with cardamom powder and saffron, is poured. This preparation is then topped with blanched almond slivers and finely chopped pistachios, refrigerated for some time and served chilled. Milk crown, in contrast, is prepared by cooking slightly flattened chhana balls in thick sugar syrup till a reddish tinge appears on their surface. These are then drained off the excess syrup and allowed to cool. Rose water and cardamom powder are mixed in sweet cream, which is spread in a thick layer over each of the flattened chhana balls. As a final touch, each piece is garnished with saffron strands, finely chopped pistachios and grated khoya. The oldest shop of Gangurams on Vivekanada Road also happens to be one of the few confectionery shops in the city that still makes the very traditional Bengali sweet, *labango latika*. Labango latika is a square-shaped sweet made of refined flour and stuffed with sweetened khoya kheer. A ball, pinched from the dough of refined flour, is rolled into a round and a small portion of khoya kheer, shaped into a square, is placed in the middle of it. The round dough is then folded over the khoya kheer from both sides and the overlapping edges are gently sealed with the fingers. The flaps of the dough are brought together and secured on the front by piercing a labango (clove) through them. This sweet envelope is deep-fried till golden in colour and then soaked for a few minutes in lukewarm sugar syrup, laced with green cardamom. The crispy textured sweet, well coated with sugar syrup, is served at room temperature. Labango latika gets its name from the single clove that is used to seal it. A bite of Gangurams' labango latika fills the mouth with the sweet taste of khoya kheer and the spicy flavour of labango.

Over the years, the sweets of Gangurams have been enjoyed by luminaries like Satyajit Ray, Pandit Ravi Shankar, Pandit Bhimsen Joshi and Pandit Hariprasad Chaurasia. The growth of Gangurams seems unstoppable. It is a confectionery business that is going from strength to strength and has established itself as a reliable name in the sweetmeat trade of Calcutta.

Beyond Calcutta

Of course, not all Bengali sweets owe their origins to Calcutta. Several regions and towns in Bengal are renowned for certain sweets. Kalo jaam originated in the area that now borders Bangladesh while Nabadwip is famous for *lal doi*. Similarly, makha sandesh traces its roots to the sweetmeat artists of Satkhira (now in Bangladesh), while manohara sandesh, to those of Janai. Malda is known for khaja, Natore and Dhaka (both now in Bangladesh) for kanchagolla and amriti respectively, Muragachha in Barrackpore for chhanar jilipi, Ranaghat in Nadia district for pantua and Murshidabad for its chhanabora. Although *rasokadambo*, a sweet ball coated with roasted poppy seeds, is also popular in Murshidabad, it actually originated in Malda. The inner core of the sweet is similar to rasogolla while its outer covering is made of hardened khoya. *Jaynagarer moa*, a soft ball made from khoi (made with the aromatic and slender-grain kanakchur variety of rice) sweetened with nolen gur, has always been a popular winter sweet and originated in the small town of Jaynagar Mazilpur in West Bengal.

There are some interesting stories surrounding the invention of certain sweets. Mihidana and sitabhog, for instance, originated in the Burdwan district of West Bengal, known as the 'Rice Bowl' of the state. Both these sweets were invented by the same sweet-maker, Bhairab Chandra Nag. In 1904, Viceroy Lord Curzon visited Burdwan to confer the title of Maharaja to Bijay Chand Mahtab, the king of Burdwan. As a special treat to commemorate the occasion, the local sweet-maker, Bhairab Chandra Nag, was asked to make something that would please both the royalty and the visiting British officials. The moira's attempts led to the discovery of mihidana, which is a finer version of the traditional bonde and is made with the semi-liquid batter of gram flour and rice flour which is sourced from the kaminibhog or gobindobhog varieties of rice. The batter is passed through a sieve, fried in ghee and soaked in sugar syrup, laced with saffron. The end product looks like fine (mihi) grains (dana).

Sitabhog was also created for the occasion by the same sweet-maker and is made from rice flour and chhana. The rice flour and chhana are mixed in a proportion of 1:4 and kneaded into a smooth dough with some ghee. The dough is grated into small fine strips, which almost look like vermicelli, with the help of a specially designed mesh or grater. These are then lightly fried in ghee and soaked in sugar syrup, laced with bay leaves, cloves and rose essence. This sweet looks like white pulao from a distance with miniature gulab jamuns tossed into it. But these gulab jamun balls are actually small dumplings called *nikuti* that are made of chhana and refined flour. The dumplings are deep-fried in ghee, soaked in sugar syrup and tossed into the sitabhog. Sitabhog probably got its name from the sitaser variety of gobindobhog rice that grows in Burdwan district. It is this variety of rice that is ground into flour and used in the original recipe of the dessert.

Langcha, a popular fried sweetmeat, was created by Langcha Dutta, a moira from Krishnanagar in Nadia, West Bengal, who had a limp. In Bengali, langcha means 'the person who limps'. It was a word that got stuck to the moira because of his condition and he came to be known by this name. Langcha is a cylindrical, brown sweet made of chhana, khoya and maida. It is deep-fried in ghee and laid to rest in a pool of sugar syrup. Langcha owes its popularity to the matrimonial alliance between the royal families of Krishnanagar and Burdwan. According to the popular story, a girl from the Krishnanagar royal family was married into the Burdwan royal family. On becoming pregnant, she expressed a desire to eat this particular sweet. She could not remember the name of the sweet, but since the moira who made it in her hometown used to walk with a limp, she called it 'langcha'. The fried sweet was such a success with her in-laws that Langcha Dutta was lured to Burdwan with the promise of land so that he could prepare delicacies for the royalty. His nickname was then transferred to the sweet, which came to be known as langcha. Today, Saktigarh in Burdwan district excels in the making of langchas in West Bengal, though Krishnanagar takes pride in the fact that the sweet was first made there.

Surjya Kumar Modak, a well-known confectioner from Chandannagar in Hooghly district invented the *jalbhara taalshansh sandesh* in 1818. The Bandopadhyay family, who were the zamindars of Telinipara, Chandannagar, wanted the moira to make a special sweet on the occasion of Jamai Shashthi for their jamai or son-in-law, intending to take him by surprise. For the uninitiated, Jamai Shashthi is a joyous occasion celebrated by Bengali Hindus in honour of their sons-in-law. On this occasion, parents-in-law bless their sons-in-law and shower them with gifts. The jamai is especially treated to a large, scrumptious meal, which is the highlight of the occasion. The result of the moira's efforts was the jalbhara taalshansh sandesh, which he filled (bhara) with sugar syrup flavoured with rose water. The sandesh is shaped like the kernel of a palm and is korapaak. Moiras all over Bengal usually fill the sweet, now popularly known as jalbhara sandesh, with sugar syrup or with nolen gur in winter. Surjya Kumar Modak's jalbhara taalshansh sandesh was a great favourite of Rabindranath Tagore, who would buy the sweet in bulk whenever he visited Chandannagar. Modak is also given credit for inventing motichur sandesh, aam sandesh and kheerpuli sandesh around the same time.

And, of course, chhanabora has its own story too and is believed to have originated during the reign of Manindra Chandra Nandi, the Maharaja of Cossimbazar, who ruled from 1898 to 1929. Today, Cossimbazar is a town in Behrampore subdivision in the Murshidabad district of West Bengal. The Maharaja was bored of eating sweets like rasogolla and pantua, and craved for something new. He ordered his cook, Patal Ustad, to make a unique sweet that would not be like either of them. Ustad gave it a lot of thought and finally came up with a sweet that was a cross between the two—chhanabora—made with chhana like rasogolla but fried brown like pantua. Flavoured with cardamom, the chhana balls were deep-fried in ghee and soaked in sugar syrup. Today, the sweet shops of Murshidabad, particularly those of Behrampore, specialize in the production of this dessert.

Sweetness of Yoghurt

Mishti doi is a very popular Bengali dessert. In Bengali, *mishti* means 'sweet' and *doi* means 'yoghurt', thereby, implying 'sweet yoghurt'. Usually served in a clay pot, it is made by boiling down full cream milk with sugar to half of its quantity. The boiled milk is then removed from the fire and left to cool. Cardamom powder may be added to it. When the milk becomes lukewarm, a small quantity of leftover plain yoghurt or curd is whisked and added to it. The curd has to be mixed well into the milk so that it is uniformly distributed. This is because it is the source of Lactobacillus, which is the main bacterium present in it and the most vital one required to ferment the milk. It is then poured into small clay pots, covered and allowed to set at room temperature until firm. This creamy dessert forms mishti doi and it tastes best when served chilled. Most Bengalis prefer mishti doi to have a light brown colour. To achieve this, they add a caramel mixture (milk mixed with warm caramelized sugar) to the milk when it is getting boiled with sugar. Some prefer using nolen gur in place of sugar in the preparation of mishti doi in winter to give it a special taste. In this case, the caramel mixture is avoided.

Bengalis, with their constant innovativeness when it comes to cooking, even prepare mishti doi by steam. A small quantity of whisked plain yoghurt is mixed evenly with sweet full cream milk that has been reduced in quantity by boiling and cooled down to a lukewarm temperature. Cardamom powder may be added to the mixture. This mixture is then steamed to form *bhapa doi* or steamed yoghurt, which is cooled down to room temperature and also tastes best when served chilled. Just like in its non-steamed version, a caramel mixture can be used in the initial stage of its preparation or nolen gur may be used to sweeten it in winter. Modern sweetmeat artists add flavours to mishti doi as well. The most popular among them is *aam doi*, which is mishti doi flavoured with the pulp of ripe mangoes. Flavoured mishti doi can also be steamed.

Jalajoga, a colonial sweet shop that opened in the year 1934, was renowned for its mishti doi, which was given the name 'payodhi' by Rabindranath Tagore. The name is derived from the Bengali word 'payesh' (rice pudding) and the Sanskrit word 'dadhi' (yoghurt). The owners of the shop, the Ray family, were among the first to open a large chain of sweet shops under the banner, Jalajoga. Another sweet shop that is famous for its mishti doi is Putiram, which was established by Putiram Modak, a confectioner from Chandannagar. He came to Calcutta in 1889, in search of better opportunities in his profession. Although the present shop of Putiram was set up in 1902 by his nephew Jitendranath Modak on Surya Sen Street, the original shop of this famous confectionery is believed to have been set up in 1889 as a shack on the same street by Putiram Modak, the exact location of which is unknown to the descendants of his family, who are the present owners. The best qualities of Putiram's mishti doi are its light texture and the right amount of sweetness, almost as if it has been made at home.

Over the years, since its discovery, flavour and colour have been added to the rasogolla and confectioners have come up with *kesar bhog* (saffron flavoured and coloured rasogolla) and *kamala bhog* (orange flavoured and coloured rasogolla). Similarly, mishti doi is also cooked to varying shades of pink by many confectioners, a creation that has been aptly named lal doi (literally meaning red yoghurt). The invention of lal doi dates back to around 1930. It is certain that the place where this form of yoghurt was first created is Nabadwip. But there is some difference of opinion about its creator. While most residents and confectioners of Nabadwip are of the opinion that lal doi is the invention of confectioner Kali Ghosh, there are some who believe that it was Kalipada Modak, popularly known as Kali moira, who made it first. It was prepared by heating full cream buffalo milk on a low wood fire for several hours till it took on a pink shade. Pandit Jawaharlal Nehru is believed to have been very fond of mishti doi, and Dr Bidhan Chandra Roy, West Bengal's chief minister, would often arrange large quantities of it to be sent to him in Delhi.

The Portuguese ventured into Bengal to gain control over the trade of the region but ended up teaching an invaluable technique that went on to revolutionize its sweet-making industry. If chhana had never come into existence, Bengali sweets might have been stuck in their monda-mithai form. The British, too, played a part in the evolution of the sweetmeat industry of Bengal because it was only when they made Calcutta the centre of trade and commerce, that moiras from all over the districts and halwais from all over the country began to enter the city. This, in turn, made the environment competitive and sweetmeat artists began attempting to outdo each other in bringing out new and improved versions of their products. Each and every one of these factors played an important role in making Bengali sweets innovative, superlative and much sought after, by the entire nation.

European Confectionery in Bengal

European confectionery also found its way into Bengal with the Portuguese settlements. It took off in the Portuguese strongholds and was later commercialized during the British reign. In Portuguese, bread is known as pao, and an oven, as forno. The baking of bread is an important part of Portuguese culinary culture. The Portuguese had the tradition of baking bread loaves in beehive ovens that were wood-fired, dome-shaped and typically made of either brick or stone. Sometimes, the ovens could be large in size and shared by the community. Such large ovens required at least four to five hours of heating and could hold as many as thirty loaves of bread at a time. Most food historians are of the opinion that *pauruti*, which is the Bengali word for bread, has its roots in the word, pao. The Portuguese made a traditional sweet bread called pao doce with refined flour, yeast, milk, sugar, eggs, salt and butter. They also enjoyed sticky cinnamon bread rolls that were dunked in liberal amounts of sugar syrup or honey.

The Portuguese baked biscuits like shortbread using refined flour, butter and sugar. They also baked mille-feuille in which the puff pastry dough was rolled out in a rectangular shape, lightly brushed with milk and sprinkled with powdered sugar. The baked, cooled and flaky puff pastry rectangle, with its caramelized surface, was then very carefully cut crosswise into three broad, even strips. Pastry cream was spread evenly on the first strip, and the second strip was placed over it. The top of the second strip was then covered with whipped cream and the third strip was placed over it and dusted with powdered sugar. Mille-feuille was served as a teatime treat.

The Portuguese also enjoyed rich egg-based cakes like the creamy pao de lo, a traditional sponge cake that was very moist at the centre, with a golden crust on top. Especially made during Christmas and Easter, the cake was baked in a round red clay pot. They loved mulosayo, a slab of fried sweet pastry dough, rich in milk, eggs and cream. Pudim, a simple egg-based custard, was drizzled with caramel. But these baking traditions and methods were confined to the homes of the Portuguese in Bengal. Mog cooks working under the Portuguese were introduced to the concept of baking with refined flour and eggs. They learnt everything about the baking of breads and cakes and mastered the techniques involved.

The British, too, couldn't live without bread. The British memsahibs taught their native cooks to make bread loaves, cakes, pastries, sweet pies and puddings. It is believed that the British introduced the pound cake to Calcutta. It is now a common feature of the city's confectionery shops. Anglo-Indians, the result of mixed marriages between British men and Indian women, accepted European baking as part of their culinary culture. Bread loaves, cookies and cakes became a regular feature in their kitchens. Other minority communities like the Armenians and Jews had their own traditional baking history, which remained confined to their homes. European baking and confectionery in Calcutta only burst free from the confines of the British and Anglo-Indian homes during the British Raj. The advent of hotels, restaurants and confectionery shops in Calcutta played a pivotal role in this regard.

David Wilson, who was born in Brilley in Herefordshire, England, in 1808, ran a bakery on Cossitollah Road in Calcutta during the 1830s. He was popularly known as 'Dainty Davie' and it was often said in jest that the society gathered at his confectionery shop for his 'dainty dishes'. Wilson's confectionery shop was very popular with the Europeans. Douglas Dewar, in his book, *Bygone Days in India* (1922), has written that the confections made in his bakery were so good that they were '[...] enough to give celebrity to any street in Calcutta [...]' (p. 273). The author further points out that it was the Europeans who sought Wilson out and not the other way around. He was one of those few men they could not do without. Dewar elaborates, 'Visit the rooms of this confectioner at tiffin, count the palanquins, garis (carriages), and buggies that set down sahibs at his door between noon and two o'clock every day (Sundays not being exceptions), and if you are a European stranger you will be astonished' (pp. 273–74).

On 18 November 1841, Wilson opened the Auckland Hotel on Old Court House Street in Calcutta. He named it after George Eden, the First Earl of Auckland, who was the then Governor-General of British India. Later, he changed its name to Great Eastern Hotel.

The Great Eastern Hotel has played host to eminent personalities like Queen Elizabeth II, Mahatma Gandhi, Ho Chi Minh, Nikita Khrushchev, Nikolai Bulganin, Rudyard Kipling and Mark Twain. In fact, the hotel was so luxurious and well managed that it prompted Mark Twain to describe it as 'the best hotel east of the Suez' and even coin the epithet, 'Jewel of the East', for it. David Wilson must have been a remarkable character because his hotel was popularly known as Wilson's Hotel among the local people, both Europeans and Indians, and particularly among the 'gharry-wallahs' (cab drivers), coolies and others belonging to the lower rung of society. If hearsay is to be believed, many visitors to Calcutta were driven around for a long time by the 'gharry-wallahs', trying in vain to search for Great Eastern Hotel because they knew the place by the name of Wilson's Hotel.

William Walker, in his book, *Jottings of an Invalid in Search of Health, Comprising a Run Through British India and a Visit to Singapore and Java*, published in 1865, makes his observation about the Great Eastern Hotel: 'They have a steam engine to grind coffee and flour; they also make all sorts of cakes and ginger nuts; and bake excellent bread'(p. 10). The bakery of the Great Eastern Hotel was famous for its cookies, puff pastries like the deem puff (egg puff), fruit cakes, plum cakes, pies and flans, puddings, chocolates, cream rolls and assorted varieties of bread loaves, sweet buns, soup rolls and sticks. Even Indians from other parts of the country would check into this hotel and enjoy the baked delights offered here. European confectionery thus slowly became accessible to a wider customer base in Calcutta.

Chevalier Federico Peliti was considered the greatest confectioner of his time. His high-quality cakes and chocolates were sought after not only by Europeans, but by aristocratic and well-off locals as well. Peliti's always had a collection of fancy cakes, fondants, dragées and crystallized fruits, fresh in stock. The master confectioner made some of the best wedding cakes in the city, complete with beautiful decorations and of any size within the range of four to a hundred pounds. One of Peliti's greatest achievements was a twelve-foot tall replica of the Eiffel Tower in sugar, for which he won an award at the Calcutta International Exhibition in December 1889. There were constant speculations in the newspapers about the subject of Peliti's future creations, making his followers wonder what his confectionery marvels in the approaching exhibitions would be: a replica of the London Bridge, or perhaps, the Buckingham Palace? An advertisement in *The Statesman*, dated October 1886, shows Peliti's catering chocolates, cakes and other confectioneries to the mofussil towns of Bengal. He would receive the orders by letter or telegram, and supply them by the first return mail. Another advertisement for Peliti's, appearing in the same newspaper in April 1905, shows the confectionery shop selling sixteen pieces of hot-cross buns for a rupee for the occasion of Good Friday. As Easter approached, the Christian community would make a beeline for Peliti's for its endless varieties of Easter Eggs.

Firpo's on Chowringhee was also renowned for its confectionery. Europeans and snooty brown sahibs were often seen in Firpo's having puffs and pastries. Firpo's' collection of breads was popular with the middle-class residents of the city and its outskirts like Howrah, particularly its milk bread and raisin bread, with the latter tasting a lot like cake. Its breads were affordable, tasted great and were made available at shops through agents.

The grand Christmas celebrations that were introduced to Calcutta by the British gave a wider visibility to European confectionery. Chowringhee was the main centre of Christmas celebrations. The entire street and all its mansions would be lit up at this time. Christians would attend Mass in the churches, which baked their own traditional Christmas cakes, rich in dried fruits and laced with flavoursome spices like cinnamon and nutmeg. Anglo-Indians would celebrate Christmas with home-made cakes, rose cookies, kulkuls, marzipan candies, plum pudding and wines. Though Christmas cake is not an integral part of the Christmas celebration in Armenia, the Calcutta Armenians celebrated their Christmas on 6 January with cakes because they were influenced by the British and Anglo-Indian customs.

Although Christmas celebrations during the Company Raj period were confined to the Europeans and Anglo-Indians, the various hotels and restaurants dotting White Town became centres of revelry during the festive season. Spence's Hotel, Great Eastern Hotel, Grand Hotel, Peliti's and Firpo's were popular haunts for grand Christmas lunches and dinners. There would be a great rush for the cakes and confectioneries made by the master confectioner Federico Peliti during the festive season. His rich Christmas plum cake, advertised by the firm as 'highly decorated in Mr Peliti's own particular style', could be bought either plain or with almond paste. Customers reached out for cakes like the almond red and the endless varieties of chocolates, toffees and confectioneries. Federico Peliti had a 'special recipe' for his plum pudding that was made only on order. A large variety of crackers and fancy baskets, and the choicest of bonbonnieres selected personally by Federico Peliti from Paris, were some of the items that were available at Peliti's, exclusively during the festive season.

As long as the ground floor of the Great Eastern Hotel was filled with shops, an enjoyable social function took place there annually during Christmas Eve. The entire central portion of the ground floor was like an emporium, lined on both sides with a continuous row of shops. A sort of carnival was held in this large central hall, which was brilliantly illuminated, beautifully decorated and festooned with flags of all nations, giving it the name, 'Hall of All Nations', on this occasion. During this time, the commercial goods in the shops were replaced with in-house cakes, of different designs and sizes, bonbons, varieties of sweets and confectioneries, crackers and all kinds of fancy products, perfect for gifting. Shortly after dark, the whole of the elite of Calcutta society gathered here to exchange Christmas greetings and small gifts. This carnival was one of the gayest sights of Calcutta during the festive season and a very enjoyable affair, which the Europeans looked forward to.

With the opening of the Sir Stuart Hogg Market, Christmas shopping shifted to this ground. Sir Stuart Hogg Market was built exclusively for the Europeans and no locals were allowed to shop in it during the Company Raj period. Everything that was required for Christmas shopping was available in the market complex, right from decorations to the ingredients required to bake cakes.

Gradually, many small bakeries sprung up across the city, making European confectioneries. The most prominent bakeries of the time were Nahoum's, M.X. D'Gama, Wyse & Co. and Saldanha. Flurys was a tea room and confectionery set up by Joseph Flury, and served well-made cakes and pastries to its large number of customers. These confectionery shops were responsible for bringing in European baked goods to the average person's home. The popularity of European confectionery grew so much that small bakeries began cropping up on the outskirts of Calcutta like Howrah, which made biscuits, bar cakes, Swiss roll cakes and tiffin cake bars. These were mainly taken as accompaniments to tea and were thus supplied in bulk to tea vendors at the Howrah railway station and elsewhere. The vendors usually stored the biscuits and confectioneries in big glass jars so that they would be visible to customers, a practice that is still in vogue. Thus, a crossover began to take place in Calcutta's culinary culture. European confectionery became sought after.

Flurys: Flurys has earned its reputation as a show-stopper when it comes to baking one-of-a-kind cakes. Around 1994, this confectionery shop baked a cake for a Lucknow nawab on his wedding anniversary. It was a plum cake of 130 lbs with icing, decorated with roses and gilt-edged double hearts pierced with an arrow, and cost nearly twelve thousand rupees. The thirty-five-square-feet cake had to be transported in a mid-sized van. Today, people flock to Flurys to order special birthday cakes for their children, from Snow White and Swiss Doll to Spiderman and Calcutta Zoo cakes. The tea room bakes some of the best cakes, chocolates and cookies in the city and the assortment is a fascinating one, from Blackcurrant Gateau, Lemon Mimosa Torte and Raspberry Ruffle to Deep Forest Cheesecake and the legendary Silvana Cake.

Joseph Flury was a native of Zurich. He and his wife, Freida, set up a tea room and confectionery like the ones in his hometown, where they served the finest teas with an assortment of breads, pastries and puffs. When he began it in 1927 in Stephen Court on Park Street, little did he realize that Flurys would go on to become a gracious tea room and confectionery where well-dressed women wearing hats and courteous men flashing pocket watches would want to be seen. The cream of society once dined here. The zamindar Sens of Rawdon Street, Sir B.C. Mitter, a member of the Privy Council, Sir P.L. Mitter, the Advocate General of Bengal and Law Member of the Viceroy's Executive Council in Delhi, and Calcutta's famous Jews, B.N. Elias and Sir David Elias Ezra, were all regular customers at Flurys. A Flurys' cake was always delivered at tea time to the verandah of Lord Sinha's house, at the demand of his wild daughter Romola, who smoked cigarillos while wearing a traditional sari and a French hat. Sir Nil Ratan Sircar, the brilliant doctor in whose name a public hospital stands in the city, would often drop into Flurys from his house on nearby Short Street. Raj Kapoor had a great love for Flurys' chicken patties, which he indulged in every time he visited Calcutta.

The Quit India notice served by Mahatma Gandhi to the British in the year 1942 saw many people of foreign origin pack their bags and leave India in anticipation of swaraj. It was in this year that Jit Paul first arrived in Calcutta on the Frontier Mail from Lahore. His family company, Amin Chand Pyare Lal, was named after his grandfather, a market-savvy businessman from the village of Chang in what is now Haryana. The company had, over the years, changed with the times and moved from the manufacturing of agricultural implements to products ranging from sanitation fittings to machines to make sevian (the Indian version of vermicelli).

In her book, *Flurys of Calcutta: The Cake That Walked* (2007), author Bachi Karkaria points out,

> The company's connection with the eastern India was already established, through the gargantuan iron and steel plants at Jamshedpur and Burnpur. His nationalist father Lala Pyarelal was one of the 14 stockists of TISCO [Tata Iron and Steel Company] products in Jullundur, and had always proudly bought his own raw material of pig iron from IISCO [Indian Iron & Steel Company], set up by Sir Rajen Mookerjee (p. 78).

Jit Paul's first visit to Calcutta was a successful one, and he began visiting the city every two months. Many of his business deals were conducted at Flurys. He remembers the hard work invested into the tea room by the Flury couple, who personally monitored every aspect of its functioning, right from the production to the serving.

Karkaria writes that at that point of time the Pyare Lals did not know '[...] that they would grow from sanitation to shipping, circle the globe with their industries, and that far more than pasta would feature in their hotels. The various holding companies would merge into the Apeejay Group, the initials standing for Amin Chand Pyare Lal, Jullundur. Surnames were never the part of the Indian traditions, but in keeping with its modernization the family adopted Paul as theirs' (p. 78).

Amin Chand Pyare Lal had set up a small office on Canning Street, a busy commercial centre of central Calcutta. Soon, the business flourished and the family shifted their office to bigger premises on Brabourne Road. By 1960, the Pauls had shifted the headquarters of their company, Apeejay Group, from Partition-fractured Punjab to their own Apeejay House on Park Street.

It was in 1965 that Flurys changed from completely Swiss to truly Indian hands. Joseph Flury was on the lookout for a buyer for his tea room and confectionery before he packed his bags. The young and ambitious Jit Paul saw a golden opportunity and expressed his desire to take over. An agreement was signed and thirty-eight years after it opened, Flurys became another man's property.

Jit Paul let the business at Flurys continue the way it had in the past. The legendary Lewis Lobo, who once had his own confectionery shop in Darjeeling before he was whisked away by Joseph Flury to Calcutta, ran the factory, located diagonally opposite to the tea room and confectionery, from 1962 to 1983. The youngest Paul brother, Surrendra, married the feisty and beautiful Shirin shortly after the tea room was acquired. Shirin, who had been working at American Express, was not too keen to give up her executive persona after marriage. On Surrendra's suggestion, she rolled up her sleeves and took Flurys under her wing. She thought up of new shapes for the cakes, new offerings, new gift box designs and new ways to decorate the festive windows. Thousands of trains were made of sponge cake, marzipan and chocolate for little boys during her time. In the late 1960s, Flurys catered for teatime at the race course's Royal Calcutta Turf Club and supplied party desserts to Calcutta's elegant homes. On these occasions, the delicacies that Shirin catered ranged from the creamy and flaky mille-feuille, each time filled and flavoured differently, to the most tempting of all Italian cakes, the Diplomat, enriched with cream, meringues and macaroons, to the delicious Brazilian pudding, made with an extra shot of rum.

As Karkaria points out, 'Flurys was the cherry on the cake, even if the Apeejay cake was made of such unconventional ingredients as steel, shipping, pharmaceuticals, tea, real estate and bookstores. The foray into hospitality was the still-skeletal Park Hotel diagonally across the street' (p. 92). The Paul brothers consolidated their slices after an amicable division in 1989. Needless to say, the ownership of Flurys now passed on to Surrendra Paul.

Over the years, the image of Flurys has been touched up a few times. The tea room and confectionery, which had been spelt Flury's, was changed to Flurys: the apostrophe done away with. The tag line, which had been 'Swiss confectionery', was altered to 'Five generations of fine confection'. In 1991, Surrendra and Shirin's daughter, Priti Paul, gave their oldest property in Calcutta a facelift by redoing the interior. In 2004, Flurys underwent a complete makeover under the management of their other daughter, Priya Paul. Even production in Flurys has undergone a change from its early days. The overhaul ranges from bringing in star chefs, who keep updating the menu, to introducing high-tech baking systems and walk-in refrigerators. The best chocolate is procured from the Callebaut and Selbourne brands. Eighty per cent of the old recipes have been retained while Ciabatta and Masala have been added to the bread range, and Vegetarian Manchurian, to the range of patties. King-sized, temperature-controlled ovens in which cookies, croissants and cakes are baked can be seen during a quick stroll through the Flurys' factory.

The best thing about Flurys is its diverse customer base. One might spot an old gentleman forking into his rum ball while perusing the crisp pages of the newspaper, or an unkempt and tattooed backpacker spending hours with a *Lonely Planet* and a Viennese coffee. Students from the nearby Loreto and St Xavier's Colleges are often seen at Flurys, bunking classes and sharing sweet buns over cold coffees. Flurys has a strong relation with the more-than-busy homemaker, who indulgently treats her child to more-than-one glass of milk shake and baba pastries (a thick cylindrical dry cake, enriched with dried fruits) while she demurely sips well-brewed Darjeeling tea and enjoys a lemon tart. The tea room and confectionery is also the ideal spot for a date. Joseph Flury's tea room and confectionery is still a very fashionable venue for meetings, big and small. Marwaris, many of whom have moved out of the noisy and crowded areas of Barabazar and north Calcutta, and settled in the spacious and leafy locales of south Calcutta, are regulars at Flurys, where they partake of the eggless cakes; the evergreen Soumitra Chatterjee was often seen at the place.

Throughout the years, Flurys has continued to be renowned for its high-quality confectioneries: its chocolate boats, triple chocolate passion and the soft and creamy almond, pineapple or strawberry cube pastries. Actress and dancer, Vyjayanthimala, would swear by the tea room's caramels, and every time she came to the city to perform, she took a large box of them back to Bombay. Uttam Kumar was a regular here. Customers love spending time in the confectionery, generously spreading fresh butter over crusty French bread at breakfast or taking bites of sweet muffins over evening tea. Flurys' creations can also be said to have earned a place in the baking history of the city, as every landmark of Calcutta, from the Hooghly river and Eden Gardens to the metro rail, was once recreated for a customer on a thirty-pound pineapple cake that was shaped into the Calcutta map and aptly named 'Kolkata Shahar' (City of Calcutta).

After Calcutta became the royal capital, the locals now not only reached for sandesh, but could also select cakes and pastries with equal enthusiasm. Bread became popular, and has now shouldered the traditional breakfast to the weekend slot. Many in the city also love to eat sausages, bacon and hash browns with eggs for breakfast. The Europeans thus changed the outlook of the locals towards food, and brought about a culinary revolution, while, ironically, a different kind of revolution brewed in Indian hearts.

4. Anglo-Indians and Their Culinary Culture

When the British officials living in the Indian subcontinent married women of Indian origin and had children with them, these children came to be called Anglo-Indians. It is difficult to point out when exactly such marriages began to happen, but it is believed that Job Charnock, regarded as the founding father of Calcutta, snatched a Hindu woman in Patna from her husband's funeral pyre and married her, renaming her Maria.

Since Calcutta was the royal capital and the headquarters of the British East India Company, the city was home to a majority of the Anglo-Indians in the country at that time. It continues to be so in independent India. Although Anglo-Indians constitute a minority of the population, they are the only community of mixed descent to be officially recognized by the Constitution of India. Today, the Constitution has expanded the definition of Anglo-Indian to include all descendants from European, and not merely British, patrilineal heritage.

For much of the latter half of the eighteenth century, Anglo-Indians were given jobs in defence and administration. They gradually grew in status in colonial Calcutta. They spoke English well and adopted a Western style of dressing, which made them acceptable for service in the British East India Company. Many of the members of this community also felt a great deal of psychological and emotional attachment to the British and were drawn to their 'fatherland' across the ocean. They often found themselves distant from other Indian communities living in the city.

The Anglo-Indians, like many others in the country, felt the need to provide their children with suitable education. To this end, a number of new institutions came up in the city, modelled on British public schools. The students, who graduated from these academies, having received a Western-style schooling and being tutored in impeccable English, had an advantage over their peers. Kuntala Lahiri Dutt, in her essay 'The Anglo-Indians of Calcutta', from the book *Calcutta—The Living City: Volume II: The Present and Future* (1990), writes, 'With the inauguration of the railways, the telegraphs and the postal system in the mid-nineteenth century, the Anglo-Indians [...] became important in the British scheme of things: they could fill the intermediate positions in these strategic sectors' (p. 68). They were also rewarded for their support to the British forces during the Sepoy Mutiny in 1857, and the men were given jobs in the police, customs, army and medical services. The women were given jobs in the education and nursing sectors. Anglo-Indians also helped the British by joining their forces during the two World Wars.

At their peak, the number of Anglo-Indians living in the city was around 4,00,000. Since the British were mainly concentrated in central Calcutta, the Anglo-Indians also congregated in this area. Park Street, Elliot Road and Ripon Street became known as bustling Anglo-Indian neighbourhoods. Many of these families still live in Bow Barracks, near Bowbazar, in central Calcutta. Over the years, Bow Barracks has come to be strongly identified with the community. It is believed that during the First World War, the British soldiers had their barracks in the place, lending it the name. Anglo-Indians began living in these barracks when the soldiers left the country. Some Anglo-Indians have shifted to localities like Behala and Picnic Garden in south Calcutta because of overcrowding.

Henry Louis Vivian Derozio (18 April 1809–26 December 1831) was among the most influential members of the community. Although an Anglo-Indian of mixed Portuguese descent, he had a great love for Bengal and was intensely patriotic about India. Derozio was a well-known academician, who taught English literature and history at Hindu College, later known as Presidency College, and now, Presidency University. Greatly admired for his intense and zealous teaching skills, his interactions with his students created a stir and were much talked about. Existing ideas and social norms were passionately discussed in debates organized by him. He was a radical thinker whose ideas strongly influenced the Bengal Renaissance movement. Even long after his untimely death from cholera at the age of twenty-two, his influence lived on among his English-educated Bengali students, who formed a group of radical free thinkers called 'Young Bengal'. These students were also known as Derozians, named after their firebrand teacher. Many of them became prominent in the fields of law, journalism and social reform. Derozio was also a poet who wrote poems in English, many of which had a patriotic flair.

After India won its independence, the members of the Anglo-Indian community felt a deep sense of betrayal when the British abandoned them and left the country. It made them feel insecure and vulnerable to remain behind in a country where the forces of Indian nationalism had taken over the centre of power. There was a large-scale exodus of Anglo-Indians from Calcutta to the United Kingdom, Canada, Australia, New Zealand and the United States of America. Those who remained in the city were relegated to an outsider status. They wore Western clothes, their religion was Christianity and their mother tongue, English. The rest of the Indian communities living in the city could not relate to them. A mutual feeling of distrust grew, which was eventually replaced by a sense of warmth and friendliness. Now, Anglo-Indians are seen as an integral part of the independent nation of India.

They run several charitable organizations that work within the Christian philosophy of social service to the poor. These work for the benefit of not only the poor sections of their own community, but also the poor of the city at large. By working in the same commercial and government sectors as the rest of the Indian communities in the city and also through increasing social interactions, Anglo-Indians have been able to assimilate themselves into the broader swathe of Calcutta society. They have learnt to speak fluent Bengali and Hindi and wear Indian clothes with grace and ease. Although, the Anglo-Indians would earlier mostly marry within their community, intercommunity marriages are a common occurrence now. Other communities now avail the services of their churches, welfare organizations and schools. The classical as well as popular form of Western music (once almost the exclusive stronghold of Anglo-Indians) has a lot of followers from other communities. Most of Calcutta's elite have studied in Anglo-Indian schools and have imbibed some aspects of their lifestyle, which has helped tremendously in bringing the communities close to each other. In recent times, Neil O'Brien, a prominent member of the Anglo-Indian community in the city, was the first to bring the quizzing culture to Calcutta by conducting its first formal well-organized quiz. There are around 20,000 Anglo-Indians living in Calcutta today.

*

When it comes to food, curry is as important to the Anglo-Indian community as stews, roasts, meaty pies and puddings. There are a few reasons for this diversity. During the early years, when the British first began settling in India, they had to eat the rice and curries cooked by the khansamas, eating whatever was available in their new environment. The khansamas only gradually began cooking European cuisine using local spices and ingredients. The taste of this cuisine varied from region to region because of the different kinds of spices and ingredients that went into the cooking, thereby giving the food different flavours. The British thus grew accustomed to a fare that included both the native staples of rice and curry and spicy European food. The cooks who worked for the British played a major role in promoting the mishmash of two cuisines. This blended cuisine of the East and the West continues in Anglo-Indian homes. The matrimonial alliances between British men and Indian women also contributed to this culinary fusion. Besides this, Portuguese cooking has left its own mark on Anglo-Indian dishes. But the predominant flavour in the cooking has always been Indian, and the food that has evolved is a lot spicier than the more traditional European cuisine.

For this reason, Anglo-Indian shepherd's pie tastes slightly different from its British counterpart. British shepherd's pie is made with minced meat, which is cooked with chopped onions and other vegetables like carrots, corn or peas, salt, pepper, tomato puree, Worcestershire sauce and meat stock. The minced meat is topped with potatoes that have been mashed with butter and milk and seasoned with salt. The pie is baked till the top starts to brown and the minced meat becomes hot and bubbles. Anglo-Indian shepherd's pie, on the other hand, is made with minced meat, which is cooked with chopped onions and other vegetables like carrots, corn or peas, pastes of ginger and garlic, ground coriander, cumin, dried red chillies and garam masala, as well as salt, pepper, Worcestershire sauce, tomato puree and meat stock.

From this, it can be seen how similar the methods of preparation are, and yet, how different the ingredients that go into the dish. Anglo-Indian cuisine is one that has been born of fusion between two cultures. It is European in spirit but local in content.

The Anglo-Indians are bread and rice eaters and rely heavily on red meat, especially pork and beef, in their dishes. Many of their staples are made with leftover cooked meat. The Anglo-Indian mince potato chop is also an adaptation from the West, except that in this preparation, the minced meat is cooked with chopped onions and the pastes of ginger and garlic, chopped green chillies, salt, pepper and chopped coriander leaves. The mashed potato is shaped into balls and depressions are made at their centres, which are then filled with the minced meat mixture. The balls are moulded in the shape of eggs and dipped into whisked eggs, coated in breadcrumbs and deep-fried.

Meat is an essential component in Anglo-Indian cooking. Even rice dishes like the junglee pulao and pish-pash are adaptations of local fare that use meat and rice as the main ingredients. Junglee pulao is called 'junglee' or wild, because this rice dish is a crazy mixture of long-grain rice, leftover curried meat such as beef, mutton or chicken, and spices and herbs that are easily available in the kitchen. It may even include vegetables. Every Anglo-Indian family prepares its own version of this one-pot meal. Junglee pulao is a very filling meal and does not require any curry dish as an accompaniment. Pish-pash is a dish of long-grain rice, meat (preferably chicken or mutton) and its stock cooked in butter with chopped onions and potatoes, and a small variety of spices like the pastes of ginger and garlic, bay leaves, black peppercorns, cinnamon, cardamom and cloves. Seasoned with salt, it is cooked till the meat becomes tender and the rice, soft and mushy. The fact that the rice is overcooked lends this dish its colloquial name.

Beef kofta curry, pork bhooni and Hussaini curry are some of the popular curry dishes made by the community. Beef kofta curry, also known as mince ball curry, is a rich and aromatic dish. The gravy is cooked with onions, tomatoes, coconut milk and a variety of spices. Meatballs or koftas made of minced beef are then cooked in the gravy. Mince ball curry is also made with mutton koftas. For pork bhooni, boneless pieces of pork are cooked with chopped potatoes and onions, the pastes of ginger and garlic, ground turmeric and dried red chillies, and meat stock till the meat is tender and the water has dried up. Chopped dill leaves are added towards the end of the cooking. This gravy dish can also be prepared with beef or lamb instead of pork. It is eaten with steamed rice and pepper water, a popular combination in Anglo-Indian households in Calcutta. Bhooni means 'to fry' and is derived from the Hindi word 'bhuna', which is a cooking process in which the spices are lightly fried in plenty of oil to bring out their flavours. The pieces of meat are then added to the spices. They are mainly cooked in their own juices along with the addition of some stock. This gives the dish a strong flavour and very little gravy. The gravy has an almost dry consistency that coats the pieces of pork. The freshness of the dill leaves gives this pork dish a distinct flavour.

Hussaini is a kebab curry made with undercut beef, and often eaten with steamed rice. The gravy is made by frying the pastes of onions, ginger, garlic, turmeric and dried red chillies along with whole cardamom and salt. Some amount of water is added to the cooking. Skewers are driven through the meat, which is arranged to alternate with thin, round slices of ginger and halved onions. The skewers are put into the gravy and it is all cooked till the meat becomes tender. A quantity of whipped curd is added to the curry as well, and the dish is kept on the stove till the oil from the curry floats to the top. Hussaini curry has always been a popular dish with the Anglo-Indians of Calcutta. Many claim that this kebab curry was the innovation of a Muslim chef named Hussain. However, the veracity of this claim cannot be confirmed.

Soups such as pepper water and stews such as buffath are eaten frequently by the community in Calcutta. Pepper water bears some influences from the southern parts of India. Similar to the south Indian rasam, pepper water is eaten with steamed rice and has a watery consistency. Some people even eat it along with a dry poultry, meat or seafood meal. The preparation of pepper water varies between regions as the ingredients may vary slightly. Despite its name the pepper water prepared by the Anglo-Indians in Calcutta does not feature any black peppercorns. Instead it is marked by the use of the Bengali five-spice mix, *paanch phoron*, an influence of the local culinary practices. The preparation of this dish requires chopped tomatoes, spices like ground dried red chillies, paanch phoron and turmeric, tamarind juice and salt, which are cooked in water at high heat. The pepper water is tempered with whole red chillies broken into bits, mustard seeds, curry leaves and sliced onions fried lightly in oil. Buffath is a meat and vegetable stew that has some Portuguese influence. In this dish, the cleaned meat pieces are boiled in water along with a variety of chopped vegetables, spices and vinegar to make a delicious stew, which is full of taste and good health.

Pamela Rebeiro, a former corporate executive and aficionado of Anglo-Indian food, says, 'There was a time when pumpkin salad was a popular dish among the Anglo-Indians of Calcutta. This salad was made of the mashed pulp of red pumpkin, to which finely sliced onions, chopped green chillies and thick coconut milk were added, along with salt and lime juice. During the 1960s and '70s, pumpkin salad was a rage in the community. But for some reason, this healthy side dish is slowly fading away from the culinary scene.'

The Anglo-Indians of Calcutta also make a small range of chutneys. Sweet mango, tomato, mint and coriander and coconut chutneys are some of the most popular varieties. The concept of chutney is very Indian and quite alien to European cuisine. One of the more famous chutneys is Devil chutney, which is made of onions, dried red chillies, salt, sugar and vinegar or lime juice. The onions and dried red chillies are ground to a fine paste and then mixed with the rest of the ingredients. The presence of dried red chillies gives it a bright red colour, which lends the sauce its fiery name. The sugar in the dish makes it quite sweet and only a little pungent in taste. It is usually eaten with pulao, meat curry and salad. A typical Anglo-Indian weekend lunch will include yellow coconut rice (made with long-grain rice, coconut milk, ghee or butter, salt, turmeric or saffron strands, bay leaves and whole spices like cinnamon, cardamom and cloves), mince ball curry and Devil chutney.

The Anglo-Indians of Calcutta have made traditional European puddings like bread-and-butter pudding, apple grunt, strawberry flummery and caramel custard a part of their cuisine as well. But there is always some room for innovation and experimentation! The flavours of the East and West continue to be blended in exciting ways, one result being jalebi pudding, in which broken pieces of jalebi are immersed in a custard mixture and baked till a golden crust appears on the surface.

*

There are some interesting stories surrounding the creation of certain dishes that feature in Anglo-Indian cuisine. At first, these dishes were served to the whites and they developed an affinity for them. The Anglo-Indians, who always had a tendency to emulate the ruling class in their lifestyle, habits and practices, including food habits, made these dishes a part of their cuisine. The Railway Mutton Curry, for instance, is a mildly spiced mutton gravy dish that was very popular with the British officers. They ordered it quite frequently while travelling by train across the country. Eminent food historian Bridget White-Kumar, who is an authority on Anglo-Indian cuisine, informs:

> The precise origin of this dish is somewhat obscure, but it can be safely inferred that it began to be prepared some time during the early 1900s by Spencer's Catering Company, a contemporary railway catering giant. During the days of the British Raj, travelling by train was considered aristocratic. Only Europeans and upper-class Indians could do so in the early years. This mutton curry dish was served in the first-class

> cabins and pantry cars on long-distance journeys along with breads or dinner rolls. It was also served in refreshment rooms in railway stations. The curry was not too spicy, bearing in mind the delicate palate of the British. The main ingredients used in preparing this curry were tender pieces of mutton and potatoes, along with either vinegar or tamarind juice, to ensure that the curry did not spoil during long journeys.

Country Captain Chicken is a chicken curry dish in which the gravy is flavoured with chopped onions, a variety of spices and vinegar. It is a semi-dry preparation with a thick gravy. This dish was very popular during colonial times. In those days, the poultry used for preparing the dish were well-fed, home-grown country chickens. It would take at least a couple of hours to cook this dish over a firewood oven. But ultimately, the chicken curry would turn out rich and delicious.

There are many versions of the story of how the dish got its name. The most popular one states that it was prepared by the grandmother of a British army captain for her favourite grandson. She made it using her home-grown country fowls, which also lent this dish the name, Grandma's Country Captain Chicken. But the most plausible version of the origin story is that it was invented by the captain of a British trade ship in India. These ships were called country ships. The captains of the ships were in turn called country captains. A certain country captain made this dish for the first time for his British officers, who enjoyed it immensely. Country Captain Chicken soon became a very popular chicken curry dish among British officers at sea, who would eat it with steamed rice, breads or dinner rolls.

The Dak Bungalow Curry was an invention of the khansamas working in the kitchens of dak bungalows. These were rest houses, maintained by the Government of India, where British officers travelling long hauls on official tours around the country, would stop and rest. The bungalow staff raised their own poultry, cows and goats for regular meat and milk supply. The cooks made the Dak Bungalow Curry with either mutton or chicken and served it to the resident British officers with steamed rice and vegetables or breads. Although the ingredients and methods of preparing this dish varied with each cook and depended on the availability of ingredients in a particular place, potatoes and hard-boiled eggs generally featured in this dish along with the meat. Dak Bungalow Curry became sought after among British officers during colonial times.

Jhalfrazie is a sautéed dish, very popular among the Anglo-Indians of Calcutta, which can be prepared with meat, poultry or seafood. The name of the dish is derived from the words 'jhal', which means spicy or pungent, and 'frazie', which means fried. Traditionally, this dish was made with leftover cooked meat. Colonial servants were instructed by their British masters to not throw away leftover cooked meat but instead make a dish out of it. These cooks applied their minds and fried the leftover Christmas turkeys and chicken roasts with spices like peppers, chillies and so on, and served it the next day. The frying removed the staleness of the meat. The original Jhalfrazie was quite bland and tasteless. Over the years, many more ingredients and spices were added to this dish to make it spicy and delicious. Jhalfrazie is synonymous with the Devil Fry and Devil Curry made in south India. In recent times, Jhalfrazie has become one of the most preferred dishes in Indian restaurants in the United Kingdom.

Vindaloo is derived from the Portuguese dish vinha d'alhos, which was mispronounced by locals as vindaloo. It was originally a vinegar and garlic-based watery stew made with pork or other meat. The dish made its way to India with the arrival of the Portuguese traders. Vindaloo is a meat-based (usually pork) curry made with the two main ingredients: vinho (wine or wine vinegar) and alhos (garlic). The Portuguese actually taught the Indians to use vinegar in their cooking and in making pickles. After the Portuguese introduced the dish in India, it was completely revamped with the addition of native spices and chillies. Over the years, it has become a spicy and popular curry dish all over the world. Vindaloo can be made with meat, poultry, seafood or vegetables. When the British arrived in India, they were surprised to see native cooks making this cross-cultural dish.

Bridget White-Kumar shares an interesting story about a dish that is often prepared in Anglo-Indian households—Bengal Lancers Shrimp Curry. Lieutenant Colonel James Skinner, popularly known as Sikandar Sahib, was an Anglo-Indian army officer who raised two cavalry regiments for the British Indian Army at Hansi (a city in Hisar district, Haryana) in 1803. These two regiments were the First Skinner's Horse and Third Skinner's Horse (formerly known as Second Skinner's Horse). The Skinner's Horse Regiment, which was renamed First Bengal Cavalry, and later as Bengal Lancers, was the most famous cavalry regiment during the British Raj. Today, it is one of the most distinguished cavalry regiments of the Indian Army. The recipe of the spicy onion-and-tomato-based Bengal Lancers Shrimp Curry originated in the mess of this regiment in Calcutta. Later, this dish, which can be made with shrimps as well as prawns and is generally eaten with steamed rice, was included in the menus of the messes of other regiments of the British Indian Army. As a tribute to the lieutenant colonel, the dish was also named as Col. Skinner's Shrimp Curry.

Mulligatawny soup was also very popular during the Company Raj and its origin can be traced back to around the eighteenth century. Soups had never been part of the local cuisine before the British introduced them to the country. British officers posted in Madras asked their Tamil servants to make soup for them. The Tamil servants made a concoction that was very similar to their pepper water. The soup was actually the anglicized version of the Tamil pepper (malagu) water (tanni) and was made with either chicken or mutton stock. This was the closest thing to soup that the cooks could make. Over the course of time, many other ingredients such as chicken, meat, coconut milk, turmeric and other spices were added to give the soup a completely different flavour. This soup began to be called Mulligatawny soup. The Mulligatawny soup of today bears little resemblance to the original Malagutanni and is made with lentils, vegetables, chicken or meat. In fact, since the time of its invention, a variety of Mulligatawny soups have come into existence. Eventually, this soup became so popular with the British that they carried the recipes with them to Great Britain and from there, it spread to the Commonwealth. Today, Mulligatawny soup has been dubbed as the 'National Soup of India' by professional chefs and connoisseurs alike.

*

Despite the huge exodus of Anglo-Indians after India's Independence, Calcutta's community remains robust and very active. This becomes especially evident during their celebration of Christmas. The quiet lanes of Bow Barracks lined with their legendary three-storeyed red brick buildings sporting green window frames are completely transformed during the festive season. The usual calmness characteristic of the place, broken now and then with a faint trace of an Elvis Presley or John Lennon number playing in one of the houses on any given day, is replaced with joyous revelry that begins two days before Christmas and continues up to the early hours of the first day of the following month. While the entire place is decorated with streamers, balloons, lights, paper snowflakes, silver bells and Chinese lanterns, a beautifully decorated big Christmas tree takes centre stage here. A crib is set up at a corner and every flat has a shining star on its balcony. The grotto where the local residents pray is spruced up and decorated. Members of the locality bake cakes and cookies and make home-made wines for residents and visitors alike. Plenty of kiosks selling a variety of food are put up in every nook and corner. Carol singers mingle with the crowd and children can be seen enjoying pony rides or their turns at the merry-go-round. For the senior citizens, there are rounds of bingo, musical chairs and dancing. Street parties, gift shops, housie games, baskets of goodies and feasts are arranged by the residents of the area. The atmosphere is enlivened with live music and revellers are not averse to breaking into jigs every now and then. Various programmes like Christmas Balls and football matches are organized. And the best part of the entire revelry is that Santa Claus arrives, not in a sleigh pulled by reindeers, but in a hand-pulled Calcutta rickshaw, digging into his toy bag and showering everybody with candies.

In Bengal, Christmas is also called 'Bara Din' (Big Day) by the locals. Christmas is a day for family reunions in the Anglo-Indian homes of Calcutta. The Anglo-Indians celebrate Bara Din with home-made wines and cakes. While many Anglo-Indian families rely on the local roti-wallah (bread man) for readymade Christmas cakes, most prefer to make their own ones. They mix the ingredients at home and then take the mix down to the local bakery for baking. Minakshie Das Gupta, Bunny Gupta and Jaya Chaliha elaborate in the chapter 'Bawarcheekhana' in their book, *The Calcutta Cookbook: A Treasury of Recipes from Pavement to Palace* (1995), 'Christmas cake with Anglo-Indians [....] is a matter of personal pride. Many kilograms of cake mixture according to an old family recipe are handed over to the local rotiwala (bread man) three weeks before Christmas. Baked in half pound bread tins, cakes are exchanged between family and friends. The ingredients: karamcha—the Calcutta cherry, a sour fruit, preserved and coloured a brilliant red—manufactured by the Kabuli dried fruit sellers in the New Market; petha, crystallized white pumpkin, another ingredient is now added liberally as it is the cheapest of the preserved fruits; green cardamoms are added to cinnamon and finally a generous measure of rum poured into the mix. The daily dousing of the cake with rum makes for a merry Christmas' (p. 207).

Wine-making is a tradition for Anglo-Indians and each family has its own stock of recipes that has been passed down through generations. The variety of homemade wines made from fruits is plenty like grape, blueberry, litchi, raisin, ginger, cherry, beetroot, gooseberry, apple and kala jamun (Indian blackberry). Wine-making is an integral part of the

Anglo-Indian Christmas celebration and Bow Barracks has its own list of wine-makers from within the community. By the time December arrives, the wines are bottled and ready for consumption. Anglo-Indians begin gifting them to family members and friends a few weeks before Christmas. Those visiting are served home-made wines and cakes. On Christmas, family members gather around the dining table for a well-spread-out meal, washed down with umpteen glasses of these wines. Not only Christmas but even weddings in the community are incomplete without home-made wines.

Chef Norman D'Silva, who had worked for many years in the five-star Park Hotel, points out that a, 'Christmas meal can be an elaborate lunch or dinner. During Christmas, Anglo-Indians in Calcutta still cook traditional British fare like roast chicken, roast turkey, roast duck and roast suckling pig. Salted beef is a must-have on the list of Christmas specials. But then our Indian roots also make us cook a rice dish like peas pulao or yellow coconut rice for the meal. Curries like kofta curry and vindaloo generally feature on the menu.' Soft bread rolls and a variety of salads from the Russian to parsley potato (tossed with bits of crispy bacon and bacon oil) to potato and mayonnaise (with small juicy pieces of pineapple and finely chopped green peppers) to the fresh vegetable salad on a bed of lettuce form part of the spread as well. 'Plum cake, rich fruit cake and plum pudding are among the confections made during the festive season', continues D'Silva. 'But confectioneries like kulkuls and rose cookies are Christmas specials that are typical to the community'.

Kulkuls are small, fried, rolled sweets with ridges. They are made of semolina and refined flour mixed with butter, powdered sugar, salt, egg yolks and vanilla essence, and kneaded with coconut milk. Rose cookies, in contrast, are deep-fried sweets that look like flowers and are made with the batter of refined flour, rice flour, salt, powdered sugar, eggs, coconut milk, cardamom powder, vanilla essence and baking soda. Generally, cast iron, aluminium or steel moulds are used to shape the sweets into flowers.

Thus, the celebration of Christmas that was begun by the Europeans is continued with as much enthusiasm by the Anglo-Indians of Calcutta. And in this celebration, they have not only remained true to their European roots but also to their Indian roots as is evident from the fare prepared during this time. Their Christmas celebration is a wonderful embodiment of the best part of both worlds. And this large-hearted and open-minded community shares the festive spirit with anybody willing to participate in the festival as is obvious from the Christmas celebration at Bow Barracks, which is open to the entire city.

*

For a long time, Anglo-Indian food was generally confined to home-made fare. But select restaurants and hotels in the city are now serving some of their curry dishes like Dak Bungalow Curry, Railway Mutton Curry, Country Captain Chicken Curry, Jhalfrazie and Vindaloo. For example, the upscale Bengali restaurant Oh! Calcutta has listed 'Classic Railway Mutton Curry' in its menu while the Kolkata Calling section in the menu of Kebab-e-Que, a restaurant in The Astor, a hotel that is very popular for its food, has the dishes 'Railway Mutton Curry' and 'Murgh Dak Bungalow'. Bhojohori Manna, another popular Bengali eatery, serves its customers both Jhalfrazie and Dak Bungalow Curry. Jhalfrazie has even crossed borders and is creating a sensation outside India.

The one of a kind Mulligatawny soup and the Anglo-Indian shepherd's pie have enjoyed a select fan following for years and can be slotted as the favourite club foods. While the former features prominently in the continental menu of the Saturday Club, the latter enjoys a special place in the aristocratic dining room of Calcutta Club. Bibi of Taaja's, a popular south Calcutta-based home delivery service, which offers dishes from across the globe and often organizes its own pop-up restaurants, cooks a steaming 'Chicken Mulligatawny', a scrumptious 'Mutton Shepherd's Pie', a delicious 'Vindaloo', a mouth-watering 'Anglo-Indian Pork Curry' and an appetizing 'Anglo-Indian Mutton Pulao' for its customers. Restaurateur Prithvish Chakravarti also organizes pop-up restaurants serving Anglo-Indian food under the banner of Calcutta Deli, a popular delicatessen that he launched in south Calcutta in April 2019. The menu features dishes like mince potato chop, brinjal mince cutlet, pantaras, yellow coconut rice, meatball curry, Jhalfrazie, Vindaloo, Dak Bungalow Curry and pepper water.

It has become customary for roast turkey to be served by hotels and restaurants of repute during Christmas. Plum cake and rich fruit cake are baked and sold by confectioneries, both big and small, and select places like Kenilworth Hotel serve plum pudding and flummeries during the festive season. Bread-and-butter pudding and caramel custard can again be slotted as popular club foods. But these are largely European fare. It is difficult to come across typical Anglo-Indian confectioneries like jalebi pudding and Christmas specials like kulkuls and rose cookies until and unless one tries them in an Anglo-Indian's home. Sometimes, one gets to hear about Anglo-Indian food festivals in the city, as was organized by the Park Hotel and restaurants like Oh! Calcutta and Chapter 2, a few years ago. It is on occasions such as these that connoisseurs and food enthusiasts are able to choose from a variety of exclusive Anglo-Indian dishes that are usually difficult to come across.

All of this has not only helped to bring to the forefront, but also keep afloat, a marginal cuisine, which is an integral part of the city. Though it began as a response to a new environment, Anglo-Indian cuisine is now an independent tradition with a strong identity of its own. It is not a dying cuisine in the city and has its fair share of admirers from outside the community as well.

5. Calcutta Armenians

Armenia, an ancient mountainous country located in Eurasia, and surrounded by Turkey, Iran, Azerbaijan and Georgia, seems a far cry from the humid port city of Calcutta. But the Armenians are known as the most ancient merchants of the world and the Indian–Armenian connection is as old as it can get. The nineteenth-century Armenian historian, Mesrovb Jacob Seth, who spent a very large part of his life in Calcutta, writes in his book, *History of the Armenians in India* (1895), '[...] they [the Armenians] were acquainted with India from remote antiquity, *perhaps* even when Semiramis, the wife of Ninus, and the warlike queen of the once-powerful Assyrian monarchy, reigned supreme in Babylon' (p. 20). There are high chances of the Armenians having accompanied Semiramis as faithful allies in her invasion of India, which took place in about 2000 BCE. It is also believed that many Armenians joined the forces of Alexander the Great during the Greek invasion of India in 327 BCE. Historical evidence proves that the powerful king and conqueror travelled through Armenia on his way to India via Persia. Hence, their commercial relations with India began from a time when the rest of Europe was yet to establish direct contact with India. Although the Portuguese explorer Vasco da Gama is believed to be the first European to reach India by sea in 1498 CE, Mesrovb Jacob Seth writes that seven centuries before this voyage, the Armenian merchant Thomas Cana arrived on the Malabar Coast in 780 CE. Cana was given trading privileges by the native ruler of Kodungallur (called Cranganore in English), a municipal town on the banks of the Periyar river on the Malabar Coast in Thrissur district of Kerala today. He amassed a lot of wealth trading in muslin and spices.

India was a treasure house and its vast wealth lured explorers, traders and conquerors from all over the world to its shores for centuries. The Armenians, too, were lured by this treasure trove and began travelling to India for trade. They took the overland route via Persia to trade for spices, muslins and precious stones. Their commercial dealings necessitated that Armenian merchants establish friendly relations with Indian princes. In this context, the Armenian king Valarsaces, who had ascended the throne in 150 BCE, provided refuge to two fugitive princes from Kannauj, who had conspired against their king. These princes were given the freedom to freely exercise their religion and worship their own gods. Their descendants formed an important colony in Armenia, which flourished till the advent of the Christian faith in the country in 301 CE.

It is believed that in the early part of the Christian era, the ancient city of Kashi (modern-day Benares or Varanasi) was the headquarters of Armenian merchants in India because of its importance as a trade centre at the time. Their interest in India was purely commercial in nature, and they didn't harbour colonial or political ambitions, unlike many other nations who would reach Indian shores in the future. The absence of other foreign commercial players in the bazars and emporiums of India enabled Armenian merchants to monopolize a large portion of the export trade. They took the merchandise to the commercial markets of Persia and China, on one side, and Venice, on the other. In her essay, 'The Armenians of Calcutta', from the book *Calcutta Mosaic: Essays and Interviews on the Minority Communities of Calcutta* (2009), Susmita Bhattacharya writes, 'They [the Armenians] carried on trade in precious stones, gems, silks, fine muslins, jutes, numerous kinds of medicinal herbs, spices and even gold, silver, copper, tin from India to Europe, and imported to India coloured leather, various dyes, cotton and iron by the overland route through Persia, Bactria (Afghanistan), Tibet, Armenia and Russia via Trabezund' (p. 76).

During the reign of the Mughal emperor Akbar, another large influx of Armenian merchants took place into India. Pomp and splendour defined the Mughal courts, particularly during Akbar's reign, and the commercial prosperity of his empire was a byword all over the world. This had attracted Armenian merchants in droves to Agra, his imperial capital. But, according to Mesrovb Jacob Seth, this merchant class first settled down in Agra only in the sixteenth century, on Akbar's invitation. The judicious emperor was well aware of their honest and hard-working ways and shrewd business sense. He wanted these merchants to settle in his kingdom instead of merely passing through because he hoped they would be instrumental in improving trade in his empire. To encourage them, he granted them quite a few privileges, including an exemption from paying taxes on merchandise that they imported and exported, and the freedom to build a church in the imperial capital. Seth even asserts that one of Akbar's queens, Mariam Zamani Begum, was an Armenian. This, he claims, is a well-known historical fact. In his more thoroughly researched book, *Armenians in India, From the Earliest Times to the Present Day: A Work of Original Research* (1937), he elaborates, 'Henry Blochmann, in his translation of the *Ain-i-Akbari* mentions in one of his notes that there is not the least doubt of "Akbar having an Armenian wife"' (pp. 151–52). By the end of Akbar's reign, Agra had a sizeable Armenian population. As Seth sums up in his book, *History of the Armenians in India* (1895), 'The Armenians flourished in that city [Agra] during the good old days of the Mogul emperors, with whom they were in the highest favour [....]' (p. 23).

In the sixteenth century, their commercial interests drove them to other places in the country, where there were possibilities of trade and profit. Permanent settlements of Armenians began to emerge, particularly in port cities like Surat on the western coast of India, which was the most important port of the country in that period. Between the sixteenth and seventeenth centuries, Armenian colonies also appeared in other places like Delhi, Lucknow, Gwalior, Narwar, Golconda, Hyderabad, Madras and Bombay. Bengal was not to be left behind and small settlements were found in Chinsurah, Chandannagar, Saidabad, Cossimbazar, Serampore and Patna. The Armenian Church in Chinsurah, completed in 1697, is the second oldest Christian church in Bengal after the Portuguese Church in Bandel. Lahore and Dhaka had their share of Armenian colonies, as did Kabul, a part of the Mughal Empire, and Rangoon, later added to British India.

Political developments in Armenia were also to a large extent responsible for the emergence of the Armenian merchants as a trading diaspora in the seventeenth century. Armenia had been a victim of the Perso-Ottoman rivalry. The Ottoman Turks had conquered a large portion of Armenia in the fifteenth century, absorbing it into the

Ottoman Empire. The king of Persia, Shah Abbas the Great, visited Julfa, a commercial city on the banks of the Aras river in Armenia. He was dazzled by the opulence of Julfa and wanted to recreate the wealth of the Armenians in his own country. He had Julfa razed to the ground, and its inhabitants were forced to move to Persia. In 1605, the Armenians reached the city of Isfahan. Shah Abbas the Great gifted them an extensive piece of ground in the suburbs of Isfahan, on the banks of the Zayanderud river. The colonists developed this place into a city and named it New Julfa. Soon, New Julfa became an important centre of Persian trade.

As long as Persia was ruled by Shah Abbas the Great and his humane and worthy political successors, the Armenians of New Julfa flourished and contributed to the prosperity of the country. They conducted trade with India but refrained from forming a permanent settlement in the country. But after Shah Abbas the Great and his successors passed away, the new religiously intolerant Persian monarch targeted religious minorities, leading to persecution and forced conversion. The new king was also angered by the considerable wealth and riches amassed by the Armenians and put an end to many of the social and economic privileges granted to them by the previous Shahs. Severe torture and extortion followed, which forced the New Julfan Armenians to flee Persia and migrate to other countries, including India.

By the late seventeenth century, the emigration of Armenian merchants from Turkey and Persia had increased tremendously. It was at the end of the seventeenth century and at the beginning of the eighteenth that the formation of the Armenian colony in Calcutta began. A majority of the early Armenian settlers in Calcutta were from the cities Shiraz and New Julfa. They had left behind politically disturbed homes and come in search of peaceful places to conduct trade.

The history of the Armenian arrival in Calcutta is controversial. It is well documented that Job Charnock invited the Armenians to settle in Calcutta between 1686 and 1690. But, in his book, *History of the Armenians in India* (1895), Mesrovb Jacob Seth writes that prior to Charnock's arrival, the Armenians had already formed a small commercial settlement in Sutanuti, where they lived with the locals. Though the veracity of this statement has been questioned by many scholars, the historian puts forth strong monumental evidence to support his theory. Seth was a noted historian and scholar, especially of Classical Armenian, and taught the subject at the Armenian College and Philanthropic

Academy in Calcutta, where he also received his education. He was invited by the British Government of India in 1894 to translate inscriptions in Classical Armenian on the tombstones of the Armenian churchyards of Calcutta, Chinsurah and Saidabad. It was then that he stumbled upon the tombstone of Rezabeebeh, upending the long-established theory that Armenians arrived in Calcutta after Job Charnock's invitation. The inscription on the tomb stone read, 'This is the tomb of Rezabeebeh, the wife of the late charitable Sookeas, who departed from this world to life eternal on the 21st day of Nakha in the year 15'. According to Seth, this date would be 11 July, 1630 CE in the Gregorian calendar. The tomb of Rezabeebeh was recorded as the oldest Christian grave in Calcutta, long before the arrival of the British.

But controversies surround the ancient tombstone. The most striking discrepancy is its discovery in a church that was built in 1724, ninety-four years after the date on the tombstone. The history of how this church was built is relevant. On 22 June 1688, an agreement was signed in London by the representatives of the British East India Company, and an eminent merchant, Khoja Phanoos Khalanthar, who was the leader and representative of the Armenian merchants in India. Besides granting certain rights and privileges, the agreement allowed the Armenians complete religious freedom. Whenever forty or more Armenians would reside in any garrison town or city belonging to the British East India Company, permission would be granted to them to freely exercise their religion and a plot of land allotted for their church. The agreement also made it mandatory for the British East India Company officials to build a basic church of timber, at their own cost, which the Armenians could later alter and rebuild with stone. In return, Armenian merchants were to ply their trade in India exclusively in British ships. This inducement and exchange of benefits proved advantageous to the British in the future.

In keeping with this agreement, the British East India Company built a small chapel of timber on Old China Bazar Street in the Barabazar area of Calcutta in 1688. But the wooden structure was completely destroyed by a ravaging fire in 1707. In 1724, the Armenian Church of the Holy Nazareth was built on Armenian Street in Barabazar, on an old burial ground of the Armenian community. Considered the oldest Christian church in Calcutta, it was built close to the previous Armenian church. Rezabeebeh's tomb is located in the graveyard of this church.

However, not a single tomb predating the year 1690 can be traced in the cemetery, apart from this one. In his article, 'Job Charnock or the Armenians: Who Founded Calcutta?' carried in the newspaper, *The Sunday Statesman* (25 August 1985), eminent scholar, Jawhar Sircar, has mentioned that in the book, *The Early Annals of the English in Bengal* (1895), the noted English. chronicler C.R. Wilson wrote that there was nothing to show. Rezabeebeh's tombstone was 'in situ'. It might as well have been brought to Calcutta from elsewhere. Wilson argued further that even if the stone was 'in situ', it did not prove the existence of an Armenian colony before the arrival of Job Charnock, due to the probability that a person would be buried at the place of death. He elaborated that if an Armenian voyager had died in a ship near Calcutta, it would have been necessary to bury the body there. The mystery of the Armenian arrival in Calcutta endures.

*

The Armenian Genocide, often referred to as the first genocide of the twentieth century, contributed largely to another major influx of Armenians into India. The date April 1915 is considered to be the starting date of the genocide, in which approximately 1.5 million Armenians were massacred by the Ottoman government. The massacred Armenians were mostly Ottoman citizens within the Ottoman Empire and its successor state, the Republic of Turkey.

The Muslim Turks and the Armenian Christians did not share an easy relationship from the very beginning. Western Armenia was under the mighty Ottoman Empire. Although the Ottoman rulers did allow autonomy to the religious minorities within their empire, they were subjected to unequal treatment. The Armenians, being Christians, were regarded as infidels. They were given very few political and legal rights, and even had to pay higher taxes than Muslims. Despite this, the Armenians thrived under the Ottoman rule. The Turks resented their success and harboured the suspicion that since the Armenians were Christians, they would be more loyal to Christian nations—like their hostile neighbour, Russia.

When the Ottoman Empire was on the decline, the Armenians began campaigning for basic civil rights. The Turkish Sultan Abdul Hamid II ordered the first massacre of Armenians between 1894 and 1896 in which 3,00,000 Armenians were murdered. These brutal murders came to be known as the Hamidian massacres and drew strong resentment from foreign governments and humanitarian organizations, labelling the sultan as 'Bloody Sultan' or 'Red Sultan' in the West. In 1908, a new government formed by a group of reformers, who called themselves the 'Young Turks', overthrew Abdul Hamid II and established a modern constitutional government. But this new government did not bring any relief to the Armenians. On the contrary, since the Turks had sided with Germany during the First World War, the Ottoman authorities declared a jihad against all Christians except their allies. Around 1915, when the war intensified, the Armenians came to the aid of the Russian army by providing volunteer battalions to help them fight the Turks in the Caucasus region. The Turkish government decided to 'remove' the Armenians from the war zones along the Eastern Front. The Armenian genocide began and, until 1922, when the country was absorbed into the Soviet Union, the Turkish government executed Armenian intellectuals and ordinary people, occupied their properties, raped women, and kidnapped and converted children. The mass killings and deportations made the surviving Armenians flee in fear of their lives to other countries. During this period, almost two thousand Armenians fled to India and particularly, to Calcutta.

*

The Armenians came to play a pivotal role in Bengal's trade and commerce. As early as 1775, the chief justice of the Supreme Court, Sir Elijah Impey wrote, 'the greatest part of the foreign trade of this kingdom [Bengal] is managed' by the Armenians and English free merchants and that, '[...] the only resource for keeping up the currency of this country lies in the honesty, integrity and perseverance of the English and Armenian independent merchants residing in Calcutta' (p. 23).

The British also sought friendship with the Armenians to further their own interests in India. Their main reason for this was the favourable position the Armenians enjoyed in the Mughal courts, due to their close association with the ruling class, and fluency in Persian, the chief language of the government and commerce. The British would engage Armenian vakils (counsels) to represent them in the Mughal courts. In the first half of the eighteenth century in Bengal, commerce and politics were closely linked. The British East India Company solicited the assistance of Khoja Israel Sarhad, an important diplomat and an extremely successful Armenian merchant in Bengal, in procuring the renting rights of the three villages that went on to form the nucleus of Calcutta. The British made him a member of the famous Surman Embassy in 1715 by appointing him as a vakil. Khoja Israel Sarhad enjoyed the good graces of the Mughal emperor, Muhammad Farrukhsiyar, and played a significant role in obtaining the Grand Imperial Firman in 1717, which granted the British East India Company extraordinary privileges like the right to trade in Bengal without having to pay the usual customs duties. In turn, the harmonious relationship that the Armenians shared with the British traders, allowed them to continue being a crucially important trading community for quite a long time, even under British rule.

Once the British had established themselves in India, they began ousting the Armenians from the trade markets. This drove the Armenians to other professions like the stock market and employment in British firms and railways. Succeeding generations went abroad for degrees in law and medicine. The community diversified from its traditional trading professions and went on to produce a number of noted scholars, architects, engineers, bankers, military personnel, armourers, wealthy landlords, ship-owners, jewellers and so on. The Armenians also found employment in seaport and governmental services. The community also had its middle class and economically weak sections, but the affluent considered it their duty to help the needy. They donated funds and properties to the Armenian churches for providing education and relief to their less fortunate countrymen. Their stupendous worldly success, combined with their philanthropic contributions, made them important members of Calcutta society.

The prosperity and social standing of the Armenian community in Calcutta is evident from the fact that certain locales have been named after them. The community was first concentrated in Barabazar in a locality that is called Armanitola (habitat of the Armenians). Armenian Street is located nearby in the same area. The Armenians were also concentrated in an area close to Free School Street in central Calcutta known as Armanipara (neighbourhood of the Armenians). The Armenian Ghat or Armani Ghat was constructed in 1734 by Manvel Hazaar Maliyan to receive shipments and facilitate the docking of Armenian merchant ships. Locally known as Huzoorimal, Maliyan was a wealthy and influential Armenian trader, renowned for his benevolence. Among his many public contributions, this wharf was the most important. From 1854 to 1874, the East Indian Railway Company had its Calcutta station and ticket reservation room at this ghat. Passengers would buy train tickets from here and cross the river on steamers or launches run by the railway company to Howrah, where they would board the trains. This arrangement came to an end after the construction of the Howrah

Pontoon Bridge (predecessor of the modern Howrah Bridge) in 1874. Instead, the Armenian Ghat became an important spot for commuters, particularly when the Calcutta Tramways Company Limited laid down tracks for horse-drawn trams to ply between Sealdah and Armenian Ghat via Bowbazar Street, Dalhousie Square and Strand Road. Today, the Armenian Ghat serves as the storehouse of the Calcutta Port Trust.

Calcutta has the privilege of having been home to many prominent Indian-Armenians. M.P. Gasper, a leading barrister of the Calcutta High Court, was the first Armenian to pass the Indian Civil Service examination in 1869. Sir Gregory Charles Paul, an Armenian born in Calcutta, was educated at Cambridge University, and holds the record as the longest serving Advocate General of Bengal. In the field of medicine, Dr Stephen Owen Moses founded the St John Ambulance courses in first aid and home nursing in Calcutta. He was also responsible for the first Red Cross ambulance in the city during the First World War. Dr Marie Catchatoor was the first woman to be appointed as the Presidency surgeon by the government of West Bengal. She was the president of the Bengal Medical Women Association as well as the Medical Women Association of India. She retired as superintendent of Lady Dufferin Hospital in Calcutta in the early 1980s. Arratoon Apcar, founder of the trading company, Apcar and Company—which operated the Apcar Line fleet of vessels in Calcutta—shifted his company to Calcutta from Bombay in 1830 and flourished in the city. His sons held positions of great distinction. Seth Apcar, was the first Armenian sheriff of Calcutta and Sir Apcar Alexander Apcar was appointed president of the Bengal Chamber of Commerce and also an additional member of the Council of the Governor-General for making laws and regulations.

Even in the field of performing arts, Indian-Armenians made their mark. Gauhar Jaan, a leading Hindustani classical vocalist and courtesan in Calcutta, was of Armenian descent. After a short-lived marriage, her mother embraced Islam and Eileen Angelina Yeoward became Gauhar Jaan. She rose to become a vocalist of great repute. In 1902, she was approached by the Gramophone Company of the United Kingdom to record a series of songs. It is commonly believed that this made her the first Indian to become a recording star.

The Armenians can be largely credited for turning Calcutta into the 'City of Palaces'. The early twentieth century saw the rise of many prominent Armenian builders and architects who constructed private residences, hotels, offices, mansions and boarding and guest houses.

Overcrowding in Barabazar drove them to other areas in central and south Calcutta. It is believed that almost the entire areas of Queens Park and Sunny Park in south Calcutta were owned by them. The Armenians helped build major portions of central Calcutta. Park Street, which had been uncharitably named Burial Ground Road, was filled with large and impressive mansions by Armenian businessmen and builders, converting it into a fashionable avenue.

Johannes Carapiet Galstaun's feats in Calcutta's real estate are legendary. He was a compulsive builder and can lay claim to about three hundred and fifty buildings in the city that have been either built or once owned by him. Max Galstaun, his descendant, lists the Freemasons' Hall on Park Street, Saturday Club on Wood Street, Royal Calcutta Turf Club on Russel Street and properties on Dharmatala Street as amongst these buildings. Galstaun beautified central Calcutta by building Galstaun Mansion on Park Street, rechristened Queen's Mansion to celebrate the visit of Britain's Queen Elizabeth II to the city in 1961, and Harrington Mansion on Harrington Street. Rawdon Street, Pretoria Street and Lansdowne Road, as well as the areas covered by Mayfair Road and Ballygunge Park in south Calcutta, once fell under his ambit. He added a touch of glamour to these areas by developing them. His biggest achievement was building a magnificent palatial residence for his wife, Rose Catherine Galstaun, on Lower Circular Road (now known as Acharya Jagadish Chandra Bose Road). He named this residence Galstaun Park. When Edward, the prince of Wales (later King Edward VIII) visited Calcutta in December 1921, he preferred to stay at this palatial residence. It is well known that, to salvage his racing debts, he sold it to the Nizam of Hyderabad, Mir Osman Ali Khan in 1933, who named it Saba Palace. Eventually this residence, now known as Nizam Palace, was taken over by the Indian government and converted into a government complex.

Like many young Armenian men of those times, Arratoon Stephen arrived in Calcutta in the last quarter of the nineteenth century as a penniless refugee. He built the Stephen Court on Park Street and the Stephen House on Dalhousie Square. The feather in his cap was building the Grand Hotel, a landmark today. He expanded his ventures outside Calcutta as well and built the Mount Everest Hotel in Darjeeling. Legend has it that the wealthy jute merchant, T.M. Thaddeus, who built Park Mansion on Park Street, had the idiosyncratic habit of travelling by rickshaws because he did not trust the local chauffeurs with his Rolls-

Royce. Another Armenian, Peter Crete, was an extremely rich merchant of Calcutta. Besides being a pioneer in the coal mining industry in Raniganj, he had huge interests in real estate and was renowned in the community for his generosity.

During the British Raj, the Armenians had a majority stake in the Calcutta hospitality industry and established many hotels in the city like the Astor, Astoria, Carlton, Lytton and Kenilworth. The flourishing Fairlawn Hotel on Sudder Street, well known for its old-world charm and for playing host to a long list of celebrity guests, was established by the Armenian couple, Minas and Rosie Sarkies. They fled the horrific genocide in Turkey in 1917. After arriving in Calcutta in 1933, they traded in jute for some time. Rosie Sarkies purchased the Astoria Hotel, also on Sudder Street, and ran it as a boarding house for the Armenians. In 1936, when business was thriving, she sold this hotel to another Armenian and bought the Fairlawn, which used to be run as a boarding house, from two English spinsters.

Mention also needs to be made of a Calcutta-born Armenian who found fame and fortune in the distant land of Hong Kong. Sir Catchick Paul Chater secured an education for himself in the school, La Martiniere for Boys, Calcutta. He arrived in Hong Kong in 1864, at the age of eighteen, and eventually became its leading business mogul and self-made multimillionaire. But none of his other business ventures could match the success of the Hongkong Land Investment and Agency Company Limited, which was co-founded by him. Land reclamations were necessary because Hong Kong was largely covered with water and had very little flat land available for building. Sir Catchick Paul Chater is best known for the Praya Reclamation Scheme, which helped build Hong Kong's central business district, and also its first permanent dock, turning Hong Kong into a major trading port. Sir Catchick Paul Chater died in 1926, leaving a lasting impression on the region. Today, there is a Chater Road, Catchick Street, Chater Garden, Chater Hall and Chater House in Hong Kong. A large portion of his estate wealth was bequeathed to the Armenian Church of the Holy Nazareth in Calcutta. The church has built a home for the Armenian elderly in Park Circus and named it the Sir Catchick Paul Chater Home.

*

The Armenian community showed unwavering loyalty to the British, who gave them the freedom to pursue their interests without much interference. In contrast, they, along with the Anglo-Indians and Jews, were kept at a distance by the majority of the locals. These ethnic communities looked European but were not quite, nor were they Indian. Except for the educated and emancipated elite, most locals viewed them with suspicion. So, the end of British rule in India was signal enough for the Armenians to leave the country, which they had called home for centuries. The departure of the British and the anti-colonial bent of mind of the general public made them insecure. The community, renowned in history as the 'merchant princes of India', left behind secure jobs and large family enterprises, which were either sold off or closed, for fresh starts in other countries.

It is difficult to provide a specific figure regarding the number of Armenians who lived in Calcutta. Susmita Bhattacharya points out in her essay that according to the French author, Doloriere, the number of permanent Armenian residents in India at the end of the nineteenth century was 25,000. But by 1947, the number had dwindled, and today, there are only two hundred Armenians in Calcutta. Armenians from Calcutta preferred to migrate to England, the United States of America, Canada and Australia. The number continues to dwindle, generating a fear that only ghostly shadows will remain behind of the community that once helped built the Second City of the British Empire. But the fact remains that Calcutta is the only city in the entire country that still has a considerable number of Armenians living in it with a distinct identity. Important Armenian institutions like the Armenian Church of the Holy Nazareth, St Gregory The Illuminator Armenian Church, Armenian Club, Armenian Sports Club, Armenian College and Philanthropic Academy and Davidian Girls' School are still functioning here, while the other places that once played hosts to Armenian colonies have to satisfy themselves with memories left behind in the cemeteries.

*

When the Armenians began coming to India as itinerant traders, they had to make adjustments to their culinary practices. They faced difficulties in getting hold of some of the typical ingredients required in their traditional cuisine. Armenia is a highland country and its cuisine is typical of such regions. The fertile volcanic soil permits the cultivation of wheat and barley, the country's major crops. Wheat is used to make a variety of breads, the most popular preparation being the thin flatbread called lavash. Freshly baked lavash bread is soft in texture but quickly becomes crispy and crunchy, giving it the name cracker bread. Wheat is also an important ingredient in many Armenian soup and stew preparations such as the harissa, a porridge-like stew usually made with chicken. Also known as keshkeg, this stew is made by boiling shredded chicken and skinless wholewheat kernels in chicken broth over low heat. When all the liquid is absorbed, the chicken and wheat are mashed till the dish resembles thick oatmeal. Seasoned with salt, pepper and freshly ground cumin, it is cooked for a few more minutes and then taken off the heat. Harissa is served in bowls with chunks of butter on top. Often, in the place of wholewheat kernels, bulgur wheat or pearl barley is used. Chicken can also be replaced with turkey or lamb. The combination of warm harissa and lavash bread makes for a perfect winter dish.

Wheat (in its refined form) is also used liberally in the preparation of cakes and other baked goods. Nazook is a flaky wheat pastry filled with a sugary and buttery crushed walnut mixture. Its dough is made with refined flour, yeast, butter, salt, sugar, oil, sour cream and egg. Flavours like vanilla, almond, sour cherry juice or a combination of flaked coconut and vanilla extract and powdered spices like cardamom, cinnamon, clove or nutmeg are mixed into the sweet filling. Although the Armenians eat this pastry (also known as gata) throughout the year with beverages like tea or coffee, the nazook is traditionally baked during Easter and eaten all through the forty days till Ascension Day. Nutmeg cake, another Armenian favourite, is not very sweet. It is flavoured with freshly ground nutmeg and sprinkled with chopped walnuts on top. Walnuts give it a nutty taste and the nutmeg lends it a delicious fragrance.

Armenians relish rice, especially in pilaf, though it had to be imported into Armenia. One such pilaf is made with vermicelli and pine nuts. Vermicelli is browned in butter and then cooked with long-grain rice and chicken broth, and seasoned with salt, pepper and lime juice. This delicious meaty flavoured pilaf, sprinkled with toasted pine nuts, is usually served with a grilled vegetable salad and a kebab preparation like shish kebab, popularly made with lamb. True to their highland roots and livestock herding traditions, Armenians prefer meat, eggs, milk and milk products, and don't eat fish very often. Grilling is a very popular method of cooking and they eat a lot of grilled meats and vegetables, which are called khorovats. Derived from the word 'khorovel', which means 'to cook over an open fire', the lightly seasoned meats and vegetables are grilled over open fires, using flat skewers called shampurs.

Vegetables such as tomatoes, potatoes, onions, carrots, cabbages, okra, aubergines, cucumbers, squash, mushrooms and green beans are used liberally in their cooking. A very popular soup dish is called bozbash, comprising a healthy mix of meat (traditionally lamb or beef), assorted vegetables like potato and onion, fruits like apple and quince, chickpeas, dried fruits like prune and herbs like mint. Armenians enjoy stuffed foods, and quite a few stuffed vegetables and stuffed edible leaf dishes are present in their cuisine. Ghapama is a stuffed pumpkin dish that is prepared by removing the guts of the pumpkin and stuffing the vegetable with half-cooked rice that has been mixed with melted butter, chopped dried apricots, prunes and apples, raisins, chopped almonds or walnuts, cinnamon powder, salt and honey or sugar. In Armenian, the word 'ghapama' literally means 'cooked in a covered pot'. A round-shaped lid that had been cut out from the top of the pumpkin is placed on it and the vegetable is traditionally baked in a tonir (a special Armenian oven, almost like a tandoor) till it becomes soft. The tender pumpkin is then cut into wedges and served. This dish is traditionally served between the New Year and Armenian Christmas, which is celebrated on 6 January.

Armenia was the first country in the world that adopted Christianity as a state religion. St Gregory the Illuminator, a leading apostle in Armenia, convinced Tiridates III, the king of Armenia, to convert to Christianity and baptized him in 301 CE. In the same year, by virtue of a royal decree, St Gregory converted the entire nation to the Christian faith. But the Armenians have always celebrated Christmas on 6 January. Although the exact date of Christ's birth has not been historically established and neither is it recorded in the Gospels, Christian churches all over the world celebrated it on 6 January till the fourth century. Instead of Christmas, the festival was called Theophany, which in ancient Greek means manifestation or revelation of God to a human. The date was later changed to 25 December by the Roman Catholic Church to override and subdue a traditional pagan festival that celebrated the birth of the sun god on this day. The ancient Romans celebrated Saturnalia, a festival to honour Saturn, the Roman god of agriculture. The festival began on 17 December and lasted for seven days. The date 25 December, which was the time of winter solstice in the Julian calendar, had added significance for the Romans as it was the birthday of Sol Invictus (Unconquered Sun).

Although the Roman Catholic Church had declared these festivals to be invalid, many Romans continued with their worship. To break their influence, the Church struck the flag of Christmas at the peak of these popular festivals and declared 25 December as the birthday of Jesus Christ—6 January was declared as the Epiphany, celebrated by Christians all over the world today as the day when the three kings or wise men known as the Magi visited the infant Jesus in Bethlehem and presented him the gifts of gold, frankincense and myrrh. But the Armenian Apostolic Church (the national church of the Armenian people, also referred to as the Armenian Orthodox Church) continued to observe 6 January as Christmas because in their religious tradition, the Armenians had never celebrated the festival honouring the birth of the sun, and the Armenian Apostolic Church was not a satellite of the Roman Catholic Church.

Christmas in Armenia is a family reunion time and the holy day is spent preparing dishes according to religious traditions and customs. Many devout Armenians observe a fast during the week before Christmas, refraining from eating animal products like meat, eggs, dairy products, fats and oils during this period. The Christmas Eve dinner, known as Khetum, is a very important part of the traditional Armenian Christmas celebrations. Those observing the week-long abstinence break their fast with this dinner. The main traditional dishes of Khetum are rice pilaf cooked with raisins, and fish. The raisins in the pilaf represent the apostles. The Armenians being orthodox practitioners of their faith, celebrate Christmas Eve with a spread that includes fish as a fixed part of the menu, harking back to the early Christian adoption of the fish symbol, ichthys, which is the Greek word for fish. In an environment where they were constantly under threat by the Romans, and feared incarceration and persecution, the Christians used fish as a secret symbol in secret meeting places, to recognize other believers and communicate with them about their faith, to recognize places where they could worship in secret and to distinguish friends from foes. Gradually, the ichthys became a sacred symbol in Christianity.

A soup made of barley and yoghurt called tanabour and nevik (a dish of Swiss chard with chickpeas) are part of this traditional menu. Kuku sabzi often features in the Christmas Eve meal and is made with plenty of herbs and a few eggs. Not to be confused with an omelette, kuku sabzi is more like a fragrant and herby appetizer. It is made by combining whisked eggs with finely chopped scallions, leek and herbs like parsley, coriander and dill, and cooking them in olive oil or butter. The kuku sabzi is cut into wedges and served with a sauce made of yoghurt and crushed garlic. The Christmas Eve spread is incomplete without red wine (symbolizing the blood Christ shed) and desserts like rojik—nut candy made of walnuts threaded on a string and well coated with thick grape or other fruit syrup, and bastegh (fruit leather made of grape juice), sugar and corn starch or refined flour.

On Christmas Day, traditional Armenian dishes like itch (salad made with bulgur wheat) and sou boreg (layered savoury pastry made with phyllo dough and stuffed with cheese) occupy the family table. Meat is reintroduced in dishes like hollowed carrots stuffed with ground lamb, rice and spices and boiled in broth, sujuk (minced meat sausages flavoured with spices), basturma (cured and air-dried spiced beef) and poulgeur pilaf (a lamb and rice dish). Ghapama, made for Christmas in Armenian households since centuries takes centre stage, and is served with turkey. Some items are standard features in both the Christmas Eve and Christmas Day spreads like cookies, baklavas, dried fruits and nuts. Although anoushabour (literally meaning 'sweet soup' in Armenian) is a popular Armenian Christmas pudding, it is also eaten on Christmas Eve. Also known as Noah's pudding, it is made with skinless wholewheat kernels or pearl barley and dried fruits. Sweetened with sugar or honey and flavoured with rose water, this porridge-like pudding is sprinkled with cinnamon powder and garnished with slivered almonds and pomegranate seeds. According to the legendary story, Noah, his family and all the animals he had crammed into the Ark began facing starvation while it continued to rain for forty days and forty nights. Food had become scarce and their supplies were nearly exhausted. To cope with the situation, Noah began boiling water in a big pot and asked his family members to give him all the leftover food items that they could find. Thus ingredients like grains and dried fruits went into the pot and the meal turned out delicious. The believers survived. Armenians recall this story during the festive season by eating anoushabour.

In Calcutta, many members of the Armenian community observe a customary fast in the week before Christmas and indulge only in light vegetarian meals. The celebration begins with a late afternoon Mass on Christmas Eve, after which a Home Blessing ceremony is held at the Armenian College and Philanthropic Academy on Free School Street. A Christmas Eve dinner is arranged for the staff members and students of the institution, which includes, among other traditional dishes, the customary pilaf with raisins and fish. The Academy also serves anoushabour.

The community celebrates Christmas on 6 January by attending Christmas Mass at the Armenian Church of the Holy Nazareth in the morning. This is followed by the festive lunch when traditional Armenian dishes occupy the family table. Unlike today, when ingredients like olive oil, thyme, parsley and oregano have become easily available in India, and even pine nuts and hazelnuts are available in high-end stores, such easy accessibility was unheard of for many years. The early Armenians in India had to make do with the locally available oils, spices, herbs and nuts. Tropical fruits and vegetables began to be incorporated into their cuisine. Wheat remained their main cereal, but the community began making pilafs more frequently, thanks to the easy availability of rice. Beef, pork and chicken continued to be their favourite meats, and lamb was replaced with mutton.

Over time, they acquired a taste for Indian cuisine and found it easier to cope with the situation by embracing it. As generations went by, Indian cuisine gradually began to replace traditional fare in Armenian households. This fundamental principle holds true even for the Calcutta Armenians. As the oldest expatriate community, their association with this city has been so long that they have adopted Bengali cuisine as their own. Barring very few traditional dishes, the current generation of Calcutta Armenians are content with the local staple diet. They have also embraced many dishes from Anglo-Indian cuisine, which is heavily meat-based. Another reason that has contributed to the replacement of their traditional cuisine is that many Armenians in Calcutta have had intercommunity marriages.

Until the 1960s, it had been a customary ritual for community members to gather for a Christmas luncheon at the Armenian Club in Queen's Mansion on Park Street after the church service was over. This was followed by a late afternoon tea party at the Armenian Sports Club on Mayo Road in the Maidan area. The Armenian Club was once nicknamed 'Bara Club' because all the prominent or bara people from the community would go there. The luncheon menu would include, besides celebratory Indian and Anglo-Indian dishes, traditional pilaf with raisins, a fish preparation, dolma, salted white Armenian cheese and kebabs. It would be a contributory feast, with each family preparing a dish. Although this Christmas luncheon at the club has been discontinued, the tea party still continues, with community members carrying home boxes of Christmas cakes and goodies.

Though Christmas cake is not a part of the traditional Armenian Christmas menu, some members of the community celebrate with home-made cakes because of the influence of the British and Anglo-Indian customs. The delicious smell of baking and nutmeg pervades some Armenian homes during this festive season. There was a time when a considerable number of Armenian bakeries conducted thriving business in the city. They catered to the community and specialized in traditional sweets. Names such as Arizona and Minas come up as favourite haunts from where cakes were bought during the festive season. But after these bakeries downed their shutters in the 1980s, their cakes have been replaced with those from Nahoum's, Calcutta's famed Jewish bakery.

The one traditional dish that the Armenians in Calcutta continue to prepare is the dolma—traditionally a dish of ground meat (usually lamb) stuffed into grape leaves. Instead of getting lost in the annals of history, the dolma has become an indelible part of the Calcutta Armenian culinary story, particularly because of the influence it has had on the culinary practices of the Bengalis. Dolmas are also made in countries like Greece, Turkey, Syria, Lebanon, Cyprus, Azerbaijan, Albania, Iraq and Iran. In short, it is a dish that is spread over the Middle East, Balkans, Central Asia, South Caucasus, Arabia and the Turkic countries. Although there are slight variations in the name of the dish between countries, it is largely known as dolma. The word originates from the Turkish 'dolmak', which means 'to be stuffed'. It is believed that the traditional Armenian name for this dish is tolma, derived from the word 'toli', which means grape leaf. But, over the centuries, the name dolma came to be used more often in Armenia. Dolma is also commonly made by stuffing cabbage leaves, bell peppers, tomatoes, onions, zucchinis and aubergines.

Chopped onions, rice, butter, tomato paste, salt, black pepper and chopped herbs are added to the minced meat (chicken or beef is largely used in Calcutta) and kneaded together with warm water. The grape leaves are blanched and small portions of the meat mixture are put into them. The leaves are rolled up like cigars—the dolmas. They are then cooked in water. The dolmas are ready when the rice is thoroughly cooked. Stuffed grape-leaf dolmas are usually served with curd mixed with garlic powder. The absence of grape leaves in Calcutta prompted the Armenians to use cabbage leaves and vegetables like patol (pointed gourd or 'parwal' in Hindi) for stuffing instead. It is widely believed that it was the Armenians who taught the Bengalis the art of making *patoler dolma* (also known as *patoler dorma*), a savoured delicacy and festive dish in Bengali cuisine today. Bengalis learnt the technique of hollowing and stuffing patol and made their own versions, with minced meat (largely chicken or mutton), fish meat or shrimp, or a vegetarian stuffing of mashed potatoes, crumbled cottage cheese or chhana. The hollowed pointed gourd was lightly coated with salt and turmeric and shallow fried in mustard oil before it was stuffed with the filling that had been cooked with local spices. Rice was omitted from the Bengali version of the stuffing and the dolmas were cooked in spicy gravy. The Bengalis eat patoler dolma with steamed rice or *polao*.

Assuming that traditional Armenian cuisine is completely forsaken by the community in Calcutta will be a mistake. Though not a part of their daily diet anymore, it is not uncommon to come across dishes like lavash bread, freshly baked from the oven, as part of the weekend meal in an Armenian home in the city. Family recipes have exchanged hands through generations, and over time, a few have survived. Attempts to revive the traditional cuisine of their homeland are being made by Armenian institutions like the Armenian College and Philanthropic Academy on Free School Street. A residential school that was established in 1821 to educate children of Armenian descent, it teaches them, besides the regular subjects, the Armenian language, literature, history, music and religion. The school makes Armenian foods throughout the year for its staff members and students.

Fairlawn Hotel once served Armenian food but slowly switched to the more saleable continental food with a curry thrown in every Sunday. With the dwindling number of Armenians, their traditional bakeries became commercially unviable and had to be shut down. These factors have left majority of the Calcuttans unaware of the Armenian culture and cuisine still extant in the city. As an example, Calcutta Stories, a one-of-a-kind restaurant, which specialized in the immigrant cuisines of Calcutta served a few Armenian dishes like lavash bread, baba ganoush (a creamy dip of roasted aubergine) and tabbouleh (a salad made from bulgur wheat, vegetables and herbs tossed in salt, pepper, lime juice and olive oil). But the concept did not work out well enough to attract a large number of customers and the restaurant had to shut down after two years. Prithvish Chakravarti, who owned Calcutta Stories, says:

> The main reason for the failure of the restaurant was that it served unusual foods and not popular ones. The Armenian dishes that we served were the least successful. Customers found them quite bland. Among all the cuisines that Calcutta Stories served, it was Anglo-Indian cuisine that picked up the most with customers. This is because the cuisine shares similarities with Indian food. It is spicy and appeals to the Indian palate.

He intends to start again with a café called Calcutta Stories, but sadly, Armenian food will not be on its menu.

PART TWO

A Culinary Melting Pot

Beth El Synagogue on Pollock Street

***Source:* Vivek Luke Mukherjee**

1. Calcutta Jews and Their Culinary Culture

It is difficult to point out when exactly the Jews began settling in Calcutta. The records of the city refer to one Shalom ben Aharon ben Obadiah Ha-Cohen arriving from Aleppo in present-day Syria on 4 August 1798, but many other Jewish traders had temporary residences in the city well before that. They traded in indigo, ivory, cotton yarn, gold leaf, silk, Venice ware, precious stones, coffee, sesame oil, jute, sugar, spices and even opium. Shalom was an ambitious young merchant who had travelled from Aleppo to Baghdad and then came via Basra, Bombay and Surat to Calcutta. He settled down in Murgighata, literally meaning 'market for chickens', near the Armenian and Portuguese settlements in Barabazar. The area around the Cathedral of the Most Holy Rosary, now commonly known as the Portuguese Church, on Portuguese Church Street is still called Murgighata. Soon, Shalom was joined by his family members and close associates. His nephew Moses Simon Duek Ha-Cohen, an astute businessman, played a pivotal role in framing the first Constitution of the community. The majority of the Jews of Calcutta consider him to be the main founder of the Jewish community in the city. The first noteworthy house of worship for the Jews in the city was Neveh Shalome (Abode of Peace), which was set up in the first half of the nineteenth century with sizeable contributions from Shalom's son, Shalom Obadiah Ha-Cohen. It was named by him in memory of his father.

Most of the Jews who settled in Calcutta were immigrants from Baghdad and Syria. They were drawn to the city by the prospect of lucrative trade and freedom from the persecution they periodically faced in the Middle East. The number of Jews in Calcutta in 1799 was a meagre fifteen. By 1813, the Jewish community was enlisted in the 'Original Calcutta Annual Directory and Calendar' and by 1825, their number had risen to 200. In their essay, 'The Jews of Calcutta', from the book *Calcutta—The Living City: Volume I: The Past* (1990), authors Pritha Chowdhury and Joyoti Chaliha write, 'With a population of 600 in 1860 and 1,900 by the end of the century, the community began to move east and later south from their original homes in the Barabazar area, close to their synagogues' (pp. 52–53).

The first thing that the Jewish community did once they had established themselves in trade and commerce in the city was to build synagogues. These also functioned as community centres for them. They spent a lot of money on their constructions, an indication of their prosperity in Calcutta. Regular services were held in the synagogues, especially on Saturdays, the day of Shabbat.

Joseph Ezra and his son, David Joseph Ezra, arrived in Calcutta in the early nineteenth century. David Joseph Ezra made his fortune trading indigo and silk and invested most of the profits in real estate. Some of the most impressive buildings in the city like Esplanade Mansions, Ezra Mansions and Chowringhee Mansions were built by him. Even Ezra Street now bears his name. His greatest contribution to the Jewish community of Calcutta was the Beth El (House of God) Synagogue, which still stands on Pollock Street. Beth El was built when it was clear that Neveh Shalome could no longer accommodate the growing Jewish community. The synagogue's construction, using funds provided by David Joseph Ezra and Ezekiel Judah, was completed in 1856.

His son, Elias David Joseph Ezra, was Calcutta's first Jewish sheriff. He built the magnificent Magen David (Shield of David) Synagogue in 1884 on Synagogue Street in honour of his father who had died two years earlier. This beautiful synagogue has been built in the Italian Renaissance style. Elias's widow, Mozelle Ezra, established the Ezra Hospital, part of the Medical College complex, in 1887 in honour of her late husband.

Towards the end of the nineteenth century, the wealthier members of the community began to adopt Western dress, manners and the English language, a far cry from their early days of speaking Judeo-Arabic (an ethnolect formerly spoken and written in various forms by Jews throughout the Arabic-speaking world) at home. They moved to select residential areas in Chowringhee, Bentinck Street and south of Park Street. The Jews of Calcutta were a small and closely knit community, many of whom became professionals like lawyers and doctors, while others flourished as opticians and confectioners. A very prominent member of the community in the twentieth century was businessman Benjamin Nissim Elias. His firm, B.N. Elias and Co. Ltd, was once a force to reckon with. He set up the Agarpara Jute Mills and National Tobacco Company in Calcutta along with a number of establishments in the fields of electricity supply, dairy farming, fertilizers, real estate, insurance, engineering and coal mining. The Elias family set up a number of charitable trusts, and added a new wing to the Chittaranjan Cancer Hospital, and a children's wing to the Medical College complex.

When Japan invaded Burma in 1942, many Jews fled to Calcutta, increasing their number in the city to 3,800. To escape Nazi atrocities during the Second World War, a considerable number of Jews fled Europe and reached Calcutta. At their peak, the number of Jews in the city was around 5,000. The Jewish Association of Calcutta was formed in 1945, and it brought out a monthly paper called *Shema*. The establishment of the State of Israel on 14 May 1948 saw the exodus of a large number of Jews. This gradual but steady relocation of the Calcutta Jews to their Promised Land and developed countries like the United Kingdom, United States of America, Canada and Australia for better prospects meant that by the 1960s, there were only four to five hundred Jews living in Calcutta, heralding the beginning of a long struggle to sustain community life in the city. Over the years, the numbers further declined. In her essay, 'The Jews of Calcutta' from the book *Calcutta Mosaic: Essays and Interviews on the Minority Communities of Calcutta* (2009), Sipra Mukherjee mentions, 'There are at present 25 Jews living in Calcutta, all of whom are above 65 years of age' (p. 88). It is sad to see this once prosperous and thriving community, which has given the city so much, slip so quietly into the background.

Jewish Cuisine

When it comes to food, Jewish cuisine is regulated by a set of dietary laws called 'kashrut', which prescribes the foods that are permitted to be eaten and the methods by which they should be prepared. Foods permitted to be eaten are called kosher. This includes, among others, cloven-hoofed animals that eat cud as well as fish that have fins and scales. The foods that are forbidden are called terefah. At first, it may seem strange that the consumption of pork is forbidden because the pig is a cloven-hoofed animal. But the pig does not eat cud. Eels and shellfish like prawns, lobsters and crabs are forbidden. Birds of prey, meaning birds who eat other animals, cannot be consumed. Thus, the consumption of the meat of domesticated birds, meaning fowls or poultry, is allowed.

In the Book of Exodus, God's command to the Jews prohibiting them from boiling a kid (meaning a young goat) in its mother's milk has been clearly mentioned. So, according to their dietary laws, meat and poultry cannot be eaten with dairy products. Butter, milk, cream or clarified butter cannot be used to cook meat dishes or served alongside. Substitutes like oil (particularly olive oil), margarine, schmaltz (rendered chicken fat) and non-dairy cream are used to cook meat and poultry dishes. The animal has to be ritually slaughtered, and the meat, drained of all blood. Before it is cooked, the meat is soaked in water for some time, and then, salted with coarse salt (which helps to draw out all the traces of blood).

In the early days, kosher meat was easy to find in the markets because of the presence of a large Jewish community in the city. The cooks in Jewish homes were mostly Muslims, many of whom had mastered the kosher way to slaughter meat. As the number of Jews in Calcutta began shrinking, the community adjusted by buying meat from halal butchers because the methods of slaughter in Islamic and Jewish dietary traditions are somewhat similar.

Although the Jewish people of Calcutta generally stuck to these dietary laws, they also began to use new ingredients from the area and bent some rules to adjust to the new environment. Their food was flavoured with ginger, chillies, garam masala and some other spices, in a departure from traditional Jewish fare. Tamarind was used for its sour taste and the liberal use of mint leaves, a fixed part of most Jewish preparations, was gradually replaced with coriander leaves in some dishes. Rice began to be seen on many Jewish tables in Calcutta, a change similar to the ways in which Sephardic Jews adapted to the staple foods of Spain and North Africa. Coconut milk began to be used in curries and desserts—an ingenious way to circumvent the prohibition against mixing meat and milk or even following each other. Bread-and-butter pudding, for example, is still cooked using coconut milk in most Jewish homes in Calcutta.

Unsurprisingly, given Calcutta's location, fish like bhekti and ilish became the staples in Jewish homes. A common stew featuring freshwater fish involves cooking flakes of the fried fish in boiling coconut milk with fresh coriander leaves and green chillies.

The Jews of Calcutta also created blends that showcased their affiliation to the local culture, such as mahashas and shooftas. Mahasha in Arabic means 'to stuff' and hence, refer to stuffed vegetables like tomatoes, onions, green or red peppers, lettuce leaves and cabbage leaves. Chicken pieces are cooked with the paste of ginger and garlic and chopped onions to make the filling. Rice and seasonings like lime juice, salt, sugar and chopped mint leaves are added to the chicken. This mixture is cooked till the rice is half done. The vegetables are then stuffed with this filling and baked till soft and the rice is fully cooked. Shooftas are kebabs made with the boneless meat of fish or minced chicken, mutton, beef or turkey.

Author Flower Silliman, a prominent member of the community in Calcutta and doyenne of Jewish cuisine, points out, '*Alu makallah* is a dish that is unique to Calcutta and not made by the Jews living in any other part of the country.' It is a sort of hybrid dish that bears traces of local influence—mainly the dish alu bhaja (fried potatoes). 'Alu' in Bengali means 'potato' and 'makallah' in Arabic means 'fried'. Whole potatoes are fried in oil until they are so crisp that one has to bite into them—using forks and knives makes them jump off the plate! Alu makallah is always served with hulba or hilbeh, a green methi chutney. A Middle Eastern relish that was brought to Calcutta from Iraq and Syria, it has been tweaked a bit and is made by grinding soaked fenugreek seeds with coriander leaves, ginger, garlic, green chillies, lime juice and salt.

The cuisine of the Calcutta Jews is a confluence of the Middle Eastern and Indian culinary cultures. Bamia khatta, for example, has been influenced by the Iraqi dish, margat bamia (okra stew), which is cooked with meat. 'Bamia' in Arabic means 'okra' and 'khatta' means 'sour' in Hindi. It is a thick, sweet and sour chicken stew made with okra. Tomatoes are an important feature of this dish. The stew is made sour by using lime juice or tamarind. Often, instead of meat, semolina dumplings called kubba, which are of the size of golf balls and stuffed with minced meat, are cooked in the hot stew. This is an influence of kubba bamia, the classic recipe of the Iraqi Jews. Both the versions are seasoned with mint leaves and served with rice or pulao.

Another typically Jewish dish, chitanee, is a cross between a curry and a sweet and sour chicken preparation. In this dish, the chicken is cooked in a gravy of spices to which tomatoes and tamarind are added. The dish is seasoned with salt and sugar and served with rice. The chicken is cooked until tender and most of the gravy has dried up.

Festive Foods

Calcutta Jews eat hameem on the day of Shabbat, which actually starts just before sunset on Friday evening and goes on till nightfall on Saturday. Cooking is not allowed on the Shabbat day and all the food needs to be prepared beforehand. To adhere to this rule, Jewish people often prepare something on Friday evening that has a long cooking period so that it can be eaten for lunch on Saturday when they come home from the synagogue. For hameem, the chicken is opened up, cleaned and stuffed with rice that is half cooked, along with spices, chopped chicken liver, nuts and raisins. The skin of the chicken is then sewn at the neck and the base. Onions, carrots, garam masala, turmeric, chicken pieces and chopped coriander leaves are then lightly cooked in a pot along with rice that has been soaked in water. The stuffed chicken is placed on top of this rice mixture. Enough water is added to the pot to cover the whole chicken. This dish is cooked with the lid on and at the lowest flame for twelve to fifteen hours. 'The whole stuffed chicken is called hashwa and the rice mixture forms a rice, chicken and vegetable soup called shorba', points out Silliman.

She further elaborates that for Rosh Hashanah, the Jewish New Year, the symbolic food of apples and honey, for the sweetness of the New Year, has been replaced in Calcutta with apple murabba, in which whole and peeled apples are cooked in sugar syrup. Traditional challah bread is also eaten on this day by Jews all over the world, including Calcutta. It is made with refined flour, yeast, warm water, sugar, vegetable oil, salt and eggs. Although typically oblong in shape, challah is made round on Rosh Hashanah to symbolize the never-ending cycle of years and seasons. Raisins are often kneaded into the dough of this festive bread. The bread is braided and brushed over with a beaten egg or egg white, and sometimes, sprinkled with poppy or sesame seeds before it goes into the oven.

Matzah, a flat unleavened bread made with only flour and cold water and without any yeast, is made during Passover in the compound outside the Beth El synagogue. 'It is rolled out into a thin round shape and baked on the side of a tandoor till crisp, when it is eaten dipped in halek, a thick date syrup,' explains Silliman. Halek is made by boiling dates, straining the liquid and then heating it over a low flame till it reduces to a thick consistency. Chopped nuts are sprinkled on top of it. During Passover, Jewish families in Calcutta come together to celebrate the story of the Exodus from Egypt, when Moses, at the command of God, parted the Red Sea to lead his people out of their slavery and into the Promised Land. The Hebrews left Egypt in such a hurry that they could not wait for their bread to rise. This unleavened bread, when baked, became the matzah, the simplest form of bread eaten by the slaves. The matzah has come to symbolize liberation and freedom in Judaic tradition. The halek symbolizes the mortar used by the Hebrew slaves to bond bricks while building cities and monuments in Egypt when they were in captivity.

Breads and More

During the rest of the year, other forms of flatbread and pancakes are eaten, though rice remains a staple as well. For example, arook tahine, another Calcutta Jewish dish, consists of small pancakes made of minced chicken breasts or fillets of fish to which finely chopped scallions, green chillies, coriander leaves, flour, whisked eggs, ginger and salt are added. It is usually eaten as an appetizer or with drinks before dinner. It can also be eaten as a light luncheon with fresh salad.

Many Muslims were professionally engaged as bakers in Calcutta in the colonial times and they also became familiar with the range of Jewish baked goods. Silliman elaborates, 'Up until the 1960s, Muslim bakers would go from door to door, visiting Jewish families in Calcutta and selling Jewish baked goods. These ranged from cacas, popular savoury biscuits eaten with tea or drinks and flavoured with caraway or fennel seeds, to babas, sweet and savoury biscuits with a date filling, and kooleechas or coconut-based cookies.' They also made and sold sweet nuggets with fillings of bindak (almonds) or fistak (pistachios) as well as halcoons or Turkish delights, which are made by boiling cornflour and sugar syrup together for a long time over low heat to form a dense and sticky jelly. It is then flavoured with rose or orange-flower water or citrus fruit juice. Once the jelly has cooled, it is cut into small cubes and heavily dusted with icing sugar. Halcoons are served with tea or coffee in Jewish homes.

Another popular bakery item, luzina, looks like a diamond-shaped barfi and is made with almonds, pistachios, coconut, guava or quince. Almond rings are circular discs made of ground almonds and castor sugar whisked with egg whites, almond essence, vanilla essence and lemon juice. The almond rings are baked till they turn golden brown. They have a crunchy exterior but are soft at the centre. The all-time favourite mulfoof is a thin nut-filled pastry. It is usually filled with pistachios, almonds or mixed nuts (Brazil nuts, walnuts, pecans and other nuts), which are pounded to a crunchy consistency, mixed with castor sugar and flavoured with rose water.

'The bakers also made and sold feta, mozzarella and rennet cheese from goat's milk. All of these items were kosher,' wraps up Silliman.

Nahoum and Sons: With the dwindling numbers of the community, the cuisine is dying in the city today. Nahoum and Sons, one of the few remaining Jewish establishments in Calcutta, which has been carrying on for years, is an iconic marker in the community that will hopefully never fade away. Its story began in the late nineteenth century, a time when the city was bustling with a potpourri of immigrants like the Jews, Armenians, Portuguese, Chinese and Parsis. This Jewish bakery in Sir Stuart Hogg Market has always been a very well-known confectionery shop, and is popularly called Nahoum's. Even today, Christmas in Calcutta is incomplete without Nahoum's signature rich fruit cake and plum cake.

Nahoum Israel Mordecai came to Calcutta from Baghdad in the year 1870. A good cook and excellent baker, he had a strong background in Middle Eastern Jewish confectionery. Mordecai decided to use his baking skills, first by baking and selling some traditional Middle Eastern Jewish confectioneries like baklava, fistak mulfoof, almond rings, challah bread, cacas, date babas, luzina, almond and cheese samosas (which are called sambusaks), plaited cheese, matza and biscuits to Jewish families, by going door to door.

In 1902, Moredcai set up his confectionery shop 'Nahoum's' in front of Sir Stuart Hogg Market, in what is the floral portion of the market today. Subsequently, in 1916, the shop shifted to its present location inside the market premises. The shop was initially meant to cater exclusively to the Jewish community and only baked Jewish confectioneries. It was the only confectionery shop in the city that sold kosher food. But after some time, Mordecai thought of catering to the European and Anglo-Indian communities living in the city and introduced European delights like sponge cakes, plum cakes, rich fruit cakes, cream rolls, fudge and chocolate bars. During Easter, Nahoum's became the favourite haunt of customers for Easter eggs and hot cross buns. The shop's plum and fruit cakes soon became bestsellers during the Christmas season.

As Europeans began leaving the country after Independence, Nahoum's changed its strategy and began baking for the cosmopolitan Indian community. They now baked more European confectioneries that catered to the tastes of the locals while retaining some of their traditional Jewish baked products. The shop has become famous for its fudges, Easter eggs and Christmas cakes. Over time, different kinds of baked goods have been added to the shop's list. Cakes in flavours like chocolate, pineapple, lemon and orange, Madeira cake, wedding cakes and brownies have gradually become part and parcel of the cake and pastry listing in the confectionery shop. Customers can find an assorted variety of breads and sandwiches in Nahoum's, along with a range of other items like puff pastries with vegetarian and non-vegetarian spicy fillings, egg or tuna cup, fish pantras, golden puff biscuits, spring onion biscuits, date sticks, gooseberry jam and pineapple pudding.

Elias Nahoum took over from his father, Nahoum Israel Mordecai, in the early 1930s. His sons Norman and Solomon ran the shop from 1948 to 1999, after which, their brother David, took over and became Calcutta's new fruit cake man. During his reign, macaroons, jam tarts and walnut brownies became some of the bestselling items at the shop. David Nahoum retained many of the old recipes and methods of baking that were passed down from his grandfather. Since his death in 2013, his younger brother Isaac manages the store.

Nahoum's is inundated with orders for wedding cakes during the Christmas season because it also happens to be the wedding season for the Christian community. For many years, orders also came for the Republic Day functions held at Raj Bhavan. Nahoum's has a long celebrity customer list, including cricketer Sourav Ganguly's family, actress Aparna Sen, singer Usha Uthup and film-maker Anjan Dutt. Even legends like the actress Suchitra Sen, singer Manna Dey and cricket commentator Pearson Surita would swear by the confectionery shop's creations. When Geoffrey Fisher, the Archbishop of Canterbury, tasted Nahoum's fruit cake during his visit to Calcutta in 1959, he remarked that it was the best fruit cake he had ever had.

*

Unfortunately, it is not easy to come across Jewish cuisine in Calcutta today. The exodus of the Jews began in the late 1940s. Their departure left a void in the cosmopolitan structure of the city. There are hardly any Jews left and many of those who have remained behind are elderly people. Even the synagogue services in the city are dwindling away. It is becoming increasingly difficult to get the minyan (quorum of ten men) required for a synagogue service to take place because the Torah (the religious text of the Jews) cannot be read in the absence of this quorum.

Other institutions, which were once particularly set up for the Jewish community of the city, now survive on the participation of other communities. The two schools primarily meant for Jewish students—the Jewish Girls' School and the Elias Meyer Free School and Talmud Torah for boys from poor backgrounds—were compelled to open their doors to students from other communities to sustain themselves. Established in 1881 and 1882 respectively, these two educational institutions are still looked after by Jewish trustees and certain Jewish traditions are still adhered to, like teaching the students Hebrew songs and traditional dances. Although teaching in Hebrew has been discontinued, the schools still observe all the major Jewish holidays and do not function on Saturday, the day of Shabbat.

Along with the dwindling Jewish population, the absence of community gatherings in these public institutions has also contributed to the fading of their cuisine. Most cooks working in Jewish homes now are Bengalis, who make rice, roti and dal. Rarely used in typical Jewish cuisine, dal or lentil has become a fixed part of the daily menu in the Jewish households of Calcutta. After having lived in the city for centuries, Jewish people enjoy eating all sorts of Indian cuisines now, as long as the meat is kosher. Several Indian dishes are cooked at home keeping the dietary laws in mind—for example, tandoori chicken is marinated with lime juice instead of yoghurt.

There has been a marked absence of restaurants in Calcutta specializing in Jewish cuisine, mainly because of the fading Jewish population. Calcutta Stories served Jewish dishes and they fared better than Armenian food. Dishes such as challah bread, kubba soup, zalata (cucumber salad), pickled okra, shooftas, mahashas, alu makallah and hilbeh, and roasted aubergines with yoghurt-tahini sauce featured in the menu. 'Out of these shooftas, mahashas and alu makallah and hilbeh performed well,' points out Prithvish Chakravarti, 'We might repeat these, along with new additions such as chitanee, in Calcutta Stories café.'

Such attempts are needed to keep alive the memories of a community that is fast disappearing.

An establishment like Nahoum's along with the synagogues, schools, mansions and the streets bearing the Jewish names, are imprints on the city that will remind the future generations of the glorious days of Calcutta's Jews.

2. Nawabi Influence

There has been a long history of Muslim presence in Bengal. Muslims from Uttar Pradesh had been living in Murshidabad since the eighteenth century, arriving during the reign of the Nawabs of Bengal (Nawab Nazims of Bengal, Bihar and Orissa to be precise), which began in 1717 with the accession of Nawab Murshid Quli Khan. The labour force of Calcutta also had a large number of Muslims, which kept increasing with the industrial development of the city.

The food cooked in the royal kitchen of Murshidabad had a strong influence on the culinary culture of the Muslims of the region. Their dishes gradually spread to the local Muslims through the royal bawarchis (chefs). Some of the dishes prepared in the royal kitchen were *murgh qorma, machli ka kalia, tikia kebab, dal gosht, seekh kebab* and *mahi pulao* (fish pulao). The royal kitchen of Murshidabad used tamarind in cooking, a culinary practice not typical of the Muslims of Uttar Pradesh.

In the Nizamat Imambara in Murshidabad, majlis or religious gatherings were held during Muharram and Safar, which corresponds to the first and second month of the Islamic lunar calendar. After the majlis were over, hissa (devotional offering) used to be distributed among the devotees, and it usually consisted of roti, paratha, tikia kebab, seekh kebab and dal gosht. The local Muslims also made these foods at home. The Muslim traders and rulers are given credit for introducing the traditional oven called tandoor as well as maida in India. Over the years, the breads they baked in this oven with this kind of flour gained widespread popularity. They tasted better than the flatbreads that were traditionally made with atta. Baking with yeast also began in India with the Muslims.

During the Battle of Plassey, the British defeated Siraj-ud-Daulah, the Nawab of Bengal, and installed a puppet nawab on the throne. They soon began demanding a great deal of money as compensation from Syed Mir Jafar Ali Khan Bahadur, the new nawab. The demands of the British East India Company were so large that Mir Jafar was forced to conspire with the Dutch to oust the British from Bengal. The British, however, defeated the Dutch in the Battle of Chinsurah (25 November 1759), and forced Mir Jafar to abdicate the throne in favour of his son-in-law, Mir Qasim. After the Battle of Chinsurah, Mir Jafar was deposed and sent to Calcutta. From 1760 to 1763, he lived in exile in the city. It was during this time that Murshidabadi Nawabi cuisine made its entry into Calcutta through the multitude of bawarchis who came along with the deposed Nawab. Murgh qorma, machli ka kalia, tikia kebab, dal gosht and seekh kebab found their way into the local Muslim kitchens. Mahi pulao also crept onto the menu of the fish-loving locals.

But Mir Qasim proved to be something of a rebel, standing against British interference in the governance of his province. This annoyed the British and they reinstated Mir Jafar as the Nawab of Bengal in 1763. A furious Mir Qasim declared war against the Company and the Battle of Buxar was fought. Despite his best efforts, Mir Qasim was defeated in the battle. Mir Jafar remained as the Nawab of Bengal till his death in 1765. Because of his short stay in the city, the influence of Murshidabadi Nawabi cuisine on Calcutta's culinary culture remained limited. It was mainly confined to the court and the local Muslims of Murshidabad.

In 1765, a system of dual governance was established in Bengal by its first Governor, Robert Clive, which permanently secured for the British East India Company the diwani rights of the Bengal Subah from the Mughal emperor, Shah Alam II. With the establishment of this dual government, the Bengal Subah, which had till then referred to the province of Bengal under the imperial rule, ceased to exist, and was replaced by the Bengal Presidency. Although the Nawab Nazims continued with their administrative authority, this new structure of governance made them subordinate to the British. But this system of dual governance was abolished in 1772 by the first Governor-General of Bengal, Warren Hastings. Bengal was now brought under the direct control of the British East India Company. In 1793, the nizamat or local rule was abolished by the British and all the powers of the Nawabs of Bengal were taken away, reducing them to mere pensioners of the Company. Sayyid Mansur Ali Khan was the last to hold the position of the Nawab of Bengal because in 1880 this title was abolished, bringing the reign of the Nawab Nazims to an end.

A wave of immigrants from Uttar Pradesh came to Calcutta in the nineteenth century, mainly to get employment in the jute mills. They also worked as sepoys, labourers, tram drivers, station masters and security personnel. Those who were well educated among them took up academic careers or went into government service. They even became professionals, like Jugal Kishore Shukla, lawyer and founder of *Udant Martand*, the first Hindi language weekly newspaper in India that was started in Calcutta on 30 May 1826. There was also a considerable number of Muslims among these immigrants who brought along their culinary practices and food habits to the city. Most importantly, the descendants of the exiled prince and the last Nawab of Awadh, Wajid Ali Shah, who settled in the city with his entourage in 1859, transformed the Muslim cuisine of the city for good.

Awadhi Cuisine in Calcutta

The journey of biryani in Calcutta began in the royal kitchen of Nawab Wajid Ali Shah, who lived in Metiabruz in the later years of his life. Nawab Wajid Ali Shah was the last ruler of Awadh. He ascended the throne in 1847 and ruled for nine years. His kingdom was annexed bloodlessly on 11 February 1856 on the ground of maladministration. Shahanshah Mirza, the great-great-grandson of Nawab Wajid Ali Shah, says, 'The nawab felt wronged by the British and decided to present his case before the Governor-General of India because he had heard a lot about the British sense of fair play and justice.' To this end, he travelled to Calcutta and met the incumbent Governor-General. But his case was not considered favourably. He then decided to travel to England and present the case to Queen Victoria, but his physicians did not think that his health would permit such a long voyage. He sent his mother, younger brother and heir apparent in his place. But before anything could be worked out, the Revolt of 1857 broke out. The mutiny spread to Lucknow and the sepoys installed one of his sons on the throne of Awadh. 'The British were afraid that Wajid Ali Shah would become a rallying figure for the sepoys in Lucknow, like Mughal Emperor Bahadur Shah Zafar had become for the sepoys in Delhi,' explains Shahanshah Mirza. This fear made them keep Wajid Ali Shah under nazarbandh (house arrest) in Amherst House in Fort William, along with his twelve courtiers, including his erstwhile prime minister, Ali Naqi Khan, for twenty-six months.

After his release from nazarbandh on 16 June 1859, Wajid Ali Shah was strongly advised by the British to settle in Calcutta. He chose the locality of Metiabruz for the panoramic view it offered. At this time, Metiabruz was a barren tract of land that lay close to the Hooghly. The British gave the Nawab an annual income of twelve lakh rupees and a number of mansions to live in along the banks of the river. Nawab Wajid Ali Shah tried to recreate the environment of Lucknow in Metiabruz. Sahebzada Wasif Mirza, great-grandson of Nawab Wajid Ali Shah and father of Shahanshah Mirza, adds, 'When Wajid Ali Shah had first come to Calcutta, he had been accompanied by nearly 500 people, including his family members, friends, close associates, physicians, musicians and bawarchis.' After he settled down in Metiabruz, more people from the Awadhi court would join him at intervals to live in an environment that would keep the sweet memories of Lucknow alive.

Wajid Ali Shah was a gifted poet and a man of considerable artistic flair. He was also a connoisseur of art and culture. The classical dance form of kathak is believed to have attained new heights of glory and popularity under his patronage. He was also a lover of good food and is known to have had a taste for rich cooking. His bawarchis cooked his food in ghee and oil with a variety of nuts and dried fruits. It is believed that his bawarchis grew so creative that they were often wooed by the other nawabs. Master chefs were patronized and encouraged by the Nawabs of Awadh and given leave to experiment in the royal kitchen. These experimentations led to innovations and what emerged were delectable spreads of food that were greatly loved by the ruling families.

It was such an experimentation that led to the creation of biryani. The term is derived from the Persian word 'beryan' which literally means 'fried before cooking'. There are many interesting anecdotes surrounding the evolution of this wonderful one-dish-meal, but it is generally believed that the credit for its creation goes to the fourth Nawab of Awadh, Asaf-ud-Daula. Food columnist and the doyenne of Awadhi cuisine, Fatima Mirza, wife of Shahanshah Mirza and descendant of Prince Mirza Hamid Ali Bahadur (the eldest son of Nawab Wajid Ali Shah), elaborates, 'He moved his capital from Faizabad to Lucknow in 1775 and built a number of monuments, including the Asafi Imambara, which is popularly known as the Bara Imambara. The construction of the Bara Imambara was undertaken as a charitable project to generate employment for people and offer them food as wages during the terrible famine of 1784 that struck Awadh. The nawabs engaged more than 20,000 workers for the construction of this grand prayer hall. To feed the construction workers, large cauldrons were filled with rice, meat and vegetables. The lids of the cauldrons were sealed with dough and the rice mixture was cooked slowly for hours. Both the style of dum cooking and the biryani emerged from this attempt.' Dum cooking, or dum pukht cooking, has become the hallmark of the Awadhi style of cooking. It implies a slow method in which meat and vegetables are cooked for a long time over low flame in sealed containers.

The construction workers were given a heavy meal so that they could work for long hours without feeling hungry. This slow method of cooking allowed the spices and the meat to release their flavours gently and retain their natural aromas. It is believed that during his rounds of the site, Asaf-ud-Daula caught a whiff of the aroma emanating from one of the cauldrons and instructed his bawarchis to serve him the dish. He loved the taste and aroma of the biryani and demanded that it be served in his dastarkhwan (dining spread) often. In order to please the nawabs, the bawarchis in his kitchen removed the vegetables from the dish and added more meat and saffron, milk and exquisite spices to create the Awadhi biryani.

This biryani reached Calcutta when Nawab Wajid Ali Shah settled in Metiabruz. Slight alterations were made to the original recipe, leading to the introduction of a new biryani dish that has, over the years, become synonymous with Calcutta. If folklore is to be believed, the bawarchis of Wajid Ali Shah tried to cut costs and replaced some of the meat in the biryani with potatoes, thus creating the Calcutta *alu biryani*. There is another tale that insists that Wajid Ali Shah's bawarchis fell on hard times after the death of the nawabs, who breathed his last in Metiabruz in 1887, and began including potatoes in the biryani in place of some of the meat for this reason. However, the descendants of the family dismiss such stories as being far from the truth. They firmly believe that with an annual pension of twelve lakh rupees, the nawab was in a position to continue to indulge in his refined taste and interest in food. Their version of the story says that like the other Nawabs of Awadh, Wajid Ali Shah gave his master chefs a free hand to experiment in the royal kitchen. While cooking biryani one day, his bawarchis added potatoes to the rice. When the nawab was served the dish, he liked the meat biryani with the potatoes so much that he ordered his bawarchis to make the vegetable a regular feature. This practice continued and the recipe of meat biryani with potatoes gradually spread from the royal kitchen to those of the commoners. Whatever its true provenance, today, the potato is a fixed ingredient in Calcutta biryani, a stark contrast to the original Awadhi version.

The bawarchis working in the royal kitchen of Nawab Wajid Ali Shah in Metiabruz often cooked yakhni pulao and muntanjan as well. Yakhni pulao is a rice preparation that features goat meat. 'Yakhni' means 'rich meat stock'; the rice is cooked in this stock. The mutton pieces are cooked in the pastes of ginger, garlic, onions and red chillies. Whole spices like cardamom, clove, cinnamon and peppercorn are used in the cooking, along with curd. The rice and mutton are cooked separately and then mixed to make this delicious pulao.

Muntanjan is believed to have been a great favourite of Nawab Wajid Ali Shah. It is a sweet rice dish cooked with meat. It is prepared by cooking mutton and rice separately and then mixing them together. The rice is half-cooked with salt and whole garam masala, while the mutton is cooked with fried onions and the pastes of a variety of spices. The cooked mutton is then mixed with the half-cooked rice. A sugar syrup of a thin consistency (to which some lime juice and rose water have been added), and some saffron strands soaked in rose water are put in the pulao. The handi used for cooking is sealed and this sweet rice pulao is cooked till the rice is done.

The legendary moti (pearl) pulao, cooked with meatballs, has an interesting story. Legend has it that the nawab's bawarchis would beat exact quantities of gold and silver foil with egg yolks and stuff these into the gullet of a chicken that had been kept ready for grilling. Once the chicken was cooked and cut open, these foils would come out in the form of shiny golden and silver beads or pearls. The pearls were then added to the pulao, lending the dish its name. The cooked chicken was served alongside the pulao.

Breads like kulcha and sheermal were often made by the royal chefs. Sheermal is a mildly sweet, rich bread made of refined flour, milk, ghee, sugar, salt and saffron strands. It is cooked in an iron tandoor. Nawab Wajid Ali Shah is believed to have loved eating breads with galawati kebab and nargisi kofta. Legend has it that galawati kebab was specially created for the ageing Asaf-ud-Daula, who had a problem chewing meat. Despite this, he continued to be an ardent meat lover and threw an open challenge to his chefs to cook a meat dish that would require very little chewing. His bawarchis came up with this kebab. 'Galawati means "melt in the mouth",' explains Fatima Mirza. The nawab could enjoy this soft meat preparation till the last days of his life. Galawati kebab is prepared by marinating minced meat with raw papaya paste and salt for about half an hour. An assorted variety of spices, the paste of sautéed onions and gram flour are then mixed with this marinated meat paste. A burning coal is placed in the middle of the container holding the meat paste. A tablespoon of ghee is poured on the burning coal. A lid is now placed over the container and it is kept aside for some time. The smoke spreads evenly and becomes infused with the meat, thus enhancing the aroma of the dish. Whisked curd is then added to the meat paste and the mixture is cooked in ghee in a wok. The meat is cooked on low heat and stirred continuously to prevent it from sticking to the wok. Some kewra water is added to the cooked meat. Galawati kebab is served garnished with mint leaves, onion rings and lime wedges. The kebab can also be shaped into patties.

'In Urdu ghazals, ample references are made to "nargisi aankhein" or "beautiful eyes" while describing the beauty of the beloved. The oval-shaped nargisi kofta is supposed to resemble the beautiful human eye,' smiles Mirza. In this preparation, the minced meat is marinated for a couple of hours with the pastes of poppy seeds, coconut, whole red chillies, whole garam masala and onions (both raw and fried). The marinated meat is mixed with gram flour, salt and chopped mint leaves. Hard-boiled eggs are coated with this meat mixture and deep-fried in ghee. The koftas are then halved and garnished with mint leaves. It is believed that even today, Muslim marriages in Lucknow are incomplete without sheermal, nargisi kofta and galawati kebab.

Other traditional Awadhi dishes, which Nawab Wajid Ali Shah is believed to have savoured, are equally elaborate and delicious. One of these, zamindoz, involves a whole fish being cleaned and its stomach slit open and stuffed with pistachios. Lime juice and salt are spread over the body of the fish. The pastes of whole red chillies, poppy seeds, ginger, garlic, aniseed, mace, cardamom, clove and peppercorn, and some curd, are applied on the body of the fish, which is then kept aside to marinate. The whole fish is placed inside a specially designed earthenware pot. This pot is sealed, buried in the ground with about four inches of earth placed over it. Smouldering cow dung cakes are placed on top of it. The heat generated by these cakes cook the fish, which takes around six to eight hours. Zamindoz is eaten with breads or rice.

Kundan kalia is a preparation of mutton with gravy. Fatima Mirza elaborates, '"Kundan" means "jewel". In the days of the Nawab, the mutton pieces were wrapped in edible gold leaves and placed on the gravy to give a touch of luxury to the dish.'

Tali arvi ka salan, a gravy dish of arvi (colocasia) and mutton, was popular in the Metiabruz household during the summer months.

Another popular dish in the Metiabruz household was machli ke shami kebab—fish kebabs made with rohu and eaten with flatbreads.

Shabdeg is a gravy preparation of mutton balls and turnips. The unique feature of this dish is that an effort is made to keep the meatballs and turnips approximately the same size. The turnips are peeled, pricked all over and marinated with salt and the pastes of turmeric and garlic, and then fried to a golden colour. The minced mutton is mixed with the pastes of a variety of spices and salt. Koftas, made of this minced meat, are then deep fried in ghee. The mutton koftas and turnips are cooked in a gravy of spices, curd and mutton stock. The gravy is seasoned with lime juice and salt. Saffron strands dissolved in rose water are added to the dish towards the end and the preparation is cooked over a slow fire. Nawab Wajid Ali Shah was known to relish a well-prepared dish of shabdeg with sheermal. In Urdu, 'shab' means 'night' and true to its name, the dish is cooked overnight in the dum method of cooking. 'Deg' refers to the vessel used for cooking. It is made of copper and suited to the dum style. Fatima Mirza points out, 'Shabdeg was originally a Kashmiri dish that was brought to Awadh by the Kashmiris who migrated to the region during the reign of the nawabs. The Nawabs of Awadh developed a liking for this dish and it became an important part of Awadhi cuisine.'

She further adds, 'Nawab Wajid Ali Shah often went on shikars and hunted birds like partridge and quail, which were then cooked into delicious dishes.' Lagan ke teetar (partridge) and lagan ke bater (quail) were two such dishes. 'Lagan' refers to the vessel used for cooking these dishes. The birds were chopped into pieces and cooked with spices in special round vessels with concave bottoms.

Along with his love for meat, Nawab Wajid Ali Shah also had a sweet tooth and his bawarchis regularly whipped up delicious desserts. One of these, ananas ke muzaffar, is a dessert preparation made with rice and ananas (pineapple). Long-grain rice is partially cooked with saffron and then lightly fried in a karahi (wok) with ghee, cloves and cardamoms. This rice is topped with pineapple pieces and sugar is sprinkled on it. The wok is covered with a lid and the preparation is cooked over a slow fire. The dessert is garnished with chopped cashews, slivers of almonds and raisins. Grated khoya is added and mixed well before serving.

Ande ka halwa was a favourite of the Nawab. This dessert is made with egg whites, milk, sugar, ghee, khoya, cardamom powder, dried fruits and saffron. The inclusion of saffron makes the cooked mixture golden in colour. The mixture is spread evenly on a flat platter, where it hardens quickly. It is then cut into diamonds and served decorated with varak (edible silver leaf).

Shakarkand ki kheer, another favourite, is made with mashed shakarkand (sweet potatoes), milk, cardamom powder, sugar and rose water. The kheer is garnished with edible silver leaves and slivered almonds.

Jauzi ka halwa is a sweet halwa made with lots of jauz (nutmeg)—hence, the name. It is made with samnak (sprouted wheat flour), milk, ghee, sugar, saffron strands dissolved in rose water, spices like nutmeg, mace and green cardamom and nuts such as almonds. This rich dessert was usually served in the Metiabruz household during winter.

Most of the dishes cooked in Nawab Wajid Ali Shah's royal kitchen slowly faded away with the passing of the nawab. The pension that he received from the British dried up after his death and his bawarchis were unable to continue making most of the elaborate dishes due to the high cost of their preparation. The royal kitchen was discontinued shortly after the nawab's death. Besides those few dishes that were tasty as well as easy and cheap to prepare, the general public of the city eschewed most of the Nawabi kitchen's fare. The only exceptions were biryani, *shami kebab* and *shahi tukda*, which spread through the royal chefs and cooks and their descendants and continue to be cooked in Calcutta today.

Shami kebab received its name in a rather peculiar manner. Awadh reached its glorious peak during the reign of the nawabs. Shahanshah Mirza explains, 'During this time, a number of soldiers from Syria came to work in the nawabs' armies. These soldiers brought along with them their dishes and styles of cooking. The Syrian soldiers made a kebab with minced mutton, chana dal and a variety of spices, which came to be known as "Shami Kebab", after the Urdu name for Syria: "Sham".' Today, shami kebab is not only sought after in the restaurants and hotels in Calcutta, but it is even prepared at home by connoisseurs.

Shahi tukda, or 'the royal crumb' has an interesting story too. It is a dish of fried bread soaked in milk and sugar syrup and topped with thickened milk. Very rich in taste and aroma, it was deemed fit for the palate of the royalty. It is believed that this royal dessert was the invention of the bawarchis of a certain Begum of Awadh. Shahanshah Mirza elaborates, 'She would regularly give leftover bread pieces to the poor, but after a little while of doing this, she decided she did not want to give them such plain fare. She dipped the pieces of bread in sugar syrup and gave them to the poor, who enjoyed them very much. After some time, she thought of innovating this dish a little further and added milk, kewra water, saffron, rose water and nuts. On observing the enjoyment of the poor, the Begum instructed her royal chefs to give this wonderful bread dessert a professional touch. The efforts of her chefs gave birth to shahi tukda.' It is now a sought after dessert in many restaurants in the city.

Unfortunately, like the cuisine of the Nawab Nazims, most of the dishes of Awadhi cuisine also failed to make their mark on Calcutta's culinary scene. The cuisine died down with the passing of the nawab and it is possible that the royal chefs and cooks and their descendants either did not have the means or the business acumen to make use of their skills to popularize this fare among the masses.

Mughlai Cuisine

Awadhi cuisine is an extension of Mughlai cuisine, which owes its origin to the Mughal emperors. When these emperors established their rule in India in the sixteenth century, they brought with them their unique style of cooking. This style was dominated by the use of whole and ground spices and a variety of essences and nuts that gave the dishes a rich taste, distinct aroma and robust flavour. Preparations like breads, pulaos, shorba, chaanp, rezala, pasanda, qorma, dopiaza, murgh musallam, nihari, paya, haleem and kebabs formed part of this vast cuisine. Mughlai cuisine was dominant in the northern parts of India, as it was in north India that the Mughals established their rule. The foray of this cuisine into Calcutta began in the nineteenth century with the influx of a large number of Muslim immigrants from Uttar Pradesh.

Mughlai cuisine was commercialized on a big scale in Calcutta in the twentieth century when food entrepreneurs began setting up restaurants specializing in it. The first few entrepreneurs were Muslim immigrants from Uttar Pradesh who had come to Calcutta in search of better opportunities. They made use of their expertise in cooking and set up eateries where the food of their native land was available to all and sundry. The cuisine that they served in these places was mainly Mughlai, but they also served a few Awadhi dishes like biryani, shami kebab and shahi tukda. Royal Indian Hotel and Aminia are the oldest restaurants that took up the daunting task of going commercial with these two cuisines, when Calcutta was still the royal capital. Although the owners of these two restaurants initially played it safe by setting up the outlets in predominantly Muslim localities, the quality of the food served at these places was so good that both Royal Indian Hotel and Aminia have, over time, turned into well-known brands in Calcutta as far as Mughlai and Awadhi fares are concerned.

Both the restaurants began their journey in an environment that was largely oblivious to Mughlai and Awadhi cuisines. The owners of these restaurants hoped that the food they offered would catch on with customers beyond their community. They made a lot of effort to popularize these cuisines, which slowly caught on with the public and established their names in the city's hospitality industry.

A Bengali Meal at Young Bengal Hotel

Photo credit: Arkaprava Ghosh

An Indian Coffee House cup bearing the signature of former Governor of West Bengal, Gopalkrishna Gandhi, in Bengali

Photo credit: Vivek Luke Mukherjee

Indira Debi (Rabindranath Tagore's niece) serving food to Jagdish Mama, Jogesh Chowdhury, Rabindranath Tagore, Jyotirindranath Tagore and Sarala Debi (Rabindranath Tagore's niece)

Image courtesy: Rabindra Bharati Museum, Kolkata

Chicken Chipolata, Magnolia
Photo credit: Vivek Luke Mukherjee

Chimney Soup Bowl at Eau Chew
Photo credit: Arkaprava Ghosh

Biryani, Tandoori Chicken and Kebabs at Royal Indian Hotel
Photo credit: Vivek Luke Mukherjee

Armenian Christmas service being held in Armenian Church of the Holy Nazareth
Photo credit: Rangan Datta

Buying Christmas decorations at Sir Stuart Hogg Market (New Market)
Photo credit: Pallab Pyne

Josephine Huang adding last minute touches to her creation at Eau Chew
Photo credit: Arkaprava Ghosh

David Nahoum with a birthday cake for cricketer Sourav Ganguly

Photo credit: Nahoum & Sons, Kolkata

Khaasdaan (receptacle for keeping paan or be leaf rolls) belonging to Nawab Wajid Ali Shah

Photo credit: Pallab Pyne

Foreign tourists indulging in club sandwiches and orange juice at Flurys

Photo credit: Arkaprava Ghosh

Amrita Kumbha Sandesh at K.C. Das *Image courtesy*: K.C. Das, Kolkata

Abar Khabo Sandesh, Baikuntha Bhog Sandesh, Dedo Sandesh, Ata Sandesh and Kanthal Sandesh at K.C.Das

Image courtesy: K.C. Das, Kolkata

Customers in Zakaria Street Aminia

Photo credit: Arkaprava Ghosh

Lachha Paratha and Channa Masala at Balwant Singh's Eating House
Photo credit: Vivek Luke Mukherjee

Shukto
Photo credit: Pallab Pyne

Grilled Prawns at Flurys

Image courtesy: Flurys, Kolkata

Pan-fried Bhekti at Magnolia

Photo credit: Vivek Luke Mukherjee

Rasogollas at K.C.Das

Photo credit: Vivek Luke Mukherjee

Peliti's (Confectionery and Restaurant) at Government Place (East), Calcutta

Image courtesy: Istituto Centrale per la Grafica, Rome, Italy, By Kind Concession of Ministero dei beni e delle Attivita culturali e del Turismo

Chinese Kali Mandir at Tangra (New Chinatown)

Photo credit: Pallab Pyne

St. Paul's Cathedral

Photo credit: Vivek Luke Mukherjee

Town Hall, Calcutta

Image courtesy: Aakriti Art Gallery Private Limited, Kolkata

White marble (Shwet pathor) plate, tumbler and bowls used by the Tagore family *Image courtesy*: Rabindra Bharati Museum, Kolkata

The Oberoi Grand

Photo credit: Vivek Luke Mukherjee

Firpo's Restaurant

Image courtesy: Enrico De Barbieri

Midnight Mass on Christmas Eve at St. Paul's Cathedral
Photo credit: Vivek Luke Mukherjee

Royal Indian Hotel: Royal Indian Hotel was the first restaurant to offer Mughlai and Awadhi cuisines. Ahmed Hussain was a cook from Lucknow who had spent a large part of his life cooking in the royal kitchens of the Nawabs. This experience had made him a master of his craft. When Lucknow saw the end of Nawabi rule, Ahmed Hussain packed his bags and travelled to the royal capital to make it on his own. He was clever enough to make use of his cooking skills and set up a small eatery on Chitpur Road in 1905 where he served rumali roti, paratha and chaanp. He was fondly called 'Pehelwan Chaanpwala' by the residents of the area. He had a shrewd business acumen, evidenced by the fact that he chose Chitpur as his base. Its closeness to the river made Chitpur a very important centre of commercial activity. On a daily basis, the area would be inundated with Muslim traders, most of whom were often on the lookout for quick, scrumptious meals.

It was khushka and alu ka salan (potato curry) that popularized this eatery beyond Chitpur. Khushka is a pulao-like preparation made with long-grain rice, onions, tomatoes, spices, herbs, ghee and lime juice or curd. Muslims usually eat it with accompanying preparations like salan (curry), qorma (a yoghurt-based curry), dahi (curd), raita (a yoghurt-based condiment) and chutney. In the colonial days, a weekly wholesale clothing market called Mangla Haat was set up in Howrah where ostagars (garment businessmen) from the suburbs of Calcutta put up stalls to sell their wares. The business-savvy Ahmed Hussain thought that this would be a good place to publicize his eatery. He put up a kiosk in Mangla Haat every Tuesday, selling khushka and alu ka salan. The ostagars loved these dishes and thus, came to know about Ahmed Hussain's eatery on Chitpur Road. Whenever they came to Calcutta on work, they would drop into Pehelwan Chaanpwala Ka Dukan.

Gradually, the range of dishes served at the eatery increased. The food gained popularity thanks to its good quality and delicious taste. The customer base was not just restricted to Muslims anymore; this was a stepping stone in promoting Mughlai and Awadhi cuisines in the city as people from outside the Muslim community gradually began trying them out.

The economy of the city was not in a good shape after Independence. The common folk did not have money to spend on luxury goods. They did not have enough to spare on eating out luxuriously, and were always on the lookout for filling, inexpensive meals. Biryani is a wholesome meal in itself and it is not necessary to ask for an accompanying dish when one orders it. Although biryani had been available in the eatery earlier, it was only after Independence that it became the most-ordered dish.

The biryani that Ahmed Hussain prepared was the authentic Awadhi kind that did not feature potatoes. It was full of kofti (meat balls), and cinnamon did not feature in the cooking as well. Cloves, cardamom and saffron were a part of the exquisite spice range that was used to cook the biryani. The dish served in the restaurant exceeded everybody's expectations and became popular, overshadowing the eatery's other dishes.

It was during Ahmed Hussain's son Mehboob Ali's tenure that the eatery (which by then had become a full-fledged restaurant) was given the name of Royal Indian Hotel. To its loyal customers, however, the restaurant became popularly known as Royal. With time, Royal's biryani, along with its chaanp, became the signature dishes of the restaurant. Customers took a great liking to this combination. The chaanp at the restaurant is prepared with mutton or chicken. Royal's chicken chaanp is rich in spices and has curd, kewra water, sweet attar, gram flour and saffron as some of the main ingredients. Customers also could not get enough of Royal's soft mutton tikia kebabs.

The location of Royal Indian Hotel has tremendously helped enhance the reputation of the restaurant. Chitpur is a busy commercial area where people are always on the lookout for quick luncheons and the quality food that Royal serves brings in customers in droves. It is believed that eminent personalities like Ustad Bade Ghulam Ali Khan, Khushwant Singh, Satyajit Ray and Uttam Kumar have graced the restaurant.

In 1997, the restaurant turned into a private limited company and is now known as Royal Indian Hotel Private Limited. At present, it is run by the third generation of the family. The owners are constantly adding new dishes to the menu like nargisi kofta and shahi tukda. The new dishes have eclipsed old ones like khushka and alu ka salan, which Ahmed Hussain had used as tools to advertise his dukan in areas beyond Chitpur. These old dishes have gradually disappeared from the menu and been replaced with more flavourful ones that have made Royal Indian Hotel a household name in Calcutta.

Aminia: Aminia, a popular eatery in Calcutta today, is well known for its biryani. The story behind the establishment of this restaurant is an interesting one because it began with a little boy named Mohammed

Amin who threw a tantrum at his father Maulvi Abdul Rahim, one day, while returning home after attending the midday prayer at the mosque.

Maulvi Abdul Rahim was the son of Abdul Karim, who lived in Dariyabad, a town in the Barabanki district of Uttar Pradesh. Abdul Karim was the descendant of a sepoy who had participated in the Revolt of 1857. After the revolt died down, the British officers were on the trail of the 'traitorous' sepoys who had participated in the mutiny. The family of Abdul Karim fled to Dariyabad and took up weaving as a profession.

Abdul Karim decided to settle in Calcutta for better prospects. He bought a house in Mechua Bazar, where he lived with his family, and set up a small eatery in the area that began doing well with time. One day, Abdul Karim came into contact with an alchemist and became enchanted with the idea of making gold. He went back to Dariyabad, leaving the business in the care of his son, Abdul Rahim. In Dariyabad, Abdul Karim turned a small room in his haveli into a laboratory. Though the eatery in Mechua Bazar was doing well under the supervision of Abdul Rahim, the money he sent to his father was blown away in gold-making endeavours. When confronted, the father became furious at the audacity of his son and turned him out of the business and subsequently, out of his property.

With his savings, Abdul Rahim set up a kiosk in Mechua Bazar. He sold snacks from this kiosk. With time, he gathered enough funds to buy over the Mechua Bazar eatery from his father and start the business all over again. Soon, Abdul Rahim had made a success out of this eatery and his entire family, which had been settled in Dariyabad, joined him in Calcutta.

It was against this background that Mohammed Amin threw the tantrum, which went on to become famous in the family, and led to the establishment of Aminia. Abdul Rahim was an indulgent father and when his son refused to budge from the ground where he had squatted and was shedding copious tears, demanding on whim that the 'Pehelwan Ka Hotel' on Zakaria Street belonged to the family, the father could not help but oblige. Maulvi Abdul Rahim bought the hotel and set up an eatery in its place that served Mughlai and Awadhi dishes. He named the eatery Aminia after his son. This was in the year 1929.

Since the inception of the restaurant, biryani has been a fixed part of the menu. Aminia can be hailed as a pioneer in commercializing the biryani alongside Royal Indian Hotel. The biryani served in Aminia utilizes alu as had been the practice in the royal kitchen of Nawab Wajid Ali Shah.

Besides the usual fare, Abdul Rahim introduced two special dishes in Aminia, which continue even today. One of them was haleem, a delicacy made with four different types of lentil, broken wheat (dalia), juice of goat trotters, boneless meat, rice, spices, onions, curd, ghee, coriander leaves, mint leaves and green chillies. This dish has the consistency of khichdi and is slow cooked over a low flame, which blends the flavours of all the ingredients. Haleem can be eaten on its own or with breads. Maulvi Abdul Rahim introduced this dish in the 1930s after a trip to Mecca. He served it only during Ramzan, when devotees from the nearby mosque would drop into the restaurant after their prayers, and buy takeaway bags of haleem. When haleem was introduced in the Zakaria Street Aminia, the restaurant would sell 300 to 400 plates of the dish every day in the month of Ramzan. Today, the orders for this dish have risen to 3,000 to 4,000 plates a day during this month.

The second special dish introduced by Maulvi Abdul Rahim was the heavily spiced stew, nihari. Nihari, at the restaurant, is made of meat (with bones), twenty-six different types of spices, onions, curd, ghee, flour, rose or kewra water, star anise and sea salt. The word 'nihari' is derived from 'nihar', which means 'morning' in Urdu. The dish is cooked overnight and served in the morning during winter when customers drop into the restaurant after fajr prayers. During this season, the restaurant remains open way past midnight, preparing the nihari for the next morning. Since the climate of Calcutta is generally hot and humid, the owners of Aminia prefer serving this heavily spiced dish during winter because the ingredients are said to generate heat in the body. The tradition of serving breakfast in the Zakaria Street Aminia has been in place since its inception and the menu includes paya (trotters curry), brain curry, mutton liver curry, keema (minced meat) curry, kidney curry and tandoori roti.

After Maulvi Abdul Rahim passed away in 1940, his eldest son Abdul Qayum took over the business. Five years later, Mohammed Amin, who had now grown into a man, joined the family business. Qayum looked after the administrative side of the business while Amin looked after the production. Soon, both brothers decided to expand the business and began searching for a new property. There was a restobar in Futnani Chambers, which was located very near to the Calcutta Corporation. The place was also a stone's throw from Sir Stuart Hogg Market. The owners of this restobar were looking for prospective buyers. Since Sir Stuart Hogg Market is a shoppers' paradise, the brothers saw this as a golden opportunity and bought the plot. On 15 August 1946, the second Aminia restaurant opened its doors to the food-loving public of Calcutta, who rechristened it as New Market Aminia.

Abdul Qayum monitored the New Market Aminia while Mohammed Amin looked after their old property on Zakaria Street. The New Market Aminia began to flourish mainly because of the Calcutta Football League. In the 1970s, football lovers would watch matches at the nearby Eden Gardens and then search for restaurants to dine in. They began dropping in at New Market Aminia. The boom in the number of Hindi films shown in the cinema halls in and around New Market (which began in the late 1970s) was another factor that bolstered the business at New Market Aminia. Many cinema lovers began dropping into Aminia for quick meals after shows.

Abdul Qayum began making certain changes in the preparation of the food served at the New Market Aminia in order to cater to the palate of its large number of Bengali customers. Bengalis are sweet-loving people and have the tendency to put a little sugar in their curries. Abdul Qayum brought down the spiciness and oiliness in the restaurant's preparations. He made the gravies sweeter by adding more onions to them. Thus, a customer will find the mutton rezala, mutton masala and mutton and chicken chaanps at the New Market Aminia to be slightly modified versions. He also advised the cooks to add a little sugar in the paratha dough. The gravy in some of the dishes was made runny to make it appear like *jhol*—the favourite Bengali curry. The Aminia Special, for instance, is a runny gravy with an egg, a piece of mutton, one potato, one onion, one tomato and a slice of carrot. The dish is full of flavours and not too many spices go into its preparation. But these changes have been made only in the New Market Aminia and not in the old one, since the customer profile at Zakaria Street Aminia still remains predominantly Muslim with very authentic and conservative taste.

There was a time when European bread pudding, shahi tukda, firni (rice-based pudding) and gajar ka halwa were served in the restaurant, but today, only firni and the pudding persist. Since 2006, beef dishes have been introduced in the Zakaria Street Aminia and vegetarian dishes in the New Market Aminia to attract more diners, taking into consideration the localities and customer profiles.

*

Both Royal Indian Hotel and Aminia are pioneers when it comes to commercially launching Mughlai and Awadhi cuisines in Calcutta. These restaurants have made biryani the favourite eating-out option of the people of the city. Aminia moved out of the confines of the traditional Muslim locality and was bold enough to branch into the heart of Calcutta, Sir Stuart Hogg Market. This attempt was a brave one and it paid off. Sir Stuart Hogg Market is the hub of shopping in the city and filled with customers nearly every day. The strategic location of the restaurant has helped tremendously in attracting new customers who simply cannot get enough of the delicious Mughlai and Awadhi dishes served here. Over the years, the restaurant has carved a niche for itself in the city thanks to the quality of its food.

Nizam's Restaurant: When discussing Mughlai and Awadhi cuisines in Calcutta, it will be a mistake not to mention Nizam's Restaurant. Nizam's, as it is popularly known, is a Mughlai and Awadhi restaurant that was set up during the Company Raj period, but its signature dish over the years has become its kathi rolls.

Rolls are to the residents of Calcutta what fish and chips are to the residents of London—an inexpensive, filling meal that they eat while walking to their next port of call. Today, in every nook and cranny of the city, there are kiosks selling rolls to customers. But the pioneer of the roll culture in Calcutta was Nizam's.

Sheikh Hassan Raza left his family in Uttar Pradesh and came to Calcutta in search of a better life. He managed to find a job in Calcutta Corporation. He had a son named Sheikh Nizamuddin. When he was on the verge of retirement, Sheikh Hassan Raza thought of starting a kiosk in Sir Stuart Hogg Market from where he would sell parathas and kebabs. The market was owned by Calcutta Corporation and the authorities were then auctioning plots to prospective buyers. Sheikh Hassan Raza bought a small plot of land in the name of his son Nizamuddin. This was in 1932, now regarded as the year of establishment of Nizam's.

It was during this time that a young cook named Khalifa came to Calcutta from Uttar Pradesh in search of employment. It is not certain how this cook came into contact with Sheikh Hassan Raza, but the two somehow crossed paths and decided to make and sell parathas and kebabs together. The kebabs were prepared by lightly marinating meat pieces with spices and curd. The marinated meat pieces were threaded onto iron skewers and cooked in a tandoor filled with burning coals.

In the days of the Company Raj, Sir Stuart Hogg Market was reserved for Europeans and locals were not allowed in its premises, except for the shopkeepers. The Lindsay Street area was always brimming with white sahibs and memsahibs. These Europeans tried the parathas and kebabs that Sheikh Hassan Raza and Khalifa made, and enjoyed them tremendously. They suggested selling the kebabs stuffed inside the parathas and not separately, so that their fingers would not get greasy while eating. The owner and his employee began stuffing the kebabs into the parathas, rolling the latter into cylinders and wrapping the ends with torn pieces of newspaper. This method of serving gave birth to the concept of Calcutta's rolls.

Soon, Nizamuddin joined his father in the business. The different kinds of kebab made at the restaurant in those days were of mutton, beef, and khiri (cow's udder). Nizam's was inundated with customers. Soon, Sheikh Hassan Raza had converted his kiosk into a full-fledged restaurant. He named the restaurant Nizam's, an abbreviation of Nizamuddin.

Nizam's rolls reached dizzying heights of popularity among the general public, particularly after Independence. In 1964, chicken rolls were introduced on the menu and kathis (bamboo sticks) replaced the iron skewers used to cook the kebabs that were stuffed in the rolls, giving rise to the new name 'kathi rolls'. Today, Nizam's is regarded as the pioneer of kathi rolls, although the dish itself has spread throughout the city.

After Sheikh Hassan Raza passed away, Nizamuddin took charge of the restaurant. He expanded the menu to include breakfast, lunch and dinner dishes. The breakfast spread included puri-sabzi, flatbreads, a chicken liver preparation, keema curry and jalebis that were served as early as six in the morning. The lunch and dinner menus included biryani and accompanying curry dishes like chaanp, qorma, masala and kassa. Firni and the traditional ice cream, kulfi, were introduced in the restaurant as these light desserts went well with the heavy meals. However, the serving of breakfast has been discontinued.

Today, Nizam's list of kathi rolls is long and varied. It includes off-beat varieties like alu roll, paneer roll and egg alu roll. The cooks at the restaurant, not content to rest easy on their laurels, have experimented with ingredients to create an impressive variety of such rolls. The kathi rolls of Nizam's are believed to have found favour with a young Shashi Kapoor and his wife Jennifer Kendal when they would visit Calcutta for their theatrical performances and check into the nearby Fairlawn Hotel on Sudder Street.

*

The cuisine of the Nawab Nazims did have some impact on the food habits of Calcuttans. Murgh qorma, machli ka kalia, tikia kebab, dal gosht and seekh kebab made their mark in the city because of Mir Jafar, who was domiciled in Calcutta for a few years. These dishes are prepared in many of the restaurants and hotels in the city today. Mahi pulao has been a new entrant in the hospitality scene of Calcutta and has now found its way onto the menu of most of its upscale restaurants and hotels. Awadhi cuisine, on the other hand, has turned out to be too elaborate, costly and time-consuming, and has hence not been included on many restaurant bills of fare. There was also hardly any effort on the part of the royal chefs and cooks and their descendants to popularize this cuisine among the general public. For these reasons, alu biryani, shami kebab and shahi tukda are the only dishes that moved out of the confines of the Nawab's kitchen and left a lasting impression on the city. Recently, however, there have been attempts in some of the restaurants and hotels to resurrect the nargisi kofta and galawati kebab. Manzilat's has also come as a ray of hope for connoisseurs and enthusiasts of Awadhi cuisine. Manzilat Fatima, the great-great-granddaughter of Nawab Wajid Ali Shah, has been organizing, since 2014, pop-up restaurants in Calcutta that serve authentic Awadhi cuisine. She has also begun a home dining service called Manzilat's in 2018. Since she has begun this journey, her dishes have been creating quite a stir. She is slowly and steadily winning a loyal following, and playing a considerable role in promoting Awadhi cuisine in the city.

The Muslims in Calcutta, who have long been part of the city's cosmopolitan landscape, have cooked their home cuisine but often kept the dishes confined to their own kitchens. It was up to the owners of pioneering restaurants to bring it to the eyes and mouths of the public, to blaze the trail and make way for other food entrepreneurs to open restaurants offering similar dishes.

3. Chinese Influences

Historical documents show that itinerant Chinese tradesmen, monks, scholars and travellers have been visiting India since a long time. The first recorded account of travel from China to India is the text by Chinese Buddhist monk Faxian (Fa-Hien). In the fifth century CE,

Faxian visited Tamralipta, an ancient city on the Bay of Bengal, strongly believed by scholars to be the site of the town Tamluk, currently the headquarters of the Midnapore (East) district of West Bengal. Tamralipta was not only a very prominent international port and centre of trade and commerce but also an important Buddhist centre of learning, abounding with monasteries and monks. Xuanzang (Hiuen Tsang) and Yijing (I-Tsing) were the other important Chinese Buddhist monks who visited Bengal in the seventh century CE.

Documents name Yang Tai Chow (also known as Yang Dazhao) as the first Chinese immigrant to settle in Calcutta. Probably a tea trader by profession, he landed near Budge Budge in 1778 with the intention of setting up a sugarcane plantation and sugar factory. Warren Hastings granted Yang Tai Chow some land to turn his plans into reality. It is a recorded fact that 110 Chinese workers joined Yang Tai Chow soon after. This was the first Chinese settlement in India.

Yang Tai Chow's goal was to save enough money from his sugar business to start off in the tea trade, but he gradually became plagued with troubles due to lack of funds. He took loans from the British East India Company, but his fortunes never looked up. Yang Tai Chow died broken-hearted around 1783. He was known by various names such as Yong Atchew or Tong Atchew. Since he signed his letters as Yong Atchew, the British called him by that name. But, locally, he had been known as Tong Achi. The area where he established his first settlement came to be known as Achipur, thirty-three kilometres from Calcutta, near Budge Budge. There are no Chinese inhabitants living in Achipur today. But Yang Tai Chow's scarlet horseshoe-shaped tomb can still be seen on the banks of the Hooghly in Achipur. The tomb has become a shrine that is visited by the Chinese community of Calcutta every year, during the Chinese New Year festival (which usually takes place in the months of January or February), to pay tribute to the man who established the first Chinese settlement in India. Yang Tai Chow's sugar mill no longer exists, but his efforts may have contributed to the new word for sugar—chini—which is derived from 'Cheen', the Bengali and Hindi word for China. After his death, his workers and associates moved to Calcutta and joined Chinese sailors who had practically been press-ganged into service in Macau. They had deserted their ship and were waiting for a friendly vessel to take them home. This is how the Chinese community made their first foray into Calcutta.

Waves of Chinese immigration to Calcutta followed. The earliest immigrants were the Hakkas, a group of shoemakers who settled in Old China Bazar Street. Their descendants continue to make reasonably priced shoes of good quality here. The community name of the Hakkas has been used to describe the most popular noodle dish in the city today, Hakka noodles. Authors Sipra Mukherjee and Sarvani Gooptu in their essay, 'The Chinese Community of Calcutta: An Interview with Paul Chung', from the book, *Calcutta Mosaic: Essays and Interviews on the Minority Communities of Calcutta* (2009), point out, 'A police record preserved in the public records of the Government of India dating back to 1788 indicates that a sizeable Chinese population settled near Bow Bazar Street' (p. 131). The Chinese book *A Maritime Record* (1820) mentions that Calcutta housed a small Chinese population from Fujian (Fukien) and Guangdong. Many of these Chinese were engaged in the opium business in the aftermath of the First Opium War, fought between the British and the Qing Empire from 1839 to 1842. During this time, a wave of Chinese nationals migrated to Calcutta. The instability and chaos caused by the Xinhai Revolution (10 October 1911–12 February 1912), the Chinese revolutionary movement against the Qing Empire that ended imperialism and established the Republic of China, brought another wave of Chinese nationals to Calcutta. By the 1930s, the number of Chinese women and children had increased considerably as entire families migrated to Calcutta. The forefathers of most of the current generation of Calcutta Chinese arrived during the turbulent days of the Kuomintang rule (1927 to 1948).

By the mid-nineteenth century, the Calcutta Chinese had made a reputation for themselves as skilled and industrious workers. The Chinese shoemakers of Cossitollah (later Bentinck Street) made shoes that were beautiful in design but reasonably priced. Even today, Bentinck Street is famous for its shoe shops. All the carpenters working on the ships that thronged the Port of Calcutta were Chinese. The skills of the Chinese mechanics and artisans were considered matchless. The only drawback of the community was its association with opium. The licensed opium dens in Calcutta were controlled by Chinese people on the whole, until they were declared illegal after Independence.

The Second World War (1 September 1939–2 September 1945) also precipitated Chinese immigration into Calcutta. The 1951 census records show 5,710 people of Chinese origin living in the city. The Cultural Revolution (1966-1976), a sociopolitical movement initiated by Mao Zedong (then chairman of the Communist Party of China), saw another wave of Chinese nationals flooding the city. With time, the number of Chinese people in the city gradually increased and a 1990 survey showed their population in Calcutta to be 20,000. A majority of them had Indian citizenship and had been given voting rights.

A City of Chinatowns

Today, Calcutta is the only city in the country that has not one, but two Chinatowns, an old one and a new one. The first Chinatown, known as Old Chinatown, is located in central Calcutta. It began as a concentration of Chinese immigrants who came to Calcutta either for better economic prospects or to escape the various sociopolitical disturbances that were taking place in China. The New Chinatown, located in east Calcutta, came up much later because of business compulsion. Today, New Chinatown has to a great extent overshadowed the old one and become an area bustling with members from the community, who have their various business establishments, residences, places of worship and academic institutions in it. New Chinatown is also the hub of Chinese eateries, making it an iconic landmark for connoisseurs and food enthusiasts.

In Calcutta, Chinese people practise Taoism (also known as Daoism), Buddhism, Confucianism and Christianity. Although Islam is also practised by Chinese people, not much is known about Chinese Muslims in Calcutta. The Chinese places of worship continue to be frequently attended in both Old and New Chinatowns. As strange as it may seem, their numerous Taoist temples in Old Chinatown are called churches by the members of the community in Calcutta. There are two plausible explanations for this. Firstly, it is believed that the grand churches built by the British colonialists in the city made a lasting impression on the early Chinese settlers. Secondly, they did not know the exact English word for their place of worship.

The community observes its own festivals in Calcutta, like the Chinese New Year, which is based on the Chinese Lunar Calendar. The first day of this festival is celebrated with lights, firecrackers, lion and dragon dances, and traditional music like beating drums and striking gongs and cymbals. The celebration lasts for fifteen days and ends with the Lantern Festival on the last day. This festival is observed by hanging colourful lanterns that are made of paper and bamboo, and eating glutinous (sticky) rice balls, traditionally made with a variety of sweet fillings. This sweet dessert is symbolic of a sweet reunion. The sticky rice symbolizes inseparability and the round shape, a never-ending unity and harmony within the family. The Chinese New Year is followed by the

Rice Pudding Festival, celebrated five months later. In mid-autumn, the full moon is worshipped, in the hope that it will bring a plentiful harvest the following year. In Calcutta, the Moon Festival sees a profusion in the production of the traditional and delicious round moon-shaped cakes.

Over the years, the contribution of the Chinese community to the economic sphere of the city has been considerable, particularly in setting up tanneries, beauty parlours, restaurants and laundries. The different Chinese groups in the city have maintained their divisions with respect to the kind of businesses they are engaged in. The Hakka community are tanners and shoemakers, the Hupeh are dentists, the Cantonese are carpenters and restaurateurs and the laundries are the stronghold of Chinese people who trace their origins to Shanghai. Chinese entrepreneurs have also ventured into the food processing industry, like the manufacturing of sauces, pickles and processed seafood. Sing Cheung is Calcutta's oldest and largest Chinese sauce manufacturing company, established in 1954. It was followed by Pou Chong, which was established in 1958 and manufactures Chinese sauces and noodles. Both Sing Cheung and Pou Chong not only supply bulk quantities of their products to a majority of the restaurants and hotels in the city, but also sell them in retail outlets. Sing Cheung has its own retail outlet on Lu Hsun Sarani in Old Chinatown while its factory is located in New Chinatown in Tangra. Pou Chong, also with its factory in New Chinatown in Tangra, has branched out into three retail outlets, two of which are located in and around the Tiretta Bazar area in Old Chinatown.

Two Chinese newspapers—*The Chinese Journal of India* and *The Overseas Chinese Commerce of India* are published in the city. The community has quite a few schools, clubs and associations in Calcutta that form an essential part of their social life, such as the Indian Chinese Association for Culture, Welfare and Development on Park Street.

Chinese Cuisine

Today, Chinese cuisine is the most popular eating-out option in Calcutta. Over the years, Chinese immigrants have adapted their cuisine to suit the tastes of the local people who simply cannot get enough of chilli garlic noodles and prawn in red pepper sauce, creating a veritable new fusion cuisine known as Indian-Chinese. But a visit to Chinese homes at mealtime is a revelation, because the food they eat is very different from that served in restaurants and hotels. Authentic Chinese food is comparatively bland, and relies more on sauces than spices to add flavour.

China is a very large country with at least fifty-six recognized distinct ethnic groups and correspondingly diverse food preferences. The people of the Szechwan, Hunan and Guizhou provinces like to eat spicy food, for which they use ginger, garlic, shallots, peppercorns, star anise and chilli peppers. Guizhou cuisine also has a mix of the sour and spicy flavours, which gives it a distinct taste. The cuisine of Beijing is marked by simpler, less spicy, salty and crisp food. Cantonese cuisine lays great stress on steaming and is famous for its dim sum. Fujian cuisine is light, flavourful, less salty and has a slightly sweet and sour taste. The cooking style is marked by the liberal use of fish sauce and peanuts.

South China boasts of a high level of rice production as the climate in this part of the country is warmer and rainfall plentiful. North China, on the other hand, with its cold and dry winters and hot summers has the highest level of wheat production. This dictates the food habits of the residents of the two regions. Wheat-based products, like noodles, dumplings, pancakes, mantou (steamed bun) and stuffed buns, form the staple food of the northerners. Dumplings are served with hot sauces for dipping and noodles are served either stir-fried or in soups. The southerners tend to eat more rice, with long-grain and glutinous rice varieties being common. The latter is also known as sweet rice and is eaten with the help of chopsticks, a pair of traditional dining tools that was first used by the Chinese and later spread to other countries in East Asia. The Chinese use chopsticks to eat noodles as well. Early chopsticks were made of bamboo or wood. Modern times have seen the entry of plastic and stainless-steel chopsticks, while restaurants prefer single-use disposable ones.

The two major elements of Chinese food are fan (grains and other starch-based staples) and the two types of cai—sucai and huncai. Sucai are vegetable dishes and huncai are non-vegetarian dishes like fish or meat. Dairy products are markedly absent in Chinese cooking. Rice, noodles, buns, vegetables, tofu, mushrooms, fish, shellfish, poultry and meat form the staple foods and are cooked with a variety of sauces and seasonings. Fruits have limited use in Chinese cuisine and lentils, none at all. It is a largely meat-based cuisine, with liberal use of chicken, pork, beef, duck and mutton, among others. Popular seasonings include soya bean sauce, vinegar, rice wine, ginger, garlic, leeks, star anise, sweet bean sauces, chilli peppers, scallions and sesame oil.

Soups of all kinds are popular, and vegetables for the main course are often served in a slightly soupy form. The hot pot is a traditional way of eating soup, which remains popular in Chinese cuisine. Hot pot is a winter meal and its concept, very simple. A large pot of simmering, mildly flavoured and fragrant soup is placed on a portable burner in the middle of the table. Plates of tofu, mushrooms, leafy green vegetables, vegetables, fish, seafood, molluscs like squid and cuttlefish, cooked and sliced eggs, meat and noodles, steamed white rice or cooked dumplings surround the pot. The food items are sliced thin so that they cook quickly and evenly when they are thrown into the soup. The soup with the cooked fillings is served in bowls, along with accompanying dishes of dipping sauces. Family and friends eat a hot pot together, making it a communal meal.

Chinese food is often roasted, braised or stir-fried, but oily and deep-fried foods are not preferred. The iconic example of a roasted Chinese dish is Peking Duck. Peking was the English name for the capital city, Beijing. Peking Duck became a popular imperial dish in the fifteenth century during the Ming dynasty (1368–1644 CE). The popularity of this roasted duck dish spread from the imperial court to the nobility and upper classes in the Qing dynasty (1644–1912 CE), and gradually to the rest of society. Today, Peking Duck is the face of Beijing's cuisine and restaurants throughout the capital specialize in this dish. A handful of Chinese restaurants in Calcutta too make Peking Duck. Among these, the fine-dining Chinese restaurant Chinoiserie in Taj Bengal, stands out for its authentic preparation of the dish. In contrast, stir-frying is a method of cooking in which the ingredients are fried in small amounts of very hot oil while being stirred in a wok. This method of cooking became popular during the Ming dynasty, when increasing urbanization required speedy methods of cooking. In stir-frying, food is cooked very quickly without wasting any fuel or overusing oil.

'Huo buo' (fire-timing) is a major factor in Chinese cooking. It basically refers to the cooking time, which varies from preparation to preparation. For example, it may take quite some time to cook few dishes or a few minutes to cook something like stir-fries. Traditionally, animal fats like lard, beef tallow and schmaltz were used as the main mediums of cooking, and they added their flavours to the food. But these mediums have now been replaced with cooking oils like soya bean oil, corn oil and peanut oil because of health considerations.

Old Chinatown

The Chinese community from Achipur settled first in Chitpur after Tong Achi's death. But when the Calcutta Corporation began making concerted efforts to develop the area, the Chinese community moved to the Sun Yat Sen Street locale near Poddar Court, named after the first President and founding father of the Republic of China. They established a miniature Chinatown in the area, where they built homes, spoke their own language, established shops and other small business establishments, constructed traditional temples, founded schools, set up social clubs and cooked authentic Chinese food. This Old Chinatown, which has been in existence since the 1800s, is located in central Calcutta around Bentinck Street, Phears Lane and the adjoining part of Rabindra Sarani (Chitpur). A street in the area has even been rechristened Lu Hsun Sarani after the Chinese literary great Zhou Shuren who wrote under the pen name Lu Hsun.

When the Chinese community first settled in Calcutta, they kept up their cuisine in the new land. They prepared everything at their homes in Old Chinatown, right from hand-drawing noodles to creating sauces from scratch, because these ingredients were not available in the local markets. Gradually, a few entrepreneurs began setting up eateries in Old Chinatown for all those who had migrated to the new land without their families and found it difficult to cook at home. Most of these eateries were set up inside Chinese homes, where they served authentic and original Chinese food like soups, hot pot, dumplings, mantou, stuffed buns, pancakes, roast duck and roast pork, steamed and fried rice, noodles and steamed chicken. A few Chinese residents began gathering every morning at Tiretta Bazar, a marketplace in Old Chinatown, to sell home-cooked food for breakfast. Hawkers would gather in a lane near the Lal Bazar police station to sell vegetables, fish, meat and other ingredients required for daily cooking. It was a morning bazar that began at daybreak and wrapped up before the business activities in the area began.

Chinese men and women began sitting by the wayside at this morning bazar. They sold hot noodles and fish or meatballs soup, crispy roasted pork belly slices, steamed dumplings called siu mai with fish or meat fillings, crispy spring rolls and oversized dumplings called baozi, with fish, chicken or pork fillings. Delicious zongzis—glutinous rice dumplings with fillings, wrapped in bamboo leaves and cooked by steaming or boiling—were available on most days. Desserts like sweet balls made of rice and sesame seeds as well as rice and grated coconut were also sold. During winter, Chinese sausages (lap cheong) made of pork and hanging from ropes beckoned customers. It became a ritual every Sunday to slice roasted suckling pigs called sau chu and serve them to eager Chinese customers. This tradition of the Chinese selling home-made breakfast at Tiretta Bazar has continued since the early years of their settlement in Old Chinatown, and has become popular with the general public.

Dominic Lee, chief executive officer and managing director of Pou Chong Food Products Pvt. Ltd, says, 'By the 1930s, Old Chinatown was filled with eateries that served authentic Chinese cuisine, and word of them began to spread beyond its boundaries. Officers working for the British East India Company and customers from the upper classes of Calcutta society decided to experiment with this kind of food. They began gathering at the eateries in Old Chinatown out of curiosity and enjoyed the dishes served. Soon, authentic Chinese cuisine in Calcutta turned into a niche affair that was enjoyed by the cream of society.' Observing this boom in Chinese cuisine in Calcutta, a couple of small units began manufacturing and selling noodles to the Chinese people based in the city. Chinese entrepreneurs also set up factories to manufacture the sauces which were used in Chinese cooking.

Customers relished the mini meals at the legendary kiosk, **Fat Mama**, named after its large lady owner, who served her customers generous helpings of fried rice and noodles for reasonable prices. Fat Mama is still remembered for some of the best breakfasts: rice noodle soup with stir-fried vegetables and chicken juliennes.

Chung Wah was the first proper Chinese restaurant to open in Calcutta. It was set up on Chittaranjan Avenue in central Calcutta by a Chinese immigrant named Au, who was a carpenter by profession. At that time, the menu not only included authentic Chinese dishes but also certain European delicacies like pickled fish, roasted pigeon, prawns on toast and fish chowder. Chung Wah was also famous for its delicious crab soup.

Nanking was the first fancy Chinese restaurant in the city, set up on Blackburn Lane in Old Chinatown. It opened its doors in 1924 and became famous for its baked crab. It was housed on the ground floor of a beautiful two-storeyed brick red building. On the first floor of the building was a Chinese temple known as the Toong On Church, dedicated to their warrior god, Kuan Ti. Dominic Lee adds, 'It is believed that British officials would arrive in their tongas to dine in the classy restaurant, whose interior was brought to life by the soulful music of violins'.

Nearly all the Chinese restaurants in Calcutta today serve dishes that are the adapted and spiced-up versions of authentic Chinese cuisine. Even Chung Wah has replaced the authentic Chinese cuisine that it once served with this adapted version to keep up with customer preferences. Chung Wah and Eau Chew are the remnants of the Chinese restaurants of the pre-Independence era of Calcutta. Fat Mama gradually came to a close after the death of the owner and Nanking closed down in the 1970s. The problem with most of the old eateries and restaurants was that the next generation was not interested in continuing the business, leading to most of them downing their shutters. For instance, Au, the owner of Chung Wah, had a son named Henry. Henry Au took over the restaurant after his father had passed away. But his children were not interested in the business and took up other professions, while his grandchildren migrated to Canada. This compelled him to sell the rights of the restaurant. Today, Chung Wah is a private limited company, but Eau Chew is still a family-owned restaurant that continues to serve its customers delicious Chinese fare.

Eau Chew: On winter days, one can see customers filling their bowls with Eau Chew's signature gyako (chimney soup). This is the most renowned of all the preparations made in this restaurant, and is similar to the hot pot. Eau Chew's chimney soup has egg drop, vegetables, chicken, pork, prawns and fish cubes cooked in the stock. Boiled noodles can be added to the soup on request. The soup is served in a special chimney soup bowl with a spout. It is cooked on a charcoal stove and a piece of hot charcoal is placed inside the spout of the soup bowl. This gives a slightly burnt taste to the soup which customers find rather appealing.

The Chinese canteen, Eau Chew, was set up in the 1920s on Ganesh Chandra Avenue and became a regular haunt of the inhabitants of Old Chinatown. The Indian Chinese Association considers Eau Chew to be the oldest family-owned Chinese restaurant in India. While walking down the crowded avenue, one comes across a petrol station, above which is a yellow board emblazoned with the name 'Eau Chew'. A flight of wooden stairs leads to the first floor of the building, which houses the restaurant.

Eau Chew was set up by Chinese immigrants Chi Thien Huang and his wife, Cheng Shih. Chi Thien Huang migrated to Calcutta in the early twentieth century from Moiyenin Guangdong province in the People's Republic of China. He rented a house on Ganesh Chandra

Avenue, where he opened a small canteen, serving home-style meals to his countrymen in this alien land. There were a number of Chinese singletons in the city at the time who longed for home-cooked food. Most of these bachelors were settled in Old Chinatown, and the news that a new Chinese canteen had opened nearby brought many of them to Eau Chew.

Eau Chew literally means 'Europe' in Mandarin. The restaurant was so named to lure British customers. A major factor that worked in its favour during the first few years was its location. Ganesh Chandra Avenue has always been an office area. Soon, Eau Chew became successful as a tiffin house, catering to the people who worked in the area. Today, their work descendants in these offices have kept up the tradition and are regular customers at the restaurant. The busiest days in the restaurant have always been weekdays, particularly the lunch hours. The business of the Huangs grew by word of mouth and they have never advertised, not even in recent times.

The restaurant went through a change in ownership after Chi Thien Huang's death, when the reins were taken over by his son, Huang Pao Lim. After the death of Huang Pao Lim, his son Joseph Huang ran the restaurant with the assistance of only one helper. The family is fiercely possessive of their recipes. That is why they do not hire any cooks in the restaurant. For a short period of time in the 1990s, the family had hired a few stewards and helpers, but no cooks. At present, the restaurant is run by the fourth generation of the Huang family, Joel Huang.

The food served in Eau Chew is different from that served in other Chinese restaurants in the city. Unlike other restaurateurs, the Huang family has refused to spice up their dishes. As a result, the taste of the food is a little bland. Regular customers are aware of the kind of food that is served in Eau Chew, but first-timers are often surprised by the look of the food, having become used to the presence of dark soya sauce in Chinese food, which imparts a 'curried' look to a dish. But the Huang family utilizes light soya sauce because they believe that it is better in quality and has less monosodium glutamate (MSG). Light soya sauce is actually used more often in traditional Chinese cooking, with the dark variety reserved for only a few particular recipes. The owners of the restaurant also abstain from adding MSG, popularly known as ajinomoto, to their dishes for health reasons.

Besides its signature chimney soup, the restaurant also serves some wonderful creations like noodle meatballs soup, burnt garlic soup and mixed mei-foon soup, using thin mei-foon rice noodles. Crunchy prawn chips and roast pork chilli are the perfect starters to any meal. The whole shoulder of the pig is roasted for three to four hours with spices and seasonings in order to prepare roast pork chilli. When a customer orders this dish, the pork is sliced into thin pieces and stir-fried with garlic, onions and green chillies before being served.

Eau Chew offers a variety of rice and noodle preparations that are off-beat and not usually found in other outlets in the city. Josephine Noodles is an in-house pan-fried noodle dish that was invented by Josephine Huang, wife of Joseph Huang. It has a gravy-like consistency, and is quite heavy and filling. The noodles are topped with a delectable preparation of seasonal vegetables, shiitake mushrooms, seafood and meat. Tomato steamed rice is a Chinese rice dish in which whole tomatoes, slices of onions and capsicums, pieces of chicken and prawns are seasoned with salt and sugar, stir-fried and mixed with steamed rice.

Chinese chop suey is also a fixture on the menu. The noodles used in this preparation can be the rice-based mei-foon noodles, or the regular kind, depending on what the customer demands. While the noodles are deep-fried, a sauce is prepared with chicken pieces, prawns and juliennes of cabbage, onions, carrots and bean sprouts. These are stir-fried and seasoned with soya sauce, pepper and sugar, thickened with cornflour and spread generously over the fried noodles.

Pork pineapple and pork ribs are the perfect side dishes to these rice and noodle preparations. In pork pineapple, slices of pork are marinated with cornflour, pepper and salt for some time. The pork slices are then deep-fried. Meanwhile, slices of cucumber, tomato, onion, capsicum and pineapple are stir-fried. Some tomato sauce and the slices of fried pork are added to these and the preparation is thickened with corn flour mixed in water. The family always buys good-quality pork ribs for use in their restaurant. The pork ribs are marinated for an hour with soya sauce, pepper and the Chinese five-spice powder, and then roasted for at least three hours. Black bean sauce and sweet chilli sauce are combined and poured on top of the roasted ribs.

For the dish, steam soyo fish, a whole piece of bhekti is deboned and steamed. Juliennes of ginger and green chillies are stir-fried with soya sauce, black beans and home-made rice wine. The sauce is thickened with cornflour and poured on top of the fish. The dish is garnished with chopped spring onions. The presence of green chillies gives a lot of flavour and fragrance to this otherwise bland dish, which the owners recommend as an accompaniment to steamed rice.

Since the 1920s, Eau Chew has been providing catering services on special occasions for the Chinese community in Calcutta. Besides a variety of dishes, the Huang family serves the roasted suckling pig with its curly tail on ornamental trays on the occasion of weddings. Traditionally, it is the first dish to be served on such an occasion. Slices of the roasted suckling pig fill the plates of the guests.

Traditionally, when a child is a month old, a ceremony is held during which some of the dishes that are served include red eggs (eggs that have been hard-boiled with red food colouring) and slices of chicken cooked in chicken broth and rice wine. Longevity noodles made with eggs and not a drop of water is the first dish that Eau Chew serves on birthdays because, according to the traditional customs in the community, the long noodles symbolize a long life.

Eau Chew is popular among the Chinese community in Calcutta because it attempts to adhere as far as possible to traditional styles. Among the Bengalis and other communities living in the city, Eau Chew's food is popular with connoisseurs, enthusiasts and upper-class customers who have acquired a taste for authentic Chinese cuisine. Customers from the nearby corporate offices are also regulars. But Eau Chew's food is yet to attain mass popularity in the city.

New Chinatown

New Chinatown, which has been in existence since 1910, is located in Tangra in east Calcutta. The area was a marshy and reclaimed piece of land on which the Hakka Chinese began setting up small-scale tanneries. It was chosen because the area was far from the main city and the pollution created by the factories would not affect the residents. Over the years, this place evolved into a predominantly Chinese-owned tannery zone. Chinese families have also built their residences here and made Tangra an important destination for sourcing finished and semi-finished leather, which is bought in bulk by shoe and other leather goods manufacturers across the country.

Once Tangra became the new home of the Hakka Chinese, it developed into a second Chinatown. Unlike Old Chinatown, which was already an established area with space constraints, Tangra, being a new area, had ample space. The Chinese settlers here not only set up tanneries and residences but also established places of worship and learning, social clubs, factories and other small business establishments, shops and even cemeteries. The area came up as a separate township with its own markets and eateries. The Chinese people living here began celebrating their festivals with as much pomp and grandeur as in Old Chinatown.

But, despite following their own religions, festivals and traditions, the Chinese settlers in New Chinatown have imbibed certain local customs after having lived in the city for centuries. Goddess Kali is the ruling deity of the Bengalis, and the Chinese Kali Temple in New Chinatown is proof of the peaceful coexistence of the two communities and acceptance of certain customs peculiar to each. Legend has it that the site where the temple stands today was once occupied by an old tree. Under the tree stood two black stones smeared with vermilion, said to represent the goddess. The local people worshipped these black stones and on observing them, the Chinese settlers began emulating the practice. When a young Chinese boy fell critically ill and doctors had practically given up on him, his parents laid him near the tree and prayed for his recovery. The boy was miraculously cured, and the Chinese people in the area developed great faith in the goddess. Every Chinese family in New Chinatown donated money to build the temple and the two idols of Goddess Kali that are now installed inside it. Over the years, the local Chinese community in New Chinatown has become devoted to the deity and a Bengali Brahmin priest has been appointed to perform aarti every day. The two black stones are still worshipped alongside the idols of the goddess. On the day of the Kali puja, the Chinese residents take the day off from work so that they can participate in the religious festival. A huge crowd gathers in front of the temple to participate in the pushpanjali. The worship is conducted by the Bengali priest in accordance with Hindu rituals. The deity is decorated with flowers, and fruits and sweets are offered as prasad. Certain Chinese traditions have crept into the worship, like the lighting of *lap chok* (red candles) and Siang incense sticks in front of the deity. Handmade paper is burned to ward off evil spirits. The bhog (devotional offering) of the day consists of noodles, chop suey, fried rice and vegetable dishes.

Today, New Chinatown has not only become famously associated with the immigrant community and tanneries, but also with Chinese cuisine. The thought of Tangra immediately conjures the image of numerous eateries serving the Indianized version of Chinese food, famously known as 'Indian-Chinese' cuisine. When Chinese settlers began to occupy the area, they also opened eateries for the members of their community. At that point of time, these eateries were small food joints that were mostly housed in homes and served authentic Chinese food. But, gradually, the non-Chinese communities in and around Tangra, became aware of these eateries and began dropping in. They either lived in these areas or worked nearby. Although they liked the food that was served to them, they found it quite bland and preferred it to be spicy. Initially, the Chinese community was reluctant to make any changes. But, as more non-Chinese people, particularly Bengalis, began thronging these eateries, their owners realized that this was a lucrative business. If they were keen to make profit, they would have to adapt their cuisine to the demands of their new customers.

Thus, the Chinese cuisine of New Chinatown began to undergo a change. More spices and sauces were added to the cooking to please the spice-loving palate of the Indians. This was the wonderful version of Chinese cuisine that customers were looking for. New Chinatown slowly became a rage with food lovers for the delectable dishes that the small eateries served at cheap prices. Gradually, with increasing profits, these small eateries were transformed into proper restaurants. They served ample quantities of good-quality Indian-Chinese food at reasonable prices, a characteristic that is still the hallmark of the restaurants of that area. By the 1970s, New Chinatown became synonymous with Indian-Chinese cuisine.

Over the years, the area has become chock-a-block with so many Chinese restaurants of good quality that customers are spoilt for choice. Yet, among this plethora of eateries, are two restaurants that stand out not only for their quality of food but also for their owner whose persona has given a whole new dimension to her ventures. Think of Chinese cuisine and one of the images that are sure to come up in the minds of Calcuttans is of Monica Liu, zooming past people in Tangra every morning on her scooter while on the way to her restaurants, Kim Ling and Beijing. The success of her restaurants as well as her life story has given the restaurateur a celebrity status not only in New Chinatown but the entire city.

Monica and Her Eateries

When Monica Liu, or rather, the 'Don of Tangra', as she is fondly called, decided to start a restaurant in New Chinatown, it marked the beginning of a difficult journey that ultimately catapulted her to fame. Born in Calcutta to Chinese immigrants, she was named Sui Ye, meaning 'beautiful jade'. Her father, Leong Ton Seong, migrated to Calcutta in 1928 when he was fourteen years old, to work at a relative's shoe shop in central Calcutta. He was the only son in a large family that was based in Canton. The financial condition of the family and the political turbulence of China compelled him to come to Calcutta. The income was meagre, a part of which he would regularly send to his family. While still making and selling shoes in his uncle's shop, he went back to China and married Wong Mu Yun, bringing her to Calcutta with him. Sui Ye was born to the couple on 14 October 1953. In a couple of years' time, when his wife was pregnant again, Leong Ton Seong was sacked from his job because his uncle feared that he would now ask for an increase in his salary to maintain his growing family. Sui Ye's father became jobless and this is when the troubles of the family actually began.

Leong Ton Seong tried to get another job in Calcutta but in vain. In neighbouring places like Darjeeling, Kalimpong and Shillong, the Chinese community had opened several small businesses like restaurants and beauty parlours that were doing very well. This made him shift with his family to Kalimpong, where he ventured into the restaurant business. With whatever little money the family had saved, he took a small place on rent and opened an eatery in it. The restaurant just had three tables and served thukpa, noodles, Chinese beef and pork curries, steamed buns called pao stuffed with minced pork and sweet milk tea. The restaurant mainly catered to the Tibetan tourists who would frequent Kalimpong to do a lot of shopping because of the wide variety of items that were available at cheaper prices. Although the earnings were not much, the family managed to pull through. But as border tensions arose between India and China regarding Tibet, the business was badly affected as the tourists stopped coming. The family had to close down the eatery. Towards the end of 1958, they shifted to Shillong because one of Leong Ton Seong's friends rented out a place to him in which he started a small eatery. The restaurant business in Shillong did better and the family earned enough to live comfortably for some time.

It was at the eatery in Shillong that Sui Ye learnt her first lesson about the hard ways of the business world. She was only nine years old and along with attending school, had started helping out at the eatery. Her father taught her how to calculate bills and put her in-charge at the cash counter whenever he would be busy in the kitchen. But she was still a novice at the job. One day, while settling a customer's bill, instead of giving him the exact change in return, she overpaid him. Taking advantage of her innocence, the customer pocketed the extra cash and went away. Her father immediately came to know about the incident and reprimanded her. Sui Ye ran out of the shop, searching for the man and managed to find him. But when she asked him to return the extra cash, he denied having dined at the restaurant. For the little girl with a young impressionable mind, this was a big lesson learnt.

And then disaster struck in 1962 when the Indo-China War (20 October 1962–21 November 1962), also known as the Sino-Indian War, broke out. It was an unanticipated attack by China and an unprepared Indian army suffered a humiliating defeat in the hands of the Chinese People's Liberation Army (PLA). Ultimately, China ended the war after a month by unilaterally declaring a ceasefire. This war wrecked havoc in the lives of the Chinese-Indians living in Calcutta and the border areas. They were not only looked upon with suspicion but also all those Chinese people who lived in the hilly areas of Darjeeling district and the Northeast of India, which are geographically located in close proximity to China, were suspected of being potential spies. In the wee hours of a cold November morning in 1962, Sui Ye's family was arrested from their home and accompanied by armed police to Shillong Jail, where they were locked up for fifteen days. After that the family, along with many other Chinese-Indians, were taken to Guwahati by bus, and from there sent by train to Jaipur, and ultimately taken to the Central Internment Camp in the city of Deoli in the Tonk district of Rajasthan. This was to be home for Leong Ton Seong and his family for the next five years.

Sui Ye was nine years old when she arrived in Deoli. Nearly 3,000 Chinese-Indian men, women and children were imprisoned without trial in an internment camp that was demarcated by barbed-wire fences and patrolled by rifled soldiers. The years were marked with absence of education and work. Although the internees were free to move about within the limited area, the quality of life they experienced took a toll on them. They lived like prisoners. Each one had a roll number and Sui Ye's was 880. As the eldest of five children, Sui Ye would wake up every morning and bathe her siblings, wash their clothes and feed them—activities that she continued from her pre-confinement days. Like others, she would stand in the queue every day for a bowl of barely edible cooked rice and potato or gourd curry. Water had to be fetched from a faraway tap within the grounds. Moreover, Rajasthan, being a desert region, is a place of extreme climatic conditions that many internees found difficult to cope with. The camp was also poorly prepared and unable to house them all. Many were forced to sleep outside, without blankets, in the cold mosquito-infested nights.

In his article, 'Without Apologies', (22 October 2012) for *Outlook* magazine, S.N.M. Abdi writes about the camp, '[...] Its origins lay in a cantonment established by the British army in Deoli in 1852; in 1942 its barracks were converted into a POW camp for German, Italian and Japanese combatants and nationals. In 1947, the military handed it over to the home ministry. When busloads of Chinese families began arriving at the camp in November 1962, they were subjected to regulations from an old military manual for administering Axis POWs gathering dust in the commandant's office. For instance, dinner was served at 5pm and lights were switched off at 7pm, plunging the prisoners' wings into darkness until daybreak. The rule was revoked when it was realised that, unlike Axis POWs, 60 per cent of the internees were children or elderly persons.'

He continues, '[...] on February 27, 1963, Union home minister Lal Bahadur Shastri gave the detainees a clean chit! He told Parliament that no internee would be tried for spying or subversion. Shastri was true to his word: nobody was prosecuted. But nobody was set free either: they simply languished behind barbed wires like POWs.' Shastri followed this up with a visit to the Deoli camp on 9 June 1963, where he met and interacted with the Chinese internees. A young Sui Ye was one of those and a photograph was even taken of her, among a group of little Chinese boys and girls, and others at the camp, interacting with the Union home minister. The photograph, carried in the newspaper *The Hindu*, had agitated the Chinese community back then who objected to their community members interacting with those who were responsible for their incarceration.

It was at the internment camp that Sui Ye understood the value of freedom because like many others, she felt like a bird in a cage. The feeling was not pleasant and induced the internees to indulge in activities to improve the quality of their lives while in confinement. They did this by making use of their talents. Those who were educated among them taught English and Chinese while those who knew singing and dancing, imparted these skills to others.

It was on 23 March 1965 in the Deoli camp that Sui Ye became Monica because at the behest of her parents, she was baptized by a Catholic chaplain. Her baptism took place in a makeshift chapel by Reverend Father Benedict Fernandez of St Joseph, the Worker's Church in Kota. Leong Sui Ye now became Monica Leong.

Between 1964 and 1966, the government began to release the detained

Chinese-Indians. In 1964, the Indian government began transporting internees who were willing to go back to China. This brought them some relief from their current predicament and many voluntarily left for their native land in ships sent by the Chinese government. Most headed to a country they had never been to before. But Monica's father did not want to go back as there was no one to return home to anymore. From 1965, the government began releasing the internees in small batches. Eventually, in February 1967, the Chinese families remaining at the camp were released. However, 150 of them were still detained and transferred to a jail in Nagaon in Assam. Monica's family was one of them. They were finally released after nine months.

Traumatized and penniless, the family returned to Shillong. They took shelter at friends' homes. For a month the children ate bone soup for lunch and dinner. But they did not complain because they were thankful to have a roof above their heads and food on their table. After about a month, Monica and her family moved into a 300-square-feet room, which was rented out to them by an acquaintance. This was their new home. It was located near two schools. Monica's mother financially helped the family by making and selling momos and thukpa to the schoolchildren every morning.

Monica started school again. She was put into Class six. But she had been out of touch with education for so long that she found it difficult to cope and managed to scrape through till Class nine. Ultimately, she dropped out of school in Class ten. She aspired to become a nurse and trained briefly. But before she could fulfil her dream, she was married off at the age of twenty to Liu Kuo Chao, a resident of New Chinatown in Calcutta.

And this is how Monica Liu stepped into Tangra—a place that would, unknown to her back then, get tagged onto her name in the distant future.

Over the next five years, three children were born to her. They were a happy family. But financial troubles began knocking on her door again. Her husband's leather tannery business was not doing very well. To supplement the income, she began buying chemicals used in leather processing from wholesalers and sold them to retailers. She did this for three years and whatever she earned was enough to buy the rations for the house.

Inspired by her brother and sister-in-law's success with their beauty parlour business in Shillong, she took a loan from a friend and started her own beauty parlour in a rented place in Lansdowne Road (now known as Sarat Bose Road) in south Calcutta. The business did moderately well. But, after three years, she rented it out to a relative because the business was taking up a lot of her time. Her children were growing up and needed attention. She kept her hold over the beauty parlour for another four years. Finally, she let go of it.

Because Monica now had other plans.

Being a good cook and having gained some experience at her parents' eateries, she wanted to venture into the restaurant business. Her earnings before had never been enough to fully support her family. They did not even have a decent place to stay and faced constant threats and harassments from the landlord whenever they failed to pay the rent. She was aware how much the local people of Calcutta enjoyed eating Chinese food. And she rightly thought that it might turn out to be a lucrative business. 'Those ten years that I spent selling chemicals and running a beauty parlour were very tough. But the entrepreneurial bug had bit me. I was my own boss, running my own show and earning my own money. I enjoyed every bit of it,' she adds.

She had an eye on a house in Tangra that belonged to her aunt-in-law's granddaughter and expressed her keenness to buy it over. Since she did not own any land or property, she could not take loan from a bank. Instead, she took loans from her parents, brothers and friends and paid the due amount that was slightly above Rs 10 lakhs. The property was immediately handed over to her. This was in March 1991, and after two months of renovation work, Monica Liu's first restaurant, **Kim Ling**, was opened. The restaurant started out with ten tables, each a four-seater, and was the first in the whole of Tangra to be air conditioned—a wise decision that proved to be gainful in the future. Unlike the elaborate menu that it now has, in the initial years, the restaurant served its customers only Chicken Hot and Sour Soup, Hakka and Cantonese Chow (noodles) and Chilli Chicken.

With the help of a few family members and one helper, Monica ran the show. But, initially, there were hiccoughs. She got into a quarrel with a customer on the first day itself. 'The gentleman seemed to be the shady kind. After finishing the meal, he refused to pay me, saying that the food is of poor quality. I asked him to either pay me or leave. But he left,' says Monica. She did come across some more shady characters like this in the future. Seeing a woman running the business, they tried to create problems by refusing to pay and blamed it on the quality of food. Then there were the local goons who often hounded her for money or 'chanda'. 'They wanted a part of my earnings. I had just started the restaurant and was not earning a lot yet. I also had loans to repay. They would particularly come on Sundays because they knew that business is more on weekends. And they would demand a chunk of my profit. Sometimes, they would also want free food. It was exasperating to deal with all this,' she adds.

But if there were people who caused problems, there were also the supporters. There were customers who tremendously enjoyed the food in her restaurant. People from nearby offices began dropping in on weekdays. On the weekends, one could find large family crowds, eating at tables that were joined together. During festive seasons like Durga Puja, the restaurants in Tangra were packed with customers from all communities. The footfall in Kim Ling was more during these times. Customers not only enjoyed the delicious food Monica served but the air-conditioned interiors of her restaurant also gave them a lot of comfort from the scorching heat outside. Gradually, as business started doing well, Monica cleared all her debts. She also expanded the menu that now included a variety of soups, appetizers, vegetable, fish, prawn, crab and chicken curries, fried rice and noodles. The food that was prepared in the restaurant was not the authentic variety but commercial Indian-Chinese. This was purposefully done to attract a large customer base and it worked. Customers began to throng Kim Ling in droves because of the good-quality Indian-Chinese cuisine that it served. The number of tables and staff members working in the eatery increased. Kim Ling was now a flourishing restaurant.

The success of Kim Ling can be gauged from the fact that the family of the former chief minister of West Bengal, Jyoti Basu, once placed an order with the restaurant. The restaurateur still cherishes the incident. 'I remember it was in November 1992,' she says, 'Kim Ling had begun making a name for itself and business had started booming. I got a call from the family. They wanted to taste Kim Ling's food. So, I personally catered the food at their home in Indira Bhavan in Salt Lake City. This happened in the initial years of the restaurant and it was a big boost for me.' Kim Ling was also once into the catering business. Three years after the restaurant had opened orders for catering began pouring in from the Chinese community in New Chinatown. Kim Ling would cater at occasions like Chinese weddings and the Chinese New Year. The restaurant would also get a lot of orders for birthday parties from both the Chinese and the non-Chinese communities in and around Tangra.

So, after many failures, Monica Liu had finally hit the jackpot. She was now a successful restaurateur and the financial condition of her family improved tremendously. But she was not the kind to rest on her laurels. Having tasted success with her first venture, she opened a small chain of restaurants in different parts of the city over the next few years. In 1993, she bought **Mandarin** from her cousin brother. It was originally started in 1970 in Lansdowne Road. But, over the years, it lost business. Monica renovated the restaurant and served good-quality food at reasonable prices. Soon, Mandarin became a hit with customers—as did **Beijing** (started in Tangra in 1998) and **Tung Fong** (started in Free School Street in 2001). If her first and second ventures, Kim Ling and Mandarin, are simple restaurants with homely surroundings, Beijing is comparatively upscale while Tung Fong is very posh. The food served in Beijing is much more elaborate than Kim Ling. Additional items like a variety of salads, duck and mutton dishes, and ice creams are listed in its menu. Renowned author Amitav Ghosh, best known for his work in English fiction, is believed to have dined at this restaurant.

In 2013, Monica Liu opened a second outlet of Mandarin in Lake Avenue in south Calcutta. Although her first three restaurants were started with financial help from her parents and friends, when it came to Tung Fong, she was financially strong enough to take a hefty loan from the bank. From starting with one helper in Kim Ling, Monica now has over a hundred staff members working in both her restaurants in New Chinatown, and altogether over 250 staff members in all her five restaurants taken together. Although keen on further expansion within Calcutta, she baulks at the idea of opening restaurants outside the city because she feels that might compromise the quality of the food. Her restaurants are well-known for the good quality and ample quantity of food that is served at fairly reasonable prices. Since she is based in Calcutta, if she opens outlets outside the city, she will have to franchise them. And she fears franchisees may not maintain the standard her restaurants are known for.

If anyone witnesses Monica at work in her restaurants in New Chinatown, they will quickly realize how warm and friendly she is with the customers, chatting with them and listening to their feedback. Her people skills, along with the great food she serves, have made the Monica Liu brand of restaurants a household name in Calcutta. Today, at the mere mention of Tangra, the first thought that comes to peoples' minds is Chinese food. And the two most famous names associated with the cuisine in that area are Kim Ling and Beijing.

Monica Liu's story is one of grit and determination. It is a story that gives hope. Her journey from the depths of poverty to becoming one of the most successful restaurateurs of Calcutta is inspiring. With a slew of awards under her belt from national and local periodicals like the *Times of India*, *Outlook* and *Anandabazar Patrika* for her entrepreneurial abilities, this tough-as-nails daughter of Chinese immigrants is also a philanthropist at heart. She did not forget her roots and extends a helping hand to the underprivileged whenever possible. This has created an aura about her that inspires a mixed feeling of fear and respect. It is this mixed feeling that has made people label her as the 'Don of Tangra'. But to all those who know her personally, she is still Sui Ye, the beautiful jade whose dreams and hopes took shape in Calcutta. 'I love Calcutta,' she ends the conversation, 'this city gave me a fresh start at life and its people have given me a lot of love and respect.'

*

Today, the Chinese community in Calcutta is dominated by the Hakka ethnic group, followed by the Cantonese. Most people from the Shanghai area have gone back to China, while the Hupehs have spread themselves across the country. The cooking styles of the Hakka and the Cantonese groups have heavily influenced the cuisine in Calcutta. Since the government of West Bengal banned tanneries in Tangra in 2001 in an attempt to prevent further pollution in the area, and ordered the tannery owners to shift their units to a place called Bantala, a neighbourhood of east Calcutta, the Hakka community living in the area has opened many more Chinese restaurants in the abandoned factory premises. The West Bengal government took this action following the order of the Supreme Court dated 19 December 1996. A leather complex, which is now one of the most important tanning centres in the country, was inaugurated in Bantala on 30 July 2005. Known as the Kolkata Leather Complex, it not only houses the relocated tanneries of the city, including those of Tangra, but new ones as well.

When Chinese cuisine was commercially launched, the majority of the locals were bold enough to experiment with it. Finally, when it was adapted to suit the local palate, customers began enjoying it tremendously. Gradually, the word about the cuisine spread throughout the city and so did its popularity. Bengalis now enjoy this cuisine so much that the majority of them have even learnt to cook quite a few of the dishes, which they often make at home. Thanks to the cuisine's popularity, there are numerous famous eateries in Calcutta today that serve it. It can be confidently said that Chinese cuisine has become the most popular immigrant cuisine in Calcutta.

The Chinese settlers too, on their part, often cook Bengali food at home using local spices. It is not uncommon to come across members of the community indulging in Bengali curry dishes with steamed rice. They also enjoy Bengali confectioneries. Dominic Lee adds, 'My family enjoys eating payesh. So, we often make it at home.'

There are around 2,000 people of Chinese origin living in Calcutta today. In the aftermath of the Indo-China War, there was a large-scale exodus from Calcutta to China. They felt insecure and vulnerable living in a city where they were now looked upon with suspicion. They had lost their jobs, their schools and businesses were shut down, and the publication of their newspapers stopped. Over the years, the number of Chinese in the city reduced further because many from the educated young generation refused to continue with the family businesses of tanneries, restaurants, beauty parlours and laundries. Instead, they preferred to migrate to Europe, North America, Canada and Australia in their quest for better lives. It is often said in jest that Toronto in Canada is the new Tangra, bustling with people from the Calcutta Chinese community.

A few like-minded people from the Indian and Chinese communities have come together and begun an initiative called the CHA Project. 'CHA' stands for Cities*Heritage*Architecture. This project, in partnership with the West Bengal Chapter of INTACH (Indian National Trust for Art and Cultural Heritage), aims to regenerate the Old and New Chinatowns and give the areas a face lift. The members want to recreate the ambience that existed when there was a sizeable number of Chinese living in Calcutta. They want to create a Chinese food street near the Toong On Church on Blackburn Lane. The plans of the project include creating a Chinese cultural centre in the Toong On Church premises, reopening Nanking, creating a heritage tourist trail connecting all the Chinese temples in Old Chinatown and building a Chinese market in New Chinatown to give the place a tourist appeal.

The project also aims to set up tea rooms in these areas as well. 'Tea rooms are very popular in Chinese culture,' says G.M. Kapur, convenor of the West Bengal chapter of INTACH, 'Each of the temples in Old Chinatown has its own association, where members of the Chinese community meet and interact. The CHA Project plans to take tourists on a tour of these temples. They could also interact with the community while drinking tea inside the premises of the temples.' These plans to turn the only Chinatowns in the country into popular tourist destinations confirm the importance of this community to the social fabric of the city.

Moving Beyond Chinatown: Indian-Chinese Cuisine

The Chinese have settled in different parts of the world due to economic and other compulsions. This has led to the growth of Chinatowns in the places they have settled. These Chinatowns are known for their eateries, which initially served the kind of food typically eaten by the Chinese. Since the cuisine on the whole is adaptable, the owners of these eateries gradually improvised the dishes for commercial purposes, keeping in mind the new surroundings and palate of the local people. The taste of Chinese cuisine varies between countries for this reason. Since the Chinese community in India first settled in Bengal, they gradually adapted their cuisine to suit the taste buds of the local Bengalis. Today, Calcutta is regarded as the birthplace of Indian-Chinese cuisine.

Authentic Chinese cuisine in Calcutta gradually turned into the spiced-up cuisine that we eat today. The motive behind this transformation was purely commercial. It was not until the 1970s that Chinese cuisine became the rage that it is today, thanks to the efforts of the succeeding generations of Chinese restaurateurs. They wanted to move out of the confines of the Chinatowns and set up businesses in other parts of the city. They were adventurous and not afraid to take risks. Like their countrymen living in different parts of the world, this new generation of Chinese restaurateurs in Calcutta wanted to turn their native cuisine into a source for business and profit. To this end, they set up restaurants throughout the city and began serving Chinese food to the local customers that was spiced-up in order to cater to their spice-loving palate. Yet, all these changes were brought about without altering the basic structure and identity of the cuisine itself.

It is difficult to figure out the exact time frame when this transformation began to take place. The process was a gradual one which gained momentum from the 1950s. Chinese restaurateurs introduced 'Chilli Chicken' and recommended that Calcuttans eat this spicy chicken side dish with a stir-fried noodle preparation called 'Hakka Noodles'. Customers loved this combination and thus, Hakka Noodles and Chilli Chicken became the signature dishes of the city.

It's interesting to note that the origin of the dish 'Chilli Chicken' has no links with China, and is completely a local creation. It is difficult to name the inventor of this dish, and the time frame in which it was created and introduced to the culinary culture of Calcutta. The Chinese inhabitants of the city who are in the hospitality industry believe that no single person can be given credit for its invention. Chilli Chicken is a dish that is the result of the prolonged efforts of the city's chefs. It has evolved from constant experimentations and turned into a dish that is unique in taste and flavour. The recipe has gone through many trials and improvisations to ultimately evolve into a standard one. Today, this standard recipe of Chilli Chicken, which has its roots in Calcutta, has become popular all over the country.

However, the same story cannot be applied to the dish 'Chicken Manchurian' because it is possible to name the person responsible for its creation as well as give an approximate time frame for its discovery. Although this dish did not originate in Calcutta, it can be said that it has some connection with the city. Chicken Manchurian is the creation of the mega successful restaurateur Nelson Wang who is the poster boy for the rags to riches story in the community. A man with a humble beginning, Wang owns the fine-dining restaurant China Garden in Bombay, which has branches spread across the country. He was born in New Chinatown in Calcutta to Chinese immigrants. His biological father died within three days of his birth and he was brought up by a foster family. His foster father was a chef and it was under his influence that Wang's love for cooking grew. He travelled to Bombay, where he began his career in the hospitality industry as an assistant cook in Frederick's, a popular Chinese eatery in Colaba.

It was during his tenure as a chef at the elite Cricket Club of India in Bombay that his career took a dramatic rise when a club member asked him one day to cook a dish that was different from anything he had tasted before. It is widely believed that this happened in the year 1975. Wang cooked chicken pieces with ingredients like onions, ginger and garlic pastes, soya sauce, cornflour, egg white, black and white pepper powders, red chilli sauce and vinegar and garnished the dish with chopped spring onions. The club member thoroughly enjoyed the dish, which was christened Chicken Manchurian by Wang. Word about it spread and the dish gained popularity and fame. Today, Chicken Manchurian is prepared by all Chinese restaurants in the country and comes a close second in popularity to Chilli Chicken.

Over the years, Chinese cuisine has made a big impact on Calcutta's culinary culture. Bengalis have turned into loyal fans and enjoy the dishes served in Chinese restaurants, whether it is the stuffed and fluffy egg omelette called foo young, or one of the many stir-fried dishes. Calcutta-based Chinese food product companies have even started manufacturing sweetened versions of their chilli sauces to cater to the Bengali palate. For example, Pou Chong Food Products Pvt. Ltd sweetens its chilli sauces with pineapple, dates or garlic so that they have a predominantly sweet flavour. The Bengali community enjoys eating these sweet chilli sauces with fried foods like samosa, which is called *shingara* in Bengali, and fritters like *alur chop*.

'Local farmers are also making attempts to grow some of the native Chinese vegetables in the suburbs of the city for the community,' points out Dominic Lee. 'Today, they grow Chinese spring onions and the Chinese cabbage called pak choi. Farmers in north Bengal and the Northeast of India have always been cultivating the glutinous variety of rice for local consumption. Since this variety is also preferred by the Chinese, it is now sold in Chinese shops in the city.'

Gradually, this modern generation of food entrepreneurs began moving out of Calcutta to cities across the country for more lucrative opportunities. They introduced the Calcutta Chinese cuisine to different parts of India. The local people in the different regions had different palate. In some places, the restaurateurs had to tone down the spice content in the dishes, while in others, it had to be increased. Today, Chinese cuisine is the most popular eating-out option not only in Calcutta, but throughout the country.

4. Parsi Cuisine

Unlike many of the communities who have contributed to the culinary culture of Calcutta, Parsis have remained distinct and exclusive in their food habits, and their cuisine has not been able to garner widespread popularity. Nevertheless, their cuisine has had a significant historical presence in the city, and as such, is an important part of Calcutta's culinary journey.

Most Parsis in India today are descendants of the refugees who fled from Khorasan in northeastern Iran in the eighth century CE in order to free themselves from religious persecution and forced conversion to

Islam. The Arabs conquered Iran (earlier known as Persia) in the middle of the seventh century CE, overthrowing the Sasanian Empire (224 CE—651 CE), which is considered to be the last great Iranian Empire before the rise of Islam in that country.

The Persians were mainly Zoroastrians. Zoroastrianism, the pre-Islamic religion in the Persian Empire, is based on the teachings of the Persian prophet and reformer Zoroaster (also known as Zarathustra). These teachings consider an uncreated deity of wisdom, Ahura Mazda (Wise Lord), as the Creator, Supreme Being and Highest Deity. Thus, the Zoroastrians worship Ahura Mazda as their God. Zoroaster chose fire as the symbol of Ahura Mazda based on the belief that it is the purest and cleanest of all elements and can never be contaminated. Hence, the fire temple became the Zoroastrian place of worship. It contains the Holy Fire, known as Atar or the ever-burning flame, which is an eternal flame that burns continuously for an indefinite period. This Holy Fire is considered to be the visible presence of Ahura Mazda and represents His light or wisdom.

But Zoroastrianism began to decline in Persia after the Arab conquest. The Arabs destroyed fire temples and built mosques in their place. They levied jizya on the Persian Zoroastrians, which is a special tax imposed by Islamic rulers on their non-Muslim subjects. Failure to pay the jizya would lead to death, enslavement or imprisonment. The Zoroastrians were subjected to unwarranted aggression, discrimination and harassment. Many laws were implemented that made life difficult for them and any form of resistance was violently suppressed. Over time, the Iranian Zoroastrians were compelled to convert to Islam to escape the systematic abuse and discrimination. By the end of the eleventh century, a majority of them had become Muslims. Those Zoroastrians from Iran who fled to India because they chose to preserve their religious identity are called Parsis. The term 'Parsi' is a derivation of the Persian word 'Parsian' (which literally means 'Persian').

The Parsis settled in Gujarat after reaching the western coast of India. 'Qissa-i Sanjan' (literally meaning the 'Story of Sanjan'), an epic poem composed in 1599 CE by the Parsi priest, Bahman Kaikobad, is accepted as the only narrative available that gives an accurate account of their ancestors by the community. When he wrote the story, Bahman Kaikobad was a Sanjana (priest) in Navsari (now a major city in Gujarat) and his full name was Bahman Kaikobad Hamjiar Sanjana. According to the narrative, when the Parsis arrived in India, they first landed in Div (commonly taken to mean the coastal town of Diu) and lived there for nineteen years. But a prophecy made by one of their priest-astrologers made them finally leave Div and seek another place of refuge as they believed that their destiny lay elsewhere. So, they headed for Gujarat, and while at sea, encountered a severe storm that endangered their lives. They promised God that they would build a temple to house the Atash Behram if they survived the terrible storm. Atash Behram, literally meaning 'Fire of Victory', is the highest grade of fire that can be placed inside a Zoroastrian fire temple as an eternal flame. Their prayers were heard and they reached Gujarat safely.

At that point in time, the kingdom of Sanjan in Gujarat is believed to have been ruled by the Hindu king, Jadi Rana. His reputation for fairness induced the Zoroastrians to seek asylum in his kingdom. Whether Jadi Rana was actually a historical figure has not been established. He might have been a Rajput ruler who ruled the region in that era. If oral lore is to be believed, Jadi Rana was initially apprehensive about granting sanctuary to these foreigners with warrior-like appearances. At first, he asked them to explain their religious beliefs and then showed them a bowl filled with milk to the brim, implying that his kingdom was full and could not accommodate any more people. The leader of the Parsis was a Dastur (a Zoroastrian high priest), who spoke to the king with the help of an interpreter. He asked for some sugar and stirred a spoonful of it into the milk, convincing the king that they would be like sugar, blending well and adding sweetness and not causing the liquid to overflow. In other words, they would adapt themselves to the kingdom and its surroundings, and not cause any disorder. All that they asked for in return was the full freedom to practise their own religion and follow their traditions. Pleased with this symbolic gesture of the high priest, the king granted them their wish and the permission to settle in Sanjan. They were also given a small piece of land to cultivate so that they could live independently.

But the king also made them promise to adhere to certain conditions: they were to give up their weapons, obey the laws and adapt to the ways of their new homeland, and adopt the local Gujarati language. Their women were to wear the sari (the garment of the local women) and their marriages were to be held in the evenings. The Zoroastrian refugees agreed to these conditions and with the passage of time, a flourishing settlement of the Parsis came up in Sanjan. It is believed that the Parsis named the town of Sanjan after the ancient city of Sanjan in Greater

Khorasan. After some time, the Zoroastrian settlers took the king's permission to build the temple which they had promised God. Today, Udvada, a small coastal town near Sanjan, houses the Udvada Atash Behram, the oldest and most sacred of the Zoroastrian fire temples in India, which dates back to 1742 CE. Also known as the Iran Shah (king of Iran), because it is symbolically supposed to represent the deposed Zoroastrian monarchy of Iran, it attracts thousands of devotees from all over the world, making Udvada an important pilgrimage destination for Zoroastrians.

Thus, we see how the members of the community learned the local language and adopted the native dress and customs of the Gujaratis before migrating to other parts of the country. Around 1750 CE, a few Parsis came to Bengal and settled in Murshidabad before finally moving into Calcutta.

As Calcutta was the land of opportunities in the eighteenth century, Parsi Seths began arriving in large numbers and settling in the city. The growing trade with China was also another important reason for their immigration. In his essay, 'The Parsis of Calcutta', from the book, *Calcutta—The Living City: Volume II: The Present and Future* (1990), Cyrus J. Madan writes, 'The earliest known and recorded history of a Parsi in Calcutta commences in 1767 with the arrival of Dadabhoy Behramji Banaji from Surat. A flourishing trader, "Banaji Seth" was patronized by John Cartier, then Governor of Bengal but earlier in charge of British commercial interests in Surat. He was the doyen of the famous Banaji family which made a deep mark in the commercial and industrial history of Bengal' (p. 62).

'After these early inroads into Bengal commerce, the person who truly raised the name of Banaji to legendary heights was Seth Rustomji Kawasji Banaji' (p. 62), asserts Cyrus J. Madan. In the city's industrial world, 'Rustomji Babu' was a personality to reckon with. He was a very successful merchant, who arrived in Calcutta on business in 1812, and grew to love the city so much that he finally settled here with his family in 1838. Seth Rustomji Kawasji Banaji had many business enterprises in the city. He is believed to have founded the Sun Insurance Office, which was an insurance firm, as well as paper and cotton ginning mills. Although, his extensive entrepreneurial activities made him a renowned name, the cornerstone of all his business ventures was shipping. Seth Rustomji Kawasji Banaji was a shipping magnate, who not only owned a fleet of twenty-seven ships with his sons, but also bought the Calcutta

Docking Company, now the Khidderpore Docks, in 1837. Well known for his social and philanthropic ventures, he was responsible for founding the first fire temple in Calcutta on Ezra Street in September 1839. It has now been abandoned. Besides the Banaji family, there were many other illustrious Parsi families in Calcutta who rose to positions of eminence in the city. Calcutta's location made shipping and the jute trade its most prosperous industries and the Parsi community flourished in both.

Another important member of the Parsi community in Calcutta was Jamshedji Framji Madan, regarded as one of the pioneers of the Indian film industry. Born in Bombay, he made Calcutta his home in 1883. In 1902, he founded the Elphinstone Bioscope Company that began producing and exhibiting silent movies. The company organized a lot of bioscope shows and produced a number of short films. In 1907, he established the first permanent show house in Calcutta, the Elphinstone Picture Palace, later known as the Chaplin Cinema. He also opened Madan Theatre and Palace of Varieties, later known as Elite Cinema. In 1919, Madan Seth, as he was known, turned his film production business into a joint stock company and gave it the name, Madan Theatres Limited, which owned movie theatres in Calcutta like Grand Opera House, Electric Theatre and Crown Cinema. These theatres, which were later renamed Globe Cinema, Regal Cinema and Uttara Cinema respectively, went on to become some of the most popular cinema halls in the city. By the time of his death in 1923, Madan Seth owned over a hundred movie theatres all over the country. He was honoured with the Officer of the Most Excellent Order of the British Empire (OBE) in 1918 and Commander of the Most Excellent Order of the British Empire (CBE) in 1923 by the British government for his help to the British Indian Army during the First World War (28 July 1914–11 November 1918).

Thus, on the whole, the Parsi community in Calcutta was well known for its prosperity. There are conflicting reports about the number of early Parsi settlers in Calcutta. In Subhajoy Roy's article 'Window to Parsi Life', carried in *The Telegraph* newspaper on 27 October 2017, it is mentioned that the number of members in this once-strong community dwindled to around 2,500 in the 1960s. According to a survey conducted by the Calcutta Zoroastrian Community's Religious and Charity Fund on March 2019, there are around 405 Parsis living in the city. Zoroastrian Anjuman Atash Adaran, the fire temple that is currently in use, was built in 1912 by Ervad Dhunjeebhoy Byramjee Mehta. He arrived in Calcutta in 1846 and soon began trading with China. He opened the Empress of India Cotton Mills in Serampore. The fire temple he built is located on Metcalfe Street, popularly known as Bandook Gali, in the Bowbazar area of central Calcutta.

After Independence, most Parsis took Indian citizenship as they had not acquired any nationality previously. The Parsis of Calcutta continued to contribute to the life of the city, whether through commercial ventures like M.N. Dastur & Company Pvt. Ltd, a renowned consulting engineering concern that was established in 1955, or individually, as in the case of businessman and philanthropist Rusi B. Gimi, who became the sheriff of Calcutta in 1974. Like Madan Seth, noted musician Vistasp Ardeshir Balsara, well known as V. Balsara, moved to Calcutta from Bombay, and gifted the music lovers of the city a range of beautiful melodies. In 1964, Dhun and Dorab Adenwalla set up the first school for the deaf in the city, known as the Oral School for Deaf Children. Since 1974, the children of the school, under the guidance of another Parsi, Zarin Chaudhuri, began making a name for themselves with their theatrical group, the Action Players. Today, this group, which began with the school students, is very well known in theatre circles and works on a big scale with hearing-impaired actors.

And, when writing on the Parsis of Calcutta, one simply cannot ignore the achievements of the most versatile sportswoman that this city has gifted to the country—Shireen Khushroo Kiash (nee Contractor). This highly respected sportswoman of the 1970s not only represented India internationally in hockey, basketball and cricket, but also excelled in other sports like table tennis, tennis, badminton and carom.

Unfortunately, many Parsis also left Calcutta, and settled abroad, or returned to Bombay in search of better prospects.

The Parsis have a tradition of rich food, the legacy of Iranian cooking. Both rice and wheat-based products form part of their diet, as these are the major crops grown in Iran. The use of flavourings, like saffron, and dried fruits, like apricots, raisins, almonds, pistachios and dates is also the result of Iranian influence. Cinnamon, cardamom and cloves, which are some of the essential spices in Iranian cooking, play an important role in Parsi preparations as well. The heavily meat-based diet of Iran has also led to the same playing a huge role in Parsi cuisine.

Apart from its Iranian origin, there have been three major influences on Parsi cuisine in India—Gujarati, Portuguese and British. The Gujarati influence is evident in the balancing of sweet and sour flavours in some Parsi curries, by using either jaggery or sugar and tamarind. The Parsi love for seafood is the result of their long historical proximity to Gujarat's coast. They have a penchant for saltwater fish like pomfret, prawns, grey mullet, Bombay duck, salmon and surmai (king mackerel). The community's new home also produced an abundance of coconut and the fruit soon began to feature in their fare. The use of Indian spices, herbs and fresh vegetables became predominant as well.

The Portuguese had established settlements in Surat and other parts of Gujarat much before the arrival of the British. It was they who were responsible for introducing many plants, like the potato, to India. This perhaps explains the penchant of the Parsis for including crisp fried potatoes in gravy dishes. The Portuguese also introduced the use of vinegar in cooking and making pickles in India, and taking cue from them, the Parsi community learned to flavour some of their dishes with vinegar. The use of cashew nuts in Parsi cuisine can also be attributed to the fact that the cashew plant was first brought to the Indian soil by the Portuguese.

The British East India Company established a factory (trading post) in Surat in the early seventeenth century. Parsi custards and puddings owe their origin to British cuisine, which began filtering into Gujarat around this time.

When the Parsi community migrated to Calcutta, they were able to stick to their original cuisine without making too many changes, thanks to the easy availability of ingredients. The freshwater fish of Calcutta did not appeal to them (they found it to have a muddy taste), but they did enjoy bhekti and hilsa. Patra ni machchi is the most popular fish preparation in Parsi cuisine that is made with either pomfret or bhekti. The fish fillets used in this preparation are marinated with salt and lime juice before being coated with a chutney or paste made with grated coconut, coriander leaves, mint leaves, green chillies, ginger, garlic, turmeric, cumin and salt. The coated fish fillets are wrapped in banana leaves and steamed. A very sought-after dish in Parsi weddings, it is generally eaten with rice preparations. The dish is similar to the Bengali *maachher paturi* because the method of preparation is the same as the fish is coated in a paste, wrapped in leaves and steamed. But the flavourings used in the two dishes vary between the communities, making it difficult to claim that the Parsi version follows the Bengali dish.

In Parsi cuisine, patio is the generic name for those curry dishes that are traditionally cooked in a vessel that has a wide, flat and thick bottom and bulging round sides. The name of the dish is derived from this vessel, which is known as patio tapeli. Patio is basically a sweet, sour and spicy seafood curry. There are quite a few patio dishes, even a solitary vegetarian one made with red pumpkin (koru no patio). But the most popular one is kolmi no patio, a prawn (kolmi) curry that has an amalgamation of sweet, sour and spicy flavours. The sweet flavour is brought about by using jaggery and the sourness by traditionally using cane vinegar. But now the latter is often replaced with other forms of vinegar and even tamarind pulp. Onions, tomatoes, coriander leaves and a small variety of regular spices are used in the cooking. But the emphasis is on the use of garlic and green chillies that impart a wonderful aroma and flavour to the preparation. The best accompaniment to kolmi no patio is steamed rice or jeera (cumin) rice and dhan dar, which is a simple lentil preparation made almost daily in Parsi homes with tuvar dal (split pigeon pea). Since chingri is the Bengali word for prawn, this dish is also known as chingri no patio among the Calcutta Parsis.

The most popular snacks or appetizers in Parsi cuisine are patrel and marghi na farcha, a crispy fried chicken dish. The latter refers to large pieces of chicken (marghi) that are marinated with spices, crumbed and deep-fried. Patrel is a dish of fried arvi (colocasia) leaves made into rolls. A sweet, sour and spicy paste made of gram flour (or a combination of a few flours like gram, wholewheat and rice flours), a variety of spices, herbs, grated coconut, tamarind pulp, jaggery and salt are spread on an arvi leaf. Three to six arvi leaves are prepared in the same manner and stacked together. The leaves are then rolled, tied securely with a string and steamed till firm. Many more such rolls are prepared and steamed. When the patrel rolls have cooled and their strings removed, they are sliced and shallow-fried till crisp. This recipe has been adapted from patra, which is a similar Gujarati preparation with colocasia leaves. Parsis also add their own touch to this dish by sometimes adding minced onions or mashed bananas to the paste. Garlic, cinnamon and cloves, spices which usually do not feature in the patra recipe, are often found in the Parsi version. Some even add chopped boiled prawns to the preparation—a clear indication of their love for non-vegetarian food.

Sali ma marghi is a popular chicken gravy dish topped with sali (thin sticks of fried potatoes). The sali is prepared by soaking the potato straws in salted water for some time. The water is then drained and the straws are fried in oil till they are golden and crisp. Sali ma marghi is served on all auspicious occasions, including Navroz, the first day of the Parsi New

Year. Another popular dish is jardaloo ma gosht, a mutton and apricot curry. This dish is strongly influenced by the cooking style of the Persians who have the tendency to cook their meat dishes with dried fruits. A combination of the above two dishes is jardaloo sali boti, a typical Parsi dish that includes both jardaloo and sali. As is evident from its name, this boti or mutton gravy dish is cooked with apricots and topped with potato strips that have been fried till crisp.

Dhansak is perhaps the most well-known dish of the Parsi community. This meat and lentil dish shows influences of khoresh, which is the generic Persian word for stew. Khoresh is always served with rice, particularly with polo (pilaf). The meat used in dhansak can be either chicken (marghi) or mutton (boti). A mixture of a few varieties of lentils is used in this dish. Besides onions and tomatoes, this gravy dish also features a few other vegetables like aubergines, potatoes, bottle gourd and pumpkin. Herbs like mint leaves, coriander leaves, dill leaves and fenugreek leaves are added to the preparation. The use of jaggery and tamarind gives a sweet and sour flavour to this dish. A spicy and salty cucumber-tomato-onion salad called kachumber and brown caramelized rice are served alongside the dhansak. This is a ritual Sunday lunch for traditional Parsi families. Despite its popularity, dhansak is never served at Parsi weddings and other auspicious occasions because, according to their custom, it is always cooked on the fourth day of mourning.

Parsi cuisine is known for its egg or eeda dishes. Weekend breakfast is incomplete without poro, the Parsi version of masala omelette. Bhaji par eeda ('par eeda' literally meaning 'egg on top') is a dish in which the eggs are cooked with leafy green vegetables, preferably with fenugreek leaves. The leafy greens are cooked with chopped onions and tomatoes, spices and salt. When the cooking is complete, eggs are broken over them. Very little salt is sprinkled over the eggs and the dish is covered and cooked on low heat until the egg whites are set and the yolks are runny. Akuri is a creamy and heavily spiced version of scrambled eggs that also features chopped onions, tomatoes, green chillies and coriander leaves. Parsis prefer to cook their scrambled eggs in butter and some even add cream to this dish, which is eaten with bread or roti. In papeta par eeda, thin slices of potatoes are cooked with chopped onions, tomatoes, green chillies and coriander leaves, a few spices and salt. The eggs are broken on top of the preparation when the potatoes are fried. The dish is covered and cooked on low heat until the egg whites are set. It is eaten with bread or roti.

Eggs serve a spiritual purpose at Parsi weddings or lagans, during a ritual called 'achoo michoo', which is a typical Parsi custom to ward off the evil eye. The achoo michoo is performed after the 'nahan' or ritual bath, just before the groom enters the sacred space in which the ceremony is going to be held. The ritual is performed by a married woman who is not a widow, usually the bride's mother or eldest female relative. She circles the head of the groom seven times with an egg, and then breaks it on the ground to his right. The ritual is repeated by the groom's mother on the bride. It is performed to protect the couple from the evil eye and prevent any impediments to a successful marriage.

The Parsis make a host of desserts as well. As the name suggests, lagan nu custard is a custard served as part of the grand feast at Parsi weddings. It is a simple yet delicious preparation made with eggs, milk, sugar, vanilla essence and nuts like cashew, almond or pistachio. Ravo is a Parsi kheer dish made with semolina, milk, sugar, eggs, butter, vanilla essence, green cardamom, nutmeg and mace. The dish is garnished with dried fruits like cashew and raisins that have been lightly fried in ghee. Parsi sev is a favourite, prepared by cooking fried vermicelli in sugar syrup to which some vanilla essence, nutmeg powder and green cardamom powder have been added. Slivered almonds and raisins are fried lightly in ghee and mixed with the cooked vermicelli. Sev, ravo and mithu dahi (sweet yoghurt) are served during the Parsi Navjote ceremony when a Parsi child is initiated into the Zoroastrian religion.

In spite of having lived in Calcutta for years, the Parsi community has not developed much of an affinity for Bengali cuisine. Bahadur Postwalla, a prominent member of the Parsi community in Calcutta and a trustee of the Calcutta Zoroastrian Community's Religious and Charity Fund, says, 'The older generation prefers to stick to traditional Parsi cuisine, and while the younger generation might try the cuisine of their adopted home, they have not brought it into their everyday cooking.' Alur dom and mishti doi are the only two Bengali dishes that have had a widespread influence on the Parsi community in Calcutta. In fact, the latter has slowly replaced mithu dahi at many celebratory occasions. To be fair, Bengalis have also not developed much of an affinity for Parsi cuisine. The absence of social interaction between the two communities and the lack of Parsi restaurants in the city has contributed to there being very little awareness about Parsi cuisine. The only dish that most Bengalis are likely to be aware of is dhansak, which has been made popular by cookbooks and cookery shows.

There was once a Parsi restaurant called **Elphinstone** on Meredith

Street, established in 1936. The restaurant catered to the Parsi community and served typical Parsi cuisine. It was sold off in 1965. The new owners named the restaurant Elfin, and it now offered a multicuisine menu.

In recent times, attempts have been made by institutions and individuals to create an awareness about Parsi cuisine. The **Calcutta Parsee Club** (established in 1908 and located on Mayo Road) organizes a Parsi food festival every winter, which is open to all communities in the city. 'This festival is advertised in the media and traditional Parsi dishes are prepared on order, as the Calcutta Parsee Club has no regular kitchen of its own', adds Bahadur Postwalla, who is also a member of the club. The festival is generally catered by Manackjee Rustomjee Parsi Dharamshala, which has been functioning as a boarding and lodging house for Parsi travellers on Bow Street in central Calcutta since 1909.

Attempts are also being made by some food entrepreneurs from within the community and outside, to popularize the cuisine by opening restaurants in the city. Calcutta Stories served Parsi dishes like masoor ma gosht, masoor ma marghi, dhansak, brown caramelized rice, kachumber, patra ni machchi, sali ma marghi, sali ma boti and kolmi no patio. According to Prithvish Chakravarti, it was Parsi food that sold the most in his restaurant after Anglo-Indian dishes. 'Parsi cuisine shares similarities with Indian cuisine. This appeals to the Indian palate,' he points out. He plans to serve both Anglo-Indian and Parsi dishes in the **Calcutta Stories** café.

Around 2007, Manchi and Supriya Mancherji launched their venture **Mancherji's** on Kyd Street. In all probability, it is the second Parsi restaurant in Calcutta after Elphinstone. It is still continuing business and serves dishes like dhansak, brown caramelized rice, kachumber, marghi na farcha, sali ma marghi, akuri, papeta par eeda and lagan nu custard. In its early days, the restaurant would serve only Parsi dishes and had quite an elaborate menu. But to broaden the customer base and keep the business afloat, the owners had to introduce Bengali cuisine in their restaurant. However, there is a ray of sunshine for Parsi cuisine in Calcutta. The connoisseurs and food enthusiasts, who are willing to try out new cuisines, are quite eager about Parsi food. Their number may be small but they have helped to keep alive the Parsi section of Mancherji's menu. Manackjee Rustomjee Parsi Dharamshala not only serves authentic Parsi cuisine to its resident guests but also welcomes outsiders to partake of the Parsi dishes cooked by its chefs. The dining room of the boarding and lodging house often gets a small number of enthusiastic visitors from outside the Parsi community. 'Bengalis are very experimentative', says Meher Hansotia, who manages the place with her husband, Dara. 'We get quite a few Bengali customers who are keen to try out the cuisine as well as groups of foodies for whom we host meals on a larger scale.'

Mancherji's is also into the catering business and caters Parsi food to Parsi families during their various functions. Meher Caterers is a successful catering business run by Dara and Meher Hansotia. Through this catering service, the couple serves traditional and authentic Parsi dishes to members of their community during their festivals and special occasions.

These attempts are praiseworthy and every little effort will help the mission to put Parsi food on the radar for the city's restaurant patrons.

PART THREE

Bengali Cuisine

Rasogollas in the process of being made in K.C. Das Factory, Calcutta

***Source:* Arkaprava Ghosh**

1. Bengali Cuisine

Bengal conjures up an image of a land full of lush green paddy fields and palm trees. The gods have blessed this region with the bounties of nature. The men in Gram Bangla or rural Bengal spend their time sowing and harvesting crops, grazing animals in the fields, and throwing large nets on the blue waters with the hope of catching shoals of fish. Meanwhile, smoke billows out of mud huts with thatched roofs built around ponds filled with swimming ducks. This is a sign that the lady of the house is cooking a delicious and nutritious meal for her family.

Over the years, these simple meals have evolved and developed into a fare that is vast and sophisticated. Undivided Bengal was made up of East Bengal and West Bengal. Later, East Bengal became the sovereign nation of Bangladesh with Dhaka as its capital city. West Bengal became an Indian state with the former royal capital as its capital. The Bengalis of West Bengal have coined the terms Opar Bangla for Bangladesh and Epar Bangla for West Bengal. In Bengali, 'opar' means 'that side' and 'epar' means 'this side', referring to the two regions of Bengali-speaking people separated by geographical and political boundaries.

East Bengal was largely dominated by Muslims and West Bengal by the Hindus. After the partition of Bengal in 1947, many Bengali Hindus from East Bengal migrated to West Bengal and made it their home. Those belonging to East Bengal have always been colloquially known as 'Bangals' and those from the West as 'Ghotis'. Today, Bengali society in West Bengal is made up of these two groups. There are a lot of cultural similarities, and yet, plenty of minor differences between them. Over the years, instead of becoming more pronounced, these minor differences have largely blended into the overall Bengali culture of West Bengal because of increased social interactions and intermarriages between the Bangals and Ghotis. Despite living in West Bengal for years, the older generation of Bangals still hold fond memories of their lives in the land of the Padma (the major river of Bangladesh). However, the succeeding generations consider the land of the Ganges river as their own and often find it hard to point out the differences that define the two groups because they have amalgamated so well. Just like its cultural amalgamation, the cuisine of West Bengal too has gradually evolved to become a fusion of the dishes of the two groups, which are largely similar with some trivial differences in the preference of ingredients and styles of cooking. Moreover, the long period of Muslim rule in undivided Bengal has made Muslims the second largest religious community, after Hindus, amongst the Bengalis of West Bengal. Their culinary practices and eating habits have largely influenced the cuisine of Bengal.

The beauty of Bengali cuisine lies in the vast array of its dishes that can be rich and exquisite as well as simple and delicious. In the chapter 'Bangla Ranna' from their book, *The Calcutta Cookbook: A Treasury of Recipes from Pavement to Palace* (1995), authors Minakshie Das Gupta, Bunny Gupta and Jaya Chaliha write, 'Monsieur Daridan, the French Ambassador to India in the 1960s, remarked to his Bengali host in Calcutta that of all the foods in the world, only Chinese and Bengali food could compare with the sophistication of his native fare' (p. 34).

A common notion about this cuisine is that its two pillars are rice and fish. This couldn't be further from the truth. The three authors (above) elaborate about the food habits of the Bengalis since time immemorial in another chapter 'A History and Philosophy of Food' from the same book, 'The Bengalis were amongst the foremost maritime people of the subcontinent. They navigated the rivers and seas and caught vast netfuls of fish and crustaceans, the freshwater variety in particular' (p. 2).

The authors further mention that of all the wild grasses that grew in profusion, rice was perhaps the only one that yielded a grain that was fit to be consumed and was, therefore, cultivated. Besides rice and fish, lentils were another staple. Ginger, long pepper, sesame and turmeric were used in cooking not only for their medicinal properties but also to titillate the palate. The diet of the inhabitants of this land also consisted of the fruits that they gathered. Ingredients like sugarcane and coconut were often used and native fruits like hog plum, the white, yellow, bitter and ridge gourds and yams were common favourites. Sesame oil and ghee served as mediums of cooking.

During prehistoric times in Bengal, the hunter's wife dug the earth for colocasia corms and gathered aquatic plants, tiny shrimps and molluscs from ponds and marshlands. Animals were hunted by men and the wife's gatherings complemented the husband's hunting of the mongoose, wild boar, turtle, iguana, hare, porcupine and sometimes, the deer.

Things began to change when the Aryans arrived from Central Asia, migrating to northern India in the second millennium BCE, and reaching Bengal in the fifth and sixth centuries BCE. They found the fertility of the soil and the abundant monsoon of the region appealing. Making full use of this rice-growing belt, the Aryans planted and reaped the natural wealth of the fertile land filled with rivers, teeming with fish. They introduced Vedic rituals in the preparation, serving and eating of food, and developed a fondness for tropical fruits, converting the bounty of Bengal into sweet and savoury dishes that were delicious enough to be served to the gods.

Rice

Although Bengal is dotted with hills and forests, most of its terrain is flat, delta land that is braided with rivers. Its location in the delta of the Ganges, fills the region with fertile alluvial soil that is well-suited for the cultivation of paddy. Most of the cultivable land is divided into lush green fields, primarily meant for growing rice—the staple food crop. In her book, *Bengali Cooking: Seasons and Festivals* (2017), Chitrita Banerji writes, 'In this fertile tropical delta that serves as a basin for innumerable rivers, rivulets and tributaries, it is rice that has been the common sustaining staple from pre-Aryan times until today' (p. ix).

Raw rice is called chaal in Bengali and cooked rice is called bhaat. In Sanskrit, the word anna (pronounced anno in Bengali) means 'grain', particularly signifying the rice grain. A popular manifestation of Goddess Parvati is Annapurna, the consort of Shiva. She is believed to be the goddess of food and nourishment. Annapurna is shown in religious pictures offering rice grains as alms to her husband. The importance of rice in the Bengali community is highlighted by certain religious rituals. Annobhog is a very important ritual observed during religious ceremonies in Bengal. This devotional rice offering is served by the Bengali Hindus to their deities during religious festivals, and forms a very important part of their worship. For example, during Durga Puja, the most important festival of the Bengalis that takes place annually in autumn, annobhog is offered to Goddess Durga; this cooked rice is eaten later as prasad by the devotees once the worship is over. It is also an essential part of the Bengali ritual to offer rice grains as naivedya (main devotional offering) during religious ceremonies. Even unhusked rice, which is called dhan in Bengali, is an important part of ritualistic offering to the gods.

Kabita Chowdhury, who belongs to a zamindari family herself and is the daughter-in-law of the famous Dutta Chaudhury family of Andul, fills the pages of her cookbook *Rajbarir Ranna* (2017) with many traditional as well as unusual recipes that were mostly made at her in-law's house. The Dutta Chaudhury family is the first zamindari family of Andul, a town in the nearby Howrah district of West Bengal. The zamindari families of Bengal lived lives of great wealth, privilege and luxury. Known for their lavish and opulent lifestyle, these zamindars (jomidars in Bengali) were patrons of art, culture and the finer things in life. 'Rajbari', literally meaning 'royal house', refers to the beautiful and stately mansions in which these families lived. These palatial houses are an integral part of Bengal's legacy of Bonedi Bari. In Bengali, the word 'bonedi' is used to describe high-born or socially distinguished families. This includes both zamindari as well as aristocratic families.

The ancestors of the Dutta Chaudhury family were Ramsharan Dutta Chaudhury, Gobindasharan Dutta Chaudhury and Harisharan Dutta Chaudhury. One school of thought credits Gobdindasharan Dutta Chaudhury for founding the village of Gobindapur, which was later merged with Sutanuti and Kalikata to form Calcutta. The story woven around this discovery is that sometime towards the beginning of the sixteenth century, while returning from a pilgrimage by boat, Gobindasharan had a spiritual dream. In the dream, Goddess Kali instructed him to dig the barren land on the riverbank. He followed the instruction and discovered an enormous amount of wealth hidden underneath. He stayed back and founded the place, which was named Gobindapur after him. This school of thought is contradicted by the second one, which firmly believes that the powerful and affluent merchant families of the Sheths and Basaks founded the village of Gobindapur. Four families of the Basaks, and one of the Sheths, were determined to profit by the growing prosperity of Betore, then a major trading centre around present-day Shibpur, a neighbourhood in the city of Howrah. This encouraged them to establish the village on the east bank of the river, which was named Gobindapur after Gobindaji (Lord Krishna), the family deity of the Sheths and Basaks.

Bengalis celebrate so many festivals throughout the year that it has given rise to the proverb, '*baro maashe tero parbon*', which means thirteen festivals in twelve months. A very interesting mention in Chowdhury's book is of Nabanno Utsab, a harvest festival that is celebrated by the Bengali Hindus of both Epar and Opar Bangla. This festival, which is of utmost importance to the agrarian community of Bengal, is celebrated in the Bengali Hindu month of Agrahayan, which extends from the middle of November to the middle of December. The word 'nabanno' literally means 'new rice'. During this festival, Gram Bangla, in an act of propitiation and also as an expression of gratitude for the bounty, first offers this harvested rice to the gods before enjoying it themselves. Chowdhury describes the naivedya that is offered to the gods at the time of worship. The harvested rice grains are coarsely ground and put in a platter with an upward curving edge. Milk is poured on these grains and peeled and chopped fruits like orange, banana, papaya, grapes, pomegranate, cucumber and dates are placed atop it. Other ingredients like grated coconut, crumbled sandesh, powdered sugar and broken pieces of patali gur are also sprinkled over. The naivedya is then garnished with grated khoya.

Beautiful white designs or alponas are drawn on the clean floor in front of the gods and the platter containing the naivedya is placed on them. After the end of the worship, all the ingredients of the naivedya are mixed together and served as prasad. Even the alpona, which is an important part of all Bengali Hindu religious ceremonies, is drawn with the paste of coarsely ground rice. The abundance of rice made it easier to use its paste for floor designs, a practice that has been prevalent for centuries.

In Bengali tradition, plain boiled rice is eaten with bitter preparations, leafy green vegetables, lentils, vegetables, egg, fish and meat curries. Chitrita Banerji writes, 'In ancient and medieval times, Bengalis did, however, sometimes moisten their rice by pouring clarified butter, ghee, over it after it was served. A succinct description of an average person's meal can be found in the *Prakritapaingala*, written around 1400 CE, in which there is a quotation from a hundred years earlier: "Fortunate is the man whose wife serves him on a banana leaf some hot rice with ghee, mourala fish, fried leaves of the jute plant, and some hot milk on the side"' (p. xvi). According to Banerji, it was not until the establishment of the Islamic rule in India that pilaf or pulao (as Bengalis call it) became a common item at feasts and banquets. The Muslim rulers, in keeping with the practice of the entire Middle Eastern region, found it unpalatable to eat rice without first frying and then cooking it.

The Bengalis who had converted to Islam embraced the Muslim cuisine. They also continued their former culinary practices and eating habits with some significant changes. Their daily fare was the same as that of the Bengali Hindus, but the influence of Muslim cuisine also made them utilize the abundant produce of vegetables and fish of the land and cook them into dishes, like *enchorer qorma* (unripe jackfruit qorma), *kancha kalar kofta* (raw banana kofta), *maachher kofta* (fish kofta) and *mahi pulao* (fish pulao), which was typical of the culinary culture of their Muslim rulers. According to Banerji, qorma is a Muslim term, meaning meat or chicken cooked in a mild yoghurt-based sauce with ghee instead of oil. Some people use thick evaporated milk instead of yoghurt. This method of cooking can be applied to vegetables and fish as well. Kofta, a Persian word, originally implies fried meatballs. After the establishment of Muslim rule vegetarian koftas also began to be made in India, and incorporated into the pan-Indian cuisine. The abundance of banana trees in Bengal led to the creation of koftas using the raw fruit of the plant. Fish meat was also used in the preparation of some koftas that were cooked in spicy gravies. While fish like bhekti, chingri (prawn), rui and katla were cooked into delectable pulaos, it was a masterstroke to use ilish, the iconic fish of Bengal, in pulao preparation.

Meat is a very important ingredient in Muslim cuisine. Goat meat has always been a favourite of the Bengali Hindus. The converts now added beef and chicken (both favourite meats of the Muslims) to their larder, which was already well stocked with goat meat, and included these varieties in many recipes. They made delicious pulaos and curries with them. When it comes to goat meat, Bengali Muslims have always preferred khashi or castrated goat meat over ordinary goat meat because the body of such a goat is more developed and fleshier. Over the years, the Bengali Hindus have also adopted this preference and purchase khashi meat mostly from the Muslim butchers. But the Bengali Hindus also enjoy eating the meat of young and tender goats, something that is largely avoided by the Bengali Muslims.

Another kind of meat eaten by this religious section is duck meat. But if given a choice between duck and chicken meat, the preference is always for the latter. Duck meat is more expensive and not as widely available as chicken meat. Moreover, it has a strong odour that needs to be neutralized, which only a competent cook can achieve. Duck meat that is prepared well can compete with any well-made chicken dish. But the pricing, availability and odour of duck meat along with the difficulty in cooking it make chicken meat, at least on a large scale, the preferred choice.

Today, duck meat is not commonly cooked in the homes of the Bengali Muslim families of West Bengal. But it continues to be cooked in Bangladesh, particularly during winter because the birds are quite plump and healthy during this season. The meat is generally cooked into a 'bhuna' dish. According to Chitrita Banerji, 'bhuna' is a Muslim term meaning fried for a long time with ground and whole spices over high heat. This method of cooking is usually applied to meat. To prepare *hansher manghser bhuna* or duck meat bhuna, the pieces of meat, preferably along with the skin and fat, are cooked in mustard oil with whole garom mashla, dried red chillies, bay leaves, plenty of chopped onions, the pastes of dried red chillies, ginger, garlic, turmeric, coriander and cumin, and salt. The spices are fried in oil for some time before the meat and water are added. The wok is covered with a lid and the meat is cooked till done. The cooked meat pieces will be surrounded by thick, rich and oily gravy. The preparation is then seasoned with garom mashla, roasted cumin powder and slit green chillies, and stirred for a few minutes before taking it off the flame.

The meat of pigeons and small birds were also eaten. In addition to duck eggs, which have always been a strong preference of the Bengali Hindus, the Muslim converts now employed hen eggs in their diet. They cooked these into curries and relished them with boiled rice. All of this made their cuisine ample because it included the best of both worlds.

Gradually, with time, the Bengali Muslims of West Bengal shifted their attention to biryani, thanks to the advent and spread of the biryani culture, after the Nawab of Awadh relocated to Metiabruz. Mahi pulao became more of a preference with the Muslims of Bangladesh. Their enthusiasm for ilish pulao is well known thanks to their obsession with the fish. The Bengali Muslim of West Bengal prefers biryani to be made with beef or mutton. The influence of the royal kitchen of Metiabruz lives on in the preparation because it features potatoes. They mostly enjoy this single dish wonder on its own or with cucumber raita or green salad or even a side dish of chicken. Of course, Bangladeshi Muslims also enjoy eating meat biryanis and out of these, the delicious *kachchi biryani* is tremendously popular. In the regular biryani preparation, half-cooked rice and fully cooked meat are arranged in alternate layers in a large container. The lid of the container is sealed and the biryani is cooked on a low flame. 'Kachchi', on the other hand, means 'raw'. In kachchi biryani, raw rice is cooked with raw meat, which lends the dish its name. The raw meat pieces are marinated with yoghurt, ground spices, fried onions and salt. The biryani is slow cooked over low heat. This makes the meat very soft and tender in texture, lending an extra flavour to the preparation. Khashi goat meat is preferred for this preparation. Since the royal kitchen of Metiabruz introduced biryani into undivided Bengal, the kachchi biryani features potato. Other additional ingredients like hard-boiled eggs and alubokhara (prunes) can also be added.

Meat pulaos and biryanis are generally cooked with long-grain basmati rice and garnished with beresta (crispy fried onions). They form an essential part of dawats or feasts in the Muslim community. Meat pulaos have continued in popularity among the Bengali Muslims of West Bengal. *Morog pulao* or chicken pulao is especially popular in both Epar and Opar Bangla. Another variety of pulao popular with the Bengali Muslims of Epar Bangla is kofta pulao (flavoured rice featuring fried meatballs). Elaborate dishes like pulaos, biryanis, kebabs, tikia kebabs (also known as tikias) and chaanp (a Mughlai dish consisting of flattened slices of boneless meat in dry gravy that is rich and spicy) are not regular fare for the Bengali Muslim. Too rich to be consumed every day, these dishes are reserved for the weekends and special occasions. While drinks like *aam pora sharbot*, a sweet and slightly spicy refreshing drink made with the pulp of roasted raw mango or kancha aam, *beler pana*, a sweet yoghurt-based drink made with the pulp of wood apple or bel and *ghol*, a light and thin sweet yoghurt drink, are popular coolers with both the Muslims and the Hindus in the community, the traditional salted and spicy yoghurt drink called *borhani* is largely confined to the Bengali Muslims. Since this drink aids digestion, it is especially served with the rich food spread and is taken after meals.

Over the years, thanks to the efforts by chefs and connoisseurs, and also because of increased social mixing between the two religious groups, many dishes in Muslim cuisine have been embraced by the Bengali Hindus. Thanks to their non-vegetarian food habits, the Bengali Hindus not only relish the delicious rich food spread of the Muslims but some of them even make attempts to cook a few of these dishes at home.

There are two primary categories of rice, depending on the method of dehusking the paddy—sheddho chaal or parboiled rice and atap chaal or sun-dried rice. Vitamins and micronutrients are retained in the thicker parboiled variety, making it more nutritious. These are lost in the milling and polishing of the fine sun-dried variety. This, perhaps, explains the reason behind parboiled rice being a favourite choice and commonly eaten for both lunch and dinner. Atap rice is preferred for making pulao, khichuri and payesh. It is ground into flour and used for making pithes. Atap rice is also considered by the Hindu section of the community to be more appropriate for its widows who are traditionally expected to be vegetarians and follow a diet that is bound by certain rules and conventions. Most importantly, it is the preferred variety of rice that is offered by the Bengali Hindus to their deities.

Each category of rice has different varieties that are known by different names and are used for different occasions. The different varieties of rice will have varying degrees of fineness and length. The finer varieties of atap rice are usually used for making payesh or pulao while the coarser varieties are used to make plain boiled rice. The Burdwan district of West Bengal is famous for sun-dried varieties like the scented small-grained kaminibhog and the fragrant gopalbhog and gobindobhog. Traditionally, the last is the preferred variety to be cooked as annobhog. Chamarmoni and dudhershar (literally meaning 'cream of milk' and so named because of its creamy colour) are the popular parboiled varieties. Bengalis also use the long-grain basmati rice from north India for making rice dishes on special occasions. It is particularly used in the preparation of biryanis.

Eating meals by sitting cross-legged on the floor was a common practice in the early days before the dining table took over. Small individual pieces of carpet, called asans, would be spread on the floor for each person to sit on. However, in the villages of Bengal, this manner of eating food still continues. Food would be served to the person in front of this seat. In the early days, food was served on banana leaves that had been cut to size or on dried sal leaves pinned together with twigs. Later, these platters made from leaves got replaced with terracotta, stone or metal plates. Although, sadly, chinaware and stainless steel have largely replaced these traditional dishes in modern homes, some people still adhere to tradition by serving food the traditional way during functions and ceremonies.

Since Bengali cuisine largely centres upon rice, the traditional way of serving food is to first heap a generous amount of piping hot rice in the middle of the plate. Some salt, a few wedges of lime and one or two whole green chillies are placed on one side of the upper edge of the platter. Sometimes, appetizers like bitter leaves and vegetable fries in summer and vegetable fritters in winter are served around the upper edge of the platter as well. The different curries and other food items are served in a number of small bowls arranged around the plate beginning with the dal or lentil on the extreme right and ending with the sweet on the extreme left. Often, a hole would be made in the middle of the mound of rice and some ghee poured into it to flavour the initial mouthfuls of rice. Since the meal is eaten with the right hand, the glass is placed on the left.

In modern times, the tremendous improvement in means of communication has led to pan-Indian influences in Bengali cooking. Today, we find a variety of pulaos, both vegetarian and non-vegetarian, being cooked in Bengali Hindu households. Pulaos are popularly made with mixed vegetables, green peas, whole cumin seeds, dried fruits, hard-boiled eggs, fish, chicken and mutton. But, if asked to write about the traditional pulao preparation of Bengali cuisine, then it has to be *basanti pulao*. This slightly mishti or sweet pulao preparation is holud or 'yellow' in colour and usually made with the fragrant gobindobhog variety of rice.

While those Bengalis, who have their roots in East Bengal, use more spice and oil in their cooking because they like their dishes to have a sharp taste, those with their roots in West Bengal have the habit of adding a little bit of sugar (about half a teaspoon) to most of their food preparations, particularly to many of their vegetable and some of their leafy green and lentil dishes because they believe that the addition of sugar improves the taste of whatever is cooking.

But there are exceptions. Basanti pulao is a unique rice preparation in which the Bengali Hindus from both sides of the border add sugar. The yellow colour, which lends this pulao its name ('basanti' means yellow colour in Sanskrit) is brought about by the use of holud or turmeric ('holud' also means turmeric in Bengali). The rice, which has been previously soaked in water for some time, is dried and mixed with ghee, turmeric, ground garom mashla, ginger paste and salt. A few pieces of whole garom mashla, bay leaves, broken cashew nuts and raisins are stir-fried in ghee. The rice is then added to the spices and dried fruits, and stir-fried with them for some time. At this juncture, water and sugar are added, and the rice is cooked till done. This pulao preparation, which is also known as mishti pulao or holud pulao, has pride of place in Bengali cuisine. Tremendous importance is attached to it by making it the only alternative to plain boiled rice in annobhog. It is the favourite pulao dish that is cooked in Bengali Hindu homes on special occasions and served during social gatherings. It is also a popular pulao preparation that is served in feasts organized on celebratory occasions, whether religious or otherwise.

Despite having many servants, the women of zamindari families would take a lot of interest in the preparation of food. The women of the

Dutta Chaudhury family particularly enjoyed cooking out-of-the-box recipes in their ranna ghar or kitchen. One such recipe was *kamala lebur pulao*, which was made with the two main ingredients of gobindobhog rice and orange juice. A variety of spices, dried fruits, ghee, sugar, salt, lime juice, grated orange rind, saffron infused milk, grated khoya and miniature pantuas or nikutis are the other ingredients that are used to make this rice dish. The pulao is garnished with orange segments. *Gajorer pulao*, made with the two main ingredients of grated carrot and basmati rice, is another rare dish cooked in the household.

The family of Maharaja Nabakrishna Deb (1733–97) of Sovabazar is one of the most renowned bonedi or aristocratic families of Calcutta. They are famous throughout the city for their grand celebration of Durga Puja. The Sovabazar Rajbarir Durga Puja was begun in 1757 by Maharaja Nabakrishna Deb and was regularly attended by Robert Clive, Warren Hastings and many other officials of the British East India Company.

The women of the household took a lot of interest in the activities of the house. They were not only skilled in the art of embroidery but were also excellent chefs. The cuisine of this bonedi paribar or family is renowned for its traditional and unique dishes. The book, *Sovabazar Rajbarir Rannabanna* (2017), has a collection of recipes from the kitchen of this aristocratic family. The recipes have been narrated by Nandini Deb Bourani, wife of Aloke Krishna Deb, a descendant of the family, to the author of the book, Sushmita Basu Singh. Chhanar pulao is one such unique rice preparation made by the women of the household that is mentioned in the book. Maida, which acts as a binding agent here, is blended well with chhana. Some salt is added to the mixture and small balls are made of it, which are then lightly fried till they turn golden brown. Meanwhile some washed and dried gobindobhog rice is mixed with plain yoghurt and ginger paste and kept aside once again to dry. The dried rice grains are cooked in ghee with bay leaves, shah jeera (caraway seeds), pounded javitri, whole garom mashla, salt, sugar, raisins and broken cashew nuts. After some time, the required quantity of water is added to this preparation. Once the rice is cooked, the fried balls of chhana are added to it. The dish is stirred well for one last time before it is taken off the flame.

Bengalis also cook rice into simple delectable dishes like khichuri—rice and lentil dish cooked together with spices. Although khichuri can be eaten anytime of the year, for some strange reason it is a dish that Bengalis mostly associate with the monsoon.

The consistency of khichuri can be thin or thick. The variety of rice and lentil used in this preparation is generally short-grained atap rice and bhaja (roasted) moong dal (split green gram). Sometimes, musur dal (split red lentil) is combined with bhaja moong dal to make this dish. Khichuri can be made plain or with vegetables like potato, tomato, green peas, carrot and cauliflower that are added to the basic rice and lentil mixture. This simple rice and lentil dish, which is seasoned with ghee towards the end, is generally yellow in colour because of the turmeric that is added to the cooking. Many also like to season the preparation with some sugar. Although khichuri is a complete meal in itself, Bengalis like to eat it with fried vegetables like aubergines, potatoes and pointed gourds or a fritter made with aubergine called *begooni*. Some even like to eat it with non-vegetarian accompaniments like fried fish, omelette and deep-fried boiled eggs. Crispy fried papors (poppadoms) are a popular accompaniment to khichuri.

The Bengali Muslims of West Bengal not only like to pair khichuri with the aforementioned accompaniments but also with highly seasoned meat dishes like *bhuna gosht* and meat koftas. 'Gosht', a Persian word, means 'meat'. Generally, beef or khashi goat meat is preferred to make the dish. In this preparation, the meat is cooked in oil with bay leaves, whole garom mashla, the pastes of onion, ginger and garlic, tomato paste, yoghurt, ground spices like turmeric, black pepper, cumin, coriander, dried red chilli and garom mashla, and salt. Since the gravy in this dish is of a thick consistency, the water added while cooking should be just enough to boil the meat. The wok is covered with a lid and the meat is cooked until it turns soft and tender. When the water dries up and the dark brown gravy releases oil, a few slit green chillies and chopped coriander leaves are added to it.

The Bengali Muslims of Epar Bangla like to make their koftas with ground beef, goat meat or chicken. The minced meat is ground to a paste with onions, spices, herbs, gram flour and salt, shaped into slightly flat circular discs and fried. These are then paired with khichuri. The meat koftas can also be cooked into rich, spicy and thick gravies and served alongside the khichuri.

Bhuna khichuri is a slightly exclusive variety, which is more popular in Opar than Epar Bangla, particularly with the Muslim community. Unlike the usual khichuri, this one has the dry and fluffy texture of pulao. Also known as *bhuni khichuri*, the two main ingredients of this dish are atap rice and bhaja moong dal. A considerable variety of spices like whole garom mashla, cumin seeds, dried red chillies, bay leaves and the pastes of turmeric, cumin, coriander, ginger, dried red chillies and garom mashla are used, making this variety of khichuri rich in taste. Traditionally, the ingredients are cooked in ghee in a manner similar to making pulao. Whole or slit green chillies and chopped coriander leaves can be added to the preparation. While Muslims add onion and garlic to the cooking, the Hindus add dried fruits like cashew nuts and raisins, and sometimes, even a little sugar. The ingredients need to be fried for a longer time than usual, lending the dish its name. Bhuna khichuri can also be cooked with vegetables, egg, fish or meat. While the residents of Opar Bangla like cooking bhuna khichuri with hilsa or beef, there is an often-heard story in Epar Bangla that Swami Vivekananda, who was an enthusiastic and experimental chef, is believed to have been fond of this type of khichuri and liked cooking it with duck eggs.

The Hindu section of the community gives a lot of importance to khichuri by offering this simple dish as bhog (devotional food offering) to their deities. *Bhoger khichuri* is mildly spiced and made with the fragrant gobindobhog variety of atap rice. Bhaja moong dal is the only variety of lentil that is used. Onion and garlic are taboo ingredients. Seasonal vegetables can also be added. The most popular accompaniment to bhoger khichuri is a mixed vegetable dish called *labra*, which is made with a variety of seasonal vegetables. Leafy green vegetables may also be added to the preparation. While onion and garlic are not used, grated coconut is usually added in bhoger labra. Some sugar is generally added to the preparation, which is also seasoned with ghee towards the end. Since this is a dry dish, water is generally not added to the cooking. The vegetables and leafy greens begin to release water when salt is added to them. The wok is covered with a lid and the vegetables are cooked in their own steam. Although this mushy vegetable dish is also eaten with steamed rice, it pairs best with khichuri.

Khichuri is especially associated with Saraswati Puja, which takes place annually at the end of January or early February in Bengal. Saraswati is the goddess of knowledge, learning, language, music and all other forms of art. In Bengal, Saraswati Puja is also celebrated on the day of Vasant Panchami (called Basanta Panchami in Bengali). Vasant Panchami is a harvest festival that is celebrated in the Hindu calendar month of Magha. The month falls between mid-January and mid-February. The festival marks the beginning of spring (vasant or basanta means spring). Since Goddess Saraswati is associated with knowledge and arts, this is an important day of worship for all those who are connected with academics, particularly children, and even those who work in artistic fields. A holiday is declared in academic institutions and students don't study on this day. On the contrary, many schools observe Saraswati Puja and much to the delight of the children, ample quantities of bhoger khichuri are prepared in the temporary kitchens constructed on their premises, which are distributed to them as prasad once the worship is over.

Another very interesting aspect of Saraswati Puja is its association with a tropical fruit known as ber in Hindi and Indian plum or Indian jujube in English. In Bengali, this small and round fruit is called kool and it appears in the market around the same time as this festival. Two types of kool are sold in the markets of Bengal—narkel kool and topa kool. Although the first one, called narkel kool ('narkel' means coconut in Bengali), tastes nothing like a tender green coconut, it is to some extent shaped like one. It is green in colour and sweet in taste. The second one, when ripe, takes on a reddish-brown hue, and is sour in taste.

Kool is considered to be the favourite fruit of Goddess Saraswati. It is offered to her during worship on the day of Saraswati Puja. In Bengali homes, it is considered inauspicious to eat the fruit before it has been offered to the goddess on the day of Vasant Panchami. Only after the worship is over, the fruit is distributed as prasad to the devotees. Henceforth, Bengalis can partake of this seasonal fruit as much as they want. Thanks to its sweet taste, narkel kool is relished on its own as prasad after the worship is over. But the sour taste of topa kool makes it difficult to relish it as a fruit. Only few can adjust their palate to its sourness. Many generally flavour it with sugar or jaggery and cook it into a sweet chutney preparation after the worship. Topa kool can also be used to make *ambole* (sweet and sour runny chutney) or a sweet, sour and spicy pickle.

It is also interesting to note that this simple rice and lentil dish called khichuri caught the attention of the British. In the chapter 'A History and Philosophy of Food' from their book *The Calcutta Cookbook: A Treasury of Recipes from Pavement to Palace* (1995), 'Calcutta's chronicle began on a hot, wet August afternoon in 1690 when a hungry Job Charnock climbed off his ship on to the steps of a muddy ghat (landing stage)[...]The river was the Hooghly and the place Sutanati, one of the three principal villages which became Calcutta[...]It is said that Charnock Sahib was served khichuri, a meal of rice and dal cooked together in a terracotta handi (cooking pot), by a flabbergasted villager' (pp. 1–2). The British grew to enjoy this dish so much that they adapted it to their own palate and cooked it in a new way with rice, lentils, fried fish flakes, hard-boiled eggs, spices and raisins. They called this dish kedgeree and took the fish kedgeree back to England, introducing it on the breakfast menu all over the Commonwealth. Minced meat was later added to bring about a variety in this dish.

Villagers in Bengal enjoy a preparation of slightly fermented cooked rice called *panta bhaat* with accompaniments like raw onions and chillies. The cooked rice is fermented by soaking it overnight in water. It is a very filling dish, making it the ideal breakfast option for farmers, who have to toil for long hours in the fields. A common way to eat panta bhaat is to add some salt and pour some mustard oil over the cold and slightly watery fermented rice, which is mixed well and relished with accompaniments like raw onions and green chillies or mashed potatoes mixed with some salt, mustard oil and minced onions and green chillies or fried and crushed dried red chillies. Some people also like to squeeze some lime juice into the rice.

Leftover vegetable dishes, vegetable mashes and lentil pastes are the most common accompaniments to this rice dish followed by vegetable fritters and *bora*s (small round balls that are deep-fried) made of lentils or edible leaves. In Bengali, 'sheddho' means boiled and 'makha' means mashed. Generally, mashes are called *sheddho makha*. They may also be casually called only 'sheddho' or 'makha'. The most common vegetable mash is made with the potato. Other vegetables, which complement the potato like bitter gourds, hyacinth beans, unripe papaya, green banana, pointed gourd, okra and colocasia corm are also used to make mashes. The vegetable is boiled and mashed with the boiled potato. But okra and bitter gourds can also be mashed on their own. A paste of bhaja chholar dal that is made by grinding the roasted dal together with minced green chillies and some salt, and then mixing it with mustard oil and minced onions, is the most popular lentil paste accompaniment. Another popular accompaniment among those villagers, who are financially better placed, is *kancha posto bata* or raw poppy seeds paste that is made in the same way. A paste of dry roasted black sesame seeds is also relished with the fermented rice.

The villagers that are better off often catch small fish from the ponds which they roast and grind with minced onions, green chillies and some salt. Mustard oil is mixed into this paste and eaten along with fermented rice. Pastes of kankra (roasted crab) meat and shutki maachh (dried fish) are also much liked accompaniments to panta bhaat. Bigger fish, particularly the carp varieties like rui and katla, are deep-fried in mustard oil, ground to a paste with the same ingredients, mixed with the oil and eaten with the rice. Some even eat panta bhaat with a semi-dry vegetable dish to which a few shrimps have been added.

Since this fermented rice dish is eaten cold, it is perfect for the hot and humid summers. Even urban households are no stranger to this summer staple and relish it on hot summer afternoons.

On Dashami, which marks the end of Durga Puja, many families observe the tradition of offering sheetal bhog to the goddess. 'Sheetal' is a Sanskrit word. It is derived from the root word 'sheet', which means cold. Sheetal bhog refers to the cold food that is offered to the goddess. The descendants of Sabarna Roy Choudhury have been celebrating their famed 'Aatchala Bari' (eight-roofed structure) Durga Puja at Barisha in Calcutta since 1610. The family members have continued the tradition of offering sheetal bhog to the goddess on Dashami since the inception of this puja, which is considered to be the oldest Durga Puja in the city. The food, which is cooked a day in advance, consists of panta bhaat, *khesari dal* (a type of lentil known as grass pea), *kochu shaak* (the stalks of colocasia leaves), *koi maachher jhal* (climbing perch cooked in spicy gravy) and *chaltar ambole* (a sweet and sour runny chutney made with elephant apple).

Durga Puja celebrates the victory of Goddess Durga over the demon Mahishasur in a fierce battle that was fought between them, thereby, epitomizing the victory of good over evil. But, in Bengal, this festival also celebrates the goddess's visit to her natal home with her children, Lakshmi, Saraswati, Ganesh and Kartik—all major deities of the Hindus. The festive season is heralded by the abundant growth of kash phul (a white and feather-like long, oversized grass native to the Indian subcontinent) in the countryside. The festival is preceded by Mahalaya, which is believed to mark the start of Goddess Durga's journey to her natal home from her husband's abode in Mount Kailash. It is on this day that the whole of Bengal has been waking up at 4 a.m. since 1932 to listen to Birendra Krishna Bhadra's recitation of the *Chandi Path* that is broadcasted by the Calcutta chapter of Akashvani (All India Radio).

Dashami happens to be the day when the goddess, along with her children, is immersed in the river as a symbolic departure from her natal home, bringing the four-day festivities to an end. She is now returning to her husband, Lord Shiva, in Mount Kailash. Sabarna Roy Choudhury's descendants, like the rest who observe the tradition of offering sheetal bhog to the goddess on this day, believe that the prospect of leaving her natal home makes the goddess sad and she has no appetite to eat. The members of the family are also sad that the goddess is leaving them and are not in a mood to cook on the last day. This explains the reason for the cold and plain fare that is offered to the goddess. Others believe that since the goddess is in such a hurry to return to her husband, there is no time to cook a fresh meal.

Another equally popular preparation in the villages and urban households of Bengal is *phana bhaat* (literally meaning starchy cooked rice). Phana bhaat is a Bengali rice gruel or porridge preparation. When the starchy rice water (phan) is not drained and eaten with the hot cooked rice, the preparation is called phana bhaat. Salt is always added to the rice while it is being cooked. Although, traditionally, some ghee is spread over the starchy cooked rice, many may add butter to it instead. Like all of the other gruel preparations in the world, phana bhaat is a staple dish for the farming community of Bengal. Since this mushy and starchy rice preparation, which is very filling, is eaten hot, it is prepared more often during winters. It is eaten with all of those preparations that accompany panta bhaat except fritters and boras. Another much liked accompaniment to phana bhaat is a seasoned mash of boiled potato and egg, known as *alu deem sheddho makha*.

Chitrita Banerji also writes about the abundance of the rice crop leading to other mutations like muri (puffed rice), khoi (popped rice) and chire (beaten rice). All these three forms of rice are enjoyed with equal fervour by the Bengalis. 'Puffed rice, muri, became a favourite occasional snack as well as breakfast food served with milk and brown sugar. Popped rice, khoi, apart from being eaten with milk, is used to make a favourite winter sweet, *moa*. It also has a distinctly auspicious significance, unlike puffed rice, for it is poured into the sacred fire in front of which the Hindu wedding takes place, as a special offering to the gods,' writes Banerji (pp. 54–55). But the most interesting mutation is chire. 'Probably no other region does as much with the chira as Bengal does,' continues the food historian. 'Soaked in water and softened, it is eaten with sugar, fruits, yoghurt or milk as phalahar. Combined with the coastal bounty of finely-ground coconut, it provides the most delicate of tastes. It can be fried very quickly in hot ghee or roasted in a dry pot, to be eaten as a savoury item seasoned with salt, pepper and chopped ginger. In winter it is combined with vegetables to make a quick pulao, or with sticky-sweet date-palm sugar to make another kind of moa. Mixed with yoghurt and milk-based sweets, the chira becomes part of the offering for the gods, and brides and bridegrooms go through the ceremony of "dadhimangal" very early on their wedding day when they are given this to eat before the day's fast begins'(p. 55).

Condiments

Bengal abounds in the shorshe (mustard) plant. This made the Bengalis switch to using shorsher tel (mustard oil) over the years as the medium of cooking thanks to its sharp taste. Despite the arrival of sunflower, groundnut and rice bran oils in modern Bengali kitchens, the preference still remains for mustard oil. Although these new oils (collectively called shaada tel or white oil by the Bengalis because of their light and transparent appearance) are considered to be a healthier option, the mustard oil is a constant feature in Bengali kitchens. The community cannot think of cooking certain items like fish in any other oil except mustard oil. Even the paste of mustard seeds is used in cooking. Different varieties of fish, and even vegetables like begoon (aubergine), sheem (hyacinth beans), dherosh (okra), uchche and karola (bitter gourds), are often cooked in this paste. This has lent these vegetable dishes the names *begoon shorshe, sheem shorshe, dherosh shorshe, uchche shorshe* and *karola shorshe*. An assortment of vegetables like alu (potato), mulo (radish), begoon and kumro (pumpkin) are often cooked with shojne danta (drumstick) and bori (sun-dried lentil blob) in mustard paste. Bengalis prefer to cook mustard paste based preparations in mustard oil because this enhances the taste.

A variety of spices is used in cooking. Whole spices are ground into pastes with the help of a traditional stone grinder called 'shil-nora'. A variant of the mortar and pestle, 'shil' is the slab of stone on which the spices are ground and 'nora' is the big and heavy pestle used to grind them. A shil-nora is a fixed feature in Bengali households, no matter how modern some of them may be. The community largely believes that grinding spices in this manner is better as it brings out their real punch. Until medieval times, the spices used in Bengali cooking were minimal. Turmeric, ginger, mustard, long pepper and jamila (sour citrus) were some of the main ones used. Gradually, long pepper was replaced with black peppercorn, which was, in turn, replaced by the cheaper chilli. The green chilli is a Central American import and found its way into

Bengali cooking through Sri Lanka, which explains the reason behind it being called 'lanka' in Bengali. Both the green chilli and dried red chilli are liberally used in food preparation. Bird's eye chilli is a small pungent chilli that is green in colour, and when fully mature, takes on a bright red hue. The sharp and severely hot taste that it imparts gives it a small number of followers who enjoy eating it with rice and curry preparations.

The memoirs of Hiuen Tsang, a seventh-century Chinese traveller who came to India, and thus, to Bengal, to study at the centres of Buddhist learning, provide some details about the food habits of those times. Onion and garlic, used a lot in cooking by the Muslims worldwide, were considered to be taboo items because of their heathen associations. They were also supposed to have a libidinous effect. It was the Muslim invaders and conquerors from Central Asia who introduced the use of onions and garlic in Indian cooking in the thirteenth century. Although, in some homes these two ingredients are still considered to be taboo, yet, they soon became essential ingredients in Indian cooking, particularly when combined with the local green ginger. The use of these two ingredients was popularized in Bengali cooking by the Nawabs of Bengal in the eighteenth century. However, the local converts to Islam accepted them before the Hindus.

This is explained in detail by Alamgir Vikramaditya Ghaffar, who not only belongs to a family whose ancestor was the diwan of Midnapore, but is also the great-grandson of Huseyn Shaheed Suhrawardy (chief minister of undivided Bengal from 23 April 1946 to 14 August 1947). Ghaffar elaborates, 'The culinary practices of the converts underwent a change. Onion, garlic and green chillies began to feature in nearly every dish. The quantity of turmeric used in preparations increased. They also began to use a lot of plain yoghurt in cooking, especially to marinate meat, as a souring agent in curries or to make raitas.' However, this senior executive with the Oberoi Group, who has been exposed to a cosmopolitan upbringing in his hometown of Calcutta thanks to his Bengali Muslim father and Bengali Hindu mother, also points out, 'I agree that Bengali Muslims use a lot of oil and spices in their cooking. This largely follows the basic pattern of Muslim culinary practices. In spite of this, I must add that our food is less rich than the food cooked by the Muslims living in the gullies of Delhi or the gullies of Karachi.'

Spices like cinnamon, cardamom and clove were brought into the region by spice traders and the mixture now known as garom mashla became popular, and was used for seasoning. As more spices like asafoetida, cumin and saffron began to be imported into the market, Bengalis learned to temper their cooking with a combination that is used by very few communities in the country—paanch phoron. While 'paanch' means five, 'phoron' means tempering. 'Paanch phoron' is a five-spice mix or a potpourri of five whole spices that are either dry roasted or fried in oil, such as fennel, nigella, fenugreek, cumin and black mustard seeds. Bengalis use this spice often for tempering preparations. Kalonji, commonly known as nigella or black cumin seeds, is used extensively and radhuni (wild celery seeds) is also used in the tempering of some preparations. The latter is barely used by other communities in a similar fashion.

'There have been exchanges as well,' points out Ghaffar. 'Muslims living in Bengal picked up the habit of using paanch phoron from their Hindu brethren and made it a part of their spice rack. The Muslims also brought "kalia" with them, which is a rich curry preparation of fish, meat or vegetables that uses ghee, oil and spices like onion, ginger, garlic and garom mashla. With the growing acceptance of onion and garlic, the Bengali Hindus adopted this gravy preparation as their own.'

Bengali cuisine is quite elaborate. Just like the service à la russe of French cuisine, the different food items in Bengali cuisine are also served course-wise rather than all at once. It is perhaps the only cuisine in the country that is served in this manner, whether at home or on celebratory occasions. Each dish is eaten separately with a little bit of rice in order to savour its individual flavour. The more delicate tastes always come first. These are gradually followed by stronger ones in order to accommodate the entire range of flavours. Leafy green vegetables or bitter preparations are the first items to be served. These are followed by a lentil preparation, which is usually accompanied by fries or fritters of fish and vegetables. After this comes a complex vegetable dish followed by a fish curry or any other fish preparation. Meat will always follow fish and the meal is wrapped up with sweet preparations. Paan or betel leaf roll provides the perfect ending to the meal. Although, in modern times, the regular fare is not so elaborate, the order of serving remains the same.

Lentils

It is interesting to note that lentils, which form an indelible part of any vegetarian cooking, was absent in the food of ancient Bengal. Banerji points out, 'The earliest examples of Bengali literature, the *Charyapada*s, dating back approximately to the eleventh century, depict fishing and hunting for game, and mention rice, sugarcane and many other crops, but there is no reference to any kind of dal. The first mention of dal and of ways of cooking it is in post-fifteenth-century literature. It seems that in this respect ancient Bengal had more in common with Southeast Asia and China, where pulses are virtually unknown, than the Bengal of today. Even now, most of the dals consumed in West Bengal come from the other states in India. Apart from the natural cropping factor, the super-abundant supply of fish made dal, as a source of protein, unnecessary. The shift in balance in medieval times can probably be attributed to the spread of the Vaishnav Bhakti cult, whose followers were vegetarian. As a result, a substitute for fish or meat had to be found and the non-vegetarians also became familiar with this new element' (pp. xx–xxi).

Today, the scenario is very different and like vegetables, lentils are also an integral part of Bengali cuisine. Although a variety of lentils is featured in the cuisine, the most popular ones eaten on a daily basis are musur dal, moong dal and chholar dal. Lentils are often simply boiled and eaten with rice. This preparation is known as *dal sheddho*. The most favourite lentil to be prepared in this manner is musur dal, which is boiled with mustard oil, slit green chillies and salt, and eaten with rice. The popularity of musur dal sheddho is followed by that of bhaja moong dal sheddho, which is prepared in the same manner. Only the mustard oil is replaced with ghee in the latter preparation.

Lentils can be cooked plain with tempering and seasonings. In Bengali cuisine, phoron is a very important part of all lentil preparations except when they are boiled. Shukno lanka, paanch phoron and whole cumin seeds are the essential tempering ingredients. Ginger paste and black mustard seeds are also used to temper some lentil preparations. Musur dal is sometimes tempered with ingredients like radhuni, green chillies, garlic and onions. While all of the lentils are seasoned with turmeric and salt, a few are also seasoned with either sugar or ghee or both.

Lentils can also be cooked with a variety of ingredients. For example, coconut meat is a popular ingredient that is often cut into small slices, fried and used in cooking chholar dal or bhaja moong dal. Bengalis enjoy having *tetor dal* (bitter lentils) and *tok dal* (sour lentils) in summer. Tetor dal is commonly made by cooking moong dal with slices of fried bitter gourds like uchche or karola. Often the bitter gourds are combined with cubes of bottle gourd (lau) in the lentil preparation. Sometimes, shojne danta (drumsticks) are also added to this combination. Bhaja moong dal is cooked with helencha shaak (watercress leaves), a bitter leafy green vegetable. Tok dal is generally made by cooking musur dal with ingredients that are tart in taste like kancha aam (raw mango), chalta (elephant apple), jalpai (Indian olive), amra (Indian hog plum) and tomatoes that are partially ripe. It is a common practice among the villagers of Bengal to add tamarind pulp to the lentil to make it sour.

Lentils are also cooked with vegetables (*shobji diye dal*). Bhaja moong dal or chholar dal are often cooked with finely chopped mocha (banana blossoms) and small slices of fried coconut meat. While bhaja moong dal can be cooked with bottle gourd, musur dal, sometimes, is cooked with gathi kochu (colocasia corm). Leafy green vegetables are also used in lentil preparations. Musur dal can be cooked with palong shaak (spinach) combined with cubed potatoes and aubergines while chholar dal can be cooked with pui shaak (Malabar spinach) and cubed potatoes. Winter is the time to have bhaja moong dal cooked with vegetables like cauliflower and green peas.

Bengali Muslims also cook meat and eggs with lentils. The former is known as *dal gosht*. Generally, beef or goat meat is used in this dish. The meat is cooked with chholar dal, onions, spices, herbs and salt into a spicy lentil dish that is relished with both rice and bread preparations. *Deem diye chholar dal*, as the name suggests, is another delectable preparation in which hard-boiled eggs are fried and cooked with chholar dal, onions, tomatoes, spices and salt.

Vegetables

The fertile soil of Bengal promotes the growth of a large variety of leafy greens, vegetables and tubers. The versatile potato, which has its origin in South America, is grown profusely by local farmers and has become a constant feature in Bengali kitchens. The Spanish conquistadors first encountered the root vegetable when they arrived in Peru in 1532 and introduced it to Spain in 1570. From there it slowly spread to the rest of Europe. The Portuguese introduced the tuber to the Indian soil on the western coast in the early seventeenth century. In spite of this, very few Indians grew or ate potatoes. It was the British East India Company officials who decided to promote the vegetable among the Indian peasants. The potato was gradually becoming a staple in Britain, particularly among the Irish. In the eighteenth century, the agents of the Company introduced the crop in Bengal. According to the Company ledgers of 1797, now housed in the India Office Records in the British Library in London, the agents in Bengal provided free seeds to the peasants to encourage them to produce and eat their crop. In its early days in Bengal, the vegetable was christened biliti alu (English potato) by the local farmers to differentiate it from the indigenous ranga alu (sweet potato). The relentless promotion across the country soon led to the potato being widely cultivated and within a century, Indians had grown very fond of it.

Even the tomato, earlier christened biliti begoon (English aubergine), has its origin in South America where it used to grow wild. It was only when the tomato gradually moved upward towards Mexico that it began to be cultivated and used as food by the Aztecs, who called it 'xitomatl'. It was during the Spanish conquest of the Aztec Empire in the sixteenth century that the Spaniards encountered the fruit (in strict botanical terms, the tomato is a fruit, and not a vegetable) for the first time and introduced the plant to Spain. Gradually, it spread to the rest of Europe and began to be cultivated.

While in Spain, the tomato was probably eaten shortly after it was introduced and was certainly used as food by the early seventeenth century, in most European countries, the plant was sought after only for its beauty in the initial years. This was because it was looked upon with suspicion by botanists, who considered it to be poisonous. Its leaves and immature fruits contain tomatine, which if consumed in large quantities, can be toxic. Many were also of the opinion that the high acidic content of its juice rendered it unfit for consumption. But the ripe fruit does not contain any tomatine. So, the tomato, which turned blood red or golden in colour on maturing, was grown in gardens and flower beds as an ornamental plant and used as ornamental decor on tables. It took a lot of time to dispel much of this suspicion and the fruit was incorporated into European cuisines only in the eighteenth century. In Britain, it was now used in soups, broths and as a garnish.

Suspicions about the fruit being poisonous even delayed its spread to India. Nobody is really sure when or by whom the tomato was introduced into this country. Eminent journalist and food critic, Vir Sanghvi, is of the opinion that it was the Portuguese who introduced the plant. But, according to the renowned Indian food historian, Dr K.T. Acharya (6 October 1923–5 September 2002), tomato made its entry into India as late as 1850. Whatever may be the case, it is a fact that local chefs began using the fruit in cooking only during the British period.

The tomatoes, which were first introduced to India, were not round. Instead, they were long and shaped vaguely like aubergines. They were also very sour. Even thirty years after its introduction to India, the tomato was grown mostly for the Europeans. But, among the Indian communities, it was the Bengalis, who first began to use the fruit, although as a souring agent, in their curries around this time. Over the years, as the tomato grown in the local soil became less sour, it began to be treated as a vegetable rather than a souring agent. It was now used to add colour and taste to curries. Today, the tomato has made its presence felt in Bengali cooking by being used in most of the vegetarian and non-vegetarian preparations.

Non-Bengalis (generally implying other Indian communities) have the misplaced notion that Bengalis are too inclined towards amish or non-vegetarian food. In reality, the community has always made extensive use of this vast variety that grows all over the land. Vegetables are eaten ground, boiled, mashed, roasted, fried or curried. Their love for vegetables finds expression in the creation of unique dishes. For example, while the paste of *maan kochu* (malanga coco), which is made by grinding chopped pieces of the root vegetable with mustard seeds, green chillies, grated coconut, tamarind pulp and salt, and then mixing some fresh mustard oil in it, is relished with steamed rice at the beginning of a meal, a semi-dry dish made with whole kalai dal (also known as biuli dal in Bengali, urad dal in Hindi and black gram in English), shish palong (as tender spinach tip is called in Bengali) and a mixed variety of unpeeled whole vegetables is also savoured with rice. Although the latter preparation, known as *gota* (whole) *sheddho* (boiled), can be eaten anytime, it is especially associated with Sheetal Shashthi.

Sheetal Shashthi and Gota Sheddho

The connection between Sheetal Shashthi and gota sheddho is an interesting one. In Bengal, Sheetal Shashthi is a religious festival that is observed by the Ghotis on the day after Saraswati Puja. Shashthi is the Hindu goddess of reproduction and fertility, and the benefactor and protector of children. She is held in high esteem by the womenfolk of Bengal and her worship is considered to be a celebration of 'Matri Shakti', meaning the power of motherhood. Mothers worship her for the well-being of their children. Sheetal Shashthi is primarily observed by Ghoti women to seek the blessings of Goddess Shashthi for their offspring.

The fortnight between a new moon or no moon (known as Amavasya) day and a full moon (known as Poornima) day is considered to be a Shukla Paksha or waxing moon phase. In Sanskrit, Shukla means 'white', 'bright' or 'pure'. This period is considered auspicious. Panchami means 'the fifth'. Vasant Panchami is observed on the fifth day of the Shukla Paksha of the month of Magha. Shashthi, on the other hand, also means 'the sixth', and Sheetal Shashthi is observed on the sixth day or the very next day. Sheetal Shashthi means 'Cold Sixth'. For those observing the festival, it is a day of 'Arandhan', which means 'no cooking'. Kitchen fires are not lit in these houses on this day. The food that has been cooked on the night before is eaten cold on Sheetal Shashthi.

On Sheetal Shashthi, the shil-nora is not used at all. Instead, the shil is wrapped in a yellow cloth and worshipped because it is believed to represent Goddess Shashthi. Once the worship is over, devotees break their fast and partake of the bhog as prasad. Religious custom demands that the food cooked for this day should be completely vegetarian. Even onion and garlic cannot be used in the cooking. Again, according to religious custom, the bhog for Sheetal Shashthi should mainly consist of bheja bhaat and gota sheddho. Although fermented cooked rice is largely known as panta bhaat in Bengal, it is also known as *bheja bhaat* (literally meaning wet rice) among the Ghotis because it is soaked overnight in water. This bheja bhaat is eaten with gota sheddho.

Gota sheddho is made with bhaja kalai dal, shish palong and a medley of vegetables. One can choose from a range of seasonal vegetables to make this dish like baby aubergine, baby potato, hyacinth beans, green peas, sweet potato and radish. It is customary to use an odd number of different vegetables in this preparation. For example, devotees can choose three or five different types of vegetables. But the number five is largely adhered to and the dish is usually made of a medley of five different types of vegetables. Six pieces of each vegetable are used in the cooking. Even the tender spinach tips have to be six in number.

The beauty of this preparation lies in the fact that the vegetables cannot be peeled or cut. Even the stalks of aubergines and the leaves of radishes have to remain intact. The green peas are cooked in their pods. The shish palong has to be whole. Even the lentil used in the preparation has to be whole and not split or skinned. All of the ingredients are boiled whole on a low flame. Salt and spices are not added to the cooking. But, while eating the dish, salt and mustard oil are added to it to make it tasty. Many add ghee instead of mustard oil and some even add chopped green chillies.

Although devotees often add gota topa kool to the cooking because it lends a tangy flavour, it is not an essential ingredient in gota sheddho. However, the ripe fruit is usually offered to the goddess. If it is not included in gota sheddho, chutney or ambole is made with it and offered as part of the bhog. In case, gota topa kool is added in the gota sheddho preparation, the mandatory rule of using six pieces has to be followed. Many families offer plain yoghurt, which has been made the day before, as part of this bhog. Other vegetarian dishes cooked on the night of Saraswati Puja can also be offered. This may include any dish that can be eaten with bheja bhaat like lentils, fritters, fried vegetables, vegetable curries or any other vegetable preparation. Chutney, payesh and sweets are offered as well.

While researching on this subject, I came across the deeper reason behind the shil being worshipped as Goddess Shashthi. The shil-nora is symbolic of sexual union, procreation and, most importantly, the mother-child relationship. The mother protects her child, gives food and takes care of all of their needs. There are quite a few conjectures about the reasons behind the rituals of this festival. Some are of the opinion that since the shil-nora cannot be used, food is not cooked on the day of the festival. Instead, it is cooked the day before.

But is there any reason behind the main bhog of Goddess Shashthi being so plain? Many feel that the onset of spring ushered in several diseases in the early days. The main bhog of Sheetal Shashthi was a symbolic gesture that consumption of healthy food, devoid of richness, would keep diseases at bay. Food writer Priyadarshini Chatterjee, in her article, 'Why do so many Indians eat cold, stale food at the start of spring?' (16 March 2019) for the news website *Scroll.in*, writes, 'This practice of eating day-old food at the onset of spring is more than simply a religious observance or a folk festival. Shital Shashti in Bengal is observed right when winter makes way for spring or basanta, as it is known in Bengal. During this time of seasonal transition, our immunity tends to weaken, making the body prone to infections and diseases. This is also the time that chicken pox, called basanta in Bengali after the eponymous season, is widespread. Keeping all this in mind, the Shital Shashti spread is constructed to cool the body and fortify the immune system.'

Conjectures are also made about the rest of the rituals. For instance, since, according to Bengali Hindu religious custom, during religious festivals, an odd number (generally five) of whole fruits are offered to the deities, this, perhaps, explains the reason behind an odd number of whole vegetables being used in gota sheddho. Moreover, since the festival is observed on the sixth day of the Shukla Paksha of the month of Magha, each ingredient is used in six pieces. Lastly, besides the seasonal vegetables, shish palong and kool appear in the markets around this time. This has made it customary to include shish palong in the preparation and offer the fruit to the goddess. But, whatever maybe the different conjectures, over the years, Sheetal Shashthi has remained a special festival for the womenfolk of Bengal. Today, in West Bengal, Bangal mothers are also seen observing this festival for the welfare of their children, thereby, breaking its confinement to Ghoti women.

Even fruits like enchor and kumro are treated as vegetables. While *enchorer kofta* implies koftas of unripe jackfruit meat cooked in rich gravy, *kumror chhakka* is a dry vegetable preparation made with ripe pumpkin and potatoes. The former is savoured as a delicacy with rice, while the latter is largely relished with luchi, parota and *ruti* (as roti is known in Bengali). In Bengali, the word 'chhawkka' means 'dice'. In all probability, the dish derives its name from this word as the cubed vegetables in the preparation resemble dice. Black chickpeas and grated coconut feature in the preparation, and hing (asafoetida), a spice that Bengalis rarely use, is an essential ingredient. Some sugar is added and the preparation is seasoned with ghee. Since onion and garlic are not used in kumror chhakka, the dish is often prepared during religious festivals and offered as bhog with luchi. Bengalis also do not spare the beechi or seeds of the ripe jackfruit, called *kanthal* in Bengali, and *kanthaler beechi* are often cooked into vegetable, leafy green and lentil preparations for an extra crunchy bite.

The Tagore Influence

Any writing on Bengali cuisine is incomplete without mentioning some of the unique dishes cooked in Thakur Bari or the Tagore household. 'Tagore' is the anglicized form of 'Thakur', which is the Bengali surname of this distinguished family who once lived in a large house spread over acres of land in Jorasanko in north Calcutta. Thakur Barir ranna (the cooking of the Tagore household) has always been a subject of great interest among Bengali food historians and connoisseurs.

The Tagore family stood apart from many contemporary zamindari families because despite being privileged, they showed great benevolence in their disposition. The men of the family were pioneers in their respective fields and made continuous efforts to institute social reforms. The most renowned of the lot was Rabindranath Tagore. His writings were of such great versatility and profound depth that they earned him a mass following and tremendous respect. The women of Thakur Bari were not traditional homemakers but pioneers in their own right. They were highly skilled in the fields of music, painting and writing. They were also renowned for their culinary skills. The family was very well travelled and collected the recipes they liked, incorporating them into their collection of family recipes. The Tagore household cooking featured dishes from Indian and European cuisines.

Rabindranath Tagore's wife, Mrinalini, and his elder brother, Hemendranath Tagore's wife, Neepomoyi, were good chefs. But Hemendranath's daughter, Pragyasundari Debi, outshone everyone else in the family when it came to expertise in the kitchen. She not only discovered new dishes but also wrote down recipes and published them, something that was uncommon among Indian women in those days. She was responsible for introducing the system of menu cards in Bengal. Although Hemendranath and Rabindranath's elder brother, Satyendranath Tagore's daughter Indira Debi Choudhurani never stepped into the kitchen to cook, she had the habit of writing down all the recipes used at home, which she liked, in her khata or exercise book.

The women of the Tagore household were innovative and experimental when it came to their food. The family made certain niramish or vegetarian dishes that were very unusual. Some of these have been mentioned in Pragyasundari Debi's cookbook, *Amish O Niramish Ahar* (1995). *Beet bata* or the paste of beetroot was one such preparation that was relished by the members of the family with steamed rice. In this preparation, the chopped and boiled beetroots are ground to a paste with a small variety of spices like black mustard seeds, poppy seeds, ginger and green chillies. The paste is then cooked in mustard oil with a phoron of kalo jeera and salt.

The Contribution of Widows

Bengali cuisine includes a wide variety of vegetarian dishes that have evolved over the years. Food historians are of the opinion that the widows of Bengal have greatly contributed to the evolution of its vegetarian cooking. They once led very repressive lives and were compelled to stick to a vegetarian diet though social progress has ensured that many of these restrictions are no longer observed or imposed. Their difficult lives included a lot of dietary restrictions. They were prohibited from eating high protein foods like meat, fish, eggs and even musur dal because these were believed to have libidinous effects. Garlic and onion were also banned for their alleged impassioning properties.

In the chapter 'Bangla Ranna' from their book, *The Calcutta Cookbook: A Treasury of Recipes from Pavement to Palace* (1995), the authors describe the plight of a Bengali widow, 'In a secluded corner of the cookhouse, a widowed relative sits over her own stove. She has added delicate nuances to the rich vegetarian cornucopia of Bangla ranna. Her role in the kitchen warrants an explanation of her situation. Up to the turn of the century, a ten- or twelve-year-old girl was sometimes widowed and lived for the rest of her life dressed in white with her hair cropped, eating a radically vegetarian diet' (pp. 35–36).

But, naturally, Bengali widows craved tasty food. Gradually, they decided to make the best of the bad bargain and began using their innovativeness to add colour to their fare. They started experimenting with the limited ingredients that went into their dishes in order to add more taste to them.

One of the things that they did was to think of different ways of making use of the wasted parts of vegetables instead of throwing them away. For example, they used the leftover peels and scrapings of vegetables to make simple but delicious preparations—something which is unique to Bengali cooking. *Lauer khosha bhaja* (fried peels of bottle gourd) is a preparation in which the thinly sliced peels of the vegetable are fried in hot mustard oil with a phoron of black mustard seeds and dried red chillies. Some salt and turmeric are added to the cooking. In *alur khosha bhaja* (fried peels of potato), the leftover potato peels are thoroughly washed, chopped and fried in hot mustard oil with a phoron of kalo jeera and dried red chillies. A pinch of salt and a small quantity of posto are added to the cooking. Both preparations are eaten with steamed rice.

Even the stalks of cauliflower and leafy green vegetables were not thrown away. Instead, *chachchari* preparations were made out of them. Chachchari usually implies a lightly spiced dry vegetable dish made with one or more varieties of vegetables. Often, the preparation is flavoured with mustard or poppy seeds paste. Sometimes, the stalks of cauliflower and leafy green vegetables, and even drumsticks, are cooked with vegetables to make this dish. Such chachchari preparations are known as *danta chachchari* ('danta' means 'a succulent stalk'). Thus, in this land of plenty, the widows made thrift an integral part of Bengali cooking.

The widows even experimented with the *bori* ('vadi' in Hindi) or sun-dried lentil blob, which took on a more important role in their kitchens. Since it is made of lentil, they welcomed it as an optional source of protein. Most importantly, it added some variety to their frugal dishes. The boris were fried and added, in either whole or crumbled forms, to many of their dishes. Some of their shaak (leafy green vegetables) preparations like palong shaak and lal shaak (red spinach), and vegetable preparations like *shukto* (a bitter and mild mixed vegetables stew), *alu begooner jhol* (a lightly spiced curry of potatoes and aubergines), and *ghanto*, made with either lau (bottle gourd) or chaalkumro (ash gourd), featured boris.

A ghanto generally means a semi-dry vegetable dish made with either one or a few complementing vegetables, which are cooked with phoron, ground spices and a little bit of sugar. Boris often feature in ghanto preparations. A mixed vegetable ghanto, in which chopped potatoes, aubergines, hyacinth beans and radish are cooked in oil with a phoron of kalo jeera and dried red chillies, the pastes of turmeric, coriander and cumin, salt, sugar and fried boris, and seasoned with ghee, is commonly eaten with rice. Palong shaak, in traditional Bengali cuisine, is popularly cooked into a ghanto dish with vegetables like potatoes, pumpkin, aubergines and hyacinth beans. Boris are often used in this dish. Kochu shaak (stalks of colocasia leaves), a very popular leafy green vegetable in the culinary culture of East Bengal, is also used to make a ghanto dish. This ghanto preparation, which originally hails from Opar Bangla, is made with the boiled and mashed stalks of colocasia leaves, and features black chickpeas and coconut meat.

Fried boris were not only added to vegetarian preparations but they were also eaten plain. The widows even devised curry dishes made only with these blobs like *borir jhal* and *bori posto*. 'Jhal', literally meaning 'hot', is generally a preparation of fish, shrimp or crab cooked in mustard paste or with the paste of dried red chillies. Borir jhal can also be made in either of the two ways. Fried boris are also cooked in a paste of poppy seeds, lending the dish the name, bori posto.

Bori—A Culinary Art

Bori-making is an art that has always been exclusively associated with women. It is a skill that is not limited to widows. Bori is popularly made with white kalai or biuli dal (split and skinned black gram). The lentil is soaked overnight in water and ground to a fine paste the next day on the grinding stone. Some salt and appropriate spices (especially asafoetida) are added to the paste. The lentil paste is whipped hard enough before boris are shaped out of it. It is believed that boris made with a well-whipped lentil paste turn out the crispiest when fried. A clean cloth or muslin is spread out on a large plate or tray and little blobs of the spiced paste are placed on it in rows. These are left to dry in the sun for several days until all the moisture has evaporated. Once thoroughly dried, they are stored in tins for later use.

Boris are also made of musur dal and motor dal (split yellow peas). Sometimes, the pastes of chaalkumro, lau or mulo may be added to the lentil paste to make *kumro bori, lau bori* or *mulo bori* respectively. In her cookbook, *Amish O Niramish Ahar* (1995), Pragyasundari Debi writes about at least fifteen kinds of boris made in her household with ingredients like kancha aam, bel, ranga alu and phulkopi (cauliflower). The Tagore women made *phulkopir bori* by blending the paste of white kalai or biuli dal with the paste of the vegetable (including its leaves). Spices like asafoetida and ground cumin seeds, dried red chillies, green cardamom, cinnamon and clove, and salt were added to it. The whipped paste was shaped into boris and sun-dried. The women of the household often deep-fried these boris in mustard oil and made gravy dishes out of them with spices.

In modern times, boris are made commercially on a large-scale throughout the year and dried in ovens. They are available in packaged forms in grocery stores. But, traditionally, in the rural areas, bori-making takes place especially in the winter months. It paints a very warm and cosy picture to see groups of women in the villages huddle together under the winter sun, making boris and gossiping.

Special mention needs to be made of *phulbori* and *goyna bori*. Phulbori is the lightest of all boris. It is made with kalai dal and is so feather-light that it nearly melts in the mouth once fried in oil. According to Banerji, the consistency of the dal, the degree of spicing and the intensity of whipping the paste before making the boris differ from women to women. Those who can whip the dal hard enough to make the lightest of phulboris tend to acquire a reputation.

Gahona or *goyna bori* ('gahona' or 'goyna' means jewellery in Bengali) is a speciality of the Purba Medinipur (East Midnapore) district of West Bengal. The women of this district, from where this variety of bori originated, are experts in its making. Also known as *naksha bori* ('naksha' means design in Bengali), these boris look like intricately designed jewellery. A fine paste of kalai dal is filled in a piping bag and nakshas of earrings (especially the traditional ear studs called 'kaan pasha'), necklaces and pendants are made on a plate full of poppy seeds. These boris, which are generally deep-fried and eaten plain, are also available in the designs of paisleys and flowers. Although nobody is sure when the humble bori began to be shaped in such intricate designs, this art has been in existence for a long time now. It definitely began before the arrival of the British and is centuries old.

Over the years, many noted personalities, including the 'Bard of Bengal', Rabindranath Tagore, have been impressed by this wonderful art. In 1913, Tagore became the first non-European and non-white to win the Nobel Prize in Literature for the English translation of his work, 'Gitanjali'. His Nobel Prize had included a medal, a citation and a cash prize of 8,000 pounds. It is widely believed that he used this money to set up his dream project Visva-Bharati University in the town of Shantiniketan (meaning the abode of peace). Shantiniketan is a town neighbouring Bolpur city in the Birbhum district of West Bengal, which was initially developed by his father Debendranath Tagore as a spiritual centre. Rabindranath Tagore believed that studying in open spaces, close to nature and free of restrictive walls and boundaries aided in better learning. With this vision he started a school called Patha Bhavan, which, in 1921, was expanded into the university. Today, thanks to this university, Shantiniketan is renowned as a vibrant and bustling university town.

In 1930, Seba Maity, a student of the university, presented a few goyna boris made by her mother and grandmother to Rabindranath Tagore. He was so impressed by the boris that he had their photographs taken and preserved in the art department (Kala Bhavan) of Visva-Bharati University for people to see. After this, goyna bori achieved the status of fine art and gained a lot of popularity. Abanindranath Tagore, a renowned artist and nephew of the poet, and Nandalal Bose, a pioneer of modern Indian art and student of Abanindranath Tagore, hailed the boris as great pieces of art. In 2016, the Intellectual Property Rights cell of IIT (Indian Institute of Technology) Kharagpur applied to get the geographical indication (GI) for goyna bori.

Thus, we see that the extensive use of boris by the widows added another dimension to the vegetarian cooking of Bengal. Thanks to these ladies, a lot of imagination, precision and refinement went into Bengal's vegetarian cooking. This has led to the evolution of an elaborate vegetarian cuisine that Bengalis are proud of today.

Some of these vegetarian dishes can be simple while others can be quite exquisite. One such simple dish is *begoon pora*, which is prepared by roasting an aubergine directly over the flame, and then peeling the skin, mashing the flesh and mixing it with chopped onions, green chillies, coriander leaves, and some salt and mustard oil. A very basic and almost rustic preparation that has a smoky flavour and aroma, and is very popular throughout Bengal, including urban homes, the begoon pora or roasted aubergine is relished as an accompaniment with steamed rice and musur dal. It is also a much-liked accompaniment to panta or phana bhaat. In modern times, begoon pora is often eaten with ruti for dinner. In contrast to this simple dish are delicacies made with aubergine like *doi begoon* and *begoon basanti*. When the fried aubergine pieces are cooked in spicy yoghurt gravy, the dish is called doi begoon, and when they are cooked in yoghurt and mustard paste-based gravy, the preparation is called begoon basanti.

Another simple dish is *alu posto* (potatoes cooked in poppy seeds paste), which is a very sought-after preparation and tastes delicious when eaten with steamed rice. This dish is cooked with poppy seeds that have been ground to a fine paste with green chillies. A phoron of dried red chillies and kalo jeera are added to mustard oil. Cubed potatoes, some salt and water are now added to the cooking. When the potatoes are partly cooked, the poppy seeds paste is added. Some fresh mustard oil is drizzled over the cooking once it is complete. The dish is stirred well and taken off the flame.

Bengal's Prized Posto

Posto or poppy seed is a popular ingredient that is used in quite a few recipes in Bengali cuisine. This may come as a surprise to many as it is a residual by-product of the opium plant. The poppy seed has been mentioned as an important ingredient in the ancient medical texts of many civilizations. For centuries, the seed had been used for its medicinal properties like inducing sleep and promoting fertility by civilizations like the Egyptians, Minoans and Sumerians. In her article, 'How British greed spurred the creation of one of Bengal's most loved dishes' (dated 31 March 2016), for the newspaper, the *Indian Express*, noted food historian, Pritha Sen, mentions that the opium poppy, from which poppy seeds are derived, has a long relation with India not as a gourmet ingredient but as a medicinal plant. Since it is a remedy for a number of ailments, it finds mention in *Dhanwantari Nighantu*, one of the oldest Indian texts dealing with the properties of drugs.

Sen goes on to add that it was during the reign of Akbar that opium slowly took over as a recreational drug and its cultivation was stepped up by royal diktat. The tiny dried white seeds formed after the drug had been extracted from the latex of the poppy seed pods were non-narcotic. Gradually, they began to be used in the royal kitchens as a texture enhancer and thickener for gravies. When, soon after the Battle of Plassey in 1757, the British discovered the lucrative market for illegal opium in China, large tracts of agricultural land in the Bengal Presidency, much to the agony of the local farmers, were converted into poppy fields, gradually turning Britain into the world's biggest drug dealer as they raked in huge profits by turning the Chinese into severe drug addicts.

The local farmer's family was now deprived of the agricultural produce that once fed it. Most of the time, the opium or aphim farmer himself was addicted to his narcotic produce. Having no choice, the farmer's wife began to look for ways to provide a basic meal for her family. Large quantities of dried out poppy seeds would be left behind as waste by the colonial masters. Her miserable plight drove the farmer's wife to consider the possibility of experimenting with the ingredient as food. She took the risk and realized, much to her delight, that a raw paste of the seeds complemented well with the family's frugal meal of panta bhaat. This is when poppy seeds or posto began to take on an important role. Thus, began the journey of this relatively new ingredient in Bengal's culinary art.

Gradually, posto inundated Bengal's kitchens. Apart from being easily digestible in the summer heat, Bengalis discovered that it has a uniquely delicate taste. The Bengali chef, with his experimental streak, came up with quite a few recipes, both vegetarian and non-vegetarian, using this ingredient, which were eaten with steamed rice. *Posto batar chachchari* is a much-liked preparation in which the ground poppy seeds paste is cooked in mustard oil with chopped onions, ground cumin and dried red chillies, salt, sugar, ghee, cardamom and cinnamon. *Posto bhapa* (steamed poppy seeds paste) is a very popular preparation, eaten as a summer cooler with boiled rice. In this preparation, the poppy seeds paste is mixed with chopped onions and green chillies, and some salt and mustard oil. It is then put in a bati or bowl. The bowl is sealed with a lid and placed inside a larger container. Although adequate water is poured into the container, care is taken that it remains at the base of the bowl containing the paste. A lid is placed over the container and the paste is cooked in steam till done. Steaming the paste in a bati also lends this dish the name *bati posto*.

Vegetables like jhinge (ridge gourd), patol, phulkopi, begoon, lau, chichinga (snake gourd), kankrol (teasel gourd), dharosh, sheem, peyanj (onion), peyanjkoli (spring onion), shojne danta, kancha pepe (unripe papaya) and French beans began to be cooked in poppy seeds paste. Vegetables like ridge gourd, pointed gourd, cauliflower, unripe papaya, okra, aubergine, drumstick and French beans were often combined with potato and cooked in the paste. Sometimes, the poppy seeds paste was combined with the paste of black mustard seeds or coconut meat to cook some vegetables.

Simpler recipes were also found in the chef's diary like *postor bora* (bora made with poppy seeds paste), *narkel postor bora* (bora made with grated coconut and poppy seeds paste) and posto chutney, a preparation made by grinding poppy seeds with coconut meat, green chillies, garlic and green mangoes (lime juice can be used instead), and then seasoning the paste with salt and sugar. Over the years, kalai dal eaten with steamed rice along with some alu posto has become one of the favourite dishes of the Ghotis for summer lunch. Even the designs of goyna bori, which was an art of bori-making that had existed from before the arrival of the British, now began to be made on a bed of poppy seeds.

While the Bengali Hindus, living on the side of the Ganges river, preferred to cook hard-boiled eggs in poppy seeds paste (deem posto) and also a small variety of fish like rui, katla, mrigel and bata (varieties of carp), pomfret, bhekti, parshe (flathead grey mullet), tilapia (cichlid), ilish, pabda (Indian butter catfish) and chingri or prawns (the poppy seeds paste was often combined with black mustard seeds or coconut meat pastes to cook some of the fish), the Bengali Muslims, living on the side of the Padma river, with their strong inclination towards poultry and red meat, preferred to pair chicken and mutton with the paste.

Sen writes, 'Recipes featuring posto are aplenty today and range from simple fritters to main courses made with hitherto forbidden ingredients in Bengali vegetarian cuisine such as the *peyanj posto*, made with onions, or the *roshun diye posto*, made with garlic. As it entered the more sophisticated portals of urban kitchens it was added to eggs, fancier fish preparations and meats. The crowning glory was its use in the jewel of Bengal's culinary legacy, the *shukto*. And, in an emulation of East European and European traditions of Jewish and British settlers in Calcutta—read poppy seed cakes and pastries and its use as a garnish on breads and savouries—the Bengali sandesh, too, was rolled in roasted poppy seeds to lend it a crunchy exterior.'

After Independence, with the government tightening its grip on opium poppy cultivation, this once residual product turned into an expensive ingredient. Over the years, despite its rising price, the unique and subtle taste of posto has made it a prized ingredient in Bengali cuisine.

In contrast to simple vegetarian dishes, there are some exquisite ones that are time-consuming to prepare, like the lentil cake gravy dish called *dhonkar dalna*. Made with small, square, diamond or rectangular-shaped fried cakes called 'dhonkas', this traditional recipe has remained the same and does not include the two heathen ingredients—onion and garlic. The dhonkas are made with the paste of chholar dal mixed with grated coconut and seasoned with salt, sugar and ground ginger. The paste is stirred in a pan over a low flame until quite dry, and then, transferred to a greased tray or dish, pressed and shaped into a large, flat square, given the desired shapes with a sharp knife, and fried in oil until they are brown. The dhonkas are then cooked in spicy gravy that is seasoned with salt and sugar, and also includes the souring agent, plain yoghurt or tomato, fried potatoes and coconut milk. A phoron of whole cumin seeds and bay leaves, and a seasoning of garom mashla and ghee are permanent fixtures in the gravy preparation.

'Dalna' generally implies a medium-thick vegetarian or egg gravy dish, seasoned with ground spices, especially garom mashla, and a touch of ghee. Although onion and garlic feature in *deemer dalna*, they are hardly used in any of the vegetarian dalna preparations. Despite the omission of these heathen ingredients, dhonkar dalna does not lack in richness and taste. Over the years, dhonkar dalna has been put on the pedestal with those vegetarian classics that rule Bengali cuisine, and is generally served on special occasions.

Similarly, *chhanar dalna*, another vegetarian classic, made of fried balls of chhana cooked in lightly spiced gravy that includes potatoes, rules feasts and special occasions. The absence of onion and garlic in its preparation makes chhanar dalna a sattvic dish like dhonkar dalna. According to Ayurvedic principles, sattvic food refers to clean and fresh vegetarian meals that are supposed to improve the health of both body and mind, and increase the purity within. It is derived from the word 'sattva', which, according to Hinduism, is the highest guna or quality in human beings, and generally implies virtues like goodness, balance, harmony, purity, positivity and peace. Onion and garlic, which are supposed to have a libidinous effect, and increase negative emotions like anxiety and aggression that upsets the balance and peace of mind, are avoided in a sattvic diet. Eaten with plain boiled rice or vegetarian pulaos, both chhanar dalna and dhonkar dalna are a part of all those feasts, both religious and otherwise, where vegetarian food needs to be served.

Often, thanks to the versatility of Bengali cuisine, even a single vegetable can be cooked into different dishes. For example, we have already seen that lau or bottle gourd, a vegetable with cooling effects, can be cooked into a ghanto or its peels, cooked into a fried dish. A spicy paste of the peels of the vegetable is relished with rice. This traditional dish is called *lauer khosha bata*. This versatile vegetable is also cooked into a dalna or with fried shrimps into a classic dish called *lau-chingri*. Many are also fond of a lightly spiced gravy dish of bottle gourd called *doodh-lau*. The unconventional part of its preparation is that instead of water, milk is added to the cooking to make the gravy. The preparation generally features grated coconut.

Kabita Chowdhury, in her cookbook, mentions the traditional dish *lau-narkel* that is cooked often in the Dutta Chaudhury family. The members of this erstwhile zamindari family made this semi-dry dish by cooking finely sliced pieces of bottle gourd in mustard oil with grated coconut, green peas, tomatoes and spices. *Lauer kofta*, another dish prepared by the family, has fried koftas, made with peeled and grated bottle gourd that has been mixed with chhana, refined flour, spices, salt and sugar, cooked in thick rich gravy. Sometimes, instead of rice, Bengalis use lau to make their famous dessert preparation called payesh. Generally, a Bengali meal is wrapped up with a small serving of a sweet preparation called chutney, which is often eaten with fried papors. The Dutta Chaudhury family also cook lau into a slightly offbeat sweet chutney preparation. Finely sliced pieces of the vegetable are cooked in mustard oil with a phoron of black mustard seeds and dried red chillies. The pieces are then boiled by adding some water and turmeric. At this juncture, a little bit of salt, some tamarind water and adequate amount of sugar are added, and the chutney is cooked to a semi-thick consistency.

The summer vegetable, patol or pointed gourd, which the Bengalis are enthusiastic about not only for its great taste but also because it is light and digestive, is another one that is cooked into different dishes. This small vegetable, which happily fits into the palm and is much firmer and less watery than the lau, becomes a favourite accompaniment to rice and dal when fried, halved and unpeeled. The vegetable is also peeled, cut into pieces and cooked with potatoes or fish like rui, bata or parshe in a jhol (generally meaning a light and thin curry) or with potatoes in a dalna or chachchari. As has been mentioned earlier, patol is often cooked in a paste of poppy seeds, lending the preparation the name *patol posto*. Although these dishes form a part of the daily fare served in Bengali households, patol can also be cooked into exclusive Bengali dishes that are served in social gatherings and celebratory occasions like *patoler dolma*, *doi-patol* (patol cooked in plain yoghurt with salt, sugar, spices and ghee) and shukto.

Nandini Deb Bourani also mentions *til patol*, another unique dish that was prepared by the women of Sovabazar Rajbari. Patol and white sesame seeds or shaada til are the two main ingredients of this simple and delicious dish that is relished with steamed rice and bread preparations. The washed and peeled pointed gourds are coated with turmeric, salt and sugar. They are then put in a wok containing a small quantity of hot oil. The wok is covered with a lid and the pointed gourds are cooked on a low flame. When they are partly cooked, the lid is removed and some more oil and a paste of white sesame seeds are added to the cooking. The pointed gourds are cooked in this paste till it releases oil at the sides.

Bengali cuisine, as has been mentioned before, is served course-wise. Usually, meals begin with either a shaak or bitter preparation that is eaten with cooked rice. The popular varieties of leafy green vegetables cooked in Bengali homes are palong shaak, methi shaak (fenugreek leaves), shorshe shaak (mustard leaves), lal shaak, kalmi shaak (water spinach), notey shaak (green amaranth leaves), paat shaak (jute leaves), motor daler shaak (leaves of split yellow peas), mulo shaak (radish leaves), beto shaak (lamb's quarters) and dhenki shaak (fiddlehead fern).

Shaak is finely chopped and fried with a phoron of kalo jeera and dried red chillies, and some turmeric and salt. The leaves let out a lot of water. The wok is covered with a lid and the leaves are cooked on a low flame till all the water dries up. This is the most popular method of preparing shaak in Bengali homes. Variety is often brought into this standard recipe of *shaak bhaja* (fry) by adding fried and crumbled boris, fried and pounded peanuts, slices of fried potatoes or chopped hyacinth beans and aubergines. However, *kalmi shaak bhaja* is prepared in a slightly different manner by frying the leafy green vegetable with finely chopped garlic and onions, slit green chillies, fried potato cubes, turmeric and salt.

As has been mentioned before, danta chachchari is also made with the stalks of leafy green vegetables. For example, the stalks of lal shaak are cooked with potatoes in a paste of poppy seeds and green chillies. But, often, both the stalks and leaves of leafy green vegetables are cooked together in chachchari preparations. *Pui shaak*, another favourite of the Bengalis, is not fried but cooked into a popular dry chachchari dish with potatoes, aubergines and pumpkin. Both the leaves and the stalks of the shaak are cooked with the chopped vegetables in a tempering of paanch phoron and dried red chillies. The other ingredients added to the preparation are salt, sugar, turmeric and shorshe bata (paste of mustard seeds). Some water is added to boil the vegetables. This chachchari preparation can also be made without the mustard paste. The stalks, leaves and vegetables are cooked in a tempering of paanch phoron and dried red chillies. Spices like the pastes of ginger, turmeric, cumin and coriander, and slit green chillies are used in the cooking, and the preparation is seasoned with some salt and sugar.

Bengalis often grind mustard seeds and poppy seeds together and use the paste in different preparations to enhance their taste. *Shish palonger chachchari* is a very popular dish in the community. Although the tender spinach tips can be cooked with a medley of vegetables like potatoes, aubergines, hyacinth beans and radish in mustard paste, a much-liked preparation of this dish is to cook them in a paste of mustard seeds and poppy seeds that have been ground together with a few green chillies and some salt. Some even add fried boris and a pinch of sugar to the cooking.

Leafy green vegetables are also cooked into tarkari preparations. According to Banerji, the word tarkari, originally from Persian, meant uncooked garden vegetables. This was naturally extended to mean vegetables cooked in some gravy. This category also includes leafy green vegetables. Lau shaak (bottle gourd leaves) and kumro shaak (pumpkin leaves) are the two varieties that are popularly cooked into tarkari dishes. The chopped leaves of lau or kumro are cooked with potato and pumpkin cubes in a tempering of kalo jeera and dried red chillies. Some salt, sugar, turmeric, and pastes of coriander, cumin and dried red chillies are added to the cooking. Many add boras or boris made of motor dal to the preparation.

The Significance of Teto

Sometimes, instead of shaak, a meal begins with a bitter preparation like *neem pata bhaja* (fried margosa leaves) or *neem-begoon* (margosa leaves fried with small cubes of aubergine). These bitter preparations of neem pata, a medicinal herb, which are eaten by mixing them with steamed rice and some salt, are spring and summer favourites as the new leaves (kochi pata) that cover the branches of the margosa tree in these times are less bitter than the older ones (buro pata) and ideal for making these dishes. As Banerji writes in her book, 'The association of healthy properties with a bitter taste and the subsequent appreciation of that bitterness as a taste is a Bengali peculiarity that outsiders find incomprehensible' (pp. 5–6).

Bitter preparations are classified as *teto*. The stress it lays on the importance of consumption of bitter ingredients makes Bengali cuisine quite scientific in nature. It not only recognizes the value of bitterness as a palate cleanser (starting a meal with a teto dish helps to appreciate the taste of the other dishes better) but, following Ayurvedic traditions, also has a high regard for its medicinal properties. Ayurveda considers bitter ingredients to be very good for health. For example, the consumption of neem leaves and bitter gourds strengthens the immune system, purifies blood, thereby boosting the health of the skin, and improves vision. Neem leaves, even when consumed, are beneficial for the scalp and hair. Being excellent for the liver, they help in improving digestion. Even bitter gourds, being an excellent source of dietary fibre, aid digestion. Their consumption heals liver problems. Most importantly, bitter gourds control insulin, making them essential for patients suffering from diabetes.

Since the availability of the bitter gourds, karola and uchche, are not confined to the spring and summer months, they are eaten throughout the year. They can be simply cut into rings, coated with salt and turmeric, and fried (*uchche bhaja* or *karola bhaja*), chopped into cubes and fried with small cubes of aubergines (*uchche-begoon bhaja* or *karola-begoon bhaja*), sliced and fried with small slices of pumpkin (*uchche-kumro bhaja* or *karola-kumro bhaja*) or cooked into a chachchari with just potatoes or a combination of potatoes and aubergines or potatoes, aubergines and French beans. The vegetables in the chachchari preparation are cooked with a phoron of black mustard seeds and dried red chillies, turmeric, salt and sugar. Cooking the bitter gourds with other vegetables like the sweet kumro downplays their bitterness to some extent.

A *bhaate* can also be made with uchche or karola. The word 'bhaate' is derived from the words 'bhaate sheddho', which literally means 'cooked in rice'. These words originated from the old practice of boiling certain food items, commonly potatoes, together with rice. This ancient technique in Bengal's culinary lifestyle has survived centuries, and is still prevalent in many homes. The food items generally boiled with rice are whole vegetables like potato, bitter gourds, hyacinth beans, pumpkin, unripe papaya, green banana, pointed gourd, ridge gourd, okra and colocasia.

The boiled vegetable is taken out from the cooked rice, mashed and mixed with mustard oil, minced green chillies and salt. The method of cooking lends this preparation the name 'bhaate' and it is eaten with the rice in which the vegetable has been cooked. Out of these vegetables, those which complement the potato are often mashed together with it to make this preparation. Bhaate is also made with oal (elephant foot yam) but in a slightly different way. The vegetable is boiled, mashed and then fried in mustard oil with a phoron of kalo jeera and dried red chillies. Some salt is added to the cooking. The vegetable can also be mashed in the wok with a spatula while it is being cooked. A bhaate of gathi kochu can also be made in this way.

Sometimes, bhaate is made with whole eggs (*deem bhaate*) or musur dal (*musur dal bhaate*) that has been boiled together with rice. Musur dal is boiled in rice in an interesting way. The washed dal is put in a clean cloth, which is knotted tightly at the top and then placed inside a pot full of boiling rice. The dal, without any water being directly added to it, gets boiled with the rice. This method results in dal that is boiled dry. Bhaate is made by mashing the dal and mixing it with mustard oil, salt and minced onions and green chillies. This is then eaten with the cooked rice.

This practice of cooking the bhaate items stems from the early days of large joint families in Bengal. Since a lot of food had to be cooked for the large number of family members, this practice evolved to save time and fuel. However, in the modern world of small nuclear families, the amount of food cooked in a single family has reduced considerably. So, the different food items are often chosen to be boiled separately and not together. Thus, the mashes, instead of being called 'bhaate', are often confusingly called 'sheddho', 'makha' or 'sheddho makha'.

The bitter gourds can also be cooked into a tarkari with either the paste of mustard seeds or the combined pastes of mustard seeds and poppy seeds. The seeds are ground to a paste with green chillies and salt. Uchche or karola can be cooked on their own or combined with complementing vegetables like potatoes, aubergines or potatoes and aubergines to make this dish. The chopped and fried vegetables are cooked in mustard oil with a phoron of kalo jeera and dried red chillies, turmeric, salt and the paste.

Although neem pata, uchche and karola are the most popular bitter ingredients cooked into dishes in Bengal, a culinary enthusiast can also come across dishes made with a few other bitter ingredients like thankuni pata and helencha shaak.

Thankuni pata, which are the leaves of the herbaceous perennial plant, Asiatic pennywort (also known as Indian pennywort), commonly found in India and Bangladesh, is used for culinary as well as medicinal purposes. According to Ayurveda, these bitter leaves are supposed to be an effective remedy for any kind of digestive disorder. It is a common practice among Bengalis to soak these leaves in water for many hours, and then strain and drink the liquid to get relief from stomach ailments. A paste of these leaves, known as *thankuni pata bata*, is relished with steamed rice. It is made by grinding the leaves to a fine paste with a few cloves of garlic and green chillies. Some salt and mustard oil are added to the paste and mixed well.

Helencha or hinche shaak is regarded by Ayurveda to be beneficial for digestive disorders and skin diseases, and promotes liver health. It can be cooked into a bhaja with a phoron of garlic and dried red chillies, a bhaate by boiling and mashing it with potatoes and into a tarkari with cubed potatoes and aubergines.

The community's appreciation for bitter ingredients even extends to using them in bora and fritter preparations. However, these are served as an accompaniment to cooked rice and lentils and not eaten at the beginning of a meal. Either the fruit or only the leaves of bitter gourds are often ground to a coarse paste with musur dal or chholar dal (which have been soaked before for a few hours), green chillies and salt. This paste is shaped into boras and fried. Sometimes, dal is omitted and the paste is simply mixed with a lightly spiced and salted batter of besan (gram flour), shaped into boras and fried. Boras are also made with thankuni pata and helencha shaak.

The night-blooming jasmine or night jasmine, known as parijat in Hindi, is considered to be a sacred tree in Hinduism because it is featured in many of its religious and mythological stories. Known as shiuli in Bengali, this tree is also considered sacred in Bengal's culture because it starts flowering in the beginning of autumn, a season which heralds the approach of Durga Puja. The tree is aptly named night-blooming jasmine because its flower, which is tiny with white petals, that are rooted in an equally tiny orange coloured corolla tube, blooms only at night, giving out a strong sweet fragrance. During the day, the tree is surrounded by its own flowers, which shed to the ground when the sun rises. Bengali Hindus weave these tiny flowers into garlands and offer them to deities during worship. In fact, this is the only tree whose flowers are permitted to be picked up from the ground and offered to deities. The flowering season is short and comes to an end with the closing of the autumn months.

The different parts of the tree like its seeds, stem, leaves and flowers are highly regarded in Ayurveda for their medicinal benefits. Bengalis use the bitter leaves of this tree in their culinary practices by mostly making boras out of them. The leaves are considered to be beneficial for treating cough, chronic fever, high blood pressure, diabetes, intestinal ailments, malaria and bone-related diseases like rheumatism, arthritis and joint pain. They are also used as a laxative. Bengalis even eat the excruciatingly bitter leaves of patol, known as palta pata, by making boras and fritters out of them.

One school of thought, vehemently disputed by the Ghotis, believes that the habit of eating teto dishes was once more prevalent in East Bengal. In the article, 'The truth about our bitter food' (18 March 2018), carried in the newspaper, the *Times of India*, Indologist and author, Nrisingha Prasad Bhaduri, points out that historically Bangladesh, apart from its capital city Dhaka, had a village-dominated economy. The villagers ate what they produced on lands owned by them. Bitter gourds were commonly grown and neem trees were found in nearly every corner, making teto dishes a popular addition to daily menus. According to the author, since rainfall in the Rarh region of West Bengal, which includes districts like Birbhum, Bankura and Nadia, is much less, production in these areas is affected and the amount of bitter gourds grown here is less compared to that in Bangladesh. So, bitter dishes, at one point of time, used to be more popular with the Bangals. The habit of eating these dishes on a regular basis developed gradually among the Ghotis. Even today, in contrast to West Bengal, where such dishes are generally reserved for luncheons, in Bangladesh, bitter dishes are even eaten at dinner. The boatmen of Bangladesh are also found to make a preparation with bitter gourd that has been stuffed with dried fish—a culinary practice not prevalent among the Bengalis of West Bengal.

Whatever the truth might be, teto dishes are an integral part of the culinary culture of Bengalis irrespective of whether they belong to the East or West of Bengal. But teto is more appreciated as a taste at home. Dishes made of bitter ingredients are generally reserved for home cooking and form a part of the daily fare. They are hardly served in social gatherings or on celebratory occasions. The only exception is shukto—a classic mildly bitter dish in which Bengalis take a lot of pride.

Chitrita Banerji explains in her book, 'The term is derived from the medieval Bengali shukuta, meaning the dried leaves of a plant, usually the bitter jute plant. These leaves were stored throughout the year and used to make a bitter dish with seasonal vegetables. From the mythical Shiva in the narrative poems to the historical figure of Chaitanya, medieval Bengalis loved shukto, and all the more so because it was believed to be an antidote for excessive mucus in the gut, a sign of dysentery' (pp. 6–7).

The dish is made with a medley of vegetables that varies according to season and availability, like potatoes, aubergines, sweet potatoes, unripe papaya, radishes, hyacinth beans, French beans, green bananas, ridge gourds, pointed gourds, pumpkin, banana stems, drumsticks and the most essential bitter gourds, which brings about the characteristic bitter taste. Shukto is a sattvic delicacy, which is prepared in mustard oil. The vegetables are cooked in a tempering of paanch phoron, black mustard seeds, dried red chillies and bay leaves. The chopped vegetables are then added to the cooking. The pastes of ginger, mustard and poppy seeds, along with a sprinkling of some salt and sugar, are added at this juncture. The vegetables are boiled in water and thereafter, some milk and a few fried whole boris are added to this cooked concoction. The preparation is seasoned with some ghee towards the end. This light, tasty and easily digestible medley of vegetables also has some gravy in it.

Shukto is not very bitter in taste. It is mildly bitter and a little sweet, making it a bitter-sweet medley of vegetables. The addition of milk and sugar to the preparation reduces its bitterness. Sometimes, the bitter taste is brought about by replacing the bitter gourds with bitter leaves or bitter leafy green vegetables. Neem pata is an often chosen alternative. The choice of margosa leaves is not confined to kochi pata in a shukto preparation. If tender new leaves of the margosa tree are not available, the dish can also be prepared with buro pata. Though more bitter than the kochi ones, their bitterness get subdued as they are cooked with an array of vegetables, spices, milk and sugar. Many use shiuli or palta pata, and even helencha shaak, to prepare shukto. Variations are also brought about by using spices like radhuni and turmeric. Sometimes, milk is omitted from the preparation.

Though it falls under the category of bitter dishes in Bengali cuisine, shukto is generally served after a shaak and before a lentil preparation. It is an integral part of summer lunch menus and is regularly served to guests on formal occasions. Considered to be a classic vegetarian delicacy that is served as part of a celebratory fare in many gatherings and functions, its sattvic nature also makes it the perfect choice for all those feasts, especially religious ones, where such dishes are served.

But this classic vegetarian delicacy is not free from controversy. There is a general belief that shukto has its origin in Portuguese cooking. Portuguese culinary practices, as we have seen before, have had some considerable influence on the food habits of Bengalis. This theory believes that the firingis had a similar dish, which they tweaked, upon their arrival on the shores of Bengal, by using the local ingredient bitter gourd, and combining it with a few other local vegetables. Gradually, the Bengalis adopted this dish into their own cuisine and brought in some variation by adding their favourite ingredients like mustard oil and seeds, boris and even milk.

But Pritha Sen is sceptical about this belief. According to her, the tradition of eating bitter food at the beginning of a meal dates back to the Ayurvedic dietary practices of ancient times. The medicinal value of eating bitter food was laid down by the great sages and physicians of Ayurveda like Susruta, Charaka and Dhanwantari. Shukto was a cooling dish that was eaten in the hot and humid climate of ancient undivided Bengal. This habit is mentioned in the *Mangal Kavya*. Sen's view is similar with Banerji on the point that shukto featured in the food habits of Sri Chaitanya Mahaprabhu of the Bhakti movement. She further adds that in one of the narrative verses of the *Mangal Kavya*, Lord Shiva requests Goddess Annapurna to cook shukto for him. Many of the women protagonists of the *Mangal Kavya* cooked elaborate meals, which included shukto. This shows that the tradition of eating shukto in Bengal existed much before the arrival of the Portuguese in the sixteenth century. So, Sen firmly believes that contrary to the misplaced theory of shukto being a dish of Portuguese origin, it was the firingis who made it a part of their fare after intermarrying with the locals, and perhaps, tweaked it a bit, and cooked it in their own way.

Lentils follow shaak or bitter preparations. The lentils are mostly accompanied by fries (bhaja) made with vegetables like potato, aubergine, pointed gourd, okra, pumpkin and cauliflower. The chopped vegetables are coated with salt and turmeric and fried. Boras made of lentils, posto, edible leaves like coriander or flowers like shojne phul (moringa flower) are equally relished. Often, certain fritter preparations like kumro bhaja, kumro phul (pumpkin flower) bhaja, bok phul (heron flower) bhaja or begooni are eaten with rice and lentils.

The last one, begooni, is a classic Bengali fritter that is not only eaten as part of a meal with rice and lentils, and even khichuri, but also as a snack. In Bengali, a fritter is called *telebhaja*, literally meaning 'fried in oil'. Telebhajas are largely made with vegetables. They are mostly popular as teatime snacks and are generally eaten with the afternoon or evening tea. Even many legends of the city like the great scientist Professor Satyendra Nath Bose (of the Bose–Einstein theory fame) were known to have been extremely fond of this humble snack.

Telebhaja as a Snack

Although Bengali cuisine boasts of a range of fritters, the commonly made ones are begooni, *alur chop* (made with potato) and *peyanji* (made with onion). The vegetable is chopped, coated with a batter of besan, which has been mixed with salt and spices, and deep fried in oil. This method of preparation lends the end product the name telebhaja. In the olden days, some chaaler guro (rice flour) was added to the gram flour and the batter was beaten long and hard so that the fritters turned out crisp and fluffy. But, in modern times, some baking soda is added to the batter instead to achieve the same result.

Telebhaja is also commonly made with coriander leaves. A few stalks of the herb are taken together, coated with the batter and fried in oil. *Fuluri*, the simplest of all telebhajas, is not made with any vegetable or herb but just the spicy batter of gram flour. Round balls are roughly made out of this batter and deep-fried. The presence of baking soda in the batter makes the balls really round and crisp.

The fritters are also eaten with great relish on rainy days. They are either eaten on their own or with a bowl of muri. Often, some bitnoon (black salt) is sprinkled over the fritters. Many also enjoy eating them with green chillies. Bengalis often make telebhajas at home in the evenings. The fritters are also made and sold in shops and kiosks, and even by vendors on carts. Today, the streets of Calcutta are dotted with such shops and most of them begin operating from the afternoon.

But, during the colonial days, fritter shops were much fewer in number. Instead, vendors would stroll through the streets with baskets on top of their heads, containing the fried snacks. It was in this climate that a few telebhaja shops came up in north Calcutta, which had the largest concentration of Bengalis. Credit must be given to the owners, who were among the first to think differently, and set up such shops. Out of these few, Mukhoruchi, which is the oldest telebhaja shop in Calcutta, and Lakshmi Narayan Shaw & Sons, which is perhaps, the most famous of the lot, deserve special mention.

Mukhoruchi: Mukhoruchi, the oldest telebhaja shop in Calcutta, was set up in 1864 by Fagu Lal Sahu. Housed on Gopal Lal Thakur Road, Mukhoruchi was the favourite telebhaja dokan (shop) of the great Bengali saint Ramakrishna Paramahansa. Fagu Lal Sahu made all kinds of fritters for the people of the neighbourhood. Much later, a proper shop was built in place of the shack by Gopi Lal Sahu, a descendant of Fagu Lal.

Ramakrishna Paramahansa would travel from Dakshineswar down Gopal Lal Thakur Road to meet the legendary figure of Bengali theatre, Girish Ghosh, at his house in Bagbazar. On the way, the saint would often stop at 'Fagu's shop' and buy his favourite kochuri and alur tarkari, which he would carry along with him. When the great saint was critically ill with throat cancer, he spent the last days of his life at Udyan Bati, a garden house located at Cossipore. The house was not far from Fagu's shop. The duration of his stay at Udyan Bati lasted from 11 December 1885 till his demise on 16 August 1886. His wife, Sarada Debi, and his closest followers, lived with him at the large garden house and looked after him. Girish Ghosh would often visit the ailing saint at Udyan Bati. Swami Adbhutananda, popularly known as Latu Maharaj, who took his monastic vows in 1887, shortly after the great saint's death, was then his personal attendant and took care of nursing him in his final days. During these visits, Girish Ghosh would sometimes ask Latu Maharaj, 'I am feeling hungry. Is there anything to eat?' Latu Maharaj would send someone to fetch telebhajas from Fagu's shop.

A board nailed to a wall inside the small shop is considered evidence enough to prove that Ramakrishna Paramahansa did indeed visit Mukhoruchi and enjoyed eating the kochuri and alur tarkari made in the shop. A translation of the Bengali writing on the board says, 'To the north of the Kali temple was Fagu's shop and Sri Sri Ramakrishna Deb would love to have the kochuris of the shop. Where there was a shed at which fritters were sold, there now stands a proper brick shop today, and the name of the shop is now Mukhoruchi'. This quotation is from page 28 of a souvenir book published in 1967, which was taken from the library of Ramakrishna Mission Ashrama in Baranagar. The Ramakrishna Mission Ashrama in Baranagar is located close to the shop and was established in 1912. Since its inception, the maharajs (monks) of the ashrama have bought telebhajas from Fagu's shop.

In 1958, Babu Lal Sahu, another descendant, named the shop 'Mukhoruchi', which when translated roughly means 'tasty for the palate'. The shop sells a variety of savouries like dhakai parota, khasta kochuri, nimki, shingara, begooni, alur chop, vegetable chop, Kashmiri chop, capsicum chop, dhonka, daler bora, fuluri, jhuri bhaja, and kochuri and alur tarkari.

Lakshmi Narayan Shaw & Sons: There is another telebhaja shop in Calcutta, which is very famous, thanks to one of its customers. Established in the year 1918, Lakshmi Narayan Shaw is popularly known as 'Netajir telebhajar dokan' (Netaji's fritter shop) because Netaji Subhas Chandra Bose enjoyed eating the telebhajas made at this shop.

Lakshmi Narayan Shaw was earlier located on Abhay Guha Road in north Calcutta. Originally from Gaya in Bihar, Khedu Shaw's parents shifted to Calcutta in search of better work prospects. Khedu Shaw began the telebhaja business in 1918 by setting up a hutment on Abhay Guha Road. Along with Fagu Lal Sahu, he can be given credit for being one of the few who set up a stationed hutment from which he made and sold telebhajas at this time.

The telebhajas he made at first were begooni, peyanji, alur chop and phulkopir chop (cauliflower fritter). When his business began to grow, Khedu Shaw decided to shift his shop to a bigger place, and chose a corner plot on Bidhan Sarani, near Hedua. He had one assistant who chopped the vegetables, and mixed the spices and the batter while he himself checked over the ingredients, fried the fritters and served them piping hot to his customers. Gradually, Shaw began adding more kinds of fritters to his shop's collection like *aamer chop* (raw mango fritter) and *narkeler chop* (coconut fritter).

The shop soon became the favourite haunt of freedom fighters. When any swadeshi meetings were held in the area, freedom fighters would place large orders of telebhajas with Khedu Shaw, who would pack them in leaf parcels and take them over to the meeting places. When messages had to be passed from one freedom fighter to another, Khedu Shaw would play the part of an emissary.

Subhas Chandra Bose began frequenting the shop during his student days at Scottish Church College, which is located close by. On February 1916, the freedom fighter, who was then an undergraduate student in Presidency College, was rusticated from the academic institution on grounds of having assaulted Professor Edward Farley Oaten for the academician's anti-India comments and racial slur against the students. Sir Ashutosh Mukherjee, who was then the vice-chancellor of Calcutta University, helped him get admission into Scottish Church College, from where he graduated with honours in philosophy in 1918.

Though he was just a student at this time, there was a spark about him that did not go unnoticed by Khedu Shaw. It made him think aloud to his family and friends, 'That boy is going to become somebody very big one day.' And when those words came true, Khedu Shaw was very proud to have had Subhas Chandra Bose, now Netaji, as one of his regular customers. He wanted to celebrate his birthday—23 January—every year, but it was not possible during the rule of the Company Raj. So, Khedu Shaw would instead indulge in a covert celebration by distributing free telebhajas to all the freedom fighters in the area, dropping into their homes and giving them the leaf parcels himself.

It was only after Independence that Khedu Shaw began openly celebrating Netaji's birthday. He put up a board that said, 'Today is Netaji's birthday. Free distribution of telebhajas to all'. This tradition has stayed in place since 1948. In recent times, Netaji's birthday celebrations in Lakshmi Narayan Shaw have reached a grand scale, with an average of 10,000 packets of telebhajas distributed to customers free of cost. A celebration takes place in the evening in his honour and residents of the neighbourhood put up skits, sing patriotic songs and recite poems.

After Khedu Shaw's death, it seemed a natural decision that his son Lakshmi Narayan Shaw would take over the business. In the last days of his life, long after India had attained its independence, Khedu Shaw named the shop after his son. Over the years, Lakshmi Narayan Shaw's popularity has multiplied. Yet, the shop is referred throughout the city by the name of its famous customer, rather than by the name of its owner.

Since Bengalis are very fond of fried foods, over the years, people with entrepreneurial abilities have banked on their fondness, and fritter shacks, kiosks and shops have proliferated in the city. A few of these shops, besides selling telebhajas, also sell a small range of other fried foods, chief among them being the 'samosa'.

The Story of Samosa

The samosa is a pan-Indian savoury, which has pride of place among all of the fried foods eaten as snacks in the country with hot beverages. Triangular in shape, the shell of this fried pastry is made with the dough of refined flour and generally stuffed with potato. Called *shingara* in Bengali, this particular type of pastry is mistakenly assumed by many to be indigenous to Indian cuisine. However, it is an adaptation of an old preparation, which is very popular in the Middle Eastern and Central Asian cuisines.

An early reference to 'sambosag', as this particular type of pastry is known in Persian, can be traced to a ninth-century poem by the Persian poet, Ishaq al-Mawsili. By the tenth century, the recipe began to feature as 'sambusak' in Arab cookbooks. These were largely filled with meat.

In his article, 'Tasty Triangles' (12 September 2009), for the newspaper *Hindustan Times*, Vir Sanghvi, writes, 'The samosa/sambusak spread all over the Middle East as conquerors and traders travelled and it took various forms and various shapes in every country. The original sambusak was probably a half-moon but as it moved, it acquired its current triangular shape. In some countries (Turkey and Afghanistan for instance) both triangular and semi-circular shapes continue to coexist.'

Although the different countries, in which this type of pastry is made, follow a standard recipe, the filling often differs. As it travelled through various countries, this fried pastry took on different names. But it is widely believed that the origin of all of these names lies in sambosag.

In all probability, the original sambusak was baked. Sanghvi continues, 'Somewhere along the way, the people of the Middle East began frying their sambusaks. It is easy to see why they would do this: you can fill a dekchi with oil and build a fire pretty much anywhere you go. An oven is much more difficult to construct.'

In the realm of culinary history, it is widely believed that in the thirteenth or fourteenth century, traders from Central Asia introduced this pastry, which they filled with meat and called samsa, to India. By this time, the Muslims had given up on the baked version and the pastry they brought to India was fried. Over time, Indians observed Muslim settlers making the meat-filled sambusak. Both Amir Khusro (1253 CE–1325 CE), a renowned scholar and royal poet of the Delhi Sultanate, and Ibn Battuta, a renowned Moroccan Muslim scholar, traveller and explorer of the fourteenth century, who was a guest at the court of Muhammad bin

Tughlaq, the sultan of Delhi, have made their observations about this particular type of pastry.

In the beginning of the fourteenth century, Amir Khusro wrote that the princes and nobles of the Delhi Sultanate enjoyed eating this pastry, which was fried in ghee and stuffed with meat, onions and other ingredients. On the other hand, Ibn Battuta described a meal at the court, which included small spicy pies that were stuffed with minced meat, almonds, pistachios and walnuts. These pies were served before the third course of pulao. As Sanghvi confirms, 'Push Indian food writers and they will eventually concede that the earliest mentions of the samosa in Indian literature can only be found after the Muslims established their kingdoms in India.' This timeless pastry remained popular even when the Mughals came to India and finds a mention in *Ain-i-Akbari*, the sixteenth-century Mughal document. Later, the Jewish settlers brought with them sambusaks with cheese or almond fillings.

The Portuguese came to India and introduced several food crops, chief among them being the potato, which they called 'batata'. With the help of the British, this small root vegetable caused a revolution in Indian cooking and began to be included in almost all of the preparations. Over time, Indians borrowed the basic recipe of sambusak and the fried pastry began to move out of the confines of the royal kitchens and homes of the foreign settlers. They filled the pastry shell with a spicy stuffing of crumbled or mashed potatoes and herbs like coriander leaves. Sometimes, green peas and dried fruits like cashew nuts and raisins were added to this basic filling. The pastry was fried till golden brown in colour and served with chutney. Thus, the meat-filled sambusak was converted into the potato-filled samosa.

But why was the potato particularly chosen for this preparation? There is no definite answer. The Hindus have always been largely inclined towards vegetarian food and upon experimentation, the potato-filled pastry definitely tasted great. Gradually, the price of the vegetable, as it became widely available, turned cheaper and the potato became the best available option to be used as stuffing. Since Indian confectionery shops run by Hindu halwais and moiras have a tradition of selling sweets and vegetarian snacks, this light and easily digestible fried pastry, gradually became a chosen savoury that was made and sold in these shops. The potato-filling made the savoury accessible price-wise and over time, the samosa gained tremendous popularity as a snack.

While the rest of the country called this pastry samosa (derived from the root words sambosag, sambusak and samsa), nobody is really sure why Bengalis began calling it shingara. There is a general belief that the name is derived from the word 'singhara', as the fruit of the water caltrop is known in Hindi. The fruit of this annual aquatic plant, which grows underwater and is widely cultivated in freshwater lakes, is called paniphal in Bengali. The snack closely resembles the triangular contours of the fruit. Bengalis made their shingaras a little differently. The fried pastry was smaller and its crust, thinner. The potatoes that went into the preparation were chopped into small cubes (although they did get mashed a bit while being cooked) and hing (asafoetida) became an essential ingredient. While the favourite Bengali paanch phoron and shukno lanka were used to temper the potatoes, both salt and sugar were used for seasoning.

Variation was brought to this standard recipe by adding green peas, fried peanuts or tiny cauliflower florets, the last being a favourite addition during winter. Over the years, Bengalis took their experimentations with the shingara a few notches higher. Their love for meat made them come up with *mangsher shingara*, a popular variety made with the stuffing of minced goat meat, and their incorrigible sweet tooth led to the creation of a sweet version called *kheerer shingara*, which is made by stuffing the pastry shell with a sweetened khoya mixture, deep-frying it and then dunking it in sugar syrup laced with rose water. Although other varieties like *maachher shingara* (made with fish meat stuffing) and *narkeler shingara* (made with grated coconut stuffing) were also created, these are now rarely made.

Chhenchki

The vegetable preparation that comes after lentils can be *chhenchki*, chachchari, ghanto, tarkari or dalna. Chhenchki is a dry preparation made with bite-sized pieces of vegetables, which are usually flavoured with a tempering of chillies and paanch phoron or kalo jeera or black mustard seeds. Ground spices are hardly used. Although these basic ingredients remain the same in different chhenchki preparations, sometimes other ingredients, like onion, ginger, garlic, coconut meat, bori, coriander leaves, sugar and ghee are also used. The vegetables that are generally used for this kind of preparation are pumpkin, potato, radish, unripe papaya and snake gourd.

Lal shaaker chhenchki is a preparation that is unique to Thakur Bari. The boiled lal shaak is sautéed in mustard oil with paanch phoron, black mustard seeds and dried red chillies. After some time, grated coconut is added and the mixture is seasoned with salt. This recipe is a deviation from the usual chhenchki preparations because it is made with a leafy green vegetable. Moreover, using both the tempering ingredients of paanch phoron and black mustard seeds in the same recipe is another exception in chhenchki preparations.

Bengali cuisine boasts of a variety of popular vegetable chachchari dishes like *sheemer* (hyacinth beans) *chachchari*, *alur* (potato) *chachchari*, *barbotir* (yard-long beans) *chachchari* and *dharosher* (okra) *chachchari*. Often, complementing vegetables are combined to create chachchari dishes like *alu phulkopir* (potato and cauliflower) *chachchari*, *peyanjkoli alur* (spring onion and potato) *chachchari*, *sheem begooner* (hyacinth beans and aubergine) *chachchari*, *kumro alur* (pumpkin and potato) *chachchari* and *sheem begoon mulor* (hyacinth beans, aubergine and radish) *chachchari*. Chachchari dishes made with shojne danta and katoa danta (a type of drumstick) are sought after in Bengali cuisine.

Bati chachchari is another very popular preparation, particularly among the Ghotis. The method of cooking the vegetable in a pot (and not in a wok) lends the preparation this name. This is a dish made with limited ingredients. The standard ingredients that are used in vegetable bati chachchari preparations are salt, turmeric, slit green chillies and mustard oil. There is no concept of phoron and frying in bati chachchari preparations. Instead, all of the ingredients, including the chopped vegetable and oil, are put into the pot at the same time, mixed together and cooked on a low flame till done. This enhances the taste of the dish. Very little water is added to the cooking and the pot is covered with a lid. *Alur bati chachchari* and *alu phulkopir bati chachchari* are popular vegetable bati chachchari preparations.

Dal is often followed by a ghanto dish. While bandhakopi (cabbage) and kancha pepe (unripe papaya) are some of the common vegetables used in ghanto preparations, dumur (cluster fig) and shojne phul are occasionally used. When bhaja moong dal is used as an ingredient in making *lau* (bottle gourd) or *chaalkumro* (ash gourd) *ghanto*, it lends the preparations the names, *moong dal diye lau ghanto* and *moong dal diye chaalkumro ghanto*. But the queen of all ghanto preparations is *chapor ghanto*, a delicacy and signature vegetarian dish from Opar Bangla. Made with a mixture of vegetables like potato, pumpkin, aubergine, hyacinth beans, pointed gourd and ridge gourd, the signature feature of this ghanto dish is the lentil patties that are added to the preparation.

The patties, made of motor dal, are known as *chapor*, thereby, lending the dish its name. The motor dal is soaked overnight in water and then, ground to a paste with a few green chillies and some salt. Round and flat patties are made with this paste, which are shallow-fried in mustard oil till they are light brown in colour. The small patties are broken into halves and added to the cooking towards the end.

Similarly, even though a variety of tarkari dishes can be made with different vegetables, the dish that stands out the most in this category is *paanch mishali tarkari*, a very popular preparation made with a medley (mishali) of five (paanch) different types of vegetables. A chef can choose from a range of seasonal vegetables available in the kitchen like ridge gourd, potato, pumpkin, aubergine, pointed gourd, radish, hyacinth beans and cauliflower to make this dish. In contrast, dalna dishes are made with limited number of vegetables like cauliflower, pointed gourd, unripe papaya, elephant foot yam, colocasia corm (gathi kochu), kohlrabi (olkopi) and unripe jackfruit (enchor). Out of these, *gathi kochur dalna* and *enchorer dalna* often feature onion and garlic in their preparations. Potato is often combined with vegetables like pointed gourd, cauliflower, colocasia corm, kohlrabi and unripe jackfruit to make dalnas.

The Importance of Bananas

In Hinduism, the banana plant is a symbol of auspiciousness and prosperity. It is one of the most important tropical plants and its fruit is available throughout the year. Bengal has an abundance of banana trees. As Chitrita Banerji writes in her book, 'Bananas were probably cultivated by the proto-Australoid peoples who originally inhabited the land. Both the fruit and the tree are abundantly represented in inscriptions and stone relics that date back to Bengal's antiquity. Like the rice plant, the banana tree also has a strong mythical significance in Bengali life. A young specimen is always placed outside the front door, together with a green coconut sitting atop an earthen pitcher, when a wedding or any other auspicious ceremony takes place. The same tree is pictured as the wife of Ganesa, elephant-headed god of success, son of the goddess Durga, Bengal's greatest deity. If a person dies on a Tuesday or a Saturday, the banana blossom has to be given as an offering' (p. xx). In the chapter 'Bangla Ranna' from their book *The Calcutta Cookbook: A Treasury of Recipes from Pavement to Palace* (1995) the authors mention, 'The outer sheath of the stem is also cut and made into artistic boat-shaped receptacles in which fruits and flowers are offered to the gods' (p. 27).

Different parts of the banana tree, which is so significant to their culture, are also used by the Bengalis in their culinary practices. Its leaves are used as plates on which food is served or small parcels are made out of them in which food is wrapped and cooked. While its ripe fruit (kala) is eaten on its own, its raw fruit (kancha kala), pith (thor) and blossom (mocha) are cooked into delectable dishes.

The raw fruit, kancha kala, is cooked into a few preparations that are relished with rice. It can be diced and curried or koftas can be made out of it, which are fried and cooked with spices into a gravy dish. The dough to make the koftas is made of boiled and mashed raw bananas that have been mixed with mashed potatoes, minced onion and green chillies, ginger paste, chopped coriander leaves and salt. The balls pinched from this dough, which are shaped into round and slightly flat discs, are called *kancha kalar kofta*s. Raw banana mash or *kancha kalar bharta* is made by mixing the boiled and mashed raw fruit with minced onion and green chillies, salt and mustard oil. Even the boiled 'khosha' or 'peel' of the raw fruit is used in culinary preparations by making a spicy paste or a chachchari dish out of it. In *kancha kalar khoshar chachchari*, boiled peels of the fruit are cooked with potatoes, pumpkin, spices, grated coconut and fried boris in mustard paste.

The most popular preparations made with the pith (the soft inner white portion of the banana stem) are chhenchki and ghanto. The pith, or 'thor' as it's called, can be cooked on its own in a variety of spices or combined with potato to make a ghanto dish. Grated coconut, sugar and ghee generally feature in the preparation. Some add boras made of motor dal to the cooking. Thor can also be cooked with bhaja moong dal, lending the dish the name, *thor diye moong dal*. In this preparation, the boiled banana pith and lentil are cooked with spices, salt and ghee.

But, in Bengali cuisine, the celebrated component of the banana plant is its tear-shaped, purple-red flower. Called mocha in Bengali, chopping it is a difficult and time-consuming task, which requires considerable skill and patience. The white or pale-coloured, tear-shaped, innermost tender portion of the flower is its centre. This centre is known as the heart of the flower and it is surrounded by the purple-red leaves. Known as bracts, these leaves are peeled off and the flower clusters found on the inside are collected. The yellow-tipped florets are plucked from each cluster. Each of these florets needs to be cleaned by removing the calyx and pistil. The remaining portion is used in cooking. In her article, 'The purple heart of the banana tree' (24 March 2018), carried in the newspaper *Mint*, Priyadarshini Chatterjee writes, 'There was a time, elders reminisce, when "cutting and cleaning the mocha" was counted among the essential skills for all Bengali girls of marriageable age.'

Bengalis have a remarkable enthusiasm for mocha. According to Chatterjee, the exalted culinary status, the cultural iconicity and sentimental value that Bengalis attach to the innocuous mocha, can hardly be seen elsewhere. Few cuisines use it as diversely and imaginatively. While, on the one hand, Bengalis make a simple bhaate preparation out of mocha, in which the boiled and mashed florets are mixed with salt, minced green chillies and mustard oil, on the other, they have crafted certain dishes out of it that are regarded as delicacies in Bengali cuisine like *mochar ghanto* and *mochar paturi*. Even koftas are made with it. These are cooked with potatoes in rich gravy. Chatterjee continues, 'The weakness of the fifteenth century Vaishnava saint Sri Chaitanya Mahaprabhu for mocha was legendary. In fact, the mocha is mentioned quite a few times in the *Chaitanya Charitamrita*, a biography of his life and teachings written by Krishnadas Kaviraja. Swami Vivekananda, too, was a fan and is believed to have proclaimed that in order to eat mochar dalna, "one could be born again and again".'

Mochar ghanto is made by cooking the chopped, boiled and slightly mashed florets with potatoes, grated coconut, boiled chickpeas, spices and salt in mustard oil. While sugar and ghee generally feature among the ingredients used, a few even add boras made of musur dal to the cooking.

The word 'paturi' is derived from 'pata', which means leaf in Bengali. The most common leaf used in paturi preparations is kala pata or banana leaf. The large banana leaf is cut into a medium-sized rectangle and the food is placed in the middle of it. The leaf is then folded into a rectangular-shaped parcel, which is secured by tying a fine thread all around it. The food is cooked in this parcel. Preparations made in this manner are called paturis. Instead of banana leaf, food can also be wrapped and cooked inside pumpkin, bottle gourd or ash gourd leaves. Banana leaf is inedible while the other varieties of leaf used are edible. When the banana leaf parcel is served, it is unwrapped, and the food cooked inside it is scooped out and eaten with boiled rice. The leaf is discarded. But when the edible leaves parcels are served, the leaves, along with the food cooked inside them, are often mixed with rice and eaten.

The food is mixed well with a paste, marinated for a short period of time, and then cooked inside the leaf parcel. Paturi is more common in

East Bengal. Hence, food cooked in this manner is generally associated with a sharp flavour and aroma. This makes mustard paste a common feature in most paturi preparations. The mustard seeds are mostly ground to a paste with a few green chillies. Additional ingredients are often added to this basic paste, the most common being grated or ground coconut or poppy seeds paste. There are also rare instances when, instead of mustard paste, other varieties of paste are used. Mustard oil is a common feature in paturi preparations and is mixed into the paste. The oil is also smeared on the leaves that are used to wrap the food.

Steaming or cooking on a tawa (griddle) is the most common method of making a paturi dish. Both the edible leaves and banana leaf can be used in the bhapa or steamed version. But, unlike kumro, lau and chaalkumro pata, which are considerably fine and delicate, kala pata is tough and can be used for rough cooking. Traditionally, a banana leaf parcel would be thrust into the unoon or earthen oven lit by wood or charcoal fire. The cooking was done on the smouldering embers when the fire was fading so that the leaf parcels would not get burnt. This method of cooking *kala pata paturi* is still practised in villages. But in urban homes, the leaf parcels are placed on a preheated tawa that has been smeared with some mustard oil. The food is cooked on a low flame till done. This second method of cooking on a tawa is applied to edible leaf parcels as well.

Fish paturis are very popular in Bengali cuisine. But the vegetarian ones are limited in number. Out of these, it is *mochar paturi* that stands out in popularity. The boiled and finely chopped florets are mixed with the paste of chholar dal, mustard seeds and green chillies paste, grated coconut or poppy seeds paste, mustard oil and salt. The mixture is then kept aside for a few minutes to marinate. A clean banana leaf is cut into a rectangle. It is smeared with mustard oil and a portion of the mixture is placed in the middle of it. A whole green chilli is placed on top of the mixture. The banana leaf is folded into a parcel. This process is repeated for the entire mocha mixture. The leaf parcels are then placed on a preheated tawa that has been smeared with some mustard oil and the mocha is cooked on a low flame till done. The dish is relished with steamed rice.

Fish

It will be an unpardonable mistake to overlook the profound role played by fish in the Bengali cuisine. The great rivers of Bengal like the Ganga or Ganges, Padma, Meghna, Jamuna or Brahmaputra, Damodar, Ajoy, Tista and Karnaphuli have always contained a wealth of life. These rivers, teeming with freshwater fish, are a source of livelihood for the fishermen. Even the lakes, ponds, canals and streams in the region teem with freshwater fish that are mild in taste. This explains the community's preference for this kind of fish. The salinity of seawater gives saltwater fish a briny taste that does not suit their palate.

The wide availability of fish has played a large role in shaping the food habits of the people. Bengalis feel incomplete if they are unable to have a fish preparation at least once a day. Fish can be eaten crisply fried or cooked into a light and thin jhol, a rich kalia or a delicious jhal. Here again, comes up a major difference between the Bangals and the Ghotis regarding the way they treat the fish before cooking it into a curry. Unlike the Bangals, the Ghotis fry the fish pieces that have been coated with salt and turmeric before adding them to the curry. Traditional Bangals frown upon this practice because they feel it ruins the flavour of the fish. However, many from the succeeding generations of Bangals living in West Bengal have gradually embraced this practice because they find it difficult to bear the smell and relish the taste of fish that has not been fried.

According to the Hindu caste system, Brahmins are the highest-ranking caste group. Traditionally, the Brahmins were purohits (priests) in temples, who conducted worship and acted as an intermediary between the worshipper and God. They were also well-versed in sacred religious texts and were acharyas (religious teachers). Hindu religious tradition dictates that these upper caste Brahmins have to adhere to a vegetarian diet. The majority of the communities in the country follow this principle. However, the Brahmin section of the Bengali community is one of those few who indulge in a non-vegetarian diet. They found the flavour of Bengal's sweet water fish irresistible and manipulated the *Shastra*s (book of religious rituals) to vegetarianize the denizens of the deep, calling fish the 'fruit of the ocean'.

The love that Bengalis have for fish is legendary. For most, maachh-bhaat (fish and rice) is an integral part of their daily food habits. Chitrita Banerji elaborates in her book, 'As the evidence of literature shows, fish has been part of life from ancient days to now. True, written evidence is scarce before the eleventh century, but as the historian Dr Nihar Ranjan Ray points out in his definitive text, *Bangalir Itihash*, the terracotta sculptures on the walls of Buddhist viharas in Paharpur and Moinamoti (now in Bangladesh), which go back to the days of the Pala and the Sena dynasty that ruled Bengal from the eighth to the eleventh centuries, provide reliable indications of lifestyle. Realistic portrayals show fish being cut, cleaned and transported in woven baskets. Nothing can be a greater testimonial to the continuity of food preference than to see the subsequent depiction of fish in folk art down the years. The nineteenth-century Kalighat pats paintings, show an abundance of fish themes, of fisherwomen selling their goods in the market and of babus carrying their fishy purchases. Throughout the intervening years, the fish has figured as a motif in the quilts embroidered by Bengali women, in the alpana or decorative patterns drawn on floors or walls or seats, as a shape for home-made sweets and in innumerable proverbs and phrases. The eighteenth-century narrative poem *Annadamangalkabya*, by Bharatchandra, gives us a list of 51 varieties of fish that Bengalis ate in those days, and a food-loving poet in the nineteenth century, Iswarchandra Gupta, said that since Bengalis lived on fish and rice, nature had given them a land full of rice fields and rivers full of fish' (pp. xiv–xv).

Fish is so important in the lives of Bengalis that the community considers it a symbol of auspiciousness. It often serves as a sign that heralds the beginning of a new cycle in a person's life. Combined with rice, its significance is reflected in many of the rituals and ceremonies of the Bengali Hindus.

On the day of the Bengali wedding, the bride's and the groom's families exchange whole fish that have been bought fresh at the market. Sometimes, a sandesh shaped like a fish is exchanged as well. According to custom, when a bride arrives with her husband at his house, she is supposed to hold a live fish in her left hand, a symbol of her being the harbinger of prosperity. This is also a test that confirms how adept she might be in her role as a wife, the person who handles such an essential food item in Bengali cooking.

During the shaadh ceremony or the Bengali concept of the baby shower, which takes place towards the end of pregnancy, the expecting mother is treated to her desired foods. The ceremony is attended by relatives, friends and other well-wishers who shower the expecting mother with blessings and gifts. The feast starts when she begins to eat the different food items placed before her. Rice and fish are compulsory among these food items. During annoprashan or the grain initiation ceremony of a baby, rice and fish are among the essential food items served. In Bengal, this ceremony is also known as mukhe bhaat (literally meaning 'rice in the mouth') and celebrates the child's introduction to solid foods. This solid food consists of a full-fledged meal that includes, among other food items, rice, fish and most importantly, payesh made with rice. The mother gives the child a small portion of soft and boneless fish meat to nibble on.

Visitors touring Calcutta's fish markets are fascinated by the large variety on display. The sight of fishmongers cutting whole fish into pieces on huge bontis greets them everywhere. Like the shil-nora, the bonti, which is a traditional cutting tool consisting of a long-curved blade attached to a slab of wood, is also a fixture in Bengali homes. Available in different sizes, it is used for cutting fish, vegetables, and even fruits.

The most widely used fish in Bengali cuisine is rui, which has a sweet taste and is eaten on a regular basis. Bengalis also like to eat other big fish like katla, mrigel, aar, boal (wallago catfish), chital (clown knifefish), bhola (Indian trout), bhola bhekti (Indian Jewfish) and shol (snakehead murrel). Small fishes like koi, bata, parshe, tilapia, pabda, bele (sand goby), kajuli (Gangetic ailia), sarpunti (olive barb) and topshe (mango fish), as well as those from the wriggling catfish family like tyangra, magur and shingi are enjoyed a lot. The big pangas tyangra is becoming an increasingly popular fish. Tiny fish are called chuno maachh in Bengali and the popular varieties that fall in this category are mourala (Indian carplet), punti (swamp barb) and kechki (minnow). Bengalis make a variety of dishes out of bhekti. Pomfret, lotey or loitta (Bombay duck) and amodi (anchovy) are some of the rare saltwater fish that are relished by the community. The Bengali Hindus of both Opar and Epar Bangla also indulge in eels like guchi, pankal, turi and chirka.

Bengalis treat ilish as the queen of all fish though the dispute between Bangladeshis and the Bengalis of West Bengal as to whether the hilsa of the Padma river is superior to that of the Ganges river or the other way around seems to be an eternal one. Chingri, on the other hand, is their king. The popular varieties of chingri eaten by the community are galda chingri (scampi), bagda chingri (tiger prawn) and kucho chingri (shrimp).

But Bangals have a stronger affinity for ilish and the Ghotis for chingri. This is jocularly highlighted in the chapter 'Bangla Ranna' from the book, *The Calcutta Cookbbook: A Treasury of Recipes from Pavement to Palace* (1995), where the authors mention about the stark difference in the reactions of the Ghotis and the Bangals to the victories of Mohun Bagan Athletic Club (the oldest professional football club of West Bengal) and East Bengal Football Club (a professional football club based in Calcutta whose founders belonged to East Bengal). The authors write, 'The monsoon is the most dramatically beautiful season in West Bengal and the emotional Bengali expresses himself through recitations, songs and eating. Football is another monsoon madness and office attendance is thin on the afternoon when the two ace rival teams, Mohun Bagan and East Bengal, kick-off on the Maidan'. Victory for East Bengal means a run on hilsa as fans get together to celebrate with shorsey ilish (hilsa in mustard). Prawns hit the high-water mark when Mohun Bagan wins' (p. 41).

In fact, the Bangals have such a strong affinity for the hilsa that on the auspicious occasion of Saraswati Puja, a large section of the community will offer jora ilish (a pair of hilsa) to the goddess. The pair of whole fish is welcomed into the house amidst joyous ululations. Some turmeric, mustard oil and shindoor (vermilion powder) are applied on the pair. These whole fish, placed on a banana leaf, are offered to the goddess. Later, this pair is cooked and eaten as prasad after the worship is over. In contrast, the Ghotis will never offer non-vegetarian food to the goddess.

The other variety of crustacean enjoyed by the community is kankra or crab. Bengalis, particularly those from East Bengal, also have a strong affinity for sun-dried fish, which they call shutki. However, the consumption of lobster, crab and eel are forbidden in Islam. Bengalis prefer using the rich and golden yellow mustard oil to cook fish. Even the health-conscious lot in the community believe that fish cooked in mustard oil has a unique taste, which shaada tel cannot achieve.

Over the years, Bengalis have used their imaginations and come up with a range of recipes for fish: from the simplest of preparations to the most exotic fare. Fish, cut into small pieces, is coated with turmeric and salt, and fried in oil till golden brown in colour. These pieces of fried fish, known as maachh bhaja, are relished on their own, often with drinks, or with rice and lentils. The fish mostly used to make maachh bhaja are rui and katla.

Topshe maachh bhaja is a delicacy served on special occasions and grand feasts. It is more like a fritter because the whole fish is coated in batter and deep-fried. The fish is more of a favourite of the Ghotis of West Bengal than those who have their roots in East Bengal where it is a rarity. The word 'topshe' is derived from 'tapaswi', which means a religious person leading an austere and ascetic life that is spent on meditation for the purpose of achieving spiritual goals. Just like the unkempt holy man, the fish too sports ample whiskers. Moreover, the mouth, fins and tail of the fish sport a saffron colour, which is the colour of the robe worn by a Hindu ascetic. These factors have contributed to its name.

The fish is small in size and has a single backbone. The bones are also soft. Hence, the whole fish, inclusive of the bones, is fried. At first, the whole fish are mixed with some lime juice and salt. Onion, ginger, garlic and green chillies are ground to a paste and a portion of it is used to coat the whole fish. They are then marinated for some time. Salt, spices, and the rest of the paste, which is used to coat the fish, are added to a batter made of gram flour. Many also add some rice flour to make the outer crust crispier and crunchier. The whole fish is coated with this batter and deep-fried till golden brown in colour. Topshe maachh bhaja tastes delicious when eaten with rice and dal. It can be relished with khichuri or eaten as a teatime snack.

Living in Bengal for years even made the British very fond of topshe maachh. They named it mango fish because it breeds in the rivers during the mango season. In *Calcutta Taverns and Hotels—Volume I* (1988), Major Harry Hobbs writes about the topshe maachh, '[...]the Fish is of great delicacy of flavour, slightly larger than a sardine, but smaller than a herring. The natives have named them *Tapaswi* (penitent) fish, (abbreviated by Europeans to Tapsi) from their resembling a class of religious penitents, who never shave, but who, like the mangoe fish, disappear during the rainy season' (pp. 157–58). Taverns, hotels, restaurants and other establishments profited from this fondness. Those were the days when a hundred pieces of the fish could be bought for four rupees and 'smoked mango fish' was a classic dish enjoyed by the sahibs and memsahibs.

In his book, *Fifteen Years in India; Or, Sketches of a Soldier's Life* (1822), R.G. Wallace eulogizes, 'Perhaps there is not in the world a greater delicacy than the mangoe fish of the Hooghly, which is as beautiful to the eye as it is delightful to the taste. With the flavour of the mangoe, which is an uncommonly fine fruit, it combines the colour and richness of the trout, and has a fine large roe which cannot be compared to anything, being a perfect original. For two months in the year this charming fish is caught in plenty, and the roes are preserved, and always appear at table' (p. 134).

Both Europeans and Indians would look forward to the season of the mango fish. Many Europeans would travel to Calcutta for their share of 'tapsi muchee' and Bengal Rum in places of fine dining. They enjoyed eating the fish so much that they felt the journeys were worth the effort. Even those who destroyed their livers in the process were glad that they had managed to eat their much cherished tapsi muchee. The authors of *The Calcutta Cookbook: A Treasury of Recipes from Pavement to Palace* (1995) point out in the chapter 'Firinghee Flavours' that even *Hicky's Bengal Gazette*, which was India's first printed newspaper that began publication in 1780, mentions topshe maachh. In this weekly newspaper, founded and published in Calcutta by the Irishman James Augustus Hicky, who is today regarded as the 'Father of Indian Journalism', the authors find mention that at meetings held in the late eighteenth century in Calcutta, the eating of mango fish was a priority on the agenda. Many swore that it was worth the journey to the city to eat the fish lightly crumbed and fried.

The daily fare involving fish includes ghantos, tarkaris, chachcharis and jhols. When applied to fish, ghantos, with the exception of muri ghanto, usually implies fish heads or shrimps cooked with vegetables. Fish ghanto preparations are semi-dry and generally spicy. Fish can be cooked with vegetables into tarkari dishes. These are spicier than jhol preparations and have some gravy in them. Young and tiny fish can be made into chachcharis. Generally, cooked with potatoes, onions and appropriate spices, the fish chachchari preparations have very little gravy in them.

Bengalis are voracious fish eaters. They eat the animal from the head to the tail. Even the deem or roe is not spared. Bengalis indulge in fish roe during monsoon because they are available in plenty at this time. The fish, whose roes are generally eaten, are rui, katla and ilish. *Maachher deemer bora* is a fritter preparation of the fish roe that can be eaten as a savoury snack or with rice. The fish roes are mixed with minced onions, spices, gram flour and salt, shaped into boras and fried. Many add rice flour, cornflour or refined flour to the batter to make the fish roe fritter crispier and crunchier. The fish, whose roe is generally preferred for this preparation, is rui. The boras can be eaten by simply mixing them with rice or as an accompaniment to rice and dal. Delicious tarkari, jhol, jhal and dalna preparations can be made with these boras. *Maachher kalia* is a very rich gravy preparation of fish. The pastes of ginger, garlic and onion are used in the cooking. Garom mashla and ghee are inevitably used for seasoning. A kalia preparation can also be made with maachher deemer bora. Since ilish or hilsa roes are the tastiest, they are often simply coated with salt and deep-fried in mustard oil. The fried hilsa roes, along with the mustard oil in which they have been fried, are relished with rice.

Even paturi and bhapa preparations are made with fish roe. Generally, in the *maachher deemer paturi* preparation, banana leaf parcels are used to cook the fish roes. The fish roes are mixed with minced onions, grated coconut, mustard and green chillies paste, turmeric, mustard oil and salt. Portions of the mixture, each garnished with a whole green chilli, are wrapped in banana leaves. The parcels are placed on a preheated tawa that has been smeared with some mustard oil and the roes are cooked on a low flame till done. Alternatively, the fish roes contained in the banana leaf parcels can be steamed or cooked in the unoon.

Bhapa is another popular method of cooking fish. Just like in paturi preparations, mustard paste is a common feature in most bhapa preparations made with fish. *Maachher deemer bhapa* or steamed fish roe is a very healthy dish that is eaten with rice. It is made by mixing the roes with grated coconut, mustard and green chillies paste, turmeric, mustard oil and salt. The mixture is placed inside a container and garnished with a few whole green chillies. This container, sealed with a lid, is placed inside a larger one. Some water is poured into the large container, taking care that it should remain at the base of the vessel containing the mixture. A lid is placed on top of the large container and the mixture is cooked in steam. The Tagore family was very fond of this dish and their women made a bhapa preparation of hilsa roes.

Other preparations like *maachher deemer jhura* (also known as jhuro or jhuri) and *maachher deemer bhuna* are also much liked. The former, more popular in Opar Bangla, is a preparation like fried spicy scrambled eggs. The only difference is that fish roes are used here instead of fowl eggs. The roes, which have been marinated with salt and lime juice, are fried in mustard oil with minced garlic, onions, ginger and green chillies, chopped tomatoes and turmeric. The preparation is seasoned with salt and chopped coriander leaves. The fish roes are scrambled while being cooked. Maachher deemer bhuna is a recipe from Opar Bangla. Although bhuna is a method of cooking that is usually applied to meat, in Opar Bangla, fish and fish roes are also cooked in a similar fashion. Chopped onions and tomatoes, ground spices like ginger, garlic, dried red chillies, coriander, cumin and turmeric, and whole green chillies are fried in mustard oil. The fish roes are added to the cooking. The preparation is seasoned with some salt and coriander leaves after which water is added to it. The wok is covered with a lid and the roes are cooked till done. This is a semi-dry dish. The fish roes can be cooked whole or scrambled while making the bhuna preparation.

Bengalis enjoy eating fish heads (*maachher matha* or *muro*) too. They not only relish chewing the whole heads of cooked fish but also cook them with other ingredients like lentils, leafy green vegetables and vegetables into delectable dishes. The heads of fish like rui, katla and ilish are generally preferred. When being used in these preparations, the fish heads are always coated with salt and turmeric, deep-fried and crushed with a spatula. Bengalis cook the fried and crushed fish heads with bhaja moong dal, pui shaak, palong shaak, bandhakopi, lau, kumro, chaalkumro, mocha or an assortment of vegetables of one's choice. While the dish *ilish maachher matha diye kochur loti* (hilsa fish head cooked with colocasia stolon) is very popular in Opar Bangla, *ilish maachher matha diye kochu shaak* (hilsa fish head cooked with the stalks of colocasia leaves) is a delicacy in both Opar and Epar Bangla.

Muri ghanto, one of the signature dishes of Bengali cuisine, is made with the fish heads of rui or katla, atap rice, of which the gobindobhog variety is the most preferred, and potatoes. Muri here means the fish head. The fish heads and potatoes are fried in mustard oil, and the rice is roasted, before being used in the cooking. This rich ghanto dish, which is meant to be eaten with rice, is made by cooking these ingredients with chopped onions and a variety of spices. The cooking is seasoned with ground garom moshla and ghee. *Chhanchra*, on the other hand, is a classic dish in which the fried and crushed fish heads are cooked with pui shaak and vegetables like potatoes, aubergines and pumpkin. The fish generally preferred are rui and katla. No water is added to the cooking. Instead, the ingredients are cooked in their own juice in a wok that is covered with a lid.

The principle of minimum wastage is followed even here. While the head, bones and tail of rui, katla or bhekti are often cooked with potatoes and aubergines into a delectable preparation called *kanta chachchari* (kanta means bone), sometimes the fat, and also the liver and intestine of these fish, are cooked with the same vegetables into another delicious preparation called *maachher teler chachchari* (tel here implies fish fat).

Bengalis cook fish into the simplest of curries. These jhol preparations are a part of their daily fare. They are cooked with minimum spices and often feature vegetables like potato, aubergine, hyacinth beans, pointed gourd, ridge gourd, cauliflower, unripe papaya and raw banana. Boris, when featured in maachher jhol preparations, lend an extra taste and bite. Special mention needs to be made of the versatile shrimp that is cooked with lentils, leafy green vegetables and a variety of vegetables.

These dishes also form a part of the daily fare. The shrimps are coated with salt and turmeric, fried and added to bhaja moong dal, lal shaak, kalmi shaak, pui shaak, palong shaak, notey shaak, kumro shaak, kochu shaak, lau, bandhakopi, peyanjkoli, chichinga, barboti, jhinge, kumro, mulo, chaalkumro, kancha pepe, gathi kochu, oal, olkopi, enchor, thor, mocha and shalgam (turnip). Shrimps can also be cooked with kumro danta, lauer danta, shojne danta, pui shaaker danta and notey shaaker danta or into a delectable preparation with dumur. Often, some of the ingredients are combined and cooked with shrimps. *Chingri maachh diye pui shaak kumro alur chachchari* is an example. Instead of boris, fried shrimps can also be added to paanch mishali tarkari.

Shrimps are cooked with kochur loti and shapla (the stalk of water lily), which are popular ingredients in Opar Bangla. *Kochu pata diye chingri*, a speciality of Opar Bangla, is a rare recipe which uses colocasia leaves. The leaves are chopped and boiled, and cooked in mustard oil with shrimps, the paste of mustard and green chillies, grated coconut, turmeric and salt. A bhapa dish is also made with kochu pata and chingri maachh. Known as *kochu pata diye chingri bhapa*, the prawns are mixed with salt, turmeric, mustard paste, grated coconut and chopped and sautéed colocasia leaves. The mixture is garnished with slit green chillies and drizzled with mustard oil. The prawns are then cooked in the manner of making bhapa dishes. Regular and big-sized prawns are cooked with vegetables like potato, pumpkin, okra, unripe papaya, cauliflower, pointed gourd and ridge gourd into delicious jhols.

Chingri maachher bati chachchari is a very popular dish. Originally a Ghoti preparation, it is relished even by the Bangals. The ingredients used in this preparation, besides salt, turmeric, slit green chillies and mustard oil, are shrimps, onions and potatoes. The method of cooking remains the same as in vegetable bati chachchari preparations. But some prefer to fry the shrimps before using them in the cooking.

The abundance of fish in the rivers of Bengal led to techniques like sun-drying to preserve the excess supplies. This sun-dried fish, called shutki maachh, is very popular with people who have their roots in East Bengal. In her article, 'I've got some fish to dry' (16 December 2016) for the newspaper, *The Hindu Business Line*, food writer Arundhati Ray explains, 'Shutki—a Bengali word that connotes dried-up or anorexic—stands for dried fish or shrimp, and it is inextricably associated with the overpowering smell that emanates when being cooked'. Generally, fish like loitta, punti, mourala, kechki and kucho chingri are turned into shutki. In Opar Bangla, particularly in Sylhet, even the prized ilish is turned into shutki. Contrary to the general belief that shutki maachh is popular with everybody on the other side of the border, the love for the fish is restricted to people belonging to certain regions like Sylhet and Chittagong.

Preparations of shutki maachh will inevitably be spicy and feature plenty of onions, garlic, ginger and chillies to give it a great taste and subdue its strong odour. It is believed that shutki maachh was a favourite of the noted singer and musician, Dinendranath Tagore, who was the grandson of Dwijendranath Tagore, the eldest brother of Rabindranath Tagore.

Shutki maachh can be prepared in many ways. It can be ground to a paste with plenty of chopped onions, cloves of garlic and dried red chillies. This paste is then fried in mustard oil with some chopped onions and tomatoes, turmeric and salt. The fish can also be roasted and ground to a paste with onions, green chillies and salt. Sometimes begoon pora is added and ground to a paste with these ingredients. Some mustard oil is mixed into this paste. These pastes, known as bata or bharta, are relished with rice. Shutki maachh is popularly cooked into a chachchari dish with potatoes and aubergines. The dried fish is also cooked into a bhuna dish with chopped potatoes, plenty of chopped onions and cloves of garlic, pastes of ginger, garlic, dried red chillies, turmeric, cumin and coriander, slit green chillies and some salt. This preparation is popular in Opar Bangla.

Richer preparations of fish include *kalia* and *jhal*, which are the perennial favourites of the Bengali Muslims. *Kankrar jhal*, a rich and spicy gravy preparation of crab meat, is very popular. In winter, koi is a popular fish sold in the markets. *Tel koi* is a much-liked rich and spicy gravy dish made with this fish. In this preparation, the fish is cooked in a slightly higher proportion of mustard oil, which lends the dish its name. Another favourite preparation of the koi in this season is to cook it into a jhol with cauliflower florets and potatoes. Bengalis are fond of mustard paste and particularly like cooking fish in it. Fish cooked in mustard paste are called *shorshe maachh*. But jhal preparations also feature mustard paste. The difference between the two is that the mustard paste gravy in shorshe maachh is not as hot and thick as in jhal dishes. A variety of fish like rui, katla, pabda, parshe, bata, bhekti, tyangra and koi can be cooked with mustard paste. Pomfret and prawns are also cooked into shorshe dishes. But *shorshe ilish* is the most iconic dish of them all. Another delicious preparation is *narkel chingri*. In this preparation, prawns are cooked in a mustard paste and grated coconut-based gravy. In Opar Bangla, a bhuna preparation of narkel chingri is made. Mustard paste is omitted from the preparation. Instead, the prawns are cooked with onions, spices and coconut paste into a dry dish.

But these are just few of the recipes created by the Bengalis. Since the community is so fond of fish, the preparations involving this aquatic animal are aplenty. The founders of the cuisine have stretched their imaginations to the greatest possible extent to craft different recipes of fish using available ingredients. Recipes are also constantly evolving and new dishes are being innovated, every now and then, by chefs, connoisseurs and food enthusiasts. But there are certain fish recipes that will always remain iconic. Over the years, these have become synonymous with Bengali cuisine and will never go out of vogue.

Maachher paturi is one such classic dish. The varieties of fish generally chosen for this preparation are those with a single backbone or very few bones. The popular ones used among these are bhekti and chingri (shrimps are preferred). In the background of this logic, it may come as a surprise to many that ilish, a fish with plenty of bones, is also popularly chosen for this preparation. But this fish is a delicacy and Bengalis always find excuses to make exotic dishes out of it.

Banana leaves are commonly used in maachher paturi preparations. In contrast, the edible leaf parcels are generally used to cook small varieties of fish. Maachher paturi can be steamed or cooked in the unoon or on a tawa. To cite an example of the last, a piece of fish is coated with salt, turmeric, paste of mustard seeds that have been ground together with green chillies, and mustard oil. Garnished with a whole green chilli, as is usually done in paturi preparations, the fish is then cooked in a banana leaf parcel on a preheated griddle or tawa that has been smeared with some mustard oil. The mustard paste gives the fish a pungent taste, while the method of cooking inside a banana leaf imparts a robust flavour. Almost inevitably made on celebratory occasions, this traditional dish has taken Bengali fine dining by storm in recent years.

Bhapa maachh is another classic dish. Ilish, rui, bhekti, bagda chingri and parshe maachh are the popular choices to make this dish. Some salt, turmeric, finely grated coconut, paste of mustard seeds that have been ground together with green chillies, and mustard oil are mixed together into a paste. The fish pieces are liberally coated with it and placed inside a container. The remaining paste is poured into the container and each piece of fish is garnished with a whole green chilli. The fish pieces are cooked in the manner of making bhapa dishes.

While *doi maachh*, a spicy yoghurt-based gravy preparation made with fish like rui and katla, is a sought-after celebratory dish, koftas made out of the same fish, cooked in spicy gravy, are also very popular. The biggest contribution that East Bengal has made to the recipes that define Bengali cuisine is *chital maachher muithya*. It is an extremely popular classic fish preparation with people from both sides of the border. The dish consists of koftas of chital maachh cooked in rich and spicy gravy. The people of East Bengal have named these koftas as muithya because they are made in the muthi or fist.

From boras or cutlets, which are served as appetizers or snacks, to dishes that are served as accompaniments to rice, the preparations made with the versatile chingri are aplenty. But there is one iconic dish made with this shellfish that stands out—*chingri maachher malakari* or prawns cooked in sweet and spicy coconut milk-based gravy. Made with bagda or galda chingri, this classy and elegant dish, which has its origin in the Ghoti kitchens, was also popular among the British in Calcutta. It is served on special occasions and is usually the toast of parties. The fried prawns are cooked with bay leaves, pastes of onion, ginger, turmeric and dried red chillies, and coconut milk. The preparation is seasoned with salt, sugar, ground garom mashla and ghee.

Chitrita Banerji elaborates in her book, 'The malaikari, which makes every Bengali salivate with pleasure, is a rich red preparation in which the sauce, enriched with thick coconut milk, ghee, spices and the oozing juices from the huge heads, serves as a background to the richer red of the shells enclosing the heads. Though considered a Bengali classic, it is doubtful if the malaikari has been in Bengal for more than 150 years. Even Iswarchandra Gupta, the poet of good food and good cooking, who died in 1860, did not mention it. There are many theories about the origins of the name malaikari, which seems linked to the English word curry. By the nineteenth century it was being used for the various dishes cooked by the people of Ceylon and southern India with coconut milk, as is the modern malaikari, and flavoured with kari leaves. Another theory argues that the dish should be called Malay curry since the people of the Malay archipelago have been cooking with coconut milk for centuries, a practice which came back to us through the emigrant Indian Tamil settlers there. To my mind, however, there is a big difference between Bengali malaikari and similar recipes in cookbooks on South-

East Asian food—this is the combination of the garom mashla flavour with the coconut milk and the pure ghee' (pp. 140–41).

No matter how relatively new the dish maybe, its popularity with the residents of Bengal became unparalleled. Even the sahibs and memsahibs could not help but be drawn to it.

Another iconic prawn preparation in Bengali cuisine is *daab chingri*. In Bengali, daab is tender coconut. In this dish, prawns are cooked inside a tender coconut shell from which the water has been poured out and the flesh has been scooped out. Mustard seeds, poppy seeds and green chillies are ground together into a paste with some salt, turmeric and tender coconut water. The flesh that has been scooped out is also ground to a paste with coconut water. These pastes are mixed together and some salt, mustard oil and tender coconut water are added to the mixture. The prawns, usually bagda chingri, are coated with salt and turmeric, mixed with this paste and kept aside to marinate for some time. The empty tender coconut shell is filled with this marinated prawn mixture. Some mustard oil and green chillies, whole or split, are put into it. The top of the shell that has been cut out is placed on it again like a lid and sealed with wheat dough. The prawns are cooked inside the tender coconut shell. Traditionally, the cooking was done by placing the tender coconut over direct fire. This could be wood or charcoal fire or a fire pit. In modern times, the prawns are cooked inside the tender coconut shell in an oven. The prawns could also be cooked like the bhapa dishes. In this case, the tender coconut shell containing the prawn mixture is generally placed inside a pressure cooker instead of a large container and cooked in steam. The dominating flavours of mustard and tender coconut give this aromatic dish a unique taste that is sharp and pungent as well as sweet and fresh. In recent years, this traditional preparation has been elevated to the status of an upscale dish in Bengali fine dining restaurants. The prawns, served in a fancy manner inside the tender coconut shell in which they have been cooked, are relished with rice.

Bhuna chingri is a dish that has its roots in East Bengal. In this dish, which is a classic of Opar Bangla, the prawns, generally bagda chingri, are cooked in mustard oil with sliced onions, chopped tomatoes, pastes of onion, ginger, garlic, turmeric, cumin, coriander and dried red chillies, slit green chillies and some salt.

Kabita Chowdhury, in her cookbook, mentions a traditional and classic prawn recipe that originated in Barisal in Opar Bangla. This recipe is *chingri maachher pithe*, a savoury dish cooked often in the

Dutta Chaudhury household. Shrimps and coconut meat are the main ingredients of this recipe. Grated coconut is ground to a smooth paste with a few cloves of garlic and green chillies. This paste is blended with the paste of shrimps. Turmeric, mustard oil and salt are added to this blended paste and mixed well. The paste should be thick in consistency. A clean piece of banana leaf, cut to a size that will fit a pan, is brushed with mustard oil. It is then placed on a pan and the shrimp and coconut mixture is spread on it in a circular shape. This is the raw pithe and it can be garnished with a few slit green chillies. Another piece of banana leaf, treated in a similar manner, is placed on the pithe and the pan is covered with a lid. The chingri maachher pithe is cooked on a low flame. After some time, it should be turned over so that both its sides are well cooked. Once done, it is cut into wedges and served. The women of the Dutta Chaudhury family serve this dish with steamed rice, musur dal and a salad consisting of onion rings, chopped green chillies and lime wedges.

An exotic dish that is made with the lobster is *chingri maachher chiney kebab*. This recipe has drawn its inspiration from the popular French dish, lobster thermidor. The scooped-out meat of the boiled lobster is cooked in ghee or oil with a variety of spices, minced onions, khoya, plain yoghurt and salt. Some shrimps are also added to this gravy and cooked. Some even add almonds, pistachios and raisins to the gravy. The shell of the boiled lobster is stuffed with some of this thick, hot, sweet and spicy gravy mixture. The rest of the gravy is poured over and around the lobster as a garnish.

The aforementioned descriptions of vegetarian and fish preparations reveal the large variety of dishes available in Bengali cuisine. Unfortunately, non-Bengalis have the impression that Bengali cuisine is a limited one. They come to this conclusion by observing the dishes that are served in restaurants, social gatherings and feasts. These are largely the rich and spicy preparations. The vast numbers of simple dishes that constitute a major portion of the cuisine are overlooked. Bengalis simply cannot bring themselves to serve the common daily items like *alu sheddho makha, neem-begoon,* khosha bhaja, alu posto, begoon pora or the thinnest of fish jhols to guests because these are regarded as too ordinary. But these common daily dishes are also some of the best the cuisine has to offer.

Meat

In an elaborate spread, fish is generally followed by a meat preparation. The popular choice of meat in such a spread has always been goat meat or mutton. Ancient culinary history has shown us how men hunted wild animals, which were cooked into dishes. In medieval Bengal, meat mainly meant rabbit, venison, turtle, goat, pigeons and small birds. Ducks were captured and bred for their meat and eggs. After Independence, the government banned the hunting of wild animals under the Wild Life (Protection) Act, 1972, bringing to an end the consumption of the meat of several animals and birds like deer, rabbit and pigeon. Consumption of the meat of turtle, which was a great favourite of the Bengalis, who endangered the species by eating them to near extinction, was also banned.

But Jawhar Sircar, in his article 'Are Bengalis Turning Vegetarian?' (9 June 2018) for *The Wire*, points out that it is not clear whether all these birds and animals were eaten by the upper social groups of Hindus as well. According to the eminent scholar, three types of flesh were taboo for the Hindus of Bengal—beef, pork and chicken. While Islam supports the consumption of beef, it is common knowledge that Hinduism prohibits it. Islam prohibits the consumption of pork and Bengali Hindus also avoided it as the pig was an unclean scavenger who survived on eating dirty waste materials. Although chicken was eaten by the Muslims, Hindus back then eschewed it as the bird was looked upon as heathen. Categorized as 'Muslim food', chicken was not touched by the Hindus for centuries. In those days, eggs meant duck or turtle eggs for the Bengali Hindu. In fact, duck eggs were very popular in West Bengal till the 1960s and 1970s. After that they began diminishing in popularity and got sidelined by the chicken egg. It was during the second half of the twentieth century in Bengal that the meat of this heathen bird began to overtake every other meat and reached a close second in popularity to goat meat.

But what caused this shift in fondness? The shift was not sudden but a slow and gradual one. It began with the arrival of the British. They relished the meat of the chicken and passed on their fondness to all those Bengali Hindus who were very influenced by their lifestyle choices. According to Sircar, these Bengalis and all those England-returned Bengali sahibs, who were together categorized as brown sahibs and were the subject of many lampoons, were eating the tasty chicken, much to the horror of the orthodox Bengali Hindus, long before the traditional middle class and other classes did. The arrival of the Awadhi brigade (Nawab Wajid Ali Shah and the retinue of people accompanying him) in the second half of the nineteenth century added fuel to the covert desire among many to eat the prohibited meat, which, if rumours were to be believed, was delicious. Their introduction of the biryani to Calcutta, which was later promoted by the Muslim chefs who came to the city from different parts of Uttar Pradesh during the British Raj, encouraged many traditional and middle-class Bengali Hindus to break the shackles of orthodoxy and try out the delicious 'Muslim dishes', which included Awadhi and Mughlai fare. This Muslim fare was an exciting and delicious departure from the traditional Bengali Hindu fare as the dishes were generally cooked with onion, garlic and lots of spices. The Bengali Hindus could not remain immune to this colourful and aromatic Muslim fare for long, which included many dishes of chicken, and began consuming them outside their homes.

It is difficult to point out precisely when the meat of the 'murgi' or 'fowl', as the bird is known in Bengal in Bengali and English respectively, began getting cooked in the home kitchens of the Bengali Hindus. The movement of the bird from Muslim homes into Hindu homes was a gradual one. The first move was made by the aristocracy, upper echelons and the educated and emancipated lot of the Hindu society. The Tagore women began to make an unusual lentil preparation with chicken and named the dish *chicken dal*. The pieces of chicken were marinated with the pastes of turmeric, dried red chillies, onions, ginger and garom mashla, plain yoghurt and salt. Sliced onions were fried in ghee along with cardamoms, cinnamons, cloves and bay leaves. When the onions turned pink and translucent, the chicken pieces were added along with some water. The pot was covered with a lid and the chicken was cooked till done. The chicken pieces were then added to chholar dal (boiled with turmeric and salt) and cooked for a few more minutes. Chicken dal had a thick consistency and went well with steamed rice and bread preparations.

By the middle of the twentieth century, many from the middle class were influenced enough to bring the meat and eggs of the fowl home. Although, murgir mangsho (as chicken meat is known in Bengali) was now cooked in Bengali Hindu homes, there was still an underlying guilt that the meat of a heathen bird was being consumed. Therefore, it was not allowed to enter the kitchen and was generally cooked at some remote corner in the house. By the 1970s and 1980s, the meat and eggs of the fowl had gained a large-scale acceptance among all classes of the Bengali Hindu society. The younger generation, always known for their experimental streak, were especially eager about the fowl and the bird ultimately gained access into the kitchen. Suddenly, there was a proliferation of poultries in Bengal, making the chicken and its eggs more affordable. Chicken broth and meat, cooked in a bland manner, even began to be recommended by doctors to patients for their high protein content.

Jawhar Sircar writes, 'It started with the fad for the omelette made from chicken eggs that came with an irresistible aroma. The more traditional eggs of ducks and turtles were also prized but they lost out eventually.' Duck and turtle eggs had to be cooked with spices into a gravy-based dalna because of their strong odour. This dalna of hard-boiled eggs or deem was served at lunch or dinner with rice. The duck egg was also cooked into an omelette and eaten at breakfast. Bengalis made the omelette in their own unique way by flavouring it with chopped onions and green chillies, and then frying it in mustard oil. Duck omelettes were often cooked into a jhol with potatoes, tomatoes, onions, green chillies and other spices. Like the dalna, this *omeletter jhol* was also relished at meals with rice.

But the deem of the fowl could be eaten boiled, fried, poached or in the form of an omelette, which could also be cooked into a thin jhol. Gradually, *murgir deemer dalna*, a preparation of hard-boiled chicken eggs cooked with potatoes in thick, rich, spicy gravy, and *murgir mangsher jhol*, a curry preparation of chicken cooked with potatoes and spices, turned into favourites. Onion and garlic, which over the years had become acceptable to the Hindus, now featured prominently in both these preparations. Today, amongst a small section of urban Bengali Hindus, the mental barrier towards pork has also disappeared and the meat is relished with a lot of fervour.

This leaves us with goat meat—a perennial favourite of the Bengalis. Both Bengali Muslims and Hindus have always enjoyed eating this meat. The British too had a high opinion about Bengal's mutton. They felt it was of excellent quality and flavour, and relished it to their heart's content. The goat meat or panthar mangsho consumed is of two types—'kochi panthar mangsho' or the meat of the young and tender goat and 'khashir mangsho' or the meat of the castrated male goat. Even the liver of the goat, called mete in Bengali, is cooked into a delectable chachchari preparation with onions, tomatoes, potatoes and spices.

Goat is also a sacrificial animal in both these religions. In the Muslim festival, known as Bakr Eid in India ('Bakr' is derived from the Urdu words 'bakra', which means male goat, and 'bakri', which means female goat while 'Eid' is derived from the Arabic word 'iwd', which means festival), well-fed goats are bought by the devout from the markets and offered as sacrifice to their god, Allah. Sunni Muslims offer castrated male goats, which they call khashis, as sacrifice. The meat of the castrated male goat is always more expensive because the hormonal change caused by castration increases the muscle content and body weight, and improves the quality of the meat. But Shia Muslims believe that the animal that is offered for sacrifice should be free from all physical defects. In castration, the natural physiology of the animal is interfered with and therefore, it turns out defective. So, they prefer offering the female goat for sacrifice instead.

According to Islamic belief, to test Prophet Ibrahim's devotion, Allah appeared in his dreams and commanded him to sacrifice his beloved son, Ismail. Although he loved his son dearly, Prophet Ibrahim decided to carry out the divine order and took Ismail to Mount Mina, which is located close to Makkah (Mecca in English), the holiest city in Islam. So that he was not overcome with emotion, Prophet Ibrahim blindfolded himself, laid his son prostrate on an altar at Mount Mina, with his forehead touching the block of stone, and sacrificed him. But when he removed his blindfold after performing the act, he saw his son standing alive in front of him. On the altar was a slaughtered ram. Allah had showered his mercy on Prophet Ibrahim and he had passed the test. Since then Bakr Eid is celebrated as the day to commemorate Prophet Ibrahim's devotion to Allah and remember his great sacrifice as well as Allah's clemency. Known as Eid ul-Zuha or Eid ul-Adha (meaning 'Festival of Sacrifice') in the Arab world, Bakr Eid has always been one of the most significant Muslim festivals in India.

The festival is celebrated over a period of three days. In Calcutta, on the morning of the first day, mass prayers are held in masjids (mosques) like the Nakhoda Masjid (most prominent mosque built in 1926) or in large open spaces especially reserved for the occasion like the Park Circus Maidan or Red Road. After the namaz (Islamic prayer) is over, the Imam, who leads the prayer, reads the Khutba or religious sermon and talks about the sacrifice of Prophet Ibrahim, the religious significance of his actions and the lessons to be learnt from them. Finally, he gives a message to the community for better living and wraps up the service. Once the prayer service is over, the men get up and embrace each other, joyously proclaiming the words, 'Bakr Eid Mubarak Ho'. The rest of the days are spent in enjoying and bonding with family members and friends.

Generally, people visit each other and even exchange gifts. The younger lot pay their respects to those from the older generation by visiting them. This older lot gives Eidi or gifts, most commonly money, to the young visitors.

The animal, which is mostly bought on the eve of Bakr Eid, can be sacrificed on the first day after the morning prayers or over the period of the next two days. The choice of animal varies between countries, depending on its availability. Since goats are widely available in India, in most parts of the country, this animal is sacrificed, lending the festival its name. In the early days, most people lived in stand-alone houses that had courtyards of various sizes. The goats would be sacrificed in these courtyards. But, in urban homes, where space has become a constraint, the community members help each other out. Those Muslims who live in stand-alone or bigger houses help out those who live in multistoreyed apartments or limited spaces by offering to sacrifice the animal on their behalf. The money is provided to buy the animal by the family who wants to offer the sacrifice. The person, who is offering the sacrifice, takes the name of Allah, reads out a short prayer and cuts the jugular vein in the neck of the animal. He then hands over the knife to the butcher who slaughters the animal. This qurbani (sacrificial) meat has to be shared, making the virtues of kindness and generosity important aspects of this festival. One-third portion of this qurbani meat has to be shared with the poor and the needy, one-third portion with relatives and friends, and the remaining one-third portion should be kept for personal consumption.

Since this meat, which is reserved for personal consumption, is quite a lot in quantity, it is stored and over time, cooked into a number of dishes like biryani, qorma and kebabs. Some Muslim families use a part of this meat to prepare khichra, which is basically a variant of khichuri. It is a basic one-pot meal of meat (generally beef or mutton), dal (generally chholar dal) and rice traditionally cooked in ghee with onions and spices. This mutton khichra is distributed mostly to the poor and the needy, and then to relatives and friends during the first ten days of Muharram, which is the first month of the Hijri or Islamic lunar calendar. The sacred month of Muharram, which is observed in mourning for the tragic Battle of Karbala, arrives just twenty days after Bakr Eid. The remaining portion of khichra is reserved for personal consumption.

Rezala and *dopiaza* are two popular celebratory dishes made by Bengali Muslims. The meat preferred for these preparations is mutton. They make great accompaniments to bread preparations like ruti, parota, rumali ruti, naan and kulcha. Rezala is a uniquely Bengali Muslim dish because it originated in undivided Bengal. However, the facts surrounding the origin of this dish are slightly obscure because no one is really sure when, where or by whom it was discovered. Shahanshah Mirza, thinking aloud, points out, 'Few are of the opinion that the birthplace of this dish is Dhaka but I would like to believe that it originated in the royal kitchen of the Nawabs of Bengal in Murshidabad. The rezala has now spread throughout the country and become incorporated into the pan-Indian cuisine.'

Chunks of meat, preferably with their juicy bones intact, are marinated with the pastes of onion, ginger, garlic and green chillies, and plain yoghurt. The pieces of marinated meat are cooked in ghee with a phoron of whole garom mashla (green and black cardamoms, cinnamon and clove), whole dried red chillies, whole black peppercorns and bay leaves, pastes of onion, ginger and garlic, cashew nuts and poppy seeds paste, sugar and salt. The quantity of water added to the cooking should be just enough to cook the meat. The wok is covered with a lid. The cooking is considered complete when the meat is soft and tender, and the thick gravy releases ghee. At this stage, ground garom mashla, saffron-infused milk and kewra water (screwpine water) are added to the cooking. The use of poppy seeds paste and sugar in this mutton dish is synonymous with the culinary practices of Bengal.

Dopiaza (literally meaning 'two onions') is a dish that was introduced to India by the Mughals. The two main ingredients of this dish are meat and onions. The onions used in this dish are of a large quantity. That is the reason behind the preparation being named as such because 'do' loosely means 'double'. This might make many think that the onions used should be twice in quantity compared to the meat. But this is not really the case and simply a large quantity will suffice.

There is a very interesting anecdote about the invention of this dish. If the popular story is to be believed then the dish dopiaza owes its origin to Mullah Do-Piyaza, who was the advisor to the Mughal Emperor Akbar. In the chapter 'Dastar Khwan' from their book *The Calcutta Cookbook: A Treasury of Recipes from Pavement to Palace* (1995), the authors introduce this character, whom most scholars consider to be completely fictional, 'The story goes that Mullah Do Piyaza was one of the nine jewels of Akbar's court. He was a gourmet and a gourmand and no mean cook to boot. The dish dopiaza is an example of his culinary ingenuity' (p. 99). The authors then go on to narrate the popular tale about the invention of this dish, which despite being an often recounted story is most likely a figment of imagination too, 'The Mullah's home was open house and by dinnertime the guests were well over the list. To keep the party going, the Mullah would clap his hands from time to time indicating to the kitchen that more onions should be added to the meat curry. And thus did Mullah Do Piyaza accidentally discover that the proportion of double the quantity of onions to meat was quite the best. And so was created the dopiaza (Do-2, piaza-onions)' (p. 99).

In this dish, the pieces of mutton are cooked in ghee with a phoron of whole garom mashla (green and black cardamoms, cinnamon and clove), cumin seeds, whole dried red chillies, whole black peppercorns and bay leaves, chopped onions, the pastes of ginger, garlic, turmeric, dried red chillies, cumin, coriander and garom mashla, kasuri methi (dried fenugreek leaves), plain yoghurt and salt. The quantity of water added to the preparation should be just enough to cook the meat. The wok is covered with a lid. The meat is cooked till it is soft and tender, and the thick gravy releases ghee. A few slit green chillies and chopped coriander leaves are stirred into the dish before it is taken off the flame.

Jhura gosht, a dry and spicy preparation of shredded meat, is also very popular among the Bengali Muslims. The dish is typically made with leftover cooked meat of either mutton or beef that is slow cooked in oil with minced onions and spices. Ghaffar feels that the slow cooking gives a burnt flavour to the shredded meat (to put it precisely in his words, '...almost like a well done steak...'). Although this dish makes a great accompaniment to bread preparations, it goes equally well with boiled rice. Ghaffar prefers to treat the dish as an accompaniment to bhaat and dal. He describes his favourite spread, 'I personally like to add chopped tomatoes and green chillies, and lime juice to the dish. I toss the shredded meat with these ingredients and serve the dish in a spread of bhaat, alu bhaate, shaak and dal. Then I put a few lime wedges, whole green chillies, onion rings and salt on the side of the plate. Voila, I am done! It is the perfect meal I can think of.'

Most Bengali Hindus are Shaktos or the followers of the tradition of Shaktism. This means that they are worshippers of Mother Goddess or Shakti and are largely the devotees of the Goddesses Durga and Kali, the two powerful forms of Shakti. In the early days of Bengal, it was customary to sacrifice goats during Durga and Kali Pujas. These sacrifices would be offered to the goddesses and the holy sacrificed meat would be eaten on the same day. This practice of goat sacrifice is called 'pantha bali'. The day before Dashami, which is known as Nabami, is the last day of Goddess Durga's stay at her natal home. Meat would be eaten as prasad by the devotees on this day and live goats would be sacrificed by a priest for this purpose. These sacrifices would take place either in temples or in the courtyards of the wealthy, who would conduct the worship in their own houses. The goat had to be a male and it could not be sick or have any physical deformities or blemishes. The priest had to be physically strong enough to sever the head of the goat from its body in one blow. After the animal was sacrificed, its head and blood were placed before the image of the goddess. The rest of the body was taken away and the meat was cooked in mustard oil into a gravy dish that did not feature onion and garlic, the traditionally forbidden ingredients. The ingredients that generally featured in this *niramish mangsho* or *niramish panthar jhol* (called niramish because of the absence of onion and garlic) were potatoes, plain yoghurt, ginger, cumin, coriander, turmeric, dried red chillies, cloves, cardamom, cinnamon, bay leaves and a pinch of asafoetida. This *bhoger mangsho* was seasoned with some ground garom mashla and ghee towards the end of the cooking. It was first offered to the goddess as bhog and then eaten by the devotees as prasad after the worship was over.

This practice of offering pantha bali was also followed in Kali Puja, another important autumn festival in Bengal, which takes place much after Durga Puja on the new moon day in the Hindu calendar month of Kartik (a month that runs from the middle of October to the middle of November). The sacrificed meat was eaten as the goddess' prasad by the devotees. During Kali Puja, the goddess is worshipped at night in temples and pandals (temporary structures that are mainly set up for community worship) all over Bengal. In temples dedicated to Goddess Kali, particularly in those that are regarded as Shaktipeeths, the goddess is worshipped with tantric rites and mantras. Shaktipeeths are the holiest and most significant shrines and pilgrimage destinations in Shaktism. There are fifty-one Shaktipeeths in this world. The temples of Kalighat and Tarapith are the most famous Shaktipeeths in West Bengal. Practitioners of tantra also worship Kali in large cremation grounds where she is believed to dwell. Kali Puja may be conducted at home as well but the practice is not very common. In pandals and homes, Kali Puja is not carried out according to tantric tradition but the mainstream Hindu Brahmanical one.

But, over the years, attitudes and perspectives are changing in Bengal.

Rising concerns over the cruelty of animal sacrifice or 'bali' among the Bengali Hindus is causing the practice to slowly fade away. Pantha bali on Nabami has nearly disappeared in the urban cities and towns of Bengal. If meat is at all cooked on this day, then it is bought from the market. But this meat is not offered as bhog. Instead, it simply forms a part of the Nabami feast. This gives the thakur or cook, the freedom to use onion and garlic in its cooking as these two ingredients have received a warm welcome in the regular panthar mangsher preparations.

In those erstwhile zamindari or aristocratic families where the practice of pantha bali was once much prevalent, the tradition is continued by many in a different manner. Vegetables and fruits like ash gourd, pumpkin, gourds, cucumber, banana, sugarcane and coconut are used as replacements and offered as sacrifice. This is because the conservatives still feel that sacrifice is an essential aspect of Durga Puja since the Goddess Durga is an embodiment of Shakti (literally meaning power) and bali invokes power. Therefore, it is essential to incorporate it in Durga Puja but it can be done in a less harsh manner by using vegetables and fruits instead, which are decorated with vermilion, turmeric and oil before being split with the knife in one blow.

Even in the barowari or community pujas, which have become the most popular, common and standard manner of conducting the worship among Bengalis, animal sacrifices have completely stopped or in some cases, been replaced with sacrificing fruits and vegetables. The barowari puja was started in the second half of the eighteenth century in Guptipara in Hooghly by twelve friends (the word is derived from 'baro' meaning twelve and 'yaar' meaning friends) when they were barred from taking part in a household Durga Puja. Today, this form of Durga Puja has become the norm all over West Bengal and among Bengalis settled in different parts of India and the world. The funds for these community pujas are raised through donations and subscriptions. The various activities of each community puja are organized by a committee of members set up exclusively for this purpose. Of course, Durga Pujas are still conducted in some individual households but they are heavily outnumbered by the barowari pujas.

But pantha bali still takes place during Kali Puja in some temples, particularly in those that are regarded as Shaktipeeths because animal sacrifice is an important feature of the tantric tradition. The time-honoured niramish version of panthar jhol is still continuing in these pujas. However, animal sacrifice is avoided in homes and places of community puja like the pandals.

Today, a Bengali Hindu cannot think of cooking goat meat without onion and garlic whether in the regular *panthar mangsher jhol* or in the immensely popular kosha mangsho. Special mention should also be made of a unique and simple dish called *shorshe mangsho*. As the name suggests, it is a preparation of meat in mustard paste. This traditional dish, which was a favourite of Thakur Bari, is quite unusual because in Bengali cuisine mustard paste is usually reserved for fish and vegetable preparations. At first, the women of Thakur Bari cooked the pieces of mutton with plain yoghurt and salt until they became tender. Meanwhile, mustard and poppy seeds were ground together with green chillies into a fine paste. The mutton pieces were then cooked for some time in mustard oil with this paste and a few whole green chillies. This preparation, which was relished with steamed rice, relies heavily on the distinct flavours of goat meat and mustard. However, shorshe mangsho gradually faded away in popularity and became a lost recipe. Modern-day chefs and connoisseurs are trying to revive the dish by including onions and an adequate variety of spices like garlic in the recipe since these ingredients have become so essential in the preparation of meat and impart a great taste to it.

In panthar mangsher jhol, the pieces of mutton are most commonly cooked in mustard oil with potatoes, onions and spices. Souring agents like plain yoghurt or pureed tomatoes are added to the cooking to enhance the taste. The preparation, which is seasoned with some ghee and garom mashla towards the end, is relished with steamed rice.

But the iconic mutton dish in Bengali cuisine is kosha mangsho, a rich preparation of goat meat in which the pieces of meat are surrounded by thick and oily gravy. 'Kosha' is derived from the word 'koshano'. The latter word is the Bengali equivalent of 'bhuna', which means that both the methods of cooking are similar. To make this dish, the pieces of mutton are marinated for a few hours with ginger, garlic and onion paste, plain yoghurt, the pastes of turmeric and dried red chillies, mustard oil and salt. The meat is then cooked in mustard oil with a phoron of bay leaves, cardamom, cinnamon, cloves and dried red chillies, finely sliced onions, green chilli, ginger and garlic paste, souring agents like plain yoghurt or pureed tomatoes, ground dried red chillies, cumin and coriander, and some salt. At first, the spices and meat are fried for some time over medium heat, stirring them at intervals to prevent them from sticking to the base of the wok. Some water is then added to the cooking. The wok is covered with a lid and the meat is slow cooked over a medium flame. At intervals, the meat is stirred and water is added in small quantities. This method of slow cooking is called 'koshano', which continues till the meat is well cooked and the water evaporates, leaving behind gravy that is thick, rich and oily. The preparation is seasoned with ground garom mashla and ghee, stirred for one last time and cooked for a few more minutes before it is taken off the flame. This method of cooking can be applied to murgir mangsho as well.

Although this delicious preparation is not particularly well known for having health benefits, Bengalis like to indulge in it occasionally with accompaniments like rice and pulaos, particularly basanti pulao. Kosha mangsho also goes well with bread preparations like ruti, parota and especially luchi.

Breads

Bengalis enjoy eating luchi, a local variant of the north Indian puri. Both puri and luchi are circular puffy breads that are deep-fried. The difference between the two lies in the dough. While the dough for puri is made of atta, the dough for luchi is made of maida. Small balls are pinched from this dough of maida. These small balls are called 'nechi' or 'lechi' in Bengali and they are rolled out into small round shapes and fried.

Kachori (Bengalis call it kochuri) is almost like a luchi but with a difference. Here, the circular puffy deep-fried bread that is made of refined flour has a filling. This filling varies between different recipes of kachoris. Luchi is the most popular variety of the famous refined bread trio of Bengali cuisine, the other two popular varieties being *radhaballabhi*, which is a kochuri stuffed with a fried and mildly spiced paste of white kalai or biuli dal, and *koraishutir kochuri* (also known as *motorshutir kochuri*), which is another variety of kochuri stuffed with a fried and mildly spiced paste of koraishuti or motorshuti (green peas). The sweet and slightly spicy preparation of chholar dal cooked with fried pieces of coconut, and alur dom (known as dum alu or alu dum in north Indian cuisine), a spicy potato curry, are the popular accompaniments to these refined bread preparations.

The fish-loving Bengalis also stuff kochuris with a spicy filling of fish meat. According to Nandini Deb Bourani, *maachher kochuri* has always been a favourite with the members of Sovabazar Rajbari. The filling is preferably made with the meat of rui or bhekti. The fish pieces are boiled and deboned. The fish meat is then mashed and cooked in a small quantity of mustard oil with chopped onions and ginger, garlic paste, salt and sugar. When this paste of fish meat is well cooked, some lime juice is added to it.

When writing about bread preparations, it is also essential to mention bakarkhani roti (*bakorkhani ruti* in Bengali). Over the years, the recipe of this roti has spread throughout the Indian subcontinent. It is most commonly treated as a breakfast dish or snack. It is also served during luncheons and dinners. In Kashmir and Hyderabad, where it is especially popular, the bakarkhani has gained so much importance that it is even served in weddings and other celebratory occasions. But how did its journey begin? Let us digress a bit and take a look at its story.

The Legend of Bakarkhani

The origin of this bread, which is exclusive to the Muslims, is in Opar Bangla. But the historical facts surrounding its invention are obscure. Many opine that bakarkhani has its roots in Old Dhaka of Mughal Bengal. The historical old city of Dhaka was the capital of Mughal Bengal (also known as Bengal Subah), which included both modern-day Bangladesh and West Bengal. But nobody knows who invented the bakarkhani roti in Old Dhaka. The date of its invention also remains unknown.

A few are of the opinion that this bread actually belongs to Central Asia and was introduced to the people of Sylhet by the Afghans. The Turks and Afghans were in power in the Indian subcontinent before the Mughals. In 1612, Khwaja Usman Khan Lohani, the last Afghan chieftain and ruler in Bengal, was killed by the Mughals in a battle in Daulambapur in Sylhet. He had ruled the northern parts of Bengal including regions like Greater Mymensingh and South Sylhet. When this brave Pathan lost to the Mughals, the remaining rebellious Afghans surrendered and the region of Sylhet got incorporated into the Bengal Subah. But these Pathans continued to live in Sylhet and mingled with the local people. They baked this particular kind of bread called bakarkhani and shared it with the locals, who took an instant liking to it. Many among them learnt the recipe and mastered the preparation of the bakarkhani. A whole new set of bakarkhani-wallahs (makers of bakarkhani roti) appeared on the scene.

Since Old Dhaka was the capital, it was the centre of trade and commerce. During the period of Mughal rule, people from all over the Bengal Subah flocked to this city for better opportunities. Many bakarkhani-wallahs from Sylhet shifted their base to Old Dhaka and set up shops that specialized in the production of the bread. The business did not require much capital investment. Gradually, bakarkhani roti became a very popular bread preparation among the locals of Old Dhaka. Bakers belonging to the city learned the recipe from the immigrants and became expert bakarkhani-wallahs. Every citizen of the city, from the members of royal, aristocratic and wealthy families to the common folk, enjoyed eating this bread. As a result, the number of bakarkhani shops proliferated in the gullies of Old Dhaka and the bread became synonymous with the city.

If legends are to be believed, there is also a popular love story surrounding the bakarkhani. Anyone who has been to Dhaka knows that the locals of the city attribute the discovery of this bread to Aga Bakar Khan. It is a legendary tale narrated in every gully of the city. He was a great warrior, army commander, military strategist, administrator and an equally proficient scholar in Arabic and Persian. He was posted as the commander of the armed forces in the district of Chittagong by Murshid Quli Khan, who was then the diwan of Bengal. While serving office there, he fell deeply in love with Khani Begum, a nartaki or dancer from Arambagh near Dhaka. Unfortunately, there appeared a villain in this love story in the form of the kotwal or local police chief. Kotwal Jainul Khan had an eye on the beautiful dancer whom he relentlessly pursued. But his advances were rebuffed by Khani Begum. Ultimately, the doomed love affair was brought to an abrupt end by the kotwal. To cut a long story short, a series of unfortunate events followed and the nartaki was killed by him. For some time, a heartbroken and distraught Aga Bakar Khan lost his mind. Finally, on the order of Murshid Quli Khan, he married a respectable Shia woman and had children with her. But he never forgot Khani Begum. Since he enjoyed cooking, he invented the recipe of bakarkhani and named it after himself and his former lady love. Both the story and the bread, which date back to the eighteenth century, survived the tides of time to become legendary. Although a famous folklore, this ill-fated love story cannot be taken seriously. It simply cannot replace historical facts. The real story of bakorkhani ruti continues to be vague.

But the fame of this bread gradually spread far and wide. From the gullies of Old Dhaka to the rest of the Bengal Subah, and from there, to the rest of the subcontinent, the recipe of bakarkhani was adopted by Muslims. The merchants and traders were mainly responsible for this spread. The bread became a favourite with the Mughals of Delhi and the Nawabs of Awadh. It is now especially popular in Kashmir, Hyderabad and Patna. Everywhere it went, the recipe was tweaked to cater to the taste buds of the local people.

In Old Dhaka, which is regarded by most as the place of its origin, the bread was commonly eaten with tea because of its crisp biscuit-like texture. It became a common practice to serve guests tea and bakorkhani ruti. The bread also began to be eaten with other dishes like kheer, payesh and meat curries. Baked in a tandoor, this thick circular flatbread has three long incisions drawn at its centre. At the time of its origin, the dough of this bread was made with the basic ingredients of refined flour, milk, butter and a pinch of salt and sugar. Over the years, milk got replaced with water and butter with oil or dalda (hydrogenated vegetable oil) in this basic recipe. But, in weddings, feasts, special occasions and social gatherings, many families serve the old version by placing advance orders with caterers or bakarkhani-wallahs.

As time went by, more varieties of this basic recipe emerged. Sweet and salted versions of this bread appeared in the market. Bakarkhanis flavoured with ghee quickly gained popularity. The dough also began to be stuffed with grated coconut, crumbled paneer (cottage cheese) or chhana, keema (minced meat) and kebabs. Bakarkhanis stuffed with jhura gosht became very popular during the two festivals of Eid. The meat used in this preparation was generally beef or goat meat.

Bakers everywhere have been constantly experimenting with the bakarkhani and a pool of recipes has emerged. Ingredients like semolina, egg, plain yoghurt, cardamom powder, screwpine or rose water, chironji (cuddapah almond) and dried fruits like almonds, raisins and pistachios are added to the dough. The use of milk and butter in the recipe has been revived. Other basic ingredients like yeast and baking powder may or may not be added. The bread may also be sprinkled on the surface with poppy or sesame seeds before being put into the oven. The appearance and texture of the bread may also vary in places.

In West Bengal, bakorkhani ruti is not as popular as it is in modern-day Bangladesh. But the Bengali Muslims in the land of the Ganges river do indulge in it at times. A variant of the bread is made over here. Says Ghaffar, 'Unlike in Bangladesh where it is a dry or shukha ruti with a biscuit-like texture, over here it is more like a parota. It is not baked but fried. Earlier the medium of cooking used to be beef tallow but now bakers have switched to using refined oil. Just like in Old Dhaka, where the bread is still more popular as a light breakfast dish that is eaten with tea, over here too, the bakorkhani is popularly eaten at breakfast with tea.' Bakorkhani ruti and jilipi is a popular combination among Muslim families of Calcutta. 'It is the perfect luxurious breakfast', continues

Ghaffar, 'when I am in a mood for it, I just forget about my frugal healthy breakfast options and stuff the bakorkhani with jilipis, roll it and have it with *pani kum chai*, which is a popular expression for tea made with less water and more milk.'

This brings us to the finale of the bakarkhani story. Although nobody is much sure of its beginning, everyone knows that this flatbread has had a marvellous ending. This versatile bread can be treated as a regular fare as well as served at grand feasts and weddings. It is also made during religious festivals like Ramzan and Eid. Old Dhaka has many bakorkhani shops in its gullies. In contrast, the number of such shops in Calcutta is few. Most of them are located in areas with a large concentration of Muslims. K Ali Bakery on Mominpore Road, which is located in Khidderpore, a Muslim-dominated neighbourhood of Calcutta, is well known for its bakarkhanis. It has been making this bread every morning for more than eighty years now.

Over the years, kosha mangsho has become a dish that is associated with special occasions and features in the menus of most grand feasts. So popular is this dish that it has become categorized as a 'weekend special' in most Bengali homes. Many Bengalis cannot think of spending their Sundays without indulging in their favourite combination of luchi and kosha mangsho. There are several eateries in Calcutta that have been serving kosha mangsho for years. But the most popular among all of them has to definitely be Golbari, which still makes the best kosha mangsho in the city since the Company Raj days.

Golbari

Golbari is immensely popular throughout the city for its signature dish, parota and kosha mangsho. The surprising part is that Golbari was not established by a Bengali but by a Punjabi from Amritsar. Ratan Chand Arora packed his bags and left his hometown for Calcutta when the economy of the city was at its peak. He rented a house in Shyambazar in north Calcutta and began searching for a place where he could open an eatery. Since he had a knack for cooking, he wanted to put his skill to professional use. He found a corner plot near the Shyambazar Five Point Crossing and opened a small eatery that he named Punjabi Hotel.

Realizing the Bengali's love for the rich and oily kosha mangsho, Arora decided to serve this dish in his restaurant. Through trial and error, he came up with his own recipe of kosha mangsho which was rich, oily and had an extra bite of taste. Word about his dish spread and people began flocking to his eatery. The food-loving public enjoyed the combination that Ratan Chand Arora served—a plate of kosha mangsho with parota, a little bit of tamarind chutney and onion salad—and this shortly became the bestselling dish in the restaurant.

Although Ratan Chand Arora had named his eatery Punjabi Hotel, the public began calling it Golbari ('gol' means round and 'bari' means house in Bengali) because of the semicircular facade of the restaurant. Even now, many people are unaware of the actual name and refer to it only as Golbari. The year of the inception of the restaurant is unknown to the current generation of owners, who run it as a joint family business. But it is a confirmed fact that Golbari is indeed a very old eatery. Most connoisseurs believe that it was set up in the early decades of the twentieth century. The owners of Golbari have continued to use the same recipe for kosha mangsho, the one that has been passed down since the inception of the restaurant. There are certain additional ingredients that go into the preparation of Golbari's kosha mangsho that has set it apart and made it famous throughout the city, but it is a heavily guarded secret, which the owners refuse to divulge.

The kosha mangsho and parota combination of this eatery was once enjoyed by some of the famous artists of Bengali cinema like Suchitra Sen, Soumitra Chatterjee and Ranjit Mallick, who would order takeaway platters. The eatery is filled with customers on a daily basis, and sees a greater rush on weekends. The restaurant has been rechristened New Punjabi Hotel but the food-loving public of Calcutta continue to call it Golbari. It has become the last word on parota and kosha mangsho in the city.

A meat dish will be followed either by an ambole or chutney preparation. Ambole is more of a favourite with the Ghotis. In the chapter 'Bangla Ranna' from the book *The Calcutta Cookbook: A Treasury of Recipes from Pavement to Palace* (1995), the authors explain 'Ambole is a sweet-and-sour dish of fish, vegetables or fruit. A sharp tasting fruit makes a tasty ambole or chutney. Amra (hog plum), chalta (elephant apple), green mango with shole maachh (murrel) make lip-smacking amboles' (p. 35). It is of runny consistency and sometimes made with fish heads or roe. It is also called tok (literally meaning sour) because the sour taste is dominating in it. In contrast, chutney is a sweeter and thicker version made with either fruits or vegetables. In Bengali cuisine, chutney is not a sauce or a relish that is used as a dip or an accompaniment to other foods. It is a dish in itself that is often served with papors. The most popular varieties of chutney are those made from green mango, tomato, unripe papaya and pineapple. While ambole is a preparation that is confined to regular meals served at home, chutney is a celebratory dish that is also served at home.

Sweets

Sweets and mishti doi will inevitably follow a chutney preparation in an elaborate meal. The Tagore women made some interesting desserts as well that were served at the end of meals. One of them was *jemon temon*, a speciality of Thakur Bari, which was basically an unconventional and delicious medley of different sweets. It was made by mixing plain yoghurt with rabri; broken pieces of rasogolla and ledikeni were added to this. Additional ingredients like slivers of almond and chopped pistachios and raisins were also part of this sweet delicacy. The dessert was sprinkled with rose water, mixed well and served. *Paka peyarar halua* (halua is a dense sweet confection called halwa in north India) is another dessert that was prepared often in the Tagore household. This ripe guava halua is made by cooking the boiled and mashed fruit in ghee with cloves, cinnamon, milk and sugar. Sometimes, payesh is served in place of mishti doi. *White Bombay onion payesh* is a unique preparation. A speciality of Thakur Bari, it is made by boiling white onions with water at least three times to remove their odour and then cooking them in milk with sugar, chopped pistachios, raisins and some rose water.

In the book, *Sovabazar Rajbarir Rannabanna* (2017), it has been mentioned that the women of Sovabazar Rajbari also made certain interesting dessert preparations that were both traditional as well as uncommon. *Peper payesh* is one such uncommon preparation. This payesh is made with unripe papaya or kancha pepe. Peeled and grated papaya is cooked in milk with sugar, raisins and cardamom powder to make this dessert. Payesh is also made with custard apple or ata. This is a traditional and time-consuming preparation. The fruit is peeled and deseeded and its soft, sweet and creamy flesh is cooked in milk with sugar and raisins to make this dish. It is interesting to note that some of the aforementioned fruits like guava, papaya and custard apple that Indians probably consider to be their own were actually introductions by the Portuguese.

The dessert that Bengalis call payesh is known as kheer in most parts of India. The latter has a different meaning in Bengali cuisine. Kheer, in Bengali cuisine, means milk that has been reduced to a very thick consistency by boiling and stirring it continuously. Sugar may or may not be added while boiling the milk. Rathindra Narayan Deb, another descendant of the family, pointed out in an interview that kamala kheer, which is a traditional and popular dessert, has always been a favourite with the members of Sovabazar Rajbari. 'Kamala' means orange. The milk is cooked to the consistency of kheer with ingredients like sugar or patali gur, cardamom powder and saffron. When the kheer is taken off the flame and cooled, orange pulp is mixed into it. The preparation is garnished with chopped pistachios. When, in place of orange pulp, aam or mango pulp is mixed into the kheer, the preparation is known as *aam kheer*, another traditional dessert that is popular with the family.

Rathindra Narayan Deb also points out that the family has always been making certain traditional sweets in a slightly unconventional manner. The regular motichur laddu is a round, orange-coloured sweet made up of fried and sweetened gram flour boondis. But the one made in Sovabazar Rajbari is pristine white in colour and lightly spiced with black pepper. Different varieties of sweets have always been a part of the bhog offered to Goddess Durga by this family, which are distributed as prasad after the worship is over. Moiras from all over the city are hired for this purpose and they spend hours making this large variety of mishti in the vien. Mammoth-sized motichur laddus have always been an essential part of this bhog. During the festival of Poush Sankranti, the family enjoys indulging in *koraishutir pithe*, another unconventional preparation in which the filling is made of a spicy fried paste of koraishuti or green peas.

Bengali Muslims have the best of both worlds because their range of desserts includes traditional Bengali sweets as well as sweet preparations typical to the Muslim cuisine. Sweet chutneys, pithes, mishti doi, rasogolla, sandesh, rasomalai as well as shahi tukda, rabri, firni, kulfi, falooda and a range of tempting haluas are few of the enticing desserts eaten by the community. They have certain sweet preparations that are particularly associated with festivals and celebrations. To understand their culinary culture better, these should be explored.

Eid ul-Fitr, Shab-e-Barat, Nikah and Mishti

Vermicelli is a very important ingredient for Muslims in the preparation of desserts. Known as 'sevai' in Urdu, this ingredient is called shemoi in Bengali. Bengali Muslims as well as Hindus make payesh with both rice and vermicelli. 'Sevai is a very traditional ingredient that is especially synonymous with Eid ul-Fitr,' points out Mirza. 'Even the poor in our community will make a dessert with sevai on this particular day.'

The holy month of Ramzan is the ninth month of the Islamic lunar calendar and lasts for a period of either twenty-nine or thirty days. Islam commands its followers to observe this month with fasting, prayers, reading the Quran and charitable acts. The main highlight of this month is the long hours of roza or fasting that lasts from dawn to sunset. The day begins with an early morning meal called sehri, which is eaten before dawn. 'Niyat or intention is very important in our religion,' explains Mirza. 'After finishing the morning meal, an intention or niyat is made in the mind about starting the roza. This niyat has to be made *fajr ke azaan ke pehle*, which means before the call for the morning prayer. Fajr is the first of the five daily prayers read by Muslims. It is a dawn prayer. The moment that niyat is made, the fast for the day begins.' The fast is broken after sunset with an evening meal called 'iftar'. 'This meal is eaten *maghrib ke azaan ke baad*, which means after the call for the evening prayer,' continues Mirza. Maghrib is a sunset prayer and the fourth of the five daily prayers required. The roza is generally broken after sunset by eating dates in keeping with Prophet Muhammad's practice of breaking the fast with dates.

There is a spiritual explanation behind this routine, which continues for the entire month of Ramzan. This practice of fasting, which also includes abstinence from sinful speech and behaviour, sexual relations and addictive substances is a process of self-purification. It requires strong self-discipline and self-control. By sacrificing the pleasure-giving actions and substances in life, focusing more on worship and acts of charity, and directing the inner consciousness towards self-introspection, self-improvement and spiritual reflection, the soul is cleansed of its impurities and a heightened sense of spiritual awareness and empathy is achieved. 'This one month of fasting also makes us realize the suffering that those living below the poverty line have to go through when they don't get enough food to eat,' points out Mirza. 'It increases our empathy towards the poor and the needy.'

The last day in the month of Ramzan is the day of the final fast. This fast is broken with the evening meal. From the next day, the tenth month of the Islamic lunar calendar begins, which is known as Shawwal. On the first day of Shawwal, the festival of Eid ul-Fitr is celebrated. This joyous and auspicious festival marks the end of the holy month of Ramzan. Life goes back to normal from this day onwards. The day begins with the morning namaz, which is known as Eid ki namaz (Eid's namaz). The main dish cooked in every Muslim house on this day is sevai or shemoi. *Shemoier payesh, sheer khurma* and *jarda shemoi* are the most popular sevai or shemoi desserts made in Muslim households on Eid ul-Fitr. Such sweet preparations are not only eaten throughout this festive day but are also served to visiting guests. Gifts are often exchanged and special attention is paid to the young who are given Eidi on this day. 'Eid ul-Fitr is considered to be a day when enmities are forgotten. As an expression of that people embrace relatives, friends and acquaintances when they pay them a visit,' points out Mirza. 'Many also visit graveyards on this day to pay their respect to loved ones who have departed and send them a message that they haven't been forgotten.'

To prepare shemoier payesh, milk is boiled with cinnamon, cardamom and sugar. Meanwhile some dried fruits like broken cashew nuts, slivered almonds, chopped pistachios and raisins are fried in ghee. The shemoi used in this preparation is generally made of refined or wholewheat flour. The vermicelli is broken into pieces and lightly fried in ghee over a low flame. The fried vermicelli is added to the boiling milk when it has slightly reduced in quantity. Once the vermicelli is cooked, the dried fruits are added. Some may add khoya to the cooking at this stage to make the payesh thicker and tastier. The vermicelli pudding is now stirred for a couple of minutes before it is taken off the flame. It is served cold.

Sheer khurma is another special dessert made with shemoi. Many consider their Eid ul-Fitr celebrations incomplete without this creamy vermicelli pudding. 'Sheer' and 'khurma' are Persian words, meaning 'milk' and 'dates' respectively. So, 'sheer khurma' literally means 'milk and dates added to sevai'. Also known as sheer khorma, this vermicelli pudding is rich in taste because it is made with lots of dried fruits and sugar. Dried dates, known as 'shukno khejur' in Bengali and 'chhuara' in Hindi, are used in this dish.

Dried fruits like dried dates, cashew nuts, almonds and pistachios are soaked in water and chopped. Along with raisins, these are then fried in ghee. Sometimes, even chironji is added to these ingredients. A variety of shemoi called nylon vermicelli is used in this preparation. The shemoi is broken into pieces and fried in ghee over low heat till golden brown in colour. The fried dried fruits and shemoi are added to milk that has been boiled with crushed cardamom seeds. After some time, sugar is added and the payesh is cooked till it slightly thickens in consistency. Although it can be served warm, most prefer eating this vermicelli pudding cold. The milk can also be flavoured with rose water. Saffron strands can be added to impart a nice flavour, colour and aroma to the dish. Many add khoya along with the sugar if they like their sheer khurma to be tastier, richer and thicker.

Zarda sevai (jarda shemoi in Bengali) is a dry and crisp vermicelli preparation. The Urdu word 'zarda' has its roots in the Persian word 'zard', which means 'yellow'. The name of this dish is something of a misnomer because the preparation is far from being yellow in colour. The shemoi (generally wholewheat vermicelli is used) is broken into pieces and fried in ghee with bay leaves, green cardamoms, cinnamon, sugar and dried fruits like almonds, cashew nuts, pistachios and raisins. Since this is a dry preparation, the amount of water added should be just enough to cook the vermicelli. The wok is covered with a lid and the shemoi is cooked over a low flame till done. The dish is served at room temperature.

Apart from these traditional desserts, Muslims also add shemoi to other sweet preparations like falooda, a delicious cold dessert that has its roots in 'faloodeh'. The latter arrived in India with the Muslims. It is a traditional Persian dessert made with rice vermicelli. The broken pieces of boiled vermicelli are mixed with scrapings of frozen sugar syrup laced with lime juice and rose water. The dessert is served in a glass bowl with some lime juice squeezed into it, and sometimes, ground pistachios sprinkled over it.

It is believed that this dessert evolved and developed into the rich and complex falooda in the Mughal Empire. The vermicelli or shemoi used in this dessert is called 'falooda sev', which is generally made of tapioca starch, sago starch, cornflour, corn starch, arrowroot starch or wheat starch. Served in a glass tumbler with a wide mouth, falooda is made with flavoured syrup, broken pieces of coloured jelly, soaked and swollen tokma dana (sweet basil seeds), broken pieces of boiled falooda sev, chopped fruits, broken cashew nuts, slivered almonds, chopped pistachios, raisins and slightly thick sweetened milk flavoured with ingredients like green cardamoms and screwpine water. Traditionally, this refreshing dessert does not feature ice cream. But, in modern times, many top it with a scoop of ice cream, which is garnished with the syrup that has been used. The syrup used may also vary. Mango syrup and chocolate syrup have turned into favourites. But traditionally, it has always been rose syrup, which is still the most popular.

However, this dessert should not be confused with kulfi-falooda. In the chapter 'Dastar Khwan' from their book *The Calcutta Cookbook: A Treasury of Recipes from Pavement to Palace*, the authors have rightly pointed out that kulfi is India's first ice cream. It is believed that this dairy-based dessert was invented by the Mughals during their rule in India. Frozen in metal cones, this rich creamy dessert is generally topped with chopped dried fruits and rose syrup along with *falooda sev*, thereby lending it the name. Alternately, when the cold dessert falooda is topped with slices of kulfi and not regular ice cream, the preparation is also called *kulfi-falooda*.

Shab-e-Barat is another festival of great significance in Islam celebrated in Shaban, the eighth month. 'Shab' means 'night' and 'barat' means 'festival'. This festival is observed during the night. For both Shias and Sunnis, it is a festival dedicated to departed souls. On this night, devout Muslims visit cemeteries where their near and dear ones are buried. It is believed that the devout are visited by these departed souls. Candles and incense sticks are lit and special prayers are read. The souls are then set free. It is considered to be one of the holiest nights in the Islamic calendar when the Almighty determines the destiny of every believer for the coming year by taking into account the deeds committed by the person in the past. Shab-e-Barat is known as the 'Night of Forgiveness' because the sins of those who follow these rituals and pray to the Almighty on this occasion are forgiven. On this auspicious night, Shias also celebrate the birthday of Imam Mehdi (a.s.), the twelfth Imam, who has not yet arrived in this world. He is considered to be the final prophet, who, the devout believe, will redeem the world when he steps into it. Candles are lit in Shia homes at midnight and special prayers are read in his honour on this occasion.

This festival is also marked by acts of compassion and charity. It is obligatory to distribute ruti and halua to the poor and the needy, who flock to the graveyards or collect them from houses on this night. The halua is generally made with chholar dal or shooji (semolina) on this occasion. Large quantities of the flatbread and dessert are prepared. After the distribution is over, the remaining food is eaten by the devouts.

Zarda pulao (*jarda pulao* in Bengali) is a rice dessert named as such because it is yellow in colour. This famous sweet rice pilaf, which happens to be the favoured dessert distributed at Sufi shrines, is a special dish served on celebratory occasions especially weddings.

This dish has its roots in 'zard biranj', which was prepared in the royal kitchens of the Mughals. It has been chronicled in *Ain-i-Akbari* that zard biranj was a rich and sweet rice dish cooked with lots of dried fruits. It was one of the dishes that belonged to the premium class of meatless food known as 'Sufiyana'. The recipe mentioned in *Ain-i-Akbari* uses rice, sugar candies, ghee, fresh ginger, cinnamon, saffron strands, dried fruits like almonds, pistachios and raisins, and salt. The dishes that fell under this category were consumed by Emperor Akbar on his days of abstinence. This zard biranj has evolved into the modern-day zarda pulao, which continues to belong to the premium class of dishes in Muslim cuisine. Hence, it is significant as a celebratory dish.

The variety of rice used in this dish has to be long-grain. Traditionally, the colour was achieved by using saffron strands. But, in modern times, most prefer to use food colour. The rice is partially boiled in water that has been laced with saffron strands, and flavoured with green cardamoms, cinnamons and cloves. Boiling the grains in saffron-infused water makes them take on a lovely bright yellow hue. Care should be taken to take the rice off the flame and drain the water when the grains are nearly cooked but not completely done. This dish is loaded with dried fruits. So, an ample quantity of dried fruits like chopped cashew nuts and pistachios, slivered almonds and raisins are sautéed in ghee. Meanwhile, the partially cooked rice grains are also sautéed in ghee for a few minutes. Sugar is then added to the grains. The vessel is covered with a lid and the rice is cooked over a low flame till the sugar melts. The rice is then stirred for a few minutes till the water let out by the sugar completely evaporates. Screwpine or rose essence is now added to the rice along with grated khoya and the fried dried fruits. The rice is stirred, covered and cooked for a few more minutes. By now, the grains will be completely cooked and fluffy.

Additional ingredients like copra or dried coconut meat slices, chopped dried dates, grated orange zest, tutti-frutti, chopped petha or ash gourd candy or miniature gulab jamuns can be added to the cooking. Many garnish the dish with the extra fried dried fruits and grated khoya. The dish is taken off the flame and served warm or at room temperature.

Paan

Paan or betel leaf roll is the perfect ending to a traditional Bengali meal and forms an important part of all Bengali feasts. It works as a mouth freshener and also helps in the digestion of spicy food. In their article, 'Betel leaf: Revisiting the benefits of an ancient Indian herb', for the

South Asian Journal of Cancer (July–September 2013, v.2 (3): 140–41), authors Rajendra Toprani and Daxesh Patel elaborate, 'In India, Betel leaf (BL) plays an important role since ancient culture. Its use in India dates back to 400 BCE. As per ancient books of Ayurveda, Charaka, Sushruta Samhitas, and Kashyapa Bhojanakalpa, the practice of chewing BL after meals became common between 75 CE and 300 CE. Toward the thirteenth century, European traveler Marco Polo recorded betel chewing among kings and nobles in India.'

Early Ayurvedic texts emphasize that a man should chew paan after taking a bath and before leaving for the day's work. The betel leaf roll is a sign of enjoyment and also, to a certain extent, of eroticism. It does not come as a surprise that students, widows and ascetics were deprived of this pleasure in ancient India. Only married men and women had a right to it. Its anti-bacterial properties are supposed to kill germs in the mouth. It can be safely inferred that paan is Ayurveda's alternative to the mint with a hole.

Over the centuries, eating paan, particularly after meals, became a common practice among all classes of Indians. A regular paan is made from a well-washed betel leaf (with its stalk removed), which has the pastes of chun (chuna or edible limestone or slaked lime) and khoyer (kaththa or catechu) spread on it. These two pastes, when combined, impart a red colour to the leaf, which is then sprinkled with finely chopped shupuri (supari or areca nuts, mistakenly called betel nuts because of their association with the betel leaf), mouri (saunf or fennel seeds), jowan (ajwain or carom seeds) and sometimes, elaich (elaichi or green cardamom). The paan is folded into a triangle, coated with edible silver leaf and pierced through the centre with a clove before being served to a customer.

There are two basic types of paan: sada (plain) paan, as described above, which may or may not have tobacco filling, and meetha (sweet) paan. In the latter preparation, known as mishti paan in Bengali, the pastes of chun and khoyer are spread on the betel leaf, which is then filled with sweet cherry jam or chutney, gulkand (a sweet preserve of rose petals), fennel seeds, dhana dal (roasted split coriander seeds), green cardamoms, tutti-frutti and rose essence. Other ingredients like desiccated coconut and chopped and ground candied and dried fruits may also be added. Meetha paan may or may not contain shupuri. If it contains the nut, then a shredded version that is saffron coloured and sweet in taste is used. And it certainly does not contain carom seeds because of their sharp, bitter and pungent taste. Although, in recent years, paan-wallahs or the makers of paan have come up with a considerable variety of innovative betel leaf rolls, the sada and meetha varieties continue to be the most popular.

Today, Calcutta's roads are filled with paan shops. But, during the Company Raj days, the scenario was very different. Vendors would stroll through the streets with baskets or boxes that contained all the ingredients required to make fresh betel leaf rolls for customers. It was Kalpataru Bhandar, the oldest paan shop in the city that changed this picture.

Kalpataru Bhandar: Kalpataru Bhandar, popularly known as Kalpataru, was established in 1946 by Radhabinod Dutta, who migrated to Calcutta from Dhaka for work opportunities. The idea of setting up a paan shop struck him because of the popularity of the betel leaf roll among all communities and classes. College Street and its surrounding areas have always been the centre of intellectual and commercial activities. The streets are crowded with people. Sensing a lucrative business opportunity in this area, the enterprising man set up his shop a stone's throw away from Indian Coffee House on Bankim Chatterjee Street. Soon, Kalpataru began doing brisk business among all those who inundated the boi-para and its neighbourhoods not only because of its location but also because of the quality of its betel leaf rolls. Customers agreed that a Kalpataru paan felt so smooth that it dissolved in the mouth within minutes and indulging in a good-quality paan in the middle of activity was a refreshing change.

Setting up his shop near the Indian Coffee House also proved to be a wise decision. Customers of the iconic institution often wrapped up their meals and addas with a Kalpataru paan. Many well-known intellectuals have been customers of Kalpataru as College Street is their hub. Renowned personalities like Dhananjay Bhattacharya (the devotional singer), P.C. Sorcar (the magician), V. Balsara (the musician), Pulak Bandyopadhyay (the lyricist), Manna Dey (the playback singer), Bhanu Bandopadhyay (the Bengali actor) and Padmaja Naidu (former Governor of West Bengal) have enjoyed the paans of this shop. The fame of Kalpataru's paans is so widespread that some of the noted aristocratic families of Calcutta have had the shop cater its collection on their functions. Radhabinod Dutta had acquired a reputation for mastering the proportion of ingredients that went into the paans, a skill that he passed on to his son, Shyamal Dutta, who had always taken an active interest in the business since childhood. Today, Kalpataru is run by him. Like most paan-wallahs, Shyamal Dutta also buys his betel leaves and other ingredients from the shops in the age-old Raja Katra Market in Barabazar. He feels this is still the best place in the city for this purpose. He hand-processes (assembling, sieving and mixing) all the ingredients in his house before putting them into jars and bringing them to the shop.

Although the dilkhush paan of Kalpataru is very popular, Shyamal Dutta recommends the badshahi paan as the best the shop has to offer. The ingredients that go into it are the pastes of muktabhashya chun (a type of edible limestone) and janapari khoyer (a type of catechu), shupuri and the most essential badshahi masala, a speciality of Kalpataru, which is a closely guarded secret. The betel leaf roll is sprinkled with rose water, coated in edible silver leaf and pierced with a clove before it is offered to the customer. The badshahi masala, which is the main ingredient of this variety, gives a special taste to it. In the days before and shortly after Independence, the badshahi paan of Kalpataru included a small portion of kasturi (commonly known as musk), a very strong-scented substance found in the male musk deer (also known as kasturi in India) of the Himalayan mountain range. This highly prized ingredient gave a powerful aroma to the paan because of which it was favoured by the aristocrats. But the Wild Life (Protection) Act, 1972 banned the hunting of this animal and it came under its legal protection. Since then this ingredient could no longer be sourced. This royal set of ingredients lent the name badshahi (meaning kingly or regal) to the betel leaf roll.

Kalpataru Bhandar has definitely been a trendsetter. Many paan-wallahs in Calcutta, drawing inspiration from its success, began setting up shops. Despite being the oldest paan shop, the quality of Kalpataru Bhandar's paans has not dropped even once. This has kept its fame afloat in a city that is now brimming with paan shops.

Home Style

There are many eateries in Calcutta that serve a basic spread of Bengali meals, cooked in homely style, on a daily basis. The decor of these restaurants is not fancy. The focus is more on providing inexpensive wholesome meals of generous portions that are scrumptious and satiate the appetite. These unpretentious eateries generally cater to the office goers. The concept of such eateries developed in the early years of the twentieth century to cater to the immigrants who came to Calcutta in search of work. There was an increase in the footfall of such immigrants during this period. They would be on the lookout for places to eat during lunch hours. There arose a demand for eateries that would serve quick filling luncheons at reasonable prices. This demand was met by a few enterprising Bengalis who began setting up such places. Gradually, this trend picked up and there was an upsurge of such eateries. These eateries were the earliest Bengali restaurants. Young Bengal Hotel, one of the oldest surviving Bengali restaurants set up in Khidderpore during the colonial days to cater to those who worked in Calcutta Port, deserves special mention.

Young Bengal Hotel: Young Bengal Hotel in Khidderpore, a port area, is undoubtedly one of the best among the oldest Bengali restaurants of Calcutta. The restaurant began serving full-fledged Bengali meals in the early 1930s to the port workers. It is designed like a hut with brick walls and a thatched roof in order to give it a certain village aesthetic. A narrow entrance leads customers to a spacious courtyard and a winding path guides them into the hut that houses the restaurant. Young Bengal Hotel still remains a flourishing business today. Its quaint ambience, old world charm and homely meals attract a large crowd of customers, many of whom work in the area. It is a heritage restaurant that finds mention in Portuguese guidebooks about Calcutta.

The restaurant was set up by Tarapada Guha, who arrived in Calcutta from a small village in Barisal district. Tarapada Guha wanted to deviate from his family profession of paddy cultivation by coming to the big city and starting a business of his own. Like most food entrepreneurs, he was a good cook and wanted to put his culinary skill to use. He set up his first restaurant in the Khidderpore dock area and named it Nandankanan. The port workers of the area were always on the lookout for kiosks that served homely and inexpensive meals. Nandankanan is believed to be the first restaurant to come up in the area that began serving such meals. With profits earned from the success of his first venture, Tarapada Guha soon set up a second restaurant nearby, which, inspired by the Derozian movement, he named Young Bengal Hotel.

This second restaurant served homely Bengali meals as well. The food was basic and a meal included rice, a shaak or teto preparation, lentil, fries or fritters, a vegetable dish, the option of a fish, chicken or mutton jhol, and chutney. Special dishes like basanti pulao, shukto, shobji diye bhaja moong dal, dhonkar dalna, patoler dolma, chhanchra, chingri maachh diye mochar ghanto, maachher jhal or kalia, shorshe maachh, bhapa maachh, maachher paturi, chingri maachher malaikari and kosha mangsho (both chicken and mutton) were also served. Sometimes, postor bora or maachher deemer bora were listed in the menu that changed every day. He advertised this restaurant through signboards and Young Bengal Hotel was inundated with customers who wanted a quick lunch before they headed back to work. With the success of the luncheons, Tarapada Guha started serving dinner to customers in both his restaurants, which by now had become flourishing businesses.

But in the 1960s, Nandankanan was shut down. The manager of the restaurant had a son of about twenty-five years of age whose life was ended by a ghastly road accident when he was on his way to a job interview. Out of sympathy, Tarapada Guha gave the proprietorship of Nandankanan to the bereaved manager so that he had something to fall back on in his old age. But the manager was too heartbroken to make the restaurant financially viable and the once profitable venture began running at a loss, eventually leading to its shutdown.

In contrast, Young Bengal Hotel was functioning well and continued to be a profit-making venture. The restaurant still does not have a fixed menu, which changes on a daily basis. Since the inception of the restaurant, food is served on a banana leaf platter and water is served in an earthen tumbler. Over the years, the restaurant has become a family concern where traditional practices are still followed in cooking the food. While modern kitchenware has taken over most restaurants, the spices used in Young Bengal Hotel's kitchen are still ground with the shil-nora. The chicken and mutton dishes in the restaurant are cooked over a charcoal fire because the owners believe that meat boils better over a slow flame. These practices make the food cooked in Young Bengal Hotel more authentic and truer to traditional Bengali cuisine.

Each of the establishments mentioned earlier were pioneers as their owners were among the first to think differently and set up restaurants or shops that specialized in a particular area of Bengali cuisine. These have played an important role in bringing to the forefront the cuisine of the land at a time when eateries were few and far between. Their owners started the trend that was gradually picked up by successive food entrepreneurs and casual, family-style and fine dining restaurants began appearing in the city.

The lure of a dual income increased the trend of working couples. These working couples now had more money to spend, but their busy schedules also meant shortage of time. The familiar scene of our grandmothers and mothers spending hours toiling in the kitchen was getting replaced by the multitasking modern woman running from pillar to post on professional and family errands. As a result, these women could not spend too much of their time and energy in the kitchen and all of those dishes that were elaborate and time-consuming to prepare were mostly given a miss.

But these factors proved beneficial to food entrepreneurs. To make up for their inability to cook fancy dishes at home, families began dining out more often. These eating-out experiences even included indulging in their own cuisine in the fancy ambience of a restaurant. This new trend encouraged entrepreneurs and more restaurants specializing in Bengali cuisine began coming up in the city.

The non-Bengalis who had been living in Calcutta for generations had developed an affinity for Bengali food. While luchi, chholar dal, alur dom and begoon bhaja had especially turned into favourites with the vegetarian section of other communities, the non-vegetarian section enjoyed eating almost everything featured in the cuisine. Over the years, these people had become so acclimatized with the Bengali culture that they even wholeheartedly participated in the festivals of this land and bhoger khichuri had become another great favourite. They flocked to Bengali sweet shops to buy their favourite mishti, particularly those made with nolen gur, before the confectioneries could fly off the shelves. And the evergreen shingara, rechristened 'Bengali samosa' by these people, became a regular feature in their homes at teatime. Driven by their love for Bengali food, these non-Bengalis also began visiting restaurants that served Bengali dishes. Thus, the growing customer base was an encouraging sign because it created a demand. And to meet this demand, restaurants serving this cuisine began mushrooming.

Like the paradoxical question that has baffled people for centuries, 'which came first: the chicken or the egg?', even with regard to Bengali cuisine, it is difficult to figure out which came first: the casual, family-style and fine dining restaurants or the demand for the cuisine? Did an existing pool of demands induce entrepreneurs to sense an opportunity and open such restaurants or did the first few restaurants encourage potential customers to try out the cuisine, which eventually created a growing demand for it? Whatever may be the answer, it is a fact that for a long time, except for confectioneries, partaking of Bengali food was confined to home-cooked meals. Fortunately, this shackle has now been broken and the tendency to eat out often in Bengali restaurants, whatever may be their category, has particularly increased from the early years of this century. This enthusiasm is also encouraging experimentation and the culinary culture of Bengal is going through a change as people are witnessing chefs, connoisseurs and enthusiasts come up with innovative dishes every now and then as well as put in hours of thought and labour into reviving recipes that have got lost in the annals of history.

Today, Bengali cuisine has become one of the coveted eating-out options. The growing curiosity and interest about this cuisine has spread through the country, catching entrepreneurs in their grip. Restaurants of different categories are cropping up almost everywhere, thereby increasing the eating-out opportunities and options in this cuisine.

But these casual, family-style and fine dining eating-out options in Bengali cuisine had a humble beginning. For a long time, since the early years of the twentieth century, eating-out options in Bengali cuisine were limited to roadside kiosks, pice hotels and small eateries. Pice hotels were actually very basic eateries that served Bengali meals, cooked in homely style, at the cheapest of prices possible for an eatery. The name 'pice hotel' has its roots in the monetary unit 'pice'. These hotels came up at a time when the pice was in use and a person could buy a full meal at these places with them. Although this monetary unit does not exist now, the name 'pice hotel' has stuck on and come to denote cheap eateries. Like the kiosks and small eateries, these places were mainly meant for office goers and were the busiest at lunch hours. There were no formal menu cards at these places and the dishes served kept changing every day.

It was in 1969 that Bengali cuisine broke the shackle that bound it to such establishments with the opening of the Suruchi Self-Help Group on Elliot Road. Popularly known as Suruchi, this Bengali restaurant was started by the All Bengal Women's Union, a non-profit organization dedicated to working for the rights of disadvantaged women, young girls and children. Some of the women under the care of the organization, after having received training as chefs and managers, began running the place. This was the first Bengali restaurant in Calcutta that was not a kiosk or a pice hotel or a small eatery. More of a cross between a casual and family-style restaurant, it targeted middle-class customers who could dine in its premises with their families. Run efficiently by a staff of dedicated women, who did everything from cooking to taking orders and serving the food, Suruchi offered its customers a menu card that initially featured a limited range of dishes priced to suit the middle-class budget. Open only for luncheons, the dishes were cooked in a simple homely style.

The simple decor of the restaurant along with the superior quality of the food that it served caused quite a stir in Calcutta society in those days. People belonging to different age groups and financial brackets, including those from well-to-do society, dined in the restaurant, shattering the notion that it was only meant for a middle-class clientele. The entire concept was new and unconventional, and it attracted people, Bengalis and non-Bengalis alike. Prior to its establishment, Bengalis could never think of eating the cuisine that they cooked regularly at home in the set-up of a restaurant and settling a bill at the end for it. Although there was a section among them who derided the idea, the majority did not seem to mind. They found the concept of a Bengali restaurant appealing and gave Suruchi a try, ultimately getting hooked and visiting it often. This made the restaurant a household name in the city.

Today, the Suruchi Self-Help Group is regarded by many as not only the first family-style Bengali restaurant in the city but also in the country. Over the years, the décor of the restaurant has been upgraded and the number of dishes featured in the menu card has increased. It has become an air-conditioned restaurant that serves breakfast, lunch as well as afternoon tea. But the dishes cooked continue to be elegant in their simplicity. This restaurant is the result of innovative thinking and an extremely bold move, taking into consideration the era and mindset of people at that time, by a well-meaning organization that was not guided by commerce but with the intent to help the disadvantaged women it had taken under its wing.

But it cannot be said that Suruchi paved the way for other entrepreneurs to set up Bengali restaurants anytime soon. It took a little over two decades for the another iconic Bengali restaurant to come up in the city. In 1993, the Peerless Inn, a top-ranking hotel located on Chowringhee Road in Calcutta, launched Aaheli, the first fine dining Bengali restaurant in the city and the country, within a month after starting operation. The restaurant, inaugurated by the then chief minister of West Bengal, Jyoti Basu, was the brainchild of industrialist Sunil Kanti Roy, who has been heading the Peerless Group since 1985.

Although, over the years, Aaheli became the flagship restaurant of the Peerless Inn, prior to its launch, doubts were expressed by the Board of Directors about how successful a fine dining restaurant specializing in Bengali cuisine would be. There were fears that the project, in which considerable amount of funds was being invested, would not take off with the public and result in failure. But Sunil Kanti Roy was adamant on going through with his plan because he believed it had a lot of potential. He felt the absence of an exclusive Bengali restaurant where diners could enjoy the delicacies of the land in a posh environment created a market for such an establishment. From a regular outfit that served homely food at lunch hours to one that offered a fine dining experience, the leap was big. There was nothing to fill the gap in between, making the move a brave and adventurous one. But the chairman of the hotel went ahead with his brainchild and in the midst of much fanfare, Aaheli was born.

The restaurant met with grand success. If the launch of Suruchi had caused a stir, the launch of Aaheli made waves throughout Calcutta society, particularly among Bengalis. It had been more than twenty years since Suruchi had been launched. People appreciated the good-quality homely meals and the clean and neat environment of the family restaurant. But a Bengali fine dining restaurant was an entirely new experience of a different level altogether. Customers enjoyed being served a range of authentic delicacies in traditional bell metal dinnerware by men clad in traditional dhutis (as dhoti is called in Bengali) and kurtas, and women in saris worn in the traditional Bengali style. Live Bengali music enlivened the atmosphere of the restaurant on weekends. On the days of typical Bengali festivals like Poila Baisakh (Bengali New Year), Jamai Shashthi and Bhai Phonta (as the festival of Bhai Dooj is known in Bengali), the comfortably placed Bengali family now made it a part of its agenda to make a trip to Aaheli to dine on expertly crafted food in its plush interiors. Corporate and personal guests visiting Calcutta from other states and countries were now proudly driven down to the restaurant to make them have a first-hand experience of exquisite Bengali fare in an exclusive environment.

Over the years, this restaurant, which is open for both lunch and dinner, has been constantly adding new dishes to its menu card. From the regular as well as elaborate dishes of Epar and Opar Bangla to exclusive ones like dishes from the Thakur Bari kitchen and goyna bori—their menu card has it all, thereby giving diners an all-round gastronomic experience.

The success of Aaheli now made many food entrepreneurs sit up and take notice. Prateep Kumar Dasgupta and his daughters Rakhi Purnima and Pia Promina converted the small garage in their house on Elgin Lane into an air-conditioned restaurant that began serving Bengali dishes.

Thus, in 1998, the iconic Kewpie's was born, thereby completing the trio of restaurants that pioneered the concept of proper restaurant style dining in Bengali cuisine. The restaurant was named after the legendary Minakshie Das Gupta, wife of Prateep Kumar and the mother of Rakhi Purnima and Pia Promina.

Fondly called Kewpie by her family and friends, Minakshie Das Gupta's name has become synonymous with Calcutta's culinary history. She was so passionate about cooking and had such profound knowledge about everything to do with the subject that she authored two acclaimed cookbooks that have received a lot of appreciation from critics and readers alike. This was a woman who loved food and her interest in the subject went beyond just knowing how to cook dishes from any part of the world. Food was a subject of research for her. Driven by her love for it, she delved deep into it, studying its detailed history to such an extent that she became a scholar in the field. The result was *Bangla Ranna: The Bengal Cookbook* (1982), the first cookbook on Bengali cuisine written in English, and *The Calcutta Cookbook: A Treasury of Recipes from Pavement to Palace* (1995), the landmark book that combines priceless information about Calcutta's culinary history with iconic recipes, which Minakshie Das Gupta co-authored with freelance journalists and writers Bunny Gupta and Jaya Chaliha. This second book, which has been an invaluable source of research and information for my work, was published after Das Gupta's demise in 1994. Both these books feature rare and lost recipes along with regular and well-known ones.

Kewpie's was the first family-owned Bengali restaurant and it served home-cooked food. Many of the dishes served in the restaurant were documented in Minakshie Das Gupta's cookbooks. This meant that regular, well-known, rare and even lost recipes were transformed into delectable dishes and served in traditional earthen dinnerware, making the entire dining experience unique and appealing. From the very beginning Kewpie's had an aura about it—even when it was confined to the garage and had not expanded and shifted to the ground floor of the house, the entire expanse of which it now occupies. This had a lot to do with the late Minakshie Das Gupta whose reputation as a knowledgeable gourmet, versatile chef and well-known author of food books had always preceded her. Curiosity to experience a restaurant that had been set up in her memory drove people to try it out at least once. And it is needless to say that everything about the restaurant got them hooked to it for years. For quite some time, since the initial years of its establishment,

Kewpie's filled the wide gap between Suruchi and Aaheli. It did not fall into the fine dining category but was always looked upon as an upscale family-style restaurant that had the unique reputation of being exclusive as well as homely. Years have gone by since its establishment but this reputation has remained intact, attracting customers who enjoy dining in the sophisticated ambience of the restaurant, which has a refined décor that is reminiscent of typical Bengali culture.

The New Era of Bengali Cuisine

The early years of the twenty-first century witnessed a sprout of Bengali restaurants in Calcutta. The trend of setting up restaurants specializing in this cuisine had now obviously picked up. Some of the earliest and the most prominent among these were Bhojohori Manna, 6 Ballygunge Place and Oh! Calcutta. Each one of these was a phenomenal success from the very beginning. Most people had got used to the idea by now that even Bengali cuisine could be an eating-out option. The credit for this largely goes to the Suruchi Self-Help Group, Aaheli and Kewpie's. These three had opened the door and shown the way to entrepreneurs and customers alike.

Today, Calcutta has plenty of such restaurants and the number seems to be growing by the day. Advertisements of new Bengali restaurants promoting themselves to potential customers can be often seen in the media. The restaurants, belonging to different categories, may be housed in malls or stand-alone buildings. People's interest in Bengali cuisine as an eating-out option cannot be called a passing phase, which can be witnessed in the increasing footfalls in these restaurants. This has encouraged further expansion and the last decade has especially witnessed a boom in the business. Some of the restaurants not only have multiple branches in Calcutta but also across the country especially in cities that have a considerable concentration of Bengalis. The growing nation-wide interest in the cuisine has also encouraged the opening of these branches. Bengali restaurants have become such profitable ventures that even entrepreneurs from outside the Bengali community are setting them up. For example, Sonar Tori, an upmarket Bengali restaurant, which opened its doors to diners in 2018, has been set up by Ambuja Neotia Hospitality. Harshavardhan Neotia, the chairman of the Ambuja Neotia Group, is a leading Calcutta-based industrialist and belongs to a Marwari business family whose forefathers made Calcutta their home sometime in the 1890s.

Then there are those few Bengali restaurants that specialize in dishes from Opar Bangla. The oldest of these restaurants is Kasturi, which was set up in 1994 on Mustaque Ahmed Street, which is located off Mirza Ghalib Street (earlier known as Free School Street). Calcutta is frequented by many Bangladeshis. Most of them are patients who come to the city for affordable and quality treatment at the local hospitals. The rest are mainly traders and tourists. Most of these visitors are always on the lookout for accommodations that are available at reasonable prices. Central Calcutta is full of such places. The neighbouring areas of New Market like Free School Street and Sudder Street have plenty of such accommodations, which are mostly taken up by the Bangladeshis. This led to a growing demand for eateries in these areas that would serve Bengali cuisine, particularly focusing on dishes from Opar Bangla. Thus, a market got created and the enterprising Gopal Chandra Saha grabbed the opportunity and set up Kasturi. The Bangladeshis, who had to adjust to the food served in hotels and guest houses, could not have been happier. They enjoyed the dishes cooked by the restaurant's chefs, which made them miss home a little less. Very soon the restaurant became a huge success, inspiring more entrepreneurs to walk on the same path. Gradually, more restaurants specializing in Bangladeshi cuisine like Prince and Radhuni came up in these localities. In fact, Mirza Ghalib Street is now popularly known as 'Little Bangladesh' because it is filled with Bangladeshis and restaurants serving their food.

Many years have gone by since Gopal Chandra Saha set up Kasturi on Mustaque Ahmed Street. The restaurant has always lacked a fancy décor. Instead its selling points have always been quality food, prompt service and hospitable staff. The Bangladeshis had always been its loyal customers. But word about the kind of food it served and the quality of cooking began spreading. This roused the curiosity of the local Bengalis and gourmets from other communities to try out the food at the restaurant. This particularly happened from the early years of the twenty-first century. Today, the name Kasturi has become synonymous in Calcutta with Bangladeshi cuisine. The restaurant has opened branches in different parts of the city, its suburbs and other parts of the country. It is a pioneer of Bangladeshi restaurants in Calcutta. In recent times, a few more such restaurants have come up in different parts of Calcutta, particularly in the central areas. The rising popularity of Opar Bangla cuisine is even making other Bengali restaurants include quite a few of its dishes in their menus.

Catering is an important part of the business activities of these restaurants. In this context, it is important to mention a Bengali restaurant that is well-known for its catering services in Calcutta. Dipti Cabin, a small eatery that served tea and snacks, was started by Debu Barick's uncle in the pre-Independence era. Debu Barick began working in this eatery, which was located just behind Bijoli Cinema Hall in Bhawanipur in south Calcutta, from the age of sixteen. By 1947, Debu Barick, who was now around twenty-three years of age, was in charge of the eatery. He rechristened it Bijoli Grill after the cinema hall. Over the years, under his leadership, Bijoli Grill became a catering giant in Calcutta. Today, this brand name is no longer confined to the small eatery behind Bijoli Cinema Hall but has many casual and family-style restaurants under its banner spread across Calcutta and other parts of the country. The food served in these is mostly Bengali while some even have multicuisine menu cards. But Bijoli Grill is still the most famous for its catering service. Be it weddings, parties, functions or other special occasions, Bijoli Grill has been the foremost name in organized catering in Calcutta for years.

Its growing popularity has made Bengali cuisine such a profitable venture that many hotels in the city have made it a part of their regular menu. For example, Sonargaon, the Indian fine dining restaurant in Taj Bengal has some of the choicest Bengali delicacies as permanent fixtures on its menu card along with dishes from north India. Similarly, threesixtythree°, the all-day fine dining restaurant of the Oberoi Grand, which specializes in world cuisines and serves an array of dishes from across the globe, has made it a point to include a section aptly titled 'Specialities of Bengal' in its menu card. This section has some of the most tempting and appetizing Bengali dishes listed in it. In contrast, Bhoomi is an exclusive Bengali fine dining restaurant in the Vedic Village Spa Resort. It serves delicacies from both sides of the border with organically grown ingredients. The restaurant follows the farm-to-table concept and uses the fresh vegetables grown in the verdant premises of the luxury health resort in cooking.

During Bengali festivals many of these fine dining restaurants bring out festive menus that feature many special dishes from this cuisine. On these occasions, the décor of the restaurants is done up in special ways that bring the Bengali culture and festive spirit alive. JW Marriott Hotel, a relatively new entrant in the hospitality scene of Calcutta, has taken this mode of celebration a few notches higher. In 2019, during the festive days of Durga Puja, the hotel organized a Mahabhoj or Grand Feast in the Grand Ballroom, a stately room in the building that is reserved for special occasions. Lavish buffet spreads featuring a wide range of Bengali delicacies welcomed diners at lunch hours. The staff members, dressed in Indian wear such as saris and dhuti-kurtas, attended to a multitude of guests while the rhythmic beat of the dhaks (a type of Indian drum) played by dhakis (ceremonial drummers) resonated in the background.

The atmosphere was further enlivened by the joyous and devotional Dhunuchi Naach, a customary dance performed by Bengalis during this occasion to thank the goddess. Dancers dressed in traditional attire swayed to the beat of the dhaks while holding flared earthen pots called dhunuchis from which billowed fragrant smoke. While the devotional songs of the Bauls, the mystical minstrels of Bengal, made diners pause for a few moments and get absorbed in the depth of their meaning, the captivating performances by masked dancers in vibrant costumes hailing from the Purulia district of West Bengal brought to life the victory of Goddess Durga through the tribal dance form of Chhau. The programme was such a grand success that it has been turned into an annual event.

The history of Bengali cuisine has thrown light on the fact that experimentation with ingredients once played a major role in its evolution. The current breed of chefs, encouraged by the owners of restaurants and driven by professional challenge, have begun experimenting and competing to bring out innovative dishes and revive lost ones. These are then highlighted as signature dishes of restaurants and become their unique selling points. By doing this, the chefs are inadvertently ushering in a second wave of evolution.

Some of these creations are given unique names. At 6 Ballygunge Place, 'Anthony Firingee' is a drink that combines the flavour of 'sahib vanilla' with 'desi nolen gur'. It has been advertised as a drink that will create magic just like the foreigner, who became a son of Bengal through his songs, did many years ago. Oh! Calcutta makes an appetizer of shallow-fried king prawns that have been marinated in vodka with chopped herbs. This 'spirited' creation has been cheekily named 'Matal Chingri' ('matal', in Bengali, means drunkard). Royal Vega, the signature pan-Indian vegetarian restaurant of ITC Royal Bengal, a Luxury Collection Hotel, satisfies the sweet tooth of Calcuttans by serving them a royal or 'shahi' sweet dish of layered sandesh and seasonal fresh fruits or 'phal' napped with rabri that has been flavoured with cardamoms. This luxurious creation, fit for the royalty, is garnished with edible silver leaves and pistachios, and served cold. It is not surprising that the chefs at this fine dining restaurant have aptly named the dessert, 'Shahiphal Sandesh'.

'The world is a small place' is a phrase that can be applied to food as well. Wider means of communication have made culinary influences common and our local chefs are not immune to it. Alfresco, the all-day fine dining restaurant of The LaLit Great Eastern Kolkata has modified the baked stuffed fish recipe of the West and come up with 'Pur Bhora Beckti', a dish of deep-fried bhekti paupiette stuffed with seafood. Pomfret, a variety liked by all fish eaters, is given a special treatment in the kitchens of Oh! Calcutta. The fish is pampered in a combination of sweet lemon paste, a favourite of the West, and pungent mustard paste, a favourite of the Bengalis. It is then char-grilled, which is a culinary technique more popular in Western countries. This makes the dish, 'Char-Grilled Lemon Mustard Pomfret', a perfect fusion of the East and the West.

Bhoomi, on the other hand, has transported Bengal's favourite fish to the coasts of Kerala. Moilee, a mildly spiced curry that has the dominating flavour of coconut, dates back to the time when the Portuguese ruled Kerala. It has drawn inspiration from a bland Portuguese stew that originally featured milk. Since Kerala is a state that abounds in coconut, spices and saltwater fish, the locals made the stew their own way by using coconut milk, local spices and different varieties of fish, the most popular choice being pomfret. Today, 'Meen Moilee' or fish moilee has become a dish that is synonymous with the cuisine of Kerala. The chefs at Bhoomi have made an unconventional move by cooking the hilsa, a fish that does not feature in the traditional recipe, into this curry. 'Ilish Moilee', which combines the flavours of south and east India, is a dish that many can look forward to at the restaurant.

Innovations continue at full steam and the latest trend is non-vegetarian pithes. Although not very common, such pithes are recently being made in a few Bengali homes. Generally, the community, as a whole, is a connoisseur of good food. This makes Bengalis experimental chefs. Their love for non-vegetarian food drives them to use such ingredients more often in cooking. It does not come as a surprise then that some of them have even begun stuffing pithes with non-vegetarian fillings, particularly fish. This developing trend is now being commercialized. Aaheli has come up with 'Rui Maacher Patishapta'. In this dish, the crepe of the patishapta pithe is filled with mashed rui maachh that has been cooked with spices, onions and herbs.

Pithe Bilashi, as is obvious from the name, is a relatively new restaurant that especially specializes in pithes. Of course, the restaurant does serve a range of regular sweet pithes like gokul pithe with kheer filling, doodh puli pithe, mohon puli pithe, mug puli pithe (also known as mug samli pithe or mug daler bhaja pithe) and patishapta pithe with kheer or coconut filling or a combination of both as well as innovative ones like baked gokul or patishapta pithe and chocolate-flavoured gokul, puli and patishapta pithes. Puli and patishapta pithes are also available in mango flavours at the restaurant.

But what is interesting is the restaurant's remarkable range of savoury pithes, which has been inspired by the French concept of savoury crepes. These may be mug puli pithes with paneer, fish, prawn, chicken or mutton fillings or patishapta pithes with vegetarian fillings like paneer and mocha as well as non-vegetarian fillings that range from bhapa ilish, mocha chingri, chingri maachher malaikari, kochi mutton to bhekti or chicken that has been flavoured with butter, cheese or the sublime gandhoraj lebu, a variety of lime with a unique and delicate fragrance. This interesting variety of savoury patishapta pithes are served with a unique combination of red sauce and yellow doi. Today, ingredients are played around with in the kitchen and chefs are coming up with unusual recipes. Paanch phoron is not a spice that Bengalis use to cook meat. But the chefs of Eden Pavilion, the twenty-four hours fine dining restaurant at ITC Sonar, one of the finest five star hotels in Calcutta, have a different opinion because they slow cook pork spare ribs with the five-spice mix. This dish, named 'Slow-Braised Paanch Phoron Pork', is served with steaming gobindobhog rice. 'Kakra Chingri Bhapa' made at Oh! Calcutta innovatively combines crab meat and chopped shrimps in a traditional bhapa preparation. This unusual combination is marinated with the paste of mustard and green chillies, and then steamed in banana leaf parcels.

Gandhoraj lebu ('gandhoraj' means 'aroma king' and 'lebu' means 'lime'), which can be given the sobriquet 'King of Indian Limes', has jumped on the bandwagon as the most popular ingredient used by modern chefs in innovations. This exotic lime is slightly scarce in juice but renowned for its refreshing citrus fragrance. It is not a matter of surprise then that it has been a common practice among Bengalis to squeeze its juice into musur dal or bhaja moong dal or maachher jhols when these are mixed with rice. Some even add its juice to rice mixed with thin meat curries. This is mainly done to add a heady aroma to the food along with lending an extra flavour to it. Some even add the leaves of this lime to a preparation of musur or bhaja moong dal and keep it aside for some time so that their flavour and aroma get absorbed. The plain panta bhaat, when flavoured with the juice and leaves of this lime, turns into an exotic feast. The aromatic juice of the lime is also added to ghol, sharbots and fruit juices to lend a delightful fragrance and flavour to them.

Gandhoraj lebu has its roots in a variety of lime known as Rangpur lime. The latter is known as Rangpur lime because it is a native of Rangpur, a region in the northern part of Bangladesh, where it used to grow wild before it was discovered. Rangpur is bordered on one side by Assam and on the other by West Bengal. The gandhoraj lebu that is commercially grown is not the pure Rangpur lime, which is a round orange fruit, but it has been cross-bred to a smaller size. The green, oblong and thick-skinned gandhoraj lebu is plucked before it ripens. If left to ripen on the tree, it will turn bright yellow in colour. This variety of lime is grown commercially in West Bengal, Assam, Tripura and parts of Andhra Pradesh and Tamil Nadu.

But, in Bengali cuisine, the juice of this prized lime was consumed raw and never added to cooking because of the prevalent notion that it tends to lose its fragrance when heated. However, our current breed of chefs stepped in and decided to change the scenario by turning the gandhoraj lebu into a star ingredient. They were keen to capitalize on its unique aroma. Since, the juice of lime complements fish, the gandhoraj lebu was first used in fish preparations. Restaurateurs and their chefs began combining both these favourite ingredients of the Bengalis and came up with unusual creations.

Oh! Calcutta pioneered the 'gandhoraj movement' and came up with the appetizer, 'Bhetki Gondhoraj', a dish of boneless bhekti fillet made delicately fragrant with the aromatic juice of the gandhoraj lebu and steamed. The main ingredients used on the fish in this preparation are a mixture of ginger and garlic pastes, and the juice of the lime. 6 Ballygunge Place made the same dish in a slightly different way. It served its customers 'Bhapa Bhetki (Gondhoraj)' by flavouring the fish with yoghurt and the juice of gandhoraj lebu, and then steaming it. The restaurant also makes a grilled version called 'Gondhoraj Grilled Bhetki'. In this dish, the fish is marinated with the unique combination of the zest of gandhoraj lebu and a variety of spices. Bhoomi, on the other hand, flavours pabda maachh with gandhoraj lebu and calls the dish 'Lebu Pabda'.

Once the experimentation with fish became successful, the chefs turned their attention to chicken. Unlike in Southeast Asian countries, the practice of flavouring chicken preparations with lime juice is not common among Bengalis. But the versatile chefs of Bengal, with their vast culinary knowledge, decided to be adventurous. They took their experimentation notches higher by flavouring chicken with gandhoraj lebu. Today, 6 Ballygunge Place serves its customers the appetizer, 'Gondhoraj Chicken', a dish of fried strips of succulent chicken in which the lime juice is used, among other ingredients, to marinate the meat while the chefs at Oh! Calcutta makes the lighter, 'Gondhoraj Bhapa Murgi', an appetizer in which the chicken is marinated with ginger paste and the fragrant juice, and steamed. 'Lebu Lanka Murgi', an innovative dish of chicken curry flavoured with green chillies and the juice of gandhoraj lebu, is served by Bhoomi. 6 Ballygunge Place, on the other hand, has revived 'Murgir Tramfrado', a traditional dish of boneless chicken, which the chefs at the restaurant flavour with the juice of gandhoraj lebu and coconut milk.

The aromatic juice of the lime is also being used to marinate cutlets and flavour chops. Even mutton has now fallen into its grip. This has led to creations like 'Gondhoraj Mangsher Chop' or crumb-fried lamb croquettes scented with gandhoraj lebu and served by Alfresco. The juice of the lime is also being used to marinate both vegetarian and non-vegetarian tikkas and kebabs.

Not just professional chefs but even connoisseurs and food enthusiasts are experimenting with this ingredient. A variety of gandhoraj lebu-flavoured fish, chicken and mutton recipes are coming up. The ingredient is experimented more with fish. While innovations like grilled ilish steaks drizzled with a spicy sauce flavoured with the juice of gandhoraj lebu, mustard and plain yoghurt can be seen, traditional recipes, which originally do not feature lime juice as an ingredient like doi maachh and maachher paturi, are also being flavoured with the aromatic juice. Bengalis love the heady aroma of this lime so much that along with its juice many add its zest and crushed leaves to preparations.

One can now come across diametrically opposite dishes flavoured with this exotic variety of lime like Gandhoraj Pulao and Gandhoraj Cake. The latter creation shows that even in desserts, gandhoraj lebu has become the avant-garde flavouring ingredient and experimentations with it are plenty. While one of the innovative creations of the popular Bengali confectionery shop Balaram Mullick & Radharaman Mullick is

'Gondhoraj Lebu Sandesh', the moiras of the new confectionery chain Mishti Katha have come up with 'Gandharaj Doi'. 'Gandharaj Lemon', on the other hand, is one of the best-selling ice creams of Pabrai's: Fresh & Naturelle, the Calcutta-based ice cream parlour chain that specializes in ice creams of natural and unusual flavours. While creations like Gandhoraj Mousse are not hard to come by, gandhoraj lebu-flavoured chocolate is an innovation that takes the cake.

Gandhoraj lebu is also being used to flavour tea. Either a slice of the lime is added to black tea or its juice is used in place of regular lime juice in lebu cha. Karma Kettle, a Calcutta-based company that sells packaged handcrafted teas has launched their signature blend 'Lebu Cha' as part of their 'Kolkata Series'. This variety combines Assam black tea with gandhoraj leaf and peel, lemon leaf and peel, and nimbu pani (lime water) flavour. The delicately fragrant gandhoraj lebu is slowly becoming a preferred ingredient in the preparation of drinks. The aromatic juice of this exotic lime and its wedges lend a refreshing touch to mocktails and mixed drinks. It is becoming a popular trend among bartenders to add wedges of gandhoraj lebu in place of the regular variety of lime to a drink of gin or vodka topped with tonic water.

Credit also goes to these enterprising chefs for reviving lost and rare recipes. Bengalis usually eat the seasonal mango fish in a fried, frittered or curried form but hardly as a cutlet. The last preparation was mostly enjoyed by the British. Oh! Calcutta has revived this recipe that had got lost in the annals of history with the departure of the British. 'Topsher Cutlet' is now a regular feature in its menu card. The fish, spiced with ginger, garlic and green chillies, is crumbed and fried. Many of these restaurants also serve smoked hilsa, which had become a lost recipe. This dish, prepared in different ways by different restaurants, is also known by different names. For example, in Oh! Calcutta, the fillets of boneless hilsa are delicately smoked with a secret sauce and served with potato fries and stir-fried vegetables. While at Aaheli, a Bengali twist has been given to this dish by cooking the boneless smoked fish in mustard, in Eden Pavilion, the boneless smoked fish goujonettes are served with yoghurt mustard gravy and gobindobhog rice. Oh! Calcutta has stuck to the original name of this dish. But the chefs at Aaheli call their creation 'Dhumrogondhi Eilish' while those at Eden Pavilion call theirs, 'Smoked Sorsey Hilsa'.

While mahi pulao, a legacy of the Nawabs of Bengal, is being revived by commercial chefs, mahi biryani happens to be their innovation. The latter, labelled with the more comprehensible words 'fish biryani', is especially featured in restaurants, particularly of the fine dining category, as part of their festive menu spread. Credit must be given to these chefs for using the river fish of Bengal in biryanis to satisfy the fish-loving palate of the Bengalis. It does not come as a surprise that Bengalis prefer this variety to be cooked with their favourite hilsa, making 'ilish biryani' their most favourite fish biryani.

More at the home level, influenced by mahashas—the stuffed vegetables dish of the Jews—the modern Bengali homemaker began stuffing deseeded and hollowed capsicums and tomatoes with vegetarian fillings, the most popular being a spicy cooked paste of mashed potatoes, crumbled chhana or grated paneer, and non-vegetarian fillings, the most popular being a cooked spicy mixture of fish meat or minced meat. A variety of fillings of one's choice can be used in this versatile dish. Some even stuff the vegetables with cooked and flavoured rice like pulao. The vegetables are slow cooked in very little oil in a pan that is kept covered. Alternatively, they can be baked. Many also cook the stuffed vegetables into a rich and spicy tomato-based gravy. While the dry version is generally eaten as an accompaniment to meals, the curried version is eaten with steamed rice. Thus, the spice- and curry-loving Bengalis transformed the mahashas and made the dish in their own way.

The chefs, in their enthusiasm to experiment and innovate, have not spared our traditional sweets as well. The founding fathers of the modern Bengali sweetmeat industry, perhaps, would never have imagined in their dreams that a day would come when sweets like sandesh, rasogolla, chamcham, pantua, kalakand, mihidana and mishti doi would be baked or the traditional nolen gur would be used to flavour the modern ice cream. While, on one hand, 6 Ballygunge Place is serving its customers the exclusive 'Aam Sondesh Paturi', a confection in which mango-flavoured sandesh is wrapped in a banana leaf parcel and grilled, on the other, its chefs are topping mihidana with rabri and then baking the dish as well as steaming sandesh flavoured with the pulp of daab.

When it comes to nolen gur, the prized possession of Bengal, the innovations are endless. If there is a general belief that this popular ingredient is exclusive to Bengali sweets, then it is time people changed their minds. The current breed of chefs, throwing caution to the winds, is treating this ingredient with unrestrained imagination. In Calcutta, nolen gur is not only being used to sweeten other Indian desserts like firni and kulfi but it is also becoming an avant-garde ingredient in the creation of Western desserts. Often, one can come across nolen gur mousse or cheese cake or baklava in high-end bakeries and restaurants.

The latest addition to the confectionery racks of Flurys in winter is 'Nolen Gur Crepe Gateaux'. In this creation, the filling is made of nolen gur that has been folded with mascarpone cheese and whipped cream. The layers are thin French pancakes. The chefs at the five-star Novotel Kolkata Hotel and Residences have introduced nolen gur to the classic French dessert crème brûlée. 'Nolen Gur Crème Brûlée', the rich yet simple egg yolks-and-cream-based custard, is flavoured with vanilla extract, sweetened with nolen gur and topped with a layer of hardened caramelized brown sugar and nolen gur. Balaram Mullick & Radharaman Mullick as well as Mishti Katha, confectionery shops well known for their innovations, has come up with Nolen Gur Soufflé.

In January 2020, 'Nolen Gurer Utshob', meaning 'The Festival of Nolen Gur', hosted by the five-star Hotel Hindustan International at their patisserie, 'Sweet Pleasures', revealed the great lengths to which chefs are being innovative with this ingredient. The creations made with the date palm jaggery ranged from nolen gurer plain, rose and fruit breads to nolen gur doughnuts that were filled with the jaggery and topped with milk and white chocolates. And then there were the elaborate confections like 'Nolen Gurer Oreo Cheese Cake', 'Nolen Gurer Tiramisu' and 'Nolen Gurer Orange Delight'. In the first creation, on the base of the cheese cake made of crushed Oreos, lay a mixture of mascarpone cheese and whipped cream, which was topped with nolen gurer jelly. The second dessert is made in a dark chocolate cup with coffee liqueur and mascarpone cheese. Instead of sugar, it is sweetened with the reduction of nolen gur. In the last creation, a casing made of orange peel that has been infused with sugar syrup to get rid of its bitterness, is filled with nolen gurer mousse, diced orange and praline. The dessert is finished off with almond flakes.

But, when it comes to innovations in Bengali cuisine, there is one particular chef who wears the crown as the 'King of Innovations'—Joymalya Banerjee. Popularly known as Chef Joy, this former executive chef of Oh! Calcutta is renowned for his avant-garde recipes. His bold and daring attempts at transforming Bengali cuisine are encouraging a mini revolution. He is responsible for ushering in the 'gandhoraj movement' with his creation of 'Bhetki Gondhoraj' when he was with Oh! Calcutta. The mega successful Anjan Chatterjee, the owner of Oh! Calcutta, who began his career as a restaurateur in a humble way, came up with the idea of this dish. Like every other Bengali, both the restaurateur and the creator were fond of gandhoraj lebu and wanted to incorporate the ingredient in cooking. Chef Joy then came up with the revolutionary recipe. Today, 'Bhetki Gondhoraj' is replicated by other restaurants, chefs and connoisseurs with many coming up with their own versions of it. His other innovations with the gandhoraj lebu include 'Gondhoraj Martini', 'Gondhoraj Julep', 'Gondhoraj Soufflé' and 'Gondhoraj Sorbet'.

Finding it difficult to contain his bohemian ideas, Chef Joy finally decided to invest in a restaurant of his own where he could explore them. This small restaurant with a charming decor, which the chef has aptly named 'Bohemian', is tucked away at the end of a by-lane in the Ballygunge area. A meal at the restaurant can begin with a smoked ilish consommé that has ilish roe shavings, shredded chillies and mustard seeds. For the appetizer, one can select pan-grilled pork spare ribs with kalo jeere and nolen gur. A fish-loving Bengali can choose from a range of fish and shellfish dishes like pabda rolls stewed in cherry tomato and spinach broth and served with bori pilaf and tossed vegetables or kajuli maachh stuffed with egg yolk mousse and stewed in aromatic orange and cumin broth or prawn and crabmeat dumplings stewed in spicy nolen gur reduction or prawns steamed with yoghurt and gandhoraj. The last three dishes are served with steamed rice and wilted greens.

For the meat-lover, there is chicken breast stuffed with kalmi greens, simmered with cheese and green chilli pickle, and served with garlic and flattened rice pilaf and tossed vegetables or sliced pork and baby turmeric in banana leaf envelopes served with steamed rice and potato mustard salad or mutton and drumsticks stew with gandhoraj leaves served with steamed rice and green salad. In the dessert section, the adventurous can choose between creations like 'Gondhoraj Lemon Pie with Ginger Brittle', which is a King of Lime-flavoured pie served with whipped cream and ginger brittle or 'Toffee Roshogolla with Green Chilli Sabayon', a dish of caramelized baby rasogollas served with fragrant green chilli sabayon or 'Malpua Cheesecake', star anise-flavoured chhana cheesecake interlayered with traditional soft malpoas or 'Pantua Baked Alaska', a dish of baby pantuas cocooned between ice cream and sponge cake and topped with meringue.

Thus, we see that Bengali cuisine has had a long and exciting journey. From a simple cuisine that was confined to home, it has evolved into a sophisticated fare served in fine dining restaurants. The journey began with ancient men hunting down animals and cooking them as food in the most basic manner to modern suave chefs blending Bengali cuisine with Western fare and coming up with fusion dishes. And the evolution continues.

PART FOUR

Pan-Indian Cuisines and Darjeeling District

South Indian Thali at Prema Vilas, Kolkata

***Source:* Vivek Luke Mukherjee**

1. Pan-Indian Cuisines

As a storehouse of wealth and riches, Bengal, which François Bernier considered to be richer than Egypt, and particularly Calcutta, after it was made the capital, was an attractive destination for anyone on the lookout for opportunity and prosperity. In *Calcutta—The Living City: Volume II: The Present and Future* (1990), Animesh Ray writes in his essay 'The Calcutta Port', 'When the British came to Bengal in the seventeenth century, they found the people prosperously engaged in exporting rice, sugar, silk, cotton, lac and amber. In the heart of Bengal there were mulberry trees nurturing silk-worms, weavers were producing silk and muslin, and the soil upstream was rich in saltpetre' (p. 123). We have seen before how its abundance drove many communities to Calcutta. They made the city their home and contributed to its culinary culture.

But there were a few more important communities that came to live in the city during the colonial rule. Some of them came in search of employment while others came to conduct trade. Over the years, these communities have contributed tremendously to the economic and social progress of the city. But the cuisines of these communities have not much influenced the local culinary culture and nor have they, in turn, got influenced by it. Instead the communities have stuck to their food habits without making any alterations or adaptations after relocating to Calcutta. Yet, it is important to make a mention of these communities as their vital presence cannot be ignored. While most of their dishes have largely remained confined to themselves, a few have gained popularity in the city.

Punjabi

One of them is the Punjabi cuisine. After having lived in Calcutta for years, the Punjabis have made a strong impact on the culinary scene of the city with their cuisine. After Chinese and Mughlai, Punjabi is the most-ordered cuisine in restaurants in Calcutta. But the Punjabis who have stayed in Calcutta have remained loyal to their food habits. The easy availability of ingredients required in their cooking made it possible for them to stick to their foods, and their dishes were not subjected to any drastic change thanks to relocation.

Sikhs from the state of Punjab began immigrating to the royal capital in the post-First World War years, settling in south Calcutta because north Calcutta had become overcrowded by this time. The introduction of modern automobiles in the city gave them the opportunity to earn a better livelihood. Except for the railways, transportation in Punjab was not well developed in those times. Most of the settlers were farmers who bought vehicles with their savings and made a living driving trucks, buses and taxis, enjoying a monopoly over the motorized public transport system till 1957. They also sold spare parts, joined private security services, operated machines and tools in factories, worked in the textile and coal mining industries, and set up small restaurants called dhabas between Bhawanipur and Hazra in south Calcutta. Sikhs from Punjab working in the city were mainly Jats from cities like Amritsar, Ludhiana and Gurdaspur. But the Green Revolution of 1965 in the states of Punjab and Haryana bolstered income growth and reduced poverty in those states, leading to the gradual exodus of Punjabi Sikhs from Calcutta. They headed back to the state of Punjab.

Many of these Punjabi Sikhs who settled in Calcutta were Akali sympathizers with bitter anti-British sentiments. Kavi Kutia was the first Punjabi literary society to be set up in Bengal. It was established in Calcutta in 1922, and published revolutionary literature. The society launched a monthly magazine called *Kavi* in 1927, and the news daily *Desh Darpan* in 1930. The latter is still in print.

Most of the rural people in Punjab work very hard in the fields and burn a lot of calories while tilling the soil and planting crops. Wheat is the staple food of the Punjabis, with rice playing a minor role. It is usually reserved for holidays and special occasions. Rajma masala, simply referred to as rajma, is a spicy curry preparation of red kidney beans (rajma) which is eaten with chawal (rice), and kadhi pakora is a plain yoghurt (dahi) and gram flour (besan) based curry preparation that has gram flour fritters (pakoras) floating in it. It is sour in taste and also eaten with chawal. Punjabi food is rich in taste and involves liberal amounts of ghee, butter and cream. Butter is used extensively in Punjabi cooking and blobs of butter are often placed on top of dishes for extra taste. Punjabi women make white (safed) butter at home, called ghar ka makkhan or safed makkhan, by churning malai (cream that floats on top of milk when it is boiled). Dal makhani, paneer makhani (popularly known as paneer butter masala) and murgh makhani (popularly known as chicken butter masala), as can be understood from their names, are cooked in liberal quantities of butter and may even have cream added to them at the end of the cooking. These three dishes are popular among most of the communities living in Calcutta.

Milk and its products like curd and paneer are also hallmarks of Punjabi cuisine. Lassi, a sweetened yoghurt drink, is very popular for its cool, refreshing and soothing taste and is served in all Punjabi dhabas and nearly all north Indian restaurants in Calcutta. The drink has taken over the city and its preparation has become a common feature in nearly all Bengali homes. The Punjabi dish, chole bhature, is also popular in Calcutta. The combination dish of makki ki roti and sarson ka saag, exclusive to Punjabi cuisine, is slowly gaining popularity in a land full of mustard plants. Alu paratha, mooli (radish) paratha, gobi (cauliflower) paratha, pyaz (onion) paratha and paneer paratha are some of the popular stuffed fried bread preparations, often eaten with pickles and curd. The parathas are topped with generous blobs of butter. Lachha paratha is a slightly large and round layered paratha that is also sought after.

A Punjabi diet consists of both vegetarian and non-vegetarian foods. Since a majority of the Punjabis settled in south Calcutta, they turned Jadubabur Bazar, the major market of the area, into their favourite shopping hub. Simply referring to it as Jaggu Bazar, they bought everything that was required in their kitchen right from vegetables like tinda (apple gourd) and kundri (ivy gourd), commonly used in Punjabi cooking that the market began to stock, to meat from the place.

The vegetarian food served in the langars (community kitchens) at the few gurudwaras in the city is simple and tasty. The langars are open to both Sikhs and non-Sikhs alike who can partake of these free meals. It is believed that the Punjabis in Calcutta have an affinity for patol, a vegetable that is not easily available in Punjab. They also love the Bengali begoon bhaja or fried aubergine and have a strong liking for luchi, koraishutir kochuri and radhaballabhi, which they eat with chholar dal or alur dom.

After living in Calcutta for so many years, they have an increased liking for fish and prefer to eat the boneless varieties available in the market like pomfret, bhekti and prawns. The Bengali fish preparations they like the most are doi maachh, bhekti maachher paturi and the classic chingri maachher malaikari. The courageous Punjabis dare to brave the bones of the hilsa and enjoy shorshe ilish. Being a mustard-loving community, they like to cook their fish preparations in mustard oil as the Bengalis do. Amritsari fish fry is a Punjabi fish preparation that is popular among the Bengalis. Although traditionally made with surmai (king mackerel), this dish can be made with any boneless fish of one's choice. In this dish, small pieces of boneless fish fillet are marinated with lime juice or malt vinegar and the pastes of ginger and garlic, and then coated with spices (especially carom seeds), gram flour and rice flour, and deep-fried till golden brown.

Goat meat and chicken are the favourite meats of the community. Since the time Kashmir was annexed to the Sikh Empire by Maharaja Ranjit Singh in 1819, its rich preparation of rogan josh (curry made with goat meat) became a part of Punjabi cuisine and turned into a great favourite. Punjabi cooking has, to a great extent, been influenced by the cuisine of the Muslim invaders, who brought with them the tradition of the tandoor. It is largely believed that this clay oven was introduced in India during the reign of the Delhi Sultanate. However, it was only during Mughal Emperor Shah Jahan's reign that the tandoor stepped out of the royal kitchen and became portable because he had a metal model constructed that could be taken along on his travels. Punjabi tandoori cooking is hugely popular in Calcutta today. Marinated fish, meat, paneer and vegetables as well as breads of different types are cooked in the tandoor. Among all the tandoori preparations, tandoori chicken is a favourite not only among Punjabis, but also Bengalis who love to eat this dish with drinks.

The Punjabis prepare kheer on special occasions with long-grain rice, milk, sugar and green cardamom. Among their other desserts, halwa is a much sought-after preparation, and the two most commonly prepared versions are gajar ka halwa (made of grated carrots) and sooji ka halwa (made of semolina). Gajar ka halwa is a popular dessert among the Bengalis. In gurudwaras, atte ka halwa, made of wholewheat flour that is cooked in ghee with water and sugar, make the kada prashad (devotional offering).

Bengali chhana-based sweets are something that the Punjabis in Calcutta are fond of and they particularly enjoy sandesh and rasogolla. The sweet chutney that the Bengalis eat at the end of a meal is a favourite among Punjabi settlers, particularly the tomato and green mango varieties. Malpoa, a fried sweet or bhaja mishti in Bengali confectionery, is eaten with kheer or rabri in Punjabi homes.

In the colonial times, a few wayside restaurants called dhabas were set up by Punjabi entrepreneurs in south Calcutta for the Sikh truck, bus and taxi drivers who wanted to stop at a place and relax over some garam chai and their local food. These dhabas brought Punjabi cuisine out of its home confines and exposed it to the general public for the first time. Bachan's Dhaba, Balwant Singh's Eating House and The Dhaba (popularly known as Ballygunge Dhaba) are Calcutta's oldest dhabas, set up in colonial times in south Calcutta to cater to the Punjabi population in the area. Gradually, Bengalis and other communities began visiting these dhabas and grew fond of the delicious food served there. Many dhabas have come up in the city since these three made their mark and have grown in tremendous popularity over the years. But Bachan's Dhaba, Balwant Singh's Eating House and The Dhaba are still considered pioneers.

South Indian

Mistakenly referred to as Madrasis in the colonial period and for some time after that because of the inclusion of the southern states in the Madras Presidency, the south Indians began immigrating to Calcutta in force in the late nineteenth and early twentieth centuries in search of jobs. Many of these people were educated. Being proficient in shorthand and typing, they were able to get jobs as secretaries, stenographers, typists and clerks in banks, government institutions and corporate sectors. Some of them had strong financial and engineering backgrounds and took up jobs in financial houses and engineering firms. Many also tried their luck in business. The community mainly settled in south Calcutta as north Calcutta had become overcrowded by then.

The first south Indian association in the city was the Calcutta South India Club established in Hindustan Park in south Calcutta in 1926. The famous south Indian scientist and Nobel Laureate C.V. Raman was the first president of the club from 1926 to 1928. He was succeeded by Dr Sarvepalli Radhakrishnan who was a renowned academician and also served as the second President of India. The Kannadigas were the smallest group of early south Indian settlers. While some of them were bureaucrats, few were members of the intelligentsia. A prominent personality from this community was B.V. Ramiah, who was a senior member of the Indian Civil Service and was later elected as mayor of the city in 1924. B.S. Kesavan was another important personality from the community under whom the National Library attained its huge standing. He was responsible for transforming the former residence of the Viceroy of India in Belvedere Estate in Alipore into the main building of the library, and played a pivotal role in the maintenance, updating and addition of books and other important documents to its stands.

Nagarathar House and Komala Vilas are the oldest south Indian lodges in Calcutta, providing basic boarding and lodging facilities to people arriving in the city from the Deccan. Nagarathar House was opened on Ezra Street in 1921, and was a pilgrimage stopover for the Chettiar community who travelled to Calcutta to visit the city's temples. Komala Vilas, on the other hand, is a south Indian lodge near Lake Market in south Calcutta. It provided basic boarding and lodging facilities to those who came to the city in search of jobs. People would check in here for a few weeks before they found a home for themselves. Komala Vilas opened its doors in the 1930s.

Today, the community is concentrated in south Calcutta. The areas around Lake Market have earned the nickname 'Madras of Calcutta' because of the heavy concentration of south Indians. South Indian newspapers and magazines are in great demand by the community based in this part of the city, like the Chennai edition of *The Hindu*, the *Malayala Manorama* and women's magazines like *Grihalakshmi* and *Vanitha*. A road in the Lake Market area has been rechristened Kavi Bharati Sarani after the great Tamil poet Chinnaswami Subramania Bharati, a pioneer of modern Tamil poetry.

Tamilians comprise the single largest south Indian community in Calcutta. The Telugu community ranks second, numerically. Kannadigas and Malayalis have dwindled in number as most members of these communities have gone back to Karnataka and Kerala respectively.

South Indian cuisine is quite diverse, and the four communities follow their own exclusive food habits. When they settled in Calcutta, each community continued with their food habits, which were not subjected to any drastic change or adaptation due to relocation. This is because most of the vegetables, grains, pulses and spices required were available in the city. But some of the ingredients that are typical to south Indian cooking were not available in the local markets. This is where the south Indian grocers stepped in as messiahs and contributed to keeping their culinary tradition alive in this alien city. They set up stores in Lake Market and the surrounding areas, and travelled frequently to south India to bring the ingredients that were not locally available.

Contrary to popular belief, Indians are not necessarily vegetarians.

The Brahmins are vegetarian because traditionally they were priests in temples. Their vocation compelled them to follow a sattvic diet that prohibits the consumption of any kind of fish, meat or egg, and even certain lentils, vegetable and spices. But the rest has the freedom to indulge in non-vegetarian food.

The Tamil community in Calcutta is largely vegetarian, the most conservative avoiding even garlic, onion, masoor dal (split red lentil) and bottle gourd or lauki. A large section in the community offer the cooked food for the day as prasadam or devotional offering to the gods in their shrines at home before eating it themselves. This compels them to cook their food according to sattvic customs. Geographical factors have also played a role in shaping their cuisine. Tamilians have migrated from a region that abounds in the growth of paddy, sesame, coconut and tamarind. Rice is eaten nearly every day with curries, and is also one of the main ingredients in breakfast preparations such as idli and dosa. Sesame seed oil, which they prefer to call gingelly oil, is the main medium of cooking and coconut and tamarind are liberally used in their dishes.

Tamil cuisine includes a wide variety of curries made with vegetables, berries and even buttermilk. Their curries are divided into kuzhambu and kootu, the difference being their consistencies. While kuzhambu is runny, kootu is a gravy that has a thick consistency. Manathakkali or black nightshade is a very small berry that is cooked into a vathal kuzhambu, a runny curry. This is a very popular preparation in the community and local female hawkers outside Lake Market are often seen selling the berries, which they call chhoto tomato (meaning 'small tomato' in Bengali). Poriyal, on the other hand, refers to a stir-fried dish. In Calcutta, the Tamilians prepare this dish with vegetables.

The community often indulges in flavoured rice preparations like thengai sadam or coconut rice which they like to eat with appalam (poppadom). Thayir sadam or curd rice needs no introduction. It is usually eaten with lime pickle and is one of the most popular sadam preparations in the community.

Pongal is a very important festival for the community. It is a harvest festival dedicated to the sun god. It is celebrated in the month of Thai (January–February) which is the reason why the festival is also known as Thai Pongal. Tamilians in Calcutta celebrate by preparing a sweet dish of semi-thick consistency called sakkarai pongal, made of lightly roasted rice and moong dal, which are cooked with milk, water, jaggery, ghee, cashews, raisins and powdered cardamom. The community also makes a savoury version of this rice and lentil dish, known as Ven Pongal, which is usually eaten with coconut chutney.

Like the Tamilians, the Kannadigas in Calcutta are predominantly vegetarian. The cuisine of Karnataka has been seen to share similarities with those of the other south Indian states, as well as Maharashtra and Goa. This is because Karnataka shares borders with all these states, which has led to a culinary crossover, particularly in the border areas. Although influences of the neighbouring states can be seen in their cuisine, the Kannadigas have a cuisine of their own which is very typical to their land. The geographical factors of the region promote the growth of rice, jowar (sorghum), ragi (finger millet), asafoetida, tamarind and a variety of lentils and vegetables. This produce is used extensively in their cooking.

Idli, dosa, utthapam, upma and vada constitute the body of the breakfast spread in the homes of the Kannadigas in Calcutta. Breakfast is also called tiffin, implying a light meal. Although the breakfast of the Kannadigas has commonalities with that of the other south Indian communities, they have certain preparations which are exclusive to their culinary culture. Kannadigas prepare a special dosa called benne dosa, which was first made in the city of Davanagere in Karnataka. 'Benne' means 'butter'. As may be surmised from the name, this soft and fluffy dosa is prepared with liberal amounts of butter and served with potato palya and coconut chutney. Benne dosa is the only dosa that is made with a batter that has ground beaten rice or poha as a major ingredient along with the usual ground rice and ground urad dal.

Neer dosa is another Kannadiga specialtiy. The word 'neer' means 'water' in Tulu, and the dish is commonly made in the Tulu Nadu region of Karnataka. The batter for this dosa is made of ground rice mixed with salt and water. No lentil is used in the preparation. The batter is so thin that it runs over the entire greased tawa when it is poured onto it. Kannadigas usually eat it with kayi-bella or jenu tuppa. Kayi is freshly grated coconut and bella refers to grated jaggery. Jenu tuppa is honey. Neer dosa is also eaten with rasayana, a sweet chutney made with the pulp of mango or mashed bananas mixed with fresh coconut milk, sweetened with jaggery and flavoured with powdered cardamom.

Both neer dosa and the evergreen masala dosa are part of the Udupi cuisine. Udupi is a city in Karnataka which is famous for its vegetarian food. The cuisine originated in the Sri Krishna Matha of Udupi, founded in the thirteenth century by Madhvacharya, a Vaishnava saint and the proponent of Dvaita philosophy. This cuisine was created by the Shivalli Madhwa Brahmins who cooked food for the Krishna deity at the matha. The Udupi cuisine travelled out of the confines of the matha and spread across the city because some members of the Shivalli Madhwa Brahmin sect decided to venture into the restaurant business instead. They set up restaurants across Udupi and made their matha cuisine famous all over the state of Karnataka.

The community loves to eat their anna (rice) with palya, a dry vegetable preparation, or gojju, a gravy dish. But the Kannadigas in Calcutta also cook certain special anna dishes, like bisi bele bath and vangi bath, which are prepared on celebratory occasions or eaten on weekly holidays. Bisi bele bath is a mushy rice, lentil and mixed vegetables preparation that is very popular while the main ingredients of the fried and fluffy vangi bath are rice and aubergines. Kannadigas make quite a few chitrannas or rice-based dishes, of which nimbekai chitranna, or lemon rice, is the most popular. These are also served during festivals and celebratory occasions.

Kannadigas also make some home-made sweets. The two most popular sweet dishes are kesari bath and Mysore pak. Mysore pak is one of the most sought-after sweets in the community that is served in celebratory occasions. Originating in the royal kitchen of Mysore, a city in Karnataka, during the reign of Maharaja Krishnaraja Wadiyar IV (28 December 1894–3 August 1940), this sweet is made with gram flour, ghee and sugar syrup and shaped like diamonds or squares. It comes a close second in popularity to the halwa-like kesari bath, which is a sweet, saffron-infused, semolina preparation.

Malayalis settled in Calcutta are largely non-vegetarians. They come from a region that is known as the spice hub of India. Kerala was a major spice exporter and attracted foreign traders like the ancient Babylonians, Assyrians, Egyptians, Arabs, Phoenicians, Chinese, Greeks and Romans because of the variety of spices that grow in the region. The Arab merchants trading in the region married local women, and thus gave rise to the Mappila Muslim community. Syrian Christians form a major group in the region and Vasco da Gama's arrival in Kappad, near Kozhikode (Calicut) in 1498, opened trade relations with the Portuguese. It is a well-known fact that foreign traders like the Dutch and the British tried to establish their hold over the region as well. This range of foreign influences, along with geographical factors, has heavily influenced the food habits of Malayalis. Seafood forms a very important part of their diet and rice, coconut, tapioca or kappa and spices are liberally used in their cooking.

If one assumes that idli, dosa and vada form the backbone of all south Indian breakfasts, one simply has to walk into a Malayali home in Calcutta to discard that notion. Their weekend breakfast is different from that eaten by other south Indian communities. On these days, appam, idiyappam and puttu are the star performers in every Malayali home.

Appam looks like a round pancake and has a soft texture. Its thin and fermented batter is made of ground raw rice, cooked rice, grated coconut, milk, yeast, sugar and salt. A special wok for making appams is brushed with oil and the batter is poured into it. A conical cover is placed on top of this wok and the batter is cooked. Appams taste delicious when eaten with hot vegetarian or non-vegetarian stews.

Idiyappam, on the other hand, looks like noodles that have been twisted and moulded into the shape of round idlis. The main ingredient is rice flour. Idiyappams are steamed and taken with a variety of vegetarian or non-vegetarian curries, coconut milk sweetened with jaggery or sugar or grated coconut mixed with ghee and sugar. The Europeans living in the region called idiyappams 'string hoppers' but locally they are also known as nool puttu, derived from the word 'nool' which means 'string' or 'thread'.

Another very popular weekend breakfast dish is the puttu. Puttu is a steamed cake made with rice flour and grated coconut, and is cylindrical in shape. It is made in a special cylindrical vessel called puttu kutti. Before the invention of the puttu kutti, puttus were steamed in cylindrical bamboo moulds that would impart the natural flavour of bamboo to the puttus. It is eaten with kadala curry, a black chickpea preparation, or bananas that have been mashed and mixed with sugar.

The Malayalis in Calcutta eat a variety of kootan (curry) with choru (cooked rice). The community loves meen (fish), even going so far as to pickle fish, and have adapted to the freshwater variety available in the local markets. One of the community's most famous vegetable curry dishes is the coconut-flavoured avial, which is made with a medley of vegetables, and eaten with choru. The classic Malabar chicken curry is a celebratory dish that is made on special occasions. It is cooked in coconut oil, the main medium of cooking of the Malayalis, and eaten with choru.

Although kappa or tapioca is almost a staple food for Malayalis, its unavailability in the Calcutta markets limits its preparation here. In Kerala, kappa was originally a poor Malayali's vegetable because it was cheap, easily available and rich in carbohydrates, but over the years it has turned into a delicacy often eaten with meen curry. In Calcutta, kappa is grown in farmlands owned by the Malayalis in the suburbs, and sold through personal contacts. The vegetable is available for sale during the autumn months, when it is bought by Malayalis.

There is one dish that unites Malayalis across religious boundaries, and that is the immensely popular Thalassery biryani. This famous biryani originated in the town called Thalassery on the Malabar coast in Kannur district in Kerala. It was the result of the confluence of Arab and Malabari cuisines. The Thalassery port was used extensively for the trading of spices and became a melting pot for different foreign cultures. Thalassery biryani is a result of the influence of Arab culture. It is believed that the Thalassery Muslims were the first batch of Malayalis to come to Calcutta when it became the royal capital. They arrived towards the end of the nineteenth century and set up small businesses that dealt with leather materials and garments. Some of them set up shops selling dry fish in Tiretta Bazar, tailoring shops and even small eateries. Although there are very few Thalassery Muslims in Calcutta now, they have left behind a legacy in the form of the biryani that is still cooked in nearly every Malayali household in the city.

Onam, a very important ten-day festival for the Malayalis, is celebrated in the month of Chingam (August–September) every year not only as a harvest festival but also to honour the homecoming of the legendary King Mahabali, an asura or demon king who once ruled the state of Kerala. Legend has it that this noble, benevolent and devout king was pushed down to patala or the netherworld by the vamana avatara (dwarf incarnation) of Lord Vishnu because he had come to power by defeating the devas or gods and taking over the three worlds. Since King Mahabali was very attached to his subjects, he requested Lord Vishnu to allow him to visit his kingdom every year. Lord Vishnu granted him this request. Since then it is believed that he visits his kingdom in Kerala once every year during the harvest festival. Malayalis of all religions honour his visit with a huge celebration. Vishu, the Malayali New Year, is celebrated on the first day of the month of Medam, which starts from the middle of April. One of the most popular sweet preparations the community makes during the festivals of Onam and Vishu is neyyappam. Neyyappam is prepared by making a batter of rice flour, jaggery or sugar, black sesame seeds, cardamom powder and pieces of coconut. The consistency of the batter is similar to that of dosa batter. A pinch of baking soda is mixed with it. Neyyappam batter requires a long period of fermentation. Small, sweet and round appams are made by frying the batter in ghee in an appam wok. This sweet is also offered as prasadam to Lord Ayyappan.

The members of the Telugu community settled in Calcutta are a blend of vegetarians and non-vegetarians. Like their south Indian counterparts, geographical factors of the region they originally came from have dictated their food habits. Rice is the staple food of the Telugus, and they prefer their kuras or curries to be spicy as well as hot, as Andhra Pradesh is the largest producer of red chillies in the country. Turmeric, tamarind and coriander are grown extensively in the region and feature prominently in their fare. The region's proximity to the Bay of Bengal makes the non-vegetarian section of the community indulgent fish eaters. The cuisine of the Telugu Muslims also has a strong presence in Calcutta. This cuisine has been influenced by the food habits of the Qutb Shahs, whose reign over the Golconda Sultanate was brought to an end by Mughal Emperor Aurangzeb in 1687, and the Asaf Jahi dynasty, who ruled as the Nizams of Hyderabad till 1948, one year after India won her independence from Britain.

While the other south Indian communities generally use mustard seeds to temper their dishes, the Telugus also grind them into paste and flavour some of their dishes with this ingredient. This cooking style is similar to that of the Bengalis. Ava pettina aratikaya kura is a vegetable dish made with green bananas cooked with mustard paste. This vegetable curry is eaten with annam or cooked rice.

The Telugus make a sweet and tangy stew called mukkala pulusu using assorted vegetables like pumpkin, bottle gourd, sweet potato and drumsticks. They eat this stew with annam and appadam (poppadom). The use of jaggery imparts a sweet taste to the curry and tamarind, a tangy taste. This kind of sweet and tangy vegetable stew is generally not found in the fare of other south Indian communities.

The non-vegetarian section of the community makes certain curry dishes which are tasteful in their simplicity like the mamsam kura (mutton curry) and chepala pulusu, which is a simple fish curry preparation. The latter dish is prepared in Calcutta using fish like the Indian mackerel, rui tilapia, pomfret, crab and prawn or shrimp. Annam is the perfect accompaniment for both mamsam kura and chepala pulusu. The famous

Hyderabadi biryani, prepared by the Muslim section of the community, needs no introduction. It is popularly made with chicken, mutton or beef.

Telugu cuisine is famous for its pachadis or chutneys. This spicy preparation is made with vegetables, and sometimes fruits, and tastes best when eaten mixed with annam and topped with ghee. Pachadis can also be eaten with breakfast dishes like idli and dosa. The most popular vegetables used in this preparation are beerakaya (ridge gourd), sorakaya (bottle gourd), vankaya (aubergine) and dondakaya (ivy gourd). Gongura pachadi, also immensely popular, is made with sorrel leaves.

The Telugus also make a fiery sambal or sauce with dried fish. In this preparation, the dried fish is washed in water to remove the excess salt and then fried in oil. The fried fish is taken out of the wok and sliced onions and whole red chillies are fried in the oil with tamarind pulp. The fried onions and red chillies are then set aside and cooled. Once this is done, they are ground with the fried fish to make a fish sambal, which the Telugus eat with their dosas or annam. The community even likes to pickle chicken.

They also make certain sweet dishes during religious festivals and on special occasions. Godhuma rava payasam is a sweet wheat pudding or kheer made of broken wheat or godhuma rava. The rava is cooked till it becomes soft and the payasam, thick and creamy. It is garnished with broken pieces of roasted cashew and raisins. It serves as the perfect prasadam for religious festivals like Maha Shivaratri, Vinayaka or Ganesha Chaturthi and Navaratri. Poornam boorelu is a sweet ball made of chana dal (split Bengal gram), jaggery or sugar, grated coconut and cardamom powder. Coated with a batter made of urad dal and rice, it is deep-fried till golden brown and crisp. It is offered as prasadam to Goddess Lakshmi and Goddess Durga.

Although the four communities that represent the all-encompassing term 'South Indian' have developed a strong bond with Calcutta, their diverse cuisines have mostly remained confined within their own boundaries. South Indian cuisine is vast. But, for a long time, the other communities living in Calcutta had eschewed a large part of it. Instead, they developed a fondness for the south Indian tiffin dishes like idli, dosa, vada, utthapam and upma. The dosa, which is a filling tiffin dish, is also treated as main meal. South Indian filter coffee has always had its fair share of admirers. Over the years, certain other south Indian preparations like lemon rice and sambar rice have grown in popularity.

Hyderabadi biryani and Chettinad chicken (a flavourful chicken curry from the Chettinad region of Tamil Nadu) are the two non-vegetarian dishes from south India that are slowly climbing the popularity chart.

Today, Calcutta is dotted with south Indian restaurants that are largely vegetarian. While most of them serve only the popular vegetarian dishes, some have a few extra items featured in their menu cards like alu bonda, pongal (more of the savoury version), bisi bele bath, curd rice, rasam rice, tomato rice, coconut rice, tamarind rice, puttu and kadala curry and puri, chappati and paratha served with masala or kurma. A few of them even serve thali meals. This is simply a platter consisting of a full-fledged south Indian meal that generally features steamed rice, rasam, sambar, a small variety of vegetable preparations, plain yoghurt and a dessert. Poppadoms and pickle accompany these meals. Additional items like vada, puri, chappati, paratha and pachadi can also feature in these platters.

The old boarding and lodging house, Komala Vilas, has also opened its own vegetarian restaurant called Banana Leaf. Along with the popular south Indian dishes, this restaurant also serves other traditional ones like appam, idiyappam, neer dosa and avial. However, these typical and traditional south Indian dishes and thali meals are popular with the south Indian community and not much with the others. In recent times, a very small number of restaurants have come up in Calcutta that have ventured into south Indian cuisine in a big way, serving a variety of both vegetarian and non-vegetarian dishes from all over southern India. The award-winning Tamarind Restaurant, an upscale south Calcutta-based eatery, is a forerunner among them. But in the early days of south Indian settlement, Calcutta was not the hub of such restaurants as it is today. It is a common story among south Indian families that food was once a major problem for the bachelors who began setting up homes in south Calcutta after finding jobs in the city. They had little time to cook at home. Many of them wished that someone would begin a small canteen that might serve south Indian food. This is how Prema Vilas, the first South Indian restaurant in Calcutta, came up at the tail end of the colonial era. It was set up in 1946 by Govindan Muthedath. It began as a canteen business and later flourished into a full-fledged restaurant in south Calcutta. In 1960, he named his restaurant Prema Vilas which means 'the house of love'. South Indians, on their part, have taken a liking to many Bengali dishes after having lived in Calcutta for years. Bengali khichuri is popular among both the vegetarian and non-vegetarian sections of the community. Other dishes like paanch mishali tarkari, shukto, mochar ghanto, alu posto, maachher kalia and kosha mangsho are also popular. In fact, south Indians and Bengalis share a love for the green banana. The green banana kofta curry featured on the Raj Bhavan menu when C. Rajagopalachari from Tamil Nadu served as Governor of West Bengal. Bengali chutneys, which the community takes at the end of meals, and Bengali sweets are also very much liked by the south Indians. The young generation, being experimental with food, is more open to trying out new cuisines, which has helped in developing a growing affinity between the two communities for each other's cuisines. The expanding customer base of Tamarind Restaurant and other south Indian eateries as well as the crowds seen at the south Indian food festivals organized by a few five-star hotels like Taj Bengal, JW Marriott Hotel and Hyatt Regency Kolkata in the recent past bear testimony to this phenomenon.

Marwari

There were two important trading communities that settled in Calcutta in large numbers around this time. The Marwaris and Gujaratis arrived in search of trading opportunities. The cuisines of these trading communities have not made much of an impact on the local culinary culture. Their food habits have remained distinct and exclusive, and have not been able to garner widespread popularity except for a few dishes. Nevertheless, the cuisines of these trading communities have had a significant presence in the city.

The word 'Marwari' is used to describe the people from the Marwar region of Rajasthan. It can be said that the history of the Marwari enterprise in Bengal began with Manikchand. He was the son of Hiranand Sahu, a jeweller by profession who left Nagaur, his hometown in Marwar in 1652, for the prosperous east. He arrived in Patna, which was a major trading hub, and ventured into the moneylending and banking business. He had all the typical traits of Marwaris, who can be called born businessmen and risk-takers, and was hard-working, practical and thrifty. Thus, it is no surprise that he prospered quickly. Gradually, he began sending his sons to other cities in order to expand his business.

One of them was his eldest son Manikchand, who proved to be particularly gifted. He arrived in Dhaka in the later years of the seventeenth century and successfully expanded his family's banking business, and also began financing large-scale trade. His financial clout helped him befriend Murshid Quli Khan who had been appointed as the diwan of the Subah of Bengal by Emperor Aurangzeb in 1700. Soon, Manikchand became his personal banker and trusted economic advisor. When Murshid Quli Khan shifted the diwani office from Dhaka to Muksudabad, his friend Manikchand also shifted the headquarters of his business to this new city. Murshid Quli Khan developed Muksudabad into a flourishing city and Manikchand is believed to have contributed enormous sums of money to its development.

Around 1704, on receiving Emperor Aurangzeb's permission, Murshid Quli Khan rechristened the city after his name as Murshidabad. The decline of the mighty Mughal Empire that followed Aurangzeb's death, witnessed the rise of Murshid Quli Khan in power and influence in Bengal. In 1717, he was made the subahdar of Bengal by Mughal Emperor Muhammad Farrukhsiyar. In the same year, Murshid Quli Khan declared himself the Nawab of Bengal. He made Murshidabad the capital of Bengal and became its first independent nawab. The city became the centre for all activities in the region.

In the early eighteenth century, the prosperity of Murshidabad attracted many Oswal Jains from Rajasthan to the city. In Rajasthan, the community of Oswal Jains trace their roots to Osian, a village in the region of Marwar. In fact, Manickchand was also an Oswal Jain. The Oswal Jains of Rajasthan were very wealthy merchants. While some of them came on the invitation of Manikchand, most came to the thriving city in search of business opportunities. These Oswal Jains made Murshidabad their home by settling near the city in the twin towns of Azimganj and Jiaganj as well as Baluchar—all parts of the district of Murshidabad today. They amassed a lot of wealth as bankers and financiers, and built palatial residences in these places. In Bengal, the Murshidabadi Oswal Jains from Rajasthan came to be known as Sheherwali (city-dwellers) Jains.

Meanwhile, Manikchand had passed away in 1714. Since he had no biological child, his adopted son, Fateh Chand, who was also his nephew, took over the reins of his business and proved to be an even better businessman. He turned out to be an expert in financial matters and an astute banker and trader. Under his leadership, the family business reached new heights and the family became one of the wealthiest in India. Fateh Chand became such a successful banker and financier that he came to be known as 'Jagat Seth' (meaning 'Banker of the World'). The House of Jagat Seth (as the family business was sometimes referred to) functioned as the nawab's treasury and operated much like a centralized bank. In short, Jagat Seth ran the economy for the Nawabs of Bengal.

With the development of Calcutta in the eighteenth century and its metamorphosis into the capital of undivided Bengal, quite a few Oswal Jains settled in the city as bankers and gem merchants. But the Marwari community in Calcutta today does not only comprise the Jains. In fact, the majority of them are Hindus. The earliest place of settlement of the Marwaris in Calcutta was Barabazar and unsurprisingly, over the years, they have converted it into the largest and richest wholesale marketplace of the city. They began their journey in Calcutta in a humble way, rising into prominence and playing a major role in its economy in the years to come.

A handful of them came to Calcutta in the late eighteenth century, and settled in Barabazar. The reason for their migration was the hard living conditions of Rajasthan, which is not only home to magnificient palaces and beautiful forts but also the inhospitable Thar Desert. A large area of its land is covered by the sandy desert and scarcity of rainfall is always a matter of concern. As a result, the major part of the state is dry, parched and arid, where greenery is scarce and shortage of water is a perpetual problem. The dearth of opportunities in Marwar was another important reason why they abandoned their hometown.

A huge, second wave of Marwaris entered Calcutta in the nineteenth century as the city grew in importance in trade and commerce. More and more from the community began settling in Barabazar and began businesses in the sectors of banking, textile and insurance. Being an extremely business-oriented community, within a short span of time, the Marwaris made their mark in the city as bankers and merchants. Later, they ventured into the businesses of jute, hessian, silver, gold, grains, oil, import and export, commission agencies and brokering.

From the middle of the nineteenth century, Barabazar grew as the stronghold of Marwari businessmen. They were responsible for starting the gaddi (literally meaning padded seat) culture in Barabazar, where they worked on mattresses in their offices instead of tables and chairs. The community gradually came to control the crucial inland trade in jute and cotton goods. By the end of the nineteenth century, they had virtually monopolized the banking system in the city.

One of the most prominent members of this community was Ghanshyam Das Birla who went on to become a leading industrialist in the country. Since Bengal was India's largest jute-producing region, he immigrated into Calcutta from Rajasthan and ventured into the jute business. In 1910, he founded Birla Jute Manufacturing Company

Limited (now known as Birla Corporation Limited), and set up several jute mills in Bengal. During the First World War, when the British were facing economic hardship, his business especially flourished and he became the leading raw jute exporter to London. After the war, Calcutta became a battleground between Indian and British business interests. The British formed the Associated Chambers of Commerce of India and Ceylon in 1920, and in retaliation, the Indians formed the Federation of Indian Chambers of Commerce and Industry in 1927, which is today the apex business organization in the country. Ghanshyam Das Birla was the main driving force behind its establishment and also served as its third president.

Over the years, the Marwaris have established themselves as a prosperous business community in Calcutta. They have gifted the city some of its best schools, colleges, hospitals, auditoriums and temples. Though the major section of the community continues to live in Barabazar, some of the more well-off have moved to posh localities like Alipore, Ballygunge and Salt Lake.

Marwaris are largely vegetarians and their cuisine forms an important part of the culinary culture of Calcutta. This cuisine first stepped into the city with the arrival of the Jain and Hindu merchants from the community. While the Marwari Hindus of Calcutta follow a simple vegetarian diet, the Jains adhere to the dietary rules of their religion that transcend simple vegetarianism. In Jain culinary tradition and belief, the principle of ahimsa or non-violence is strictly applied to their diet.

For example, the consumption of root vegetables and tubers or rather, foods grown under the ground like onion, garlic and potato are avoided because of the belief that tiny life forms such as small insects and microorganisms get injured when these vegetables are pulled up from the soil. Moreover, the entire plant gets killed when it is uprooted and the bulb is also a living being as it is able to sprout. Similarly, the consumption of honey is prohibited as its collection amounts to violence against bees. Fermented foods such as wine, beer and other varieties of alcohol are not consumed since a large number of microorganisms get killed during the fermentation process. Some take these dietary principles to a severe extent and avoid eating foods that have been stored overnight like yoghurt because they contain a higher concentration of microorganisms compared to the food that is prepared and eaten on the same day. During certain religious festivals and specific periods of fasting, Jains avoid eating green coloured vegetables as well as fruits because they contain uncountable lives. On these occasions, the Rajasthani Jains eat dried vegetables.

The geographical and climatic conditions of Rajasthan have also dictated the food habits of its people to a large extent. Oil-producing plants are scarce in Rajasthan and cattle are in abundance, which has led to ghee becoming the main medium used in their cooking. The three important crops grown in the state are bajra (pearl millet), wheat and corn. The community uses bajra to make rotis, preferring it to wheat since the latter was not easily available in Rajasthan in the early days. It is only over the last seventy to eighty years that wheat cultivation has increased in the state.

Rice still continues to be scarce in Rajasthan, as the geographical and climatic conditions do not promote the cultivation of paddy. As a result, rice does not feature prominently in Marwari cuisine. Lentil is the main source of protein. The scarcity of water has made this community accustomed to using very little of it in their cooking. This has led to a greater reliance on milk, buttermilk and curd in its place. Digestives like asafoetida, rock salt, ginger and carom seeds are added to preparations to combat the flatulence-producing effect caused by the use of milk and its products. The land did not promote the growth of many vegetables, except for a few ones like potatoes, and it is because of this that fresh green vegetables are not used extensively in Marwari fare. Local berries and beans like ker (a small and sour berry), sangri (a long and thin green bean) and gwar phali (cluster beans) are used liberally in cooking. In fact, ker and sangri are the two most natural and popular produce of the region. While both fresh and dried ker is sold in the markets, sangri is available only in the dried form. On the other hand, gwar phali is generally eaten fresh.

Ker and sangri hold a special place in the hearts of the people of Rajasthan because they saved many lives at the time of the Great Rajputana Famine of 1868. The large bush or shrub on which ker (often referred to as the desert berry) grows is more like a small and evergreen tree that has a thick bunch of thin and light green branches that bear no leaves and has conical thorns. Since these fruits, locally known as ker, are very sour and peppery in taste, they are eaten in the cooked form. The small, tender and immature green fruits are more in demand than the large, hard and mature pink ones because they are tastier and succulent. Ker is either pickled or cooked into tasty vegetable dishes. On the other hand, sangri, the desert bean of Rajasthan, grows on the moderate-sized and evergreen khejri tree that has the ability to survive in the dry, arid and tough desert region. Sangri is pickled, prepared as snacks and cooked into curries. During the famine, when all the scarce natural vegetation of the land had died and disappeared, the ker and sangri were still surviving on their trees. It is widely believed that this is when the famine-stricken villagers first noticed these berries and beans, and used them in cooking. Thus, the unassuming ker and sangri helped them survive the famine and went on to become the two most important ingredients of Rajasthani cooking.

One of the more commonly prepared dishes is ker sangri ki sabzi. This is a combination of the berry and the bean. It is a simple vegetable dish that is made with easily available spices and is eaten with either atte or bajre ki roti. It is so mouth-watering that it has become a fixed part of the menu at every Marwari wedding. Some connoisseurs even add raisins to the cooking to give a sweet touch to the dish. Ker sangri ki sabzi is one of the most popular vegetable dishes in Rajasthan, especially among the Jains, as it does not feature any of their forbidden ingredients like onion and garlic. They also indulge in it on those specific days when the consumption of green coloured vegetables is prohibited.

Dried mango powder or aamchur, as it is called, and curd are often added to the dishes to lend sourness to them, due to the non-availability of vegetables like tomatoes. Gram flour is also a major ingredient in their dishes as chickpeas are grown in abundance in Rajasthan, inducing many food historians and chefs to believe that the gram flour droplet called boondi originated here. The favoured spices are fenugreek seeds, fennel seeds, kasuri methi and nigella seeds. Red chilli is used as well, and lentils, particularly moong dal, are used to make papad (poppadom) and mangodi (vadi in Hindi and bori in Bengali). In fact, moong dal is quite the popular lentil in Rajasthani cuisine and is used in place of the usual urad dal in their preparation of vadas in the dish, dahi vada. Since the Marwari community in Calcutta is largely vegetarian and adheres to the traditional Rajasthani vegetarian diet, this has led to a common misconception that all people from Rajasthan are vegetarians. But this is not necessarily true. Rajasthan has a sizeable number of Muslims and Rajputs who follow a non-vegetarian diet. Calcutta is home to a modest number of Rangrez, the Marwari-speaking, Muslim community of dyers, who function from the Chitpur area. The cuisine of the Rajasthani Muslims includes the range of food that is typical of the culinary culture of the majority of Muslims residing in the country. The Rajputs (warrior class) are meat eaters, and chicken and goat meat are eaten during their meals. During their reign, the Rajput kings and members of the court even ate the spoils of their shikar (hunting), which included the meat of wild boar, deer, camel, rabbit, peacock, pheasant, quail, pigeon and duck. The royalty guarded their recipes closely and spent a lot of time and money preparing exotic dishes. Lal maans, which when translated literally means 'red meat', is a famous dish in Rajasthan, a product of the royal kitchens. It was traditionally made with wild game meat like boar or deer. It is a very hot and spicy meat curry whose preparation involves a lot of red chillies. Thanks to the ban on hunting, this dish is now made with goat meat.

It must have been baffling at first for the Marwaris to move into a city that has an abundance of rice and green vegetables. In spite of this, the community longed for their ker, sangri and gwar phali, the berries and beans they were accustomed to using. This gave rise to a number of Marwari traders in Barabazar, who would travel frequently to Rajasthan to buy the ingredients typical to their cuisine. With the development of the railways, the traders began travelling more frequently and bought ingredients in bulk, making it easier for the Marwaris in Calcutta to continue to cook their local cuisine in an alien land. Every area in which the Marwaris have settled today has a Marwari grocer, who buys commodities in bulk from the traders in Barabazar that still remains the domain of the Marwari community in Calcutta. The Marwaris have made certain adjustments in their cooking style after having lived in Calcutta for years, including using less ghee and relying more on refined oils, using more fresh green vegetables and eating more atte ki roti than bajre ki roti. However, a great deal of the traditional fare is still cooked in the age-old manner.

Dal baati churma is another dish that has become a staple wedding fare. Baatis are balls that are about the size of table tennis balls, and are made with wholewheat flour. They are slightly flattened and then roasted or baked. The baatis are eaten with panchmel dal and churma. As the name suggests, panchmel dal is prepared with five different kinds of lentils. Churma is prepared by coarsely grinding roasted or baked balls of wholewheat flour or simply a few of the cooked baatis, and then frying them in ghee with some cardamom powder, slivered almond and chopped pistachio. The fried churma is taken off the flame, slightly cooled and mixed well with powdered sugar. The fresh warm baatis are soaked in ghee before being served with the dal and churma. Dal baati churma is the perfect winter dish that warms up the body, thanks to the combination of freshly baked crunchy baatis, warm lentils and sweet churma.

In gatte ki sabzi, the gatta is prepared with gram flour. Balls pinched from a gram flour dough are shaped into finger-breadth long cylinders that are put into boiling water, cooked for some time and then cut into small pieces of about half an inch in size. The boiled gatte are then cooked in spicy yoghurt gravy. The preparation is generally garnished with chopped coriander leaves and eaten with roti. This is another dish that is popularly prepared in Rajasthani Jain homes on those days when the consumption of green coloured vegetables is prohibited. They just avoid the use of coriander leaves. On these specific days, the Jains also make a pilaf dish using gatte, which is known by the names of gatte ka pulao, gatte ki khichdi and even Ram khichdi. Papad ki sabzi, a dish of broken pieces of roasted moong dal papads cooked in yoghurt gravy, and papad mangodi ki sabzi, a dish of coarsely crushed and sautéed moong dal mangodis and broken pieces of roasted papads cooked in yoghurt gravy, are the other dishes generally prepared on such occasions by the Jains.

Marwaris make quite a few spicy chutneys which are eaten with paratha and roti. Chutneys made from turmeric and garlic make the perfect accompaniments. Lahsun ki chutney (garlic chutney) is particularly well liked. The community also makes a popular sweet and sour relish using raw mangoes called kachche aam ki launji. It is prepared by cooking peeled and chopped raw mangoes in very little oil with turmeric, red chilli and coriander powders, asafoetida, water, salt and lots of sugar or jaggery. The preparation is tempered with whole spices like fennel, cumin, fenugreek, black mustard and nigella seeds. The Marwaris in Calcutta replace these whole spices in the cooking with paanch phoron. Since their cuisine is spice-dominated, they find the use of this five-spice mix handy. Kachche aam ki launji pairs well with roti, paratha and puri.

Marwari sweets can be stored for a long time and are prepared with easily available and rich ingredients like khoya, ghee and dried fruits to combat the extreme climatic conditions of Rajasthan. Over the years, gur or jaggery, a traditional ingredient in their sweet preparations, have been replaced with sugar. Laddus are an important feature of the sweet culture of this community, and are prepared on most auspicious occasions. Out of these, boondi ke laddu (laddu made with boondi) is the commonly prepared one. Gond ke laddu, another traditional Rajasthani sweet, is commonly prepared during the severe winter that plagues the state. This is because the gond (literally meaning 'gum' in Hindi) used here is the edible acacia gum that generates heat in the body when consumed. While mawa kachori, implying a sweet kachori stuffed with a mixture of mawa and dried fruits, is very popular, mawa gujiya is a festive sweet that is especially made during Holi and Diwali and looks liked fried half-moons. In contrast, the disc-shaped ghevar resembles a honeycomb and is made with refined flour, ghee and sugar syrup. Rajasthani ceremonies are incomplete without this sweet that can be made plain or topped with rabri.

Moong dal ka halwa (also known as moong dal ka sheera) is especially prepared on winter and auspicious occasions like Holi, Diwali and weddings. It is made with rich ingredients like moong dal paste, ghee, milk, water, sugar, cardamom powder, saffron strands, pistachios and almonds. Badam ka halwa or sheera is a dessert that is typically Rajasthani. Badam, over here, means almonds, implying that this sweet halwa is made with the paste of almonds. Considered to be a rich and exotic dish, it is prepared often during winter and popularly served in weddings. In the Rajasthani culture, women are quite often given this halwa to eat after childbirth. Having lived in Calcutta for generations, the Marwaris have taken to rice and different vegetarian pulao preparations with more enthusiasm. The community has developed a liking for the Bengali khichuri and certain vegetarian dishes like labra. Light Bengali dishes like luchi, radhaballabhi, chholar dal, alur dom and begoon bhaja are particularly popular. They thoroughly enjoy the Bengali sweet chutney preparations like the tomato, green mango, date and tomato, and pineapple varieties. Over time, the community has grown to love Bengali chhana-based sweets, especially sandesh and chamcham. They are also fond of rasogolla and are responsible for spreading the word about this sweet and aiding its meteoric rise.

In the colonial times, there were a number of basas in Barabazar that provided boarding and lodging facilities to bachelors and families from the Marwari community. These basas served Rajasthani vegetarian cuisine to their guests. Many of them have shut down, and only a few basas continue to function, like those within the Bangur building which is located at the M.G. Road and Chitpur Road crossing. The basas within the Bangur building began functioning before 1947, and continue to serve Rajasthani vegetarian food. Rajasthan Guest House located on Zakaria Street in the Barabazar area deserves a mention as well. It is another establishment that has been playing host to visitors from Rajasthan for a long time now.

Over the years, a modest number of Rajasthani restaurants have opened in Calcutta in different localities, attracting not only a large Marwari crowd, but also customers from other communities, including Bengalis. Rajwada, housed in the posh hotel, The Sonnet, in the neighbourhood of Salt Lake, is a new entrant. This upscale restaurant has a fair share of customers who are not Marwaris.

Confectionery shops have been established as well by Rajasthani entreprenuers in different parts of the city, particularly in those areas that have a large concentration of Marwaris like Barabazar. The majority of these shops came up in the city after 1947 to cater to the growing Marwari community and most of them still conduct flourishing business. Some among them, have risen above their modest beginnings to become prominent and have several branches spread across the city. The confectionery shop Haldiram's, which has its origin in the city of Bikaner in Rajasthan, is a prime example.

The large Marwari community in Calcutta flock to these shops to buy the traditional sweets of their land. For their commercial interests, the shops not only stock traditional Rajasthani sweets but also sweets from all over north India that also find favour with the Marwaris. However, except for a few ones like boondi ke laddu, the Bengali community does not have much of a liking for most of the Rajasthani confectioneries, which they find to be rich in taste. In contrast, the confectionery shops set up by entrepreneurs from Rajasthan have begun stocking quite a few Bengali confectioneries because they have many takers from the Marwari community. In winter, the nolen gur variety of chhana-based sweets find their way to the racks of these shops because Marwaris are fond of them. On an ending note, it has been interesting to discover that few Bengali confectionery shops have begun stocking a limited variety of Rajasthani sweets. For example, gond ke laddu can now be seen on the racks of Balaram Mullick & Radharaman Mullick.

Gujarati

It is believed that the Gujaratis first began migrating to Bengal during the reign of Nawab Siraj-ud-Daulah. They came as cannon experts in the beginning. However, it was the prospect of business that began to drive them to the royal capital in the early twentieth century. When the community first migrated to Calcutta, they concentrated in Barabazar, Chitpur and Ezra Street. Being a business-oriented community, the Gujaratis began trading in textile, tea, hardware, leather, jute and coal in the city. The community later diversified into manufacturing and there also came a time when the Calcutta Stock Exchange was dominated by the Gujaratis. They shared a common publication with the Parsis called *Navroz*, which was printed in Gujarati. Subsequently, many from the community moved into Bhawanipur in south Calcutta. Today, this area remains the main hub of the Gujaratis in Calcutta.

After Independence, a number of Gujaratis arrived in Calcutta, raising their number to over two lakhs. Over the years, a few Gujarati institutions have come up in the city which act as a binding force to the community like Lakshmi Narayan Temple, the Bhawanipur Education Society College, Shree Calcutta Gujarati Samaj, Shree Bhawanipur Gujarati Stree Mandal, Gujarat Club, Friends Sporting Union and the publishing house Halchal whose magazines are a big success. However, the rapid development of Gujarat in recent times has led to an exodus of many members from the community back to their own state.

Although Gujarat is a coastal state that has an abundance of fish, its inhabitants are largely vegetarians. At first, this might seem paradoxical. But it is important to understand that the main influence on Gujarati cuisine is religious in nature. The region was once a flourishing centre of Jainism and the religious philosophy of Vaishnavism always had a major influence on the community. One of the tenets of the Vaishnava philosophy is abstinence from non-vegetarian food. Many monarchs and members of the royal families of Gujarat were influenced by Jainism and adopted the religion as a way of life, King Vanaraja of the Chavda dynasty and King Kumarapala of the Solanki dynasty being prime examples. During the reign of these kings, vegetarian cuisine became predominant in the region. Those who had converted to Jainism began adhering to the dietary rules of their religion. Today, Gujaratis are largely Hindus and Jains who have maintained the practice of eating a vegetarian diet. There is also a section in the community who are Muslims and they follow a non-vegetarian diet. But the Gujarati community in Calcutta is heavily dominated by Hindus and Jains who shun non-vegetarian food.

When the Gujarati Hindus and Jains began migrating to Calcutta, they found it easy to continue their food habits in this alien city. Gujarati cooking involves the use of simple and easily available ingredients that can be found anywhere in the country. The community was delighted to find the markets of Calcutta selling their favourite spices like asafoetida, fenugreek seeds, mustard seeds, sesame seeds and dried mango powder. The local markets stocked good quantities of gram flour which is used a lot in their cooking. Fresh green vegetables were available in plenty and cereals like rice, wheat and maize were sold in abundance. Other cereals like sorghum, pearl millet and finger millet were already being sold by the Marwari grocers in Barabazar. A majority of Gujarati curries have a sweet and sour taste. The sweetness in the curries is brought about by the use of jaggery or sugar and the sour taste is a product of tamarind or dried kokum. Kokum is a plant native to the Western Ghats region of India. The dried fruit of this tree, which has the same function as tamarind, is a popular ingredient in the western coastal cuisine of the country.

'But why do Gujaratis sweeten their curries?' is perhaps a common question in the minds of most Indians. The reason for this lies in geography. Thanks to the coastline, the drinking water of the state contains a high percentage of salt that does not lend a particularly pleasant taste to curries. To counter this effect, Gujaratis sweeten their curries and also add a souring agent in them to bring about a balance in the preparations. Over the years, this has turned into an established practice and irrespective of where they settle, Gujaratis simply cannot do without their sweet- and sour-flavoured curries. Fortunately, both jaggery and tamarind were available in abundance in the Calcutta markets when they settled here.

Gujarat abounds in the growth of coconut and the Gujaratis use its pulp to flavour many of their dishes. The Calcutta markets sold plenty of coconuts as well as dried fruits that are used in the making of Gujarati sweets. Gujarat is a leading state in the production of peanuts. Unsurprisingly, the Gujaratis are fond of peanuts and use them in many preparations. Peanut oil or shengdana tel is the community's favourite medium of cooking. Both the peanut and the oil were also available in the markets of Calcutta.

Gujarati cuisine offers an extensive variety of farsan (meaning salty snacks). The most popular snack is the dhokla, which is available at many confectionery shops in the city. Dhoklas are small and savoury steamed cakes. The Gujaratis make three varieties of this snack—khaman, safed and khatta. The main ingredient that goes into the batter of khaman dhokla is gram flour while for safed dhokla, the pastes of ground rice and ground urad dal are used. The pastes of ground rice, ground urad dal and ground chana dal are the main ingredients of khatta dhokla. Bengalis have a liking for khaman dhokla, which is served with coriander and tamarind chutneys as dips.

Snacks like khandvi, khakhra, fafda and chorafali have remained confined within the community and have not been able to garner much of a following in the city. Khandvi, for instance, is made with a batter of gram flour, curd and spices, and look like strips, rolled and cut into small pieces. A tempering of mustard and sesame seeds is poured over the khandvis and chopped coriander leaves and grated coconut are finally sprinkled over them before they are served as teatime snacks or starters at parties. Some confectionery shops in Calcutta sell khandvis as well.

Khakhra is a popular teatime snack prepared with wholewheat flour and spices. It is a round, crispy and crunchy roasted flatbread. Traditionally, the Calcutta Gujaratis have made their khakhras at home, but now, many of the supermarkets in Calcutta sell different varieties of readymade khakhras like plain, methi, masala, pudina (mint), jeera (cumin) and garlic khakhra.

The most noticeable feature of Gujarati cuisine is its dryness. Most Gujarati curries are not runny but semi-thick in consistency. This is due to long years of water shortage in the region. The water crisis compelled the Gujaratis to economize in this fashion. Gujaratis team their bread preparations with small portions of rice during meals and mattha (spiced buttermilk) is always drunk at these times. Besides the plain roti, fried paratha and scrumptious puri, Gujaratis have an extensive range of bread preparations which are so tasty that they are often eaten on their own, without any curry dishes as accompaniments.

Thepla is a prime example of such bread preparations. Round breads that are fried in oil, theplas could be made from muli (radish), dudhi (lauki or bottle gourd), mixed vegetables, masala and haldi (turmeric), or be sada (plain). The most popular preparation is the methi thepla, which is made with a dough of wholewheat flour to which spices like turmeric, red chilli powder, sesame seeds and asafoetida, curd, oil, the required quantity of salt and chopped fenugreek leaves are added.

Bhakri is a thick bread preparation that is made with wholewheat flour. They are coarser than rotis and eaten for both breakfast and dinner. For breakfast, bhakri is eaten with home-made curd, pickles, chutneys and cups of steaming tea. For dinner, it is usually eaten with vegetable curries. Dhebra is like a paratha, and can be made with wholewheat, bajra or makai (maize) flour. This flour may be mixed with the pastes of vegetables like radish, beetroot or cauliflower or a combination of them.

Among all the dhebra preparations, dudhi na dhebra is the most popular. Rotla is another popular Gujarati flatbread that is made with jowar, bajra or ragi flour. These are rotis that are baked on a tawa and served with ghee spread on top. It is a common practice among Gujaratis to give their women plenty of rotlas to eat after childbirth because of their nutritious value.

Besides their steamed rice and a variety of pulaos like cumin, peas, onion, coriander, green (cooked with the paste of spinach or coriander leaves) and stuffed vegetables pulao, the Gujaratis have their own version of fried rice known as 'vagharelo bhaat'.

The khatti-meethi dal is an everyday lentil preparation for the Gujaratis. It is prepared with tuvar dal (split pigeon pea), and the inclusion of jaggery and tamarind or dried kokum gives the dish, eaten with steamed rice or roti, a sweet and sour taste. The Gujaratis also have an interesting lentil preparation called dal dhokli. Dal dhokli is garnished with chopped coriander leaves and grated coconut. It is a filling dish and Sunday luncheons in Gujarati homes are usually incomplete without a bowl of steaming dal dhokli accompanied by rice, theplas and pickles. Dal dhokli also happens to be the most preferred preparation for winter picnics.

Undhiyu, a mixed vegetable curry, is the most celebrated dish in Gujarati cuisine. Methi muthiyas (muthiyas are small pakoras) are cooked into this curry. Undhiyu is associated in Gujarati culture with all auspicious occasions. Semi-thick in consistency and generally eaten with steamed rice, puri, paratha or roti, it is a fixed part of the menu on Gujarati New Year and weddings.

Unlike Bengali sweets, whose making is a highly technical process, Gujarati sweets are relatively easy to prepare. It is for this reason that the women of the community often make the sweets at home.

Shrikhand is a sweet delicacy that is prepared by adding lots of sugar to a solid mass of home-made curd from which all the whey has been completely drained. The curd is thoroughly whisked till the sugar dissolves completely. Saffron strands dissolved in milk and cardamom powder are mixed in the curd. The inclusion of saffron gives the dish a yellow colour. The shrikhand is cooled and garnished with slivers of almonds and chopped pistachios before it is served. This sweet delicacy is a fixed part of the menu in Gujarati weddings. In recent times, readymade shrikhand has become available in the market and Bengalis have developed a liking for it.

Basundi, on the other hand, is a creamy and thick sweet milk dessert that is flavoured with cardamom powder and saffron strands. Garnished with slivers of almonds and chopped pistachios, this sweet milk dessert is served cold and eaten on its own or with puris. Mohanthal, a square or diamond-shaped gram flour fudge, is also prepared often in Gujarati homes.

Although a considerable number of Gujaratis have been living in Calcutta for years, the community has not taken much of a liking to Bengali cuisine. The Calcutta Gujaratis are very strict vegetarians. The Bengalis, on the other hand, are hard-core non-vegetarians. They enjoy rice and runny gravies. The dryness of Gujarati cuisine and the sweet and sour flavouring of most of their curries do not suit the Bengali palate. However, that is not to say that they do not appreciate some features of each other's cuisine. The Calcutta Gujaratis, for one, enjoy the light Bengali dishes like luchi, radhaballabhi, koraishutir kochuri, chholar dal, begoon bhaja, alur dom, alur chop and khichuri. They enjoy the taste of mustard oil in Bengali cooking. The Bengali 'jhal muri' is gaining popularity over 'bhel puri' among Gujaratis as well. They are also regular customers at Bengali confectionery shops and buy mishti doi and chhana-based sweets like sandesh and rasogolla.

For their part, there are two dishes from Gujarati cuisine that have caught on with Bengalis: khaman dhokla and shrikhand. Bengalis like eating khaman dhokla as a light snack and their incorrigible sweet tooth gives them a soft spot for shrikhand. Lately, it has been noticed that Bengalis have begun to take a liking to more of their snack items, particularly the fafda, which is a gram flour-based fried snack that looks like a long and thick strip and is served with gram flour chutney, fried green chillies and grated papaya pickle.

There were no Gujarati restaurants or eateries in the city prior to 1947. The community did have a few basas in Barabazar, which offered boarding and lodging facilities to Gujarati immigrants. These basas served homely Gujarati vegetarian meals. Most of these basas have shut down, with only one on Rupchand Roy Street continuing to function. This particular basa serves Gujarati vegetarian meals.

In recent times, few Gujarati restaurants have come up in Calcutta that not only serve Gujarati vegetarian dishes but also a considerable number of vegetarian dishes from Rajasthani cuisine. Both the Marwari and Gujarati communities are regular customers at these restaurants, which also have a small section of customers from the Bengali community visiting them occasionally for a varied experience. Most of these visitors are from the younger generation. Khandani Rajdhani on Park Street, which began its journey in Bombay and has branches spread across the country, is one such restaurant. Famous for its delicious vegetarian thalis, this restaurant also makes it a point to cook food for its Jain customers according to their dietary rules. Lakshmi Narayan Temple has a canteen that serves Gujarati breakfast, lunch and dinner. Shree Calcutta Gujarati Samaj and Gujarat Club also serve Gujarati meals.

However, the number of shops selling Gujarati sweets and farsan have always been on the higher side. Barabazar, one of the early areas of Gujarati settlement, has quite a few of these. Today, one can find shops selling Gujarati sweets and farsan items all over the city. However, the concentration of such shops is much more in south Calcutta, particularly in Bhawanipur, because they cater to the large number of Gujaratis who are mostly based in this part of the city. On the positive side, these shops are witnessing a slow and steady rise in Bengali customers.

Bihari and Oriya

The Biharis and Oriyas are also an integral part of Calcutta. In the nineteenth century, the three states of Bengal, Bihar and Orissa together made up what was called 'Greater Bengal'. The proximity of these states to each other and the absence of geographical barriers encouraged the movement of people among these states and the migration of Biharis and Oriyas to Calcutta became a regular phenomenon.

During this time, the economy of Bihar was not so developed. On the contrary, Calcutta was a growing city and needed labour. This made the Biharis migrate to the city as labourers. Moreover, the abundance of raw jute in Bengal had led to the opening of jute mills, most of which have always been located on the banks of the Hooghly. This industry too needed a lot of labour and a large concentration of Biharis was soon found in Rishra (home to Hastings Jute Mill, the first jute mill in India under the British Raj), Liluah and Bally. The jute mills of Naihati and Murshidabad drew a large number of Bihari immigrants. Also, when the Howrah railway station began service, many Biharis arrived in droves to work as coolies (porters) at the station. They particularly came from the villages to earn a decent livelihood, a good part of which they earmarked for their families back home.

Today, the Biharis are spread all over Calcutta and its neighbouring areas like Howrah and Kamarhati. There are so many Biharis settled in north Howrah that it is known as mini-Bihar. Cossipore (a neighbourhood in north Calcutta) has a fair concentration of Biharis. The Barabazar-Posta area, renowned as central Calcutta's business hub, is also the city's Bihari heartland. The Bihari Muslims are mainly concentrated in the Muslim-dominated areas of the city like Park Circus, Rajabazar, Khidderpore, Metiabruz and Mechua Bazar. The neighbourhood of Kazipara in Barasat (an urban town in the vicinity of Calcutta) also has a large concentration of Bihari Muslims.

Their main intention of coming to Calcutta and the other areas was to earn and not to settle down forever. Income from migration proved to be a very important part of their households, particularly for the poor and those based in rural areas. Also, a part of the money earned would be reserved for buying land back home because the idea was always to go back. But the increase in the crime rate in Bihar and the Naxalite problem in the 1960s that never really came under control (unlike in West Bengal) made many Biharis change their minds about ultimately settling in the state. Years of living and working in Calcutta had earned them many friends and acquaintances. Many of their relatives had also come to Calcutta with the same purpose and settled down in the city for similar reasons. So, family and friends were another reason for ultimately not wanting to move out. Moreover, the current generation of Biharis are very comfortable in Calcutta. They appreciate the tolerant nature of the city and most have no desire to return to their hometowns.

The commercial and cultural interaction between the people of Cuttack (in the Orissa division of the Bengal province) and Calcutta was prevalent from the seventeenth century. But the Oriyas began migrating to Calcutta in large numbers during the colonial period. The economic reason was the main factor for their migration. The desire to earn a better livelihood induced them to come to this industrially developed city. Calcutta Port was a premier port in British India in the nineteenth century with docks in Khidderpore. It was at these docks that a few members of the community initially engaged themselves in the loading and unloading of ship cargo when they first came to Calcutta. These workers, in turn, invited relatives, friends, neighbours and acquaintances from their hometowns in Orissa to join them in their work at the docks. Soon, a settlement grew in the area and today, the largest settlement of Oriyas in Calcutta is in Khidderpore.

They even have a Shree Jagannath Temple in the area which has been built in the style of its namesake in the holy temple city of Puri in Orissa. Shree Jagannath (an avatar of Lord Vishnu), Shri Balabhadra (his brother), Devi Shubhadra (his sister) and the Sudarshana Chakra (his disc-like weapon) are worshipped daily at this temple. This is in keeping with the traditions and rituals observed at the main temple in Puri. The temple at Khidderpore, the most prominent among all the Lord Jagannath temples in Calcutta, is run by a committee consisting of the members of the community settled in Calcutta. In some ways, the inception of this temple began in 1948, when the Oriyas of the locality, particularly those working in the Calcutta Port Trust, decided to start a small communal worship of the venerated deities by keeping their photographs under a neem tree in the spot where the temple is located today. Years later, the photographs were replaced with small statues. In 1969, a small temple was built with limited finances and all its activities were funded by the local Oriya community. Over the years, the temple went through a few changes in its structure. In 1999, armed with enough finance, the temple committee, with the help of a few well-placed members of the community in Calcutta, decided to rebuild the structure. The construction work was completed in 2003 and the temple took the beautiful shape and form as we see it today. And just like the Puri temple, the one in Khidderpore celebrates the Ratha Yatra or the annual ten-day Chariot Festival of Lord Jagannath every year amidst a lot of fanfare.

The large settlement of Oriyas in Khidderpore is followed by the ones in Liluah (a neighbourhood of Howrah) and Titagarh (a neighbouring town of Calcutta) that have a high concentration of members from the community. Some of them even live in Creek Row. Orissa has always been vulnerable to natural calamities like droughts, epidemics, floods and cyclones. One of the worst natural calamities to strike Orissa was the Great Famine of 1866 which caused severe socioeconomic problems for the people. During this time, a good number of Oriyas migrated to Calcutta.

The Bihari migrant population mainly started out as manual labourers in this city. Some of the jobs they engaged themselves in were ferrying loads, pulling rickshaws, pushing carts and working at construction sites and as railway station coolies. Many Biharis have an entrepreneurial spirit in them and will open up small establishments like a paan or grocery shop. The ironing man or the barber of the neighbourhood may just turn out to be an affable Bihari. But, gradually, many people from this community educated themselves and climbed up the social ladder. Today, one can come across many Bihari bureaucrats, doctors, engineers and professors in the city. The relationship between Biharis and Calcutta seems to be a continuous one. With the disappointing economic, political and social scenario of Bihar, more and more people are heading out of the state and into Calcutta.

The Oriyas, initially, were mostly the domestic workers. They were the gardeners and plumbers employed by households in Calcutta. It is believed that during his tenure as the chief executive officer and later as the mayor of the Calcutta Corporation, Subhas Chandra Bose employed many Oriyas to work as plumbers in the corporation building. It is a well-known fact that he was born in Cuttack. Since he grew up in the city and secured a good schooling for himself there, he had an affinity for the people of the region. The Oriyas are such excellent cooks that most households in Calcutta once employed them as chefs. Their magical cooking skills find mention in many novels of the Bengali literary greats. Gradually, the educated class and the intelligentsia of Orissa also came to the city for better opportunities. But the number of Oriyas in Calcutta has never been as many as the Biharis. Today, one can come across Oriya bureaucrats, doctors, engineers and professors in the city. But, unlike Bihar, the economic, political and social scenario in Orissa has improved tremendously over the years. While those Oriyas who have established themselves in Calcutta for generations have remained behind, fresh migration from the state for the purpose of settling down has nearly come to an end.

Even though these two communities have been residing in Calcutta for a long time, their cuisines have not had much of an impact on the culinary culture of the city. This is particularly true for Bihari food, a cuisine that is not difficult to pursue outside Bihar because of the simple ingredients that are required in its cooking. Bihari cuisine shares similarities with both north Indian and east Indian (particularly Bengali) cuisines. It is broadly defined by Bhojpuri and Maithil cuisines. Bhojpuri cuisine is found in the Bhojpuri region of Bihar while the Maithil cuisine originates from the Mithila region of north Bihar. Besides its cuisine, Mithilanchal (the Mithila region) is also famous as the place of origin of Madhubani painting, a renowned form of art.

Bihar is a land of fertile soil and abundant water that encourages the growth of food grains, fruits, vegetables and spices. Nearly 80 per cent of its population is engaged in agricultural pursuits. Rice grows in abundance in the state, making the Biharis predominantly rice eaters.

Traditional Bihari food is incomplete without rice. Raw rice is known as chawal and cooked rice is known as bhaat. Their rotis (flatbreads) are made of wheat (gehu), maize (makai), finger millet (ragi) and sorghum (jowar). A small-grained cereal known as marua (similar to millet) is commonly used for making rotis that turn out chocolate brown in colour. But the preference is always for rice, particularly among the Maithils.

Lord Buddha attained enlightenment under the Bodhi tree in Bodh Gaya in Bihar which has become a major religious and pilgrimage site for Buddhists from all over the world. Buddhism, which propagates vegetarianism, has had a considerable impact on the food habits of the Biharis. The age-old Hindu values which largely concentrate on vegetarianism have also had their influence. The Biharis eat a lot of lentils, vegetables and green leafy vegetables. A typical meal will consist of bhaat or roti, dal (lentil preparation), tarkari (vegetable preparation) and achaar (pickles). Chopped vegetables fried with salt and a few spices are called bhujia. They are a common feature in Bihari thalis, particularly alu bhujia. Spiced buttermilk or mattha often accompanies their daily meals. They also enjoy drinking bel ka sharbat, a drink made from wood apple.

Khichdi, a medley of rice, lentils and vegetables, is given a lot of importance in Bihari cuisine. It is part of the Bihari tradition to eat khichdi once a week and Saturday is the day that is usually reserved for the dish. During winter, Bihari households prepare khichdi quite often. The Biharis have a deep-rooted tradition of worshipping the sun. Makar Sankranti is a Hindu festival which is observed every year in the month of January. It is dedicated to Surya Bhagawan (the sun god). Biharis observe this festival with a lot of devotion and piousness. It is customary for them to eat khichdi on this day.

They enjoy eating vegetable fritters which they call tarua or bachka. These are mostly made with potatoes, aubergines or pointed gourds. The vegetable fritters are served in the evening with tea and can also be eaten as a side dish with cooked rice and lentils.

But that does not mean non-vegetarianism is not prevalent in the region. Fish and goat meat have been part of their cuisine for a long time. The Maithils are especially fond of fish because of the presence of many rivers in their land. Freshwater fish and prawns are eaten. They enjoy indulging in maachh-bhaat (fish curry and rice) often. The Maithils share quite a few similarities with the Bengalis. The Maithili language uses the script, Mithilakshar or Tirhuta, which is quite similar to the Bengali script. Even some of the numbers are quite similar. The most renowned author and poet in Maithili literature was Vidyapati (1352–1448) who was mainly noted for his lyrics of love and devotion. He developed an artificial literary language called Brajabuli which was the Maithili language of the medieval period whose forms had been modified to look like Bengali. His lyrics about Radha and Krishna written in Brajabuli are considered to be some of his best works. This language became established in the sixteenth century. Many medieval Bengali poets were so influenced by it that they wrote in Brajabuli. Vidyapati was one of the favourite poets of Rabindranath Tagore and his works influenced the bard to a great extent. The poet composed his work *Bhanusingha Thakurer Padabali* in Brajabuli. It is a collection of Vaishnava lyrics that was published in 1884.

When it comes to food, the similarities get particularly pronounced. Like the Bengali Brahmins, the Maithil Brahmins are one of those few Hindu Brahmin communities of India who are non-vegetarians. Fish plays a very important role in the Maithil culture just the way it does in the Bengali culture. Some of their customs are also similar. In their weddings, it is customary for the bride's family and the groom's family to send fish to each other. After marriage, when the bride enters the groom's house for the first time, she is asked to cut a fish with the help of a hatu (a traditional cutting tool) to test her ability to handle household duties. The inclusion of chicken and eggs into the diet of the Biharis happened much later with the arrival of the British. Although the younger generation enjoy eating dishes made of chicken, many from the older generation still prefer abstaining from it. The Bhojpuris are fond of vegetables and goat meat, which they prefer to fish and poultry.

Bihari food is generally quite spicy and is defined by the liberal use of spices. Paanch phoran (five-spice mix), garam masala and whole spices feature prominently in their cooking. Even in modern times a lot of importance is given to freshly ground spices. Garlic is generously used. The spice quotient in their non-vegetarian dishes, particularly in chicken and mutton curries, tend to be on the higher side. Since mustard plants are cultivated a lot in Bihar, mustard oil is the traditional medium of cooking. Even today, most Bihari families, including those living outside Bihar, prefer using mustard oil to cook dishes. They are of the opinion that refined oil imparts a sweet taste to the food. Certain green leafy vegetables (saag) and vegetables are also cooked in mustard paste, the most common being kusum saag (safflower leaves) and aubergines. The Maithils particularly enjoy eating fish cooked in mustard paste. The fish generally used for this purpose are carps like rauh (rohu) and bhakur (katla), hilsa and small river fish. Ghee is also a preferred medium of cooking but it is mostly reserved for frying puris and parathas and making desserts.

If there is one ingredient in Bihari cuisine that has become synonymous with its culinary culture, then it has to be sattu. Although there is more to Bihari cuisine than just sattu, the entire country especially associates the food habits of the community with this one ingredient. But it cannot be denied that sattu has been the mainstay of the Bihari farmers for years. It is inexpensive and full of nutrients, making it the ideal food for the poor. Sattu is roasted gram flour. High in protein, fibre, vitamins and minerals, it is believed to be a powerhouse of energy.

Sattu did not remain confined to the food habits of the farmers and the poor of Bihar. It became deeply ingrained in the culinary culture of the Biharis because of its qualities. Having dishes made of sattu is an essential part of their food habits. And it is a habit that they have carried with them to the different parts of the country where they have settled. Today, the qualities of sattu have made it a popular ingredient which has crossed borders and become infused in the food habits of the people belonging to other states.

One of the most common uses of this staple food product of Bihar is to make a sharbat that can be salty or sweet. Although this high energy drink is more like a breakfast food in Bihar, it can be consumed any time during the day. This drink also protects the body from sunstroke.

Sattu is rich in iron, manganese and magnesium and has a small amount of sodium in it. It is also eaten in porridge form. Workers and farmers particularly prefer having sattu porridge as a midday meal because it keeps them full for long periods of time, provides the energy required to work under the direct sunlight and prevents lethargy. The sattu porridge is made with salt, mustard oil, onions and green chillies. It is part of the Bihari culture to feed babies and children with a sweet version of sattu porridge because it is nutritious. The sattu is mixed with water or milk and powdered sugar or jaggery. Fruits like bananas can be mashed and mixed into the sweet porridge. Sattu is also recommended for pregnant women and old people.

Sattu can also be stuffed into puris and parathas. Parathas stuffed with sattu are known as makuni rotis. The stuffing is made of sattu mixed with mustard oil, finely chopped onions, green chillies, ginger and garlic, aamchur, dried red chilli powder, kalonji, ajwain and some salt. The makuni rotis are served with curd, raitas, pickles, chutneys, sauces or butter. Similarly, the Biharis stuff kachoris with sattu. The stuffing is prepared by frying the sattu in mustard oil with some salt and spices.

If the ingredient, sattu, has become synonymous with Bihar's culinary culture, then the dish, litti chokha, can be regarded as the ambassador of its cuisine to the rest of the country. Although this legendary dish is eaten throughout Bihar, it is given greater importance in Bhojpuri cuisine. Balls of wholewheat flour that are stuffed with sattu (mixed with mustard oil, pickle masala, salt, lime juice, grated ginger, minced onions and chopped green chillies and coriander leaves) and baked are called litti. Traditionally, the littis are roasted on dried cow dung or charcoal fire. But, in modern homes, they are baked in the oven, roasted on a pan or a charcoal-based open grill or grilled in a tandoor. A few Biharis even prefer deep-frying the littis. The littis are dipped in ghee before being served with chokha, which is a mash of roasted potatoes, tomatoes and aubergines. Some mustard oil, salt and chopped onions, coriander leaves and green chillies are added to the mash of roasted vegetables and mixed well. Some Biharis also squeeze some lime juice into the mash to give it a sour flavour. Traditionally, chokha is made with all these three roasted vegetables mashed together. But many folks prefer preparing the chokha with any one of these three vegetables.

Like most north Indian communities, the Biharis are also fond of kadhi-badi which is a preparation of gram flour fritters (badi) floating in a spicy yogurt and gram flour curry (kadhi). Usually eaten with rice, the quantity of gram flour in the Bihari kadhi is on the higher side. Dal puri is a traditional dish of puris made of wholewheatflour that are stuffed with a cooked spicy mash of chana dal. The dal puris are most popularly paired with kheer (creamy rice pudding). This combination is offered to the gods as prasad during religious festivals like Diwali and Chhath Puja (the biggest religious festival of the Biharis which is dedicated to the sun god). The dal puris are also eaten with curries, particularly with alu dum curry. The Biharis also make dal pitha, another traditional dish that resembles a stuffed dumpling. The wrapping of the dumpling is made with balls pinched from the dough of rice flour although wholewheat flour can also be used. It is filled with a cooked spicy chana dal paste. The dal pithas are given crescent shapes and are steamed or cooked in boiling water. They are mostly treated as a snack item and served with tea and chutneys. Just like the Gujaratis have dal dhokli in their cuisine, the Biharis have a spicy version of the dish which is known as dal pitthi. While the dhoklis are shaped like diamonds or squares, pitthis are shaped like flowers. They are served with cooked rice, chokha and pickles.

Like the Bengalis, the Biharis also enjoy eating jhal murhi. Chane ki ghugni (chickpeas cooked in mustard oil with salt, spices, chopped onions, tomatoes and coriander leaves and some water) is a favourite dish that can be served with steamed rice, puris, rotis or parathas. It can also be paired with fried chura (beaten rice) and roasted tomato chutney. Chura is a very important part of the Bihari culinary culture and when mixed with milk (doodh-chura) or curd (dahi-chura), it becomes a favourite breakfast dish. Some sugar or jaggery is mixed into the preparation. Some folks may make the preparation more elaborate by mixing chopped fruits (commonly apple or banana is used) and even chopped dried fruits into it. Just like khichdi, it is customary for the Biharis to eat dahi-chura on Makar Sankranti.

Bihar was also under the Mughal rule for a long time and that had a considerable influence on the cuisine of the Bihari Muslims. They have their own distinct cuisine but, at the same time, follow the general Bihari food pattern, particularly the non-vegetarian portions. Bihari kebab, a famous kebab preparation indigenous to the region, is said to originate from the camps of the Afghan and Turkish invaders. These soldiers would roast chunks of meat in an open fire by skewering them to the edges of their swords. What evolved were rustic kebabs, cooked in animal fat, that were simple in taste and had no fancy spices in them. Over the years, this Bihari kebab has upgraded itself and is nothing like the kebab that was made by the Afghans and the Turks. The Biharis have added their touch, transforming it into a delicious preparation that has a soft texture. The kebab is traditionally made with goat meat and it is in the marinade that the uniqueness of this dish lies. The marinade is made of the paste of spices, fried onions, grated raw papaya, mustard oil, curd, poppy seeds, salt and a special Bihari kebab masala. The meat is marinated for an entire day before being grilled. The kebabs are eaten with rotis, parathas and even cooked rice.

Bihari cuisine has an impressive range of desserts that are rich in taste and created from easily available ingredients. Halwas made of semolina (suji), gram flour (besan), wholewheat flour (atta), carrots (gajar), bottle gourd (lauki or dudhi), poppy seeds (posta dana) and water chestnut flour (singhare ka atta) are an integral part of their dessert menu. Chhuare ka halwa (made with dried dates) and ande ka halwa (made with eggs) are enjoyed by the Bihari Muslim community. Kheer made of makhanas is very sought after. Makhanas are fox nuts or lotus seeds and their production is the highest in Bihar. This has made them an important part of Bihar's culinary culture. Biharis use makhanas extensively in their cooking. Makhane ki kheer is made by cooking makhanas (chopped and roasted in ghee) in milk with sugar, dried fruits like almond slivers and raisins, and crushed green cardamoms. This kheer is often made during religious festivals when it is offered to the gods as prasad. It is also eaten a lot while fasting during the Hindu religious festival of Navratri.

Sweets like sattu ke laddu (sweet balls made of sattu, milk, sugar or jaggery and dried fruits) and tilkut (sweet flat discs with upward curving edges made of roasted and coarsely ground white sesame seeds and jaggery) are not only eaten any time as snacks but are also offered to the gods as prasad during worship. Makar Sankranti is incomplete without tilkut. Thekua is considered to be an auspicious sweet in the Bihari culture. It is made during religious festivals like Holi and Teej. It is especially associated with Chhath Puja when it is compulsory for every Bihari household to make the sweet. Wholewheat flour, grated coconut, fennel seeds, green cardamom powder, ghee and melted jaggery are mixed together to make a dough. Balls pinched from this dough are shaped into thick, flat, round discs. Incision marks are made on the discs. They are then deep-fried till golden brown in colour. Thekua is also eaten as a cookie with tea and can be stored in airtight containers for weeks.

Lai are sweet balls of roasted puffed rice (murhi) that have been mixed with melted jaggery. Sometimes, the roasted puffed rice is replaced with roasted beaten rice in the preparation. Lai is made a lot as prasad during Makar Sankranti.

In contrast, Oriya food is defined by less oil and spices and simple ingredients. Yet, connoisseurs feel that it is a cuisine which is filled with flavoursome dishes. It is this very simplicity that lends the dishes a unique taste. Located in eastern India, Orissa (now named Odisha) is surrounded by the states of West Bengal, Jharkhand, Chhattisgarh and Andhra Pradesh. Certain influences from these states can be seen in its cooking and dishes. But, overall, it has a distinct cuisine of its own which is elegant in its simplicity.

Since rice is the main crop grown in the state, the inhabitants of the region are rice eaters. Raw rice is known as chaula and cooked rice is known as bhaata. On a daily basis, their most preferred variety of rice is usuna chaula (parboiled rice). The gobindobhog variety of rice, known as arua chaula, is mainly used in temples. Long-grain rice like the basmati variety, known as basumati arua chaula, is reserved for special occasions and dishes. Kanika, a sweet rice preparation made with the gobindobhog variety, forms an important part of the Chappana Bhoga of Shree Jagannath Temple. Chappana Bhoga comprises fifty-six dishes prepared everyday at the temple in Puri for the three deities and forms a part of the Mahaprasada. Puffed rice (muri) and beaten rice (chura) are eaten often by the community, particularly for breakfast. In some parts of Orissa like the northern cities of Balasore and Baripada, muri and mansa jhola (goat meat gravy) is a popular combination dish eaten for breakfast, lunch and dinner. Chura, which has been soaked in water and mashed with ripe bananas, sugar and a little salt, makes the perfect breakfast dish in many Oriya homes.

Another popular breakfast dish is chakuli pitha, a crepe made of the slightly salted batter of rice flour (preferably of arua chaula) and split black gram or urad dal (known as biri dali). Chakuli pitha is often paired with something sweet like sugar or jaggery or savoury like coconut chutney, fried potatoes or ghuguni (spicy yellow peas curry) for breakfast. Chakuli pitha and goat meat gravy is an extremely popular combination throughout Orissa, served in many celebratory occasions, especially weddings.

There is an abundance of vegetables in the state which are used in dishes. Raw vegetables are known as pariba, the fried ones are called bhaja and the ones cooked into curries are called tarkari. Curries are also called jhola or rasa in Oriya. Green leafy vegetables are known as saaga. Although saaga can be cooked as tarkari, saaga bhaja (stir-fried green leafy vegetables) is the more popular preparation. Fried badi (sun-dried lentil blobs) are added to most saaga preparations in whole or crumbled forms.

Oriyas are largely Hindus and non-vegetarians. Even the Brahmin caste in the community is allowed to eat non-vegetarian food. Traditionally, only widows and priests are supposed to observe a pure vegetarian diet. The Hindu religious tradition excludes ingredients like onion, garlic and masura dali (split red lentil) from a pure vegetarian diet. Following the Vaishnava tradition, the prasad cooked in the Shree Jagannath Temple is purely vegetarian. The restriction on the ingredients to be used in the prasad preparations is much more. Besides onion and garlic, vegetables like potato, tomato, okra, colocasia, cabbage, cauliflower, bottle gourd, ash gourd and drumstick, herbs like coriander leaves and spices like dried red chillies are excluded from the preparations. When it comes to lentils, the only one used in the temple's dishes is harada dali (split pigeon pea). Kosala saaga (red spinach) and leutia saaga (green amaranth leaves) are the only two green leafy vegetables used.

Machcha (fish), mansa (goat meat), kukura mansa (chicken) and anda (egg) dishes feature quite a lot in Oriya cuisine. But among these non-vegetarian food items, Oriyas eat fish the most. This is only natural as the state is filled with many rivers like the Mahanadi, Brahmani and Kathajodi, and even lakes, the most famous being the Chilka Lake. All these rivers and lakes are home to a large variety of fish. Some of the popular varieties of freshwater fish eaten by the Oriyas are carps like rohi, bhakura and mirikali, chitala (clown knifefish), pohala (flathead grey mullet) and mourali (Indian carplet). The eastern part of the state is lined with the beautiful seashore of the Bay of Bengal. This not only makes the people living in the coastal areas but also the rest of the state fond of saltwater fish like pamplet (pomfret) and shellfish like chingudi (prawns), and kankada (crab). Bhekti is also eaten a lot by the community. Oriyas are generally very religious people and a majority of them follow a vegetarian diet on Mondays, Thursdays and Saturdays to show their reverence to different deities. But, on other days, they indulge in non-vegetarian food with great relish.

When it comes to spices, mustard seeds (sorisa or rai) and poppy seeds (posta) are used quite often in their cooking—a similarity they share with the Bengalis. Like the people from Jharkhand and Chhattisgarh, Oriyas too use garlic a lot in their dishes. Garam masala is used liberally and the five-spice mix, which the Oriyas call paanch phutana, is also used often. The latter is a culinary practice which they share with the Bengalis and Biharis. The influence of Andhra Pradesh can be seen in the use of ingredients like tamarind and curry leaves. Coconut meat adorns many of their dishes which is another influence of the neighbouring southern state of Andhra Pradesh. Interestingly, it is part of Shree Jagannath Temple's tradition to add grated coconut to all the bhog preparations while the use of tamarind and curry leaves is prohibited.

A powdered spice that is a constant feature in all Oriya kitchens is the jeera lanka gunda (gunda means powder). It is made by grinding roasted jeera (cumin seeds) and sukhila lanka (dried red chillies) into a fine powder form. This spice is used in flavouring many of their dishes. Another popular flavouring agent is ambula—pieces of raw mango coated basically with salt, and sometimes, even with spices like turmeric or red chilli powder, and sun-dried. Ambula is added to curries to give it a sour and tangy flavour. When the cooking is complete, the flavouring agent is taken out of the gravy.

Although in villages and traditional Oriya homes, rice is a two-time affair, served for both lunch and dinner, the modern generation prefers having the light and easily digestible roti for dinner instead. In contrast, parathas and puris are treats reserved for special occasions, weekends and holidays. Like the rest of eastern India, mustard oil is their traditional medium of cooking and is still preferred over refined oil by most Oriyas. Ghee is also liberally used in cooking dishes and is the preferred medium of cooking in temples.

Oriya cuisine is filled with a variety of dishes and if one has to choose the most unique of them all, then it has to be dalma, a lentil and vegetable dish cooked in ghee or oil. The variety of lentil used in its preparation is usually harada dali or muga dali (split green gram), the former being the popular choice. Vegetables like potato, aubergine, colocasia, green banana, pointed gourd, pumpkin and beans are generally used. Unripe papaya is used only in harada dali dalma and is the main vegetable in its preparation. The combination of lentil and vegetables cooked in less oil and spices makes dalma a nutritious dish that is eaten with rice. Onion and garlic are not used in its cooking. In contrast, tomato and ginger are essentials. The dish can be seasoned simply with coriander leaves or grated coconut can be mixed into it after the cooking is complete. A part of Mahaprabhu Shree Jagannath's Chappana Bhoga, it is widely believed that dalma originated in the Shree Jagannath Temple in Puri. A basic version of the dish was offered as Mahaprasada, which later evolved and is prepared in keeping with the temple's traditions.

If dalma is regarded as one of the special dishes in Oriya cuisine because of its uniqueness, then the very raw and basic dish called pakhala is eulogized by the community for its qualities. Although originally a farmer's food, pakhala has become the most popular summer dish throughout Orissa. Orissa is largely a very warm state with scorching summer months. To beat the heat, almost every household in the state prepares this dish as much as possible. Pakhala is basically a rice dish that is made by adding water to cooked rice. There are two types of pakhala—basi (stale) and saja (fresh). When water is added to cooked rice and the dish is allowed to ferment overnight, it is called basi pakhala. This is eaten more by the farmers. The unfermented version is called saja pakhala. Some salt and lime juice are added to both the versions and mixed well. A third type, known as dahi pakhala, is made by adding dahi to either of the versions. In fact, so revered is this dish in the community that 20 March is observed as Pakhala Dibasa (Pakhala Day) every year. Pakhala is also a part of the Mahaprasada in the Shree Jagannath Temple.

Another summer cooler, which comes close second in popularity to pakhala, is kanji. It is made with torani (pakhala water). Basi pakhala torani is used in its preparation and it is fermented for a few days. At first, the torani is boiled with some arua chaula powder, turmeric and salt. Spices like paanch phutana, grated garlic, curry leaves and broken dried red chillies are fried and the torani is added to this tempering. This summer cooler is popularly eaten with rice or can be just drunk plain.

Although khichdi, known as khechudi in Oriya, is eaten throughout the year, it is also a dish that is reserved for the vegetarian days, particularly Thursday, a day dedicated to Goddess Lakshmi. Pampad (poppadom), pickle, curd, raita, dalma, baigana or alu poda (roasted and spicy mash of aubergine or potato) and dhania patra chatani (coriander leaves chutney) are popular accompaniments. Variations are often made to this plain rice and lentil dish that is cooked with spices in ghee. When vegetables are added, it becomes pariba khechudi. The addition of ginger and asafoetida to the dish converts it into adahengu khechudi. A sweetened version, which features dried fruits like cashew nuts and raisins, and sometimes even grated coconut, is also popular in Oriya homes and is called meetha khechudi. In Orissa, khechudi is offered as bhog to Lord Shiva during Maha Shivaratri in temples and homes observing this festival. It is also prepared as prasad during the auspicious occasion of Kartik Purnima (full moon day in the month of Kartik). Most importantly, it is a part of the Mahaprasada at the Shree Jagannath Temple.

Oriya cuisine has quite a variety of non-vegetarian dishes in its repertoire. Fish, eggs, chicken and goat meat are cooked into spicy and delicious curries. The fish preparations stand out the most. Dahi machcha is a popular curd-based fish curry, usually made with rohi or bhakura. Chingudi jhola and kankada jhola are delicacies relished by the community. Oriyas share a liking for fish heads with the Bengalis. The heads of rohi or bhakura are used in the preparation of machcha munda chenchda, also known as machcha munda ghanta. While big fish like rohi or bhakura are used to make machcha chudchuda, small fish like mourali are used to make machcha chadchadi. The former is a thick spicy gravy dish made with deboned fish meat and the latter is a thick mustard paste-based gravy dish consisting of small whole fish. Machcha chadchadi is more popular with the villagers of Orissa because it goes well with pakhala. Besara and mahura are two dishes that can be cooked with both vegetables and fish. Besara is a mustard paste-based gravy dish. Onion, garlic and dried red chillies can be used liberally in the machcha besara preparation. In the machcha mahura preparation, deboned fish meat is cooked with a variety of chopped vegetables, black chickpeas and spices.

And then there are the sweets—some of them renowned not just in Orissa but throughout the country. Chhena poda, literally meaning burnt casein, is one such sweet. Sudarshan Sahu, a confectioner from the town of Nayagarh, shot to fame when he invented this sweet in the twentieth century. Little did he know then that his invention would not only become the most sought-after sweet in Orissa but its fame would also cross the borders of the state. Today, chhena poda is available in all of the confectionery shops across Orissa throughout the year. It is also commonly available during religious festivals, particularly Durga Puja and Diwali. The sweet is made with chhena, semolina, green cardamom powder, ghee and sugar. The ingredients are kneaded well with chhena water (whey). Dried fruits like cashews, almonds and raisins can be mixed into it. The kneaded chhena is baked into a brown round. The edge of the baked sweet is dark brown in colour and crisp while the inner part is soft and lighter in colour. The sweet is cut into slices and served. Chhena poda is also commonly served during celebratory occasions like weddings.

The Oriyas share a great love for the rasagola with the Bengalis. In fact, so much is their love for this spongy and syrupy, round chhena sweet that it has led to a prolonged battle between the two about who invented it first. Kheeri, khaja and gaja are not only relished by the community for their delicious flavours but are also sweets that have religious uses. Chaula kheeri or creamy rice pudding is a part of Lord Jagannath's Chappana Bhoga.

Khaja and gaja have become synonymous with Shree Jagannath Temple. It is a tradition in the temple to serve these two sweets as prasad. Mahaprabhu Shree Jagannath's Mahaprasada is divided into sankudi bhoga and sukhila bhoga. Sankudi bhoga includes rice, lentil and vegetable prasad preparations while sukhila bhoga includes dry prasad varieties. Khaja is a part of the sukhila bhoga that is offered to the residing deities in the temple. Since it is dry and remains fresh for a few days, it is convenient for the devotees (both locals and tourists) to carry it back home for their family members and friends. Besides its delicious taste, this factor also accounts for its popularity as a prasad at the temple.

Gaja is a deep-fried sweet shaped into a cube. There are different types of gaja and the most popular varieties are chhena gaja (made with casein and semolina), khasta gaja (made with refined flour) and khira gaja (made with mawa and refined flour). Khasta gaja shaped into small sticks becomes kathi gaja.The gaja offered as prasad in Shree Jagannath Temple is made with biri dali and known as pheni. Pheni is also a part of the sukhila bhoga. Once they are fried, gajas are soaked in sugar syrup for a long time. Although the sweet is served dry, the sugar crystals remain on its surface.

Oriya cuisine, with the exception of the savoury chakuli pitha, has a wide range of sweet pithas in its repertoire—a similarity it shares with Bengali cuisine. Some of the popular varieties are poda, enduri, manda, arisa and kakara pithas. Rice flour is the most commonly used ingredient in the preparation of pithas followed by split black gram and semolina.

Just like the Biharis, the Oriyas were able to continue with their culinary culture upon relocation. Ingredients were easy to find and they had settled among people with almost similar food habits. Calcutta roadsides had vendors selling their favourtie snack, jhal muri, which reminded them of home. Their favourite gupchup was made in a similar fashion in Calcutta. Only the name had changed to phuchka (the Bengali word for 'panipuri'). And just like its namesake in Puri, the Shree Jagannath Temple in Khidderpore has always been makeing bhoga for the deities following all the rules and traditions. In the early days, before the construction of the present temple, fruits would be distributed as prasad to the devotees. Today, the Mahaprasada made daily at this temple is not as vast as that made in the main temple in Puri. Chappana Bhoga is reserved for only once a year, during Kartik Purnima, and on the rest of the days, a select range of Mahaprasada, consisting of both sankudi and sukhila bhoga, is offered to the deities at the temple. Shree Jagannath Temple in Khidderpore organized its first Ratha Yatra in 1989. In the early days, the celebration would take place on a small scale. Since the beginning of its Ratha Yatra celebration, the temple has been making poda pitha and chhena poda as part of the bhoga for the deities on this auspicious occasion.

Years of living in Calcutta have made both the Biharis and Oriyas accustomed to Bengali cuisine. They share quite a few similarities in their culinary practices and food habits and preferences with the Bengalis. Their affinity for non-vegetarian food, particularly fish, has helped to foster a greater bond. Whether it is savoury dishes or confectioneries, Bengali food is eaten with great relish. In fact, so much is their liking for this cuisine that the authorities at the Shree Jagannath Temple in Khidderpore have made a slight deviation and included the Bengali dish, radhaballabhi, as one of their prasad preparations. For the devotees, especially the Bengalis, who want to partake of the Mahaprasada, baigani (as aubergine fritter is called in Oriya) is listed as begooni for their easy understanding.

As for the local Bengalis, their affinity for Oriya cuisine is much more because of its similarity with Bengali cuisine. This has prompted a few entrepreneurs to open restaurants in the city that specialize in Oriya cuisine, which have become fairly successful. A prominent example is Dalma, which is located in Sector V, the IT hub of the city. Since its inception in 2001 in the bustling office para or neighbourhood, this restaurant has seen a regular flow of both Oriya and Bengali customers. However, not all of its customers are office workers from the area. On any given day, Dalma also has its fair share of food enthusiasts who arrive at the restaurant from different corners of the city to try out the scrumptious delicacies from the land that is home to the Konark Sun Temple, an architectural marvel of this country. Although there are no Oriya confectionery shops in Calcutta, some of their dessert preparations are served in these restaurants, which are popular with the Bengalis, especially chhena poda.

However, when it comes to making a mark in Calcutta, Bihari cuisine has not met with much success. For a long time, the spread of this cuisine was restricted to the sattu drink and litti chokha stalls and kiosks scattered across the city, particularly in those areas where there is a higher concentration of Biharis. However, in recent times, a few restaurants have come up in the city that specialize in north Indian cuisine but are also committed to serving some Bihari dishes, the primary focus being on the quintessential Bihari dish, litti chokha. A majority of these restaurants are based in the posh localities of Calcutta.

A look at some of their names will reveal why the humble dish 'litti chokha' is regarded as the ambassador of Bihari cuisine to the world. While the takeaway joint, Litti King, serves an innovative variety of littis like tandoori litti, achari litti, paneer litti, cheese litti, corn litti and even ghugni litti chaat, Litti Express, which is perhaps one of the first few restaurants that introduced this cuisine to the city, serves the highly innovative and exotic 'mutton keema litti sizzler'. Some of the other Bihari specialties available in the restaurant are 'sattu paratha', 'makhana kheer' and 'sattu cooler', the last referring to the salted version of the sattu drink spiced with cumin powder, black salt and mint.

Litti Inbox, with multiple branches in the city, takes the innovativeness a step further and stuffs its littis with sautéed mushrooms or a mixture of sattu and dried fruits. While it makes an innovative fusion version called 'burger litti', a dessert version that is overloaded with chocolate also has its fair share of takers. And a closer look at the description below the item 'Indian Cookie' listed in its menu card reveals that it is actually the thekua. But when it comes to creativity with the litti chokha, shot glasses filled with vodka-infused pear salsa and topped with baked littis, take the crown. Hakuna Matata, a one-of-a-kind restaurant famous for its fusion dishes, is the proud owner of this unique creation, which it has christened 'Litti-Chokha Shots'.

Although there are no Bihari confectionery shops in Calcutta, lai is sold by a few snack shops, again in those areas with a large concentration of Biharis. But, overall, both the cuisines are still to gain favour with the majority.

Sindhi

Finally, when writing about the different communities of Calcutta and their food habits, it will be a mistake to leave out the Sindhis, a community which has contributed much to the economic growth of the city, though, most of it happened after the Partition of India. The Sindhis are originally from the Sindh province of Pakistan. The region was named after the Indus river, which is also known as Sindhu. There is a tribe called Baloch who live in the Sindh province. The Balochs originally migrated from Balochistan to the Sindh province, and assimilated themselves with the Sindhis. The extremely cold climate of Balochistan and the difficult living conditions during winter were the reasons behind their immigration. The Baloch Sindhis speak the Sindhi language as their mother tongue now.

From the middle of the eighth century, large parts of Sindh and Balochistan fell within the dominion of the Arab Caliphs. Islamic invasions of northwestern India began taking place from the twelfth century. These factors led to a great Islamic influence on the region.

Sindhis can be Muslims, Hindus or even Sikhs. Most Sindhis in India are Hindus, and there is a prominent minority of Sindhi Sikhs living in the country as well. The Sindhi Hindu community in India consider themselves 'Nanakpanthis' who follow the teachings of Guru Nanak. Some of the Sindhi Hindus were so influenced by his teachings that they went to the extent of adopting Sikhism as a religion.

The Sindhis also have a community god or Ishta Devata (most revered god) whom they call Jhulelal, Dariyalal or Zinda Pir (meaning 'Living Saint'). He is believed to have lived in the tenth century. Both the Hindu and Muslim sections of the community worship this god. Thus, we see that this community shows a wonderful blend of many religions and cultures. Even the Sindhi language used in India is a Sanskrit-based one with many Arabic and Urdu words thrown in. Their script can be either Sindhi-Arabic or Devanagiri. It is not uncommon to come across words that are common to both the Arabic and Sindhi dialect like 'bedo', which is the word for egg.

The Sindhis distribute misri (crystallized sugar lumps) as a token of bonding during betrothal and marriage. This ritual and the word itself can be traced to ancient links with the Arabs. There are two main festivals that the community celebrates annually. One of them is Cheti Chand, which is not only the Sindhi New Year but also the day when Sindhis celebrate the birthday of Jhulelal, and the other is the birthday of Guru Nanak, which is observed in November.

The Sindhis come from a region that is bound by the Thar Desert on the east and the richly irrigated valley of the Indus in the centre. The community can be divided into three groups—the Amils, who have descended from the tribe of ironworkers called Lohanas, the Bhaibands who are the baniyas or merchants, and the Shikarpuris, who are an in-between group. The Amils became an educated class and served as revenue officials for the Mughals and then for the British. They formed the educated middle class, though some of them ventured into business during the time of Partition when jobs became scarce and educations remained incomplete. The Bhaibands traded along the Silk Route, travelling on camels and in dhows. In modern times, they have traded in goods that have scarcity value like transistor radios, television sets, calculators and computers. The Shikarpuris are from north Sindh and are traders too. They have also entered middle class professions now.

The earliest Sindhi settlers in Calcutta arrived in the late nineteenth century. It is believed that before the Partition in 1947, there were roughly ten Sindhi families settled in Calcutta. The community was largely involved in trade and was very well travelled. They set up a network of shops and traded in silk and jewellery. The renowned Park Street jewellers, Satramdas Dhalamal, was among the early settlers and founded their company in 1880. One of the first from the community to set up a jewellery shop in Sir Stuart Hogg Market was B. Motiram. There were also silk merchants whose descendants are still running the business and own some of the large old shops in Sir Stuart Hogg Market.

Sindhis arrived in large numbers in Calcutta during Partition. At first, they stayed with relatives, friends or other people they had connections with. The fresh arrivals were always on the lookout to start over on their own, and gradually acquired or created new means of employment. Most of the Sindhi Bhaiband traders set up shops in the Sir Stuart Hogg Market area and lived very close to their places of work. Some of the oldest and biggest shops selling saris, jewellery and watches in the area belong to Sindhis. The bulk of the community still lives in central Calcutta, while the more affluent among them have moved to south Calcutta. Being mainly in the retail business, a large part of the community has moved out of the city to Dubai and Hong Kong, where they have set up successful retail stores. Today, there are about 15,000 Sindhis in Calcutta, a stark contrast to the ten families which had settled in the city prior to Partition.

There are four major influences on Sindhi cuisine—Persian cooking, the proximity of the sea and river, the climatic conditions of the region and the cooking styles of the neighbouring states of Punjab and Gujarat. Since Sindh was controlled by Muslim rulers for long, meat plays an important role in the fare of this region. The food of the Balochs, who are of Iranian descent, has also played a significant role in influencing the culinary culture of the Sindhis. Sindhi Muslims do not eat pork and strictly observe the dietary guidelines of halal. Beef, goat meat, chicken, fish, vegetables, lentils, fruits and dairy products are consumed by the Sindhi Muslims. The Sindhi Hindus eat similar foods, except that they eschew beef. Pork does not feature in the cuisine of the Sindhi Hindus as they come from a region where there is a religious ban on the consumption of pork. The Sindhi Hindus savour goat meat more than poultry and enjoy eating biryanis and kebabs. Additives like saffron and rose water and rich dried fruits like almonds, walnuts, raisins, pistachios and dates, used liberally in Persian cooking, add a touch of luxury to some of the main course dishes and sweet dishes in Sindhi cuisine.

Sindh is bordered by the Arabian Sea to the south. This proximity has allowed the community to indulge in saltwater fish like surmai and pomfret and shellfish like lobster. The proximity of the region to the Indus ensured a fertile land, one that produces vegetables like potatoes, onions, tomatoes and okra. The proximity to the river also provided the inhabitants of the region with abundant freshwater fish like hilsa, which the Sindhis call palla or pallo. Sindh is inundated by the Indus river in the summer months, which helps to irrigate the rich alluvial soil and promotes the growth of paddy. The climatic conditions of Sindh also favour the cultivation of wheat during the winter. This makes the Sindhis both rice and wheat eaters.

Lotus grows in abundance in Sindh thanks to the numerous ponds. This has led to the crunchy, fibrous and nutty flavoured lotus stem (bhee) becoming an indelible feature of Sindhi cooking. The proximity of the region to Punjab in the north and to Gujarat in the east has led to some influences from those quarters as well. The Sindhis use souring agents like dried mango powder and dried pomegranate seed powder, just as the Punjabis do, as well as the souring agents, tamarind and dried kokum, in the manner of the Gujaratis. They enjoy eating plain and stuffed parathas, an adaptation of Punjabi cuisine.

When the Sindhi Hindus migrated to Calcutta during Partition, they carried their food habits with them. The few Sindhi families who had been settled in Calcutta before also made the cuisine typical to their native land. Sindhi cuisine is a simple one, prepared with easily available ingredients. Most of the cereals, pulses, vegetables, spices and herbs that are used in the cooking have long been available in the city. Even the lotus stem began to be sold in a few vegetable shops in Sir Stuart Hogg Market. The easy availability of ingredients made the Sindhi community in Calcutta continue cooking their home cuisine with ease.

The Sindhis eat their food spicy and enjoy phulko (roti) as much as rice. They have an extensive variety of bread preparations besides phulko. Dodo, for instance, is a kind of roti made by the community. These are made either with bajri (pearl millet) or juar (sorghum). The dodos are not rolled out into round shapes with a rolling pin, but with the palms instead. They are baked on a tawa and served with ghee spread on top. There is another method by which the Sindhis make bajri jo dodo. They spice up the dough by adding chopped garlic, green chillies and coriander leaves and salt. The bajri jo dodo made using this method is not baked but fried in ghee, which is the main medium of cooking of the Sindhis, and eaten hot with home-made curd, making it a nutritious breakfast.

Juar jo dodos are generally not spiced and made plain. Satpuro phulko is a flaky layered paratha that is eaten with cooked lentils, curries or simply with curd. As the name suggests, this paratha has seven layers. Dal jo phulko is a paratha that is stuffed with moong dal. This stuffed paratha is usually eaten with curd or pickle, although it goes best with boondi jo matho (boondi raita).

The dough of koki, another bread preparation, is made of wholewheat flour to which some ghee, salt and black pepper powder have been added. Kokis are thick and round breads that are fried in ghee. The Sindhis eat them with cooked lentils, vegetables or other gravy preparations. The most popular combination of koki is with chai (tea) and koki-chai is a popular breakfast spread in Sindhi families. Another popular breakfast dish is the loli, which is made with a dough of wholewheat flour to which chopped onions, green chillies and coriander leaves, carom seeds, ghee and salt are added. Lolis are round and fried in ghee. They are consumed with home-made curd to which some salt and black pepper powder are added. Kokis and lolis have long shelf lives and were carried by Sindhi traders on long journeys along the Silk Route.

Lolo is the sweet version of the loli. It is also known as meetho lolo. Here, the wholewheat flour is kneaded with sugar syrup, ghee and crushed green cardamom into a hard dough. Although lolos are generally baked, some Sindhis prefer frying this sweet bread. Lolos are eaten during the Satai or Satam festival, which is also known as Thadri, when Shitala Mata is worshipped. Thadri is derived from the words 'thadi' or 'thado', which mean 'cold' in the Sindhi language. According to the Thadri rituals, the stove cannot be lit and food cannot be cooked on the day of the festival. As a result, the food is cooked the previous day and eaten cold on the day of the festival.

The Sindhis make a very popular breakfast dish called dal pakwan, which is quite heavy and filling. Pakwan is a crisp flatbread made of wholewheat flour that is fried in ghee. It is eaten with dal or lentil which is cooked, churned and sprinkled with ghee and spices like aamchur, coriander, cumin and red chilli powders, and crushed whole garam masala. The lentil used to make the dal is either chana dal or moong dal.

Seyun patata, a sweet and savoury dish, is also eaten for breakfast. It is prepared by heating ghee in a wok, to which crushed green cardamoms are added and sautéed. The seyun (vermicelli) is thrown into the cooking and fried till it takes on a reddish hue. Some water and sugar are added at this juncture. The vermicelli is cooked till it becomes absolutely dry and golden brown in colour. This sweet vermicelli is eaten with fried chunks of patatas (potatoes). Some spices are sprinkled over the fried potatoes, including aamchur, coriander powder, cumin powder, red chilli powder and some salt.

While onions and tomatoes are used extensively by the Sindhis to flavour their curries, the community makes a lot of dishes out of lotus stem and okra which are perhaps their most commonly used vegetables. Bhee basar and seyal bhee patata are two of the most popular lotus dishes. Bhee basar is lotus stem cooked in onions. In this preparation, chopped onions are sautéed in ghee to which some chopped bhee is added. Chopped tomatoes, ginger, garlic and green chillies and spices like turmeric, coriander and red chilli are added to the dish, which is seasoned with salt and garam masala. The dish is garnished with coriander leaves and eaten with rice or phulko. It is interesting to note that the Sindhis do not eat steamed rice plain. Instead, they always boil the rice grains with a little salt and then add melted ghee to the cooked rice after draining the water. The dish, seyal bhee patata, in contrast, is eaten with phulko and as its name suggests, features bhee and patata. 'Seyal' refers to a method of cooking food with very little water or no water at all. This means that seyal dishes have a semi-dry or dry consistency. Thick and round slices of lotus stem and potato are cooked in ghee with onion paste, chopped tomatoes, spices and very little water.

Sai bhaji is a healthy dish made from spinach, lentil and seasonal vegetables. 'Sai' means 'green' in Sindhi and in this dish, the word refers to the colour of the spinach. The lentil used here is chana dal. Vegetables like carrots, aubergines and potatoes can be used. The spinach, lentil and vegetables are cooked in ghee with onions, tomatoes and spices. Very little water is used in the cooking. When the lentil becomes soft, the vessel is taken off the fire and salt and tamarind water are added. The whole mixture is churned till the consistency becomes smooth. A tempering of garlic paste that has been sautéed in ghee is added to the churned sai bhaji and mixed into it. Sai bhaji is a dish which is exclusive to the Sindhis and very popular with the community. It is always served either with steamed rice or pulaos, fried papad (poppadom), fried potatoes and plain yoghurt.

Although the Sindhis are happy with their simple and non-fussy vegetarian dishes, they also cook a lot of meat and fish preparations.

Foto bhuno gosht is an exquisite mutton chop dish that is made with lots of green cardamoms. No onions or garlic are used in its making. This deliciously juicy and tender mutton dish is a delicacy in the community. It is eaten with phulko.

The Sindhis share their love for the hilsa with the Bengalis. Dishes made of pallo are served as delicacies on most celebratory occasions. But pallo is not just a favourite fish of the community. It is iconic to such an extent that it is regarded as the vehicle of Jhulelal. The Zinda Pir sits on a large pink lotus that is perched atop the pallo and comes riding on it. Sindhis cook the pallo in many ways and the popular dish seyal pallo is one of them. Seyal pallo is a dry preparation in which pieces of the fish are cleaned and marinated with salt for at least two hours. Onions, tomatoes, green chillies, ginger and garlic are chopped and spices like turmeric, coriander, cumin and red chilli are added to them. These are then mixed well. After the marination, the fish pieces are washed to remove the excess salt and coated with this mixture. The coated fish pieces are arranged inside a pot and ghee is poured over them. The pot is covered with a lid while the fish pieces are being cooked. No water is used in the cooking and the little soupiness that remains is the result of the juices of the cooked onions and tomatoes, as well as the oil that is released by the fish. Seyal pallo tastes delicious when eaten with dodo, phulko or steamed rice.

Like every other community, the Sindhis also have their exclusive collection of sweets. Milk, ghee, sugar, khoya, flour, poppy seeds, green cardamom, dried fruits and saffron are some of the commonly used ingredients in their sweet preparations that tend to be rich in taste. A popular Sindhi winter sweet is the golden brown and square-shaped majoon that is prepared with milk, sugar, ghee, mawa, green cardamom, poppy seeds, grated dried coconut (copra), coarsely ground dried dates (chhuara), and chopped dried fruits like almonds, pistachios, walnuts, cashews and raisins. The richness of this soft fudge-like sweet makes it perfect for consumption during the cold winter months.

Khorak, another rich fudge-like sweet, is also popular during winter. It is made with lots of ghee and other ingredients like wholewheat flour, gond, green cardamom, poppy seeds, sugar and dried fruits like almonds, cashews and raisins. Golden brown in colour, it is shaped into a square or a diamond. Khorak is also a popular wedding sweet that is presented to the bride and groom by their relatives. Instead of buying sweets from confectionery shops, Sindhis prefer making khorak and gifting it to the newly-weds.

Tosha, on the other hand, is a golden brown sweet that is shaped like an oblong cylinder. Balls pinched from a dough of refined flour are given the shape of the sweet and deep-fried in ghee. Sugar syrup is prepared and the toshas are soaked in it while the syrup is still on the flame. After some time, the sugar syrup is taken off the heat but the toshas are allowed to remain in it for some time to soak up the sweetness. Tosha is traditionally a Punjabi sweet but it has been adapted to Sindhi cuisine.

Tehri is a sweet rice preparation that is made on auspicious occasions and festive days. It is especially made during Cheti Chand when it is distributed as prasad. It is prepared by sautéing rice in ghee with a few green cardamoms. Some water and a very small quantity of salt is added to the cooking. When the rice is half-cooked, sugar is added to the preparation along with chopped dried fruits like almonds, cashews and raisins and some saffron. The pot in which the tehri is being cooked is covered with a lid and the mixture simmers on the lowest flame. Tehri is ready when all the water from the sugar is absorbed and the rice is soft and fluffy. The Sindhi Hindus, being Nanakpanthis, also make a sweet wholewheat halwa (atte ka halwa) like the Punjabis which they call kanha prasad on Guru Nanak's birthday.

The Sindhis of Calcutta have not developed much of an affinity for Bengali cuisine. The majority of the Bengalis in Calcutta still cook their food in mustard oil, but the Sindhis do not relish the taste at all. Bengalis also season some of their curries with sugar, which goes against the spice-loving Sindhi's palate. There are only a few savoury dishes from Bengali cuisine that the Sindhis have developed an affinity for, such as luchi, radhaballabhi, koraishutir kochuri, alur dom and begoon bhaja. The sweet chutneys which are served at the end of Bengali meals are relished by the Sindhis. They also enjoy Bengali chhana-based sweets, particularly rasogolla.

The Bengalis, on the other hand, are not very well aware of Sindhi cuisine. The Sindhi community in Calcutta is small and close-knit. The absence of social interactions between the Bengalis and the Sindhis is a big factor that has contributed to the lack of awareness. Another important reason for this ignorance is the absence of Sindhi eateries in the city. A small Sindhi eatery had opened on Sudder Street, close to Sir Stuart Hogg Market, after 1947 to cater to the Sindhi community. Two Sindhi confectionery shops were also set up in the vicinity of the market. Both these shops sold dal pakwan for breakfast and the Sindhi alu ki tikki (potato patty) alongside typical Sindhi sweets. But these confectionery shops and the small eatery closed down a long time ago.

In recent times, food enthusiasts, writers and bloggers have stumbled upon Kandoi Sweets and Snacks, which is actually quite an old shop located on Canning Street in the Barabazar area. Since most of the early settlers of Calcutta made Barabazar their home, the area continues to be the hub of people from different cultures. Unsurprisingly, quite a number of modest shops in the area sell an interesting variety of sweets, snacks and savouries, particularly from north India and Gujarat. One such shop is Kandoi Sweets and Snacks, which also may be the only one in the city that has been selling dal pakwan for some time now. However, this lone attempt has failed to make any impact.

On an ending note, it can be said that although their cuisines might not have made much of an impact on the culinary culture of Calcutta, it cannot be denied that each of these seven communities have contributed a lot to its cosmopolitan nature and structure. Their presence and growth as communities have added a lot of value to the social and economic fabric of the city. Even their diverse food habits have added a touch of vibrancy to Calcutta's culinary culture. Having been an indelible part of the city for centuries now, their bonding with it is one of permanence. Their relationship with its people is one of mutual acceptance, trust, dependability and harmonious coexistence. And as an author of a book on culinary history, I consider it to be a positive trend that the cuisines of these communities are slowly and steadily gaining appreciation.

2. Influences of Darjeeling District Cuisine

Until now this book has elaborated on the influences on the culinary culture of Calcutta that took place prior to India winning her independence. However, there have been other influences that took place after the country won its freedom and it will be an error to leave those out. The movement of immigrants from Darjeeling into Calcutta post-Independence greatly influenced the city's culinary culture and habits. Against this backdrop, it becomes essential to explore this cuisine and its effect on the culinary scene of the city so far.

The Darjeeling district is in the northernmost part of West Bengal. It is located at the foothills of the Himalayas and is famous for its hill stations. The district comprises the major towns of Siliguri, Darjeeling, Kurseong, Mirik and Kalimpong. The official language of the district is

Bengali. The town of Darjeeling, renowned as 'The Queen of Hills', is its headquarters. The earliest records of the town date back to the early nineteenth century when the British colonial administration set up a sanatorium for the ailing British troops and a military outpost there. But the cool climate of the entire region also made the British consider it a wonderful place to settle in as well as make a quick getaway from the heat and humidity of the plains. Gradually, as the colonialists began settling down, many English medium public schools were set up, some of which are renowned academic institutions even today. Geographically speaking, the district can be divided into the hills and the plains. Although Kalimpong became a separate district as of 14 February 2017, for the sake of convenience, the Darjeeling district refers to the erstwhile composition that includes Kalimpong, throughout this chapter.

To study the culinary trends prevalent in the region, it is important to understand its demography. Darjeeling district is home to many immigrants. These immigrants are mainly from Nepal, Tibet, Sikkim and Bhutan. The Lepchas (also known as Rongpas, meaning 'the dwellers of the valley') are the original inhabitants of the district. Although now a minority, they are still an important part of the Darjeeling district and have their own exclusive language called 'Rong-Ring'. But most Lepchas now speak Nepali. They are mostly agriculturists that rear cattle and other farm animals, like goats and pigs. They are excellent at bamboo craft and carpentry and are known for their weaving and spinning abilities. Most of them are Buddhists while some have converted to Christianity.

When the British started developing the region, the original land was full of dense forests. So, they encouraged immigrant workers from the neighbouring places to settle in the region and work at its development. The immigrants came in large numbers and were mostly from Nepal. Gradually, these immigrants made up the bulk of the hill people. The Nepalese now largely dominate the Darjeeling district. They are mostly Hindus and speak Nepali, a language that happens to be the co-official language in the Darjeeling and Kurseong subdivisions. Since 1950, many Tibetans have fled China and settled in the district. However, over the years, they have established themselves, particularly in the hospitality industry. These Tibetan immigrants are mainly Buddhists and speak their own language called Tibetan. The Tibetans and the Bhutias (Sikkimese of Tibetan ancestry) make up the second largest bulk of the population. Some communities from the plain of West Bengal like the Bengalis and the Marwaris also reside in the region making the Darjeeling district a multiethnic place to live in. Each of these communities brought with them their own culinary culture and practices. The food scenario in the region is an amalgamation of all their cuisines. But the Nepalese, followed by the Tibetans, dominate the culture of the district and have left a lasting impression on its culinary culture. In recent years, Tibetan cuisine has become popular in Calcutta.

All over the world the name Darjeeling is famously associated with one thing—tea. The soil and climatic conditions of the region combined with the sloping terrains are ideal for the production of tea. The tea industry in the Darjeeling district is a major source of employment for its people. Renowned for its natural beauty, the Darjeeling district is replete with beautiful hill stations. This ensures a regular flow of tourists, giving the region a flourishing tourism industry. But the district is industrially backward. As a result, it does not offer too many job opportunities to its educated youth, a situation that is similar with most hill stations. Its poor infrastructural facilities do not promote the growth of medium and large-scale industries. This leads to its dependence on small-scale and cottage industries to generate employment. The scope of the professional life of the educated youth is largely restricted to the tourism and hospitality industries. Government offices, public sector undertakings and academic institutions are also some of the major sources of employment. A large number of youngsters take up jobs in call centres and the beauty and wellness sector.

But when it comes to the matter of wider career choices and opportunities and even better chances at higher education, the residents have no choice but to move out of their hometowns. Calcutta provides the best possible answer to their woes. It is a developed city with better career opportunities and located very close to their homes. Since Independence there has been a steady flow of immigrants from the Darjeeling district to Calcutta, particularly from Kurseong and Kalimpong. They enrol themselves in colleges and universities in Calcutta for higher education and are constantly on the lookout for job opportunities with better prospects and salaries. A fair number of food enthusiasts and connoisseurs among these immigrants have ventured into the restaurant business, setting up both small and medium-sized eateries that serve Tibetan cuisine, the most successful immigrant cuisine in Calcutta post-Independence.

Doma Wang, a Tibetan restaurateur in Calcutta, has blazed the trail by being among the first few connoisseurs to serve Tibetan dishes to curious customers when the cuisine was relatively new in the city. Her journey as a restaurateur had a humble beginning and an initial food home delivery service led to the establishment of the canteen, Blue Poppy, in Sikkim House (a government guest house for the visiting government employees and officials from the state of Sikkim) in central Calcutta. Set up in the early years of this century, the location of the canteen contributed a lot to its success, as central Calcutta is the most commercial and cosmopolitan area of the city. Not only did guests from the guest house dine in Blue Poppy, but also students and professionals from the schools, colleges, offices and markets located nearby. Today, Blue Poppy has become a brand name in Calcutta that mostly specializes in the Tibetan cuisine of the Darjeeling district. Doma Wang's business is no longer confined only to the canteen service but is gradually expanding. The entrepreneur has started a small chain of Tibetan restaurants, most of which are under the Blue Poppy brand name. The success of her restaurants also proves the success of the cuisine with the city people.

Today, thanks to the efforts of restaurateurs like Doma Wang, Tibetan cuisine has become so widespread and loved in Calcutta that even the food entrepreneurs among the local residents who do not belong to the Darjeeling district have set up kiosks and small eateries specializing in it or incorporating it as part of a multicuisine menu. This is a cuisine that has gradually grown and boomed in the last few years. The plausible reason behind its success could be its uniqueness. Tibetan cuisine is very different, healthy and tasty. The city youth, with whom this cuisine is especially popular, is a health-conscious lot but at the same time they are experimental with their food habits. They enjoy indulging in Tibetan food, making it an often ordered, quick, healthy and light meal.

It becomes important at this juncture to understand this cuisine and the factors that have shaped it. Tibet is a mountainous country with an average elevation of 16,000 feet and long cold winter months when the temperature falls well below zero. The high altitude of the Tibetan plateau, the dry cold climate and the traditions and religious beliefs and customs of the Tibetans have influenced their cuisine to a great extent. Only hardy crops that can survive the harsh climate grow in such a high altitude. The lower areas are relatively warm and suitable for growing fruits like apples, bananas, apricots, oranges, lemons, plums and walnuts. Rice is also grown in very limited amounts in the river valleys in southern Tibet. But most of the plateau is unsuitable for its cultivation. The main crop in Tibet is the resilient highland barley. It grows all over the region and is a major part of the Tibetan staple diet. The cultivation of barley is followed by that of wheat and buckwheat, two other crops that grow well in the country and are the mainstays of its cuisine. Potatoes, onions, cabbages, radishes, turnips, broad beans and peas are among the few vegetables that always grew in the region. Mustard seed has always been well cultivated. Mushrooms are also commonly used in Tibetan cooking. The region has quite a variety of them that grow in the wild. Spices like garlic, chillies and emma or erma (Sichuan peppercorn) are grown and feature widely in the culinary practices. Groundnut oil is the traditional medium of cooking.

Non-vegetarianism always seemed like a natural choice for the Tibetans till Buddhism got introduced into the country towards the end of the eighth century by their king, Trisong Detsen. Before the advent of Buddhism, most of the Tibetans were followers of Bon, a religion based on animistic and shamanistic beliefs. Today, the majority of the Tibetans are Buddhists and their fondness for meat may seem contradictory to the principles of their religion. Buddhism strongly advocates vegetarianism as a dietary choice. But in this region where the climate is extreme and crops are difficult to grow, vegetables are scarce. The inhabitants cannot survive on vegetarianism alone. Moreover, meat provides the energy required to cope in the plateau with such a high altitude and very cold climate. Even the Tibetan Buddhist monks and nuns are meat eaters. But there are certain restrictions on their meat consumption practices. They are allowed to eat the meat of only cloven-hoofed animals, but they cannot be implicated of killing them. This means that they can eat the meat of dead animals without being directly involved in their butchery. So, the Tibetan Buddhists buy meat from the local Muslim butchers.

The lakes and rivers in the region teem with fish. But Tibetans do not touch fish as there is a religious ban on its consumption. Killing other living beings for food is an act of survival by the Tibetans. They do it out of necessity. The belief that 'every animal is a life' prevents Tibetans from killing fish for their dietary needs. A fish is a small living being and a single fish can feed only one person. So, for a large family to survive, many fish will have to be killed. This means the selfish taking of more lives. On the contrary, a single large animal can feed many members in a family for a long time. This means less lives are killed here.

Tibet is the land of yaks. These large hairy sturdy animals can climb steep elevations, making them a necessary mode of transportation in the country. They are also used to plough the farmlands.

But most importantly, yaks are a major source of food in Tibet. The local Tibetans survive a lot on meat and dairy products, high protein foods essential for survival in the tough living conditions. Yak meat is the staple meat of the Tibetans and the dri (the female yak) is the main source of milk and its by-products like butter, cheese and yoghurt that are eaten on a regular basis. Chhurpi is a special kind of cheese that Tibetans love to eat and an excellent source of protein. It is made from buttermilk and comes in two forms—soft and hard. The soft chhurpi is a white crumbly mass that is used as an ingredient in dishes. It is particularly popular as a momo filling. The hard variety is prepared by completely filling jute bags with the soft lumps of cheese, laying them on a flat surface and piling stone slabs over them. In this way, the cheese gets pressed hard and the excess water drains out. Finally, a slab of dried cheese emerges that is cut into small candy-like cubes. These cubes are dried by either keeping them under the sun or hanging them over an open low fire till they become very hard. The candies are sucked on and can last for hours in the mouth. Tibetans snack a lot on hard chhurpi, particularly while walking on the rugged mountains, as it keeps the body warm by keeping the mouth busy.

Most Tibetan dishes will feature yak meat in them. It is eaten in various forms like dried, boiled, fried, stewed, roasted and sometimes, even raw. It is cooked into soups, curries and fillings. Dried meat is known as shakambo in Tibetan, sha meaning meat and kambo meaning dried. But instead of sun-drying the yak meat, Tibetans dry the meat in winters in sub-zero temperature. By doing so the original distinctive flavour of the meat is preserved. Yak jerky, a form of dried meat, is a favourite, particularly among the nomads.

Tibetans also like to eat the fresh as well as the air-dried meat of sheep. They eat a variety of sausages—blood sausage or gyuma is the most famous preparation. Tibetan blood sausages are made with ground beef, cooked rice or roasted barley flour, salt and erma mixed in yak or sheep blood and filled into yak or sheep intestine casings and boiled. Sometimes, they indulge in goat meat too. It is difficult to raise other farm animals in the environment of Tibet.

But there are some differences in the food habits of the Tibetans in Tibet and those living in the Darjeeling district. The main difference is in the kind of meat they eat. Yaks are found in high altitudes and are not available in the Darjeeling district. So, while the Tibetans in Tibet eat a lot of yak and sheep meat, those living in the Darjeeling district eat a lot of beef and pork instead. Beef jerky is their favourite. Even the source of their blood sausage is the cow. Earlier, since the Tibetans were poor refugees in the Darjeeling district, they could not afford goat meat given its high price, which is why even today it does not feature much in their cuisine. Unlike in Tibet, the main source of milk and its by-products for these exiled Tibetans is the cow. Another very big deviation in their food habits is that they eat a lot of rice. Rice is grown extensively in the plains of the Darjeeling district, particularly in Siliguri, and also happens to be a major item of import from other parts of West Bengal. This makes the people of the region, including the Tibetans, major rice eaters. A considerable number of fruits (the district is renowned for its oranges) and vegetables are sold in the markets leading to their inclusion in the diet of the Tibetans. Moreover, the Tibetans living in the district use a little bit more spice in their cooking compared to their countrymen in Tibet. Erma is not available and only a few shops stock the spice by mostly importing it from Bhutan.

If there is one dish that can be called the national food of Tibet, then it has to be tsampa or roasted barley flour. Tsampa is mostly eaten with po cha or butter tea, the national beverage of Tibet. The flour and butter tea are mixed together in a bowl and kneaded into a dough. Sometimes, other ingredients like dried dri cheese, butter or sugar are added to this mixture. Small balls are then made out of this dough. These balls are called pa and they are eaten plain or enjoyed with a spicy sauce or gravy. Although tsampa is now more of a morning food, there was a time when it was eaten every day and at every meal, a practice still common in Central Tibet. Tsampa is also eaten in porridge form for breakfast. This version, known as cham-dur, is made by mixing the flour with butter, sugar or honey and hot water or milk or black tea.

Like most foods of Tibet, tsampa is calorie-rich and a vital source of energy necessary for survival in the harsh plateau. Doma Wang points out that instead of tea, tsampa mixed with milk, unsalted butter and sugar and made into semi-thick porridge-like consistency is the perfect nutritious meal for babies. 'It is extremely good for health,' she says, 'and is also eaten by pregnant women and old people.' Tsampa is also a very important part of the Tibetan culture. It is considered auspicious and during many Tibetan religious festivals, the flour is tossed high into the air as an offering to the gods and praying for peace and prosperity. This is especially done during Losar or the Tibetan New Year. During weddings and other traditional ceremonies, it is thrown into the air as a mark of joy and celebration. But, along with the traditional roasted barley flour, Tibetans in the Darjeeling district also use the flour milled from other roasted products like maize, dried yellow peas and black chickpeas because they are widely available in their adopted home. They call these flours tsampa as well. So, there is makai (maize) tsampa, matar (dried yellow pea) tsampa and chana (black chickpea) tsampa. They all serve the same purpose in the immigrant Tibetan cuisine as the traditional tsampa.

Tibetans drink a lot of tea. As mentioned before, they drink butter tea or po cha and make it with black tea that comes in the form of bricks. Butter tea is made by crumbling off some tea from a brick, putting it into boiling water and brewing it for a few minutes. The strained tea is then put into a traditional cylindrical churn, along with the required quantity of salt, dri butter and milk. All the ingredients are churned together to make a perfectly blended liquid that is poured into a teapot. The tea is then warmed before serving and not boiled, as Tibetans believe that boiled butter tea loses its flavour. The concept of butter tea may read very strange at first but it is very popular as it warms the body and provides the vitamins and minerals necessary to deal with the cold weather. Tibetans living outside Tibet make butter tea using black tea in the form of loose tea leaves. Sweet milk tea is also popular among the Tibetans, particularly among those living in India.

If tsampa is the national food and butter tea, the national beverage of Tibet, momo and thukpa can be regarded as the ambassadors of its cuisine to the world. Momo is one of the major influences of Chinese cuisine on the food habits of the Tibetans and refers to a dumpling with a filling. There is a theory that the origin of the Tibetan momo can be traced to the Chinese dumplings, baozi (round-shaped filled dumpling) and jiaozi (crescent-shaped filled dumpling). When their concepts reached Tibet, a single dish evolved that took on the name, momo. The filling and flavour of the dish took on a more localized definition. Although the dough for the momo wrapping is usually made of refined flour, it can also be made of wholewheat flour. The most common way to make momos is by steaming. Momos can be round, but these days crescent-shaped momos are mostly seen everywhere.

Momos generally have minced meat or vegetable fillings that have been seasoned with ingredients like onion, ginger, garlic, soya sauce and salt. Tibetans mostly use yak meat for the non-vegetarian version that is known as sha momo or meat dumpling. Traditionally, meat fillings have defined momo in Tibetan cuisine. But, over the years, vegetarian momos began to appear on the scene. For the vegetarian version, known as shamey momo, the main fillings used are generally cabbage, onions, squash, spinach, mushrooms, chives, potatoes and chhurpi. 'Shamey' means 'without meat'. Although these are the standard ingredients that go into the dumpling, every Tibetan home makes their momos slightly differently. Some families make their sha momos with minced meat while some may add additional ingredients like erma, celery and coriander. Making momos is a time-consuming affair. Since it is a labour-intensive dish, its preparation is mostly reserved for the weekends, holidays and special occasions. Family members and friends gather together in the kitchen and spend a day making these dumplings amidst a lot of chitchat and laughter.

Since yak meat is not available in the Darjeeling district, the Tibetans living there make do with beef or pork fillings for their non-vegetarian momos. In Calcutta, where momos have caught on like wildfire with the general public, they are mostly available with chicken or pork fillings. Non-vegetarian steamed momos are served with soup (meat broth) and sepen (a spicy sauce). Doma Wang points out, 'Readymade minced meat is not available in the markets in Darjeeling district. So, the Tibetans there mince the meat at home. Then they put the bones in a vessel, pour water into it and put it on boil. Some salt, chopped onions and spices like ginger and black peppercorns are added to the boiling broth to give it flavour. While the broth is being made, the momos are steamed above in a large colander or porous container that has been greased with some oil and fitted on top of the vessel with a cover placed firmly over it. The cooked broth is strained and served separately as clear soup with the momos. Spring onions are commonly used as garnish for momo soups. Traditionally, soup is not supposed to be served with steamed vegetarian momos. But most do not follow this and the broth of the vegetables is served as soup.' 'Sepen', meaning 'chilli' in Tibetan, is a generic word for chilli sauces in the cuisine. Since steamed momos are slightly bland, the spicy sepen makes the perfect accompaniment, balancing the taste. The traditional version of sepen is always made with dried red chillies that give it a red colour. The paste is made by grinding dried red chillies with garlic and salt. But there is also a non-traditional version of it that is popular and is made by grinding fresh green chillies with garlic, coriander leaves, roasted tomatoes and salt.

Although there are quite a few varieties of momos, Doma Wang asserts that steamed momo, fried momo and kothey momo are the most authentic Tibetan momos. A fried momo is made by frying a steamed momo. Kothey momo has been influenced by the Chinese dumpling preparation called potstickers, which is a combination of steamed and fried dumplings. In the preparation of kothey momo, one side of the momo is pan-fried and the other side is steamed. Both fried and kothey momos are served with spicy sauces. There are other varieties like tingmo, also known as ting momo or T-momo. It is a big and puffed up steamed momo with no fillings on the inside. It is rolled or folded to give it a layered appearance. Since tingmo has no fillings, Tibetans treat it like a steamed bun that can be eaten any time with a variety of foods depending upon personal choice. Spicy sauces and meat curries are the perfect accompaniment to this kind of momo. 'The Tibetans in the Darjeeling district hills like to have it with chicken, beef or pork curries,' points out Doma Wang. Tibetans also eat tingmos for breakfast with drethuk or rice porridge. They can be dipped into almost anything. 'My dad enjoys eating them with honey for breakfast,' continues Doma Wang with a nostalgic smile.

Blue Poppy not only serves all these momos to its customers but also a few others that are slight variations from the traditional Tibetan momos. These variations are chilli momo or C-momo (steamed dumplings tossed in a spicy sauce) and pan-fried momos tossed in hot garlic sauce. Momos are particularly popular with the youth in the city and they enjoy spicy food. Doma Wang made these introductions in her restaurant keeping this in mind. Mothuk (momos served in soup) is another preparation that is much liked by Tibetans across the world. Tsi-tsi momos or mouse-shaped momos are cooked in a delicious broth to make this dish. Although Blue Poppy does not serve mothuk, a few of the other restaurants specializing in Tibetan cuisine in Calcutta make this dish. A very big version of momo that is popular in Darjeeling district is thaipo. It is round in shape, has a flat bottom and comes in both vegetarian and non-vegetarian versions. To make it so big, some baking soda is added to the dough. It has been observed that some Tibetan restaurants in Calcutta have begun serving thaipo. But there is some controversy about the origin of the dish. Although it is generally believed that thaipo is a Tibetan dish, Doma Wang asserts that it is Chinese. But its popularity in the hills cannot be denied.

Tibetans simply love momos and yet they do not indulge in them during Losar or the Tibetan New Year. The festival is a celebration of generosity and prosperity and the closed shape of the momo is looked upon as inauspicious. Tibetans abstain from non-vegetarian food during Saka Dawa, the month honouring Buddha's entire life right from his birth to his enlightenment and finally, his death. Even onions, garlic and radishes are avoided during this time. This is a solemn month of prayers, pilgrimages and charitable actions. So, during this holy month, vegetarian foods, including vegetarian momos, become a part of their daily eating habits.

The Tibetans share a few similarities in their culinary practices and eating habits with the Chinese because of the proximity of the two countries. One of them is the liberal use of soya sauce in cooking and the others are the use of chopsticks and the fondness for dumplings and noodles. Nothing can be more comforting in the harsh cold climate of the Tibetan plateau than a bowl of steaming thukpa. Thukpa is generalized as warm soups that have noodles of different shapes and sizes floating in them. This soupy noodle dish also has either vegetables or a combination of meat pieces and a few vegetables cooked into it. But Doma Wang has a slightly different definition of thukpa. 'Thukpa,' she clarifies, 'is a generic Tibetan name for raw noodles. It includes both soupy and dry noodle dishes. Even starchy porridges fall in this category.' Whatever maybe the case, it is a dish that is one of the cornerstones of Tibetan cuisine and the second most popular one after momos in Calcutta. However, most eateries and takeaway joints in Calcutta serve only the basic form of thukpa with long noodles floating in a bowl of soup that has either vegetarian or non-vegetarian fillings. And the general public is of the opinion that this is the only version of the soupy noodle dish. But this is a fallacy because thukpa can be of several types. Thenthuk, for example, is one such variety and when translated, it literally means 'pull noodles' ('then' means pull and 'thuk' means noodles). In this dish, hand-pulled noodles that are bite-sized and square-shaped are thrown into a broth that is cooked with meat, vegetables like chopped onions, carrots and cabbage, seasonings and soya sauce and finally, garnished with chopped spring onions. In the vegetarian version of the dish, the meat is left out.

Gyathuk, on the other hand, means Chinese noodles. Thukpa gyathuk is a soupy noodle dish made with Chinese-style long and thin egg noodles. Along with thenthuk and thukpa gyathuk, Blue Poppy also serves mentsetse and phakthuk, two soupy noodles dishes that are very popular in the Darjeeling district and not made anywhere else in Calcutta. Mentsetse has long and flat egg noodles floating in the soup while phakthuk has handmade small-sized ones instead that are similar to conch shells in shape. Phakthuk is also known as cowrie thukpa among the Nepalese. Though thukpa bhathuk is not served in Blue Poppy, it is very popular among Tibetans. It is a soupy noodle dish that consists of handmade bhatsa noodles that are small and oval-shaped. Komay thukpa is made with thick vegetarian noodles and comes in both vegetarian and non-vegetarian versions. A rice porridge dish like drethuk will also be included in the category of thukpa. Dre means rice and thuk means thukpa. When rice is replaced with wheat in this dish, it becomes drothuk. Dro means wheat.

In the Darjeeling district, momos and thukpas are widely available in restaurants and roadside eateries. The Tibetans living there generally eat cooked rice with meat curries for lunch while they reserve the thukpa dishes for dinner. Momos are more of a weekend or Sunday lunch treat and they are generally eaten steamed. Making momos becomes quite a family affair with everyone gathering in the kitchen, sitting on the floor and making the dumplings. The leftovers are fried the next morning and eaten at breakfast.

Tibetan cuisine has a considerably large variety of breads. Flatbreads like phalay (made of wholewheat flour), yu-shang phalay (made of refined flour) and balep (made of tsampa or wholewheat flour or refined flour) are some of them. Logo momo, another popular Tibetan bread preparation, is made of refined flour. Not to be confused with the regular momo, this bread preparation is unique both in its appearance and method of preparation. Logo momo is both pan-fried and steamed. The bread is round in shape with a large circular depression in its centre that is fried while the rest of the bread is steamed. It is generally eaten at meals with vegetable or meat dishes.

Shaphalay is a very popular Tibetan meat bread (sha means meat and phalay means bread). It is actually a fried minced meat pie with a crimped border. It comes in two shapes—round and crescent. The meat used in Tibet is yak meat while in the Darjeeling district beef and pork are commonly used. Although it is supposed to be eaten as a meal, Doma Wang points out that the lovers of Tibetan food in Calcutta generally eat it as an appetizer with sepen. They cut it into pieces and share it among themselves. When it is eaten as a meal, shaphalay is generally taken with rutang soup (meat bone soup). It can also be eaten with a basic fresh salad dish called trang tsel (meaning cold vegetables). Since vegetables and cold foods are rare in the harsh cold climate of Tibet, trang tsel is not a dish that most Tibetans in Tibet have eaten. This is more of an invention of Tibetans in exile. Shaphalay is a popular picnic dish and most Tibetans carry it while travelling.

The concept of desserts is missing in traditional Tibetan cuisine. Tibetans enjoy eating sho (yoghurt) every day. In Tibet, yoghurt is mainly sold in small shops or by villagers in the markets in the mornings. It is eaten plain with a little bit of sugar added to it. Tibetans often eat it as a snack while travelling.

Khapse is made a lot during celebratory occasions like Losar and weddings. It is a biscuit or a cookie (some even call it a pastry) that is very unique to Tibetan cuisine. The dough for khapse is made with refined flour, milk, water, oil and sugar. Balls pinched from this dough are then rolled out into thin round flatbreads. Long thick strips are cut out from this flatbread. Tibetans dexterously and patiently mould these strips into different shapes, sizes and designs with their hands. These khapses are then deep-fried, often dusted with powdered sugar and served with sweet tea or Tibetan butter tea.

It is also important to mention two sweet preparations that are much loved and prepared by Tibetans across the world including those settled in the Darjeeling district and Calcutta. Tibetans are heavy meat eaters and hardly indulge in vegetarian food except for certain times of the year like in the holy month of Saka Dawa. Bhatsa marku is a very popular dish made during this time. This is a lightly sweetened and very buttery noodle dish. Boiled bhatsa noodles are stir-fried with some butter and sugar. An adequate quantity of grated cheese (traditionally dried dri cheese) or chhurpi is added to the cooking. The dish is stir-fried for some more time and served as a meal. Bhatsa marku is very rich in taste because of the combination of butter and cheese. But it is this richness that is much loved by Tibetans all over the world.

Dresil is a lightly sweetened rice dish in Tibetan cuisine. The three most important ingredients in this dish are rice, butter and raisins. Tibetans make it by mixing cooked rice with dri butter, sugar, droma, raisins and cashew nuts. Droma is a small root that grows underground in the grasslands of Tibet. It is dark brown in colour and has a naturally sweet flavour. This ingredient is so widely used in Tibet in preparing dresil that the sweetened rice dish is often called droma dresil. But Tibetans living outside Tibet, where the ingredient is not available, make their dresil without it. They also use cow butter instead of dri butter. Some Tibetans do not use sugar as the raisins lend enough sweetness to the rice. Other varieties of nuts and dried fruits can also be used in the preparation. Dresil is a celebratory dish especially made during Losar. It is also served on Buddhist festivals and special occasions like weddings.

Then there is chura (cheese) momo, a dish that is mostly confined to the Tibetans in Tibet. The filling is of grated dried dri cheese that is sweetened with some sugar. Sometimes, chhurpi is used in the place of dried dri cheese and walnuts can also be added to the filling.

Any writing on Tibetan cuisine will remain incomplete without mentioning chang, a popular alcoholic drink of the Tibetans. It is a fermented drink that is traditionally made from the grains of barley. Chang has very little alcohol content in it and floods the body with warmth. This makes it a popular drink in the cold and harsh environment of Tibet. According to folklore, it is the favourite drink of Yeti, the mythical Himalayan snowman. It is both a celebratory (barring religious celebrations) and leisure drink. Chang is traditionally home-made and the Tibetans have carried its recipe to all the places they have settled in. In the Darjeeling district, the Tibetans prepare chang with either rice or millet. The chang made from rice (drechang) is a celebratory drink that is made during Losar and other festivals. Tibetans enjoy having changkol with dresil and khapse for breakfast on the first day of Losar. It is made with drechang and is prepared by melting some butter in a pot and adding the chang (often with the rice in it), some grated cheese (traditionally dried dri cheese), sugar and water to the cooking.

To say that most of the Tibetan dishes that are prevalent in the Darjeeling district have made their presence in Calcutta will be far from the truth. The Tibetan dish that has made the most impact is momo. The dumpling is so popular with the residents of the city that it has prompted restaurateurs to experiment with the dish. Today, customers can come across momos stir-fried with fish or satay sauces or with fillings that are flavoured with basil or black bean. One can also come across a momo with a combination of chicken-mushroom-cheese filling. Tandoori momos, momo burgers, momos slathered in Punjabi-style butter masala sauces or stir-fried in Chinese-style Sichuan, garlic or hoisin sauces, momos with cheese, fish, prawn or goat meat fillings, chicken tempura momos, baked momo au gratins and chocolate momos are a few of the experiments that can be seen. The popularity of the dumpling is followed by that of the thukpa. Although a standard version of this soupy noodle dish is available in most restaurants, a few (other than Blue Poppy) have started serving some specific varieties like thukpa gyathuk and thenthuk.

But that does not mean Tibetan cuisine in Calcutta is only confined to momo and thukpa. The restaurateurs from the Darjeeling district, particularly, are trying hard to popularize the cuisine by gradually introducing other dishes. Doma Wang and a few other restaurateurs are serving the dishes called shapta (a stir-fried meat dish) and shaphalay in their eateries. Since the residents of Calcutta are very fond of chicken, pork and mutton, it has made the restaurateurs include these meats in the preparation of the dishes. Blue Poppy also makes a vegetarian version of shaphalay to suit the taste buds of its vegetarian customers. So far, it is the only Tibetan restaurant in the city to serve laphing, a dish of cold, spicy and slippery bite-sized noodles, and the unique Tibetan butter tea. This shows the continuous effort that the restaurateurs from the district are putting in to promote their cuisine. And the enthusiasm with which their customers are responding to it speaks of its bright future in the city.

If Tibetan cuisine enjoys a lot of prominence in the Darjeeling district, then Nepali cuisine dominates the food scene because there are a large number of Nepalese residing in the region. There are quite a few similarities between the Nepalese and the Indians, the main one being that though their countries are secular, a large number of the citizens are Hindus. Lord Shiva is a very important deity in the Nepali Hindu culture and his incarnation, Pashupatinath, is much revered. The Nepalese also give a lot of importance to the worship of the Goddesses Durga, Kali and Lakshmi. Their religious festivals are quite similar, the biggest among them being Dashain (Dussehra or Bijaya Dashami) and Tihar (Diwali). Also, just like Sanskrit and Hindi, Nepali follows the Devanagari script.

Nepal is geographically close to India and Tibet. It does not come as a surprise that its cuisine has been influenced by the culinary practices of both these countries. Despite these influences, Nepal has a well-developed cuisine of its own that is distinct and unique. Like the Tibetans, they enjoy momo and thukpa. Chhurpi, which the Nepalese also call durkha, is an equally important part of their cuisine. In the Darjeeling district, the source of chhurpi is cow's milk and its soft version is known as kachcha chhurpi. The soft chhurpi is prepared in both the hilly area and the plain land of the region. The hard chhurpi, on the other hand, is confined to the high altitudes.

The Nepalese share similarities with the Indians in not only the kind of food they eat but also in their culinary practices. They eat a lot of rice, wheat and lentils. Vegetables, eggs, fish and meats are cooked into curries. Most Nepalese, being Hindus, abstain from eating beef since the cow is their sacred animal. They use the animal only for its milk.

Although the meat of water buffalo, popularly known as buff, is enjoyed, staunch Hindus abstain from eating it because a water buffalo is also a bovine animal. The Nepalese living in the Darjeeling district eat a lot of pork, chicken and goat meat. The spices and herbs used in cooking are also similar like turmeric, ginger, garlic, cumin, coriander, chillies, black pepper, cinnamon, cardamom, clove, mace, asafoetida, sesame seeds, mustard seeds, fenugreek seeds, bay leaves, coriander leaves, curry leaves, garam masala and padkaune masala (paanch phoron or the five-spice mix). In the Nepali language, chillies are known as khursani and dalle means round. Dalle khursani is considered to be one of the hottest chillies in the world. Widely grown in Darjeeling district, it is a cherry-sized chilli that is almost round and takes on a bright red colour on ripening. Also known as cherry pepper, it is consumed fresh and never in the dried form. Dalle khursani is used in making chutneys, cooked into curries and also pickled. Mustard oil is the traditional medium of cooking by the Nepalese. Ghee is also used quite often.

But, at the same time, they use certain ingredients that are special to their culinary practices like tama (bamboo shoots), jimbu (an aromatic herb, most commonly used dried) and timmur (Sichuan pepper, commonly used in marinades and pickles). However, in the Darjeeling district, the Nepalese don't use jimbu as it is unavailable. Timmur and erma mean the same thing. It is a spice that is not available in the district and has to be imported from Bhutan. The Nepalese always use fresh bamboo shoots in cooking unlike in the northeast region of India where fermented bamboo shoots are mainly used.

Also, like most residents of the hilly regions, the Nepalese believe in preserving certain ingredients for future use either by dehydrating or fermenting them. For example, sukuti is edible dehydrated meat. It is generally made with buff or goat meat although in recent times, chicken, pork, duck and even fish are used. Sukuti is prepared by cutting the meat into thin long strips and removing the fat. The strips are then spread on a flat surface and sun-dried for many days. At night, the meat strips are wrapped in paper. Once the meat has completely dried it is considered ready for use. The meat strips can also be dried by spreading them under the sun for a short while and then hanging them above a charcoal fire. Sukuti can be eaten in many ways: as meat jerky or cooked into soups, noodle dishes and curries. In Nepali, a curry preparation is known as jhol or tarkari. Sukuti ko tarkari is prepared by cooking the chopped bite-sized pieces of the dried meat with vegetables of one's choice like chopped onions, tomatoes and potatoes, spices, herbs and some salt. It is served as a side dish with cooked rice or chiura (beaten rice). Sukuti can also be pickled (sukuti ko achaar).

Sukuti can also be eaten as sukuti sandheko. Although in Nepali sandheko means 'marinated', the preparation actually involves mixing with spices and other ingredients and making a salad dish out of it. Here it refers to the strips of meat that are spiced up. Sukuti sandheko makes a perfect appetizer.

The Nepalese also ferment many vegetables. These are fermented naturally and without adding any salt. Gundruk is, a fermented and sun-dried leafy vegetable product commonly made in Nepalese households, especially during winter when there are plenty of leafy vegetables around. It is prepared by fermenting the fresh green leaves (saag) of mustard (rayo), radish (moola), turnip (salegum), cauliflower (kauli), cabbage (banda kovi) or spinach (palungo). The leaves are plucked from the garden and allowed to wilt for a few days. They are then washed and pounded. The same can also be done with turnip. The water is then squeezed out thoroughly and the pounded leaves are filled in an airtight container, allowing them to ferment by putting the container in a sunny place. The fermented leaves are taken out of the container and sun-dried for a few more days by spreading them on a flat surface. The end product is called gundruk, a sour, acidic and flavoursome ingredient that is stored for future use. Gundruk is used to make both curries and pickles (achaar).

Sinki, another fermented and sun-dried vegetable product, is also used to prepare dishes. It shares similarities with gundruk in its method of preparation. The only difference lies in the ingredient used to make it. Sinki is made with the taproots of radish. The next fermented product that the Nepalese make quite often is kinema or fermented soya beans. The soya beans are soaked in water overnight and boiled the next morning. Water is drained out and the beans are lightly cracked with a pestle in a mortar to aid the process of fermentation. They are then kept in a bamboo basket whose walls are lined with fresh fern leaves. The basket is covered with a jute bag and kept above a warm earthen kitchen oven for a few days. Alternatively, they could be wrapped in banana leaves. This banana leaf wrapping is further wrapped with layers of thick cloth and put in a container that is kept in a warm room. Once the kinema is thoroughly fermented, it becomes sticky in texture and develops a pungent smell. It can now be used in cooking or sun-dried and then used. Fresh kinema has a short shelf life and needs to be used soon but the sun-dried one can be stored for months. Kinema is used to make curries (kinema ko jhol) and pickles (kinema ko achaar). 'The Nepalese particularly enjoy eating a curry preparation of pork cooked with kinema,' points out Doma Wang. They also like to stir-fry pork with fresh mustard leaves and kinema.

Young shoots of edible bamboos are also fermented. These are called mesu and they are prepared by peeling off the outer inedible casings and then chopping the inner parts. These inner parts are washed in water, cut into small pieces, pressed tightly into an airtight bamboo vessel or glass container and kept aside for a few days. Mesu has a sour taste and a strong odour. The Nepalese generally pickle it. When matured cucumbers are fermented, they are known as khalpi. Fermentation of cucumbers is rare and hard to find in other Himalayan cultures. This product is made with locally grown big-sized cucumbers that are washed, deseeded, cut into small pieces and sun-dried for a few hours. Khalpi is basically a fermented cucumber pickle preparation. The sun-dried cucumber pieces are then mixed with spices like cumin, coriander, red chilli, mustard and turmeric powders, salt, fried fenugreek seeds and mustard oil. The preparation is stored in an airtight container and kept aside for a few days in room temperature for the fermentation to take place. The fermentation is considered complete when the pickle takes on a typical sour flavour. Although khalpi is generally served at meals with steamed rice, the Nepalese follow a tradition of serving it with masu chiura (meat and beaten rice) during the Dashain and Tihar festivals.

While writing about the food habits of the Nepalese, one simply cannot leave out their staple meal—dal bhaat (lentil and rice). The Nepalese all over the world are addicted to this simple dish that is usually eaten twice a day and can be described as their national dish. Cooked rice is eaten with lentils prepared in a soupy form with some salt and turmeric and seasoned with spices that have been fried either in oil or ghee. The spices can vary according to personal choice like cumin seeds, coriander seeds, ginger, garlic and dried red chillies. Sometimes, sliced onions, chopped tomatoes and coriander leaves are added to the preparation. The Nepalese use a variety of lentils but the most commonly used ones are split red lentil or masoor dal and split black gram or urad dal. Often, some saag and tarkari is added to this thali (platter) of dal and bhaat. Saag over here refers to the preparations of green leafy vegetables like mustard, spinach and radish. Tarkari refers to both vegetable and meat curries. Other additions to this platter can include some fresh salad, a few chillies (dalle khursani is a common feature in the Darjeeling district), poppadom and yoghurt. A small amount of achaar is always included in the platter. In Nepali cuisine, the word achaar includes pickles, chutneys and even salad preparations. So often, a small amount of a spicy pickle, chutney or salad is served. Pickles and chutneys based on sesame seeds (til) are the most popular. The rice in the thali is sometimes replaced with rotis.

A very unique dish in Nepali cuisine that has its roots in rice is sel roti. Sel roti, a very popular preparation, is a deep-fried sweet rice bread that is golden brown and ring-shaped. It is quite thin and big in size and made with the batter of rice flour, sugar and ghee or butter that is fermented for a few hours. Some prefer using milk instead of water to make the batter. It is a celebratory dish that is not only essential in most social functions and gatherings but also prepared a lot during religious ceremonies and festivals, particularly Tihar and Dashain. Sel roti can be eaten any time during the day as a snack by itself or with yoghurt, butter, cheese or chutneys. It is also eaten with hot beverages, particularly with chia (tea) for breakfast. Although it is slightly sweet, this rice bread is mostly eaten with curries and pickles.

The most popular vegetable curry preparation is kauli ra alu ko tarkari (cauliflower and potato curry). Other popular preparations include those made with mixed vegetables (misayeko tarkari), bottle gourd (lauka ko tarkari), unripe jackfruit (katahar ko tarkari) and even kidney beans (rajma ko tarkari). Another sought-after accompaniment to cooked rice is alu bodi tama, a simple potato curry dish made with black-eyed peas (bodi) and bamboo shoots (tama). Alu bodi tama and chiura also make a great khaja dish (khaja means snack in Nepali).

Soft chhurpi is cooked into curries (chhurpi ko jhol) or pickled (chhurpi ko achaar) and served with rice. In the Darjeeling district, the most popular curry preparation of chhurpi is with ninguro, an alpine fiddlehead fern. It is also used as an ingredient in chutneys. The Nepalese are extremely fond of alu dum, which they cook with lots of dried red chillies and garlic. They may make either a dry version of this spicy dish or cook it with a little gravy and enjoy eating it with cooked rice, rotis or puris. Alu dum is also eaten as a snack with some bhujia (thin potato wafers) sprinkled on top or with bhuja (puffed rice) as an accompaniment. It is not only a popular celebratory dish in Nepali cuisine that is served during parties and festivals but also a popular street food in the Darjeeling district with vendors selling it as a snack item.

Quite a large number of Newars, the original inhabitants of the Kathmandu Valley, live in the Darjeeling district. Traditionally, this community has been involved in the professions of priesthood, business and agriculture. They have their own exclusive language called Newari. But the Newars living in the Darjeeling district speak Nepali. They have a few traditional dishes that are very unique to them. Kwati is one of those dishes. Kwati (kwa means hot and ti means soup) or kwati ko jhol is a mixed beans curry dish made with nine different types of sprouted beans, chopped onions and tomatoes, spices and salt and garnished with chopped coriander leaves. The beans used in this dish can vary according to personal choice. Some of the commonly used ones are red kidney beans, chickpeas, soya beans, black-eyed peas, green gram, black gram, field beans, garden peas, field peas, cow peas and rice beans. Kwati ko jhol makes a delicious accompaniment with cooked rice or rotis. Although kwati originated from the Newar community, Nepalis all over the world make this dish. It is also a festive dish because it is customary to prepare it during Janai Purnima, a festival of great significance among the Nepali Hindus.

When it comes to non-vegetarian dishes, the Nepalese have an affinity for meat (masu) preparations over fish (machcha) or egg (anda or phool). The Nepalese in Nepal don't eat much fish. Whatever little they eat of it, they generally deep-fry or cook into curries, pickles and chutneys. Trout is a common fish eaten over there. But it is a different story for those living in the Darjeeling district. After living for years in West Bengal, the fish-eating habit of the Bengalis have caught on with the Nepalese. They enjoy eating machcha bhaat (fish curry and rice). 'The Nepalese in the district make simple fish curries inspired by the Bengali maachher jhol,' smiles Doma Wang. They cannot handle too many bones and prefer varieties like rui and katla. Small river fish are deep-fried and eaten as snacks with alcoholic drinks. They have also picked up the habit of making fish curries with shorshe bata from the Bengalis. It is a preparation that they enjoy a lot.

Buff (ranga ko masu), goat meat (khasi ko masu), pork (sungur ko masu) and chicken (kukhura ko masu) are cooked into curries and served with rice or rotis. The curry preparations are simple and delicious and generally made with basic ingredients like onions, tomatoes, spices and herbs. Some variety can be brought into the preparations like cooking pork in a curry form with green leafy vegetables or bamboo shoots. The trotters (khutta) of the pig are cooked into curries. Pork pickle is popular with the Nepalese and can be prepared with the meat or the trotters of the pig.

Duck (haans) is also much liked by the Nepalese in the Darjeeling district. They cook its meat in many ways like deep-frying, roasting or into curries.

Kheer is a very popular dessert prepared by the Nepalese at home. It is easy to make and at the same time very important in their culture. This creamy rice pudding is made with basic ingredients like long-grain rice, milk, sugar, ghee or butter, cloves, cardamoms, coconut and dried fruits. Perceived to be a pure and holy food, it is considered auspicious and offered to the gods during worship and served in religious festivals and other auspicious ceremonies. Kheer is also a celebratory dish served in social functions and gatherings.

It has been mentioned before that Tibetan cuisine also has an influence on the food habits of the Nepalese. This particularly includes their fondness for momo, thukpa and chhurpi. It is believed that these Tibetan dishes reached Nepal because of the Newar traders who travelled back and forth between Kathmandu and Lhasa trading in goods. The journeys increased after a treaty was signed between King Lakshminarasimha Malla of Nepal and Tibet in the seventeenth century that permitted the establishment of thirty-two trading houses by the Newar traders in Lhasa. These traders would sometimes live in Tibet for years at a time. The inevitable happened and influences in food habits began to take place. They learned to prepare the local dishes and on their return to Nepal would teach their family members the methods of preparation. Other Tibetan dishes like shaphalay and logo momo also found their way into Nepal through these traders. However, there is another theory that certain Tibetan dishes became an integral part of Nepali cuisine because of the Tibetan immigrants who settled in Nepal. This belief particularly holds true for the dish laphing, which is very popular in Boudha, a Buddhist religious site in Kathmandu. Boudha is home to the Boudhanath Stupa and a large number of Tibetan settlers.

The Nepalese made some adjustments in their momo preparations keeping their culinary habits in mind. The yak meat filling was replaced primarily with buff and then with chicken, pork and goat meat. While Tibetan momos generally have the basic ingredients of finely chopped onions and coriander leaves, the pastes of ginger and garlic, soya sauce, black pepper, salt and water mixed with the minced meat, the Nepalese spice up their momos by adding additional ingredients like turmeric, cumin, coriander and red chilli powders and sometimes even garam masala. Soya sauce and black pepper are omitted from the ingredients and in place of water some oil (particularly mustard oil), ghee or butter is mixed with the filling. The popular ingredients used as fillings in vegetarian momos include potatoes, cabbage, carrots, capsicums, spinach, mushrooms, soya beans, cheese, paneer, tofu and khuwa (khoya). The spicy sauce that is paired with momos is called achaar. The momo ko achaar that is made with the three main ingredients of tomatoes, sesame seeds and chillies is a favourite dip. The momo sauces are also called chutneys.

But when it comes to the Darjeeling district, Doma Wang points out that the Nepalese living there make momos the Tibetan way. 'They prefer it that way,' she says, 'there is a lot of merging of cultures between the Nepalese and Tibetans in Darjeeling district. These two communities mingle a lot. The Tibetans living there speak fluent Nepali and intercommunity marriages often take place between the two. We know that Tibetan cuisine is inclined towards Chinese culinary practices like steaming and stir-frying and Nepali cuisine is inclined towards Indian culinary practices like using a lot of masalas. But, in the district, the two communities not only try out each other's cuisine but most also know how to cook the other community's dishes. Using dalle khursani is an equally important part of the Darjeeling Tibetan culinary practice.'

The Nepalese living in the Darjeeling district enjoy eating Tibetan momos so much that they don't make some of the momo preparations that are popular back home in Nepal like buckwheat momo and jhol momo. When the dumpling is made of buckwheat flour, it is known as buckwheat momo or phaphar ko momo. When the momos are dipped in a pool of spicy and tangy tomatoes, soya beans and sesame seeds-based gravy sauce (jhol achaar), the preparation is known as jhol momo. The Nepalese in the Darjeeling district frequently use dalle khursani in making momo sauces.

Restaurateurs have come up with many new varieties of momos in Nepal. Since it has become such an important dish in the country, innovations are constantly taking place in the standard recipe. For example, an open momo is a very modern concept in momo making. The Gangri Sui Mai restaurant in Kathmandu is the pioneer of this particular type of momo preparation. A single piece of momo is stuffed with the filling and then shaped in such a way that it has four slots that are open on top, giving it the look of a flower. A small variety of spicy sauces are served with this momo. The sauces are poured into the different slots and the momo is eaten.

Although the Gangri Sui Mai restaurant is the pioneer of the concept of the open momo, it does not have a monopoly over the dish. Open momo is not only prepared by other restaurants in Nepal but also by food enthusiasts and connoisseurs across the country. It is such a popular preparation that Doma Wang included it in the menu of Blue Poppy Thakali, one of her many ventures in Calcutta, which mainly concentrates on the Himalayan range cuisines of Nepal and Tibet.

Just like the momo fillings, the Nepalese spice up their vegetarian and non-vegetarian thukpa preparations with ingredients like ginger, garlic, garam masala and turmeric, cumin, coriander and red chilli powders.

Doma Wang, with the ambition of promoting the culinary culture of the Darjeeling district, launched Blue Poppy Thakali in Sikkim House. Thus, it is of no surprise that the dishes served in this restaurant are not confined to Tibetan cuisine alone. An enthusiast of Nepali food will be pleased to discover sel roti, alu dum and even chicken choila listed in the menu. Choila is a Newari dish that is traditionally prepared with buff but can also be prepared with chicken, pork, mutton and even duck meat. Although the Newars in the Darjeeling district do not prepare choila, Doma Wang has included it in the menu of Blue Poppy Thakali. Choila means smoked meat in Newari. In this preparation, long strips of boneless meat are threaded onto skewers and barbequed till the meat is black and tender. This is known as haku choila (haku means black). The meat is then cut into bite-sized pieces. Spices like fenugreek seeds, turmeric and whole red chillies are fried in mustard oil. The pieces of meat are mixed with salt, spices, coriander leaves and the fried spices. The oil in which the spices have been fried is also poured on the meat and mixed well, completing the preparation.

Alu thukpa, a Nepali preparation very popular in Kalimpong, is available in the restaurant. Generous servings of steamed rice accompany curries like alu bodi tama, anda ko jhol, kukhura ko masu, sungur ko masu with rayo ko saag and khasi ko masu. Spicy pickles such as alu ko achaar and sungur ko khutta ko achaar (pickled pork trotters) can be eaten. The daring customers can choose small portions of sandheko gundruk and kinema (cooked in mustard oil with onions, garlic, ginger, chillies and salt) from the menu. Customers also have the choice of opting for thali meals. Dalle khursani pickles are available for sale in Blue Poppy Thakali and they come in paste form or with bamboo shoots or with spices or in brine.

Many other restaurateurs from the Darjeeling district have also opened eateries in Calcutta that now offer a small spread of Nepali dishes alongside the Tibetan ones.

Jhol momo, cowrie thukpa, chamre rice (a Nepali fried rice preparation) and a variety of tareko (meaning deep-fried) and choila preparations can be seen in these restaurants. Sekuwa is a grilled meat delicacy that is very popular in Nepal. Although the Nepalese in the Darjeeling district do not make this dish, one can find it in a few restaurants in Calcutta.

Doma Wang points out that many Bhutanese live in the district, particularly in Kalimpong. This has made Bhutanese cuisine prevalent in the district and a few restaurateurs like herself are trying to promote it in Calcutta by serving a few prominent dishes. Different kinds of cheese-based soups called datshis are eaten in Bhutan which are also popular in the Darjeeling district. The most famous of these datshis is ema datshi, ema meaning chilli and datshi meaning cheese, implying a dish of large chilli peppers cooked in a cheese-based sauce. Looked upon as the national dish of Bhutan, ema datshi is eaten with rice or tingmo. Doma Wang serves ema datshi in Blue Poppy Thakali as well as other datshi varieties, like kewa datshi (potatoes in cheese sauce) and shamu datshi (mushrooms in cheese sauce). But the mission does not end here. 'I plan to gradually introduce more Bhutanese dishes,' she ends the discussion. This shows that the efforts are clearly there. While a few restaurateurs have been brave enough to solely concentrate on Darjeeling district food, most have played safe by also including Southeast Asian and East Asian cuisines in the menu. But their hard work and the positive response of the customers make the future of this cuisine look promising.

3. Conclusion

I remember, many years ago, on returning to Calcutta after spending weeks abroad, the first thing that struck me about my country after being away from it for so long was its colour. There is truly never a dull moment in India. Its diversity and vibrancy add to its colour—not to mention the crowded streets, dust, dirt and smell, which also perhaps, add their own shades to the overall package that we call India.

The diversity of our country also extends to the food habits of the people of the different states. Each state has its own cuisine, style of cooking, variety of dishes, food habits and preferences. The differences may be governed by geography, religion or other factors, but they make the cuisines exclusive and unique. These different cuisines, combined together, fit into the broad term, 'Indian Cuisine'. Whether they live in the plains, hills or near rivers or seas, Indians have always celebrated this diversity. They have never shied away from enjoying each other's cuisine, just the way they have never shied away from participating in each other's festivals, irrespective of the customs, traditions and religions they individually follow.

It is then no surprise that Indian cuisine today is so sought after by foreigners. To them, Indian cuisine is complex, unique, elaborate and bursts with flavours. It is also, like many things to do with India, considered 'exotic'.

In this book, so far, I have given a ringside view of the diversity of the culinary culture of Calcutta by exploring its prevalent food trends. But, the experimental nature of the residents of the city, keeps the door ajar for newer food trends to walk into the market in the future. The food business is lucrative in Calcutta, encouraging entrepreneurs to invest in the market, and capitalize on the enthusiasm of its foodies.

There are already visible signs of the Northeast Indian cuisine having made its foray into Calcutta. Although this cuisine is in a nascent stage and yet to make any impact due to its blandness, it deserves a mention because it has stepped into the city.

The northeast region of India is a haven for lovers of non-vegetarian food. The cuisine of each state is unique with its own special flavour and is an amalgamation of the different cuisines of the various tribal groups living in the state. In the pre-colonial days, the market for food products in the northeast was not developed because of the transport bottleneck and poor purchasing power of the people. This made the villagers self-sufficient as they heavily relied on the natural produce of the land. Since rice is the main grain crop grown in the region, they are major rice eaters. Ample fresh green vegetables and leafy green vegetables are used in their cooking. The locals, particularly the inhabitants of Assam and Tripura, enjoy eating fish. Although different animals and birds are eaten, a majority of the tribes in the region prefer pork, and for this reason, pigs are reared and slaughtered in village households. Northeast Indian cooking does not feature the liberal use of the two pillars of Indian cooking—oil and spices. On the whole, they use very little oil and minimum spices in their cooking, and manage with locally grown herbs and spices. The use of garam masala does not feature in their culinary practices. On the contrary, ginger and garlic are the essential spices. The spiciness in their food usually comes from the use of chillies. It is part of their culinary culture to use dried and fermented ingredients in cooking. Bamboo shoots feature a lot in their cuisine. Although mustard oil is their main medium of cooking, lard is used most often by the tribes in the villages for cooking dishes. They also enjoy imbibing fermented alcoholic drinks.

Although Northeast India is blessed in many ways, life is not easy for the inhabitants of the state, particularly the youth. The natural beauty of these states ensures some flow of tourists, giving the region an active tourism sector. But, otherwise, industry in most of the northeastern states of India is underdeveloped, leading to unemployment and frustration in the youth. The lack of infrastructure prevents industries from investing in the states. The number of private enterprises and small and medium businesses in this region is very few. Locals are left to seek work mostly with government organizations and academic institutions, making options very limited. Frequent conflicts between the different ethnic groups often bring normal life to a standstill. These circumstances force the youth of this region to abandon their land and come down to the plains in search of better job opportunities and better chances at education.

Although there are many settlers from Northeast India in Calcutta, not many among them have made the attempt so far to set up canteens or restaurants. The governments of the different states in the northeast have provided boarding and lodging facilities for government officials and employees from their homelands in the city. These guest houses are called 'Bhavans' or 'Houses' and they have full-fledged canteens that serve authentic meals from their homelands at reasonable prices. Although outsiders are welcome to try out the food in many of these canteens, they are mainly meant for the visiting officials and employees. Also, the canteens have not been set up with the objective of commercializing or popularizing these regional cuisines, thereby restricting their visibility.

However, it will be a mistake to assume that no attempts are being made at all to promote the cuisine. In recent years, the owners of a full-fledged Assamese restaurant, a pop-up Naga restaurant and a restaurant that primarily focuses on the cuisine of Meghalaya are making some serious attempts not only to cater to the members of their communities but also serve the authentic dishes of their homelands to enthusiasts and connoisseurs willing to experiment. These restaurants are Jaluk—The Taste of Assam, a traditional Assamese restaurant in Calcutta and the first of its kind in the city so far started by Sanker Prasad, El's Kitchen, a pop-up restaurant organized by Chef Elika Awomi that offers full-fledged authentic Naga meals, and Shillong Point, a small multicuisine restaurant set up by restaurateur Raja Joy Phookan that has a few Khasi dishes from Meghalaya as well as Naga dishes featured in its menu. For this purpose, the restaurateurs frequently travel all the way to their hometowns and bring back loads of the indigenous ingredients required for cooking their dishes. Sometimes, they even get the ingredients shipped. By investing so much capital, time and effort in these ventures, these restaurateurs have managed to attract a loyal clientele outside their own communities.

Perhaps, it is the possibility of a future for this type of cuisine that has induced few restaurateurs who do not belong to the Northeast region of India to set up a restaurant serving this fare as well. It came as a pleasant surprise when three Bengalis opened a restaurant named Santa's Fantasea in Calcutta, specializing in seafood and the tribal cuisines of India. These tribal cuisines include a few dishes from the Northeast region of the country.

Kaushik Ghosh, one of the three partners of the restaurant, explains, 'we lived in Chandipur in Orissa for around fifteen years, where we ran a hotel. The tribal food of Orissa is very tasty. Together, we would travel to the forests, interact with the tribal folks and enjoy their food. Even visitors from Calcutta relished their food very much. This gave us the idea of starting a restaurant in Calcutta that would specialize in tribal cuisines. The dishes would be off-beat and different from what is usually served in the restaurants in the city.' This thought made them return to Calcutta and open their first outlet in Golpark in the southern part of the city.

They decided to serve tribal dishes from all over the country. And this included Orissa and the Northeast region of India as well. Santa's Fantasea does not concentrate on the food of any particular state of the Northeast region. As of now, it serves dishes from states like Nagaland, Meghalaya, Mizoram and Manipur. Usually, the cuisine of the Seven Sister States is bland but in order to cater to the taste buds of the local people, the owners of the restaurant chose to serve only those dishes from these states that are spicier than usual. They have also tweaked the dishes a bit to cater to the taste buds of Calcuttans.

Since this book explores the culinary story of Calcutta, it will be a gross mistake to overlook a largely unknown aspect of it—Burmese cuisine. There is a certain section of Bengalis who have had a strong connection in the past with Burma, or rather Myanmar, as it is now known, while it was under the British rule from 1824 to 1948.

In her article, 'Burmese Food in Kolkata' for *Mint* (16 September 2018), Arundhati Ray points out, 'Although Kolkata's cosmopolitan table has been extensively chronicled, one strand remains overlooked: the story of thousands of Bengali families who went to Myanmar during colonial times, starting from the end of the nineteenth century, and settled there for two or three generations. Many went as part of the government service—as doctors, professors, officials in the post and telegraph department and railways—while others established lucrative businesses there. This community of migrant Bengalis flourished, maintaining their social and cultural identity in their new homeland without difficulty.' But the Japanese invasion and subsequent occupation of Burma in the early 1940s and the imposition of military rule in the early 1960s compelled the Bengali immigrants to relocate to Calcutta.

While these immigrants gradually found their feet in the city of their origin, fond memories of their lives in Burma remained with them—memories of the homes they had built, the wonderful lives they had led and even the food they had eaten. It had not been too difficult for them to adjust to life in Burma, especially when it came to culinary practices and food habits. The Burmese are largely rice-eating people and the Irrawaddy and its tributaries teem with fish like the hilsa, carp and catfish—all favourite choices of the Bengalis. The immigrants also became gradually aware of the cuisine and cooking style of their new environment. They became familiar with the popular breakfast food—mohinga—rice vermicelli in a fragrant catfish-based broth cooked with shallots, spices, lemon grass, fish sauce, ngapi (salted, fermented and dried fish or shrimp paste), sliced banana piths and rice or chickpea flour, and garnished with toppings of one's choice that range from condiments like chilli flakes, coriander leaves, lime wedges, halved boiled eggs and beresta to vegetable (like bottle gourd) fritters and deep-fried fish cakes. They began indulging in it often as they did in the different varieties of healthy thokes (salads), especially the fermented or pickled tea leaves salad called laphet thoke (laphet means fermented or pickled tea leaves) made by mixing the leaves with chopped tomatoes, cabbage and red chillies, dried shrimp powder, fish sauce, lime juice, crushed peanuts, assorted fried bean seeds, sesame seeds and garlic infused peanut oil, as well as the delicious khow suey (noodle) preparations like ohn no khow suey—a spicy and soupy, coconut milk-based egg noodles dish, consisting of chicken pieces, and served with toppings like chilli flakes, coriander leaves, lime wedges, halved boiled eggs and beresta.

Once the immigrants developed a taste for Burmese dishes, they also learnt to prepare them. Soon, ingredients typical to Burmese cuisine began to enter their kitchens like fish sauce, peanut oil, shallot oil, lemon grass, chilli flakes, chickpea flour, ngapi and powdered dried shrimp. Jars of balachaung, a spicy shrimp relish, began to be seen on dining tables while hinjos (soups) and non-vegetarian sipyans (curries) began to be eaten with steamed rice. Even Bengali cuisine put on a different garb in these homes. The Burmese style of cooking and ingredients crept into otherwise authentic Bengali preparations. For example, meat began to be cooked with vegetables, sourness from agents like lime juice and tamarind pulp began to infuse curries, additional doses of pounded garlic and dried red chillies added an extra punch to preparations, and crushed peanuts were now added to lend crunchiness to plain salads.

The Burma-returned-Bengalis have continued with these culinary practices. This holds true even for their succeeding generations who have kept alive the recipes. Over the years, many of them have also tried to stay connected with each other on the common grounds of fond memories and food. Arundhati Ray points out an interesting fact, 'Every January, an abandoned gymnasium in Kankurgachi, Kolkata, comes alive with a gathering of some 200 Bengalis. Doctors, retired public servants, professors and businessmen congregate to celebrate their shared history of a foreign country that generations in their families had considered home: Myanmar—or Burma as most still call it. Over typical Burmese dishes like mohinga, [ohn] no khow suey and laphet thoke, slipping effortlessly between Bengali and Burmese, they recall people, places and flavours of the "land of golden pagodas".' This annual gathering is a way of keeping in touch with each other and staying connected to their erstwhile homeland.

For a long time, Burmese cuisine in Calcutta remained a home-confined cuisine till Chanda Dutt, a third generation Bengali Burmese, who had lived in Burma till 1977, decided to take the risk, upon encouragement by family members and friends, and began organizing pop-up restaurants at her home, serving this cuisine. She had always been a good chef and had mastered the recipes carried back home by her mother. Chanda Dutt has played a leading role in bringing some visibility to the largely unknown Burmese cuisine in Calcutta. Since Bibi Sarkar of Bibi of Taaja's offers her customers dishes from across the globe, her menu also features a few Burmese dishes.

The efforts of these ladies have been followed by the recent establishment of the pan-Indian initiative called Burma Burma Restaurant and Tea Room in Stephen Court on Park Street. Needless to say, the classy ambience of the restaurant and its menu have begun attracting a fair number of diners who are liking the spiciness and tanginess of the dishes.

With this, I bring to a close my chronicle of the culinary story of Calcutta. Fortunately, the bright side of the story is that it will not end here because the culinary journey of Calcutta is a continuous and ever-evolving one.

Recipes

British Influence

Rose Malai: Serves 6 (Courtesy: Paramount, Kolkata)

Ingredients

Milk 300 ml
Extra milk 1 cup
Khoya 250 gms
Sugar 200 gms
Salt ½ tsp
Rose syrup 2 tbsp per glass
Broken cashew nuts 100gm
Halved raisins 50 gms
Crushed ice

Mix the khoya and half the quantity of sugar with the extra milk and keep it in the refrigerator. Now mix the salt and the remaining sugar with 300 ml of milk. Fill a tall glass with crushed ice (up to half the level of the glass). Put 2 tbsp of rose syrup in the glass and pour some of the sweetened milk in it. Layer the top of the juice with some of the khoya mixture. Put a few pieces of broken cashew nuts and halved raisins on the khoya layer. Serve chilled.

*

Tipsy Pudding: Serves 4 (Courtesy: Ashish Bagul, former executive chef, Novotel Kolkata Hotel and Residences)

Ingredients for the Pudding:

Vanilla sponge cake ½ lb
Milk ½ cup
Red wine 200 ml
Brandy 100 ml

Mixed jam 50 gms
Marmalade 50 gms
Fruit jelly 100 gms
Snow egg 1 (optional)
Almond slivers for garnishing

Ingredients for the Custard:

Milk 1l
Egg yolks 10
Cream 100 ml
Sugar 200 gms
Vanilla essence 5 ml

Mix all the ingredients for the custard and cook on a double boiler. Cook the custard till it becomes thick.

Cut the vanilla sponge cake in half. Soak the halved pieces in milk, red wine and brandy. Place a piece of the cake in a bowl. A mixture of the mixed jam, marmalade and fruit jelly is applied in a layer on the sponge cake. Place the other piece of the sponge cake on this jellied piece and repeat the process. Spread the custard in a layer over the sponge cake and apply the last layer of mixed jam, marmalade and fruit jelly over it. Spread the snow egg (if using) over this last layer and sprinkle the slivers of almonds on top of the pudding. Serve chilled.

*

Portuguese Influence

Rasogolla: 25 Pieces (Courtesy: Dhiman Das, director, K.C. Das Pvt. Ltd, Kolkata)

Ingredients

Chhana 250 gms
Sugar 2 kgs
Water

Take 1 litre of water and add 500 gms of sugar to it. Boil the water and the sugar mixture to make sugar syrup of a thin consistency.

Take 1 litre of water and boil 1½ kg of sugar in it to make a thick sugar syrup. Drain the chhana of all its whey and knead it into soft dough. Make small equal-sized balls from this dough. Put these chhana balls in the thick sugar syrup and cook them on simmer heat for 15 minutes. The balls will double in size.

Take the cooking off the fire when the chhana balls have completely soaked up the sugar syrup. Immerse the chhana balls in 1 litre of lukewarm water for some time. Then take them out of the lukewarm water and put them in the thin sugar syrup. Serve the rasogollas with the syrup when they turn cold.

*

Anglo-Indian Influence

Jalebi Pudding: Serves 4 (Courtesy: Pamela Rebeiro, former corporate executive and food enthusiast, Kolkata)

Ingredients

Milk 500 ml
Eggs 3
Jalebis 3 (broken into pieces)
Vanilla essence a few drops
Sugar as per taste

Whisk the eggs along with some sugar. When the sugar dissolves completely, add the milk. Now add a few drops of vanilla essence. Put the broken pieces of jalebis in a pudding dish that has been greased. Pour the custard mixture over the jalebis. Cover the pudding dish and place it in a pan that is filled with water that comes halfway up the sides of the dish. Preheat an oven to 180 degree Celsius and bake the pudding till the custard is set. The jalebi pudding is now ready. Serve warm.

*

Jewish Influence

Cheese Sambusak: 20 Sambusaks (Courtesy: Flower Silliman, author of *Three Cups of Flour*, Kolkata)

Ingredients for the Dough

Self-rising flour 1½ lbs
Sugar 2 tsp
Salt 1 tsp

Oil 6 oz
Water

Ingredients for the Filling

Cheese (Gouda or Cheddar) 3 lbs
Flour 3 tbsp
Eggs 9

Mix the flour, salt and sugar. Add the oil and some water to make a dough. Cover the dough and allow it to stand for half an hour. Meanwhile make the filling. Grate the cheese (if using Gouda, cut into cubes and leave in the refrigerator for one or two days to dry out before grating). Mix the grated cheese, beaten eggs and flour.

To make each pastry, pinch a ball from the dough and roll it out into a thin ¼-inch circle. Put 1 tablespoon of the filling in the centre and turn over to form a half-circle, sealing the edges with water. Bake till the pastry is light brown in colour and the cheese filling is risen and puffy. Serve warm.

*

Nawabi Influence

Galawati Kebab: Serves 4 (Courtesy: Fatima Mirza, descendant of Prince Mirza Hamid Ali Bahadur (the eldest son of Nawab Wajid Ali Shah) and food columnist, Kolkata)

Ingredients

Minced mutton 500 gms
Raw papaya paste 50 gms
Roasted gram flour (sattu) 50 gms
Curd 50 gms
Kewra water 2 tbsp
Salt as per taste
Ghee 100 gms

Ingredients for Grinding

Whole red chillies 5
Coriander seeds 1 tbsp
Poppy seeds 1 tbsp
Cinnamon ½ piece

Almonds 10
Dry coconut, a big piece
Lightly roast the ingredients and grind them into a fine paste.

Ingredients for the Masala Paste

Medium-sized onions (sliced, fried and crushed) 2
Small onions 2
Ginger 20 gms
Garlic 15 gms
Cloves 5
Green cardamoms 5
Mace, a small piece
Nutmeg, a pinch
Black pepper ½ tsp

Secret Ingredient

A piece of burning coal

For Garnishing

Mint leaves, a few sprigs
Onion rings, a few
Slices of lime, a few

Grind the minced meat to a fine paste and marinate it with the raw papaya paste and some salt for 30 minutes. Mix the ground masala, the paste masala and the gram flour with the minced meat. Place a burning coal in the middle of a container holding the minced meat. Pour a tablespoon of ghee on the burning coal. Immediately put a lid on the container and keep it aside for about 20 minutes. Now allow the smoke to spread evenly and get infused with the meat. This enhances the aroma of the dish.

Now heat the rest of the ghee in a pan. Add the minced meat to the ghee along with the beaten curd and the required quantity of salt and cook on a low flame. Stir continuously to prevent the meat from sticking together. Once the meat is cooked, add the kewra water to it. Garnish with the mint leaves, onion rings and slices of lime. Serve hot with paratha or rumali roti.

*

Chinese Influence

Chicken Manchurian: Serves 2 (Courtesy: The Saturday Club Limited, Kolkata)

Ingredients

Boneless chicken 150 gms (8 pieces)
Egg white 1
Onion (sliced) 1
Ginger-garlic paste 1tbsp
Soya sauce 1 tsp
Cornflour 1 tsp
Black and white pepper 1 tsp
Salt as per taste
Chopped spring onions for garnishing
Oil

Ingredients for the Sauce

Soya sauce 1½ tsp
Red chilli sauce 2 tsp
Vinegar 1 tsp
Cornflour 2 tsp mixed with 3 tbsp of water
Salt as per taste

Marinate the chicken pieces with the cornflour, soya sauce, one tsp of ginger and garlic paste, egg white, pepper powders and some salt. Keep the marinated chicken aside for some time. Make the sauce by mixing all the ingredients listed under 'Sauce'. Heat some oil in a pan and deep-fry the marinated chicken pieces and keep them aside. Fry the sliced onion till soft but not brown. Add the remaining ginger and garlic paste and fry till aromatic. Now add the fried chicken and the sauce and fry for another five to six minutes. Some water may be added if the sauce becomes too thick, keeping a little gravy. Serve the Chicken Manchurian garnished with chopped spring onions.

*

Bengali Cuisine

Ilish Maachher Paturi (Hilsa Paturi): 8–10 Paturis (Courtesy: Utpala Kanjilal, former bureaucrat and food enthusiast, Kolkata)

Ingredients

Hilsa pieces 8–10
Turmeric powder 2 tsp
Mustard paste 6 tbsp
Green chilli paste 2 tsp
Green chillies 8–10
Banana leaves
Salt as per taste
Mustard oil 150 ml

Make a mixture with the mustard paste, green chilli paste, turmeric powder, salt and mustard oil. Coat the hilsa pieces with this mixture. Cut the banana leaves into big rectangular pieces and grease them with some mustard oil. Take two such leaves and arrange them, one on top of the other. Place a piece of coated fish in the middle of the arranged leaves and add a little more of the mixture to it. Garnish the fish with a whole green chilli. Fold the leaves to make a parcel and secure with a string. Repeat this process with the remaining fish pieces.

Grease a griddle or tawa with some mustard oil. Place the parcels on the preheated griddle and cook the fish pieces over low flame. It takes about twenty minutes to cook the fish well. Ilish maachher paturi is served with steamed rice. The fish is taken out from its parcel and eaten with the rice.

*

Chingri Maachher Malaikari (Prawn Malai Curry): Serves 4 (Courtesy: Utpala Kanjilal, former bureaucrat and food enthusiast, Kolkata)

Ingredients

Prawns 500 gms
Onions 3
Chopped cinger 2 tbsp
Turmeric powder 1½ tsp
Red chilli powder 1 tsp
Garom mashla 1 tsp
Bay leaves 2
Coconut milk 2 cups
Sugar 1 tsp
Ghee 2 tsp
Salt as per taste
Mustard oil

Shell and devein the prawns. Slice one onion and keep aside. Roughly chop the other onions and grind them into a paste with the ginger. Coat the prawns with a pinch of turmeric powder and salt. Marinate them for a few minutes. Now heat some oil in a wok. Lightly fry the prawns in it. Remove the fried prawns and keep them aside. Pour some more oil into the wok. Add the bay leaves and onion slices and fry them till the slices are soft but not brown. Now add the onion and ginger paste, and the turmeric and red chilli powders. Sauté the spices. Add the fried prawns and cook them for a few minutes, allowing the spices to mix well with the fish. Finally, add the coconut milk is added and season with some salt. Cook till done. As a final touch, add the sugar, garom mashla and ghee. Stir for a few minutes and take the cooking off the flame. Serve with steamed rice.

*

Darjeeling District

Shaphalay (Tibetan): 5 Pieces (Courtesy: Blue Poppy, Kolkata)

Ingredients for the Filling

Minced meat (chicken, mutton, pork or beef) 100 gms
Chopped onions 50 gms
Ginger paste 1 tsp
Soya sauce 1 tsp
Chopped spring onions or coriander leaves optional
Salt as per taste

Ingredients for the Dough

Refined flour (maida) 200 gms
Water

Ingredient for Frying

Oil

Mix the refined flour and some water and knead into dough. Pinch balls from this dough and roll them out into medium-sized flatbreads (rotis). Meanwhile mix all the ingredients for the filling. Put two to three tbsps of the mixture on a flatbread and spread it well, leaving out the edges. Put another flatbread on top of it and crimp the edges together to seal them. Repeat this procedure for the remaining flatbreads. Heat the oil and deep-fry the shaphalays till they are golden brown on both sides. Serve with momo sauce (sepen).

Acknowledgements

Writing this book has been a long and interesting journey. It has been more of teamwork between me and all those who have contributed to the contents of the book. This includes the authors who have documented the history of the city and its different communities, food historians, writers, connoisseurs and enthusiasts as well as the owners of the several eateries featured in the book. I take this opportunity to extend my heartfelt gratitude to them for sharing with me their knowledge about the city and its culinary story either over lengthy interviews, interspersed between with much-needed tea and coffee breaks or by lending me extensive material. A special note of thanks goes out to Maria Letizia Peliti, the great-grand-daughter of Chevalier Federico Peliti, and Diya Basu, then director of public relations and communication at the Park Hotels, for being of much help in the writing of this book. I have greatly appreciated the help offered to me by the owners, curators and authorities of art galleries, museums and libraries by allowing me to use photographs from their priceless collections for this book and in this regard, I extend my thanks to Istituto Centrale per la Grafica in Rome and Rabindra Bharati Museum and Aakriti Art Gallery in Kolkata. I would also like to thank Enrico De Barbieri, descendant of Angelo Firpo, for allowing me to use images from his family heirloom photo collection for the book. The willingness of the various establishments, chefs and food enthusiasts to share their favourite recipes has also been much appreciated.

I especially want to extend my heartfelt gratitude to some individuals who have played very significant roles in the shaping of this book. First, my parents, to whom I am indebted for not only being my biggest source of emotional strength and support, but also providing constructive criticism that was required while writing the book. I extend my sincerest thanks to Himadri Banerjee, well-known researcher and former professor of history, who held the chair of Guru Nanak professor of Indian history at the department of history in Jadavpur University, for lending me the profound work of research on the different communities of the city, *Calcutta Mosaic: Essays and Interviews on the Minority Communities of Calcutta*, which he has authored and edited with other scholars. This book has been a major source of research and information while exploring the histories of the different communities for my work. Finally, I fall short of words to express the gratitude I feel towards my brother-in-law, Abhik Ray, a banking professional, heritage enthusiast and one of the few banking historians in the country, who has authored acclaimed books on the subject. His profound knowledge and priceless collection of materials about the heritage of Kolkata has helped me tremendously in the writing of this book.

Bibliography

Abdi, S.N.M. *Without Apologies*, Outlook, October 22, 2012. https://www.outlookindia.com

Acoos. *Why do we (Armenians) celebrate Christmas on January 6th*. www.acoos.org

Aghajanian, Liana. *Anoush Abour or Noah's Pudding*, Dining in Diaspora: Documenting the Armenian Food Experience in the Diaspora, January 1, 2018. https://www.diningindiaspora.com

Ahmed, Ershad. *Dhakai Bakarkhani and the legend*, Dhaka, September 29, 2007. www.dhakadailyphoto.blogspot.com

Ahmed, Salahuddin. *Bangladesh: Past and Present*, A.P.H. Publishing Corporation, 2004.

Ajantrik. *Armenian Ghat, Calcutta, 1734*, puronokolkata: Calcutta: as she was—a visual documentation of socio-cultural ethos spanning over three centuries, May 28, 2015. https://puronokolkata.com

_____*Hall and Anderson Store, Chowringhee, Calcutta, c1925*, puronokolkata: Calcutta: as she was—a visual documentation of socio-cultural ethos spanning over three centuries, April 25, 2014. https://www.puronokolkata.com

Alter, Joseph S. *Yoga in Modern India: The Body between Science and Philosophy*, Princeton University Press, 2004.

Amarot srl. *1872: Peliti's Vermut*, Peliti's, 2017. www.pelitis.com

Amit, Dassana. *Litti Chokha Recipe, How to Make Litti Chokha/Litti Recipe*, Veg Recipes of India, September 20, 2019. https://www.vegrecipesofindia.com

Amr, Samir S.; Tbakhi Abdulghani. *Abu Bakr Muhammad Ibn Zakariya Al Razi (Rhazes): Philosopher, Physician and Alchemist*, July–August, 27 (4): 305–07, Annals of Saudi Medicine (ASM), PMC: US National Library of Medicine, National Institutes of Health, NCBI, 2007. https://www.ncbi.nlm.nih.gov

AncientPages.com. *King Charles II of England Banned Coffeehouses in 1675*, Ancient pages, June 18, 2018. https://www.ancientpages.com

Apcar, Alexander Apcar. *Supplement to the London Gazette (Of Friday, the 29th of December, 1905)*, India Office, January 1, 1906. https://www.thegazette.co.uk

Archuleta, Nadia. Leaf Group Ltd./Leaf Group Media, *Armenian Culture & Traditions on Christmas*, Classroom, https://www.classroom.synonym.com

Armeniagogo. *Armenian Christmas/What are the Traditions & Date?, How to Say Merry Christmas in Armenian?* November 12, 2016. https://www.armeniagogo.com

Arshtad. *The Story of Sanjan: The Qissa-i Sanjan*, Arshtad. https://www.arshtad.wordpress.com

Avey, Tori. *Coffee—A Caffeinated History*, Tori Avey: Every Day Inspired By The Past. April 4, 2013. https://www.toriavey.com

Bag, Shamik. 'Blue Santa and fruit-less Armenian cakes', *Mint*, December 23, 2016. https://www.livemint.com

_____'Kolkata Chromosome: The last emperor', *Mint*, December 13, 2012. https://www.livemint.com

_____'Yesterday once more at Trincas', *Mint*, March 16, 2010. https://www.livemint.com

Bagchi, Nondon. 'Beef it up', *The Telegraph,* June 3, 2008.

_____'Yesterday once more', *Tongue Twister, The Telegraph*, March 14, 2006.

Bali, Rajen. *Chef and the City—The Tastemakers of the 1940s Calcutta*, Hungry Thirsty Wot, Kolkata & Bengal, Window On Travel, 2018. https://www.wotweb.com

Bandyopadhyay, Debashish. 'Keo Lal Keo Dudh-Shada, Doi Diye Jai Chena', *Anandabazar Patrika*, November 18, 2017.

Bandyopadhyay, Raghab. 'The Inheritors: Slum And Pavement Life in Calcutta', *Calcutta: The Living City—Volume II: The Present and Future.* Ed. Sukanta Chaudhuri. Oxford University Press, 1990.

Banerjee, Dibyendu. *Firpo's Restaurant—The Legend of the Lost*, Tutorial At Home, March 14, 2019. https://www.tutorialathome.in

_____*Legend of the Lost—Firpo's Restaurant*, NoiseBreak, September 22, 2016. www.noisebreak.com

Banerjee, Gautam. *Robert Bruce Opened the Door to Assam's Great Tea Industry*, Khabar Samay, April 7, 2017. https://www.khabarsamay.com

Banerjee, M.K., 2004, 'Parsi', *People of India: Maharashtra*, Part Three, Volume 3, Anthropological Survey of India. Eds. B.V. Bhanu, B.R. Bhatnagar, D.K. Bose, V.S. Kulkarni, J. Sreenath. Popular Prakashan, 2004.

Banerjee, Poulomi. 'Church Children', *The Telegraph*, Kolkata, West Bengal, India, May 23, 2010.

Banerjee, Sudeshna. 'Kitchen Queens', *The Telegraph,* Kolkata, West Bengal, India, May 11, 2012.

Banerji, Chitrita. *Bengali Cooking: Seasons and Festivals*. Aleph Book Company, 2017.

Banka, Neha. 'Street-wise Kolkata: How Park Street got its name', *The Indian Express*, December 3, 2019. https://www.indianexpress.com

Barua, Ananya. *King of Lemons: How the Gondhoraj Lebu Literally Remains True to Its Roots*, The Better Home, The Better India, June 17, 2019. https://www.thebetterindia.com

BBC, *Daily life: food laws*, Practices in Judaism, Bitesize, BBC. https://www.bbc.co.uk

Bethell, Leslie. *Brazil: Empire and Republic: 1822–1930*, Cambridge University Press, 1989.

Bhandari, Bhupesh. 'It started with Plassey…', *Business Standard*, June 12, 2014. https://www.business-standard.com

Bhasin, Raaja. 'Chevalier' Federico Peliti and Carignano, *Jottings from Himachal, Himachal Tribune, The Tribune: Voice of the People*, August 3, 2019. https://www.tribuneindia.com

Bhattacharya, Arundhati. 'Friends in need: Parsis care for their elderly', *The Telegraph*, Kolkata, West Bengal, India, September 13, 2019.

Bhattacharya, Bhaswati. *Much Ado Over Coffee: Indian Coffee House Then and Now*, Routledge, 2018.

Bhattacharya, Nandini. '"South Indians" in Calcutta: Experiences in Cultural Processes', *Calcutta Mosaic: Essays and Interviews on the Minority Communities of Calcutta*. Eds. Himadri Banerjee, Nilanjana Gupta, Sipra Mukherjee. Anthem Press, 2009.

_____'The Anglo-Indians of Calcutta: An Interview with Rudolph L. Rodrigues', *Calcutta Mosaic: Essays and Interviews on the Minority Communities of Calcutta.* Eds. Himadri Banerjee, Nilanjana Gupta, Sipra Mukherjee. Anthem Press, 2009.

Bhattacharya, Raj. Copyright Darjeeling-Tourism.com, *People & Culture of Darjeeling*, Darjeeling Tourism. https://www.darjeeling-tourism.com

Bhattacharya, Susmia, 2009, 'The Armenians of Calcutta', *Calcutta Mosaic: Essays and Interviews on the Minority Communities of Calcutta*. Eds. Himadri Banerjee, Nilanjana Gupta, Sipra Mukherjee. Anthem Press, 2009.

Bhattacharya, Tania. *How the 20 Jews left in Kolkata are using food to keep their culture alive*, Namaste/Shalom, Quartz India, September 12, 2016. https://www.qz.com

Bhattacharya, Urvashi. 'Sweet Surprise at the HHI's Nolen Gur Fest, With t2', Food, t2, *The Telegraph*, January 20, 2020. https://www.epaper.telegraphindia.com

Bhuyan, Avantika. 'From antique barnis to bowls, vintage utensils tell a hundred tales'. *Panache*, *The Economic Times*. October 1, 2018. https://www.economictimes.indiatimes.com

_____'How the humble potato has a more personal resonance for most', *Panache*, *The Economic Times*, March 18, 2018. https://www.economictimes.indiatimes.com

Biswas, Prabodh. 'Job Charnock', *Calcutta: The Living City—Volume I: The Past*. Ed. Sukanta Chaudhuri. Oxford University Press, 1990.

Biswas, Premankur. 'Kolkata's 195-yr-old Armenian College and Philanthropic Academy: The last bastion of the rapidly declining community in India', *Lifestyle, The Indian Express*, April 10, 2016. https://www.indianexpress.com

Blue Bottle Coffee. *Origins: Brazil*, Blue Bottle Coffee Lab, December 5, 2017. https://www.blog.bluebottlecoffee.com

Bose, Rakhi. *What Did Rabindranath Tagore Do with the Nobel Prize?*, Buzz, News 18, May 11, 2018. https://www.news18.com

Boyce, M. *Ahura Mazda*, Encyclopaedia Iranica, July 29, 2011. https://www.iranicaonline.org

Boyd, Joshua Danton. *How Britain's tea economy pushed the world to boiling point*, Crunch. July 29, 2014. https://www.crunch.co.uk

Brown, Katherine Butler. 'Did Aurangzeb Ban Music? Questions for the Historiography of His Reign', *Modern Asian Studies*, 41 (1): 79. Cambridge University Press, 2007.

Calcutta Law Times. 'Sabarna Roychowdhury Paribar Parishad Vs. The State of West Bengal & Ors. on 16 May, 2003'. *Calcutta Law Times*, Vol. 2, p 625, W.P. No. 1484 of 2001, HC Bench Judgement, Ashok Kumar Mathur (CJ), Jayanta Kumar Biswas (J), R. Cambray & Co. Private Ltd., 2003.

Capricornio Coffees (Specialty Relationships Brazil). *Brazil—Coffee History*, All about coffee, https://www.capricorniocoffees.com

Chakrabarti, Kunal; Chakrabarti, Shubhra. *Historical Dictionary of the Bengalis*, Scarecrow Press, 2013.

Chakraborty, Rakhi. 'The Bengal Famine: How the British engineered the worst genocide in human history for profit'. *Your Story*. August 15, 2014. https://www.yourstory.com

Chakraborty, Riddhi. 'The Story of Gauhar Jaan: India's First "Pop" Star', *Rolling Stone India*, June 26, 2018. https://www.rollingstoneindia.com

Chakraborty, Samhita. '55 years young Chowringhee', *The Telegraph online*, June 11, 2017. https://www.telegraphindia.com

Chakraborty, Satyesh C. 'The Growth of Calcutta in the Twentieth Century', *Calcutta: The Living City—Volume II: The Present And Future*. Ed. Sukanta Chaudhuri. Oxford University Press, 1990.

Chakraborty, Shamayita. 'Saraswati Puja officially kicks off the season of ilish', *E Times: Entertainment Times*, *The Times of India*, January 28, 2020. https://www.timesofindia.indiatimes.com

———'The truth about our bitter food', *E Times: Entertainment Times, The Times of India*, March 18, 2018. https://www.timesofindia.indiatimes.com

Chaliha, Jaya; Gupta, Bunny. 'Durga Puja in Calcutta', *Calcutta: The Living City—Volume II: The Present and Future.* Ed. Sukanta Chaudhuri, Oxford University Press, 1990.

Chaliha, Jaya; Gupta, Bunny. 1990, 'The Armenians in Calcutta', *Calcutta: The Living City: Volume I: The Past.* Ed. Sukanta Chaudhuri. Oxford University Press, 1990.

Chapman, Jeff. *The Impact of the Potato, History Magazine*, https://www.history-magazine.com

Chater, Liz. *Sir Paul Chater: Brief Biography*, Sir Catchick Paul Chater Kt. C.M.G. (1846–1926). www.freepages.rootsweb.com

Chati, Amrusha. *Lady Kenny: A Sweet Legacy*, Live History India, June 19, 2017. https://www.livehistoryindia.com

———*The Samosa Trail*, Live History India, April 26, 2017. https://www.livehistoryindia.com

Chatterjee, Arup K. 'How chai arrived in India 170 years ago', *The Hindu*, August 18, 2018. https://www.thehindu.com

Chatterjee, Garga. *'In my religion, meat is Ma Kali's prasad': A Shakto Hindu objects to enforced vegetarianism*, Scroll.in, September 16, 2015. https://www.scroll.in

Chatterjee, Partha. 'The Political Culture Of Calcutta', *Calcutta: The Living City—Volume II: The Present and Future.* Ed. Sukanta Chaudhuri. Oxford University Press, 1990.

Chatterjee, Priyadarshini. 'One country, many "wadis", *Mint*, September 24, 2018. https://www.livemint.com

———'The purple heart of the banana tree', *Mint*, March 24, 2018. https://www.livemint.com

———'The universe of Bengali sweets was vast even before the roshogolla arrived with the Portuguese', Food, *Scroll.in*, November 24, 2017. https://www.scroll.in

———'Nobody in India is as mad about mangoes as the Sheherwali Jains of Bengal', Food, *Scroll.in*, May 19, 2017. https://www.scroll.in

———'Not just khichuri: Durga Puja food is a lot more vibrant than you think', Festival Season, *Scroll.in*, October 6, 2016. https://www.scroll.in

———'Why do so many Indians eat cold, stale food at the start of spring?' Food, *Scroll.in,* March 16, 2019. https://www.scroll.in

Chatterji, Monidip. 'Before Calcutta', *Calcutta: The Living City—Volume I: The Past.* Ed. Sukanta Chaudhuri. Oxford University Press, 1990.

Chatterji, Shoma A. *Antony Firingee and his poignant question that haunts us even today*, Cinestaan, November 9, 2018. https://www.cinestaan.com

Chaudhary, Pranav. 'Job Charnock married Patna's young widow', *The Times of India*, September 4, 2014. https://www.timesofindia.indiatimes.com

Chaudhuri, Moumita. 'Boston Ice Party', *The Telegraph online*, March 28, 2020. https://www.telegraphindia.com

Chaudhuri, Sukanta. 'Calcutta: The Name', *Calcutta: The Living City—Volume I: The Past.* Ed. Sukanta Chaudhuri. Oxford University Press, 1990.

Chaudhury, Sushil (University of Calcutta). *Trading Networks in a Traditional Diaspora—Armenians in India, C. 1600–1800*, Paper submitted for presentation at the Session 10, 'Diaspora Entrepreneurial Networks, C. 1000–2000' of the XIIIth International Economic History Congress, Buenos Aires, July 22–26, 2002. www.eablanchette.com

Chavan, Akshay. *The Sweet Journey of Sandesh*, Live History India, April 26, 2017. https://www.livehistoryindia.com

Chen, Liu Chuen. *53 years of Indo-China war: Indian-Chinese prisoners recount horror behind barbed wires, India Today*, October 20, 2015. https://www.indiatoday.in

Cherry Coffee Beans. *The History of Coffee in Brazil*, The Brazilian Coffee. https://www.cherrycoffeebeans.com

China Tibet Online, 2013, 'Do Tibetan monks eat meat?' Eds. Huang Beibei, Yao Chun. *People's Daily Online*, July 11, 2013. chinatibet.people.com.cn

Chisti, Main Uddin. 'Sports library salute to Cooch Behar king', *The Telegraph online*, January 6, 2014. https://www.telegraphindia.com

Choudhury, Ranabir Ray. *Early Calcutta Advertisements: 1875–1925: A Selection from the Statesman*, Nachiketa Publications Ltd, 1992.

Chowdhury, Kabita. *Rajbarir Ranna*, Ananda Publishers, 2017.

Chowdhury, Pritha; Chaliha, Joyoti. 'The Jews of Calcutta', *Calcutta: The Living City—Volume I: The Past.* Ed. Sukanta Chaudhuri. Oxford University Press, 1990.

Coffee Board Of India. *Coffees of India*, Coffee Board: Government of India: Ministry of Commerce and Industry, https://www.indiacoffee.org

CoffeeResearch.org. *Arabica and Robusta Coffee Plant*, Agriculture, coffeeresearch.org, www.coffeeresearch.org

Coffman, Elesha. *What is the origin of the Christian fish symbol?: A closer look at the ancient Ichthys*, Christian History, CT: Christianity Today, August 8, 2008. https://www.christianitytoday.com

Cole, Adam. *Drink Coffee? Off with Your Head!*, The Salt: What's on Your Plate, NPR, January 17, 2012. https://www.npr.org

'Commercial Calcutta: Federico Peliti, Confectioner and Court Caterer, 11, Government Place', *Seaports of India and Ceylon: Historical and Descriptive, Commercial and Industrial, Facts, Figures and Resources.* Ed. Allister Macmillan. W.H.&L. Collingridge, 1928.

Contractor, Farzana. 'That's Entertainment on Park Street', *Upper Crust: India's food, wine and style magazine*, www.uppercrustindia.com

Cooper, James. *Christmas in Armenia.* https://www.whychristmas.com

Cotton, H.E.A. *Calcutta: Old and New: A Historical and Descriptive Handbook to the City*, W. Newman & Co., Calcutta, West Bengal, India, Digital Library of India, Internet Archive, 1907. https://www.archive.org

Courtney, David. *Biography of Gauhar Jan*, Chandrakantha.Com, 2017. https://www.chandrakantha.com

Cringle, Tom. *Jottings of an invalid in search of Health, comprising a run through British India and a visit to Singapore and Java. A series of letters reprinted from "The Times of India"*, Times of India Office, 1865.

Crosland, Philip. 'A Spell in Hindustan', *Sahibs Who Loved India*, pp. 65–75. Ed. Khushwant Singh. Penguin Random House, 2010.

D'Souza, Ornella. 'Ushering in winter, Anglo-Indian style', *The Sunday Standard, The New Indian Express*, November 24, 2019. https://www.newindianexpress.com

Dainik Jankantha Staff. 'Bakorkhani: Amar Premer Kahani', *Dainik Janakantha*, January 21, 2017. https://www.dailyjanakantha.com

Dalrymple, William. 'The East India Company: The original corporate raiders'. *The Guardian*, March 4, 2015. https://www.theguardian.com

Dandekar, Parineeta. *Jhulelal or Zinda Pir: Of river saints, fish and flows of the Indus*, Scroll.in, January 30, 2016. https://www.scroll.in

Daniyal, Shoaib. *Who deserves credit for the rasgulla? Bengalis, Odiyas…or the Portuguese?*, Food Fight, Scroll.in, August 4, 2015. https://www.scroll.in

Das Gupta, Minakshie; Gupta, Bunny; Chaliha, Jaya. *The Calcutta Cookbook: A Treasury of Recipes from Pavement to Palace.* Penguin Books, 1995.

Das Gupta, Siva Prasad. 'The Site of Calcutta: Geology and Physiography', *Calcutta: The Living City—Volume I: The Past.* Ed. Sukanta Chaudhuri. Oxford University Press, 1990.

Das, Sibendu. 'The big fat biryani battle', Metro on Sunday, *The Telegraph,* Kolkata, West Bengal, India, November 23, 2014.

Das, Arka. 'A taste of history with tea and toast', *The Telegraph,* Kolkata, West Bengal, India, May 11, 2010.

Das, Mohua; Paul, Mathures. 'Original diva of Park Street goes silent', *The Telegraph online*, August 15, 2013. https://www.telegraphindia.com

_____'A landmark blends old and new Park Mansions makeover', *The Telegraph*, December 14, 2013.

Das, Soumitra. '100 years of city's only Parsi fire temple', *The Telegraph*, Kolkata, West Bengal, India, October 5, 2011.

Das, Srijana Mitra. 'Bengal vs. Odisha: Whose rosogolla is it anyway?', *The Indian Express*, November 17, 2017. https://www.indianexpress.com

Das, Suranjan. 'The Politics of Agitation: Calcutta, 1912–1947', *Calcutta: The Living City—Volume II: The Present and Future.* Ed. Sukanta Chaudhuri. Oxford University Press, 1990.

Dasgupta, Biplab. *European Trade and Colonial Conquest: Volume I*, Anthem Press, 2005.

Dasgupta, Piyasree. 'Those Were the Days, My Friend', *The Indian Express*, December 25, 2011. https://www.indianexpress.com

Dasgupta, Priyanka. 'Of love, lust and Miss Shefali: Why did Ray's Bengal find it difficult to accept its Queen of Cabaret?', *The Times of India*, February 9, 2020. https://www.timesofindia.indiatimes.com

Dasgupta, Rakhi Purnima. 'Local flavour', *India Today*, March 15, 2008. https://www.indiatoday.in

Datta Rangan. *Bandel Cheese: The Taste of Portugal in Bengal*, Rangan Datta: Travel writer and photographer, October 2, 2013. https://www.rangandatta.wordpress.com

_____*Bandel: Church & Imambara*, Rangan Datta: Travel writer and photographer, September 11, 2013. https://www.rangandatta.wordpress.com

_____*Chinese Breakfast: Old China Town (Tiretta Bazar), Calcutta (Kolkata)*, Rangan Datta: Travel writer and photographer, June 12, 2013. https://www.rangandatta.wordpress.com

_____*Guptipara: Chariots & Temple*, July 6, 2011. https://www.rangandatta.wordpress.com

_____*Neveh Shalome Synagogue, Kolkata (Calcutta): Rebirth of Kolkata's (Calcutta's) Oldest Synagogue*, Rangan Datta: Travel writer and photographer, October 9, 2014. https://www.rangandatta.wordpress.com

_____*Parsi (Zoroastrian) Fire Temple, Calcutta (Kolkata)*, Rangan Datta: Travel writer and photographer, January 25, 2012. https://www.rangandatta.wordpress.com

_____*Rangrez, A Muslim Marwari Dyeing Community of Kolkata*, Rangan Datta: Travel writer and photographer, June 19, 2016. https://www.rangandatta.wordpress.com

_____*Toong On Church, Calcutta (Kolkata): Rebirth of a Chinese Temple*, Rangan Datta: Travel writer and photographer, April 24, 2013. https://www.rangandatta.wordpress.com

Datta, Sandeepa Mukherjee. *Bhuni Khichuri—with a twist of spice*, Bong Mom's CookBook: A Bong, a Mom & a Cook…, August 29, 2011. www.bongcookbook.com

Davids Kenneth (Editor). *Serving: Milk and Sugar*, Coffee Review, Coffee Review: Since 1997. https://www.coffeereview.com

Deb, Chitra. 'The "Great Houses" of Old Calcutta', *Calcutta: The Living City: Volume I: The Past.* Ed. Sukanta Chaudhuri. Oxford University Press, 1990.

Deb, Ipsita. 'Baisakh bite at its best', *The Telegraph online*, April 14, 2005. https://www.telegraphindia.com

Debi, Pragyasundari. *Amish O Niramish Ahar*, Ananda Publishers, 1995.

Dewar, Douglas. *Bygone Days in India*, John Lane, The Bodley Head Ltd, 1922.

Dharmananda, Subhuti (PhD, director). *The Lessons of Shennong: The Basis of Chinese Herb Medicine*, Institute for Traditional Medicine, Portland, Oregon, January, 2004. www.itmonline.org

DiStefano, Joe. *Butter Tea, Yak Jerky, and Momos Galore: An Introduction to Tibetan Cuisine*, Serious Eats, September 29, 2015. https://www.seriouseats.com

Doctor, Vikram. 'India's affair with tomatoes', *Panache*, *The Economic Times*, September 10, 2010. https://www.economictimes.indiatimes.com

Dugar, Sujata. 'Slice of Bangladesh', *The Times of India*, February 8, 2003. https://www.timesofindia.indiatimes.com

Duggal, Girija. 'Lovely triangles', *Hindustan Times*, August 23, 2008. https://www.hindustantimes.com

Dutt, Kuntala Lahiri. 'The Anglo-Indians of Calcutta', *Calcutta: The Living City: Volume II: The Present and Future*. Ed. Sukanta Chaudhuri. Oxford University Press, 1990.

Dutta, Amrita. 'The fiery flavours of East Bengal's dried and fermented fish are all the notes of life', *The Indian Express*, December 23, 2018. https://www.indianexpress.com

Dutta, Krishna. 'Company Calcutta: The White Town and the Black Town', *Calcutta: A Cultural and Literary History (Cities of the Imagination)*. Signal Books Limited, 2003.

Edulji, Phiroze. *Shireen Khushroo Kiash: India's Most Versatile Sportsperson*, Posted By arZan, Parsi Khabar—Parsis: The Zoroastrians of India Pakistan and the World, October 30, 2015. https://www.parsikhabar.net

Ellias, Rafeeq (writer, director, producer); Yang, Yen-Thaw (narrator). *The Legend of Fat Mama* (Documentary), BBC World, YouTube (IN), December 28, 2012. https://www.youtube.com

Ellis, Markman. *The Coffee House: A Cultural History*, Phoenix, 2005.

Encyclopedia of Early Cinema, First Edition, Routledge, 2005.

Fine, Julia. *In India, the British Hyped Potatoes to Justify Colonialism*, Atlas Obscura, April 9, 2019. https://www.atlasobscura.com

Forbes, Andrew; Henley, David. 'The Rise of Tea', *China's Ancient Tea Horse Road*, Second Edition. Cognoscenti Books (Kindle Edition). October 4, 2011.

Galstaun, Max. *Nizam Palace and the Legend of J.C. Galstaun*, The Concrete Paparazzi: Architecture…History…Travel, January 7, posted by Ghosh Deepanjan, 2015. www.double-dolphin.blogspot.com

Gangopadhyay, Uttara. 'Burma Burma has Arrived in Kolkata', *Outlook Traveller*, November 24, 2020. https://www.outlookindia.com

_____'Goyna Bori: Food Art from Bengal', *Outlook Traveller*, September 25, 2019. https://www.outlookindia.com

_____'Heritage with High Tea', *Outlook Traveller*, April 22, 2018. https://www.outlookindia.com

_____'Kolkata's Well-Kept Christmas Secret', *Outlook Traveller*, December 21, 2018. https://www.outlookindia.com

Ganguly, Amrita. *Sipping on Ancient Flavours of Home Made Wines from the Bow Barracks*, The Optimist: Promoting Peace and Positivity, January 9, 2020. https://www.theoptimist.news

Ganguly, Nandini. 'A trip down memory lane as Aaheli turns 25', *The Telegraph online*, June 14, 2018. https://www.telegraphindia.com

Gao, Sally. *A Brief History of Peking Duck*, Culture Trip, December 6, 2016. https://www.theculturetrip.com

Gavin, Philip. *Armenians in Turkey 1915–1918: 1,500,000 Deaths*, The History Place: Genocide in the 20th Century. https://www.historyplace.com

Gentilcore, David. *Pomodoro!: A History of the Tomato in Italy*, Columbia University Press, 2010

Ghazarian, Salpi; Chater, Liz. *Sir Paul Chater and Armenians in Hong Kong*, CIVILNET, YouTube (IN), May 27, 2013. https://www.youtube.com

Ghose, Amita. 'The last bastons of Parsi food in Kolkata', *The Times of India*, Kolkata, West Bengal, India, May 27, 2017. https://www.timesofindia.indiatimes.com

Ghosh Paramita. 'From Canton to Kolkata', *Hindustan Times*, March 10, 2018. https://www.hindustantimes.com

Ghosh, Chandra. *Biology of tea garden weeds in Darjeeling district of West Bengal, India*, Department of Botany, University of North Bengal, Shodhganga: a reservoir of Indian theses @ INFLIBNET. https://www.shodhganga.inflibnet.ac.in

Ghosh, Deepanjan. *Peliti's Restaurant, 11 Government Place East*, The Concrete Paparazzi: Architecture…History…Travel, April 2, 2014. www.double-dolphin.blogspot.com

_____*Spence's Hotel and the Treasury Building*, The Concrete Paparazzi: Architecture…History…Travel, May 31, 2014. www.double-dolphin.blogspot.com

_____*United Service Club, Chowringhee*, The Concrete Paparazzi: Architecture…History…Travel, April 4, 2016. www.double-dolphin.blogspot.com

Ghosh, Kamalika. 'The disappearing Jewish community of Kolkata', *Business Standard*, November 1, 2014. https://www.business-standard.com

Ghosh, Opashona. 'Mime and the mind', *The Telegraph*, Kolkata, West Bengal, India, September 3, 2007.

Ghosh, Paramita. 'Fatima and Fatima', *Hindustan Times*, February 26, 2019. https://www.hindustantimes.com

Ghosh, Somrita. *Savour Kosha Mangsho at Kolkata's 92-yr-old Golbari eatery*, Indo-Asian News Service (IANS), The News Minute, March 21, 2015. https://www.thenewsminute.com

Ghosh, Suktara; Bhattacharya, Tania. 'A merry journey', *The Telegraph online*, December 25, 2011. https://www.telegraphindia.com

Goode, S.W. 'Markets, Slaughter-Houses, and Dhobikhanas: Sir Charles Allen Market', *Municipal Calcutta: Its Institutions in Their Origin and Growth*, The Corporation of Calcutta, Calcutta, West Bengal, India, Digital Library of India, Internet Archive, 1916. https://www.archive.org

Gooptu, Pradeep. *Party Time—Lost Rhyme*, Kolkata on Wheels, https://www.kolkataonwheels.com

Gordon, Stewart. *When Asia Was The World: Traveling Merchants, Scholars, Warriors, and Monks Who Created the "Riches of the East"*, Da Capo Press, 2009.

GQ. *The legend of Mumbai's China Garden*, Food, GQ, October 20, 2015. https://www.gqindia.com

Griffiths, James. *India's Forgotten Chinese Internment Camp*, China, The Atlantic, August 9, 2013. https://www.theatlantic.com

Guha, Susenjit. 'Iconic Jewish baker Nahoum passes away', *The Sunday Guardian*, March 16, 2013. http://www.sunday-guardian.com

Gupta, Amitabha. 'Durga Puja of "Bonedi Families" at Howrah', Amitabha Gupta: photographer and travelogue writer, October 27, 2015. https://www.amitabhagupta.wordpress.com

Gupta, Ashoka. *Noakhalir Durjoger Dine*, Naya Udyog, Kolkata, West Bengal, India, 1999.

Gupta, Jayanta. 'It's Christmas in January for Armenians', *The Times of India*, Kolkata, West Bengal, India, January 7, 2017.

Haines, Dena. *What Is Arabica Coffee? Arabica vs. Robusta: 11 Tasty Differences*, EnjoyJava!: Because Coffee Is Awesome, November 14, 2019. https://www.enjoyjava.com

_____*What Is Robusta Coffee? Robusta vs. Arabica: 12 Differences*, EnjoyJava!: Because Coffee Is Awesome, September 18, 2020. https://www.enjoyjava.com

Hales, Sally. 'A history of afternoon tea: why we love it and how to host your own', Afternoon tea, *loveFood*. August 14, 2019. https://www.lovefood.com

Haraniya, Krutika. *Tamralipti—The Ancient Copper Port*, Live History India, June 26, 2017. https://www.livehistoryindia.com

_____*The Curious Case of Coffee*, Live History India. May 19, 2017. https://www.livehistoryindia.com

Hardgrave, Robert L. Jr. 'A Portrait of Black Town: Balthazard Solvyns in Calcutta, 1791–1804, *Changing Visions, Lasting Images: Calcutta Through 300 Years*. Ed. Pratapaditya Pal. Marg Publications, 1990.

Hary, Benjamin. *Judeo-Arabic*, Jewish Languages. https://www.jewishlanguages.org

Headsman. *1872: Sher Ali Afridi, assassin of the viceroy*, ExecutedToday.com, March 11, 2013. www.executedtoday.com

Hebbar, Neria H. *First Europeans in India: The Portuguese and the British*, History, https://www.boloji.com

Hein, David. 'Archbishop of Canterbury, 1945–1961: The Anglican Communion', *Geoffrey Fisher: Archbishop of Canterbury*, The Lutterworth Press, James Clarke & Co. Ltd, 2008. https://www.jamesclarke.co

Hindustan Times. 'Kolkata's "Queen of Cabaret" Miss Shefali dead at 76', *Hindustan Times*, February 6, 2020. https://www.hindustantimes.com

Hinnells, John R. *Parsi Communities i. Early History*, Encyclopaedia Iranica, July 20, 2008. https://www.iranicaonline.org

History.Com Editors. *Boston Tea Party*, H-History, October 27, 2009. https://www.history.com

Ho, Yong. 'Food and Eating: Cultural Insights', *Hippocrene Beginner's Series: Beginner's Chinese*, Hippocrene Books, INC., New York, United States of America, 2005.

Hobbs Harry Major (MBE, VD). *Calcutta Taverns and Hotels (A new, enlarged, illustrated edition of John Barleycorn Bahadur)—Volume II*. Ed. P. Thankappan Nair, Bibhash Gupta (Microform Publication Division), 1988.

_____'Federico Peliti', *Talkeetalkeewallahs and Others*, H. Hobbs & Co. Ltd, 1938.

_____*Calcutta Taverns And Hotels (A new, enlarged, illustrated edition of John Barleycorn Bahadur)—Volume 1*. Ed. P. Thankappan Nair, Bibhash Gupta (Microform Publication Division), 1987.

_____*Calcutta Taverns and Hotels (A new, enlarged, illustrated edition of John Barleycorn Bahadur)—Volume 1*. Ed. P. Thankappan Nair, Bibhash Gupta (Microform Publication Division), 1987.

_____*Calcutta Taverns and Hotels (A new, enlarged, illustrated edition of John Barleycorn*

Bahadur)—Volume II. Ed. P. Thankappan Nair, Bibhash Gupta (Microform Publication Division), 1988.

_____*Calcutta Taverns and Hotels (A new, enlarged; illustrated edition of John Barleycorn Bahadur)—Volume 1*. Ed. P. Thankappan Nair, Bibhash Gupta (Microform Publication Division), 1987.

_____*Calcutta Taverns and Hotels (A new, enlarged, illustrated edition of John Barleycorn Bahadur)—Volume II*. Ed. P. Thankappan Nair, Bibhash Gupta (Microform Publication Division), 1988.

Hoh, Anchi; Khatoon, Nuzhat. *The Delhi Durbar and the Proclamation of Queen Victoria*, 4 Corners of the World International Collections, Library: Library Of Congress. November 1, 2017. https://www.blogs.loc.gov

Hossain, Muhammad Faruque. *Bakorkhani*, Banglapedia: National Encyclopedia of Bangladesh. Eds. Sirajul Islam, Sajahan Miah, Mahfuza Khanam, and Sabbir Ahmed. Asiatic Society of Bangladesh, 2012. www.en.banglapedia.org

Hussain, Deluar. *Marginalization and the tea tribes of Assam: A study on Mulk Raj Anand's* Two Leaves and a Bud and Umakanta Sarma's Ejakh Manu Ekhan Aranya, Department of Modern Indian Languages, Gauhati University, Shodhganga: a reservoir of Indian theses @ INFLIBNET, 2018. https://www.shodhganga.inflibnet.ac.in

Hutchinson, Sean. *Who Discovered Coffee?* Mental Floss, April 29, 2016. https://www.mentalfloss.com

Hyman, Mavis. *Indian–Jewish Cooking*, Hyman Publishers, London, England, United Kingdom, Recalling Jewish Calcutta: Memories of the Jewish Community In Calcutta, 1992. http://www.jewishcalcutta.in

IANS. *At Jagannath Temple, 700 Cooks for Mahaprasad*, Food & Drinks, NDTV Food, July 18, 2017. https://www.food.ndtv.com

India Today Web Desk. 'Why do people refrain from eating baer (jujubes) on Basant Panchami?', *India Today*, January 19, 2018. https://www.indiatoday.in

_____*India-China War of 1962: How it started and what happened later*, November 21, India Today, New Delhi, India, 2016. https://www.indiatoday.in

Indian Jewish Heritage Center. *West Bengal—Beth El Synagogue*, Research, IJHC: Indian Jewish Heritage Center. https://www.indianjews.org

_____*West Bengal—Neveh Shalom Synagogue*, Research, IJHC: Indian Jewish Heritage Center. https://www.indianjews.org

Indo-Asian News Service (IANS). 'IIT Kharagpur facilitating filing of GI application for "Goyna Bori", *Business Standard*, July 31, 2016. https://www.business-standard.com

'Introduction', *Calcutta Mosaic: Essays and Interviews on the Minority Communities of Calcutta*. Eds. Himadri Banerjee, Nilanjana Gupta, Sipra Mukherjee. Anthem Press, 2009.

Iqbal, Asif. 'Head to These Five Places to Enjoy Litti Chokha in Kolkata, What's Hot', December 11, 2020. https://www.whatshot.in

Itiriti. *Biography of Langcha—Burdwan Or Krishnanagar*, itiriti: Eat to Write and Write to Eat…, November 3, 2011. https://www.itiriti.wordpress.com

_____*Exploring the Romance of Bengali Sweets with J. Haldar*, itiriti: Eat to Write and Write to Eat…, November 14, 2013. https://www.itiriti.wordpress.com

_____*Sweet Biographies of Bengal*, itiriti: Eat to Write and Write to Eat…, July 30, 2011. https://www.itiriti.wordpress.com

Jain Foodie. *Jain Food Restrictions*, Michchami Dukkadam: Jain Foodie. https://www.jainfoodie.com

Jain, Saudamini. 'The case of the vanishing Armenians', *Brunch, Hindustan Times*, September 20, 2014. https://www.hindustantimes.com

Janeja, Harpeet. *Christmas in Bow Barracks, Kolkata*, Savaari Blog, December 24, 2019. https://www.blog.savaari.com

Jharia, Harish. *Rajasthani Delicacy 'Ker Sangri': The Leafless Colourful Beautiful Bush 'Ker'... Desert Shrub Capparis Decidua*, Discover Life, February 9, 2012. www.harishjhariasblog.blogspot.com

Johnson, Ben. *Afternoon Tea*, Historic UK: The History and Heritage Accommodation Guide, https://www.historic-uk.com

Johnson, George W. (ESQ). *The Stranger in India; Or, Three Years in Calcutta*, Henry Colburn, 1843.

Justin. *History and Science of Coffee (Documentary),* Exploring coffee, from its origins to the modern day, Fire of Learning, YouTube. May 9, 2018. https://www.youtube.com

Kakoty, Monali, IndianYouth.Net, 1999-2021.

Kalajian, Robyn; Kalajian, Doug. *Ghapama—Stuffed, Baked Pumpkin*, The Armenian Kitchen.com, February 23, 2012. https://www. thearmeniankitchen.com

Kapadia, Rukshana A. *My Ode to Skyroom*, The Culinary Commentator, March 7, 2018. https://www.theculinarycommentator.com

Kapoor, Sanjeev. 'Author's Note', *Marwari Vegetarian Cooking*, Popular Prakashan, 2009.

Karkaria Bachi J. *Flurys of Calcutta: The Cake That Walked*, Flurys, Kolkata, West Bengal, India, 2007.

_____*To a Grand Design,* The Oberoi Grand, Kolkata, West Bengal, India, 2009.

Karki, Tika; Ojha, Pravin; Panta, Om Prakash; Tamang, Jyoti Prakash. 'Ethnic Fermented Foods of Nepal', *Ethnic Fermented Foods and Alcoholic Beverages of Asia*, Springer Nature, 2016.

Karmakar, Kalyan. 'The Iconic "Cabin" Restaurants of Kolkata and Why They Are Worth a Visit', *Food & Drinks, NDTV Food.* June 5, 2017. https://www.food.ndtv.com

Karmakar, Sreemati Sen. *Maa Shashthi: Bengal's Deity of Womanhood*, Hinduism, Sanskriti, 2018. https://www.sanskritimagazine.com

Katti, Madhuri. *Bakarkhani: An Ode to Lost Love*, Live History India, March 14, 2019. https://www.livehistoryindia.com

Khatchaturian, Anthony. *The Armenians of India*, Live History India, August 30, 2017. https://www.livehistoryindia.com

Kifner, John. The New York Times Company, 'Armenian Genocide of 1915: An Overview' (Archived Page), *Times Topics, The New York Times.* https://www.nytimes.com

Kinnear, Michael S. *The Gramophone Company's First Indian Recordings (1899–1908)*, pp. 17–20, Popular Prakashan, 1994.

Konig, Franz Cardinal. *Zarathustra: Iranian prophet*, Britannica, July 20, 1998. https://www.britannica.com

Kopi Luwak Direct. *Coffee Culture and History in the Middle East.* KOPILUWAKDIRECT. https://www.kopiluwakdirect.com

Krishnakumar, P.K. 'Monsooned Malabar' coffee: A distinguished variety from the Mangalore coast', *The Economic Times*, July 13, 2013. https://www.economictimes.indiatimes.com

Krondl, Michael. *Sweet Invention: A History of Dessert*, Chicago Review Press, 2011.

Kulkarni Vishwanath; Kumar V. Sajeev. 'The iconic India Coffee House brewing plans for revamp, expansion', *The Hindu Business Line*, May 10, 2017. https://www.thehindubusinessline.com

Kumar, Karo Christine. 'Aaheli at 24', *The Telegraph online*, May 18, 2017. https://www.telegraphindia.com

Kumar, Madhuri. 'Pumpkins, cucumbers replace animal sacrifice in Puja', *The Times of India*, October 16, 2010. https://www.timesofindia.indiatimes.com

Kuriakose, Antony. 'A tradition of hospitality', *Spectrum, The Sunday Tribune, The Tribune*, June 28, 2009. https://www.tribuneindia.com

Kusnur, Narendra. 'Play It Again, for Pam!', *mid-day.com*, August 16, 2013. https://www.mid-day.com

Lahiri, Indrajit. *What Do I Get to Eat at Chinese Breakfast, Tiretta Bazar*, Food Blog Mohamushkil—a bong foodie's quest about best foods in India, December 19, 2015. https://www.moha-mushkil.com

——*Dacres Lane—The Blue Eyed Boy of Kolkata Street Food*, Food Blog Mohamushkil—a bong foodie's quest about best foods in India. May 6, 2019. https://www.moha-mushkil.com

——*Best Veg Street Food in Kolkata Burrabazar*, Food Blog Mohamushkil—a bong foodie's quest about best foods in India, October 25, 2018. https://www.moha-mushkil.com

——*Mutton Pantheras—Baruas*, Food Blog Mohamushkil—a bong foodie's quest about best foods in India, March 16, 2020. https://www.moha-mushkil.com

Lahiri, Ishadrita. 'Remembering Miss Shefali, Kolkata's Cabaret Queen of the 70s', *The Quint*, February 21, 2020. https://www.thequint.com

Law, Abhishek; Pramanik, Ayan. 'Re-visiting the rich legacy of Bonedi Bari', *Variety, The Hindu Business Line*, October 10, 2012. https://www.thehindubusinessline.com

Lentin, Sifra. *Exploring Calcutta's multi-ethnicities*, Gateway House: Indian Council on Global Relations. February 25, 2016. https://www.gatewayhouse.in

Lodrick, D.O. 'Lepchas', October 5, 2019. https://www.encyclopedia.com

Lutgendorf, Philip (Division of World Languages, Literatures and Cultures, University of Iowa, USA). *Making tea in India: Chai, capitalism, culture*, Thesis Eleven: Critical Theory and Historical Sociology, 113 (1): 11–31, Sage Publications. December, 2012. https://www.researchgate.net

Lynch, Nick; Lynch, Laura. *Top 10 Tibetan Foods You Must Try in Lhasa*, Food, Savored Journeys, May 17, 2018. https://www.savoredjourneys.com

Madan, Cyrus J. 'The Parsis of Calcutta', *Calcutta: The Living City—Volume II: The Present and Future*, Ed. Sukanta Chaudhuri. Oxford University Press, 1990.

Majumdar, Ramesh Chandra; Pusalker, A.D.; Majumdar, A.K. *The History and Culture of the Indian People: The Delhi Sultanate*, Volume VI, pp. 515, Bharatiya Vidya Bhavan, Bombay, 1960.

Malhotra, Shakuntla. *Mama's Punjabi Recipes—Mithe Chawal (Sweet Rice)*, Indo American News, February 12, 2015. www.indoamerican-news.com

Manoli. *The vermouth loved by the queen was created by a man from Piedmont in India*, Italy Service: A Taste of Italy, July 20, 2018. https://www.italyservice.co.uk

Mantegazza, Paolo. *India*, Fratelli Treves, Editori, 1884.

Massey, Montague. *Recollections of Calcutta for over half a century*, Thacker, Spink & Co., 1918.

Maur, Harsh. *Assam Tea or Darjeeling Tea?* Tea Wars, TEAFLOOR, April 24, 2017. https://www.teafloor.com

Maverickbird. *The Special Bow Barracks Christmas of Calcutta*, Maverickbird: Travel, Food, Culture, Expat, Lifestyle, December 17, 2017. www.maverickbird.com

Mazumdar, Jaideep. 'A Passage in Kolkata', *Open*, December 30, 2009. https://www.openthemagazine.com

_____'Sita's Sweet Tooth', *Outlook: The Fully Loaded Magazine,* January 15, 2007. https://www.magazine.outlookindia.com

_____'Presidency Takes Back Rusticated Netaji', *Honours, Open*, February 10, 2010. https://www.openthemagazine.com

_____*The 1962 jailing of Chinese Indians, Open*, November 21, 2010. https://www.openthemagazine.com

McDaniel, June. *Offering Flowers, Feeding Skulls: Popular Goddess Worship in West Bengal,* Oxford University Press, 2004.

McDonald, Skye. *The Origins of Coffee Houses*, April 10, 2018. www.keyscoffee.com

McGee, Harold. *Accused, Yes, but Probably Not a Killer*, The Curious Cook, *The New York Times*, July 28, 2009. https://www.nytimes.com

_____*On Food and Cooking: The Science and Lore of the Kitchen*, Scribner, 2004.

Mehrabian, Mane. 'The India-Armenia connection', *The Statesman*, Kolkata, West Bengal, India, September 26, 2015. https://www.thestatesman.com

Memoirs of William Hickey, Volume II (1775–82), Seventh Edition. Ed. Alfred Spencer. Hurst & Blackett Ltd. Courtesy of Digital Library of India, Internet Archive. https://www.archive.org

Mendiratta, Sidh Losa; Rossa, Walter. *Porto Grande de Bengala: Historical Background and Urbanism*, Heritage of Portuguese Influence, June 29, 2015. https://www.hpip.org

Menon, A. Sreedhara. *A Survey of Kerala History*, DC Books, 2007.

Meyer, Jen (assistant to the curator of rare books, Princeton University Library), *1785: The English Tea Trade at Work*, Princeton University Library. February 12, 2013. https://www.blogs.princeton.edu

Michael, Christopher M. *Calcutta & Nahoum—A Sweet Love Affair*, In Nahoum's, my school—i wish, March 26, 2008. http://www.goethals1907-2007.blogspot.com

Mint Staff. '8 interesting facts about the Nobel prize in literature', *Mint*, October 9, 2014. https://www.livemint.com

Mirza, Fatima. 'Awadhi biryani: From the land of Nawabs', Food for Thought, *Kolkata on Wheels*, Kolkata, West Bengal, India, June, 2013.

_____'ID feast', Goodlife, T2, *The Telegraph*, Kolkata, West Bengal, India, October 27, 2012.

Mirza, Meher. *Colocasia Leaves (Arbi Patta): A Green Leafy Veg You Should Try*, Food & Drinks, NDTV Food, June 12, 2017. https://www.food.ndtv.com

Mirza, Shahanshah. 'The house where the last Nawab of Awadh lived', *The Telegraph*, Kolkata, West Bengal, India, May 13, 2017.

Mishra, Asit Ranjan. 'After West Bengal, Odisha gets GI tag for its version of Rasagola', *Mint*, July 30, 2019. https://www.livemint.com

Mishra, Smita. *The 1000-Year History of the Kebab on Your Plate*, February 27, News, India Times, 2016. https://www.indiatimes.com

Mitra, Sukumar; Prasad, Amita. 'The Marwaris of Calcutta', *Calcutta: The Living City—Volume II: The Present and Future*, Ed. Sukanta Chaudhuri. Oxford University Press, 1990.

Mohanty, Gopinath; Patnaik, Jeeban Kumar; Ratha, Santosha Kumara. *Cultural Heritage of (Orissa): Katak District*, Volume 8, Parts 1–2, p. 650, State Level Vyasakabi Fakir Mohan Smruti Samsad, Orissa, 2003.

Mookerji, Madhumita; Chaudhuri, Sumanta Ray. '*Bow Barracks Forever* hurts Anglo-Indian sentiment in Kolkata', *DNA (Daily News & Analysis)*, August 8, 2007. https://www.dnaindia.com

Morshed, Abul Kalam Manjoor, *Brajabuli, Banglapedia: National Encyclopedia of Bangladesh*, Second Edition. Eds. Sirajul Islam, Ahmed A. Jamal. Asiatic Society of Bangladesh, 2012.

Moxham, Roy. *A Brief History of Tea: The Extraordinary Story of the World's Favourite Drink.* Constable & Robinson Ltd, 2009.

Mukerjee, Shikha. *Eight Decades Later, the Original Mahalaya Still Unites Bengalis in Communion*, Culture, *The Wire*, October 7, 2019. https://www.thewire.in

Mukherjee Subhadip. *Chinese Temples and Churches of Kolkata, Indian Vagabond*, March 12, 2018. https://www.indianvagabond.com

Mukherjee, Arundhati. *Poush Parbon and Delicious Pitha*, January 13, 2018. https://www.speakingtree.in

Mukherjee, Siddhartha. *The Mughlai the Mughals Knew Nothing About*, Flavours, Farbound. Net: Go Far, March 6, 2014. https://www.farbound.net

Mukherjee, Sipra; Gooptu, Sarvani. 'The Chinese Community of Calcutta: An Interview with Paul Chung', *Calcutta Mosaic: Essays and Interviews on the Minority Communities of Calcutta.* Eds. Himadri Banerjee, Nilanjana Gupta, Sipra Mukherjee. Anthem Press, 2009.

Mukherjee, Sipra. 'The Jews of Calcutta: An Interview with Michael Ezra', *Calcutta Mosaic: Essays and Interviews on the Minority Communities of Calcutta.* Eds. Himadri Banerjee, Nilanjana Gupta, Sipra Mukherjee. Anthem Press, 2009.

———'The Biharis Of Calcutta: An Interview with Sachchidand and Indu Rai', *Calcutta Mosaic: Essays and Interviews on the Minority Communities of Calcutta.* Eds. Himadri Banerjee, Nilanjana Gupta, Sipra Mukherjee. Anthem Press, 2009.

Mukherji, Sajni Kripalani, 2009, 'The Sindhis of Calcutta', *Calcutta Mosaic: Essays and Interviews on the Minority Communities of Calcutta.* Eds. Himadri Banerjee, Nilanjana Gupta, Sipra Mukherjee. Anthem Press, 2009.

Mukhopadhyay, Ashoke Kumar, 'Sweet Talk of Calcutta'. *Bengali Food on the Web.* www.angelfire.com

Mulmi, Amish. 'Momo: the one dumpling that rules them all', *Mint*, September 22, 2017. https://www.livemint.com

Nag, Ashoke. '130 years young: Kolkata's Raj insignia is still "New"'. *The Economic Times.* September 17, 2005.

Nagchoudhury, Subrata. 'Coming from Kolkata's business hub, trains full of votes for poll-bound Bihar', *The Indian Express*, October 8, 2015. https://www.indianexpress.com

Nair, P. Thankappan. 'The Growth and Development of Old Calcutta', *Calcutta: The Living City—Volume I: The Past.* Ed. Sukanta Chaudhuri. Oxford University Press, 1990.

Najarian, Tamar. *Armenian Traditions—Christmas Celebrations*, Traditions and Celebrations, Notes of a Spurkahye Finally Come Home, December 31, 2012. https://www.tamarnajarian.wordpress.com

Nambiar, Sridevi. *A Brief History of South Indian Filter Coffee*, Culture Trip. May 17, 2018. https://www.theculturetrip.com

———*The Story Behind India's Most Historic Coffee Chain*, Culture Trip, March 2, 2018. https://www.theculturetrip.com

Nanda, J.N. *Bengal: The Unique State*, Concept Publishing Company, 2005.

Nandy, Ajay Kumar. *The Last Days of Ramakrishna Paramahamsa*, A.K. Nandy's NEWS VIEWS ON YOUR PALM, December 5, 2016. https://www.aknandy.wordpress.com

Nandy, Pritish. 'Don't let the music die', *The Times Of India*, December 25, 2010. https://www.timesofindia.indiatimes.com

NDTV Food. *The Himalayan Chewing Gum—Churpi*, Food & Drinks, NDTV Food, December 6, 2017. https://www.food.ndtv.com

Niyogi, Subhro. 'The schools are Jewish, its students Muslims', *The Times of India*, Kolkata, West Bengal, India, October 3, 2009. https://www.timesofindia.indiatimes.com

Noorani, A.G. 'Persecution of Chinese Indians', Essay, The Nation, *Frontline*: India's National Magazine, January 9, 2015. https://frontline.thehindu.com

O'Yeah, Zac. 'Ben there, done that', *The Hindu: Business Line*, December 29, 2017. https://www.thehindubusinessline.com

Our Bureau. 'Great Eastern Hotel set for a new beginning', *Companies, The Hindu: Business Line,* November 19, 2013. https://www.thehindubusinessline.com

Pal, Sanchari. 'Care for Some 'Monsooned Malabar'? You'll Love This Celebrated Coffee!', *The Better India*, May 14, 2018. https://www.thebetterindia.com

_____'TBI Food Secrets: The Fascinating History of Rasgulla and the "Sweet" Battle Over its Origin', January 18, 2017. https://www.thebetterindia.com

Pal, Santanu. *Cooch Behar Trophy Championship*, Upcoming, January 1, 2009. https://www.archive.upcoming.org

_____'For this Kali, bhog is noodles and chopsuey', *The Times of India*, Kolkata, West Bengal, India, October 17, 2009. https://www.timesofindia.indiatimes.com

_____'Exotic sweets back on shelves after decades', *The Times of India*, October 17, 2015. https://www.timesofindia.indiatimes.com

_____'Louis Banks to belt out unheard Pancham tunes', *The Times of India*, June 23, 2013. https://www.timesofindia.indiatimes.com

_____'Swanky new Great Eastern may be thrown open by year-end', *The Times of India*, Kolkata, West Bengal, India, May 17, 2012.

_____'Flower power pushes Kolkata Jewish population up by 1', *The Times of India*, Kolkata, West Bengal, India, April 29, 2016. https://www.timesofindia.indiatimes.com

Pandey, Kirti. 'The British thought they would rule India forever; capital was shifted from Calcutta to Delhi'. *TimesNowNews.Com*. August 14, 2020. https://www.timesnownews.com

Panigrahi, Subhashish. '8 Things You Didn't Know about Rasagola!', Guest Posts, Food, Discover Bhubaneswar, July 30, 2015. https://www.discoverbbsr.com

Pant, Pushpesh. 'Savoury Temptations', Food Talk, Spectrum, *The Sunday Tribune, The Tribune*, September 5, 2004. https://www.tribuneindia.com

Parzor Foundation, *The Kisseh-i-Sanjan*, Parzor: The UNESCO Parsi Zoroastrian Project. https://www.unescoparzor.com

Paster, Emily. *Round Challah for Rosh Hashanah*, The Inspired Home, September 11, 2015. https://www.theinspiredhome.com

Patel, Perzen. *The Parsi Patio Diaries*, Stories, IFN: India Food Network, June 12, 2015. https://www.indiafoodnetwork.in

Paul, Sumit. 'How Kolkata got its parantha', *The Hindu*, November 15, 2014. https://www.thehindu.com

Pawar, Yogesh. 'Louiz Banks, thank you for the music…', *DNA (Daily News & Analysis)*, January 1, 2018. https://www.dnaindia.com

Pendergrast, Mark. 'Part One: Seeds of Conquest: Chapter 1: Coffee Colonizes the World', *Uncommon Grounds: The History of Coffee and How It Transformed Our World*, Basic Books, 2010.

Plaban. *Grilled Ilish with Gondhoraj Lebu and Mustard Sauce*, Taste Matters, Plaban's Food Photography: Food, Photography & Life!, June 29, 2018. www.plabansfoodphotography.com

Press Trust of India. *Our Claim Only on a Variety of Rasogolla, No Dispute with Odisha: West Bengal*, NDTV, July 27, 2016. https://www.ndtv.com

Professor Peaberry. 'The History of Coffee'. *Go Coffee Go*, 2021. https://www.gocoffeego.com

Purohit, Devadeep. 'Gujaratis tread the exit route: Trade slump, labour stalemate drive away business community', *The Telegraph*, Kolkata, India, April 30, 2003.

R. Charles. *A Proclamation for the Suppression of Coffee-Houses*, Ancient pages, June 18, 2018. https://www.ancientpages.com

Raghavan, Susheela. *Handbook of Spices, Seasonings, and Flavorings*, CRC Press, 2006.

Rahman, Azera Parveen. *Youth from Northeast India Talk of Hardships, Conflicts and Their Hope for Lasting Change*, YKA, February 24, 2014. https://www.youthkiawaaz.com

Raichlen, Steven. 'A Tandoor Oven Brings India's Heat to the Backyard', *The New York Times*, May 10, 2011. https://www.nytimes.com

Rajagopalan, Ashwin. *Nolen Gur Specialities You Must Try in Kolkata this Season*, NDTV Food, February 6, 2019. https://www.food.ndtv.com

Raksit, Priyadarshinee. 'On the fruit cake trail at Nahoum's, Kolkata's last Jewish bakery', Food, *The Week*, December 22, 2017. https://www.theweek.in

Rana, Sarika. *What is Makhana (Fox Nuts) and Where Does It Come From?*, Food & Drinks, NDTV Food, April 24, 2018. https://www.food.ndtv.com

Rappaport, Erika. *A Thirst for Empire: How Tea Shaped the Modern World*. Princeton University Press, 2017.

Ray, Animesh. 'The Calcutta Port', *Calcutta: The Living City—Volume II: The Present and Future*, Ed. Sukanta Chaudhuri. Oxford University Press, 1990.

Ray, Aniruddha. 'Portuguese, The', *Banglapedia: National Encyclopedia of Bangladesh*. Eds. Jamal A. Ahmed, Sirajul Islam. Asiatic Society of Bangladesh, 2012. www.en.banglapedia.org

Ray, Arundhati. 'Burmese food in Kolkata', *Mint*, September 16, 2018. https://www.livemint.com

_____'I've got some fish to dry', *The Hindu: Business Line*, December 16, 2016. https://www.thehindubusinessline.com

Ray, Dalia. *The Parsees of Calcutta*, Sujan Publications, 2005.

Ray, Somdyuti Datta. 'From war-survivor to the "Don of Chinatown", how Monica Liu turned her life around through her restaurant business', *Outlook Business*: Wow. https://www.wow.outlookbusiness.com

Ray, Utsa. *Culinary Culture in Colonial India: A Cosmopolitan Platter and the Middle-Class*, Cambridge University Press, 2015.

Reddy, Catherine. *All About Kair (Capparis decidua) in India*, The Earth of India, March 18, 2013. www.theindianvegan.blogspot.com

Roberts, Emma. *Scenes and Characteristics Of Hindostan, with Sketches of Anglo-Indian Society*, WM. H. Allen and Co., 1837.

Rosen, Laura Siciliano. 'Top 5 Tibetan Foods in Tibet', *Eat Your World*, January 17, 2018. https://www.eatyourworld.com

_____'What Is Tibetan Cuisine?' *Eat Your World*, January 3, 2018. https://www.eatyourworld.com

Rowlatt, Justin (South Asia Correspondent). *The dark history behind India and the UK's favourite drink*, India, BBC News. July 15, 2016. https://www.bbc.com

Roy Pratap Kumar. 'The Food and Sweets of Calcutta', *Calcutta: The Living City: Volume II: The Present and Future*, Ed. Sukanta Chaudhuri. Oxford University Press, 1990.

_____'The Food and Sweets of Calcutta: Calcutta and the Sandesh', *Calcutta: The Living City: Volume II: The Present and Future*, Ed. Sukanta Chaudhuri. Oxford University Press, 1990.

Roy, Priyanka; Banerjee, Malini. 'People in Pockets: Gujarat Capital', *The Telegraph*, Kolkata, India, March 16, 2008.

_____'People in Pockets: Southern Comfort', *The Telegraph*, Kolkata, India, March 16, 2008.

Roy, Subhajoy. 'Window to Parsi Life', *The Telegraph*, Kolkata, West Bengal, India, October 27, 2017.

Rozario, Joseph. *Carving His Own Destiny*, PressReader, December 12, 2018. https://www.pressreader.com

_____*The Rise and Fall of the Jagat Sheths*, Marwar India, June 12, 2015. www.marwar.com

Saha, Sambit. 'British-Armenian era checks out', *The Telegraph*, Kolkata, West Bengal, India, February 20, 2018.

Saikia, Arani. 'Food Habits in Pre-colonial Assam', *International Journal of Humanities and Social Science Invention*, pp. 1–5, Issue 6, Volume 2, Nagaon, Assam, India. June, 2013. www.ijhssi.org

Sanghvi, Vir. 'Tasty Triangles', *Hindustan Times*, September 12, 2009. https://www.hindustantimes.com

_____'The Portuguese contribution that usually goes unheralded', Brunch, *Hindustan Times*, January 17, 2015. https://www.hindustantimes.com

_____*Bread and Better*, Ask VIR, Vir Sanghvi, August 6, 2016. https://www.virsanghvi.com

_____*How did the Portuguese pav become one of Bombay's most recognisable breads?*, Ask VIR, Vir Sanghvi, January 17, 2015. https://www.virsanghvi.com

_____*You can't get good tomatoes in India*, Ask VIR, Vir Sanghvi, September 11, 2010. https://www.virsanghvi.com

Sankar. 'Ray and his grilled fish', *India Today*, September 4, 2008. https://www.indiatoday.in

_____*Bangalir Khaoa Daoa*, Sahityam, 2005.

_____*Bangalir Khaoa Daoa*, Sahityam, 2005.

Sarkar, Indranil. 'Sweets of Burdwan set for global plate', *The Telegraph online*, December 28, 2013. https://www.telegraphindia.com

Sarkar, Jadunath. *Military History of India*, M.C. Sarkar & Sons Pvt. Ltd., Calcutta, West Bengal, India, West Bengal Public Library, Digital Library of India, Internet Archive, 1960. https://www.archive.org

Sarkar, Petrina Verma. *Country Captain Chicken Curry*, The Spruce Eats, July 24, 2019. https://www.thespruceeats.com

Sarma, Gadapani (assistant professor). *A Historical Background of Tea in Assam*, Pratidhwani the Echo: An Online Journal of Humanities & Social Science, Volume–I, Issue-IV, ISSN 2278-5264, Dept. of Bengali, Karimganj College, Karimganj, Assam, India. April, 2013. https://www.theecho.in

Sen, Pritha. 'The sweet legacy of Durga Puja', *The Times of India*, September 29, 2014. https://www.timesofindia.indiatimes.com

Sen, Colleen Taylor. 'I: India: Eastern India', *The Oxford Companion to Sugar and Sweets*, Ed. Darra Goldstein. Oxford University Press, 2015. www.dl.booktolearn.com

_____*The Portuguese Influence on Bengali Cuisine: Food on the Move: Proceedings of the Oxford Symposium on Food and Cookery 1996*, A Devotee and Chronicler of South Asian Cuisine. http://www.colleensen.com

Sen, Paromita. 'Ber: The first taste of spring', *The Telegraph online*, February 9, 2019. https://www.telegraphindia.com

_____'Scent of a lemon', *The Telegraph online*, May 20, 2018. https://www.telegraphindia.com

_____'When away from home, stay home', *The Telegraph*, Kolkata, West Bengal, India, April 9, 2017.

Sen, Pritha. 'How British greed spurred the creation of one of Bengal's most loved dishes', *The Indian Express*, March 31, 2016. https://www.indianexpress.com

Sengupta, Nitish. *Land of Two Rivers: A History of Bengal from the Mahabharata to Mujib*, Penguin Books, 2011.

Sengupta, Somini. 'Calcutta: Mocambo', *The New York Times*, August 28, 2008. https://www.nytimes.com

Sengupta, Sudipto. *The Too Few People. The Jew Community of Kolkata*, Probashi, January 22, 2015. http://www.probashionline.com

Sengupta, Sushmita. *6 Amazing Benefits of Chewing Neem Regularly*, NDTV Food, July 6, 2018. https://www.food.ndtv.com

_____*Basant Panchami 2018: Why Do Bengalis Refrain from Eating Ber (Jujube) Fruit Before Saraswati Puja*, Food & Drinks, NDTV Food, January 22, 2018. https://www.food.ndtv.com

_____*Boondi: The Rajasthani Drop-sized Gram Flour Balls Perfect for Both Sweet and Savoury Delicacies*, Food & Drinks, NDTV Food, July 4, 2017. https://www.food.ndtv.com

_____*Kala Jaam: The Sweet That Looks Like Gulab Jamun but Isn't*, Food & Drinks, NDTV Food, March 7, 2018. https://www.food.ndtv.com

_____*Shingara Versus Samosa: 5 Ways the Bengali Snack Is Different from the North Indian Samosa*, Food & Drinks, NDTV Food, April 26, 2017. https://www.food.ndtv.com

_____*Shukto: Why Can't Bengalis Start Their Meal Without This Bitter Medley of Vegetables*, NDTV Food, August 10, 2017. https://www.food.ndtv.com

Seth, Mesrovb J. *History of the Armenians in India*, Luzac & Co. (Publishers to the India Office), London, England, United Kingdom, American Libraries, Harvard University, Internet Archive, https://www.archive.org

_____*Armenians in India, From the Earliest Times to the Present Day: A Work of Original Research*, Asian Educational Services, 2005.

Seth, Bharat Lal. *Kolkata tanners unhappy with new relocation site*, Down to Earth, July 4, 2015. https://www.downtoearth.org.in

Shacket, Sara, *British Tea History: From Tea Bowl to Teacup*, Tea Happiness. October 4, 2018. www.tea-happiness.com

Shah, Manali. 'Health benefits of bitter gourd, 5 reasons why it must be in your diet', *Hindustan Times*, May 1, 2018. https://www.hindustantimes.com

Sharma, Jayeeta. 'Making Garden, Erasing Jungle: The Tea Enterprise in Colonial Assam', *The British Empire and the Natural World: Environmental Encounters in South Asia*, pp. 119–41, Eds. Deepak Kumar, Vinita Damodaran, Rohan D'Souza, Oxford University Press, 2010.

Shukla, Shreya. 'Icing on the cake', *The Telegraph*, Kolkata, West Bengal, India, December 21, 2013.

Shutterstock.com. *What is sattu? 12 reasons why it is the new superfood*, Times Food, June 28, 2018. https://www.recipes.timesofindia.com

Silliman, Flower. 'Calcutta Jewish Recipes', *Three Cups of Flour, Recalling Jewish Calcutta: Memories of the Jewish Community in Calcutta*. http://www.jewishcalcutta.in

Silliman, Jael; Tramz, Mia. *Meet the Last Jews of Calcutta*, Portfolio, Lightbox, Time, April 1, 2015. https://www.time.com

Silliman, Jael. *David Joseph Ezra, Business*, Notable Members of and from the Community, Recalling Jewish Calcutta: Memories of the Jewish Community in Calcutta. http://www.jewishcalcutta.in

Simply Tibetan. *Ko-kun Bhaley, Yu-shang Bhaley, Logo-Momo (3-in-1)*, Simply Tibetan, Simply Delicious, October 28, 2013. https://www.simplytibetan.com

Singh, G. 'I Had Become a Refugee in My Own Country in a Span of Few Hours', 'Amazing Entrepreneurs' Series, Volume 8, Issue 33, The Weekend Leader.Com: Pioneering Positive Journalism, August 17, 2017. www.theweekendleader.com

Singh, Mohinder. 'Keeping cool'. *The Hindu*. January 19, 2002. https://www.thehindu.com

Singh, Sushmita Basu. *Sovabazar Rajbarir Rannabanna: A Book of Recipes in Bengali by Nandini Deb Bourani in Conversation with Sushmita Basu Singh*, Rritobak, 2017.

Sinha, Pradip. 'Siraj's Calcutta: 1756–57', *Calcutta: The Living City—Volume I: The Past.* Ed. Sukanta Chaudhuri. Oxford University Press, 1990.

Sircar, Jawhar. 'The Chinese of Calcutta', *Calcutta: The Living City—Volume II: The Present and Future*. Ed. Sukanta Chaudhuri. Oxford University Press, 1990.

_____'Armenians: Merchant-Princes of the Past', *The Sunday Telegraph*, Calcutta, West Bengal, India, May 29, 1983. http://www.jawharsircar.com

_____'Job Charnock or the Armenians: Who Founded Calcutta?' *The Sunday Statesman*. August 25, 1985. https://www.jawharsircar.com

_____'The Tomb of the Unknown Chinaman', *The Telegraph*, Calcutta, West Bengal, India, March 27, 1983. http://www.jawharsircar.com

_____*Are Bengalis Turning Vegetarian?*, Food, *The Wire*, June 9, 2018. https://www.thewire.in

Smith, Andrew F. *The Tomato in America: Early History, Culture, and Cookery*, University of South Carolina Press, Columbia, South Carolina, United States of America, Internet Archive Books, Internet Archive, 1994. https://www.archive.org

Smith, K. Annabelle. *Why the Tomato Was Feared in Europe for More Than 200 Years, Smithsonian* Magazine, June 18, 2013. https://www.smithsonianmag.com

Smith, Woodruff D. 'Complications of the Commonplace: Tea, Sugar, and Imperialism', *The Journal of Interdisciplinary History*, Volume 23, No. 2, The MIT Press, Cambridge, Massachusetts, United States of America, 1992. https://www.jstor.org

SNS Web. 'Durga Puja: What Is Dhunuchi Naach?', *The Statesman*, October 7, 2018. https://www.thestatesman.com

_____'When is Eid al-Adha; Significance of celebration', *The Statesman*, July 7, 2020. https://www.thestatesman.com

Sonalis. *Chhena Poda: Showstopper Dish Of Orissa*, Swadesi, July 26, 2017. https://www.swadesi.com

Sood, Akhil. 'The chords that bind', *The Hindu*, December 3, 2016. https://www.thehindu.com

Spirit, Wojtek. *About how a Pole opened the first cafe in Vienna and came up with coffee and milk*, June 22, 2011. https://www.historia.org.pl

Sreedharan, Das. 'Samosa: The star of snacks', *The New Indian Express*, November 11, 2018. https://www.newindianexpress.com

Stumm, Albert. 'Learning traditional barbeque in the Armenian countryside', *The Week*, June 21, 2020. https://www.theweek.com

Sukhadwala, Sejal. 'Diwali drinks: sharbat to champagne', *The Guardian*, November 12, 2012. https://www.theguradian.com

Suny, Ronald Grigor. *Armenian Genocide: Turkish-Armenian History*, Britannica, July 20, 1998. https://www.britannica.com

Surai, Sumit. *Allen Kitchen Restaurant—Great Food, History and the Special Prawn Cutlet*, Sumit Surai: a blog on travel…food…photography…and more, July 20, 2011. www.sumitsurai.com

_____*Armenian Christmas Celebration On 6th January in Kolkata (Calcutta)*, Sumit Surai: a blog on travel…food…photography…and more, January 6, 2016. www.sumitsurai.com

Swami, Chetanananda. 'Swami Adbhutananda', *God Lived with Them: Life Stories of Sixteen Monastic Disciples of Sri Ramakrishna*, Vedanta Society of St Louis, St Louis, Missouri, United States of America, 1997.

Swamy, Rohini. 'Family behind Mysore Pak "invention" to seek GI tag after row over joke', *The Print*, September 17, 2019. https://www.theprint.in

Sweeney, Stephanie. 'For Kolkata's Anglo-Indian families, Christmas brings back the old-world charm', *Hindustan Times*, December 20, 2019. https://www.hindustantimes.com

Taleb, Mohammad Abu. 'Oitijhyer Bakorkhani Jachche Bideshe', *Dainik Ittefaq*, 28 February, 2015. https://www.archive1.ittefaq.com.bd

Tamang, Jyoti Prakash; Sarkar, Prabir; Hesseltine, Clifford W. 'Traditional fermented foods and beverages of Darjeeling and Sikkim—A review', Journal of the Science of Food and Agriculture, 44 (4): 375–85, January, 1988. https://www.researchgate.net

Tanusree and Shehzaad. *Tanusree's Shaad (Bengali Baby Shower) Ceremony!*, One Time Fashionista: Vogue.Voyage.Voracity, January 9, 2019. www.onetimefashionista.com

Tchilingirian, Hratch. *Armenian Christmas: Why Do Armenians Celebrate Christmas on January 6th?*, Little Armenia. www.littlearmenia.com

Tea Coffee Spices of India. *Origin of Coffee in India,* Tea, Coffee, and Spices of India, Coffee, https://www.teacoffeespiceofindia.com

Tea Research Association, Tea Research Association C, *Tea Classification*, TOCKLAI, 2017. https://www.tocklai.org

Tea World, Copyright 2018–19 Tea World, *The Evolution of Tea's Scientific Name*, Lesson 5, Tea World: an initiative of KKHSOU. www.teaworld.kkhsou.in

Tenphel Sonam, 2019, *The Significance of Yaks for Tibetan People*, Tibet Vista: Tibettravel.org, November 16, https://www.tibettravel.org

The Armenian Genocide Museum-Institute, *Armenian Genocide*, www.genocide-museum.am

The editors of *Encyclopaedia Britannica. Opium Trade: British and Chinese history*, Britannica. July 20, 1998. https://www.britannica.com

_____*Boston Tea Party: United States History*, Britannica, July 20, 1998. https://www.britannica.com

_____*East India Company: English trading company*. Britannica. July 20, 1998. https://www.brtiannica.com

_____*Henry Louis Vivian Derozio: Indian poet and educator*, Britannica, June 9, 2006. https://www.britannica.com

_____*Keshab Chunder Sen: Hindu philosopher and social reformer*, Britannica, July 20, 1998. https://www.britannica.com

_____*Tamluk: India*, Britannica, July 20, 1998. https://www.britannica.com

_____*Tomato: fruit*, Britannica, July 20, 1998. https://www.britannica.com

The Englishman. 'Federico Peliti: Christmas Orders Advertisement', *The Englishman*, Calcutta, West Bengal, India, December 31, 1895.

_____'Federico Peliti: Christmas Presents Advertisement', *The Englishman*, Calcutta, West Bengal, India, January 12, 1903.

_____'Federico Peliti: Specialities For Christmas & New Year's Festivities', *The Englishman,* Calcutta, West Bengal, India, January 12, 1903.

_____'Grand Hotel: Advertisement', *The Englishman*, Calcutta, West Bengal, India, December 31, 1895.

The Food Heritage Foundation. *Khetum—Armenian Christmas dinner*, Eat Local, https://www.food-heritage.org

The Telegraph. 'A-brewing, a recipe for revival—Coffee house set for year-end reopening'. May 13, 2003.

_____'Eye-poppers of nawab land', *The Telegraph online*, September 3, 2012. https://www.telegraphindia.com

_____'Hotel Awaits Court Order', *The Telegraph*, March 22, 2002.

Tibetan Trekking Travel. *Dried Yak Meat*, Tibetan Trekking, May 17, 2016. https://www.tibetantrekking.com

Times News Network. 'It's Xmas time for Armenians', *The Times of India*, Kolkata, West Bengal, India, January 3, 2012. https://www.timesofindia.indiatimes.com

Tirmizi, Bisma. 'Food Stories: Zarda', *Dawn*, May 5, 2015. https://www.dawn.com

TNN. 'Have you tasted these nolen gur temptations yet?', *E Times: Entertainment Times, The Times of India*, December 12, 2018. https://www.timesofindia.indiatimes.com

Toprani, Rajendra; Patel, Daxesh. *Betel leaf: Revisiting the benefits of an ancient Indian herb, South Asian Journal of Cancer*, PMC: US National Library of Medicine; National Institutes of Health, NCBI, v.2 (3): 140–41, July–September, 2013. https://www.ncbi.nlm.nih.gov

Toumaian, Besak (Archbishop). *Why Do We Observe Christmas on January 6?*, St Thomas Armenian Church. www.stthomasarmenianchurch.com

Tucker, Catherine M. 'Part I: Coffee Culture, Social Life, and Global History: Coffee and the Rise of the World System', *Coffee Culture: Local Experiences, Global Connections,* Routledge, 2011.

'Ukers' William H., M.A. *All About Coffee*, The Tea and Coffee Trade Journal Company, New York, United States of America, The Medical Heritage Library, Gerstein Science Information Centre, University of Toronto, Internet Archive, 1922. https://www.archive.org

Unemployment in North East India, Society, Indian Youth: Coming Together to Build the New India, www.indianyouth.net

Ushakova, Maria. *Khorovats (Armenian Grilled Vegetable Salad)*, Curious Cuisiniere: Travel the World from Your Kitchen, April 29, 2019. https://www.curiouscuisiniere.com

Vanamali. *Shakti: Realm of the Divine Mother*, Inner Traditions—Bear & Company, 2008.

Verma, Rahul. 'Feast for a king', *Graphiti, The Telegraph,* Kolkata, West Bengal, India, May 10, 2009.

Walia, Srishti. *7 Health Benefits of Bitter Gourd (Karela) Juice*, NDTV Food, August 22, 2018. https://www.food.ndtv.com

Walia, Varinder. 'Historical Harmony: Bengali and Punjabi revolutionaries scripted Independence together', *Amritsar Plus, The Tribune*, July 28, 2005. https://www.tribuneindia.com

Wallace, Robert Grenville. *Fifteen Years in India; Or, Sketches of a Soldier's Life*, Longman, Hurst, Rees, Orme, and Brown, London, England, United Kingdom, California Digital Library, American Libraries, University of California Libraries, Internet Archive, 1822. https://www.archive.org

Wallin, Nils-Bertil. *Coffee: A Long Way from Ethiopia*, YaleGlobal Online, Yale University, November 5, 2002. https://www.yaleglobal.yale.edu

Wangdu, Lobsang. *Changkol Recipe: To Start Losar Morning Off Right*, Yowangdu: Experience Tibet, February 2, 2013. https://www.yowangdu.com

_____*Dresil Recipe: Easy Tibetan Sweet Rice*, Yowangdu: Experience Tibet, October 20, 2012. https://www.yowangdu.com

_____*Saka Dawa: A Month Honoring the Buddha's Life*, Yowangdu: Experience Tibet. https://www.yowangdu.com

_____*Tibetan Food: A Visual Guide*, Yowangdu: Experience Tibet, April 21, 2012. https://www.yowangdu.com

_____*Your Guide to Momos (Tibetan Dumplings)*, Yowangdu: Experience Tibet, July 14, 2012. https://www.yowangdu.com

Weinberg, Bennett Alan; Bealer, Bonnie K. 'Part I: Caffeine in History: Coffee: Arabian Origins', *The World of Caffeine: The Science and Culture of the World's Most Popular Drug*, Routledge, 2001.

White-Kumar, Bridget. *Bengal Lancers Shrimp Curry or Col. Skinner's Shrimp Curry*, Anglo-Indian Cuisine, August 14, 2014. www.anglo-indianfood.blogspot.com

_____*Coconut Rice, Ball Curry (Bad Word Curry) and Devil,* Anglo-Indian Recipes by Bridget White, August 20, 2015. www.anglo-indianrecipes.blogspot.com

Wiener, Gerald; Jianlin, Han; Ruijun, Long. 'Products from Yak and Their Utilization', *The Yak*, Second Edition, RAP Publication, Regional Office for Asia and the Pacific, Food and Agriculture Organization of the United Nations, Bangkok, Thailand, June, 2003. www.fao.org

Wilson, C.R. *The Early Annals of the English in Bengal*, W. Thacker & Co., 1895.

Yummraj. *Kapila Ashram*, October 20, 2014. https://www.yummraj.com

Index

Note: Pages which contain illustrations are noted in *italics*.

C

J

L

M

N

O

P

S